Food for Family is dedicated to
Sheelah Baxter
(1945–2011)

Your love, light and laughter
live on in Jo, Billy and Eri.

PROUDLY SUPPORTING
NATIONAL
BREAST CANCER
FOUNDATION

Royalties from the book will support
the National Breast Cancer Foundation

Food for Family

GUILLAUME & SANCHIA BRAHIMI

PHOTOGRAPHY BY
ANSON SMART & EARL CARTER

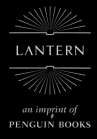

LANTERN

an imprint of
PENGUIN BOOKS

FOREWORD

———+———

Eating as a family is not only about food: it's about the experience we share with the people we love. When I'm at the stove, dinner is usually ready when the smoke alarm goes off, so you can imagine my surprise when Guillaume and Sanchia asked me to write the foreword to *Food for Family*. Of course, I was delighted to accept.

One of the most popular dishes in our home celebrates produce from the pantry, with just three basic ingredients: tinned tuna, packet pasta and any vegies I can find. *Et voilá*, dinner is served! My regular customers, aged four, eight and ten, will tell you it's worthy of four Michelin stars. In fact, it's famously become known as 'Mummy's Special Pasta'. But a shared meal is a special meal, even pantry pasta. For me, family time around the dinner table is essential. It is an opportunity to talk with our children about the world around us, to debate, laugh, and share our love for each other.

I have been privileged to know Guillaume and Sanchia for many years and their generosity of spirit and love of family is beautifully illustrated in this book, royalties from which will support the National Breast Cancer Foundation. More than 15000 women are diagnosed with breast cancer each year in Australia; as the Foundation's Patron for over 15 years, I've witnessed that life can pass too quickly. Without funds to support research, we simply cannot find answers to treat cancer. Thank you, Guillaume and Sanchia, for giving us a good reason to gather our families, share delicious food and cherish this precious time together.

Sarah Murdoch

CONTENTS

—+—

INTRODUCTION

Delighted with the response to our first book, *Food for Friends*, my wife, Sanchia, and I relished the opportunity to write a follow-up. In *Food for Family* we again feature different chapter hosts, a diverse group of interesting and dynamic Australians who are all devoted to their families. Each of the hosts devises a dream menu and my job is then to make that dream an appetising reality!

Justin Hemmes opens the doors to his home, The Hermitage. With uninterrupted views of Sydney Harbour, we idle the afternoon away with Justin, his beloved mother, Merivale, and sister, Bettina, as well as a close-knit bunch of friends. We eat buffet style, enjoying mud crab, split prawns with romesco sauce, and roast chicken with truffle, finishing with a decadent raspberry and pistachio trifle.

A seasoned entertainer and matriarch to a large and loving family, Toni Ryan's Easter luncheon features recipes that are close to perfect. It's a great thrill to get into the kitchen with her and prepare a lunch for a small army of guests i.e. the Ryan clan. We enjoy lobster and leek terrine, glazed ham, roast turkey (with Toni's mother's secret stuffing) and, as there are lots of children on board, two desserts: frozen lemon nougat and an apple tart tatin.

Mollymook is Kellie Hush's space to unwind and reboot with her family and friends. Kellie organises a *très chic* picnic for the little ones, while I prepare a leisurely seafood lunch for the parents. The day comes to a fun-filled end in the garden with a plate of cheese, a little more burgundy and game of bocce.

Cate Blanchett is someone who wears many hats: award-winning actress, philanthropist, environmentalist and of course devoted mother. But talking to Cate you forget all the accolades and just enjoy the company of a woman who is funny, candid and refreshingly real. Andrew and Cate host a lunch in a woolshed property for good friends and family. Over duck ragout with green olives and coriander, Cate reveals that Andrew is in actual fact a wonderful cook. She also tells me the family have a weakness for sticky date pudding and brussels sprouts!

A charming heritage cottage in Watson's Bay is home to Mark Bouris and his family. Overlooking Camp Cove, it is a tropical paradise that loses none of its sparkle even in the winter months. Mark's four sons and father, George, come together for a Mediterranean feast al fresco. The day involves much ribbing, hugging and laughter, not to mention impromptu Greek dancing.

Gillon McLachlan's schedule as CEO of AFL is fast-paced, so making time for family and good friends is paramount. Gillon and I enjoy preparing an Argentinian-inspired barbecue. (As his wife, Laura, says, if Gillon is cooking, it usually involves 'meat and fire'.) I serve kingfish ceviche with lime, coriander and chilli and a plate of pork, spinach and manchego empanadas to begin, followed by beef short ribs served with an irresistible barbecue sauce.

According to Marco Meneguzzi, he'd quite happily spend every weekend at his bolthole in Bowral, and after spending a riotous afternoon with Marco's good friends, I understand why. We spice things up with a Marrakesh moment in the Southern Highlands. The aromas of herbs and spices entice everyone into the kitchen, where plates soon become laden with meatballs, lamb tagine and fresh peas with feta and mint.

On New Year's Eve 2013, I delivered my very last service at Guillaume at Bennelong. As they say when one door closes, another opens . . . and for me this was true. Chapter 1 features the very first time we opened the doors of Guillaume's. As royalties from this book will support the National Breast Cancer Foundation, we asked our good friend and NBCF patron Sarah Murdoch to help us host a pink-hued luncheon. As guests assembled for a glass of champagne and crab sandwich, you could still smell the fresh paint lingering in the air. It was a day that will forever be etched in my mind.

Our Brahimi family life has changed too, most specially with the addition of a new member, Loïc. The girls often say they can barely remember life without him, a sentiment I share. Balancing the demands of a busy family life, with an intense restaurant schedule, can create its own set of unique challenges. Also at chez Brahimi it feels like we cater for completely different age brackets (think toddler and teenager) – so suddenly the set menu is becoming à la carte! Hopefully some of the recipes in our family chapter will help simplify your Monday to Friday madness too . . . and make downtime on the weekends exactly that. So with a little help, you too can enjoy good food and spend more time with the people who count most – *votre famille*.

Bon appétit!

RESTAURANT *Guillaume*

I always dreamed of opening a local restaurant that delivered the best in fine dining in a setting that was welcoming and not too formal. The space had to be sophisticated, elegant and comfortable, like you were entering a beautiful home. I saw a room timeless in its design, alongside food that was ever-changing. The service would be impeccable yet at the same time friendly, the atmosphere lively and animated, but never too noisy or overbearing. It would be a restaurant that would reflect my French sensibilities, in a distinctly modern Australian setting.

This idea bubbled along for a long time. Then in 2013 my career path changed dramatically and I began to look for a site that would become my signature local restaurant. I was overseas on a work trip when it came to me: *What about Darcy's?*

Attilio Marinangeli, a wonderful restaurateur, opened the doors to Darcy's Italian restaurant in 1975 and made it a much-loved Sydney institution. It's not surprising then that since we moved into the historic site – a 1920s terrace in a lovely tree-lined Paddington street – many people have shared the special connection they have it. I can relate, as I too have an emotional attachment to the restaurant. In 2000, when our first child was born, the hospital at that time gave new parents a 'night out': you left the hospital at 6 pm with the newborn happily ensconced in the nursery and went for dinner somewhere, returning promptly by 8 pm. We chose Darcy's and we toasted the arrival of our baby daughter Constance with a glass of pink Salmon Brut Rosé Billecart champagne, generously offered by a smiling Attilio.

My wife, Sanchia, had spent many occasions with her family at Darcy's and being one of five children, the private dining room was often booked for special occasions. She fondly remembers being just fifteen when her father, Charles, took her to dinner, one on one. It made her feel quite the adult and she basked in having a parent's attention all to herself, even though she was probably behaving like an intolerable teenager at home. It's a tradition we try to continue with our three daughters, Constance, Honor and Violette (as Loïc is still a toddler dining out is still too fraught with spillages and dummy spits . . . literally).

With the creation of Guillaume in mind, I immediately contacted my good friend Matthew Csidei to help me with the interior design. His vision was clear cut – plush Pierre Frey fabric on the walls, Matisse prints simply framed in gold, reupholstered chairs in a French blue, and herringbone flooring in the entrance which then gives way to Tuscan Casina Sisal carpet throughout the restaurant. For the private dining room, now known as the Balcony Room, an elegant Hermès 'Circuit 24' wallpaper, chairs upholstered in Hermès terre d'h Gris ponce, with a statement chandelier found at Les Puces de Saint-Ouen flea markets. Tamsin Johnson came on board to oversee the project and she did a wonderful job turning our vision into a functional, working 86-seat restaurant. My father-in-law, Charles Curran, was also instrumental in the renovation.

With the renovation underway, my team and I began sourcing those smaller details that really underpin the whole look and feel of a restaurant. The linen we use is featherleaf and clothed three times on the table. I became slightly obsessed with bespoke plates and dinnerware from Mud, and still marvel at the delicacy of the product. Laguiole cutlery and Riedel glassware are brands that are undeniably luxurious yet refined. The lighting needed to be flattering, right down to the Queen B tealight candles for the table, which are made from beeswax and provide the restaurant with a sweet, soft glow.

At Guillaume's, I wanted to cook the food that I am known for, but still let the patron choose between the eight-course degustation, or one or two courses. The menu would be seasonal – and yes, some of my signature dishes have travelled with me from the Sydney Opera House (along with much of my wonderful team). You will see my basil-infused tuna and turban of scampi, among others.

The luncheon that features on these pages is the very first time we opened our doors. It was an exciting day for everyone, with the smell of freshly painted walls still lingering in the air as guests arrived, promptly at midday. We invited close friends and family to celebrate with us and as the royalties from this book are supporting the National Breast Cancer Foundation, we invited former CEO Carole Renouf and patron and friend Sarah Murdoch.

In the kitchen, it was all systems go. The menu included an entrée of baby vegetable salad, a main of john dory with carrot and ginger purée, pommes allumettes and coriander; and for dessert, chestnut cream with Valrhona chocolate, cassis and pear purée.

With a room full of very busy people, I loved that almost everyone cleared the afternoon and just enjoyed themselves, all for a good cause. It was a day that will forever be with me and I am so grateful that my friends and my family here in Australia were with me. My family in France were with us in spirit.

The luncheon was the perfect celebration of (I hope) a new Sydney institution and our book, which has been very much a labour of love. My only wish is that both Guillaume and *Food for Family* brings happiness to many, many people. If it does, I have done my job and that in turn makes me happy.

MENU

———+———

Vegetable salad with beetroot purée and soubise

Salmon with lemon purée, fennel and apple
with wasabi emulsion

Globe artichoke royale with
barigoule vinaigrette and mud crab

Marron and pork cheek with cauliflower
purée and anchovy dressing

John dory, carrot and ginger purée,
pommes allumettes and coriander

Pigeon with onion purée, witlof and foie gras

Passionfruit soufflé with vanilla anglaise
and passionfruit and banana sorbet

Chestnut cream with Valrhona chocolate,
cassis and pear purée

Vegetable salad with beetroot purée and soubise

SERVES 4

At the restaurant, we source all our baby vegetables from local growers. In this recipe, they are dressed simply to allow their full flavours to really shine. I love the presentation of this dish: it looks like a beautiful garden. The artfully placed dots of soubise and beetroot purée work to complement the vegetables' vibrant colours.

4 baby beetroot, trimmed
4 baby golden beetroot, trimmed
4 baby carrots, peeled and trimmed
4 baby purple carrots, peeled and trimmed
2 bulbs baby fennel, trimmed and quartered
1 baby leek, trimmed and cut into four pieces
⅓ cup (80 ml) olive oil
sea salt and cracked white pepper
20 g baby peas
¼ bunch baby kale, stalks discarded
100 g snow peas (mange-tout), trimmed
90 ml Shallot vinaigrette (see Basics)
6 very thin slices French breakfast radish (about 1 radish)
8 very thin slices baby white radish (about 2 radishes)
baby herbs, to garnish (optional)

SOUBISE
30 g butter
1 onion, thinly sliced using a mandolin
table salt
1 tablespoon pure cream

BEETROOT PURÉE
1 beetroot (about 200 g), scrubbed
1 tablespoon sherry vinegar

For the soubise, heat the butter in a small saucepan and when foaming add the onion. Sweat the onion with a little salt and cook over low heat, stirring regularly, for 15 minutes or until the onion is soft but has not coloured. Add the cream and reduce for 5 minutes over low heat. Transfer the mixture to a blender and blend until smooth. Set aside.

Preheat the oven to 190°C. For the beetroot purée, wrap the beetroot in foil and bake for 1 hour or until soft in the centre when tested with a knife. Peel and chop the beetroot, then place in a blender with the vinegar and blend until smooth. Place in a squeezy bottle or piping bag.

Wrap the baby beetroot individually in foil and bake for 35 minutes or until soft in the centre when tested with a knife. Peel the beetroot and slice in half. Place in the fridge.

Place the carrots, purple carrots, fennel and leek in separate saucepans and add enough water to just cover. Add a tablespoon of olive oil and salt and pepper to each pan and bring to the boil over medium heat. Reduce the heat to low and cook for 10–12 minutes or until the vegetables are soft. Remove from the heat and cool slightly, then place in the fridge to chill.

Bring a large saucepan of water to the boil with a pinch of salt. Cook the peas, kale and snow peas separately for about 2 minutes each then refresh in iced water. Place in the fridge to chill.

Place the chilled orange carrot, golden beetroot, fennel, peas, kale and snow peas in a bowl, season with salt and pepper and dress with ¼ cup (60 ml) of shallot vinaigrette. Season and dress the red beetroot and purple carrots (separately to prevent their colour running into the other vegetables) with a tablespoon of shallot vinaigrette. Arrange all the vegetables neatly on plates and place the radish over the top. Dress the baby herbs (if using) with the remaining vinaigrette and place on top. Using a squeezy bottle or a spoon, place dots of soubise around the plate. Finish with dots of beetroot purée.

Salmon with lemon purée, fennel and apple with wasabi emulsion

SERVES 6

This sashimi-style entrée is a wonderfully healthy option on my menu. The recipe calls for Lecite, a lecithin-base emulsifier used by chefs to create culinary foams or airs. This great product is available at Simon Johnson (simonjohnson.com), but if you can't get hold of it, you can just use lecithin instead, which is stocked by health food shops and some supermarkets.

2 bulbs baby fennel, outer leaves discarded, fronds reserved
50 ml Teraoka shiro shoyu (light Japanese soy sauce)
450 g piece alpine salmon or sashimi-grade king salmon, skin removed, trimmed
sea salt and cracked white pepper
2 small granny smith apples
1 tablespoon chardonnay vinegar
2 sprigs bronze fennel (or reserved fronds from baby fennel)

LEMON PURÉE
peeled rind of 3 lemons, white pith removed
100 g sugar
juice of ½ lemon

WASABI EMULSION
150 ml sauternes
25 g wasabi paste
4 g Lecite or lethicin

To make the lemon purée, place the lemon rind in a saucepan and cover with cold water. Bring to the boil, then strain. Return the rind to the saucepan and cover with fresh cold water. Bring to the boil, then strain again. Repeat twice more. This will remove any bitterness.

Place the sugar and 175 ml of water in a saucepan and bring to the boil. Add the lemon rind and simmer for 25 minutes, then strain, reserving 2 tablespoons of the syrup. Place the lemon zest and syrup in a blender with 2 tablespoons of water and the lemon juice. Blend until very smooth with a gel-like consistency. Set aside.

To make the wasabi emulsion, place the sauternes in a small saucepan and bring to the boil, then remove from the heat and whisk in the wasabi and Lecite or lethicin. Allow to cool, then combine with a stick blender for about 2 minutes or until a foam forms.

Thinly slice the fennel using a mandolin and place in iced water for 15 minutes. Place the soy sauce in a bowl. Slice the salmon 1 cm thick and place in the soy sauce for just 2 minutes. Drain the fennel and season with salt and pepper.

To assemble, place three drops of lemon purée 2 cm wide on the plate and using a teaspoon swipe it in a circular direction. Remove the salmon from the soy sauce. Arrange a slice of salmon on top of each lemon swipe. Using a mandolin, very thinly slice the apple and dress with the vinegar. Place the fennel in between the salmon and arrange the apple in the centre. Place a scoop of wasabi emulsion each piece of salmon and on the apple. Garnish with bronze fennel (or fennel fronds). Serve immediately.

Globe artichoke royale with barigoule vinaigrette and mud crab

SERVES 6

On a recent trip to Paris, I sampled a particularly delicious *royale* (savoury custard) and was inspired to add one to my restaurant menu. I sometimes vary this recipe by using peas or asparagus instead of the globe artichoke. You can also replace the mud crab with yabbies or lobster if you like.

1 small mud crab (about 600 g)
20 g black truffle, finely chopped
¼ bunch chives, finely sliced

GLOBE ARTICHOKE ROYALE

7 globe artichokes
1 litre chicken stock
2 eggs
2 egg yolks
½ cup (125 ml) milk
½ cup (125 ml) pure cream
sea salt and cracked pepper

BARIGOULE VINAIGRETTE

½ cup (125 ml) extra virgin olive oil
6 golden shallots, cut into 3 mm dice
1 carrot, peeled and cut into 3 mm dice
2 sticks celery, peeled and cut into 3 mm dice
½ small leek, peeled and cut into 3 mm dice
¼ bunch thyme, leaves picked
1 bay leaf
50 ml white wine
50 ml white wine vinegar

To make the globe artichoke royale, remove the outer green leaves of the artichokes and cut the top where the heart starts. Remove the choke with a melon baller. Peel the stem until it becomes yellow, then cut the artichokes in half and place them in a saucepan. Cover with the stock and a cartouche (a round of baking paper cut to fit) and bring to the boil over medium heat. Reduce the heat to low and cook for about 40 minutes or until the artichokes are completely soft. Remove and drain. Place the cooked artichokes in a blender, and blend until smooth. Remove from blender and pass through a fine sieve. Set the purée aside.

Combine the eggs and yolks in a bowl and add the artichoke purée, milk and cream. Season to taste, then mix together well. Leave to rest for 30 minutes in the fridge. Divide the mixture among six 300 ml capacity heatproof bowls and cover with plastic film. Cooking in batches, if necessary, place in a large steamer and cook over the lowest heat possible for 20–25 minutes or until the mixture is just set. The water should be barely moving; if the heat is too high and the water simmers, the custards may split. Remove from the steamer and place the bowls in the fridge to chill for at least 1 hour.

For the barigoule vinaigrette, place a saucepan over medium heat and add ⅓ cup (80 ml) of olive oil. Add the shallot and carrot and cook for 2 minutes or until the shallot is becoming translucent, then add the celery, leek, thyme and bay leaf and cook for another 5 minutes. Add the white wine and vinegar and cook for a further 5 minutes or until reduced by half. Remove from the heat, add the remaining olive oil and allow to cool.

Place a large saucepan of water over high heat and bring to the boil. Add salt and the crab and cook for 12 minutes, then remove and place in a colander over a bowl and allow to cool down at room temperature. After 1 hour, break the shell of the crab and remove all the meat.

Remove the royales from the fridge and allow to come to room temperature. Place a couple of dessertspoons of barigoule dressing over the top of each royale and smooth to cover the surface of the royale. Sprinkle over the truffle, add a tablespoon of crab meat and finish with a sprinkling of chives.

Marron and pork cheek with cauliflower purée and anchovy dressing

SERVES 4

Kevin Solomon, my very talented Head Chef, created this dish with me in mind.
It showcases all my favourite ingredients – marron, anchovies, lemon and rosemary.
The dressing works perfectly to balance the richness of the marron and pork.
Sea spray is available from specialist greengrocers. It can be exchanged for any
sea vegetable or you can simply leave it out.

60 g Trisol (see page 22)
65 g plain flour
small pinch of dried yeast
pinch of sugar
salt
2 tablespoons olive oil
4 pork cheeks, all sinew removed
200 ml Pork jus (see Basics)
2 star anise
30 g ginger, peeled and thinly sliced
4 marrons
1 small head of cauliflower, cut into florets with stalks attached
2 cups (500 ml) milk
2 cups (500 ml) pure cream
50 g podded broad beans (about 4 pods)
125 g butter
vegetable oil, for deep-frying
2 sprigs sea spray
15 g preserved lemon, finely diced (about one-eighth
    of a preserved lemon)

ANCHOVY DRESSING

2 anchovies
juice of ½ lemon
1 sprig rosemary, leaves finely chopped
70 ml extra virgin olive oil

Place the Trisol, flour, yeast, sugar and a pinch of salt in a bowl. Make a well in the centre and slowly pour in 100 ml of warm water. Cover with plastic film and rest for 2 hours.

Preheat the oven to 140°C. Place a small ovenproof saucepan over high heat. Add the olive oil and the pork cheeks and seal for about 4 minutes on each side until golden. Add the pork jus, star anise and ginger and bring to the boil. Cover with a cartouche (see page 17) and place in the oven to cook for 1½ hours.

Place the marrons in the freezer for 30 minutes to put them to sleep.

Bring a large saucepan of water to the boil, then add salt. Add the marrons and cook for 90 seconds, then transfer to a bowl

of iced water to cool. Remove the claws and place them back in the boiling water for a further 5 minutes, then return to the iced water. Peel the marrons and set aside; crack the claws and leave to the side.

For the anchovy dressing, whiz the anchovies, lemon juice and rosemary in a blender, then slowly drizzle in the olive oil with the motor running. Set aside.

Set aside 16 small cauliflower florets. Thinly slice the rest of the cauliflower and place in a saucepan with the milk and cream. Bring to the boil over high heat, then reduce to a simmer and cook for 30 minutes or until the cauliflower is just tender. Remove the cauliflower from the saucepan and place in the blender with 50 ml of the cooking liquid and blend until smooth. Strain through a fine sieve, season to taste, then set the cauliflower purée aside.

Bring a saucepan of water to the boil. Blanch the broad beans for 2 minutes, then remove and place in iced water. Peel and set aside.

Bring ¼ cup (60 ml) of water to the boil in a small saucepan and gradually add 75 g of butter. Remove from the heat and combine with a stick blender until the butter is emulsified. Place over low heat and add the peeled marron so everything is covered in the butter. Slowly cook the marron for 6 minutes; turn and cook for a further 6 minutes, then add the marron claws.

Pour vegetable oil into a heavy-based saucepan or deep-fryer until two-thirds full and heat to 170°C. Lightly coat the reserved cauliflower florets in the batter. Fry for 2–3 minutes or until crisp. Drain on paper towel.

Meanwhile, reheat the cauliflower purée. Drain the pork cheeks.

Place a frying pan over medium heat and add the remaining butter. Fry the sea spray and broad beans for just 30 seconds, then remove from the pan and drain on paper towel.

To assemble, place a quenelle of cauliflower purée on the plate, then add the pork cheek. Place the marron opposite. Dot around the broad beans and drizzle with the anchovy dressing. Add the sea spray and cauliflower florets. Place preserved lemon on the pork cheek and serve.

John dory, carrot and ginger purée, pommes allumettes and coriander

SERVES 4

This is one of the restaurant's most popular dishes and I'm not surprised. Diners especially love this served with my famous Paris mash! John dory has a lovely delicate flavour. Here it works beautifully alongside tender heirloom carrots and a sweet purée of carrot with a hint of ginger.

2 baby orange heirloom carrots, peeled and trimmed
2 baby yellow heirloom carrots, peeled and trimmed
110 ml olive oil
sea salt and cracked white pepper
2 baby purple heirloom carrots, peeled and trimmed
2 desiree potatoes, peeled and cut into very fine matchsticks
vegetable oil, for deep-frying
4 small flat-leaf parsley leaves
150 g unsalted butter
juice of ¼ lemon
4 × 170 g john dory fillets, skin removed
¼ bunch coriander, leaves finely chopped

CARROT AND GINGER PURÉE
40 g unsalted butter
20 g ginger, peeled and coarsely grated
250 g carrots, peeled and thinly sliced
sea salt and cracked white pepper

For the carrot and ginger purée, place a saucepan over medium heat and add the butter. When foaming, add the ginger and lightly fry for 4 minutes. Add the carrot and 100 ml of water, cover with the lid and cook for 25 minutes or until the carrot is soft. Drain off excess liquid, then place the carrot in blender and blend until smooth. Season to taste and set aside.

Place the orange and yellow carrots in a small saucepan and cover with water. Add 15 ml of olive oil and a pinch of salt. Bring to the boil over high heat, then reduce to a simmer and cook for 10 minutes or until the carrots are just tender. Strain and set aside. Repeat with the purple carrots.

Using a mandolin, cut the potatoes into fine matchsticks, then place in a bowl of cold water to stop them discolouring. Pour vegetable oil into a heavy-based saucepan or deep-fryer until two-thirds full and heat to 170°C. Drain the potato matchsticks and pat dry well. Divide the matchsticks into four batches. Lower into the oil and form a ball of potato using a slotted spoon. Fry for 2 minutes or until golden, then remove and place on paper towel to drain. Season with salt. Fry the parsley leaves for a few seconds or just until crisp, then remove with a slotted spoon and place a leaf on each potato ball.

Place a tablespoon of water in a small saucepan and bring to the boil over low heat. Add a quarter of the butter and whisk with a small whisk or fork. Continue to add the butter a quarter at a time. Blend in gradually until emulsified. Remove from the heat, add the lemon juice and season with salt and pepper. Set the beurre blanc aside.

Place two large frying pans over medium–high heat. Season the fish, then add 2 tablespoons of olive oil to each pan and fry the fish for about 4 minutes or until nicely coloured, then turn over and seal the other side for 1 minute.

Gently reheat the purée. Cut the carrots in half lengthways and place in a saucepan with 50 ml of the beurre blanc. Cook over low heat until warmed through, and keep the carrots warm until serving. Stir in the rest of the beurre blanc with the coriander.

Place a quarter of the purée on each plate, spoon the beurre blanc around the carrot purée and place one of each colour carrot on the sauce. Put the john dory on the purée and arrange the potato on top.

Pigeon with onion purée, witlof and foie gras

SERVES 4

With its classical flavours, this dish is a nod to my heritage. It celebrates ingredients synonymous with French fine-dining – pigeon, foie gras and truffle. I use a fantastic wheat-derived product called Trisol in my batter, available from Simon Johnson (simonjohnson.com). It is well worth seeking out, as it makes deep-fried food super-crisp.

2 pigeons
200 g duck fat
150 ml chicken stock
2 witlof, halved lengthways
4 asparagus spears, trimmed and peeled
2 cabbage leaves (middle leaves)
2 tablespoons olive oil
40 g butter
160 ml Chicken jus (see Basics)
20 g black truffle, finely chopped
50 g duck foie gras, chopped
green elk, to garnish (optional)

PICKLED SHALLOTS

50 g caster sugar
100 ml white wine vinegar
2 golden shallots, peeled

ONION RINGS

60 g Trisol
65 g plain flour, plus 20 g extra for dusting
small pinch of dried yeast
pinch of sugar
pinch of salt
100 ml warm water
2 large golden shallots, sliced into 5 mm rings, centres discarded
vegetable oil, for deep-frying

WHITE ONION PURÉE

75 g unsalted butter
1 large white onion, very finely sliced using a mandolin
1 teaspoon table salt
50 ml pure cream

For the pickled shallots, place the sugar, vinegar and 100 ml of water in a saucepan. Bring to the boil. Add the shallots and cook for 25 minutes on a low simmer. Remove from the heat and leave in the pickling liquid for at least 12 hours in the fridge.

For the onion rings, combine the Trisol, flour, yeast, sugar and salt in a bowl. Make a well in the centre, pour in the water and whisk to combine. Cover with plastic film and leave the batter to rest for at least 2 hours in a warm place.

Preheat the oven to 150°C. Remove the legs from the pigeons, keeping the breast in place. To do this, run a knife along the skin at the bottom of the breast cutting down to legs, then break through the bone and trim the legs off. Heat the duck fat in a small ovenproof saucepan over low heat until melted.

Place in the pigeon legs in the duck fat, cover with a cartouche (see page 17) and place in the oven. Cook for 1 hour or until tender. Remove from the oven and leave to rest in the fat.

Meanwhile, for the white onion purée, melt the butter in a frying pan and when just starting to foam, add the onion. Sweat for 20 minutes over low heat or until the onion is soft but not coloured, then add the salt. Cook for another 5 minutes, then add the cream. Allow the cream to reduce a little for 5 minutes then transfer to a blender and blend until smooth. Set aside in the fridge.

Place the chicken stock in a saucepan with the witlof and cover with a piece of baking paper. Bring to the boil, then reduce the heat to low and cook for 15 minutes or until the witlof is just tender at the core when a knife is inserted. Remove from the stock and set aside in the fridge.

Bring a large saucepan of water to the boil and add salt. Blanch the asparagus for 2 minutes, then remove and place in iced water. Blanch the cabbage leaves for 4 minutes or until just tender, then remove and place in iced water. Drain the asparagus and cabbage, and place on a tea towel to dry.

Preheat the oven to 180°C. Place an ovenproof frying pan over medium heat and add the olive oil. Add the pigeon, breast-side down. Fry one side for 1–2 minutes or until the skin is completely and evenly coloured, then turn and cook until golden. Place in the oven, breast-side up, for 10 minutes, then leave to rest for 15 minutes in a warm spot on top of the oven. Drain the pigeon legs from the duck fat, then place in a large frying pan with the witlof. Fry over medium heat for 3–4 minutes or until coloured.

To cook the onion rings, pour vegetable oil into a heavy-based saucepan or deep-fryer until two-thirds full and heat to 175°C. Lightly flour the shallot and dip into the batter. Fry for 2 minutes or until just starting to colour. Drain on paper towel.

Melt the butter in a frying pan and when starting to foam, add the asparagus and cabbage to heat but not colour. Remove and drain off any excess butter. Reheat the white onion purée. Bring the chicken jus to the boil, then remove from the heat and add the truffle to the jus.

To assemble the dish, slice the pickled shallots into 3 mm thick slices and place on each plate. Carve the pigeon breasts from the bone and trim. Arrange the cabbage on the plate and spoon over some onion purée. Lay the witlof on top. Place a pigeon breast and leg on the plate with some asparagus. Place the foie gras into the jus at the last minute and spoon over the top. Add the onion ring and green elk (if using) and serve.

Passionfruit soufflé with vanilla anglaise and passionfruit and banana sorbet

SERVES 6

This beautifully light soufflé is a staple on my menu over the summer months. The sorbet is delicious too: passionfruit and banana is one of my favourite flavour combinations. The recipe will make slightly more passionfruit base then is required – you will need to weigh the amount required in order to ensure the soufflés will rise perfectly.

PASSIONFRUIT BASE

30 g cornflour

65 g caster sugar

1 cup (250 ml) strained passionfruit juice (about 22 passionfruit)

¼ vanilla bean, split and seeds scraped

VANILLA CRÈME ANGLAISE

2/3 cup (160 ml) pure cream

2/3 cup (160 ml) milk

2 vanilla beans, split and seeds scraped

4 egg yolks

50 g caster sugar

BANANA AND PASSIONFRUIT SORBET

125 g caster sugar

35 ml liquid glucose

5 bananas (400 g peeled banana)

1 cup (250 ml) strained passionfruit juice (about 22 passionfruit)

1 tablespoon orange juice

SOUFFLÉ

30 g softened unsalted butter

120 g caster sugar, plus extra for dusting

250 g Passionfruit base

300 g egg whites (from about 9 eggs), at room temperature

For the passionfruit base, whisk together the cornflour and sugar in a bowl. Pour in the passionfruit juice and mix well to ensure there are no lumps. Stir in the vanilla seeds. Pour the mixture in a saucepan and bring to the boil over medium heat, whisking regularly to ensure it doesn't stick to the bottom. Reduce the heat to low and cook for 2–3 minutes until thick, whisking continuously. Transfer to a bowl and cover closely with plastic film. Leave to cool at room temperature.

For the vanilla crème anglaise, place the cream, milk and vanilla pods and seeds in a saucepan over medium heat and bring to the boil. Whisk together the egg yolks and sugar in a large bowl until combined, then pour the hot milk and cream mixture on top. Whisk together, then return the mixture to the pan over low heat. Cook, stirring with a wooden spoon, for about 3 minutes or until the anglaise coats the back of the spoon. Strain through a sieve into a bowl, then leave to cool in the fridge.

For the banana and passionfruit sorbet, place the sugar, glucose and 210 ml of water in a saucepan and bring to the boil. Once boiling, remove from the heat and set aside to cool. Place the bananas, passionfruit juice and orange juice in a blender and add the syrup. Blend until smooth, then transfer to an ice-cream machine to churn immediately.

Preheat the oven to 200°C.

To make the soufflé, lightly and evenly brush six 330 ml capacity soufflé moulds with the butter. Dust the moulds with sugar, shaking off any excess. Place the passionfruit base into a large bowl and whisk until totally smooth. Place the egg whites in the bowl of an electric mixer and begin to whisking on the fast setting. When the whites start foaming, slowly add the sugar and continue to whisk until just firm, then turn off immediately.

Add a quarter of the egg white to the passionfruit base and whisk together to combine. Gently fold in the remaining egg white using a spatula. Pipe the mixture into the moulds and flatten with a palette knife. Gently run your finger around the rim of soufflés to stop the edges sticking to the ramekin. Place in the oven and cook for 8 minutes or until risen and lightly golden.

To serve, place the anglaise in a jug and the sorbet in small bowls. Serve immediately with the soufflé.

Chestnut cream with Valrhona chocolate, cassis and pear purée

SERVES 4

Chestnut and chocolate is a classic French duo. In this stunning dish, created by my Sous Chef, Jeremy Pace, the combination is artfully lifted by the cassis. It is a complex dish to create at home, but your dinner guests will be so impressed by the results, it will be worth the effort! Valrhona chocolate and chestnut purée is available from good delicatessens. You can buy acetate for the chocolate cylinders at art-supply shops or specialist kitchenware stores.

1 beurre bosc pear, peeled and halved
200 g caster sugar
1 vanilla bean, split
125 g blackcurrants
20g pure icing sugar
300 g Valrhona Guanja chocolate, finely chopped
100 g blackcurrant purée
gold leaf, to decorate
8 candied chestnuts, diced
200 ml chestnut ice-cream (or vanilla-bean ice-cream)

CHESTNUT CREAM
250 g sweetened chestnut purée
1 cup (250 ml) pure cream
2 gold-strength gelatine sheets, soaked in iced water

For the chestnut cream, place the chestnut purée in a bowl. Bring 100 ml of cream to the boil in a saucepan. Remove from the heat, then stir in the gelatine until dissolved. Pour the cream over the chestnut purée. Allow to cool to room temperature. Meanwhile, whip the remaining cream until firm peaks form. Fold the whipped cream into the chestnut mixture and place in the fridge to set for at least 2 hours.

Place the pear in a saucepan with 200 ml of water and the sugar and vanilla bean and cover with a cartouche (see page 17). Bring to the boil, then reduce the heat to low. Cook for 20 minutes or until soft. Remove the pear from the liquid with a slotted spoon. Remove the core and seeds, then place in a blender. Blend until smooth, then transfer to a squeezy bottle.

Combine the blackcurrants and icing sugar in a blender and blend until smooth. Strain through a fine sive, then set aside.

Using scissors, cut two A4 sheets of acetate into nine 20 × 10 cm rectangles. (This is more than you will need but it's better to have a few extra in case the chocolate cylinders break.) With one short side facing you, roll the cylinders up so they are 3 cm in diameter, then secure with tape along the join.

Place 200 g of chocolate in a heatproof bowl over a saucepan and cook over very low heat until the chocolate reaches 45°C on a thermometer. Make sure the water does not boil or the chocolate will overheat; the water surface should be barely moving. When the chocolate has come to temperature, remove it from the heat and stir until completely melted and smooth. Add the remaining chocolate, then stir with a rubber spatula until the chocolate cools down to 27°C. Return the chocolate to the heat and stir until shiny and the temperature increases to 32°C. The chocolate is now ready to pour into the cylinders.

Pour the chocolate into a small jug. Working with one at a time, hold each acetate cylinder upright but on an angle and pour in enough chocolate to coat the inside, turning as you pour. Place on a wire rack in a cool place until set, then remove the chocolate from the cylinders.

Spoon the chestnut cream into a piping bag fitted with a 1.5 cm nozzle. Pipe it into the chocolate cylinder until full, then smooth the ends. Place a small dot of cream on the plate to hold the cylinder. Decorate the cylinder with the gold leaf. Dot the pear purée and blackcurrant purée down the plate. Place the diced chestnuts alongside. Quenelle the ice-cream and place on top of the chestnut.

HEMMES
Family

Justin Hemmes is a paradox. Arguably Sydney's most influential restauranteur and hotelier, he is responsible for the city's most beautiful, luxurious and exciting party destinations and restaurants. Unsurprisingly, his life is indeed glamorous: think Sir Terence Conran meets André Balazs meets James Bond. Yet here I am at chez Hemmes, and instead of drinking a marathon of margaritas (or martinis shaken not stirred), Justin is in the kitchen brewing mint tea. Meanwhile, I am getting up close and personal with two of his birds – a couple of silky chickens called White Russian and Black Russian. 'My great joy is rustling around my chicken coop collecting eggs,' says Justin. 'I also have a wonderful veggie patch and herb garden.'

As CEO of Merivale, Hemmes runs a growing portfolio of more than 50 restaurants, pubs, bars, hotels and function spaces across Sydney, including ivy, est., Hemmesphere and Felix, to name just a few. He is a bona fide perfectionist, verging on the obsessive, and thrives on the adrenaline that comes from creating new million-dollar ventures from a single idea. Justin effortlessly brings international flavours to his venues – when you visit them, you feel instantly transported to London, New York, Paris, Miami or Mexico. Yet it is Sydney that always enjoys top billing, a city Justin firmly calls 'the best in the world'. 'I've travelled extensively both for pleasure and work, yet I still can't find a city that rivals Sydney,' he says. 'You can work in the CBD, then drive to the beach and within ten minutes you are swimming in our beautiful ocean.'

Justin's parents, Merivale and John Hemmes (who Justin calls a 'loving and powerful influence') were adamant that he understand the hospitality industry from the ground up. 'Dad wanted me to know all the different aspects behind a business,' Justin says. 'So after uni I went to work at their old Potts Point restaurant, first as a dish hand, then as a waiter and barista. To understand figures I did the bookkeeping on the weekend. When I started my first venture, Dad put me to work onsite for eighteen months as a brickie's labourer. I didn't get it at the time and of course being in my twenties I would have preferred being with my mates having fun, but now I see the lessons – hard work, stamina and, most importantly, knowing and understanding your business. That's what breeds success and longevity and ultimately keeps you humble.'

The hard work and training has paid off. The Merivale empire under Justin's leadership is not only growing but thriving. 'I have never measured success by just looking at the bank balance. I like the idea of building something. Ultimately it is the creative side that I find the most rewarding,' he says.

Family has always played an integral part in Justin's life. He eats with them once a week and often invites close friends to join in. Justin loves to have fun with all different types of cuisine, as seen with ventures Mr Wong and the Mexican cantina El Loco, and at home he tends towards simple and organic, grazing-type dishes. 'When I have family and friends here, I like lots of big platters so guests can help themselves,' he says. 'I live a frenetic life so I want everything to feel easy and relaxed at home. I like how my kitchen allows me to interact with my guests. I would hate to be closeted away cooking on my own!'

Justin lives at The Hermitage, an expansive waterfront property at Vaucluse. His home has a laidback feel, the natural materials giving it warmth and texture. Guests arrive after 12.30 pm and mill around the kitchen, enjoying gin and tonics with lime. Some wander out into the garden and soak up the spectacular and uninterrupted Harbour views. Merivale sits on the couch as Thunder, Justin's beloved dog, laps up her undivided attention.

For today's lunch I have been guided by Justin's love of variety and the menu is quite the smorgasbord: mud crab, ceviche of snapper, prawns with romesco sauce, artichoke barigoule, roast chicken and baby kipflers with black truffle, roasted root veg . . . And finally dessert, a trifle of raspberry and pistachio.

An air of informality reigns as guests grab plates, top up wine, change music and chat around the dining table. Justin's entertaining philosophy at home is one I very much admire – the *casa mia è casa tua* style (or in my lingo *ma maison et votre maison*). And I must admit come late afternoon, it's hard to peel myself away from the view and leave this wonderful sanctuary that Justin has created. 'I work really hard,' Justin says, 'but I don't let that distract me from what is important. My family, my friends, my dog – they count the most. They are my happiness.'

MENU

———+———

Anchovy, buffalo mozzarella and basil baguette

Mud crab with avocado cream and finger lime

Ceviche of snapper with pomegranate and chilli

Split prawns with romesco sauce

Artichoke barigoule

Roast chicken with black truffle and baby kipflers

Roasted root vegetables with truffle

Raspberry and pistachio trifle

Anchovy, buffalo mozzarella and basil baguette

SERVES 6

This simple recipe is all about top-quality ingredients. I like to use Ortiz anchovies and Iggy's bread. This is a great starter – and it's also a perfect late-night top-up dish if you're hosting drinks and canapés.

1 thin baguette, cut into 6 portions
1 × 110 g ball buffalo mozzarella, each cut into 6 slices
6 large basil leaves
6 high-quality anchovies
extra virgin olive oil, to drizzle
cracked black pepper

Slice the baguettes open. Arrange a slice of mozzarella on the base of each baguette slice and top with a basil leaf. Add an anchovy to each and drizzle over the extra virgin olive oil. Season with cracked black pepper. Enclose with the baguette tops and serve.

36

Mud crab with avocado cream and finger lime

SERVES 6

Mud crab has to be my favourite crab. You'll need to buy two whole crabs for this dish and pick the meat from the cooked crabs, as the meat isn't sold separately. If you prefer something easier to prepare, you can just buy blue swimmer or spanner crab meat instead – the dish will still be delicious.

500 g mud crab meat, picked to remove any shell
2 golden shallots, finely diced
2 tablespoons mayonnaise
50 g finger limes, split (or ruby grapefruit, segmented)
½ bunch coriander, leaves finely chopped
juice of ½ lime
baby coriander, to garnish

AVOCADO CREAM
2 avocados, peeled and pitted
100 ml milk
juice of ½ lime
3 drops of tabasco
sea salt and cracked black pepper

For the avocado cream, place the avocado, milk, lime and tabasco in a blender and season with salt and pepper. Blend until smooth, then pass through a fine sieve.

Combine the crab meat, shallot, mayonnaise, finger lime (or grapefruit) and coriander in a bowl. Add the lime juice and mix well.

Spoon the avocado cream onto a serving plate and arrange the crab mixture on top. Garnish with baby coriander.

Ceviche of snapper with pomegranate and chilli

SERVES 6

You'll need sashimi-grade snapper for this elegant starter. Some advice though: snapper can be difficult to slice when raw, so you may want to ask your fishmonger to do it for you.

1 side (700 g) sashimi-grade snapper, thinly sliced
1 pomegranate, seeds removed, juice reserved
2 red chillies, seeded and finely diced
juice of 1 lime
2 tablespoons extra virgin olive oil
1 bunch coriander, leaves finely chopped
sea salt
baby coriander, to garnish

Lay the snapper on the serving plate. Place the pomegranate seeds, chilli and lime juice in a bowl, then add the pomegranate juice and extra virgin olive oil and mix to combine. Add the chopped coriander. Pour the pomegranate, chilli and lime dressing over the snapper.

Sprinkle with salt and baby coriander and serve immediately.

Split prawns with romesco sauce

SERVES 6

I love serving fresh prawns with vibrant romesco sauce. Bursting with flavour, it features classic Spanish ingredients such as smoked paprika and sherry vinegar. Any leftover sauce will keep for up to a week in the fridge; it also goes well with chicken.

18 prawns, shells on, head removed
olive oil, for brushing
chopped flat-leaf parsley, to garnish

ROMESCO SAUCE
2 red capsicums (peppers)
100 ml olive oil
4 roma (plum) tomatoes, halved
100 g roasted blanched almonds
1 teaspoon smoked paprika
1 teaspoon garlic powder
1 teaspoon sherry vinegar
⅓ cup (80 ml) olive oil

Preheat the oven to 180°C.

For the romesco sauce, place the capsicums on a baking tray and baste with 1 tablespoon of olive oil. Place the tomatoes on a baking tray, cut-side down. Roast the tomatoes for about 30 minutes until soft, and the capsicum for about 40 minutes until slightly blackened. Transfer the capsicum to a bowl, cover with plastic film and leave to cool a little, then peel off the skins and remove the seeds. Pat dry with paper towel. Leave the tomatoes to cool and then peel off the skins.

Blend the almonds in a food processor to a chunky paste, then transfer to a large bowl and set aside.

Place the roasted capsicum and tomato in a food processor and blend until almost smooth. Add the paprika, garlic powder and vinegar and slowly drizzle in the remaining olive oil with the motor running. Add the capsicum mixture to the blitzed almonds and fold them together.

Split the prawns in half and remove the legs using scissors. Brush with olive oil and place on a barbecue grill-plate or in a chargrill pan over medium–high heat. Grill, flesh-side down, for 2 minutes or until almost cooked through, then turn the prawns over and leave for 30 seconds. Remove from the grill and brush with the romesco sauce. Garnish with parsley and serve.

Artichoke barigoule

SERVES 6

Barigoule is a classic Provençal dish made by braising artichokes with white wine,
white wine vinegar, vegetables and herbs. I like to use broad beans in my version,
as they add a lovely colour and texture.

12 globe artichokes
a squeeze of lemon juice
50 ml olive oil
1 carrot, peeled and cut into 2 cm dice
1 stick celery, peeled and cut into 2 cm dice
2 golden shallots, cut into 2 cm dice
½ leek, cut into 2 cm dice
150 ml white wine vinegar
600 ml white wine
2 sprigs thyme
1 bay leaf
1 teaspoon white peppercorns
200 g broad beans, podded
100 ml extra virgin olive oil

To prepare the artichokes, remove the outer green leaves, then peel the stem. At the top of the heart cut off the leaves with a bread knife and scoop out the furry choke. Place the peeled artichokes in a bowl of water with lemon juice until ready for cooking.

Heat the olive oil in a large saucepan over medium heat. Add the carrot, celery, shallot and leek and sweat for 3 minutes, then add the artichokes. Pour in the vinegar and reduce for 5 minutes, then add the wine, thyme, bay leaf and peppercorns. Cover with a cartouche (see page 17) and simmer for about 40 minutes or until the artichokes are just tender. Leave to cool in their cooking liquid.

Bring a large saucepan of water to the boil and blanch the broad beans for 2 minutes. Remove from the pan and chill in iced water. When cold, drain and shell the beans.

Remove the artichokes from their cooking liquid and arrange on a serving platter. Strain the cooking liquid and pour 100 ml into a bowl, discarding the rest. Add the extra virgin olive oil and whisk to combine, then add the broad beans and coat well. Dress the artichokes with the broad bean and olive oil mixture, and serve.

Roast chicken with black truffle and baby kipflers

SERVES 8

What a truly indulgent dish, just perfect for a special occasion! Truffles appear in abundance in this recipe: gently pushed under the chicken skin, shaved over the top, and also served with the accompanying potatoes. Luckily, in Australia we are very fortunate to have access to world-class truffles. I source mine from Truffle and Wine Co, a Western Australian company that supplies truffles to restaurants all over the world.

2 × 1.8 kg chickens
50 g black truffle, thinly sliced, plus extra to garnish (optional)
2 cloves garlic, halved
1 bunch thyme, in sprigs
50 ml olive oil
sea salt and cracked white pepper

BABY KIPFLERS
1 kg small kipfler potatoes
⅓ cup (80 ml) olive oil
1 head of garlic, cloves separated
¼ bunch thyme, in sprigs
sea salt and cracked white pepper

Preheat the oven to 200°C.

Pat the chickens dry with paper towel. Lift the skin away from the flesh and gently slide truffle slices under the skin on each breast. Place two half cloves of garlic into each cavity. Divide the thyme sprigs between the cavities.

Place the chickens in a roasting tin, rub in the olive oil and season with salt and pepper. Roast for 1 hour or until the juices run clear. Remove the chicken from the oven and leave to rest for 20 minutes before carving.

Meanwhile, combine the potatoes, olive oil, garlic cloves and thyme, and season with salt and pepper. Place on a baking tray and roast for about 50 minutes or until cooked through, then serve with the chicken. Garnish with more truffle, if you like.

Roasted root vegetables with truffle

SERVES 6

Truffle is the star of this side dish. I keep everything else simple, flavouring the vegetables with just garlic and thyme, to let the truffle really shine.

4 carrots, peeled and cut into batons
1 large head celeriac, peeled and cut into batons
4 parsnips, peeled and cut into batons
⅓ cup (80 ml) olive oil
½ bunch thyme, in sprigs
1 head of garlic, cloves separated
sea salt and cracked black pepper
50 g black truffle, shaved

Preheat the oven to 180°C.

Place the vegetables on a baking tray and add the olive oil, thyme and garlic. Season with salt and pepper and mix thoroughly. Roast for 1 hour or until the vegetables are tender.

Remove from the oven and remove the thyme and garlic. Serve with shaved black truffle.

Raspberry and pistachio trifle

SERVES 10–12

This irresistible dessert seems to be universally adored whenever I make it – people tend to ask for seconds … and then thirds! You'll need to start preparing this well in advance: make the gateaux, jelly and vanilla cream first, then assemble the trifle the following day, before leaving it all to set. But I promise your guests' delight will make all the effort worthwhile.

3 × 125 g punnets raspberries

PISTACHIO GATEAUX
250 g unsalted butter, at room temperature
200 g caster sugar
1 vanilla bean, split and seeds scraped
50 g pistachio paste
150 g marzipan
4 eggs
250 g ground pistachios
75 g almond meal
½ teaspoon salt
50 ml kirsch

RASPBERRY JELLY
750 g fresh or frozen raspberries
100 g caster sugar
5 gold-strength gelatine sheets

VANILLA CREAM
500 g thickened cream
500 g crème patissiere (see page 159)

RASPBERRY PURÉE
500 g fresh or frozen raspberries
25 g pure icing sugar

Preheat the oven to 160°C and line two 25 cm springform cake tins with baking paper.

To make the pistachio gateaux, place the butter, sugar and vanilla seeds in the bowl of an electric mixer with a paddle attachment. Mix until the mixture is pale and fluffy, then add the pistachio paste and marzipan and mix to combine. Add the eggs one at a time, beating well between each addition. When incorporated, add the ground pistachios, almond meal and salt. Slowly mix in the kirsch. Once everything is incorporated, transfer the mixture to the prepared tins. Bake for 35 minutes or until a skewer inserted into the centre comes out clean. Once cooked, remove from the tins but leave on the bases and allow to cool. Place in the fridge and leave to set overnight.

Meanwhile, to make the raspberry jelly, combine the raspberries and sugar in a heatproof bowl and cover tightly with plastic film. Bring a small saucepan of water to a very gentle simmer and set the bowl of raspberries and sugar on top. Simmer for about 2 hours to release all the juice from the raspberries, topping up the water in the saucepan if it runs dry. Strain the raspberry juice into a bowl, pressing down to extract as much juice as possible. Soak the gelatine in iced water, and when soft squeeze out as much excess liquid as possible and add to the juice. Stir until well dissolved. Place the jelly in the bottom of a trifle bowl about 28 cm in diameter at the top and 15 cm high. Place in the fridge to set.

For the vanilla cream, whip the thickened cream until soft peaks form. Place the crème patisserie in a separate bowl and whip until smooth. Fold the thickened cream into the crème patissiere.

For the raspberry purée, place the raspberries and icing sugar in blender and blend until smooth. Strain through a fine sieve, pressing down to extract as much liquid as possible, then discard the seeds.

To assemble the trifle, cut around one of the cakes so that it fits on top of the jelly and place it on top. Follow with a layer of vanilla cream, then the raspberry purée. Cut the other piece of gateaux to fit on top, then finish with a layer of cream. Allow to set in the fridge for 3 hours. Decorate with fresh raspberries just before serving.

Shortly after arriving in Sydney as a young French chef, I had the privilege of meeting a family who have left a lasting and indelible mark on my life. My first impression of John Ryan was of a strapping man, both charismatic and self-assured, who just couldn't resist a good ribbing from the sidelines. Through the well-worn avenue of football, John introduced me to many of his friends and my moniker Guillaume quickly became Gui Gui. Struggling with little English but immediately understanding the currency of Crown lager and Toss the Boss, I spent many happy and carefree nights getting to know a bunch of Aussie lads who would become lifelong mates.

I soon met John's parents, Peter and Toni, and siblings Julian, Patrick and Amber. For more than 50 years, Peter has run a thriving hotel and pub business, which his sons John and Patrick have now expanded in and around Sydney. Mother Toni, as beautiful today as she was when I first met her 20-odd years ago, is the matriarch of a close and loving family. My life really changed course when I met my future wife, Sanchia, at one of Toni and Peter's famous Christmas parties. John was appointed Best Man at our wedding and godfather to our first child, Constance, a role he has taken on with great love and affection.

Being of Irish Catholic stock, the Ryan clan is a large one. Toni and Peter's children have expanded the family with the introduction of eleven grandchildren. The Ryans break bread often, always coming together to celebrate a family member's birthday, anniversary or Holy Communion. And of course the family comes together at Christmas time, either at Toni and Peter's home or on a rotating system among their children. However, as Toni explains, they often just have lunch on a Sunday 'just so we can put something in the diary and all catch up together'.

This particular get-together falls at Easter and Toni has planned a delicious menu. My job is to put my French flair to work, but really Toni's recipes are near perfect and I love how they are born from family members, past and present. Toni litters the document with personal notes such as 'Mummy's turkey stuffing', and son-in-law Derek's 'Irish soda bread, which I serve with Patrick's smoked salmon entrée'.

Guests make their way to a table heavily laden with food. The younger children are encouraged by Toni to 'try a bit of everything', which they do – lobster and leek terrine with tarragon vinaigrette, roast turkey with truffle, foie gras and thyme and a delicious glazed ham. Sides include a sweet potato, parmesan and sage gratin and an iceberg salad with radish, tomato and herbs. As there are kids galore today, we prepare two desserts: a frozen lemon nougat with walnut praline and raspberries and an apple tarte tatin with vanilla crème anglaise. Dessert is served outside on the terrace and the little ones head to the garden in search of Easter eggs.

Toni loves a full house. 'I love seeing the grandchildren and with eleven, when we get together as a family I have to think big,' she says. 'But I never stress too much – it's spending time together that's important, not that someone got chocolate on the sofa!' At a Ryan gathering there will always be much laughter and merriment, good food and chilled drinks. Adults talk well into the night, children run around, or enjoy a twilight swim, teenage cousins disappear for some gossip, toddlers doze in parents laps. The sun sets on what has been another Perfect Ryan Family Get-Together . . .

MENU

—+—

Lobster and leek terrine with tarragon vinaigrette

Glazed ham

Roast turkey with truffle, foie gras and thyme

Sweet potato, parmesan and sage gratin

Iceberg salad with radish, tomato and herbs

Kipfler potato salad with speck

Frozen lemon nougat with walnut praline and raspberries

Apple tarte tatin with vanilla crème anglaise

Poppy seed lavosh

Lobster and leek terrine with tarragon vinaigrette

SERVES 12

If you're looking for an impressive dish for a special occasion, this is the one. It requires patience and skill, but it is truly stunning. You'll need to begin it two days in advance, making the stock two days before, and then assembling the terrine the day before serving in order to allow it to set. Tarragon is a wonderful accompaniment to seafood and this vinaigrette is delicious drizzled over fish for an easy dinner.

8 small lobsters
4 large leeks, trimmed
24 baby leeks, trimmed
olive oil, for greasing

LOBSTER JELLY

8 lobster heads and legs, reserved from above
2 tablespoons olive oil
2 onions, chopped
2 carrots, peeled and chopped
3 celery sticks, chopped
5 ripe roma (plum) tomatoes, chopped
2 tablespoons tomato paste (purée)
2 bay leaves
½ bunch thyme, in sprigs
½ bunch tarragon, leaves picked
1 teaspoon white peppercorns
4½ gold-strength gelatine sheets

TARRAGON VINAIGRETTE

1 tablespoon dijon mustard
2 tablespoons white wine vinegar
1 bunch tarragon, leaves picked and finely chopped
200 ml extra virgin olive oil

First place the lobsters in the freezer for an hour to put them to sleep. Place each lobster on a chopping board and insert a sharp, heavy knife through the head. Run the knife around the top of the tail and head of the lobster to separate them. Push a butter knife down the bottom side of the lobster tail in between the shell and the meat to keep the tail straight. (Keep the knife in place as when you cook the lobster tail it prevents curling.)

Bring a large saucepan of water to the boil over high heat. Add the lobster tails and cook for 6 minutes, then remove from the pan and place in iced water to chill. Break the shell and peel the lobster tails, then place them on a tea towel to dry. Slice the tails in half straight down the middle, then place them in the fridge.

To make the lobster jelly, coarsely chop the lobster heads and legs into 2 cm pieces. Heat the olive oil in a large saucepan over high heat. Add the lobster heads and legs and sweat for 5–10 minutes or until the shells change colour, then add the onion, carrot, celery and tomato. Cook for 10 minutes until everything is nicely coloured, then add the tomato paste, reduce the heat to medium and cook for a further 3 minutes. Add the bay leaves, thyme, tarragon and peppercorns. Add 1.5 litres of cold water and bring to the boil, then reduce the heat and simmer for 30 minutes, skimming the top occasionally. Remove from the heat. Strain the stock though a fine sieve and leave for 30 minutes at room temperature. Set aside 2 cups (500 ml) of stock and freeze the remainder for another use.

Soak the gelatine in iced water. Heat 100 ml of the reserved stock, add the gelatine and stir until dissolved. Add to the remaining 400 ml of stock. Set the jelly aside at room temperature to cool completely.

Chop off the green top of the large leeks, leaving the leeks about 15 cm in length. To remove the outside leaves of the leek (these will line the terrine mould), using a knife, slice down the length of the leek and around the circumference of the base but only half the depth. Carefully remove the leaves to keep them as large as possible and in one piece. Bring a large saucepan of water to the boil over high heat. Add salt and then the separated leek leaves. Boil for 2–3 minutes, or just until starting to soften. Place them in iced water to refresh. Place the baby leeks and the peeled large leeks in the boiling water and cook for 3 minutes or until tender. Remove and place in iced water. Remove and drain the leek leaves and place them on a chopping board. Use the back of a knife to scrape the inside skin, until the leek is very thin. Place on a tea towel to dry. Remove and drain the baby leeks and the peeled leeks, squeezing firmly but gently to remove as much excess water as possible. Place on a tea towel to drain.

Lightly grease a 30 cm × 8 cm terrine mould with olive oil, then line with plastic film leaving the sides overhanging. Lay the leek leaves across the terrine mould, slightly overlapping

and ensuring there are no gaps, leaving the leek overhanging. Add 3 tablespoons of lobster jelly mixture, then add six halves of the lobster tails, with as few gaps as possible. Add another 5 tablespoons of jelly, until the lobster is covered. Add 12 baby leeks, again leaving as few gaps as possible, and then cover with jelly. Repeat this process with another layer of lobster and jelly, and then the remaining leeks and jelly. Pour in any remaining jelly at the end to make sure all is covered, and then fold over the leek to encase the terrine. Bring the sides of the plastic film up to cover the top, then place a piece of cardboard on the terrine with a carton of milk on top as a weight. Place in the fridge for at least 12 hours to set.

To make the tarragon vinaigrette, place the mustard, vinegar and tarragon in a bowl and slowly whisk in the olive oil.

To serve, remove the terrine from the mould and slice. Serve with tarragon vinaigrette.

Glazed ham

SERVES 14

I recommend buying the best-quality ham you can afford for this. I love using Kurobuta Berkshire ham as its flavour is simply incomparable. And take your time with scoring the fat: keeping the diagonals even makes all the difference to the presentation.

200 g brown sugar
40 g dijon mustard
2 tablespoons maple syrup
1 tablespoon sherry vinegar
7 kg ham, skin removed
1 tablespoon cloves

Preheat the oven to 170°C.

Combine the sugar, mustard, maple syrup and vinegar in a bowl to make a glaze.

Diagonally score the fat of the ham to create diamond shapes all over the surface. Place the ham on a baking tray and brush all over with the glaze. Spike a clove into each diamond.

Roast the ham for 1 hour and 30 minutes, brushing with the glaze every half an hour. Remove from the oven and allow to rest for 30 minutes before carving.

Roast turkey with truffle, foie gras and thyme

SERVES 8

The Ryan family love French food and travel annually to Paris to enjoy its culinary delights, as well as its beauty. This stuffing is very French – and very rich! Once you have stuffed the turkey, make sure you cross the legs and tie them together tightly as this will help to keep the stuffing moist.

½ loaf day-old white bread, torn
4 golden shallots, diced
250 g foie gras, chopped into 1 cm dice
80 g black truffle, finely chopped
1 bunch thyme, leaves picked
1 × 6 kg turkey
50 ml olive oil
sea salt and cracked black pepper

Preheat the oven to 175°C.

Combine the bread, shallot, foie gras, truffle and thyme in a large bowl. Place the stuffing into the cavity of the turkey and truss the bird by crossing the legs over and tying them together with twine.

Place the stuffed turkey in a roasting tin and pour over the olive oil. Season with salt and pepper and roast for 2 hours.

Rest the turkey for 30 minutes before carving and serving.

Sweet potato, parmesan and sage gratin

SERVES 12

A classic gratin with a twist. You can of course use regular potato if you're not a fan of the sweet variety, and you can also substitute the parmesan for gruyere, which gives a lovely nutty flavour. Unless you have exceptional knife skills, I suggest using a mandolin to slice the potato: even slices will cook consistently, yielding superior results.

1.5 litres pouring cream
1 bunch sage, leaves picked
5 sweet potatoes, peeled and thinly sliced using a mandolin
sea salt and cracked black pepper
200 g parmesan, finely grated

Preheat the oven to 170°C.

Place the cream and sage leaves in a saucepan and bring to the boil over medium heat. Remove the pan from the heat and set the cream aside to infuse.

Line the base of a baking dish with a layer of sliced sweet potato. Ladle 100 ml of cream over the sweet potato, then pick a couple of sage leaves from the cream and place them on top. Season, then add another layer of sweet potato, ladle over more cream and sprinkle with parmesan. Repeat, alternating between sage leaves and parmesan. When you reach the final layer of sweet potato, pour over the remaining cream, decorate with sage leaves and sprinkle with the remaining parmesan.

Cover the top layer with baking paper. Bake for 1 hour or until top is golden and the potato layers are tender, then serve.

Iceberg salad with radish, tomato and herbs

SERVES 8

This light and crunchy salad helps to cut through the creaminess of the accompanying mains!

1 iceberg lettuce, cut into chunks and leaves separated
1 × 250 g punnet cherry tomatoes, halved
1 bunch radishes, thinly sliced
2 bunches chives, trimmed and cut into 2 cm lengths
1 bunch flat-leaf parsley, leaves picked
⅓ cup (80 ml) Shallot vinaigrette (see Basics)

Place the lettuce, tomato, radish, chives and parsley in a bowl, dress with the shallot vinaigrette and toss gently to coat. Serve.

Kipfler potato salad with speck

SERVES 12

The Ryans serve Julia's potato salad every Easter. This is my version using kipflers, which I love for their nutty flavour and firm texture. It is important that the potatoes are cold when you dress them, otherwise the mayonnaise may split, so make sure they are well-chilled: you could even cook them the day before.

2 kg small kipfler potatoes
1½ tablespoons olive oil
400 g speck, sliced into matchsticks
6 eggs
200 g mayonnaise
20 g seeded mustard
¼ bunch spring onions, green parts thinly sliced
1 bunch flat-leaf parsley, leaves finely sliced

Place the potatoes in a large saucepan, cover with cold water and add salt. Bring to the boil and cook for 20 minutes or until tender. Drain the potatoes and when cool enough to handle, peel them and leave in the fridge to chill.

Heat the olive oil in a frying pan over medium heat. Add the speck and fry for 5 minutes until coloured all over. Remove from the pan and place on paper towel to drain.

Place the eggs in a large saucepan, cover with cold water and bring to the boil. Once at boiling point, boil the eggs for 8 minutes, then remove them from the pan and place them under cold running water. Once cold, peel the eggs and cut them into quarters.

Combine the mayonnaise and mustard. Slice the potatoes into 3 cm pieces.

Place the potato, speck and egg in a large bowl. Add the mustard mayonnaise and mix well to coat. Add the spring onion and parsley and toss again. Serve.

Frozen lemon nougat with walnut praline and raspberries

SERVES 12

This recipe is inspired by Toni Ryan's exceptional cold lemon soufflé. You'll need to start this the day before to alllow the nougat to set. Garnish with the candied lemon slices just before serving, as they will drop over time.

5 × 125 g punnets raspberries

LEMON PURÉE
rind of 7 lemons, white pith removed
125 g caster sugar
juice of 2 lemons

FROZEN LEMON NOUGAT
2 cups (500 ml) thickened cream
2 gold-strength gelatine sheets
4 egg whites
150 g caster sugar
50 ml liquid glucose
100 g lemon purée (see above)

WALNUT PRALINE
150 g caster sugar
1½ cups (150 g) walnuts
sea salt

LEMON GARNISH
500 g caster sugar
3 lemons, sliced into very thin rounds

First, make the lemon purée. Place the lemon rind in a saucepan and cover with cold water. Bring to the boil over medium heat, then strain. Repeat twice more to remove any bitterness. Combine the lemon rind, sugar and 1 cup (250 ml) of water in a saucepan. Bring to the boil over medium heat, then reduce to a simmer and cook for 20 minutes. Remove from the heat and strain, reserving the rind and the liquid. Place the rind in a food processor with ⅓ cup (80 ml) of the reserved liquid and add ⅓ cup (80 ml) of water and the lemon juice. Blend to a smooth purée.

For the frozen lemon nougat, whip the cream until soft peaks form. Soak the gelatine in iced water. Place the egg whites in the heatproof bowl of an electric mixer. Place the sugar, glucose and 50 ml of water in a saucepan and bring to the boil over high heat. When the syrup reaches 118°C on a sugar thermometer, start whisking the egg whites. When the sugar reaches 121°C, pour the syrup over the egg whites. Add the soaked gelatine and whisk the mixture for about 8 minutes until cool. Fold in 100 g of the lemon purée and then the cream. Transfer the mixture to a 20 cm cake tin. Place in the freezer to set overnight.

The next day, make the walnut praline. Line a baking tray with baking paper. Place the sugar and 50 ml of water in a saucepan over high heat. Cook for 10 minutes, stirring occasionally, until the sugar turns to caramel. Stir in the walnuts and sprinkle with salt. Remove from the heat and pour over the prepared tray. Leave to cool for at least 1 hour. Once cold, roughly chop the praline into 5 mm pieces.

To make the lemon garnish, place the sugar and 2 cups (500 ml) of water in a saucepan and bring to the boil. Add the lemon slices, then reduce the heat to low and simmer for 20–30 minutes or until the lemons are nicely glazed. Remove from the syrup and place in the fridge to chill.

Arrange the walnut praline on a serving platter and place the frozen lemon nougat on top. Decorate the top with raspberries and the sides with glazed lemon slices.

Apple tarte tatin with vanilla crème anglaise

SERVES 8

The trick to achieving a lovely deep, rich colour for this tatin is to leave the apples to cool in, and absorb, the delicious caramel. If you prefer, you can serve this with a good-quality vanilla bean ice-cream instead of the anglaise.

12 small granny smith apples, peeled
200 g caster sugar
200 g butter
2 vanilla beans, split and seeds scraped, beans reserved
375 g puff pastry

VANILLA CRÈME ANGLAISE

1 cup (250 ml) milk
1 cup (250 ml) pure cream
4 vanilla beans, split and seeds scraped
5 egg yolks
⅓ cup (75 g) sugar

Cut the apples in half, then use a melon baller to remove the core, tip and bottom. Place 100 g of sugar in a large frying pan over medium–high heat, and when it begins to colour, stir it to ensure it colours evenly. When the sugar is dark, add half of the butter and vanilla seeds, mix together for 1 minute and then add half of the apples. Coat the apples in caramel and cook for 5 minutes. Remove the apples from the pan and place in a heatproof container to cool in the caramel. Wash the pan clean and repeat with the remaining sugar, butter, vanilla seeds and apples.

Once the apples are cool enough to handle, pour the caramel into a 24 cm non-stick ovenproof frying pan. Place the reserved scraped vanilla beans on the bottom of the pan. Arrange the apples, cut-side up, on top in a circular pattern, packing them tightly. Leave to set in the fridge for 1 hour.

Meanwhile, to make the vanilla crème anglaise, place the milk, cream and vanilla seeds in a saucepan over medium heat and bring to the boil. In a bowl, whisk the egg yolks and sugar until combined. Pour the hot milk mixture over the eggs and sugar and stir to combine, then return the mixture to the pan. Cook over low heat for about 5 minutes, stirring continuously, until the custard coats the back of a wooden spoon. Remove from the heat and pass through a fine strainer, then place in the fridge to chill immediately.

Roll out the puff pastry into a 28 cm square about 5 mm thick and place over the apples in the pan, trimming the corners, then tucking the pastry down the side of the apples like you're tucking in a blanket. Return the tart to the fridge for at least 1 hour to set.

Preheat the oven to 180°C. Using a paring knife, place a 5 mm hole in the middle of the tarte tatin. Place the pan over high heat and when the caramel starts to bubble (about 4 minutes] remove the pan from the stovetop and place it in the oven. Bake for 25–30 minutes or until golden brown. Remove from the oven and leave to rest for 15 minutes, then carefully flip it over onto a serving plate.

Cut the tatin into wedges and serve with crème anglaise.

Poppy seed lavosh

SERVES 12

Making your own lavosh is easy – not to mention much cheaper and tastier than the bought variety! For the best finish, roll the dough through a pasta machine to achieve perfectly thin sheets.

325 g plain flour
1 teaspoon salt
1 teaspoon sugar
30 g butter
1 egg white
1 teaspoon poppy seeds

Place the flour, salt and sugar in the bowl of an electric mixer fitted with a dough hook. Add the butter and mix on medium speed, then slowly add 150 ml of water, mixing until the dough is smooth. Remove the dough from the bowl and wrap it in plastic film, then leave it in the fridge for at least 1 hour.

Preheat the oven to 190°C and grease a baking sheet.

Remove the dough from the fridge and roll it out. Pass it through a pasta machine, gradually reducing the settings until the dough is 2 mm thick.

Lay the rolled dough on the prepared baking sheet. Brush with egg white and sprinkle with poppy seeds. Bake for 8 minutes until lightly golden, then remove from the oven and leave to cool before breaking into small pieces.

HUSH

Family

As editor-in-chief of *Harper's BAZAAR*, Kellie Hush is a *tour de force* in the fashion industry. Prior to *BAZAAR*, Kellie was the editor of *Grazia* magazine, the fashion editor of *The Sydney Morning Herald*, and executive editor of *WHO Weekly* and *In Style*. She has a following of women who covet her every outfit, travels to Paris and Milan for the shows twice a year, and has received a dozen pink-hued roses from the Kaiser of Fashion, Karl Lagerfeld.

She is stylish, erudite and impressive, all the things that you would expect a fashion editor to be, but it is her warmth that makes Kellie so appealing. Her heels may be sky-high, but her feet are firmly on the ground. Her sense of style is 'classic with a twist'. Kellie exudes an air of getting things done – but doing so with a lot of panache.

As a chef, I live and breathe food, and Kellie, by her own admission, lives and breathes fashion. Over one long weekend in June, these two worlds collided (of course, very stylishly) at Kellie's beachside property in Mollymook, New South Wales.

Kellie and her husband David Bugg's house is one of those little hideaways you yearn to have, set just metres from the beach. It is what Kellie describes as 'cosy and low maintenance'. Mollymook is an absolute retreat from their busy professional lives. Their daughters, Amelia and Lola, are just young enough so the weekends are free from the rigours and restraints of Saturday-morning sport, so the family can be spontaneous. They sometimes head south just the four of them, or invite close friends who relish a break from city life.

*h*aving a drink on their deck before the other guests arrive, it isn't long before the conversation turns to 'who cooks'. My wife, Sanchia, volunteers that she has only ever cooked for me once (which was in fact in the last century, but I don't dare remind her of this). Kellie admits she too is no domestic goddess, and is more than happy that Dave has taken over the cooking duties for the family. She laughs, 'When Dave goes away on a surf trip, the girls ask me in alarm, "Who's going to cook?" I remind them that I *can* cook, just that Daddy enjoys it more than Mummy!'

Family life at home in Sydney's Eastern Suburbs is certainly busy but it's a pace that suits the pragmatic Kellie. 'When I get home I go straight into mum mode – is all the homework done, where's that form that needs signing, do we have fresh rolls and strawberries for lunch tomorrow? As any working mother will tell you, it's a juggling act. Some weeks I'm a master and other weeks all of the balls fall on the ground. You just have to try to keep your sense of humour.'

Kellie and Dave have invited their close friends to join them for a late lunch. The guests assemble on the deck ready for a glass of champagne and my tempura prawns. After setting the table for lunch, the white orchids in striking contrast with the orange hand-blown glass vases, Kellie disappears into the garden to prepare a relaxed but still *très chic* blue-and-white themed picnic for the children.

Lunch is a riotous affair, with topics ranging from the French rugby team to hotel misadventures and gastronomic-inspired surfing trips (and bucks nights!). The menu of ocean trout gravlax followed by snapper and mussel pie is inspired by Kellie's love of seafood. I've also prepared a braised lamb parmentier, and a selection of fresh salads and baby veg. The children are coaxed into eating their carrots when they hear mille feuille of poached quince and cinnamon ice-cream is on offer for dessert.

When the last of the snapper pie is cleared, Kellie, David and their friends head to the garden for a game of bocce and some cheese. Kellie reflects, 'Mollymook is no Milan but it really is my idea of heaven . . . that and a pair of Prada heels.'

MENU

—|—

Tempura prawns with soy mayonnaise and yuzu flakes

Ocean trout gravlax with celeriac remoulade and toasted sourdough

Snapper and mussel pie with baby vegetables, chervil and tarragon

Braised lamb shoulder parmentier

Beetroot and goat's cheese salad with pickled onions

Tabbouleh with chickpeas

Baby heirloom carrots

Mille feuille of poached quince and cinnamon ice-cream

Tempura prawns with soy mayonnaise and yuzu flakes

SERVES 8

Yuzu flakes, made from the Japanese yuzu fruit, bring a splash of citrus to this dish. They're available at Japanese supermarkets, but you can always use lemon or lime juice instead.

vegetable oil or canola oil, for deep-frying
16 large green (raw) prawns, peeled and deveined,
   tails intact
sea salt
yuzu flakes, for sprinkling

BATTER
60 g Trisol (see page 22)
65 g plain flour
small pinch of yeast
pinch of salt
pinch of sugar

SOY MAYONNAISE
1 tablespoon soy sauce
¼ cup (75 g) mayonnaise

To make the batter, combine the Trisol, flour, yeast, salt and sugar in a bowl. Make a well in the centre and slowly whisk in 100 ml of water. Cover with plastic film and leave it to rest for at least 2 hours.

For the soy mayonnaise, whisk together the soy and mayonnaise and set aside in the fridge.

Pour the vegetable or canola oil into a deep-fryer or deep saucepan until two-thirds full and bring it to 175°C.

Dip the prawns into the batter, leaving the tail exposed, and allow the excess batter to drip off. Carefully lower the prawns into the oil and fry for 3 minutes or until golden brown, gently tossing them around to ensure they colour evenly. Remove the prawns from the oil and drain on paper towel.

Sprinkle the prawns with salt and yuzu flakes. Serve with the soy mayonnaise.

Ocean trout gravlax with celeriac remoulade and toasted sourdough

SERVES 8

Homemade gravlax is far superior to the bought variety. If you've never tried making it, give it a go. And if you really want to impress your guests, save the slicing until you have an audience.

8 slices sourdough, toasted
lemon slices, to serve
mâche, to serve

GRAVLAX
500 g caster sugar
500 g salt
100 ml gin
1 bunch dill, leaves roughly chopped
1 bunch chervil, leaves roughly chopped
1 bunch coriander, leaves roughly chopped
1 kg side of ocean trout, skin on, pin-boned

CELERIAC REMOULADE
1 celeriac, peeled and sliced into thin strips
¼ bunch flat-leaf parsley, leaves finely sliced
¼ cup (75 g) mayonnaise
juice of ¼ lemon

To make the gravlax, combine the sugar, salt, gin and herbs in a bowl. Place two sheets of plastic film, long enough to wrap the ocean trout in, on the work surface. Spread with half of the salt mixture. Place the ocean trout on top, skin-side down, and cover with the remaining salt mixture. Wrap tightly in plastic film, then place in a large, deep tray. Place a weight on top and refrigerate for 12 hours. Turn the fish over, place the weight on top and refrigerate for another 12 hours. Repeat again and leave for another 12 hours.

Wash the trout and pat it dry. Place on a chopping board at room temperature until serving.

For the celeriac remoulade, combine the celeriac and parsley in a bowl. Stir through the mayonnaise and lemon juice and mix to combine.

Thinly slice the ocean trout lengthways. Spoon the celeriac remoulade over the sourdough toast and top with a slice of gravlax. Serve with a slice of lemon and mâche.

Snapper and mussel pie with baby vegetables, chervil and tarragon

SERVES 8

This soulful dish is a great winter warmer. It can be easily prepared the day before
and then baked just before serving. Grab a glass of burgundy and enjoy.

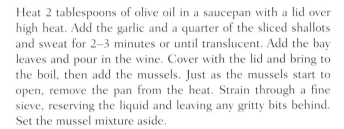

⅓ cup (80 ml) olive oil

4 cloves garlic, sliced

8 golden shallots, sliced

2 bay leaves

3 cups (750 ml) white wine

2 kg mussels, scrubbed and debearded

½ bunch thyme, in sprigs

600 ml pure cream

100 ml Noilly Prat

300 g crème fraîche

300 g baby potatoes

2 bunches baby leeks, trimmed

5 bulbs baby fennel, trimmed and each cut into 6 wedges

200 g fresh or frozen peas (about 470 g unpodded)

1 bunch chervil, leaves picked

1 bunch tarragon, leaves picked and chopped

8 × 140 g thick snapper fillets, skin and bones removed

500 g puff pastry

1 egg, lightly beaten

Heat 2 tablespoons of olive oil in a saucepan with a lid over high heat. Add the garlic and a quarter of the sliced shallots and sweat for 2–3 minutes or until translucent. Add the bay leaves and pour in the wine. Cover with the lid and bring to the boil, then add the mussels. Just as the mussels start to open, remove the pan from the heat. Strain through a fine sieve, reserving the liquid and leaving any gritty bits behind. Set the mussel mixture aside.

Wipe out the pan and place it back over high heat. Add the remaining olive oil and shallots and sweat for 2 minutes until soft. Add the reserved mussel liquid and the thyme and cook over medium–high heat for 30 minutes or until reduced by half. Add the cream and cook over medium heat for 30 minutes until reduced by half or to about 600 ml. Meanwhile, heat the Noilly Prat in a frying pan over high heat and cook for 10 minutes or until reduced by two-thirds.

Remove the saucepan from the heat and strain the sauce through a fine sieve, pressing to extract as much flavour as possible from the shallots and thyme. Discard the solids, then stir in the reduced Noilly Prat and the crème fraîche. Refrigerate the sauce until cold.

Place the potatoes in a saucepan and cover with cold water. Add salt and bring to the boil. Once the water boils, drain the potatoes, then halve and leave to cool.

Bring a saucepan of water to the boil over high heat and add salt. Blanch the leeks for 30 seconds, then refresh in iced water and drain. Blanch the fennel for 30 seconds, then refresh in iced water and drain. Blanch the peas for 10 seconds, then refresh and drain.

Remove the mussel meat from the shells and place it in a large bowl with the potato, leeks, fennel, peas, chervil and tarragon. Pour over half of the sauce and mix well. Place three-quarters of the mixture in a large baking dish about 33 cm × 22 cm (or two smaller dishes about 22 cm round) and lay the snapper fillets on top in a single layer. Add the remaining mixture and pour over the remaining sauce. Roll out the puff pastry on a lightly floured surface until large enough to cover the dish with the sides overlapping. Place the pastry over the fish and press down the sides to seal well. Brush the puff pastry all over with beaten egg. Place the pie in the fridge to rest for 30 minutes.

Preheat the oven to 180°C. Bake the pie for 45 minutes or until hot in the centre. Serve.

Braised lamb shoulder parmentier

SERVES 12

This is my French version of shepherd's pie, in which I braise the lamb shoulder and then pull the meat apart. I actually prepared this just for the kids as an alternative to the snapper pie, but all the guests, young and old, ended up digging in!

⅓ cup (80 ml) olive oil
sea salt and cracked black pepper
2 kg lamb shoulder
2 onions, chopped
4 carrots, peeled, 2 chopped, 2 finely diced
5 sticks celery, 2 chopped, 3 finely diced
1 head of garlic, cut in half
2 litres chicken stock
1 bunch thyme, sprigs separated
4 bay leaves
5 golden shallots, finely diced
100 g parmesan, grated

POTATO PURÉE
1.4 kg desiree potatoes
sea salt
120 ml milk
100 g butter

Preheat the oven to 150°C.

Place a large saucepan over high heat and when hot add 2 tablespoons of olive oil. Season the lamb and place it in the pan. Seal on each side for 4 minutes or until brown, then transfer to a casserole dish. Add another tablespoon of olive oil to the pan. Add the onion and the chopped carrots, celery and garlic and sauté for 4 minutes or until brown and translucent. Add the chicken stock and bring to the boil.

Pour the stock and vegetables over the lamb in the casserole dish and add the thyme and bay leaves. Cover with a lid, then place in the oven and cook for at least 3 hours or until the lamb is falling off the bone. Once cooked, break off the meat and place it in a large bowl or saucepan. Strain the cooking liquid into a saucepan (discarding the herbs and veg) and reduce over high heat for approximately 30 minutes until it reaches a sauce consistency.

Place a frying pan over medium heat and add the remaining olive oil. Add the shallot, diced carrot and celery and sauté for 4 minutes until soft. Add the sauce and bring to the boil. Pour the mixture over the lamb and use a large spoon or your hands to combine.

For the potato purée, place the unpeeled potatoes in a large saucepan and cover with cold water. Add a pinch of salt and bring to the boil, then reduce the heat and simmer for 25–30 minutes. (Test the potatoes by piercing them with a sharp knife. If they are ready, the blade will come out clean with no residue.) Drain well. Peel the potatoes while they are still hot, using a tea towel to protect your hands. Pass the peeled potatoes through a mouli and then a sieve. Place in a saucepan and use a wooden spoon to stir the mash until all the moisture is removed (you want the potato to be dry to the touch). Bring the milk to the boil, then reduce the heat to a simmer. Place the mashed potato over low heat and add a quarter of the butter, stirring until combined. Add a quarter of the milk and stir until combined. Repeat until three-quarters of the butter and milk has been added and the mash is creamy and light, then pass it through a sieve.

When you are ready to cook the lamb, place the mash in a saucepan and warm it over low heat. When warm, add the remaining milk and butter and beat to combine. Season with salt to taste.

Preheat the oven to 180°C. Transfer the lamb mixture to a pie dish and spoon over the potato purée. Sprinkle with the parmesan. Bake the lamb parmentier for 1 hour or until the lamb is hot in the centre and the purée is golden brown on top. Serve.

Beetroot and goat's cheese salad with pickled onions

SERVES 8

Everybody should have a good beetroot salad recipe in their cooking repertoire, and this is a favourite of mine. Be mindful of the presentation here: don't mix the salad once the red beetroot has been added as the colour will bleed, and add the cheese right at the end so that it retains its creamy whiteness.

3 bunches baby beetroot
2 bunches golden beetroot
40 g walnuts, roughly chopped
¼ cup (60 ml) extra virgin olive oil
sea salt and cracked black pepper
100 g goat's cheese, crumbled
1 × 100 g punnet mâche

PICKLED ONIONS
1 cup (250 ml) balsamic vinegar
250 g caster sugar
8 pickling onions

Preheat the oven to 180°C.

Wrap the beetroots separately in foil. Roast for 50 minutes or until tender, then peel the beetroots while they are still warm. Cut them into halves or quarters and set aside.

For the pickled onions, place the balsamic vinegar, sugar and 1 cup (250 ml) of water in a saucepan and bring to the boil. Add the onions and cover with a cartouche (see page 17). Reduce the heat and simmer for 20 minutes or until the onions are tender when pierced with the tip of the knife. Leave the onions to cool in the liquid before cutting them into quarters. Reserve the pickling liquid.

Place the beetroot in a bowl. Add the walnuts and pickled onions, along with 2 tablespoons of the pickling liquid. Pour over the olive oil and toss to combine. Season with salt and pepper. Transfer to a serving bowl and finish with the goat's cheese and mâche.

Tabbouleh with chickpeas

SERVES 8

This is my take on tabbouleh, using capsicum and chickpeas, and cous cous instead of burghul. I think it's much easier to prepare than the original recipe, and it is definitely full of flavour. The chickpeas also make it a more substantial salad than its traditional counterpart.

100 g dried chickpeas, soaked overnight in cold water
sea salt and cracked black pepper
1 bay leaf
1 cup (200 g) couscous
1 teaspoon olive oil
1 bunch flat-leaf parsley, leaves roughly chopped
1 bunch coriander, leaves roughly chopped
1 bunch mint, leaves roughly chopped
2 red capsicums (peppers), cut into 5 mm dice
2 green capsicums (peppers), cut into 5 mm dice
1 telegraph (large) cucumber, peeled and cut into 5 mm dice
1 tablespoon lemon juice
¼ cup (60 ml) extra virgin olive oil

Drain the chickpeas and place them in a saucepan with 1 litre of cold water. Add salt and the bay leaf and bring to the boil. Reduce the heat to a simmer and cook for 45 minutes or until just tender, then drain and leave to cool.

Place the couscous in a bowl and pour over 1 cup (250 ml) of boiling water and the olive oil. Cover with plastic film and leave to steam for 10 minutes, then use a fork to fluff up the couscous.

Place the herbs, capsicum and cucumber in a bowl and toss together, then add the couscous and chickpeas and combine.

In a separate bowl, whisk together the lemon juice and extra virgin olive oil.

Toss the salad with the dressing, season with salt and pepper and serve.

Baby heirloom carrots

SERVES 8

This is so simple yet so delicious. Just make sure you cook the purple carrots separately from the other carrots, so that they all retain their colour.

100 ml extra virgin olive oil
1 bunch baby purple carrots, peeled and tops trimmed
2 bunches baby orange carrots, peeled and tops trimmed
1 bunch baby yellow carrots, peeled and tops trimmed

Place a lidded saucepan over medium heat and add 2 tablespoons of olive oil. Add the purple carrots and fry for 5 minutes until starting to colour. Add ¼ cup (60 ml) of boiling water to the pan and place a lid on top. Cook for 10 minutes or until the carrots are tender. Remove the carrots from the pan and keep in a warm spot.

Place the saucepan back over medium heat and add 2 tablespoons of olive oil. Add the yellow and orange carrots and fry for 5 minutes until starting to colour. Add ¼ cup (60 ml) of boiling water to the pan and place a lid on top. Cook for 10 minutes or until the carrots are tender. Place the purple carrots back in the pan to heat through.

Arrange the carrots on a serving plate and serve.

Mille feuille of poached quince and cinnamon ice-cream

SERVES 8

I just love this dessert. After cooking, it is important to leave the quince in its poaching liquid
for 24 hours to create a rich colour and intense flavour. You must also assemble this at the last
moment to ensure your pastry layers remain crisp.

750 g puff pastry
120 g caster sugar

POACHED QUINCE

2 kg quince
juice of 1 lemon
1 kg caster sugar
4 star anise
2 cinnamon sticks
2 vanilla beans, split
grated zest of 1 orange

CINNAMON ICE-CREAM

2 cups (500 ml) milk
2 cups (500 ml) pure cream
6 cinnamon sticks
170 g caster sugar
12 egg yolks

For the poached quince, peel and halve the quinces; reserve the peel. Remove the seeds and set them aside. Place the halved quinces in a bowl of water with the lemon juice. Place the sugar and 1 litre of water in a saucepan and bring to the boil, then add the star anise and cinnamon, split vanilla beans and orange zest. Drain the quinces, and add to the saucepan with the peel and seeds. Cover with a cartouche (see page 17) and reduce to a very slow simmer. Poach for at least 6 hours or until almost soft, then remove from the heat and allow to cool in the liquid. Place in the fridge and leave for 24 hours.

For the cinnamon ice-cream, place the milk, cream, cinnamon and 60 g of the sugar in a saucepan and bring to the boil. Place the egg yolks and remaining sugar in a bowl and whisk until thick and pale. Pour the yolks and sugar into the hot cream mixture and stir over low heat until it reaches 84°C or until the mixture coats the back of a spoon. Strain into a bowl, then chill immediately in the fridge, whisking occasionally. When cold, place in an ice-cream machine and churn according to the manufacturer's instructions.

Preheat the oven to 200°C and line a baking tray with baking paper. Roll out half the puff pastry on a lightly floured surface until it is 5 mm thick. Place on the prepared tray, top with another piece of baking paper, then a heavy-based baking tray (this will keep the pastry flat) and place in the oven. Bake for 9 minutes, then remove and use an 8 cm cutter to cut out into rounds. Return to the oven between trays and bake for another 6 minutes or until golden brown. Repeat with the remaining pastry until you have 24 rounds.

Cut out quince balls using a melon baller. Sprinkle sugar over eight pastry rounds and heat gently with a blow torch just until the sugar caramelises.

Remove the ice-cream from the freezer 20 minutes before serving and place in the refrigerator to soften slightly, then spoon it into a piping bag fitted with a 2 cm plain nozzle.

Place eight pieces of plain puff pastry on individual plates and top with balls of quince. Pipe the ice-cream into the centre and around the quince. Top with another piece of plain puff pastry and repeat again with quince and ice-cream. Top with the sugar-coated puff pastry and serve immediately.

UPTON

Family

Some years ago, I had the privilege to cook for the award-winning actor Cate Blanchett, along with her husband, director Andrew Upton, and their three sons, Dashiell, Roman and Ignatius (Iggy). They were everything I hoped they would be – intelligent, funny and above all very real. They struck me as people who are fiercely passionate about the world in which we live, be it the environment, the arts, politics or social justice but they are still just as happy talking about Dashiell's drum practice and the dreaded packing of lunch boxes the night before school.

When my wife, Sanchia, wrote to Cate asking if she would appear in our book, we were a little sceptical as to how successful we might be. As one of the world's most coveted actresses *and* mother to young children *and* with her continued engagement with the Sydney Theatre Company, we assumed that whilst the project might appeal to her philanthropic side, it could be a case of just 'too much on'.

So you can imagine our surprise when we received her email – on a typical Friday night with four tired children battling over the remote control and one equally tired mother confiscating it – saying she'd love to be involved. Sanchia's piercing scream finally managed to silence the fighting children, two yapping maltese terriers and almost caused shockwaves that could be felt at my new restaurant premises.

The whole Brahimi family is invited to a lunch, hosted by Cate and Andrew, in an iconic woolshed in rural New South Wales. The woolshed is home to The Corridor Project, a regional not-for-profit company that supports education, cultural pursuits and research. Andrew and Cate are patrons of The Corridor Project and are passionate about providing regional space for the creative industries.

It is a bitterly cold July day, but as soon as we arrive the atmosphere feels homely and inviting. Cate is joined for lunch by good friends and extended family. Three rustic trestle tables are set for twenty-four, dressed simply with white Mud plates, miscellaneous old bone-handled cutlery and bunches of yellow wattle and blue gum in glass preserving jars.

We start with pear martinis, which do a very good job of warming us up, with cheese toasties for the kids. Soon all the children are racing off to explore the woolshed, parents forgotten in the pursuit of fun and adventure.

*Y*ou soon notice that much laughter intersperses Andrew and Cate's conversations. Home life at chez Upton, which includes two dogs that think they are cats and one cat that believes it's a dog, is busy to the point of chaotic but Cate thrives on the energy and stimulus of an ever-evolving household, feline and canine confusion and all. It is decreed that Andrew is a great cook – 'Well, within my own family,' he laughs. When I ask Cate if she likes to cook, she answers thoughtfully: 'Yes I do, but I think everyone puts far more expectation on Andrew to prepare something fabulous than me. So when I do, they are pleasantly surprised,' she smiles.

Today I have devised a menu born from some suggestions from the Upton family – to please include duck, sticky date pudding and brussels sprouts! (I make a mental note to enforce this slightly unfashionable vegetable in my own home, as I've always had a soft spot for a sprout.) Soon the table is laden with food: truffle sandwiches and mushroom velouté, duck ragout with green olives and coriander, roast pumpkin with harissa and herb salad, sprouts with parmesan and balsamic, broccolini with anchovy and lemon dressing, and pearl barley risotto. I have also created my version of sticky date pudding.

After one bite of the main Andrew turns to Cate and solemnly says: 'Darling, I might have to leave you for this duck.' Then Roman proposes a toast: 'Guillaume, the duck was delicious and has surpassed all my expectations. I give it a 10 out of 10.'

After lunch, Cate suggests a walk down to the river. The children dart like mountain goats and the adults slip and slide down moss-stained rocks. It is worth the effort, as the river is spectacular. As darkness descends, and with a slight mist setting in, the mood and atmosphere of the countryside becomes reminiscent of the old movie *Wuthering Heights*.

Andrew, Dashiell and Iggy set about starting an enormous bonfire and soon all the children are warmed by giant embers and are talking marshmallow toasting. The children, all sixteen of them, seem happy and content and the younger ones are becoming tired. Not so Loïc, who after too much dessert, has now morphed from Spiderman into the Hulk, showing Cate both his versatility and dramatic range. Cate assures me that if the producers of her next movie are scouting for a 2-foot, curly-haired action hero (who is more likely to lift dummies than dumbbells), she will most certainly recommend Loïc: 'Failing that, he could always play Heathcliff to my Cathy.'

119

MENU

Truffle sandwich

Field mushroom velouté with chive emulsion

Roast pumpkin with harissa and herb salad

Duck ragout with green olives and coriander

Pearl barley risotto

Brussels sprouts with parmesan and balsamic

Broccolini with anchovy and lemon dressing

Sticky date pudding with butterscotch sauce

Truffle sandwich

SERVES 6

My truly decadent take on the humble sandwich. It is especially sublime served alongside the mushroom velouté.

4 large slices sourdough
100 g unsalted butter
1 black truffle, thinly sliced

Preheat a sandwich press.

Spread both sides of the sourdough slices with the butter. Arrange the truffle slices on top of two slices, then top with the remaining slices.

Toast in a sandwich press for 6 minutes or until golden brown.

Cut into fingers and serve.

Field mushroom velouté with chive emulsion

SERVES 6

A perfect starter to a winter's lunch. The chive emulsion adds a wonderful creaminess to the soup, but if you're short on time, you can simply garnish it with chopped chives – *et voilá*!

100 g unsalted butter
3 golden shallots, sliced
6 large field mushrooms, roughly chopped
1 litre chicken stock
100 g crème fraîche
sea salt and cracked white pepper
4 cloves garlic, peeled
150 ml pure cream
2 bunches chives, chopped

Melt the butter in a large saucepan over medium heat, add the shallot and sweat for 3 minutes or until soft and translucent. Add the mushroom and cook for 10 minutes until almost soft. Pour in 800 ml of the chicken stock and bring to the boil over high heat, then reduce the heat to low and simmer for 30 minutes. Transfer the mixture to a food processor and blend until smooth, then add the crème fraîche, season with salt and pepper and blend until well combined. If the soup is a bit thick, add a little extra stock, crème fraîche or water to thin it down to your desired consistency. Set the mushroom velouté aside.

Meanwhile, place the garlic in a small saucepan and cover with the remaining chicken stock. Bring to the boil, then reduce the heat to low and simmer for about 20 minutes or until the garlic is soft. Add 100 ml of the cream. Bring to the boil and then allow to reduce for 3 minutes. Bring a saucepan of water to a rapid boil over high heat. Add the chives and blanch for 1 minute, then remove and place in iced water to chill. Drain thoroughly and place in a food processor with the garlic and cream. Blend until smooth.

Gently reheat the mushroom velouté. Whip the remaining cream and fold it through the chive emulsion.

To serve, garnish the mushroom velouté with a spoonful of chive emulsion.

Roast pumpkin with harissa and herb salad

SERVES 6

This is my kid-friendly version of harissa, without the usual chilli! You can add the heat if you want to, however: simply roast a large red chilli with the capsicum, then peel and blend it along with the other ingredients.

1 kent pumpkin (2–3 kg), peeled, seeded
   and cut into large wedges
2 tablespoons olive oil
sea salt and cracked white pepper
baby herbs, to garnish

HARISSA
3 red capsicums (peppers)
1 teaspoon cumin seeds
1 teaspoon coriander seeds
1 clove garlic, crushed
1 tablespoon olive oil

For the harissa, first roast the capsicum according to the method on page 44, then peel off the skin and discard the seeds. Place the cumin and coriander seeds in a dry frying pan over medium heat and toast, tossing regularly, for 3 minutes or until aromatic. Grind the toasted seeds using a mortar and pestle. Place the capsicum, ground spices, garlic and olive oil in a food processor and blend until smooth.

Preheat the oven to 180°C.

Toss the pumpkin in the olive oil and place on a baking tray. Roast for 30 minutes, then turn the pumpkin over and roast for another 30 minutes or until tender.

To serve, brush with the harissa, season with salt and pepper, and garnish with baby herbs.

Duck ragout with green olives and coriander

SERVES 8

When I found out Andrew Upton loves to eat duck, I knew it had to feature on my menu.
With the location of the woolshed in mind, I decided to confit the duck – I wanted to
bring the French countryside to the Australian countryside! The olives and coriander offer
freshness to counterbalance the richness.

8 duck marylands (leg and thigh portions)
1 tablespoon fine salt
¼ bunch thyme, in sprigs
2 cloves garlic, thinly sliced
1 kg duck fat
3 eggplants (aubergines)
170 ml extra virgin olive oil
2 red capsicums (peppers)
200 ml Chicken jus (see Basics)
100 g gordal olives, cheeks removed
1 bunch coriander, leaves picked and roughly chopped

Lay the duck on a tray and sprinkle with salt, then add the thyme and half of the garlic. Cover with plastic film and leave overnight in the fridge.

Preheat the oven to 150°C. Pat the duck dry with paper towel and remove any excess salt and herbs. Melt the duck fat in a saucepan over medium heat. Place the duck in a casserole dish and cover with the fat. Roast for 4 hours or until the meat starts to fall away from the bone. Remove from the fat using a slotted spoon.

Increase the oven temperature to 200°C. Halve the eggplants lengthways and score the flesh with a sharp knife. Soak the eggplant in 150 ml of olive oil for 5–10 minutes.

Place on the eggplants on a baking tray and roast for 40 minutes or until coloured and soft. Place the capsicums on a baking tray and baste with the remaining olive oil. Roast for about 40 minutes until slightly blackened. Place them in a bowl, cover with plastic film and leave to cool a little. Once cool enough to handle, peel off the skins and remove the seeds. Pat dry with paper towel, and cut into 5 mm strips.

Scrape the eggplant flesh into a strainer and leave to drain and cool, then chop to a chunky paste. Fold together with the capsicum and reheat in a saucepan over medium heat, stirring regularly.

Place a frying pan over medium heat and add the duck, skin-side down. Cook for 3 minutes or until the skin becomes golden brown.

Bring the chicken jus to the boil.

To serve, place the eggplant and capsicum mix on a serving platter and arrange the duck on top. Sprinkle over the olive cheeks and coriander, then spoon the jus over the top.

Pearl barley risotto

SERVE 6

Brussels sprouts with parmesan and balsamic

SERVES 8

This is a hearty risotto made with pearl barley rather than traditional arborio rice. It is also great served with a rich meat stew, as the barley will absorb the sauce beautifully.

1.3 litres chicken stock
50 g butter
1 onion, diced
1 clove garlic, finely diced
450 g pearl barley
100 g crème fraîche
sea salt and cracked black pepper

Bring the chicken stock to a simmer in a saucepan over medium heat.

Melt the butter in a saucepan over medium heat, then add the onion and garlic and sweat for 3 minutes or until soft. Add the pearl barley and stir to coat, then add a ladle of hot stock and cook, stirring, until absorbed. Continue adding a ladleful of stock at a time until all the liquid has been absorbed and the pearl barley is tender, about 50 minutes.

Remove the pan from the heat and stir the crème fraîche through the pearl barley. Season and serve.

Discovering the entire Upton household loves sprouts was music to my ears. I am a big fan of these underrated vegetables, but I've not met many Australians who are. The trouble is that most people overcook them, leaving the sprouts soggy. In this recipe, however, the sprouts are served raw and remain crispy – give them a try.

500 g brussels sprouts, outer leaves discarded, very finely sliced
100 g parmesan, shaved
⅓ cup (80 ml) extra virgin olive oil
1½ tablespoons aged balsamic vinegar
sea salt and cracked black pepper

Place the brussels sprouts in a bowl, add the parmesan and toss together.

Place the olive oil and balsamic vinegar in a separate bowl and whisk to combine.

Just before serving, dress the salad and season with salt and pepper.

Broccolini with anchovy and lemon dressing

SERVES 8

Even kids devour their broccolini when it's served with this delicious dressing. It's versatile too – try drizzling it over other green veg, salads and shellfish. It will keep in the fridge for a few weeks.

3 anchovies
juice of 1 lemon
100 extra virgin olive oil
1 sprig rosemary, leaves finely chopped
4 bunches broccolini, trimmed

Whiz the anchovies in a blender, then add the lemon juice. Transfer to a bowl and whisk in the olive oil to just bring the ingredients together. Add the rosemary and mix through.

Bring a large saucepan of water to the boil, then add salt. Blanch the broccolini for 2 minutes or until just cooked, then refresh in iced water and drain.

Place the broccolini in a bowl, pour over the anchovy and lemon dressing and toss to combine.

Sticky date pudding with butterscotch sauce

SERVES 8

The Upton boys' favourite dessert is sticky date pudding. In my version, I soften the dates
by cooking them in crème fraîche and water, making the pudding extra-rich. I also add
caramelised banana for a truly indulgent treat.

250 g fresh dates, pitted and roughly chopped
250 g crème fraîche
60 g soft unsalted butter, chopped
225 g brown sugar
4 eggs
1½ cups (225 g) self-raising flour
100 g sugar
3 bananas, halved lengthways, then widthways
1 vanilla bean, split and seeds scraped
30 ml pure cream
pinch of sea salt
vanilla bean ice-cream, to serve

BUTTERSCOTCH SAUCE
100 g unsalted butter
200 g brown sugar
400 ml pure cream
1 vanilla bean, split and seeds scraped

Place the dates, crème fraîche and 1 cup (250 ml) of water in
a saucepan. Bring to the boil, then reduce the heat to low and
simmer for about 15 minutes, stirring occasionally to prevent
sticking, until the dates are tender and the consistency of jam.
Remove the pan from the heat and stand until cool.

Preheat the oven to 160°C and line a 20 cm cake tin with
baking paper.

Place the butter and brown sugar in an electric mixer fitted
with a paddle attachment and cream together. Add the eggs
one at a time, incorporating well before adding the next.
Add the flour and mix slowly, then add the date mixture.
Mix together quickly, then pour the batter into the prepared
tin. Bake for 25–30 minutes or until a skewer inserted into the
centre comes out clean.

Meanwhile, for the butterscotch sauce, place the ingredients
in a saucepan and bring to the boil, then reduce the heat to
low and simmer for 10 minutes until thickened.

Place the sugar in a saucepan over medium heat and, when
golden brown, add the banana and vanilla seeds. When the
banana has coloured, removed it from the pan, then add
the cream and bring to the boil. Reduce the heat and simmer for
2 minutes, then remove from the heat and add the salt.

Pour the butterscotch sauce over the cake whilst everything
is still warm. Serve with caramelised banana and vanilla bean
ice-cream.

BOURIS

family

Mark Bouris has been a great friend of mine for many years. We train together most Saturdays (despite Mark having a good decade on me he still beats me on the rowing machine every time). We are also Roosters supporters, Mark sitting on the board as a director since 2003 and me as a very enthusiastic club member. He lives a stone's throw from my house and we often run into each other by chance, which often leads to a beer or two.

Mark is what many would call a man's man – someone who likes a beer and his footy. He is sharply intelligent and of course he is successful in business. After selling his company Wizard to General Electric in 2004, Mark is now Executive Chairman of Yellow Brick Road, a wealth management company that challenges the big players. He is a successful author, columnist and host of *The Apprentice* and *Celebrity Apprentice*. He is a household name. But how is he in the house?

Mark lives with partner, Lise, and son James in a heritage cottage overlooking Watson's Bay. The house is a lovely labyrinth of rooms wrapped in sandstone, with 100-year-old frangipanis littered throughout the garden. I've been here often for lunch or an afternoon drink, and I still think it is one of the most charming houses in Sydney. Mark splits his time between the Sydney residence and his farm in Byron Bay. 'I lived in the city for many years and I loved the energy and the convenience,' Mark says. 'But this little seachange has been a huge shift. I smell the salt in the ocean, I swim, I bike ride. Investing in my health is very important to me. I think that's why I'm drawn to the water. It has a calming effect on someone who can suffer from idea overload!'

Today we have three generations of Bouris men for a Greek-style alfresco lunch, with Mark's dad, George, and his sons, Dane, Alex, Nick and James. Mark sheds his public persona and is just the 'old man'. Mark tells me, 'My dad came from Greece in the 1940s. My mother, Marsha, is from an Irish-Catholic background. We lived in Punchbowl and my parents gave me, my brother and sister unconditional love and support. It was a very happy family life. However, hard work and discipline were the cornerstone of our upbringing. We grew up with the belief that you had to put in the hard work to achieve in life.'

The younger Bouris clan arrive at 1 pm and all say they are 'starving'. The close bond between father and sons is soon evident and the love palpable. Mark laughingly checks up on who has 'bludged out' of swimming training this week, tussles hair, throws faux punches, cracks joke after joke. He clearly puts the same dedication into his personal life as he does his professional career. 'They don't get more hands-on than Dad,' says Dane. 'We all speak every day. He still comes to any event we have going on and we always go and see the Roosters play together. And he makes a point of having a meal with us a few times a week. Maybe that's the Mediterranean blood in him – that desire to keep close by breaking bread.' Mark likes cooking and by all accounts from members of his family, he is pretty damn good at it. His sons also cook. Mark says proudly, 'All my boys can get around a kitchen pretty well. I think it's important for a man to be able to cook.'

Today's menu centres on seasonal produce and has a Greek feel. I had to think fast and abandon my usual French fare and instead focus on chargrilled octopus, suckling meat and lots of good olive oil. Mark and his family enjoy a catch up in the garden, with lots of laughter and ribbing going on, while I serve deep-fried prawns with garlic and olive mayonnaise and mini lamb brochette.

The table is set outside and we enjoy a warm winter's day lunch. The milk-fed lamb has been cooking on the spit most of the morning, brushed with olive oil, thyme, rosemary, garlic, cumin and fennel seeds. The rustic table soon fills up with dish after dish: chargrilled octopus salad; wild rice with capsicum, pomegranate, mint, goat's cheese and pine nuts; my version of eggplant parmigiana and potatoes with cucumber and mint yoghurt.

After some Greek music (and some impromptu Greek dancing), the lunch comes to an end. The boys give my team a hand cleaning up and afterwards announce that they have to leave. Each son gives their grandfather and father a hug and kiss. George says, 'I've always been very proud of Mark's achievements, and there have been many. However it is as a brother, son and father that I think he has truly succeeded.'

MENU

———+———

Mini lamb brochette with olive oil, oregano,
garlic and parsley

Deep-fried prawns with garlic and olive mayonnaise

Chargrilled octopus salad with black olives,
red onion and cherry tomatoes

Wild rice with capsicum, pomegranate, mint,
goat's cheese and pine nuts

Lamb on the spit with herbs, cumin and fennel seeds

My version of eggplant parmigiana

Potatoes with cucumber and mint yoghurt

Fig tart with balsamic ice-cream

Mini lamb brochette with olive oil, oregano, garlic and parsley

SERVES 8

A perfect *amuse-bouche*, this always reminds me of relaxing in Greece, watching the sunset with a glass of ouzo. You will need to soak the skewers in cold water for 2 hours before threading the marinated meat. This will stop them burning on the barbecue.

2 cups (500 ml) olive oil
½ bunch oregano, leaves picked
1 bunch flat-leaf parsley, leaves roughly chopped
½ head of garlic, cloves finely chopped
750 g lamb fillet, cut into 2 cm pieces

Soak the wooden skewers in warm water for 2 hours.

Combine the olive oil, oregano, parsley and garlic in a large container. Place the lamb in the oil and leave to marinate for 2 hours in the fridge. Remove the lamb from the fridge and drain any excess oil.

Thread the lamb onto the wooden skewers. Preheat the barbecue to medium. Cook the lamb skewers for 3 minutes on each side until cooked medium–rare. Serve.

Deep-fried prawns with garlic and olive mayonnaise

SERVES 8

This is a one-bite dish: you eat the entire prawn after scooping it in the mayonnaise to coat.
The secret to this mayonnaise is to ensure you blend the potato only until just smooth – it
will become gluey if you over-blend it – and to drizzle in the oil gradually and consistently.

vegetable oil or canola oil, for deep-frying
1⅓ cups (200 g) plain flour
salt
1 kg harbour prawns

GARLIC AND OLIVE MAYONNAISE
1 small potato, peeled and sliced
4 cloves garlic, peeled and halved
200 ml pure cream
2 egg yolks
200 ml olive oil
juice of ½ lemon
2 tablespoons pitted black olives, roughly chopped

For the garlic and olive mayonnaise, place the potato and garlic in a small saucepan and cover with the cream. Bring to the boil over medium heat, then reduce the heat to a simmer and cook for 20 minutes or until the potato is tender. Place the potato, garlic and cream in a food processor and blend until just smooth. Add the egg yolks and blend to combine, then gradually drizzle in the olive oil with the motor still running. Add the lemon juice. Place the mayonnaise in a bowl and top with the olives.

Pour vegetable or canola oil into a heavy-based saucepan or deep-fryer until two-thirds full and heat to 175°C.

Combine the flour and 1 tablespoon salt in a large bowl. Add a third of the prawns and gently coat with the flour, then dust off any excess. Place in the hot oil and fry for 2 minutes until crispy, then remove with a slotted spoon and drain on paper towel. Sprinkle with salt. Repeat with the remaining prawns.

Serve the deep-fried prawns with the garlic and olive mayonnaise.

Chargrilled octopus salad with black olives, red onion and cherry tomatoes

SERVES 6

You can marinate the octopus for up to 24 hours before serving, as the flavour will intensify nicely. Once marinated, make sure you chargrill it quickly though – overcooked octopus can be dry and chewy.

1 kg baby octopus, cleaned and beak removed
150 ml extra virgin olive oil
1 clove garlic, chopped
¼ bunch oregano, leaves picked
grated zest and juice of 1 lemon
2 × 250 g punnets cherry tomatoes, halved
1 red onion, thinly sliced
50 g black olives, pitted
½ bunch basil, leaves picked
1 tablespoon aged balsamic vinegar

Place the octopus in a shallow bowl and add 100 ml of olive oil, garlic, oregano and the lemon zest and juice. Mix to combine. Marinate in the fridge for 24 hours.

Preheat the barbecue to medium.

Combine the tomatoes, onion, olives and basil in a large bowl.

Place the octopus on the barbecue and grill for 3 minutes, then turn and grill for another 3 minutes.

Add the octopus to the bowl, dress with the remaining olive oil and balsamic vinegar and serve immediately.

Wild rice with capsicum, pomegranate, mint, goat's cheese and pine nuts

SERVES 8

A summer crowd-pleaser, this colourful salad is a healthy accompaniment to any meal. It contains everything you want in a salad: cheese, nuts, vegetables *and* fruit!

1½ cups (270 g) wild rice
2 red capsicums (peppers), cut into 1 cm dice
2 green capsicums (peppers), cut into 1 cm dice
1 pomegranate, seeds removed, juice reserved
50 ml extra virgin olive oil
⅔ cup (100 g) pine nuts, toasted
½ bunch mint, leaves roughly chopped
1 × 320 g jar marinated goat's cheese

Rinse the wild rice thoroughly, then place it in a saucepan with 1.125 litres of water. Bring to the boil, then reduce the heat to a simmer and cook for about 40 minutes or until tender. Set aside to cool.

Place the diced red and green capsicum and pomegranate seeds in a large bowl. Add the cooled rice and mix together.

Mix together the pomegranate juice and olive oil in a small bowl. Pour the dressing over the salad and gently combine. Sprinkle with toasted pine nuts and mint, then top with crumbled goat's cheese.

Lamb on the spit with herbs, cumin and fennel seeds

SERVES 8

Patience is key to this impressive centrepiece. Allow the lamb to cook slowly and check in at regular intervals, brushing it with the oil and herbs. For a smaller crowd, you can use a 2 kg lamb shoulder. For the marinade, use 200 ml olive oil and half the amount of garlic, herbs, cumin and fennel seeds below. After marinating, cover the lamb with foil and roast in a preheated 160°C oven for 2 hours, then remove the foil and roast for another hour. Rest the lamb for 20 minutes before serving.

1 lamb
1 litre olive oil
2 heads of garlic, halved
1 bunch thyme, leaves picked
2 tablespoons cumin seeds
2 tablespoons fennel seeds
sea salt and cracked black pepper
½ bunch rosemary, sprigs separated

Place the olive oil in a bowl with the garlic, thyme, cumin seeds and fennel seeds. Mix well, then leave for 1 hour.

Rub the lamb with the oil marinade and season with salt and pepper. Place the lamb on the spit. Using the rosemary as a basting brush, dip it into the remaining oil and brush the lamb regularly whilst it is on the spit.

Cook the lamb for about 3 hours. Remove from the spit and leave to rest before carving.

My version of eggplant parmigiana

SERVES 12

My take on eggplant parmigiana is all about time and layers – a lot of both! It always brings to mind a little Italian *cucina*, with every available surface covered with finely sliced eggplant left to drain! The longer you leave the eggplant, the better. This dish can be served hot or cold or even made the day before and reheated before serving.

12 eggplants (aubergines), cut lengthways into 5 mm slices
sea salt and cracked black pepper
olive oil, for shallow-frying
2 onions, finely diced
2 kg tinned peeled tomatoes
1 bunch basil, leaves picked
130 g parmesan, grated

Place the eggplants on a baking tray and sprinkle with salt. Leave for 8 hours or overnight to allow the liquid to come out of the eggplants. Drain and pat the slices dry with paper towel.

Heat 1 tablespoon of olive oil in a large saucepan over medium heat and sweat the onion for 3 minutes or until translucent. Add the tomatoes, stir and reduce for 1–2 hours to create a thick sauce. Remove from the heat and set the tomato sauce aside.

Place a frying pan over high heat and add 2 tablespoons of olive oil. Working in batches, fry the eggplant slices for 3 minutes on each side or until the eggplant is golden brown. Remove from the pan and leave to drain on paper towel.

Preheat the oven to 160°C.

Line a 32 cm × 26 cm × 6 cm baking dish with baking paper. Add a layer of eggplant then pour over about an eighth of the tomato sauce. Add a few basil leaves and sprinkle lightly with parmesan. Repeat this process until all the eggplant is layered – you should have about eight layers in all. Sprinkle the remaining parmesan over the top.

Bake for 45 minutes or until hot in the centre and browned on top.

Potatoes with cucumber and mint yoghurt

SERVES 6

If you are cooking the lamb on the spit (see page 155), I suggest you take advantage of the coals and wonderful juices and cook this dish under the lamb. I accompany the potatoes with a cucumber and mint yoghurt, which also pairs perfectly with the lamb.

1 kg small kipfler potatoes
¼ bunch thyme, leaves picked
¼ bunch oregano, leaves picked
4 cloves garlic, separated
⅓ cup (80 ml) olive oil
sea salt and cracked black pepper
1 lebanese cucumber, peeled and seeded
100 g sheep's milk yoghurt
1 clove garlic (extra), finely grated
½ bunch mint, leaves thinly sliced

Preheat the oven to 180°C.

Place the potatoes in a large bowl with the thyme, oregano, garlic and olive oil. Mix well to coat the potatoes with the herbs and oil, then season with salt and pepper. Transfer to a baking tray and roast for 1 hour.

Finely grate the cucumber and lightly salt it. Gently squeeze away any excess moisture with a clean tea towel. Combine in a bowl with the yoghurt, grated garlic and mint. Season with salt and pepper.

Place the cucumber and mint yoghurt in a bowl and serve alongside the roast potatoes.

156

Fig tart with balsamic ice-cream

SERVES 8

Really ripe fresh figs are surely one of life's simple pleasures. If figs are not in season, you can replace them with banana or any stone fruit. You can also cheat and buy vanilla ice-cream, then fold through a reduced balsamic vinegar.

1 sheet puff pastry
1 egg, lightly whisked
10–12 figs, halved
60 g caster sugar

BALSAMIC ICE-CREAM
100 ml balsamic vinegar
2 cups (500 ml) milk
2 cups (500 ml) pure cream
3 vanilla beans, split and seeds scraped
170 g caster sugar
12 egg yolks

CRÈME PATISSIERE
300 ml milk
2 vanilla beans, split and seeds scraped
3 egg yolks
60 g caster sugar
1 tablespoon plain flour
¼ cup (35 g) cornflour

For the balsamic ice-cream, bring the balsamic vinegar to the boil over high heat, then reduce the heat to medium and cook until reduced by half. Set aside. Place the milk, cream, vanilla beans and seeds, and 60 g of sugar in a saucepan and bring to the boil, then reduce the heat to low. Meanwhile, place the egg yolks and remaining sugar in a bowl and whisk until thick and pale. Pour the yolk mixture into the warm milk mixture and stir to combine. Cook until the mixture coats the back of a spoon, then strain into a bowl. Chill immediately in the fridge, whisking occasionally. When cold, place in an ice-cream machine and churn according to the manufacturer's instructions.

For the crème patissiere, combine the milk and vanilla beans and seeds in a saucepan and bring to the boil over medium heat. Meanwhile, whisk the egg yolks, sugar, flour and cornflour in a bowl until smooth. When the milk boils, pour it over the egg mixture, then return the combined mixture to the pan. Bring to the boil over medium heat, whisking continuously, then cook for a further 3 minutes. Remove the vanilla beans and transfer the mixture to a container. Place in the fridge to cool.

Preheat the oven to 180°C and line a baking sheet with baking paper. Cut the puff pastry into a 30 cm circle and place on the sheet. Create a 4 cm border by making a slight indentation with a knife to score but not cut through the pastry. Using a fork, dock the inner circle of pastry. Bake the pastry for 15 minutes, or until golden brown, then remove from the oven and brush lightly with egg.

Remove the crème patissiere from the fridge and whisk until smooth. Spread it over the inner circle of pastry. Dip the cut side of the figs in the sugar and place on a baking tray, then use a blowtorch to caramelise them. When cool enough to handle, arrange them over the crème patissiere. Swirl the balsamic through the ice-cream and serve with the fig tart.

MCLACHLAN

Family

*M*eeting Gillon McLachlan for the first time caused me to experience an unexpected bout of friend envy. As Gillon towered over me, I had to question whether it was his height causing me to feel more green than Gallic – or his job. As CEO of the Australian Football League, Gillon is regarded as the most powerful man in football. Being football mad, I fantasise about a life where talking and watching football is akin to breathing. Hence the 'frenvy'...

Gillon was born and raised on the land in South Australia, at the family farm near Mount Pleasant, an hour's drive from Adelaide. While growing up at Rosebank Gillon came to know and appreciate the value of a full day's work. If he wasn't at school, he was helping out with the shearing or mustering. Gillon says he often feels nostalgic for the simplicity of kicking a footy about with one of his three brothers until his mother called out for dinner. He describes in loving detail his mother's tuna pie, for which he and his brothers would line up for seconds, thirds and sometimes fourths.

Gillon is by all accounts a man of passions. Obviously football is a big one, yet Gillon is also an avid polo player. Growing up riding stock horses to practise polo, he is now a 4-goal handicap and has represented Australia and Victoria a number of times. Above all though, Gillon is a family man. He and his wife, Laura, met at university and their enduring partnership has produced three children, Edie, Cleo and Sidney. As Gillon's job involves attending all the football matches (jealousy now rears its head again), I was curious to know how he manages the demands of a young family with his work commitments. His response is quick: 'I bring them with me.' In fact, he says: 'The thing I relish most in this job is when I look out across the stands and see families there together, all wearing their team's colours. The look on their faces says it all.'

Gillon and Laura's home in Melbourne's Prahran is warm and inviting. On the weekend, they often have friends over with children of similar ages to theirs. This, says Laura, usually involves Gill cooking, which means 'meat and fire' (perhaps due to his love of polo, which heralds from Argentina). During the week, however, eating as a family can sometimes prove difficult as Gillon is often home too late. Then there are the demands of cooking for young children. Laura and Sanchia swap war stories about what they label 'Chronic Fatigue Cooking' for the family. Granted, preparing meals for children can at times feel like a relentless and unrewarding job, even for a chef like me. However, I believe it is still possible to appeal to a fussy five year old or an overtired toddler. It just takes time, careful preparation and an abundance of patience!

Laura likes to feed her family 'good, honest food'. As she tells me: 'Pasta is a favourite . . . plus the sauce means you can hide as many vegetables as possible!' But, she says, family mealtimes are about more than just food. 'The girls often help set the table or have a job filling up the water cups. It's these little rituals that I think are so important. As really mealtimes are not just about feeding your children – they are about teaching them how to behave at the table, how to carry a conversation. Some nights it runs smoothly, others not so much. But I try and persevere as I think it's so important to have that time together. You are creating lifelong memories.'

As is soon discovered, Gillon makes a mean margarita, which we enjoy with kingfish ceviche with lime, coriander and chilli, while the kids tuck into guacamole and corn chips. With Gill's love of 'meat and fire' in mind, my lunch menu is barbie-inspired: wagyu with chimichurri; beef ribs with barbecue sauce; green bean, chorizo and roasted pepper salad; squid with morcilla, apple and brazil nuts; barbecued corn, and rice pilaf. We are hosting a horde of children with, I'm assuming, very sweet teeth, so I serve a decadent dessert of churros with chocolate sauce, and chocolate and dulce de leche tart with hazelnut ice-cream.

After a long and leisurely lunch, Gillon disappears to check on work emails, and I kick a football in their garden with my children Loïc and Violette. My frenvy has subsided and been replaced by one of life's most enjoyable emotions – that of sheer contentment.

But if Gillon needs an AFL chief executive chef, he knows where to find me.

MENU

Guacamole

Kingfish ceviche with lime, coriander and chilli

Wagyu flank with chimichurri

Pork, spinach and manchego empanadas

Beef short ribs with barbecue sauce

Green bean, chorizo and roasted pepper salad

Squid with morcilla, apple and brazil nuts

Barbecued corn with tomatoes, spring onions and black beans

Rice pilaf

Churros with chocolate sauce

Chocolate and dulce de leche tart with hazelnut ice-cream

Guacamole

SERVES 8

I like to use hass avocados for guacamole as they contain less liquid than other varieties, but any type will do – just make sure they're ripe. Don't be shy with the seasoning here, and feel free to add chilli if you prefer your guacamole with a kick.

5 ripe avocados, peeled and stone removed
juice of 1 lime
1 red onion, finely diced
sea salt and cracked black pepper
corn chips, to serve

Place the avocado in a bowl and mash using a whisk. Add the lime juice, then fold through the onion. Season well with salt and pepper.

Serve with corn chips.

Kingfish ceviche with lime, coriander and chilli

SERVES 6

A light, elegant starter that shows off top-quality sashimi-grade fish. Finger limes are native to Australia and are available in summer from speciality grocers and farmers' markets. If you can't find them, you can use regular limes (you'll need an additional one) or you can substitute pink grapefruit segments.

600 g sashimi-grade kingfish, skin and bloodline removed, thinly sliced
2 finger limes, pearls removed
2 golden shallots, finely diced
½ bunch coriander, leaves finely sliced
1 large red chilli, seeded and finely diced
juice of 1 lime
1½ tablespoons extra virgin olive oil
sea salt and cracked black pepper
baby coriander, to garnish

Lay the sliced kingfish on a serving plate.

Place the finger lime, shallot, coriander and chilli in a bowl and mix well. Combine the lime juice and olive oil, then pour it over the lime mixture.

Season the kingfish with salt and pepper. Spoon the lime mixture over the top and serve garnished with baby coriander.

Wagyu flank with chimichurri

SERVES 8

This wagyu flank cooked beautifully on the Argentinian-style barbecue at Gillon's home.
I have since been fortunate enough to receive my own version of this *parilla* from Gillon.
It makes my regular everyday barbie seem very boring! You can replace the wagyu flank
with sirloin or rib eye if you like.

3 kg wagyu flank
sea salt and cracked black pepper

CHIMICHURRI
1 red capsicum (pepper)
1 jalapeño pepper (optional)
½ clove garlic, finely diced
1 teaspoon garlic powder
1 teaspoon onion powder
2 teaspoons smoked paprika
1 teaspoon ground coriander
1 tablespoon sherry vinegar
¼ cup (60 ml) extra virgin olive oil
2 bunches coriander, leaves finely chopped
2 bunches flat-leaf parsley, leaves finely chopped

For the chimichurri, preheat the oven to 180°C. Roast the capsicum according to the method on page 44, then peel and discard the seeds. If you are using the jalapeño, roast it for about 20 minutes until nicely browned, then transfer it to a bowl and cover tightly with plastic film. Leave to stand for 20 minutes, then peel the skin and discard the seeds.

Finely dice the roasted capsicum and jalapeño. Place in a bowl with the diced garlic, garlic powder, onion powder, smoked paprika and ground coriander. Mix well, then stir in the vinegar and olive oil. Add the chopped coriander and parsley, and combine.

Remove the flank from the fridge and bring up to room temperature.

Preheat the barbecue to medium–high. Season the wagyu with salt and pepper. Place on the barbecue and seal for 4 minutes on one side, then turn the beef on an angle (to achieve a criss-cross pattern) and leave for 4 minutes. Flip the beef over and seal other side for 4 minutes and then turn again to criss-cross and leave for another 4 minutes. Remove and allow to rest for 10 minutes.

Cut the steak into 1 cm thick slices on an angle, spoon over the chimichurri and serve.

Pork, spinach and manchego empanadas

MAKES 12

If you're entertaining, you can prepare this dough and filling the day before and simply assemble the empanadas just before your guests arrive. These are delicious served with the chimichurri on page 173.

vegetable oil, for deep-frying
Chimichurri (see page 173), to serve

DOUGH
1⅔ cups (250 g) plain flour
1 teaspoon fine salt
80 g cold unsalted butter, diced
90 ml room-temp water

FILLING
sea salt
1 bunch English spinach, stalks discarded, leaves washed well
150 g pork mince
70 g manchego cheese, grated
1 clove garlic, finely diced
1 teaspoon ground cumin
1 teaspoon ground coriander

To make the dough, place the flour in a bowl with the salt. Add the butter and rub in using your fingertips. Once sandy in texture, gradually add the water and knead to make a smooth dough. Wrap the dough in plastic film and leave to rest in the fridge for at least 3 hours or overnight.

While the dough is resting, make the filling. Bring a saucepan of water to the boil and add salt. Blanch the spinach for 1 minute, then remove and chill in iced water. Drain the spinach well on paper towel and squeeze out as much excess water as possible, then chop it and place it in a bowl with the rest of the filling ingredients. Mix to combine and season to taste. Place the filling mixture in the fridge until the dough is rolled and ready.

Lightly flour your work surface and roll out the dough until about 3 mm thick. Use an 11 cm cutter to cut out 12 pastry rounds, re-rolling the scraps as needed. Place a heaped tablespoon of filling on one half of each round. Dab a little water around the edge of the pastry, then fold it over to make a half-moon shape. Roll the edges in and twist gently to seal.

Preheat the vegetable oil in a deep-fryer to 170°C. Working in batches, add the empanadas and fry for 3 minutes or until golden brown. Drain on paper towel and serve immediately with chimichurri.

Beef short ribs with barbecue sauce

SERVES 6

These beef ribs may be mouth-watering, but it is the barbecue sauce that really makes the dish! The shop-bought stuff just doesn't compare. It will keep for a week in the fridge. The ribs take time, but the method results in wonderfully tender meat that just falls off the bone.

6 beef short ribs
sea salt and cracked black pepper
3 teaspoons smoked paprika

BARBECUE SAUCE
10 roma (plum) tomatoes, halved
1½ tablespoons olive oil
1 onion, diced
2 cloves garlic, chopped
1 cm ginger, chopped
100 g speck, chopped
1½ cups (375 ml) cola
2 teaspoons smoked paprika
1 teaspoon onion powder
1 teaspoon garlic powder
100 ml tomato ketchup
75 ml worcestershire sauce

For the barbecue sauce, preheat the oven to 200°C. Place the tomatoes on a baking tray and brush with a tablespoon of olive oil. Roast for 40 minutes until soft and coloured, then remove and set aside. Heat the remaining olive oil in a saucepan over medium heat and sweat the onion, garlic and ginger for 4 minutes or until the onion is translucent. Add the speck and cook for 15 minutes until nicely caramelised, then deglaze the pan with the cola and leave to reduce by half. Add the roast tomatoes and spices, then reduce the heat to low and cook for 40 minutes. Stir in the tomato ketchup and worcestershire sauce, then remove from the heat and allow to cool to room temperature. Transfer the sauce to a food processor and blend until smooth. Set aside.

For the ribs, preheat the oven to 150°C. Place the beef ribs in a roasting tin, season with salt and pepper and sprinkle over the paprika. Cover with foil and roast for 6 hours. checking occasionally.

When the ribs are soft, turn the oven to 180°C, remove the foil and baste with the barbecue sauce. Return the ribs to the oven and roast for 1½ hours, basting with barbecue sauce every 20 minutes.

Preheat the barbecue to medium. Add the ribs and cook for 6 minutes on each side until nicely coloured, then baste again with sauce and serve.

Green bean, chorizo and roasted pepper salad

SERVES 8

Squid with morcilla, apple and brazil nuts

SERVES 6

This salad is great partnered with beef or chicken, but is just as delicious by itself. I love the way the smoked paprika in the chorizo sausage is enhanced by the piquillo peppers.

The key to this simple dish is to ensure the squid remains beautifully tender. The apple adds freshness and acidity. Morcilla is a Spanish blood sausage; if you can't find it, try chorizo instead.

500 g green beans, trimmed
50 ml extra virgin olive oil
1 red onion, cut into 1 cm thick slices
100 g chorizo sausage, cut into 1 cm thick slices
1 tablespoon aged balsamic vinegar
1 × 200 g jar piquillo peppers, chopped into 2 cm pieces
¼ bunch basil, leaves sliced
¼ bunch flat-leaf parsley, leaves roughly chopped

1.5 kg squid, cleaned
¼ cup (60 ml) extra virgin olive oil
200 g morcilla sausages, peeled and broken into 2 cm pieces
juice of 1 lemon
2 green apples, cut into matchsticks
20 g brazil nuts
¼ bunch flat-leaf parsley, leaves roughly chopped

Bring a large saucepan of water to the boil and add salt. Add the green beans and blanch for 2 minutes until just cooked, then refresh in iced water and drain.

Heat the olive oil in a frying pan over medium heat. Add the onion and sauté for 4 minutes until just softened, then add the chorizo and fry for 5 minutes or until starting to crisp. Add the balsamic vinegar, then remove the pan from the heat and set aside to cool.

Place the beans and piquillo peppers in a bowl and toss together. Add the onion and chorizo and toss again to combine. Finally, add the basil and parsley, and serve.

Cut the squid tubes in half and open out with the inside facing up. Using a butter knife, scrape the inside of the squid to remove excess sinew – this will also help to tenderise the squid – then cut into 2 cm wide strips.

Place a frying pan over high heat. Add 2 tablespoons of olive oil and the morcilla and fry for 5 minutes. When crisp, remove the morcilla from the pan and drain on paper towel. Set aside.

Wipe out the pan and return it to high heat. When hot add the remaining olive oil and the squid. Fry for 1–2 minutes until just cooked, then remove from the pan and place in a bowl.

Squeeze the lemon juice over the squid, then add the apple and toss together. Add the morcilla and toss again. Grate the brazil nuts over the top using a fine grater, garnish with parsley and serve.

Rice pilaf

SERVES 6

Barbecued corn with tomatoes, spring onions and black beans

SERVES 8

Don't be fooled by its simplicity: this crowd-pleasing pilaf packs a lot of flavour. The secret is to cook the rice in great-quality chicken stock – of course homemade stock is even better.

3 cups (750 ml) good-quality chicken stock
40 g butter
1 onion, chopped
2 cups (400 g) long-grain rice
2 bay leaves
sea salt and cracked black pepper
¼ bunch flat-leaf parsley, leaves very finely chopped

Preheat the oven to 180°C.

Bring the chicken stock to the boil. Melt the butter in a flameproof casserole over medium heat, then add the onion and sweat for 3 minutes until soft. Add the rice and stir to coat with the butter. Pour in the chicken stock, then season with salt and pepper, add the bay leaves and cover with the lid.

Place the casserole in the oven and cook for 15 minutes or until all the liquid has been absorbed. Serve sprinkled with parsley.

This is an ideal dish for the barbecue, but works just as well in a chargrill pan. Soaking the corn in cold water ensures it will steam through as it grills.

4 corn cobs, in their husks
200 g dried black beans, soaked overnight, then drained
2 × 250 g punnets cherry tomatoes, halved
1 bunch coriander, leaves chopped
4 spring onions, thinly sliced
juice of 1 lemon
100 ml olive oil

Soak the corn in cold water for 1 hour.

Place the black beans in a large saucepan and cover with cold water. Add salt and bring to the boil, then reduce the heat and simmer for 1 hour or so until the beans are just tender. Drain and place in the fridge.

Preheat the barbecue to medium.

Place the corn on the barbecue and reduce the heat to low. Cook the corn, turning regularly to blacken all sides, for 30 minutes. When cool enough to handle, run a knife down the cobs to cut off the kernels.

Place the corn kernels in a bowl and combine with all the remaining ingredients. Serve.

Churros with chocolate sauce

SERVES 6

As you can imagine, this dessert was a huge hit with everyone at Gillon's barbecue
– little and big kids alike! My son, Loïc, loved it. Serve it with dulce de leche (see page 186)
as well as chocolate sauce if you're feeling especially indulgent.

300 g dulce de leche, to serve (optional)

VANILLA SUGAR
100 g caster sugar
½ vanilla bean, split and seeds scraped

CHURROS
60 g soft unsalted butter
1 vanilla bean, split and seeds scraped
1⅔ cups (250 g) plain flour
1 teaspoon baking powder
pinch of salt
1 litre vegetable oil

CHOCOLATE SAUCE
150 g dark chocolate (70 per cent cocoa), finely chopped
200 ml pure cream

To make the vanilla sugar, combine the sugar and vanilla seeds in a large bowl and mix together. Set aside.

For the churros, place 350 ml of boiling water in a jug and stir in the butter and vanilla seeds until the butter has melted. Place the flour, baking powder and salt in a bowl and make a well in the centre. Pour the boiling water mixture into the flour and mix with a wooden spoon to make a dough. Beat until smooth. Place the dough in a piping bag with a 2 cm star nozzle and leave to rest for 1 hour at room temperature.

Heat the vegetable oil in a heavy-based saucepan over high heat until it reaches 170°C. Working in batches and making sure you don't overcrowd the pan, pipe the mixture into the oil, cutting at 3 cm intervals using scissors. Using a slotted spoon, mix the churros around until evenly coloured; this will take 3–4 minutes. Remove and drain on paper towel, then place the churros in the bowl of vanilla sugar and toss whilst still warm.

To make the chocolate sauce, place the chocolate in a heatproof bowl. Bring the cream to the boil and pour it over the chocolate. Mix with a spatula until melted and smooth.

Serve the churros with the warm chocolate sauce and dulce de leche (if using) in bowls alongside for dipping.

Chocolate and dulce de leche tart with hazelnut ice-cream

SERVES 12

As far as I'm concerned, chocolate and caramel is a match made in heaven.
Dulce de leche is a sweetened milk cooked to consistency of caramel. It takes
this chocolate tart to another level. You have been warned!

300 g dulce de leche

PRALINE
1/3 cup (75 g) caster sugar
75 g hazelnuts

HAZELNUT ICE-CREAM
300 g caster sugar
12 egg yolks
2 cups (500 ml) pure cream
2 cups (500 ml) milk
3 vanilla beans, split
150 g praline, chopped

SWEET PASTRY
150 g unsalted butter, at room temperature
85 g caster sugar
1 vanilla bean, split and seeds scraped
35 g almond meal
pinch of salt
1 2/3 cups (250 g) plain flour
1 egg, lightly beaten

CHOCOLATE GANACHE
200 g dark chocolate (70 per cent cocoa), chopped
1 cup (250 ml) pure cream
25 ml liquid glucose
50 g cold unsalted butter, chopped

To make the praline for the hazelnut ice-cream, line a small baking tray with baking paper and set aside. Place the sugar in a saucepan over low–medium heat and cook, tilting the pan occasionally to make sure the syrup browns evenly, until a dark caramel forms. Add the hazelnuts and stir to coat. Remove from the pan immediately, pour onto the lined baking tray and leave to cool. Coarsely chop the praline with a serrated knife. Store in an airtight container.

To make the hazelnut ice-cream, place 200 g of sugar and the egg yolks in the bowl of an electric mixer fitted with a whisk attachment and beat until thick and pale. Meanwhile, place the cream, milk, vanilla beans and the remaining sugar in a saucepan. Bring to the boil, then reduce to a simmer. Slowly add the egg yolk mixture to the saucepan and heat for 2 minutes or until you see the first bubble, then remove from the heat and quickly strain through a sieve. Place in the fridge to chill immediately. Once cool, churn in an ice-cream machine according to the manufacturer's instructions. Sprinkle over the chopped praline at the end of churning.

For the sweet pastry, place the butter, sugar and vanilla seeds in the bowl of an electric mixer fitted with a paddle attachment. Mix for about 2 minutes on medium speed until pale, then add the almond meal and salt. Gradually add the flour and the egg. Be careful not to over-mix the dough. Wrap the dough in plastic film and place in the fridge to rest for at least 1 hour.

Roll out the pastry between two sheets of baking paper to 3–4 mm thick. Line a 30 cm tart tin with a removable base with the pastry and place in the fridge for 1 hour.

Preheat the oven to 170°C. Remove the tin from the fridge and cut off the pastry overhang. Line the pastry with baking paper and fill with baking beads or rice. Blind-bake for 15 minutes or until starting to turn golden brown, then remove the paper and beads or rice and bake for a further 5 minutes or until evenly coloured. Remove from the oven and allow to cool. When the pastry is cool, spoon the dulce de leche on top and spread evenly. Allow to set in the fridge for 20 minutes.

Meanwhile, to make the chocolate ganache, place the chocolate in a large heatproof bowl. Bring the cream and glucose to the boil, then pour it over the chocolate and mix well until smooth. Add the cold butter and mix to incorporate. Stand until cooled to room temperature but not set.

Pour the ganache over the dulce de leche and leave the tart to set at room temperature for at least 1½ hours. Serve with hazelnut ice-cream. Best eaten on the day of making.

MENEGUZZI *family*

first met Marco Meneguzzi some ten years ago. I remember thinking he looked like he had walked straight off a Ralph Lauren magazine shoot: think navy cashmere jacket, Tod loafers, crocodile-leather watch, and thick, lustrous hair. I on the other hand had just returned from the gym: think black nylon running shorts, soggy socks with runners in hand, an oversized exercise top that made me appear more expectant mother than triathlete, and hair . . . well if they say 'less is more', that is the philosophy my hair follicles subscribe to. So here was Marco, perched on a stool in my kitchen, drinking an espresso with my wife, Sanchia, and talking wingback chairs. I muttered a quick *bonjour* before running up the stairs, wondering, *What the hell are wingback chairs?*

Over the years I have got to know Marco much better (*and I am happy to report I am much more interior-design savvy*). To this day he is still immaculate and his hair is still way better than mine. However, even though he is a man of considerable talent and impeccable good taste, Marco is not afraid to laugh out loud, at life or himself, and that is why he is so much fun to be around. He is also very good at making a house a home, not a showpiece. He will custom-make an oversized couch that not only looks good but is ridiculously comfortable.

Sanchia says, 'My favourite thing is having Marco over for a consult. We always have a little catch up before getting down to business. And while we chit chat, he walks around the house doing "his thing" – he elegantly drags a wingback chair an inch to the right, he pulls a lone ginger jar and positions it with another group somewhere else, he quietly rearranges books on the coffee table, putting the excess ones in another spot, he straightens a picture, he fluffs up the cushions, he hides a power cord. I feel like locking him in and getting him to tweak the whole house.'

'I do like to move things around,' agrees Marco, 'and the mood can strike day or night. I've been known to rearrange a whole room at 2 am. I think life is ever changing and sometimes interiors reflect those little ebbs and flows. And at times life changes in big ways and you want the interiors to reflect those changes by creating a whole new mood in your living space.'

Marco's weekend retreat, Headwater in Kangaloon, works both as a mini sanctuary and a fun-filled party house. When he is there alone, he spends his time reading, catching up on sleep or pottering in the garden. When friends are over, the former still happens but it is interspersed with lots of good food and pinot noir. 'The house was built in 1910 and has the most wonderful bones. I wanted to highlight the architectural features but still create an atmosphere that is relaxed and contemporary,' explains Marco. This weekend it is a full house and Marco is excited when I tell him that we are creating a Moroccan-inspired feast. 'Would me arriving on a camel be too much?' he deadpans.

We arrive late morning on Sunday and are amused to see Marco inside doing 'his thing' with cushions on the sofa. 'Perfect,' he announces as he surveys the room. And it is – the house is filled with big, soft furnishings, blue and white china, custom-made lamps, wicker baskets and a stack of coffee-table books. Every room has a view of the wisteria-framed garden, which is lush and mist-tinged. The result is a house that is both luxurious yet homely, intimate rather than minimalist.

The quiet house becomes increasingly noisy as guests trickle in. Marco serves as head bartender, and he deftly takes everyone's drink orders as guests sink into the sofa. Others stand by the fire to warm their hands. After a stint indoors, everybody rugs up and heads for drinks alfresco. Marco is no stickler for time, and is not fussed when I say lunch may be a little later than first thought. 'Wonderful, then there's no need to cook dinner,' he says.

The aromas of Moroccan spices bring a herd of guests into the kitchen. Soon everyone is trying the filo triangles with beef, tahini and pine nuts or making their way through hummus, baba ganoush and marinated olives. By 2 pm we are ready to go and guests help themselves to dish after dish: meatballs, pickled baby veg, peas with feta and mint, and a capsicum and tomato salad. The hero of the day though is a lamb tagine with apricots, figs and chickpeas.

Over lunch we talk about Marco's family, who herald from Victoria. 'I am very, very close to my family,' he says. 'But I moved to Sydney when I was twenty-three, and in many respects, it's my friends who have taken on the role of family. When you've been friends as long as we have, there's a lot of shared history. I feel very fortunate to have them in my life,' he says with a smile.

To further make the point, Marco makes an impromptu speech and thanks everyone around the table for being with him today for this Marrakesh moment in the Southern Highlands. He finishes with a toast: 'Someone once said friends are the family we choose for ourselves. Well, I count myself very lucky to have such a wonderful family . . . even if you do drive me crazy half the time.'

MENU

Hummus

Baba ganoush

Mixed marinated olives

Filo triangles with beef, tahini and pine nuts

Meatballs with garlic and yoghurt sauce

Pickled baby vegetables

Lamb tagine with apricots, figs and chickpeas

Fresh peas with feta and mint

Capsicum and tomato salad

Hummus

SERVES 6

Baba ganoush

SERVES 6

Hummus is such a versatile dip and really easy to whip up. My kids love it served with chopped raw vegetables for an afternoon snack. At Marco's, I served it with flatbread alongside the baba ganoush.

I love to make my own baba ganoush. I like it smooth in texture, but if you prefer it chunky, you can just chop the eggplant flesh with a knife rather than blending it.

½ cup (100 g) dried chickpeas, soaked overnight
2 cloves garlic, finely diced
½ cup (140 g) tahini
100 ml extra virgin olive oil
juice of 1 lemon
sea salt and cracked black pepper

2 eggplants (aubergines)
2 cloves garlic, thinly sliced
100 ml olive oil
sea salt and cracked black pepper
½ bunch thyme, in sprigs
50 ml extra virgin olive oil
juice of ¼ lemon

Drain the chickpeas and place in a dry saucepan over medium heat. Stir continuously for 3 minutes, then pour 1 litre of water over the chickpeas and bring to the boil. Reduce the heat to a simmer and cook for 45–60 minutes until tender, then drain.

Transfer the drained chickpeas to a food processor and blend until almost smooth, then add the garlic. Slowly add the tahini and olive oil and then the lemon juice. Season with salt and pepper.

Place the hummus in a bowl and cover with plastic film. Leave to rest for 30 minutes at room temperature before serving, or place in the fridge to serve later.

Preheat the oven to 180°C.

Slice the eggplants in half and score the flesh into 1 cm diagonals. Insert the garlic into the slits. Place the eggplants on a baking tray, then sprinkle with olive oil and salt. Top with thyme.

Roast the eggplants for 1 hour or until tender, then remove from the oven and leave to cool a little. Discard the thyme. Scoop out the flesh from the eggplants and place in a sieve to drain. Place the drained eggplant flesh in a food processor and blend until smooth. Slowly add the extra virgin olive oil and lemon juice. Season with salt and pepper, and serve.

Mixed marinated olives

SERVES 6

The perfect nibble to accompany drinks. Warming the olives in the marinade makes them lovely and tender, and the flavours more intense. The olives will keep for up to 1 month.

100 ml extra virgin olive oil
1 sprig rosemary
1 long red chilli, split
1 teaspoon mustard seeds
300 g mixed olives

Place the olive oil, rosemary, chilli and mustard seeds in a saucepan over medium heat and heat for 2 minutes. Place the olives in a 2 cup (500 ml) sterilised heatproof jar and pour over the hot oil. Leave to marinate overnight.

Filo triangles with beef, tahini and pine nuts

MAKES 15

Start this dish the day before to give you more time with your guests. I also recommend cooking a small piece in the frying pan before filling the pastry, just to check your spices and seasoning are correct. You can substitute the beef mince for your preferred choice of meat. The tahini brings a lovely nuttiness to the dish.

200 g beef mince
2 tablespoons tahini
2 tablespoons toasted pine nuts
1 egg
20 g dried breadcrumbs
½ bunch coriander, leaves finely chopped
sea salt and cracked black pepper
5 sheets filo pastry
⅓ cup (80 ml) clarified butter

Place the beef mince in a bowl with the tahini, pine nuts, egg, breadcrumbs and coriander, then season to taste. Use your hands to combine well.

Cut the filo lengthways into three strips. Place a tablespoon of the beef mixture on a strip of filo at the bottom to the side of the strip. Brush the remainder of the filo strip with clarified butter. Fold the filling and filo into a triangle, then continue folding all the way to the top. Place on a paper-lined tray and place in the fridge for 40 minutes to allow the butter to set.

Preheat the oven to 200°C. Brush the filo triangles with more clarified butter and cook for 15 minutes or until golden. Serve.

Meatballs with garlic and yoghurt sauce

SERVES 6

This is my mother's recipe, one of the many dishes she has passed onto me.
I think of her every time I make it, and of times spent with my whole family,
sharing meals around the table.

2 slices white bread
⅓ cup (80 ml) milk
500 g beef mince
1 onion, diced
1 bunch coriander, leaves finely chopped
1 bunch flat-leaf parsley, leaves finely chopped,
   plus extra to garnish
1 clove garlic, crushed
½ teaspoon ground cumin
½ teaspoon ground ginger
½ teaspoon quatre-épices
1 egg
sea salt and cracked black pepper
100 g plain flour
100 ml olive oil

GARLIC AND YOGHURT SAUCE
100 g Greek-style yoghurt
2 cloves garlic, grated
1 teaspoon table salt
cracked white pepper

To make the garlic and yoghurt sauce, combine all the ingredients in a small bowl and set aside.

Soak the bread in the milk for 15 minutes, then place in a food processor. Place in a large bowl and add all the remaining ingredients. Combine well, then roll into 3 cm balls and coat with the flour.

Place a frying pan over medium heat and add the olive oil. Fry the meatballs for 2 minutes on each side until golden brown.

Serve the meatballs sprinkled with parsley, with the garlic and yoghurt sauce alongside.

Pickled baby vegetables

SERVES 6

Baby vegetables are perfect for serving canapé-style with drinks. They will keep in the pickling liquid for up to 1 month.

1 bunch baby orange carrots, peeled and trimmed
1 bunch baby yellow carrots, peeled and trimmed
1 bunch baby purple carrots, peeled and trimmed
1 bunch baby turnips, trimmed
¼ head of cauliflower, florets trimmed
1 × 120 g punnet baby cucumbers

PICKLING LIQUID
600 ml white wine vinegar
250 g caster sugar
2 cloves garlic
1 teaspoon mustard seeds
1 tablespoon fennel seeds
1 teaspoon white peppercorns

To make the pickling liquid, place all the ingredients and 800 ml water in a saucepan and bring to the boil.

Place all the vegetables in a large heatproof bowl. Pour over the boiling pickling liquid. Cover the bowl tightly with plastic film and leave for at least 24 hours.

Drain the vegetables and serve.

Lamb tagine with apricots, figs and chickpeas

SERVE 6

I made Marco this dish to bring some North African flavour and warmth to the winter of his Southern Highland home. Tagine is traditionally a combination of meat, dried fruits and spices. I use dates and apricots in mine and add them halfway through cooking to avoid the fruit breaking up too much and losing shape.

2 kg lamb shoulder, cut into 2 cm cubes

2 tablespoons ground allspice

1 tablespoon ground cinnamon

1 teaspoon ground cumin

2 tablespoons olive oil

¾ cup (150 g) dried chickpeas, soaked overnight and drained

2 litres chicken stock

5 roma (plum) tomatoes, roughly chopped

100 g dried figs, cut in half

100 g dried apricots, cut in half

100 g fresh dates, pitted and cut in half

1 bunch coriander, leaves roughly chopped

Preheat the oven to 150°C.

Toss the lamb in the allspice, cinnamon and cumin to coat.

Place a casserole over high heat and when hot, add the olive oil. Sear the lamb for 3 minutes on all sides until golden brown, then add the chickpeas. Add the chicken stock, then the tomatoes and figs and bring to the boil. Cover with a cartouche (see page 17) and the lid and place in the oven. Cook for 45 minutes, then add the apricots and dates and mix well. Return to the oven and cook for a further 45 minutes or until the lamb is tender. Rest for 30 minutes before serving.

Sprinkle with chopped coriander and serve.

Fresh peas with feta and mint

SERVES 6

Creamy feta is perfect with sweet peas and fresh mint. The beauty of using a good-quality jar of Persian feta is that you can use the oil for the salad dressing.

400 g peas
180 g marinated Persian feta
3 golden shallots, finely diced
1 bunch mint, leaves sliced

Bring a large saucepan of water to the boil and add salt. Boil the peas for 2 minutes, then drain and refresh in iced water.

Drain the feta, reserving the oil. Drain the peas and place them in a bowl with the shallot, mint and reserved oil from the feta. Mix to combine. Crumble the feta through the salad and serve.

Capsicum and tomato salad

SERVES 6

This recipe comes from my grandmother, who was born in Algeria. It was a staple in my grandparents' fridge and always used as a condiment for meats, sandwiches and fish. You can prepare this salad a couple of days in advance.

4 roma (plum) tomatoes
½ cup (125 ml) olive oil
1 clove garlic, finely sliced
1 sprig rosemary, leaves finely chopped
4 sprigs thyme, leaves finely chopped
4 red capsicums (peppers)
1 bunch flat-leaf parsley, leaves picked
¼ bunch basil, leaves picked

Preheat the oven to 120°C and line a baking tray with baking paper.

Bring a saucepan of water to the boil over high heat. Score the tomatoes on the tip and remove the eye. Blanch them for 15 seconds, then remove and place in iced water. Once cold, peel off the skins and cut into quarters. Place a tablespoon of olive oil in a bowl with the garlic, rosemary and thyme. Add the tomatoes and mix well to coat, then drain the oil. Place the tomatoes on the prepared tray and roast in the oven for 2 hours. Reserve the juices.

Increase the oven temperature to 180°C.

Place the capsicums on a baking tray and baste with 2 tablespoons of olive oil. Roast for about 40 minutes or until slightly blackened. Place them in a bowl, cover with plastic film and leave to cool a little. Strain the reserved tomato and capsicum cooking juices into a bowl. Once cool enough to handle, peel the skins off the capsicums and remove the seeds. Pat dry with paper towel and cut into 2 cm strips.

Place the roast capsicum and tomato in a bowl and toss. Add the parsley and basil and dress with the strained juices and remaining olive oil. Serve immediately.

BRAHIMI *Family*

*M*uch has changed in our family since my last book, *Food for Friends*. With the arrival of our son, Loïc, we are now a household of six, and our girls, Constance, Honor and Violette, are growing up fast. We now have a toddler *and* a teenager, and their lives are full to overflowing.

Loïc is a wonderful addition to our family, and makes us laugh at any given moment. With his three older sisters tending to his every need, he is the quintessential SNAT (Sensitive New Age Toddler). I think he may also have inherited my love of food – and possibly my waistline. The walk-in pantry is now referred to as Loïc's office, as we often find him there quietly pondering what to eat next. We also have our nephew, Clement, from Paris living with us. He has become more big brother than cousin to Consie, Honor, Violette and Loïc.

Family life is certainly busy. Weekdays are run with army-like precision. What with staying on top of schoolwork, driving to and from various after-school activities, and ensuring the kids are eating well throughout, life can be both exhilarating and exhausting. Come Saturday, we try to turn down the intensity but, as many parents can attest, weekends can seem busier than weekdays and TGIF becomes more TGIM (Thank God It's Monday!).

MENU

BREAKFAST

Bircher muesli with almond milk and strawberry jam

Sourdough toast with avocado and smoked salmon
or buffalo mozzarella, oxheart tomato and basil

AFTERNOON TEA

Roast capsicum, zucchini, olive and feta frittata
with red onion jam

Caramelised apple and roasted oat muffins

SCHOOL DINNERS

Veal and parmesan meatballs in tomato
and bacon sauce with coquillette pasta

Chicken risotto with peas and lemon

WEEKENDS

Chargrilled sirloin steaks with salsa verde

Roast jerusalem artichokes with balsamic, honey and baby herbs

Crispy potato cakes with speck, garlic and thyme

Spinach and kale salad with red pimentos,
gordal olives and goat's curd

Pineapple crumble

breakfast

Some days, breakfast, the meal universally acknowledged as the most important of the day, can be anything but. Trying to get four children dressed, with hats on and bags packed, before 7.30 am can feel like an impossible mission. Breakfast suffers as a result, often being eaten in the car en route to school: not a great start to a long day and one that of course makes me feel slightly guilty.

So following an internal review, and knowing that while I'm not always around at dinnertime, I am usually home in the morning, I have stepped in as head chef for our *petit déjeuner*. Preparing breakfast is something I can do to make the school run just that little bit smoother. Nutritious bircher muesli can be made the night before and is especially delicious served with homemade jam. Another family favourite, sourdough toast with a healthy Mediterranean-style topping, is as quick to prepare as it is to eat. So when Sanchia has the sometimes unenviable task of waking up the children, I disappear into the kitchen, strike up the coffee machine and prepare a breakfast not quite fit for a king, but for three pretty princesses and one petit prince.

Bircher muesli with almond milk and strawberry jam

SERVES 6

When making this muesli, you can opt for toasted oats instead; just add a little more juice before soaking. A good way to test the jam is set is to remove a spoonful and smear it onto a plate, then turn the plate on its side – the jam will be jelly-like if it's ready.

3⅓ cups (300 g) rolled oats
2 tablespoons raisins
2 tablespoons diced dried apricots
300 ml apple juice
¼ cup (70 g) natural yoghurt
300 ml almond milk
2 granny smith apples, grated

STRAWBERRY JAM
300 g strawberries, trimmed
300 g caster sugar
¼ teaspoon pectin

For the jam, place the strawberries and 250 g of sugar in a bowl and leave to macerate overnight in the fridge.

The next day, place the remaining sugar in a separate bowl and stir through the pectin. Transfer the macerated strawberries to a heavy-based saucepan with all the sugar and liquid in the bowl. Add the sugar and pectin mixture. Place the saucepan over medium heat and cook slowly, stirring occasionally, for about 30 minutes or until the strawberries break down. Take the jam to 106°C (or use the plate method above!). Pour the jam into a 500 ml sterilised jar, then place in the fridge and allow to set overnight. This makes approximately 400 g.

For the muesli, place the oats, raisins and dried apricots in a bowl and add the apple juice. Leave in the fridge to soak overnight.

In the morning, stir the yoghurt, almond milk and grated apple through the soaked oats.

Divide the bircher among bowls and add a spoonful of strawberry jam to serve.

Sourdough toast with avocado and smoked salmon or buffalo mozzarella, oxheart tomato and basil

SERVES 4

Good-quality sourdough is essential for these quick, healthy and filling breakfast sandwiches. They are also a great source of fibre, omega 3 and monounsaturated fat.

1 avocado
juice of ¼ lemon
sea salt and cracked white pepper
2 × 110 g balls buffalo mozzarella, sliced
4 slices smoked salmon
lemon-infused extra virgin olive oil, to drizzle
4 large slices sourdough, toasted
basil leaves, thinly sliced, to garnish
1 large oxheart tomato, sliced

Place the avocado in a bowl, add a squeeze of lemon juice and mash together with a fork. Season with salt and pepper.

For the salmon sourdough, spoon crushed avocado over two slices of sourdough and top with mozzarella. Fold smoked salmon on top and drizzle with lemon-infused olive oil. Garnish with basil.

For the buffalo mozzarella sourdough, spoon avocado over two slices of sourdough and arrange the tomato, mozzarella and basil over the top. Season with salt and pepper, and drizzle with lemon-infused extra olive oil.

afternoon tea

Schoolkids in France always eat *le goûter* (a snack) when they arrive home. Growing up, my brothers, Gael and Renaud, and I would rush into the house to see what *Maman* had prepared for us. *Le goûter* would give us that energy boost we needed to tackle the nightly homework, without spoiling our appetite for dinner. My mother often made us a frittata using ingredients found in the fridge on the day. Other times it was just the standard Nutella on toast (France's answer to Vegemite!). Sadly I'm rarely home from work at that time, but I do like to have something prepared and ready to go. So when my daughters come home from school and get changed out of their uniform, they can eat something delicious and have that moment's pause to just . . . chillax.

Roast capsicum, zucchini, olive and feta frittata with red onion jam

MAKES 30 PIECES

This favourite after-school snack or brunch dish is also very portable, making it ideal for picnics and packed lunches. Experiment with different fillings – it's a great recipe for using up leftover vegetables in your fridge.

2 red capsicums (peppers)
1 green capsicum (pepper)
⅓ cup (80 ml) olive oil
2 zucchini (courgettes), thinly sliced
100 g black olives, pitted and sliced
1 bunch flat-leaf parsley, leaves chopped
1 bunch chives, finely sliced
6 large eggs
50 ml pouring cream
150 g marinated Persian feta

RED ONION JAM
1 tablespoon olive oil
3 red onions, thinly sliced
2 sprigs thyme
2 tablespoons balsamic vinegar
20 g sugar

For the onion jam, heat the olive oil in a heavy-based saucepan over medium heat. Add the onion and thyme and sweat for 5 minutes or until soft, then add the balsamic vinegar and sugar. Cook for a further 5 minutes or until the vinegar is reduced and just sticky. Remove the thyme sprigs and set the onion jam aside.

To roast and peel the capsicums for the frittata, preheat the oven to 180°C. Place the capsicums on a baking tray and brush with 2 tablespoons of olive oil. Roast for 30–40 minutes or until the capsicums are coloured and beginning to collapse. Remove from the oven, place in a bowl and cover with plastic film. Leave to steam for 1 hour, then when cool, remove the plastic film. Peel the capsicums and remove the seeds, then pat them dry and slice into 2 cm strips.

Preheat the oven to 180°C and line a 30 cm × 20 cm baking tray with baking paper.

Place a frying pan over high heat and add the remaining olive oil. Fry the zucchini for 3 minutes or just starting to soften, then stir in the capsicum and olives. Transfer the capsicum, zucchini and olive mixture to a bowl and stir through the parsley and chives.

Break the eggs into a separate large bowl, add the cream and whisk together. Add the capsicum mixture and combine. Transfer to the prepared tray and sprinkle in the feta.

Bake for 35 minutes or until the frittata is firm. Remove from the oven and allow to cool and set aside for at least 1 hour.

Gently tip out the frittata onto a serving plate and cut into 5 cm × 4 cm pieces. Serve with the onion jam.

Caramelised apple and roasted oat muffins

MAKES 16

My children love this afternoon treat. Caramelising the apples softens them and using yoghurt gives the muffins a lovely tartness.

⅔ cup (60 g) rolled oats
50 g caster sugar
20 g unsalted butter
2 granny smith apples, peeled and cut into 1 cm dice
160 g self-raising flour
160 g plain flour
1 teaspoon baking powder
160 g brown sugar
2 eggs
110 ml olive oil
380 g vanilla yoghurt, at room temperature

Preheat the oven to 180°C. Place the oats on a baking tray and roast for 10 minutes or until nicely coloured.

Place the caster sugar and a tablespoon of water in a small frying pan and place over high heat. Cook, tilting the pan occasionally, for 5 minutes or until brown, then add the butter and apple. Stir the apple with a wooden spoon over high heat for 5 minutes until evenly coloured and slightly soft. Remove the caramelised apple from the pan and allow to cool.

Preheat the oven to 180°C and line 16 holes of two regular muffin trays with muffin papers.

Sift the flours and baking powder into a bowl and add the brown sugar and most of the roasted oats, reserving some to decorate the muffins. Mix well. In a separate bowl, combine the eggs, olive oil and yoghurt. Pour the liquid into the dry ingredients, add the caramelised apple and mix to combine.

Spoon the batter into the muffin papers and sprinkle the remaining oats over the top.

Bake for 20 minutes or until a skewer inserted into the centre comes out clean.

School dinners

School dinners at chez Brahimi are at strictly 7 pm. The table is set, and phones and gadgets are not invited! Monday to Thursday we eat as a family. As parents, we often feel time-pressured, so we try and make school dinners a mix of meals that are tasty and healthy but most importantly quick and easy to prepare.

Friday is invariably an Italian dish, which is a crowd-pleaser, not least because the children are allowed to watch TV with dinner on their laps. When I'm not working, Sanchia and I share a drink on the terrace, chatting about the week's news, before a casual dinner *á deux*.

Veal and parmesan meatballs in tomato and bacon sauce with coquillette pasta

SERVES 6

This is one of Loïc's favourites. Make it your own: you can serve the sauce with any pasta, with or without the bacon, or change the veal to beef mince. If you have any leftovers, they make a great lunchbox meal.

500 g coquillette pasta
shaved parmesan, to serve

VEAL AND PARMESAN MEATBALLS
2 slices white bread, torn
200 ml milk
500 g veal mince
100 g parmesan, grated
2 golden shallots, finely diced
2 eggs
½ bunch flat-leaf parsley, leaves roughly chopped
sea salt and cracked black pepper

TOMATO AND BACON SAUCE
4 × 250 g punnets cherry tomatoes
2 tablespoons olive oil
2 onions, finely diced
1 clove garlic, finely chopped
200 g bacon, cut into matchsticks
1 stem basil, leaves picked
sea salt and cracked white pepper

To make the meatballs, place the bread in a bowl, cover with the milk and leave to soak for 20 minutes. Drain away the excess milk, then place the soaked bread in a large bowl with the mince, parmesan, shallots, eggs, parsley, salt and pepper. Mix together thoroughly to combine, then roll the mixture into 3 cm balls and place in the fridge for set for 1 hour.

For the tomato and bacon sauce, first blanch the tomatoes. Bring a large saucepan of water to the boil over high heat and add the tomatoes. Blanch for 30 seconds, then remove and place in iced water. Once cold, drain and peel the tomatoes. Heat the olive oil in a large saucepan over medium heat and sweat the onion for 2 minutes or until translucent, then add the garlic and bacon and cook for 7 minutes or until most of the liquid has evaporated. Add the tomatoes and reduce the heat to low. Cook slowly until the tomatoes have broken down and the sauce has come together. Add the basil and season with salt and pepper.

Place the meatballs in the sauce and cover with the lid. Simmer for 10–15 minutes or until the meatballs are cooked all the way through.

Meanwhile, cook the pasta in salted boiling water until al dente, then drain. Stir the pasta through the sauce and meatballs, divide among bowls and sprinkle shaved parmesan over the top.

Chicken risotto with peas and lemon

SERVES 6–8

This dish takes a little time, but I assure you the end result is worth it! Adding the peas
brings a touch of sweetness – and it's also a good way of getting my girls to eat greens!

1.8 kg chicken
1 head garlic, halved
1 onion, roughly chopped
1 carrot, peeled and roughly chopped
2 sticks celery, roughly chopped
½ bunch thyme, in sprigs
2 bay leaves
200 g fresh or frozen peas
2 tablespoons olive oil
4 golden shallots, finely diced
2½ cups (500 g) carnaroli rice
150 g crème fraîche
150 g parmesan, grated
sea salt and cracked white pepper
½ bunch flat-leaf parsley, leaves roughly chopped
grated zest of 2 large lemons
extra virgin olive oil, to drizzle

Place the chicken in a large stockpot and cover with about 4 litres of water. Add the garlic, onion, carrot, celery, thyme and bay leaves and bring to the boil, skimming the top to remove any impurities and foam. Reduce the heat to as low as possible, then cover with a lid, leaving it slightly ajar, and simmer for 2 hours. Remove the chicken from the stock and leave to cool. Once cool, pick the chicken from the bones, shred half the meat and set it aside. Reserve the remaining meat for salads or sandwiches. Strain the stock, discarding the veg and herbs, then return 1.8 litres of stock to the pan and bring to a gentle simmer.

Meanwhile, bring a saucepan of water to the boil and blanch the peas for 1 minute, then refresh in iced water. When cold, drain the peas and set them aside.

Heat the olive oil in a saucepan over medium heat and sweat the shallot for 3–4 minutes until almost soft, then add the rice and stir to coat. Add the boiling stock to the pan a ladle at a time, stirring regularly and allowing the rice to absorb the stock before adding another. (You may not need all the stock.) Continue until the rice is al dente, about 25 minutes, then stir through the crème fraîche and parmesan. Add the peas and chicken and gently stir through. Season to taste and add the parsley.

To serve, sprinkle the risotto with freshly grated lemon zest and drizzle with extra virgin olive oil.

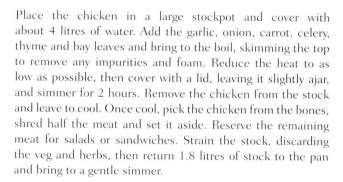

weekends

Weekends are a busy blur of playdates, drop-offs, pick-ups and of course Saturday-morning sport. On weekends we often have an even fuller house than usual, with the girls' friends popping by or sleeping over. Friends are such a lovely and important mix within our family.

Before long, it's Sunday night and everyone starts to get organised for the week ahead. Sanchia prepares school lunches and the girls go hunting for hockey sticks, shin pads and mouth-guards. Uniforms are laid out, teeth are brushed and the Sunday-night bedtime curfew is enforced, with at times totalitarian-type methods.

The house finally rests . . . before it *all* begins again.

Chargrilled sirloin steaks with salsa verde

SERVES 6

I use Rangers Valley 300-day grain-fed sirloin for this dish. It's a superb, high-quality product. You can serve the salsa verde with any cooked meat, fish or chicken and it will store in an airtight container for up to two weeks.

6 × 250 g sirloin steaks

SALSA VERDE
75 ml extra virgin olive oil
50 g ligurian olives, pitted
1 bunch flat-leaf parsley, leaves picked
1 clove garlic, peeled
1 anchovy
sea salt and cracked white pepper

To make the salsa verde, place all the ingredients in a food processor and blend until smooth. Set aside.

Preheat the barbecue or chargrill pan. When hot, place the steaks on the grill on the diagonal, and leave on medium high heat. Once coloured (about 2 minutes) turn to the other diagonal to create a criss-cross pattern on the steak. Leave for another 2 minutes and then turn steaks over. Repeat this process on the other side. Place the steaks on the barbecue rack or in a preheated 160°C oven and leave for 3 minutes.

Remove the steaks from the barbecue and rest for 10 minutes, then slice each steak into four and brush with salsa verde. Serve.

Roast jerusalem artichokes with balsamic, honey and baby herbs

SERVES 6

In France, Jerusalem artichokes were once considered the 'poor man's potato'. I love to roast them with balsamic, butter and honey.

600 g jerusalem artichokes
⅓ cup (80 ml) olive oil
¼ bunch thyme, in sprigs
1 head of garlic, cloves separated
20 g butter
¼ cup (60 ml) balsamic vinegar
20 g honey
baby herbs, to garnish

Preheat the oven to 200°C.

Place the artichokes in a bowl and add the olive oil, thyme and garlic. Mix well. Transfer to a baking tray and bake for 45 minutes or until the artichokes are tender.

Heat the butter in a small saucepan over high heat. When golden brown, add the balsamic and cook for 5 minutes until reduced by half, then stir in the honey.

Place the roast artichokes on a serving platter and drizzle with the balsamic honey sauce. Sprinkle over baby herbs to garnish.

Crispy potato cakes with speck, garlic and thyme

SERVES 6

One of my favourite recipes to cook at home. Maybe not one for the weight-watchers, but the flavour is amazing – your family will wolf these down!

4 large desiree potatoes
1 clove garlic, finely chopped
½ bunch thyme, leaves picked
sea salt and cracked white pepper
12 thin slices speck
¼ cup (60 ml) olive oil

Place the potatoes in a saucepan, cover with water and add a pinch of salt. Bring to the boil, then reduce to a simmer and cook for about 20 minutes to par-cook them. Drain, then peel the potatoes and grate them into a bowl. Add the garlic and thyme, and season with salt and pepper.

Shape the potato mix into 12 cakes about 5 cm round and 1.5 cm high. Wrap a slice of speck around each potato cake and allow to set in fridge for 1 hour.

Heat the olive oil in a frying pan over medium–high heat. When hot, add the potato cakes (in batches if necessary) and fry on each side for 3 minutes until coloured. Serve.

Spinach and kale salad with red pimentos, gordal olives and goat's curd

SERVES 6

I love the combination of the raw and cooked leaves in this healthy salad. Add goat's curd for creaminess, olives for saltiness and pimentos for sweetness, and you've got a beautifully balanced dish.

2 bunches kale, stems removed
200 g baby spinach leaves
1 small jar red pimentos, sliced into 2 cm strips
50 g gordal olives, cheeks cut away
juice of 1 lemon
¼ cup (60 ml) extra virgin olive oil
150 g goat's curd

Bring a saucepan of water to the boil, then add a pinch of salt. Add the kale and blanch for 2 minutes or until just tender, then refresh in a bowl of iced water. Once chilled, drain the kale well.

Place the baby spinach in a serving bowl with the kale, pimentos and olives. Combine the lemon juice and olive oil, add to the salad and toss gently to coat. Add the goat's curd and serve.

Pineapple crumble

SERVES 6

This family favourite can be made and assembled the day before and then placed in the oven before serving. It is especially delicious served with coconut sorbet.

200 g caster sugar
30 g unsalted butter
2 pineapples, cut into chunks
1 vanilla bean, split and seeds scraped
coconut sorbet, to serve

CRUMBLE TOPPING
200 g cold unsalted butter, diced
1½ cups (225 g) plain flour
225 g raw sugar
1 cup (75 g) shredded coconut

Place a heavy-based saucepan over medium heat and add the sugar. Cook for about 5 minutes, stirring occasionally, until it is a dark caramel, then carefully stir in the butter. Add the pineapple chunks and vanilla seeds, ensuring the pineapple is coated in the caramel. Cook for 5–10 minutes, stirring occasionally, until the pineapple is just soft. Remove the pineapple from the pan and place it in a baking dish.

Preheat the oven to 170°C.

For the crumble topping, place the butter and flour in a bowl and rub the butter into the flour with your fingertips until the mixture resembles breadcrumbs. Add the sugar and coconut and mix well to combine. Sprinkle the crumble over the pineapple in the baking dish.

Bake for 35–45 minutes or until golden brown. Serve with coconut sorbet.

Chicken jus

MAKES 650 ML

Store in the fridge for up to 3 days or freeze for up to 1 month.

---

2 tablespoons olive oil
2 kg chicken wings, roughly chopped into 2 cm pieces
1 onion, roughly chopped into 2 cm dice
1 stick celery, roughly chopped into 2 cm dice
1 carrot, peeled and roughly chopped into 2 cm dice
½ head of garlic, cut in half across the middle
¼ bunch thyme
1 bay leaf

Heat 1 tablespoon of oil in a large saucepan over high heat. When hot, add half of the chicken and leave for 3–4 minutes before stirring. Cook, stirring, until the chicken is brown all over, then remove from the pan. Add the remaining oil and repeat with the remaining chicken. Place the onion, celery, carrot and garlic in the pan and cook, stirring occasionally, for 6–8 minutes or until soft and coloured. Return the chicken to the pan, add the herbs and 4 litres of water and stir to combine.

Bring to the boil, skimming off the top layer of fat. Reduce the heat and simmer for 4 hours to release all the flavour from the meat and vegetables, occasionally skimming the top. Strain the chicken stock through a fine chinois or sieve and chill immediately.

Place the chicken stock in a saucepan and simmer over medium heat, regularly skimming the top, for 1 hour or until reduced to 650 ml. Strain through a fine chinois or sieve (do not press down on the solids or the jus may become cloudy).

Pork jus

MAKES 650 ML

Store in the fridge for up to 3 days or freeze for up to 1 month.

---

2 tablespoons olive oil
2 kg pork neck, cut into 3 pieces
1 onion, roughly chopped into 2 cm dice
1 stick celery, roughly chopped into 2 cm dice
1 carrot, peeled and roughly chopped into 2 cm dice
½ head of garlic, cut in half across the middle
¼ bunch thyme
1 bay leaf

Heat 1 tablespoon of oil in a large saucepan over high heat. When hot, add the pork and cook for 3–4 minutes until very brown all over, then remove from the pan. Add the remaining oil and the onion, celery, carrot and garlic to the pan and cook, stirring occasionally, for 6–8 minutes or until soft and coloured. Return the pork to the pan, add the herbs and 4 litres of water and stir to combine.

Bring to the boil, skimming off the top layer of fat. Reduce the heat and simmer for 4 hours to release all the flavour from the meat and vegetables, occasionally skimming the top. Strain the pork stock through a fine chinois or sieve and chill immediately.

Place the pork stock in a saucepan and simmer over medium heat, regularly skimming the top, for 1 hour or until reduced to 650 ml. Strain through a fine chinois or sieve (do not press down on the solids or the jus may become cloudy)

Shallot vinaigrette

MAKES 150 ML

Shallot vinaigrette is my staple dressing: I've used it for years, at home and in my restaurants.

---

3 large golden shallots, finely sliced
2 tablespoons good-quality red-wine vinegar
1/3 cup (80 ml) good-quality extra virgin olive oil
sea salt and freshly ground white pepper

Place the shallot and red-wine vinegar in a blender. Blitz until combined, but the shallots should not be too finely chopped. Continue to blend while slowly adding the oil. Season with salt and pepper to taste.

ACKNOWLEDGEMENTS

Firstly, thank you to our formidable chapter hosts: Justin Hemmes, Toni Ryan, Kellie Hush, Cate Blanchett, Mark Bouris, Gillon McLachlan and Marco Meneguzzi. You welcomed us into your private worlds with great warmth and generosity of spirit. Every shoot was so memorable. It is impossible to choose a favourite!

Thank you to the team at Lantern, headed by publishing dynamo Julie Gibbs. Julie again found herself at our homestead in Canowindra when she volunteered her services for the Cate Blanchett shoot. Julie's resolve was duly tested when we arrived home after a 10-hour shoot to find the only bottle opener in the place had gone missing. Thank you to Ariane Durkin for your expertise in editing and to Holly McCauley for your wonderful art design and ability to remain calm with all our last-minute changes. Thank you to Cass Stokes for your efficient co-ordination of each and every shoot. Thank you also to Christine Osmond. And *merci* to Mud Australia for generous supplying their beautiful range of ceramics.

It was wonderful to team up again with photographer Anson Smart, after working together on *Food for Friends*. Again, you have produced work that is poignant and beautiful, as well as appetising. Thank you also to Earl Carter for your photographic work in the Cate Blanchett chapter. You captured the mood perfectly, right down to the yellow wattle in the glass preserving jars.

Thank you to Sarah Murdoch, who has been a great supporter of our book and who has worked tirelessly for the National Breast Cancer Foundation.

To my family: thank you to my wife, Sanchia, who has co–written both books with me and to our children, Constance, Honor, Violette and Loïc, who are our eternal inspirations. To my other family, my restaurant team: in Sydney, Kevin and Kirsty Solomon; my maître d'hôtel, Daniel Laurence-Rogers, who has been with me for 14 years and provides unwavering support; and my sommelier, Chris Morrison. In Melbourne, Graeme McLaughlin and Marina Pranjic, and in Perth, Benoit Rivault. Thank you also to my personal assistant, Aisha Cooper, who keeps everything on track.

Thank you to the patrons of my restaurants, Guillaume in Paddington and Bistro Guillaume in Melbourne and Perth Crown Resorts. And thank you to those who have bought our books. I hope they bring you great joy and pleasure, as well as tremendous success in the kitchen.

INDEX

LANTERN

UK | USA | Canada | Ireland | Australia
India | New Zealand | South Africa | China

Penguin Books is part of the Penguin Random House group of companies
whose addresses can be found at global.penguinrandomhouse.com.

First published by Penguin Group (Australia), 2015

1 3 5 7 9 10 8 6 4 2

Text copyright © Guillaume Brahimi 2015
Photographs copyright © Anson Smart 2015, except pp 4 (top left), 110–137 © Earl Carter 2015

The moral right of the author has been asserted.

Cover design by Holly McCauley © Penguin Group (Australia)
Internal design by Holly McCauley and Emily O'Neill © Penguin Group (Australia)
Styling by Cassandra Stokes
Page 56–57 features 'Panoramic Wallpaper' by Dadoune McMahon.
Typeset in Monotype Modern Std and Fairfield LH by Post Pre-press Group, Brisbane, Queensland
Colour separation by Splitting Image Colour Studio, Clayton, Victoria
Printed and bound in China by Printed and bound in China by Toppan Leefung Printing Limited

National Library of Australia
Cataloguing-in-Publication data:

Brahimi, Guillaume
Guillaume: food for family

ISBN: 9781921383854 (hardback)

Includes index.

Cooking.
Entertaining--Australia.

Smart, Anson, photographer
Carter, Earl, 1957- photographer

641.5

penguin.com.au/lantern

To Genny,

The importance of Family
cannot be overstated.

ALL the Best!

Frank Knier

WAITE PARK

by

Frank Knier

First Edition

Cover painting by Alexandra Putzer

Publisher: Frank Knier

For my wife, Mary,
and my children: Anna, Alexandra, and Benjamin,
my son-in-law, Steven, and grandchildren, Joseph and Jane.

And for my parents, Clifford and Theresa,
and my brothers and sisters: Jeanne, Mary, Dan, Chuck,
Jim, Tom, Lisa, Susan, and Paul, and their loved ones.

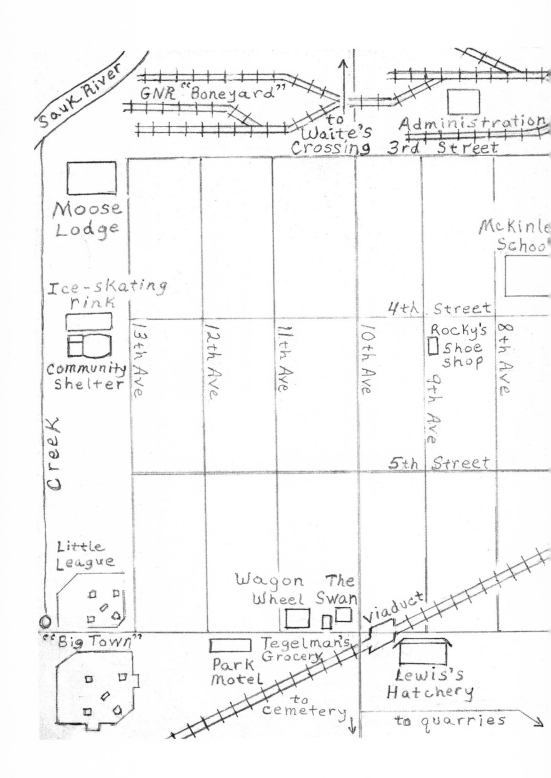

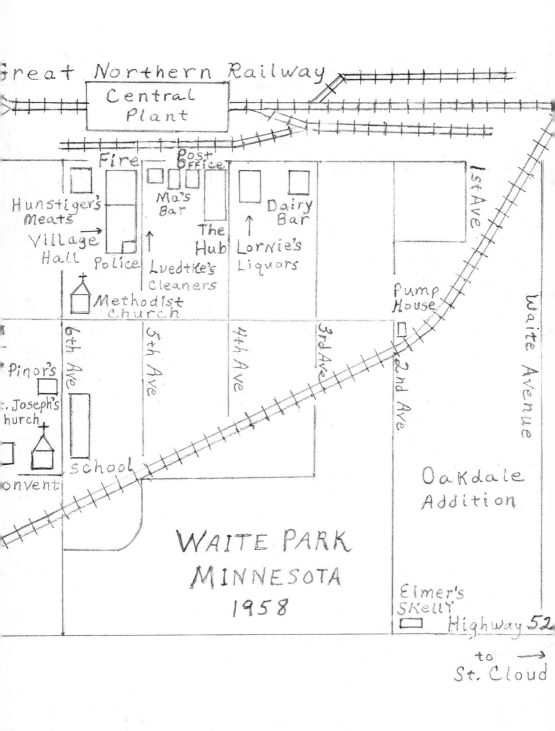

Great Northern Railway

Central Plant

Fire

Post Office

Hunstiger's Meats

Ma's Bar

Dairy Bar

Village Hall

The Hub

Police

Lornie's Liquors

Luedtke's Cleaners

Methodist Church

1st Ave

Pinor's

6th Ave

5th Ave

4th Ave

3rd Ave

Pump House

2nd Ave

Waite Avenue

St. Joseph's Church

Convent

school

Oakdale Addition

WAITE PARK
MINNESOTA
1958

Elmer's Skelly

Highway 52

to →
St. Cloud

SPRING

CHAPTER ONE

MAY, 1958

The loud blast from the railroad's yard whistle dipped across the tracks and into the village. Its low drone, like that of a thousand train whistles, interrupted the late afternoon stillness. The great sound reverberated in every direction. It glided east five blocks up 3rd Street, past the post office and The Hub supper club to the Dairy Bar. There it swerved right and drifted into the Oakdale Addition, where there were, as yet, no sidewalks. At the same time, it rushed west eight blocks down 3rd Street past Ma's Bar and Luedtke's Cleaners, past the village hall and Hunstiger's meat market to the Moose Lodge across 13th Avenue. It ventured all the way down Sauk River Road to the Cloud Drive-In Theater at the edge of town.

But most of the volume carried due south and southeast and southwest, past McKinley school and the Methodist church, past St. Joseph's Catholic Church and school and Pinor's Market across the street, past Rocky's Shoe Shop up to Highway 52. There it brushed against Waite Park's commercial strip, featuring Elmer's Skelly, the Swan Café, Tegelman's Grocery, and the Wagon Wheel supper club. It crossed the highway and wafted through Lewis's Hatchery, perched on top of a hill just beyond the viaduct. The last remnants of the sound continued out nearly a mile toward the granite quarries in the distance.

Reversing the compass, north of the Great Northern Railway's yard lay wasteland that was not part of the village. It heard nothing. Only striped gophers and grasshoppers paused to consider the blast.

It was precisely 4:30 p.m., and streams of exhausted men, lunch pails under arms, poured south through the wire gates into 3rd Street. Today was Friday, pay day, lawn-mowing day. Once outside in the sunlight, small clusters formed. One or two proceeded directly across the street to Ma's Bar to wet their whistles in sudsy beer drawn by Fat Frannie or by her husband, Hank. But the others scattered, on foot mostly, sifting through Waite Park toward their homes. In twos and threes they strolled, telling the day's stories, grinning as they stopped at street corners to wave goodbye for the weekend.

Al Ryngsmuth trudged east along 3rd Street, his black lunchbox dangling from his hand. His pace quickened as he neared his yellow two-story house. He could see Jack Shogreen, next door, already mowing his yard into neat strips. Al had built the house in 1946, after the war, on property adjacent to his dad's. It dwarfed the little one-story shanty on the corner. How well he remembered those days when that shanty had stood alone on the block, in solitude, with an enormous garden protecting its back. More than anything, the garden reminded him of his mother. His father had first plowed it two days before she stepped off the train.

* * * * * * *

Johanna Halbauer had grown into young womanhood in Dansig, Germany. The daughter of a petty clerk, she was a pretty sixteen-year-old who possessed her mother's features. Despite the unsettling times, she was looking forward to her final year of grammar school. She dreamed of becoming a teacher. School would start in the fall.

And she was in love... with a boy named Franz. Joanna liked to sit beside him in his father's carriage. There was nothing wrong with a summer fling. But she felt something deeper for him. He was the young man of her dreams. In time he would ask her to marry him, and she would accept his proposal. His father was well-to-do, and they would live comfortably. Perhaps one day Franz would inherit his father's estate, and she might become a baroness. She would bear his children! It was such fun to speculate, but the possibilities were all in the future. For now, their romance would remain a summer lark.

Franz played the gentleman. At the end of each date, he pecked his goodbye on her cheek. It was a formality they would appreciate when they were wed. There was an indication of wanton passion in them both, but it would be better to control their fiery urges and abide by the rules of propriety. "It is better to wait," her mother had told her, smiling at her daughter's fierce longing. Their consuming love would be sweeter when manifested later on.

Franz petted her, and she liked the feel of his strong hands on her back and the brush of his lips against hers. His eyes were merry, full of desire, and sent her overtures of his love. Occasionally his breathing became deeper, and she felt herself tingling when she touched his skin. These were moments when they both found it difficult to calm themselves. She kissed him on the cheek, and then she withdrew her lips, preserving the delicate balance that was theirs.

The year was 1914, and the entire country was restless. Rumors of war circulated in the local newspapers daily. Everyone was nervous.

"There will be no war!" her father had proclaimed. "Kaiser Wilhelm has promised us this. He will keep the Fatherland out of war."

But Johanna's mother did not share her husband's belief; she feared the worst. She doubted that the Kaiser would fulfill his promise. Soon, she was sure. When her two oldest sons, Friedrich and Werner, were taken from her, conscripted into the Kaiser's navy in Dansig, she knew. She overruled her husband.

"We must go, Otto..., soon... now... to America before it's too late. Think of the children. We must protect the children."

Bitterly shaken, he agreed.

Johanna cried. "I will not go," she protested. "I will not leave Germany. This is my homeland; my future is here. I will not leave Franz! I will never leave him!"

"Say goodbye to him," her mother had told her. "Our future is not here. These are times of turmoil. There will be a war with France; it's coming soon. Look at what has happened to Friedrich and Werner. The same fate awaits Franz; he, too, will be conscripted into the Kaiser's navy. We must leave before leaving becomes impossible." Johanna felt her mother's arms around her. "We must travel to Hamburg tomorrow. The ship for America sails in three days. Your father has already bought tickets for the passage.

I'm sorry that it has to be this way, Johanna. But you must go with us. There will be other boys in America."

Johanna bristled in her arms. Her tears flowed freely.

"Say goodbye to him, my darling, and do not hate us for it."

Johanna met Franz in the garden behind his house, and he swept her into his arms. The moon shone brightly, and Johanna hugged him with a fervor that he had not expected. She snuggled into his embrace. Her lips sought his. Silently she kissed him, over and over. Her passion fueled his own. She pulled him closer, and then his breath felt steamy on her neck. He pulled her body to him and felt for her breasts.

She tried to push him away. Then she pulled him closer. She groped for him. And then she saw a rising terror in his eyes. He took hold of her hands and held them steady. "What's wrong?" he asked.

She was still silent and sought to free her hands. Her tears were flowing. "Oh, Franz," she wailed, "I love you so much!"

"But what is wrong, Johanna? You must tell me now."

"Just hold me, and never let me go."

"Tell me."

She looked at him tenderly, miserable in the knowledge that a vast ocean would soon separate them. "We're leaving, Franz, for America…"

"No, you can't go! Don't leave me…" And then he stopped. "When?"

"Tomorrow."

Dazed, he let go of her hands. "Will you come back?" he questioned. "Will you ever come back?"

She fought back her tears and gazed into his tormented eyes. "If I can," she promised. "If I ever can."

The F. Lorenz Shipping Company, domiciled in Hamburg, Germany, was a business that specialized in shipping, trade, and insurance. In June of 1914 young Ferdinand Carl Lorenz sat in his office at company headquarters in Hamburg and speculated on his company's future. As heir to the company fortune, he was proud of its lengthy heritage. To him, continuity was important. He looked about him and smiled. This was the same office that he, his father Carl, and his grandfather Ferdinand, the company's founder and his namesake, had used for ninety years.

The pride of the Lorenz fleet were ten Flying L-Liners, four-masted barques, huge sailing windjammers with royal sails over double top and topgallant sails. Most of the voyages were destined for the western coast of South America, where the ships would be loaded with Chilean nitrate.

Young Ferdinand was a shrewd businessman. The west to east voyage with holds full of saltpeter was profitable. But why not increase profits on the outward passage to the Americas?

By the turn of the 20th Century, opportunity was knocking. Immigration to America had risen to a fever pitch. Now, disillusioned by the threat of war, many Europeans, including Germans, sought escape. Ferdinand Lorenz seized the opportunity to transport human beings to America—for a sizeable fee.

The detour to New York was costly, but the profits far exceeded the expense. Once the ship was unloaded of its human cargo, it would make its way south to Cape Horn, pass through the treacherous waters of Tierra del Fuego and then sail up the coast to Valparaiso or Iquique.

Otto and Sophie Halbauer and four children departed their beloved Deutschland on the Flying L-Liner, *Leipzig*. The huge sailing ship left the port of Hamburg and entered the Baltic Sea in mid-June, bound for America. With a traveling speed of eight to nine knots, the ship was scheduled to dock in New York by the end of July. The passage had cost them most of their life savings, but Johanna's mother did not care. They had escaped the war.

Two weeks later, the Austrian archduke was assassinated. Now war with France was a certainty. In school Johanna had been taught a simple lesson in history: France was the arch-enemy of Germany—and always would be.

Then the unthinkable happened. People in steerage on the lower deck fell victim to fever, followed by spells of coughing. Suddenly one man died... and then another. "Diphtheria...

diphtheria…" whispered the passengers. "Shark bait… shark bait…" whispered the crew.

The conditions were crowded; the boat was overloaded. The immigrants aboard grew fearful. "What can we do?" they asked.

"There's nothing that can be done," they were told by the Second Mate, calling down from the deck above them. "Stay down on the lower deck. Do not try to come up here. If you do, you will be shot."

One afternoon Johanna's father began to sweat profusely. He felt light-headed and nauseous. That night the coughing began. He vomited. His wife held him tightly to her bosom, sponging his forehead with a wet kerchief. "Don't die, Otto!" she pleaded. "You mustn't die. We will be there soon." But he could not stop the coughing, and he grew pale and weak in her arms. Four days later, he died. Johanna watched his burial at sea. Off the starboard stern and in the ship's wake, sharks feasted. Johanna felt numb.

Two days after her father's death, her mother coughed up blood. She perspired with a fever. Her throat swelled, and her tongue was covered with a gray membrane. Johanna held the woman's head in her arms and cried. "Oh, Mother, I want Franz."

Her mother clutched her daughter's hands. "Johanna, don't look back… never back… always forward. Promise me. I want to die knowing you have a chance for happiness."

And then Johanna saw her mother close her eyes and gasp. She labored to breathe. The girl held her mother close to her bosom throughout the night. Before the day broke, Johanna's mother opened her eyes wide and stared at the stars overhead. She clutched her daughter and tried to lift her head. Her breathing was shallow and spasmodic. She labored to find her voice and spoke haltingly: "Protect your brother and sisters," her mother instructed her. "You are all they have now."

The end came swiftly, mercifully.

Johanna observed her mother's burial, saw the body slide overboard into the deep dark ocean. She witnessed the splash of the body and watched the brackish water swallow it up. "Momma! Poppa!" the girl screamed. She wanted to die with them. She was an orphan.

But she was not alone in her grief. Across the planks of the steerage floor, she saw a huddled body. It was that of a young girl, perhaps in her early teens. The girl looked so forlorn. Johanna approached her and knelt down beside her. The young girl looked up into the older girl's face. Her blue eyes were puffy and bloodshot; it was obvious that she had not slept in days. She was weeping uncontrollably, in agony. "Maman! Papa! lls sont morts!" She spoke in French. "They are dead!"

Johanna put her arms around the girl's shoulders to stop their shaking. "Haben Sie gegessen?" she asked in German. "Have you eaten?" The girl pulled back from her, afraid.

"She knows you are German," a young man seated on the floor next to them informed her. "She hasn't eaten for three days. Her parents have died of the disease. And she is sad, so sad. She doesn't want to be an orphan. She will die if she doesn't eat."

Johanna stuck her hand into her coat pocket and brought out a small loaf of bread. "Wir teilen, du und ich," she told the girl in German. "We will share, you and I." And she tore off a piece of the loaf.

The girl shook her head. "Non!"

Johanna took a bite of one half and held out the other half. "Essen," she urged while she chewed. The young mademoiselle stared up into the young fraulein's face. Then she took the bread and began to nibble on it. "Wir sind keine feinde. Wir sind keine feinde," stated Johanna softly. "We are not enemies. We are not enemies."

The next morning they entered New York's harbor. She looked up. Gleaming skyscrapers rose into the heavens. What magnificent buildings in this land of promise! The ship was about to dock when Johanna saw a sight that left a lasting impression on her. A small island lay off the port bow. On it stood a statue of a woman, a Roman goddess, holding a torch in her hand and raising it over her head.

"It's called the Statue of Liberty," stated the young man. "It's a gift from the people of France."

The woman was welcoming her to America, this land of new opportunity. She saw words on a plaque beneath the statue's feet. They were English words. She asked the young man to read them to her and to translate them:

...CRIES SHE
WITH SILENT LIPS. "GIVE ME YOUR TIRED, YOUR
  POOR,
YOUR HUDDLED MASSES YEARNING TO BREATHE
  FREE"...

Her mother had yearned to be free. Here she was across the Atlantic Ocean, far from home, an orphan with a little brother and two small sisters—and no idea of what her future held.

Johanna felt the young man's arms around her shoulders, squeezing them to his chest. Mortified, she pulled away and disengaged herself from him. She shrank away from him. He looked puzzled. He was not Franz. She would save herself for Franz.

They were quarantined for two weeks. The authorities at Ellis Island tried to be understanding. They spoke kindly to her, but they deemed that the four children had to be separated. The oldest girl could not raise them alone. She had pleaded with them. "Rudolf... Amelia... Emma...!" She cried when her brother and two young sisters were taken from her. She could not be consoled.

Johanna Halbauer was one of seventy-five orphans who departed from Ellis Island on August 22nd, 1914. Their confined stay had ranged from four weeks to eight months. The train rumbled along the tracks, moving steadily to the west. Out of her pocket Johanna pulled a photograph that her mother had given her before she died, a picture of their family. She looked at the images of her brother and sisters who had been taken from her. The memory of their dimpled faces framed itself in her mind as she pressed her face to the window glass of the train. "Rudolf... Amelia... Emma...!" The agony in her voice shook her, and her tears flowed. She was certain that she would never see them again. "Ich werde Sie nie vergessen!" "I will never forget you!"

For several hours Johanna slept. When she awoke, she felt the sway of the train beneath her. She was moving across the midsection of a land she did not know into a world that was foreign to her. One thing was certain: she must now start her new life alone.

Johanna kept track of the empty miles that passed: the rolling hills of Pennsylvania, the swaying rows of corn in Indiana and Illinois, the stockyards of Chicago, and then the undulating dairy land of Wisconsin. Perhaps she would remember her way back to Ellis Island... to Dansig... to...

She was shaken awake by a porter, who tugged gently at her arm. Minnesota… They were crossing a mighty river at a place called St. Cloud. She and five others would be disembarking at the next depot in a little village to the west. They would arrive in fifteen minutes.

Johanna shifted her gaze. Far below she saw a clear expanse of water swirling beneath the train bridge. She raised her eyes to study the solid masses of pine forest on either side of the river. An occasional structure dotted the landscape. The train rumbled steadily on.

Father Charles Grunewald, pastor of St. Joseph's Catholic Church, had been fidgeting on the platform of the Waite Park depot for nearly an hour. He checked his watch and snapped the gold lid shut before sliding it into his vest pocket. "What's keeping the train?" he muttered under his breath. He knew that he had suggested this project to Bishop Busch as a gesture of Christian charity. But he hadn't expected to be so personally involved. Mother of Mercy—orphans! Luckily, he had found homes for the five youngest, but not for the sixth, a young German girl.

Behind him in the shade on the left side of the platform sat young Mathias Ryngsmuth. He had heard Pastor Grunewald's pleas each Sunday for good families willing to adopt the orphans. Curiosity— and a touch of loneliness—had brought him out this day.

At 10:45 a.m. the Great Northern Empire Builder pulled into the Waite Park depot. The massive diesel engine puffed billows of charred smoke as it crossed the threshold of the station. Moments later, the long connecting rods on the train's wheels stiffened as the brakemen applied the brakes and the passenger cars ground to a halt.

Inside, Johanna felt suddenly bleary-eyed. The anxious faces outside her window became mere blurs. She sighed heavily and rose somewhat stiff and wobbly. She guided five small children down the aisle to the door and pushed it open. A wild rush of air, pungent with the scent of apple blossoms, greeted her. She felt welcomed. It freshened her spirits as she entered Waite Park for the first time. Seldom in her eighty-five years would she leave the village.

Mathias Ryngsmuth fell in love with Johanna Halbauer when she stepped off the train into the morning light. He was twenty-two. She was only sixteen and rail thin, but her eyes betrayed a defiance born of hardship. She went to work as a housekeeper for Pastor Grunewald and boarded there.

Young Matt, who attended church regularly, was soon even more frequent in his visits to St. Joseph's. Quite often he served at mass. He was intrigued by the young German girl who sat in a side pew, and his heart skipped a beat when she came up for Holy Communion. Carefully he placed the paten under her chin. He noticed her pious face as she closed her eyes and tilted her head back. He watched as Father Grunewald placed the sacred wafer on her tongue. How saintly she looked!

At first, she seemed to ignore the young man, to avoid eye-contact, but one time he saw her eyes flicker in his direction. They were penetrating eyes, searching into his soul, and it confused him more. What did she want? Had she ever been in love? There was no way to know her secrets, no way to fathom what was in her heart.

One morning Matt found an odd occasion to enter the rectory. There stood Johanna, ironing Father Grunewald's purple chasuble. Purple, the color of suffering. The young man approached her. The look in her eyes was distant, but knowing. She did not shrink back from him. Instead, she turned toward him and peered into his face.

Matt Ryngsmuth was moved to pity. How lonely she must be! We are two lonely birds in the same cage. She nodded, almost imperceptibly.

On impulse, he knelt down on one knee. He took her hands in his and kissed them tenderly. "I love you, Johanna. Marry me. Oh please, marry me."

She could not understand all the words, but she knew their meaning. She blushed and tried not to think of Franz. She remembered her mother's words: "Johanna, don't look back… never back… always forward." She had promised. Heartbroken, she stared at the young man kneeling in front of her. When he looked up at her, she saw his tears. She knew that she must give him her strength.

Later that evening with shovel in hand, young Matt Ryngsmuth stole to the back of his garden and next to the cabbages buried a purple chasuble with a hole burned accidentally into the silk fabric. The following week Father Grunewald questioned Johanna. Embarrassed, she was at a loss to explain the missing vestment.

A six-month-long courtship ensued. Groom and bride were married without fanfare the Saturday after Easter the following year.

Al was born on Christmas Day that year, two-and-a-half weeks premature. Johanna had just returned from midnight mass when she felt an uncommon twinge. Methodically she lit the woodstove and placed the iron kettle on the back burner to boil before she told Matt. He wept. She placed her hands on his shoulders to calm their shaking.

Mathias raced over the snow drifts to fetch Doctor Simpson. The moon was creamy and still aglow with a soft translucent light, but the wind was bitter across his face, a northwest front that foreboded a drastic change in season. The doctor was in, snoring snuggly on the sofa in the parlor. Mathias leaped past Mrs. Simpson to the doctor's side, his eyes wild and urgent. "She's *borning* him!" he shouted.

Doc Simpson grunted. He was too ornery, even on his good days, to dwell on this peculiar phrasing or on the coincidental timing of the delivery. Groggily he sat up and growled, "Hold your horses, young devil, at least until I put on my trousers."

Twenty-two hours later, Alcuin John Ryngsmuth entered Waite Park as its 564th resident. Doc Simpson, turning his collar up against the icy wind, dragged himself home to his parlor bed. All that night, while his wife slept, Mathias held his tiny son in his arms and just smiled and smiled.

The seasons turned into years, childhood years for Al. He remembered his mother's love for her garden. As a boy, he would find her there when he needed her. Even now, he could picture her weather-beaten face and leathery skin as she held back her own tears to comfort him. In the evenings she would rock him on the porch swing and admire her handiwork: crisp rows of carrots and beans and beets and onions, with the cabbages at the back, cabbages that always brought a wisp of a smile to her mouth, cabbages with a purple hue.

But he also remembered her anguished prayers and muffled cries in her bedroom at night, always in German, in Deutsch. "Momma, Poppa, lassen Sie mich nicht! Ich mit ihnen gehen will." In the morning he had asked her what it meant. She refused to answer. So, he had asked Father Grunewald. Finally the priest had agreed to translate it. "Mama, Papa, don't leave me! I want to go with you." Those cries still agonized him. They had terrorized him at the time, but they had also made him strong and self-reliant.

Al had followed in his father's footsteps. When the time came, he crossed 3rd Street and sought employment as a tinsmith at the Great Northern Railway's car shops. He married June Spieker from across the alley. She was expecting their sixth child any day now.

* * * * * * *

As he mounted the steps to the front porch, Al waved to Jack Shogreen. He skipped lightly through the kitchen to the back porch, dropping his lunchbox on the counter. He spotted June's red print house dress some fifty feet away. She was crouched on all fours, weeding a row of radishes. Al moved under the ancient elm tree that shaded the back yard near his house. A series of rickety steps had been nailed into the trunk. From above, in the tree house in the elm branches came a mixed chorus of children's voices.

Al grabbed the garden hose and tiptoed toward the garden in a mock surprise attack. When he came within range of his target, he twisted the nozzle of the hose, making it spray.

"They don't need watering, just weeding," volunteered June without looking up.

He twisted the nozzle shut.

She rocked back on her heels and wiped her forehead with the back of her hand. Her eyes flirted openly with him.

Al dropped the hose and lifted her to her feet. He mopped her perspiring brow with his hanky. "You look pretty when you're pregnant," he grinned.

She tried to twist away, but he pulled her in. "Don't I always?" she countered, arching her chin away from him, pretending to be miffed. But soon, she relented and nestled into his arms.

They shielded their eyes and gazed skyward. The first streaks of sunset were showing in the west, ribbons of orange that would gradually fade to crimson and finally to plum. Earlier, the clouds had been restless buffaloes stampeding through the airy grasslands above. But now they had settled for the night, content to graze the heavenly pastures.

"Finished Grandma's garden this morning," she whispered. She motioned toward the figure rocking gently on the shanty porch. "She's so pleased that it's spring again. I took over a vase of lilacs. They smell so sweet, like perfume, this time of year."

Al riveted his eyes on the lonely woman next door. "Dad always loved this time of year, too." At length, he turned toward the garden. "You should have the kids help you with this," he chided.

"Or my husband," she snapped. She tried to retain her angry pose, but the façade melted into an amused giggle. Almost as an afterthought, she added, "Or the mayor!" And then they both slapped their thighs in beefy laughter.

Al Ryngsmuth had been elected to his third consecutive term as mayor the past November. The tally had been 328 to 3. His opponent, Councilman Amos Borg, and probably Amos's wife had accounted for two of the negative ballots. But Al occasionally found himself wondering who that third dissenter might be. "I have a council meeting tonight," he announced to June.

"Not another one," she moaned. "I'd better start supper." She tugged at her dress and brushed away the dirt. "Why is the village council meeting on Friday night?"

"It's a special meeting on the new sewage plant. Amos Borg thinks it's important."

She reacted. "He thinks everything he does is important." Then she scuttled away into the house.

Out over the Great Northern's yard, a late flock of Canadian honkers was winging its way north along the Great Central Flyway to Canada. Al noted that the V-shaped formation was following the natural route along the Sauk River to the rapids north of St. Cloud, where the tributary joined the larger Mississippi. Their persistent, repetitive call floated down softly to him as they progressed along the northern horizon.

Without warning, his children's voices charged toward him in greeting. "Horsey! Horsey!" they demanded. He felt pleasure in allowing himself to be wrestled to the ground, his face pressed into the soft, lush grass. To show affection in public, even to family members, was not customary in a German Catholic community. But the straining hands at his arms and neck and legs and the agile bodies squirming on his back were all Al needed. He felt secure in their warmth. Although Al had never consciously formulated the thought, his family and the village community were concentric circles surrounding him, protecting him. It was all he had ever asked for, ever wanted. Five minutes later he yanked the cord on his lawnmower, and the Briggs and Stratton engine roared to life.

Down the road west on 3rd Street, three Knights of the Round Table gathered at a corner table in Ma's Bar. It was a long tradition that had been established before these men's time, and they had been entrusted to carry it on. They had grown to like the Romantic nature of the game, the fantasy and the intrigue of pretending to be someone nobler than they were. It was a welcome diversion from their mundane work at the car shops; *that* was reality.

The men reveled in their own cleverness. They pretended to be Sir Thomas Mallory's characters performing heroic deeds. For in their own lives they were anything but heroic. In Waite Park there were no dragons to fight and no damsels in distress. There simply were their wives at home, waiting for them to finish their beers and come home and help put the children to bed.

Howard Kappas, Sir Lancelot, sat at the table with his boyhood friends, Cortney Johanson and Herman Braun. They were good men, as loyal as the day was long. They had grown up together in Waite Park, playing pranks on one another in school during the fall, winter, and spring, and playing baseball for the Parkers in the summer. Together they had won, and together they had lost.

When the time came in 1945, together they joined the marines, and together they were shipped across the Pacific to fight the invading Japanese. Cortney was wounded in the leg. When they returned stateside, they married Waite Park girls.

The original Knights of the Round Table was a secret Masonic order. The knights of legend would rather have had their tongues cut out than disclose the nature of their business. The knights in Waite Park followed their example. Without taking any formal oath or making any formal vow, they knew they were sworn to secrecy. Not that there was anything to keep secret. But it was the code they lived by on Friday afternoons when the Knights met.

Fat Frannie, Ma's daughter, brought over a third round of beers. The men watched her sashay around the table, swiveling her hips for them to see. She was light on her feet for a big woman. Cortney, Sir Gawain, nodded approvingly. "Thank you, kind lady," he stated. He was trying to be as gallant as he could be. He saluted her by raising his glass and tipping it toward her.

Herman, Sir Pellinore, held out a five-dollar bill, which Frannie collected and deposited in the crevasse of her bosom. She sashayed away, for she knew enough not to listen openly to their banter. Behind the bar she busied herself, pretending not to eavesdrop. "Silly boys," she said to herself, "playing a silly game of make-believe."

Sir Gawain leaned forward toward his friend, Lancelot. He addressed his fellow knight. "Lancelot, do we have any business to conduct?"

"No, we have no business to conduct" came the reply. The questioner nodded several times. He searched the face of his brother knight.

He maintained his charade. "Sir Lancelot, you look disturbed. Cheer up. 'Tis almost summer. The baseball season will soon be upon us. What say you to the outlook? Do we have any decent prospects?" Sir Lancelot was silent.

"Art thou angry?" asked Sir Pellinore. He poked his moody friend's elbow. "I believe so. But 'tis time to put old grudges aside."

"Cut the crap," stated Howard suddenly. "The job should have been mine." It was an old wound that surfaced from time to time. "It should have been mine."

"They gave it to Paul Rausch," stated Cortney, dropping his Medieval facade. "Paul's a good man, a good foreman. He's fair." He paused and looked across the table at his friend. "But you're right; they should have given it to you. It should have been yours."

"The old man, Superintendent Steichel, went to school with Paul. That's why he promoted him, not you, Howie. It wasn't fair, but I understand it," surmised Herman. "It's still *who* you know, not *what* you know. That's the way the world works. Drink your beer, Sir Lancelot. Drink up. Your Guinevere is waiting for you at home in your bed." They liked to tease him about his character's infidelity. "Our maidens are at home, too."

Cortney laughed. "They're not maidens any more, Sir Pellinore." He looked at Frannie's voluptuous bosom and nodded approvingly. "And they're not in our beds!"

"Soon, they'll be old maids," Sir Pellinore joked. He, too, was gazing at the buxom woman behind the bar. Several customers on barstools were vying for her attention. At the far end of the bar, Hank, not a noteworthy man, was busy washing empty beer mugs in the sink.

The two men raised their glasses and tapped them lightly together. They waited for Howard to join them. "To the Knights of the Round Table!" they toasted. And then it was time to go.

CHAPTER TWO

Big Ben Tegelman perspired heavily as he slit through the last of twenty-four chicken breasts. Mrs. Stein wanted them delivered by 7:00, and that gave him only half an hour to spare. He wielded the carbon steel butcher knife with great delicacy, slicing through fatty skin tissue and bone to clean the entrails from the carcass. The head had already been removed and lay with twenty-three others, scattered in the pit out back. Ben's sons, Butch and Tommy, had butchered the birds that afternoon. Each of the twenty-four chickens had died squawking. They had run madly after decapitation, leg muscles twitching involuntarily.

* * * * * * *

Earlier that afternoon…

Butch Tegelman barely acknowledged the 4:30 whistle from the Great Northern Railway's yard. He was fighting to choke down his revulsion. Inside the pit the stench of warm blood hung low and still in the late afternoon heat. It stood pungent in his nostrils, and he breathed through his mouth to ease his discomfort.

Butch still remembered how his first experience at killing chickens had nauseated him and forced him to vomit in the weeds near the back fence. His dad had assured him that the birds felt no pain, that it was all part of the business; but he still found it repugnant. He also found it difficult to accept young Tommy's laughter. His brother's callousness shocked him. Butch swore softly while he plucked feathers. The heads in the dirt at his feet glared up at him, mocking him. "One more year," he muttered, "and I'm leaving—just one more year."

* * * * * * *

The little bells above the front door of the grocery tinkled as Mrs. Carter entered. Three small boys with runny noses dragged at her heels. "Another pint of cough syrup for them and a bottle of aspirin for her," Ben wagered to himself. "Those brats would give anyone a headache."

Marge Carter rounded the corner of the first aisle and caught sight of Ben Tegelman behind the meat case. She winced at his blood-stained apron and his soggy, sleeveless t-shirt that only partly covered his barrel chest. Ben paused in his carving and arched a bushy eyebrow in her direction. Ill-at-ease, she turned away and hastened toward the medicine rack. The clacking of her low-heeled shoes magnified the awkwardness of the moment. She towed the two small twins along, clasping them tightly in her grip.

Suddenly agitated, the mother turned back roughly. "Buster, get away from those chickens!" But the largest boy ignored her and pressed his nose against the glass case for a closer look. A small oval of steam formed just below his nostrils.

Ben's meat cleaver rocketed downward and struck the chopping block a mighty whap. The boy yelped and jumped back. A severed chicken wing lay on the cutting board next to the breast. Fascinated, the boy returned, and Ben watched a bubble of mucous smear his display case window.

"Buster Carter! You get away from him right now," Marge Carter croaked. But a pleading tone had entered her voice, and it took two threatening steps before the boy retreated in her direction. Grinning, he leaped past her half-hearted cuff into the last aisle.

Ben glared at them as they crossed to the checkout, where his daughter, Rose, would ring up the cough syrup and aspirin. He felt irritated. If only they would pay their bill, he could put up with those brats. But $110 was enough. He waited for the clamor to begin.

Up ahead, Marge Carter pushed the children through the checkout gate. Across from her stood a brown-eyed girl of fifteen, whose tender expression and jet black hair contrasted sharply with her own. Marge felt resentful. Pretty girls were always spoiled. She thought about herself. She had been called many things, ugly things, and not always behind her back. Some people had had the gall to say them to her face. Her eyes narrowed. The worst was being told she was the wife of a drunk. That hurt her the most. It inflicted a deep wound that scarred her and left her bitter.

Rose punched the numbers into the till: cough syrup... $1.27, aspirin... 79 cents. "Mrs. Carter, that'll be two dollars and six cents, ma'am." She tried to smile.

Marge Carter's temper flared. Not a formal woman, she was unaccustomed to routine courtesy. The sound of "ma'am" stung her ears. Her back stiffened. She was determined to teach this young hussy a lesson—not to be like her father.

"Put them in a bag," she ordered.

Rose bit her bottom lip and reached for a small brown bag. She felt a lump in her throat tighten.

"And charge it," Marge added dryly.

Rose stopped and her smile evaporated. She fumbled with the box of aspirin. "I'm sorry, Mrs. Carter, but we aren't charging any more. Dad said, 'Cash only... until you pay up.'"

Marge Carter's upper lip quivered. She clenched her hands tightly to keep them from trembling. "But my boys are sick; they need medicine," she complained, her voice rising in intensity. "You can't do this to us and get away with it!" she wailed. "Everyone else still charges. You're picking on us because we haven't got what you've got." She stared at the girl. "Don't be like him!" she hissed, jutting her chin over her shoulder toward the meat case.

Rose cast a helpless glance at her father. Ben saw her tears. He untied his apron and draped it over his arm as he marched up a middle aisle. "Mrs. Carter!" he bellowed with all the force of a raging bull. "If you have a complaint, I want to hear it. But leave my daughter out of it!"

Marge Carter wheeled, her frustration strained to its limit. Her snarl was abrupt and feline, a mother protecting her young. "Don't you dare!" The words bit the air between them and caused Ben to stop in his tracks. Even the three boys stood, mouth agape, watching her unexpected flare-up.

She pressed her attack. "My husband's out of work, and you won't give us credit. I know we're poor, but that ain't a reason to disrespect us." Her eyes sparked with belligerence, and her voice had a jagged edge. "I won't take that from you... or from her." She jerked her thumb toward the girl behind the counter.

Ben fought to control his anger. Now it was his turn to protest. He spoke bluntly. "This whole village knows that Pete doesn't have a job because he can't hold one. And you know it, too! When will you ever be able to pay your bill?"

Marge Carter protected her dignity. "When the check comes, we'll pay you... some."

Ben removed the spectacles from his round, balding head and pointed them directly at her. "That's just what you said last time. Your husband drinks up most of your welfare check, so how will you pay?" His small beady eyes punctuated his message.

She shrank under the weight of this truth, turned from him, and staggered against the counter. The big man shifted to a fresh theme. "You think I'm rich. This is a business I'm running. I have my own bills to pay and a family to feed."

Suddenly his outburst subsided. A curious swaying motion caught the corner of Ben's eye. He turned his attention to the three boys toying near the candy rack, but he was too late to prevent the crash. The wooden rack tottered under Buster's weight and then arched past its center of balance. Boxes of lemon gum drops and Snickers bars and Nut Goodies toppled to the floor. Jaw breakers scurried in thirty directions. Root beer barrels wobbled down the last aisle. Strings of twisted licorice fell under the checkout gate and lay crisscrossed like pick-up-sticks in intricate design. Three bags of M and M's split open, showering the green and cream checkered floor tiles with bright drops of red and orange and green and yellow.

At the crest of this avalanche rode five-year-old Buster, whooping excitedly. Seconds later he sat unharmed, somewhat awed by his own masterpiece, exhilarated by a strange mixture of fear and daring. A slow grin rippled his face. The other two children howled their delight and began stuffing their mouths with M and M's.

Ben Tegelman threw up his hands in disgust. They fell helplessly to his sides and flapped against his thighs. The boy's smirk reminded him of the smeared window in the meat case. His frustration surfaced. "Stay off the shelves!" Ben growled. Buster looked up at him, wide-eyed. His mother stepped between them.

"Don't you scold my children!" Marge Carter warned, lashing out at the store's owner. Her eyes were full of fire.

Ben looked at the woman and shook his head. His decision jelled. "This is my store," he stated flatly, defiantly, "and I'll run it the way I see fit. You had better look for charity elsewhere."

Marge Carter stared at him, her eyes hot with shame. It was at this moment that the bells above the door tinkled again, and two women entered. Lorraine O'Brian and Val Krause were just in time to see Marge Carter rise to full height, square, and deliver a large wad of spit to Ben Tegelman's face. They were stunned. Hastily they stepped aside as the woman and her three children brushed past them and exited out the door.

Outside, Marge Carter allowed her tears to form. They swelled in her eyes as she walked west along the highway toward her house. She clutched a small child fiercely in each hand. The largest boy, free of restriction, skipped along at her side as happy as a lark, grinning, fingering a loose tooth. He was thinking of the dozen Tootsie Roll Pops stuffed secretly inside his shirt.

Ben Tegelman wiped his face on his apron. He felt the huge weight of conscience on his shoulders. He had allowed that woman to goad him, to get under his skin. Feeling frustrated, he had lost his temper. Now he regretted his outburst deeply and was ashamed. In silence he wrapped the last chicken and carried the entire order into the ten-ton walk-in freezer, where the air was cold. The time was 6:46. Tommy would just have time to make the delivery.

At 7:00 o'clock Ben locked the front door. Still embarrassed, he waved a feeble farewell through the window to Mrs. O'Brian and Mrs. Krause as they departed. Rose had already gone, after restoring order to the candy rack. Ben looked up and down the four aisles of well-stocked shelves. On this day he felt no pride. He collected the contents of the till, switched off the lights, and climbed wearily up the staircase at the back.

Ben's family lived above the grocery store. His wife, Sarah, glanced at him as he entered. After twenty-two years of marriage, that was all she ever needed to judge his moods accurately. She knew that he was troubled. Rose had filled in the details.

Sarah was busy frying potatoes and pork chops for supper. The sizzling from the steaming pans lifted Ben's spirits. He patted Sarah's wide rump and sat down at the kitchen table. The usual pile of mail, bills and advertisements mostly, was stacked on the corner.

Little Susie crawled onto her father's lap. She was only eight and loved to glide her fingertips along Ben's arms, back and forth, combing the thick, matted hairs. It was her way of talking to him. Ben found her touch soothing and always looked forward to their daily routine.

Ben reached for the letters and shuffled through them rapidly. Near the bottom of the pack, he halted when one particular long envelope caught his eye. It had a California postmark that had been cancelled two days earlier. Ben broke the seal.

Sarah approached the table and scooped the potatoes into a large, green porcelain serving bowl. She craned her neck toward the letter, straining for a closer look.

"It's from Tweet," said Ben, and then he began to read in earnest. Sarah watched him. Long before he turned the page, his bushy eyebrows furrowed deeply.

* * * * * * *

Tweet Thorsten was Ben's nephew, the son of Ben's sister, Bernadette. He was the baby of the family and also its black sheep. His parents, already tired of raising children, had lost their ability to control him. So, they spoiled him instead. They had given in to his demands for years.

Ben tried to help and be a steadying influence. Uncle Ben was the only one the boy trusted. But his uncle was a generation older and had an old-fashioned attitude. Against Ben's advice, Tweet had quit school at age sixteen. No one was surprised when he announced one day that he was leaving Waite Park for a life of adventure.

A traveling circus troupe had passed through during the Benton County Fair. Two carnies, youths his age, had lured the teenage boy to them. They had dark complexions, and both were wearing gold earrings in the lobes of their ears. "Come with us," they invited. Tweet noticed a young gypsy girl in the next booth eyeing him as she worked.

"That's Esmeralda. She's mine," stated Jal. He had flashing white teeth. "But you can have one of your own," he offered. His male companion, Kem, simply grinned and shrugged. Their invitation intrigued Tweet. A wink was all it took. He had no friends in Waite Park. Blinded by thoughts of a glamorous, carefree life, Tweet Thorsten joined the circus as it headed north and west on its summer circuit.

For two months he traversed the Great Plains states of North Dakota and Montana, just south of the Canadian border. He saw their rolling wheat fields and massive stretches of prairie grassland. These eventually gave way to the Dakota Badlands and then to the foothills of the mighty Rockies. The air was hot and humid that summer, and the list of towns seemed endless: Fargo, Minot, Billings, Butte, Spokane. The glamour faded into reality.

The carnies lived as nomads. They swarmed into each town and assumed control over it. Theirs was the power of the spectacle, of illusion. By day, they masqueraded under the charm of the street fair and childish gaiety. By night, they ravaged the town as lawless gypsies. Behind them they left a slim but well-defined trail of bloodshed and tears. Occasionally they told their stories in the wee morning hours around an open campfire of crackling birch logs. The flames danced. Drink made them bold, and they bragged of their exploits. They boasted of theft and knife fights and murder and rape.

One night, as the campfire grew dim, Tweet sat by the dying embers with several young carnies. The young men and women were soon absorbed in one another. Couples rolled away from the fire into the shadows of the night.

Tweet watched with envy as Jal and Esmeralda kissed and fondled. He saw Esmeralda's fine metallic skin shimmer in the moonlight, glistening with sweat.

Then Tweet felt someone touch him, someone with soft feminine fingers that stroked his chest. A young girl caressed him, and then she fell into his arms. Her black eyes were enchanting. Her olive skin gleamed in the waning firelight.

"Here, drink this," she instructed. "It will calm you." She offered him drink from a goat skin. Her breath itself was intoxicating, and as he drank, he relaxed and the smoke from the fire made his head swim.

The light was dying. Across the fire he watched Jal and Esmeralda embrace. Tweet's lips sought contact with the girl's.

"Another sip," his companion urged. She continued to massage his chest down into his abdomen. He complied.

The world began to swirl around him, and he settled into the young girl's arms, comforted by her caress. Her mouth closed on his. He relaxed.

When he opened his eyes, it was almost daylight. The fire had burned out, and only a few glowing cinders among the ashes remained. She was gone as were Jal and Esmeralda. So was his wallet.

His head ached from the drink as he dragged himself to his tent.

His complaint fell on deaf ears. Jal and Kem turned away in the throes of sleep. Finally Jal turned to face him.

"Ah, she's a tricky one," acknowledged the boy. Patya has a reputation, but that is to be expected—of all gypsies."

"Tweet cursed himself. "I was a fool to trust her."

"You are not the first young man to fall prey to the gypsy spell. Nor the last. I'll see what I can do," stated Jal. Right now, there's nothing to do but sleep."

The next morning the young carnie with the flashing white teeth approached him, wallet in hand. It was empty.

"Where did you find it?" asked Tweet.

"Under a rock near the fire. She's jealous of Esmeralda. It's a common trait among gypsies. I am to see her tonight. But, my friend, your money is gone."

The carnies lived as they pleased in the towns they served. They conformed to no external laws. But the internal code of law within the camp was severe and unforgiving. A day later, outside of Butte, Montana, Tweet saw the law challenged and justice administered.

Jal, the young carnie with flashing white teeth, had found Patya tempting. He did not resist her advances. Instead, he chose an ill-fated hour to satisfy his lust for a fifteen-year-old gypsy girl. He was caught, and this was held by most observers to be his worst crime.

The victim was the daughter of a long-standing member of the inner clan. Tweet recognized her olive skin and piercing black eyes. Patya's testimony hung bitterly in the shadows of the night.

"She trapped me," Jal argued, protesting his innocence. She's jealous of Esmeralda. I tried to resist her charms. I *did* resist her...," he cried out, "...at first."

He looked about the tent, and his eyes caught those of his friend. "Tweet! Speak to them," cried the boy. "You were with her by the fire. She charmed you, too. Tell them!" he screamed. "She stole your wallet. You're as guilty as I am!"

Tweet trembled. All eyes shifted his way. He felt them stare at him, the weight of generations of tribal law. Among those eyes were Patya's, black and penetrating. It could easily have been him they were trying—his fate they were deciding. He lowered his eyes and could not speak.

All eyes shifted back to the young man on trial. Tears swelled in the eyes of the accused, but his fate was sealed. He was now a captive, a hunted animal at bay. The faces surrounding him were merciless and unbending.

Jal's black eyes searched the room and found those of Patya staring at him, harsh and unforgiving. She had stalked him and trapped him in her gypsy lair. His anger flared. Suddenly, like a wounded animal, he lunged for the door. But he was caught and restrained by many hands. Foremost among those hands were Kem's.

The gypsy boy fought to free himself. "Esmeralda!" he shrieked, looking directly at Patya. "Esmeralda!" She saw the fierce light in his eyes, and she knew that he wanted to torment her. Only Tweet saw the snarl that formed on her upper lip.

Jal tried to cry out again, but his captors gagged him with a silk scarf and bound their prisoner with rope. The gypsy girl watched Jal struggle against the rope, writhing like an untameable animal.

Outside the tent, the campfire burned low. A procession of men left the camp. Fearful, Tweet Thorsten stole away. No one had invited him to witness the culminating ritual. But then, overcome with guilt, he followed them in secret.

He kept a safe distance. When the human caravan stopped, Tweet climbed high up a limestone knoll and, crouching down, hid himself behind a rocky outcropping. Perched atop the knoll, he looked on in disbelief. The solemnity with which the ritual was acted out made a lasting impression.

Somber-faced men dug a pit seven feet deep in the sand in a ravine beyond the camp. As the first streaks of pink daylight rippled in the eastern sky, the young man was lowered into the pit and buried to his neck. The gag was removed, but Jal's screams were momentary. A length of radiator hose—just short—was thrust into his mouth and down into his throat. He was forced to bite the hose to stop it from gagging him.

The girl's father watched impassively. His eyes, like those of some great war bird, riveted themselves on the face of the convicted boy. His work would come last.

More sand was shoveled into the pit, burying the head. The ground was level once again with only the life-supporting tube protruding inches above the ground. The hose emitted shallow reverberations as air was sucked into it and then expelled. The sound echoed rhythmically and dissipated into the night.

The father stood up and advanced until he hovered over the spot. He was older and more patriarchal than the others. He crouched on his haunches over the pipe and then clawed the ground beside him, scooping up sand, filling his great hands with thousands of tiny grains. He allowed them to stream downward, in single file, through the hollow of the hose.

Instantly the pulsations inside the tube turned to gurgling. The pace of breathing quickened. Within ten seconds the throat of the prisoner gagged and the stomach belched. A vaporous stench rose upward, filling the old man's nostrils. But his eyes never wavered. He continued pouring sand into the tube long after the breathing stopped.

At last, the sand neared the brim. The old man knelt. Ceremoniously he unhitched the buckle of his belt, lowered his trousers, and dribbled urine into the end of the hose. Then he left. The other carnies followed in procession, urinating violently, even defecating, heaping their tribute to the code of law by which they lived.

Tweet sat back trembling. Not a word had been spoken. This made the deepest impression on him. He had just witnessed a civilized species destroy one of its own. No animal would do the same, and yet, like animals staking claim to territory, they had marked the spot. One icy thought pervaded: these were no longer his brethren.

When they were gone, Tweet scrambled to his feet. The new day was fast approaching. The ghostly half-light was giving way to a gray dawn. Small pebbles of the rocky knoll beneath him gave way as he kicked his way down the hillside. He stole close to the burial grave. The length of rubber hose had been removed, perhaps to be used again. All that remained was a shallow impression, filled with dirt. It blended in with the stark landscape around it, a wasteland. In the distance lay the buttes of Montana.

Tweet stepped back in revulsion. The young carnie was his friend. He felt deeply disturbed. A human being was buried here on this spot; they had killed him in cold blood. It could have—would have—been him.

Hasty noises from not far away told him the camp was on the move. By morning they were gone, heading west, but Tweet Thorsten was not among them. He was nestled in an empty car of a Great Northern freight train, heading east, back to Minnesota, back to Waite Park, back to his people, where he belonged.

The rumbling of the boxcar on the iron tracks comforted him. It would be well over thirty hours until the train lumbered into the Waite Park depot—ample time to ponder past and future. He shivered slightly at the thought of the young carnie's flashing white teeth. That would haunt him forever. But now he allowed his thoughts to drift ahead. Tweet's tenure with the carnies had spanned a mere two months. Yet, they had bequeathed him their legacy; they had taught him to hustle.

The passenger car swaying gently beneath him spawned an idea. A wisp of a smile, devilishly minute, formed at the corners of his mouth. There had always been an itching in Tweet's belly. Years of humiliation had transformed it into a gnawing hunger. Now it would be satisfied. His brain suddenly was racing; the idea was struggling to take form. Carefully he nudged the details into place. When the idea finally crystallized, Tweet shot bolt upright in his seat. His smile broadened into a sly grin. He knew what he must do.

When Tweet returned to Waite Park, there was no hero's welcome. His parents had grown accustomed to his absence. Tweet applied for, and secured, a job at the car shops. Ben's influence had helped.

The Great Northern Railway's car shops spanned thirteen city blocks. The yard itself was crisscrossed with an interlocking network of steel ribbon. This intricate pattern consisted of a series of tracks and switches that enabled dozens of impaired cars to be worked on at the same time. Crews were assigned to various details. They swarmed over each boxcar or engine, inspecting damage, measuring, determining what repairs were needed.

At the east end of the car shops stood a massive steel building that housed the welders and tinsmiths who reconstructed broken parts and manufactured new ones, if necessary, and assembled them. Together, these men constituted a self-sufficient lot. Skilled craftsmanship bred a confidence that no task was too large an undertaking, that no problem was insurmountable.

The first frost arrived early that November morning. The branches of the elm trees along 3rd Street were wrapped in an icy glaze that made them click as, swaying together in the wind, they brushed together. Paul Rausch and his crew had been on the job for over two hours. Their task was to salvage parts from a thirty-ton freight car that had been demolished in a twenty-car derailment near Little Falls. Paul's experienced eye told him that even though the boxcar's frame was twisted, most of the hardware could be salvaged and reused.

Paul jerked his head skyward as the sun peaked out for the first time that morning. The sun's rays felt warm on his bull neck. A good foreman, Paul trusted his men. He had worked side by side with all of them before he was promoted. Howard Kappas was one of the best. So were Cortney Johanson and Herman Braun—good drinking buddies too. Paul thought to himself: that Fat Frannie always gives us all a laugh over a two-bit bottle of Hamm's on Friday afternoon. But his thoughts sobered as he watched the new man wrenching lug nuts from the lumber that had already been stripped from the boxcar's paneling. Tweet Thorsten... Big Ben's nephew... moody... spoiled. They must have put him on my crew because Ben and I are neighbors.

The weather was still cold. Atop the boxcar Howard was fretting. Paul eyed the narrow rungs of the ladder leading to the roof. If he had been younger, he would have shinnied up them himself. He looked around. Cortney and Herman were inside the boxcar. "Thorsten, come over here."

Tweet dropped the wrench to the ground. How long would he take orders from that obese Paul Rausch? The morning coolness seized him, making him shiver.

"Go up top and help Howard." Paul's voice was commanding. Tweet reached for the lowest rung and swung his weight upward.

Neither Howard nor Paul, the one man who actually saw it, could describe accurately what happened next. Tweet's right hand slipped on the top rung. His left foot slid off its rung and shot out at a right angle from his body, throwing him off balance. Tweet's whole body lurched away from the boxcar. Stretched flat, it struck the ground squarely and bounced a foot into the air. Then it settled in a heap in the frozen mud.

Tweet groaned in pain. Paul rushed to his side. Howard scampered down the rungs. Cortney and Herman heard the cry and appeared in the doorway of the freight car. "Don't touch me!" Tweet screamed, agony twisting his face. "Call a doctor. I can't feel my legs. I can't walk."

* * * * * * *

Ben Tegelman put down the letter out of little Susie's reach. Her inquisitive hands reached for it but then contented themselves with combing along Ben's arms. Sarah sat down heavily opposite him, her eyes prying for information. Unwilling to speak first, she searched her husband's troubled face.

Ben knew the rest of the story all too well. An ambulance had arrived and taken Tweet into St. Cloud for x-rays. Curiously, nothing abnormal had revealed itself—no broken bones, no cracked vertebrae, nothing. Suspicion surfaced. For six months Tweet strapped himself into a wheel chair. Insurance investigators arrived from Minneapolis and St. Paul. One undercover agent with a hidden camera even spied on Tweet's home, day and night, for any telltale sign of fraud. Finally, North Star Life and Casualty had been forced to pay off—$10,000. A week later Tweet disappeared, perhaps for good.

Sarah stabbed a pork chop with her fork and placed it on her plate. She shoved the platter of steaming meat toward Ben. "Well?" she coaxed.

Ben shifted Susie onto her chair beside him. Suddenly he felt so tired. He met his wife's gaze with trembling lip. "Tweet's in California. He says he's found a miracle doctor. He's been cured!"

CHAPTER THREE

The small boy rolled onto his stomach. He lay in the dirt alone in the alley behind his dad's garage. For the time being, he busied himself watching a column of red ants crawl into a sandy hole along the driveway. All around him the ground was checkered with a shifting pattern of shadows caused by the big elm trees overhead. Suddenly the western sun struck him full in the face. He squinted into it, squeezing the light into vertical rays. This absorbed him immensely, pleasurably. He relaxed and squinted again, closing his eyelids until the entire world turned hazy.

The 4:30 whistle from the Great Northern Railway's car shops brought him out of his reverie. At last, he stood up. His blue jeans were grass stained, especially the patches over the knees. He was tall for his age, with a shock of blond hair falling over into his eyes. He could hear other children in the distance from across the alley in the screen house at the O'Brians'. Big boys, plotting misadventures. They were beyond his years, so he ignored them.

The hum of a motor caught his attention. The sound was loud, heavy, and pulsating. A red Chevy approached. As it rumbled down the alley, it pushed a cloud of dust in front of it. The car sped up, and the boy stepped out of its path. The driver had one flabby arm draped out the window. His red hair matched the Chevy's fire engine color. Bertie Norton chuckled openly as he passed by, the sun bouncing off his thick glasses. The boy squinted. Bertie laughed. He flicked his middle finger upward and punched the accelerator down. The Chevy's white sidewalls spun counterclockwise, spitting gravel behind them.

The bigger boys emerged from the screen house and strolled toward an old house three doors away. The house itself, long abandoned, served as a haven away from parental eyes; its yard was the neighborhood ball field. They were led by Timmy O'Brian, a squat, pudgy nine-year-old of Irish descent. In his fist he carried a menacing stick. The other five were armed with baseball bats and gloves.

Timmy glowered and feigned an attack. The small boy stepped back onto family property. He kept his eye on the stick. Timmy picked up a rock and slung it at a power pole. *Clunk*. The rock connected viciously. Timmy picked up another jagged piece of granite. The boy squinted. He did not see the rock graze his arm, but he soon became aware of the stream of bright blood that was trickling down his forearm. He did not feel any pain, only a sense of alarm and dread. Emboldened, the other boys stooped for rocks of their own. Timmy pointed his stick at him to hex him.

But the ballyhoo stopped abruptly, and one of the boys turned. Across the many yards his mother's voice rang out. "Doug…las!" Her cry wafted over the entire neighborhood, commanding an immediate response. The six boys dodged behind the boy's garage, angled across the front of his house, and disappeared up 11th Avenue toward the highway. The boy, squinting into the distance, watched them. Then, for some reason, he followed them.

He followed them up to Highway 52, where they turned left. Massive trucks heading west buzzed by, picking up speed. Timmy threw a rock. It clanked off a semitrailer as the rig's path intercepted the rock's trajectory. The driver slowed momentarily, and the truck lurched. Then he punched the accelerator to the floor, sending a burst of black smoke out of the dual exhausts that extended vertically behind the cab.

Timmy's band watched the semi carefully. Occasionally a driver would turn right on 12th Avenue and give chase. But an angry truck driver was no match for fleet-footed urchins who knew the territory.

The boys crossed 10th Avenue and climbed the arching viaduct. There they joined another band of three boys, Ray and Robbie

Stein and their cousin from St. Cloud, Clayton Zern. Clayton was holding a gunnysack that wriggled in his hands. A red gasoline can lay at their feet. The young boy tailed them to within seventy-five yards. Then he crouched down against a cement pillar while cars and trucks roared by. He observed carefully. What he saw was Robbie Stein twist the cap from the red can.

A loud train whistle sounded to the west. Clayton Zern's movements quickened. He untied the sack's drawstring and reached inside the pouch. A tail emerged. Robbie raised the can and poured a stream of yellow liquid into the sack. Another blast from the west told them that the train was approaching—fast.

Clayton yanked the tail out and exposed a cat, its black fur drenched in gasoline, its face a mixture of feline anger and terror. It screeched a blood-curdling meow. Clayton grabbed the loose fur behind the cat's neck and pinned it. The cat arched its body and stretched its limbs. It splayed its claws, striking futile blows.

The train came suddenly into view, a bulging black mass of iron. Just as it entered the tunnel beneath the viaduct, Ray Stein lit a stick match. He flicked it into the cat's face and the whiskers ignited. In a moment a ball of flame erupted, and Clayton Zern let go of the cat's neck. A second later he let go of the tail, and the cat, flailing helplessly, plunged down toward the tracks below.

The boys leaned in a row over the railing to watch. The fireball was swallowed by the jaws of the passing train. The cat's piercing shriek was stilled by the locomotive's metallic rumbling as the wheels rolled over the carcass.

In the distance the young boy shuddered. The flaming cat had left its imprint on him. In the stillness that followed, he could still hear its screams. He turned to go home. The last word he heard was from Robbie Stein. "Purrfect... Purrfect..." the rebel boy crowed over and over, much pleased with his clever play on words.

After supper the young boy drifted up the alley. A crowd of spectators had gathered around the woodpile in the Rausches' back yard. Atop the woodpile, hands clenched into fists, stood Joe Rausch and his brother, Frannie. Frannie, one year younger than Joe, had the crowd on his side, except for Ray Stein, who stood stolidly in Joe's corner. Their punches were real and sharp. *Crunch… crunch…* "ow!" *crack…* Gradually Joe, older and more powerful, was gaining the upper hand. Tears were forming in Frannie's eyes.

On the steps sat their young sister, Barbie. Her hair was matted; her skin, unwashed and full of grime. She had been crying, and tears stained her cheeks. A forceful clip on Frannie's chin sent her into spasms of rage.

"You killed my cat," she ranted. "You killed my cat. You killed Fluffy."

She looked daggers at Ray Stein. "You're a murderer!" she bawled. The boy from across the alley tilted his head and shrugged, but said nothing.

Seeing his sister's agony, Frannie unleashed a vicious attack. He leaped. But Joe deftly countered it. He caught Frannie off balance and landed a decisive punch. It sent the younger lad off the woodpile headfirst. It was over, except for the recriminations.

Frannie's face was puffy around the eyes, and his cheeks were bruised. He was bleeding from the nose. He pinched his left nostril shut as he spoke, crying out his accusation. "You gave them Barbie's cat."

"So what? I hate cats," was Joe's retort. All eyes were on him. "It was a stray," he added. And after an awkward pause… "I didn't kill it."

"Look at her cryin'. You shouldn't 'a done that. You're a pea brain!"

Joe's face turned ugly. "Come up here, and I'll beat the piss out of you again."

"Pee brain!" screamed Barbie from the steps. "You piss from your brain."

"I'll show you who's a pea brain," growled Joe. He leaped off the woodpile in her direction.

The girl jumped to her feet and aimed one final barb at him. "Murderer!" she hissed. "I'm telling Mom." And she retreated into the relative safety of the house.

"Well, I'll tell Dad!" he blurted to no one in particular. Then he and Ray Stein marched off across the highway toward the granite quarries in the distance. Dead Man's or Camel or Granite City, they were safe havens for rebellious young outlaws.

The granite quarries south of the village were places where teenagers hung out. Out on the granite rocks or in the water, adolescent boys and girls were free to do as they pleased. There they were free from adult intervention; their parents could not interfere.

A month earlier "Chigger" Hoffman had wanted to prove it. Chigger had dived from an outcropping one hundred feet above the surface of Dead Man's quarry. He had landed—a perfect belly flop—with a thunderous clap into the water. The impact had torn open his gut and ruptured his spleen, but he had proved his point: no one had stopped him. An ambulance was summoned. It carted the teenaged boy off to the St. Cloud Hospital, where he was confined for two weeks.

"Hey, pea brain!" yelled Timmy. He was speaking to the young boy at the fringe of the crowd. The boy immediately took two steps back. He squinted into the sun and blinked hard. "Let's fight," suggested Timmy, "up on the woodpile, you and me."

The younger boy said nothing. He did not immediately run away, but he kept his eyes riveted on Timmy. They were nearly the same size. Perhaps one day he might fight him… when the older boy didn't have his gang around him. Timmy's younger brother, Terry Joe, came up beside the young boy. He stepped past him and faced his brother. "You're the pea brain."

This unexpected support from his best friend strengthened the young boy's spine. Today he was not alone and would not let this older boy bully him. Together, they could stand strong against attack.

Timmy, not quite sure what to do, picked up a rock. But he knew that if he hit his brother, he would be in serious trouble at home. Lorraine O'Brian had an Irish temper and a harsh way with sons who provoked her. "You're both pansy asses," he blurted out. He spat and then left, followed by his pack of young hounds.

The bystanders split up. "Come on, Frankie; let's go ride our bikes," suggested Terry Joe.

As the sun set, the evening sky grew delicious, a taffy of flavors: lemon and orange, then cherry fading into plum. The two boys pedaled their Schwinns up and down the side streets in the west end of the village. Their boundaries were McKinley Elementary to the east and the community park to the west. Their northerly course took them past a white two-story structure with a brick facade, Rocky's Shoe Shop. A sign in the window read

REPAIR YOUR SHOES OR ELSE in bold black letters. It had been taped onto the glass years ago, and no one ever asked "Or Else What?" Next to it hung a poster advertising this year's Fourth of July soap box derby. And next to that, official notice of a quilting party to be held the following Thursday at St. Joseph's Catholic Grade School, Room 104, sponsored by the Ladies Guild.

"Let's stop here," suggested Terry Joe. "I've gotta take a leak." He jumped off his bicycle, letting it fall, and darted behind Rocky's shrubbery.

Just then the door of the shoe shop opened, and Tillie Kuchenmeister stepped onto the top step. She was a large, big-breasted woman. Always attentive, she noticed the white blob in the bushes. It was Terry Joe in midstream.

"Stop that, you fool!" she blurted.

Suddenly conscious of a woman's presence, Terry Joe looked at her helplessly. He couldn't stop. But he could turn. Unfortunately he turned toward her. Also unfortunate was that her sharp words sent a sudden burst of adrenaline coursing through his urinary tract. The result was an immediate increase in both the length and intensity of the stream.

"My shoes!" she gasped. She leaped back and surveyed the damage. "You squirted all over my leather shoes. They're ruined!" She lunged to grab the boy, but he broke free from her clutches. Still unzipped, he scrambled onto his bike and pedaled.

"Your wiener's showin'," said his friend as they sped down the block. "And your pants are wet." They heard a woman's shriek in the distance behind them. "Come back, you little squirt!"

"She'll call my mom," said Terry Joe huskily. His face was glum. "They're both in the Ladies Guild at church."

"I know," said Frankie. "My mom's in it too, Circle 13." Religious affiliations created a transparency: Lorraine O'Brian would know before they arrived home.

At 3rd Street the railroad depot loomed in front of them, protected by a wire mesh fence. Secondary spikes of railroad tracks branched off from the primary track alongside the central plant. A long section of train with an engine and boxcars colored orange and green stood silent on one of the spikes. Stamped on the front of the engine was a picture of a goat climbing a mountain. "That's a Great Northern Empire Builder," noted Terry Joe. "It climbs the mountains in Montana like a billy goat."

The boys turned right onto 3rd Street and, after pedaling half a block, detoured from the streets into the alleys. These were dirt: sandy loam covered with gravel. The alleys opened onto the back yards, exposing the underbellies of the properties. They were totally different from the front yards. Here is where the people lived. Here is where they worked and played.

Nearly every yard contained a rectangular garden plot, which would soon be laden with produce. Many had already been tilled. In the coming weeks the women of the village would plant rows of lettuce and beans, radishes and carrots, onions and potatoes and snap peas. They would plant patches of cucumbers and squash and a few pumpkins and watermelons. At one end of the garden, they would dig in kernels of corn, which grew profusely and whose tall stalks would provide sweet golden ears. At the other end they would sow the seeds and bulbs of flowers: zinnias, petunias, gladiolas, irises, and hollyhocks. A rose bush would be prominently placed to complete the display. All summer long, these housewives would venture out into the garden to water the tender crops and to hoe the weeds. Naturally, they would call to each other in the neighboring yards to sing the praises of summer's bounty and to gossip. They shared the news of the day, *tsk-tsking* that of which they did not approve. It was a morning routine, for the afternoons were too hot.

The men of Waite Park worked in their garages. Built into most of them was a shop with a work bench. It was handy for home construction and repair and for automotive maintenance. These men were skilled with their hands, able to weld iron and saw wood and hammer nails. They were craftsmen. That fact bred confidence. They spent their evenings and weekends in retreat, refinishing furniture and mending broken household furnishings and children's toys. Refurbishing old cars was both practical and economical. A man's tinkering in his garage served a dual purpose; it provided both satisfaction and an escape.

The children of these men and women played in the back yard. Some occupied forts from which they ruled the neighborhood. Some of the older ones, seeking the advantage of height, built tree houses, up high enough where they could test their adolescence in secrecy. Still others, less domesticated, less evolved, merely perched on the branches of trees like birds or wild monkeys. Below them the younger children swayed in a pendulum motion on a swing set or a tire swing, pumping their legs for elevation. Then suddenly they would shift in pairs to the teeter totter, riding in unison up and down, up and down, springing like bullfrogs for leverage. These hungered for motion.

Most of the yards were empty. But several shops were lit. The boys raced south on this leg of their journey, pretending to be jockeys on thoroughbreds. The finish line was Walter Unger's backyard shop. A man of sixty, gray-haired and mild-mannered, Walter had found his niche in the community as a bicycle repair man. Children on bikes stopped in as a matter of routine; he always had a piece of candy handy for potential customers.

"Hi, Walt," said Terry Joe as he reined his metal pony to a stop. "What're ya doin'?"

Walt Unger eyed the boy patiently. "Just relaxing."

"Can't you relax inside the house?" was the boy's next question.

The man looked amused. "Not really." He chuckled, looking left and right at no one in particular.

"Is Jerry home?" asked the other boy, Frankie? "He's in my class at school, Sister Mary Andrew's First Grade.

"If you'll excuse me, I'll see" was his reply. The bicycle repairman stopped abruptly. He was staring at the front of Terry Joe's pants. Terry Joe turned sideways; he seemed embarrassed. Then Walter left.

The bike shop was a curiosity of treasures. Against one wall lay a metal work bench, above which hung the tools of Walt Unger's trade: rows of open-ended wrenches, a socket set, Allen wrenches, screw drivers, pliers, different-sized vise grips, an oil can, and a grease gun. A fifty gallon drum containing oily rags stood in the corner at one end of the work table with a large box of clean rags above it. On a second wall was suspended a network of wooden shelves holding a vast assortment of chains and sprockets and brake levers and replacement wheel spokes. Below these shelves lay boxes of handle bars and fenders and seats and new wheels. The third wall was a display of mirrors, reflectors, new seat covers and the latest handle grips. In front of the wall stood a glass counter, on top of which rested an old metal till. A wooden water bucket, filled with packages of streamers for children's bikes and tricycles, decorated the counter. Frankie noted that most of the streamers were red, white, and blue; the Fourth of July parade, fast approaching, was only two months away.

But it was the fourth wall that drew the boys' attention most. Sheets of plywood held a dozen large, framed pictures of trains: trains glistening in the morning sunshine on journeys west through the badlands of North Dakota and over the mountains of Glacier National Park, Montana. They were glossy, black and white pictures of Great Northern Railway trains puffing black smoke, crossing train bridges over vast rivers in Idaho and Washington, and snaking along the iridescent Pacific Ocean in that paradise, California. On each engine the boys saw the goat climbing a mountain, moving along the skyline. And there in the pictures was Walter Unger, the engineer of those trains, wearing a gray-striped uniform, smiling from the engine's window and waving a gloved hand in salute.

Above the gallery was a two-by-ten plank, painted black. This shelf housed train engines and boxcars and cabooses, miniature replicas of the originals.

The young boys' eyes shifted. The focal point of the room was a glass case displaying a life-sized mannequin in a train engineer's outfit. The face was that of Walter Unger. He was dressed faultlessly in coveralls and a jacket, in the daunting gray pinstripes of the trade. There, on his head sat his engineer's cap. On his feet, black boots. A red-checkered kerchief was knotted around his neck. The chain of a gold pocket watch was attached to the front pocket of the jacket; the watch lay in the mannequin's hand. He was smiling.

"Would you like a piece of candy?" was Walt Unger's first question when he returned from the house. "Jerry is indisposed at the moment, but he'll be out in a jiffy."

"What does that mean—indisposed?" asked Terry Joe.

"He's in the bathroom," answered the engineer without a hitch in tempo." He pulled out two pieces of hard butterscotch candy. Terry Joe forgot all about his embarrassment. "Is that you, Walt?" He pointed at the mannequin.

Walter Unger paused. "That *was* me," he corrected, his eyes nostalgic. "I'm retired." He took out his handkerchief to blow his nose. It was identical to the red kerchief in the display. When he finished, his eyes were still a bit misty.

"Those are sure *purty* pictures," stated Terry Joe. The man nodded at the compliment.

"How are your bikes working?" Walt asked. He fiddled with the chain on Terry Joe's bicycle. "Hmm... it's a bit loose." The boys watched him search in his rows of tools for a particular socket wrench. He loosened a nut on the back sprocket and tightened the tension on the chain. "A little oil up front here on the chain will help, too." He applied the lubricating oil.

Jerry appeared. "Hi, Frankie," he muttered.

"Hi, Jerry."

"Would you like to see my train set again?"

The boys nodded. The three marched down the basement steps into the family room. All around them lay sets of tracks and an entire layout of a Bavarian landscape, replete with Alpine mountains, tunnels, even a glacial lake with a stream and a waterwheel. "This is Germany," proclaimed Jerry. "Unger is German." He flipped a switch and dimmed the ceiling lights. A European continental scene appeared.

"Dad helped me set it up." He flicked another switch.

A miniature train engine sprang to life. It pulled a complement of tiny boxcars down the opposite side of the tracks and up a winding mountain at the far end of the room. It disappeared behind the mountain and re-emerged up high in time to pass through a dark tunnel. The little Lionel engine's headlight swept the tracks before it. Its horn sounded. Triumphantly the train pushed forward at full throttle. The train passed in front of the boys and over a stout metallic bridge that spanned an artificial lake. As it entered the miniature town, music erupted, *The Bavarian Waltz*. The train twisted down its main street, passing toy shops with toy shopkeepers pivoting back and forth, each holding a tool of their trade: the mustached mason, a trowel; the burly barber, a clippers; the buxom baker woman, a rolling pin; the merry musician, a concertina. He yodeled as he played, and his neck stretched upward on the highest note.

The train chugged to the opposite end of the room and curved along the far wall, completing its circuit. The music continued while the train rounded the mountain again on its second lap, navigated the tunnel, crossed the bridge, and reentered the town.

The boy looked at Jerry, whose eyes were alight. Then an intruder on the steps drew the boy's attention. Jerry's sister, Caroline, entered the room. She was two years older than her brother. On her right arm she balanced a tray containing a pitcher and three glasses. "Want some Kool-Aid?" she asked. "Mom said to pour you some."

Frankie's eyes stared at the girl. She seemed somehow off balance. Her left arm did not match the right. It was only twelve inches long, a little baby's arm. It hung limp at her side, useless, dead weight. One-handed, Caroline poured the purple liquid into the glasses and departed.

"It never grew," volunteered Jerry. "I hope she cuts it off someday and gets a fake hand."

"Maybe it would grow back," suggested Terry Joe. "If you cut a leech in half, it'll grow back the other half."

"Regenerate" stated Jerry flatly. "Dad says that soon anything will be possible."

"Grape Kool-Aid," smiled Terry Joe, changing the subject. "Grape is my favorite."

Frankie tried to watch the train circling the room once more, but all he could think about was the tiny baby arm dangling from the girl's shoulder. He heard the music and watched the train, but for some unknown reason he wanted to leave the house.

"Let's go, Terry Joe," he muttered. The boys waved goodbye to father and son.

They pedaled south to the railroad tracks and then biked west, parallel to them. Just before the viaduct, they came to a little one room shanty no bigger than a one stall garage. "Watch out for Crazy Milo," warned Terry Joe. "He comes out at this time of night."

The house was roughly a cube with a pyramid sitting on top. Both the roof and the siding were shingled: charcoal on the top, honey on the sides. It had two windows on each side.

A shutter blinked. "Did you see that?" Terry Joe's pedaling had slowed to a crawl. His imagination was aflame. "He eats squirrels and rabbits that he catches after dark," asserted Terry Joe. "Grandma says she's seen him do it," he added, pointing to his Grandma's house across the street and three houses down.

At that moment the door opened, and a little man stepped out. Everything about him was diminutive, except for his matching set of mutton chop whiskers that covered both sides of his face. He wore wire-rimmed glasses that were overly large, and he had a missing front tooth.

"Whatchoo boys up to? You get away from my property or I'll call the cops." He talked rapidly, his speech nearly gibberish.

Crazy Milo's spectacles caught the day's last rays of sunlight and glinted. Frankie squinted at the reflected light.

"Quit making faces at me or I'll whip ya," Milo screamed. His voice had risen to a high-pitched screech. More gibberish poured from his lips.

"My brother teases him," said Terry Joe, "every chance he gets."

Frankie thought about Timmy O'Brian and his cohorts. He could see how they would drive the little man mad. A bully like Timmy was always bolder with his friends behind him.

"Milo is crazy," asserted Terry Joe, finalizing his assessment. They left Milo on his step, chattering to himself.

Across the road lived the Rader family. "Hey!" said a voice from out of nowhere. The boys stopped but saw no one. "I said 'Hey!' I'm up here." It came from up in a tree, a girl's voice.

They were right under it, and Frankie looked up. A cross-eyed creature stared down at him. Her deformities startled him. She had a clown's face with a white complexion, as if it never saw the sun. Atop her head were just a few wisps of hair in a tuft.

With practiced ease, Joyce Rader swung onto a limb and then dropped to the ground. She was a large girl with a happy laugh. The boy immediately felt sorry for her.

Inside the house her twin sister, Janice, looked just like her. She, too, was an albino. "Janice doesn't come out of the house much," Terry Joe had told him. "She's shy."

Joyce had red lipstick on her lips, and her movements were flirtatious. "Hey, Terrance Joseph O' Brian!"

"What's that under your eyes?" asked Terry Joe, ignoring her brazen remark and pointing at something blue.

"Eyeliner," she answered. "The black on the lashes is mascara."

By village standards, because of their looks, the Raders were loners. Yet, despite her physical shortcomings, this girl had a positive air about her. Frankie was amazed at her friendliness. She was outgoing and had approached them with a reckless trust, as equals. She exuded a feminine softness. He wondered if she had any friends.

"She knows me from Grandma's," said Terry Joe as they climbed a slight incline to 10th Avenue.

Beside them to their left lay Highway 52. They were at the base of the viaduct, which led east back up over the railroad tracks. Across the street stood the Swan Café, famous locally for its Friday specialties: turtle and frog legs.

* * * * * * *

Two days ago Frankie and Terry Joe had been playing with their army men in the O'Brian's screen house when Timmy came up to them with an idea. They eased their way into the house and breathed a sigh of relief—Lorraine O'Brian was nowhere in sight.

Timmy unhooked the receiver of their telephone. "Erhrrm…" he coughed, trying to modulate in a deeper voice. "Erhrrm…" he repeated.

A woman's voice stung his ears. Val Krause, next door, snapped at him. "Get off the phone. I'll be done in a minute." Timmy placed his hand over the mouthpiece and listened. Party lines were sources of juicy gossip.

Then he hung up abruptly. "She said if I don't hang up, she'll hang me up!"

Three minutes later the line was clear. Terry Joe dialed as Timmy read him the number. Then he handed the receiver to his brother.

"Hello?" Timmy lowered his voice. "Is this the Swan Café? I want to order dinner for four. Tonight…" he squeaked. "7:00 o'clock... Jones…" he muttered. "Blackburn 1 – 2828." Timmy hung up and chortled.

"That's our number," Frankie blurted, terror in his voice.

"They won't check," said Timmy, his voice an air of certainty.

"Not until after," echoed Terry Joe.

Suddenly a shadow loomed over them—Lorraine O'Brian. She eyed the telephone suspiciously. She did not trust her sons. "What are you up to, Timothy?"

"Nothin, Ma." He bolted from her grasp, but she caught him and delivered a swift Irish cuff on his temple.

"Owww!" he cried. "Lay off," he commanded. But he realized his mistake too late.

"What did you just say?" She leaped at him. "What did you say to me?" It will be the belt for you tonight when your dad gets home," his mother warned. Her face formed a crooked smile. "You're getting too big for your britches."

He knew her vow of punishment was true, and he exited the house. Back in the screen house, he let fly and scattered the younger boys' army men. "I'm the general," he asserted. "Someday I'll show her." But tonight he would have to face his father. And he knew that Bill O'Brian was one tough sergeant.

The thought of his prank softened his misery. That night, shortly before the appointed hour, the three boys walked casually into the Swan. Sure enough, by the window there was a table set for four with place settings, silverware, and four lettuce salads. The boys grinned and giggled until Schwan Ober, the owner, had to shoo them out.

*   *   *   *   *   *   *

The lights on the Swan Café blinked their welcome. The two boys on bicycles cut behind the café and through the small parking lot that the Swan shared with Tegelman's Grocery. Ben Tegelman had already closed his door and trudged up the back stairs to supper. The boys zipped into the larger parking lot behind the Wagon Wheel supper club. It adjoined the Rausch home. Frannie Rausch was sitting alone on the woodpile. His sister, Barbie, was back at her station on the back steps. She was holding what looked like a kitten.

Darkness was fast approaching. The boys made one final detour along the highway. They passed the Rox Liquor store, brightly lit and busy, and turned right at 12th Avenue. Halfway down the block, they passed the Carter residence. Pete Carter was sitting on his porch swing, rocking gently. He was holding a small child in each arm while sipping from a Schmidt's beer can. His son, Buster, sat next to him, his pockets bulging with root beer barrels and his mouth working on a jaw breaker.

Near the end of the block and across the street, they passed Phil Schultz's blue Crispy Chips truck that was parked in the driveway, empty now but ready to be loaded and make deliveries the next day. Rumors of Phil's marital infidelity floated about the village. He was a good-looking man. Phil's son, Freddy, was three years older than the two boys. Brash like his father, he was part of Timmy O'Brian's circle of friends.

After the two riders crossed 5th Street, they biked down a lengthy hill. Frankie felt the wind in his face and the thrill of speed. The lights in the windows were like cat's eyes, glowing yellow in the blackness outside.

Turning right, they puffed hard as they pedaled up the slope of 4th Street toward the top of the hill where the annual soap box derby commenced each Fourth of July. "This way," Terry Joe called. He was gasping for breath and falling behind. He detoured right into an alley, and his friend reversed course and followed him.

Their legs churned. Upward they climbed until at last the gravel leveled off. Finally the home street, 5th Street, came into view. They stopped to regroup at the top.

Before them lay a short steep hill that descended into the street. This would be the day's finale. On both sides of the alley, the lots were elevated. The front sides were separated from the sidewalks and the streets by rock retaining walls. On the back side, a border of tall trees shielded each lot from the alley. The trees were lanky poplars, planted close together. Mrs. Beebehauser's old brick house, to the left, was barely visible beyond her garden. The poplars created a chute through which the rider would pass before emerging into the street.

"You go first, Frankie," Terry Joe urged.

"No, you," his friend replied.

"You go, I'll follow," Terry Joe reiterated.

"No, you."

"Okay."

Frankie watched as his friend accelerated down the slope and sailed into the street. Just then a black sedan, approaching from the right, catapulted into view. The car intersected Terry Joe's line of flight. It reached the meeting point a moment before the bicycle's front tire crashed squarely into the driver's door.

In an effort to stop, Terry Joe flung his legs outward. But the impact sent him airborne, and he landed with a thud on the asphalt road. The crunch of a bone breaking was audible.

At the top of the chute, Frankie watched in amazement. Then he skidded down the incline to where his young friend lay moaning, writhing in pain.

CHAPTER FOUR

His mother's garden was abloom. It had been an early spring with an early thaw. She reserved one end of her garden for flowers: zinnias, tall gladiolas, petunias and daffodils. At the forefront of the display was the marigold plant her son had given her, maroon and gold, ordered from a fundraiser catalogue at a cub scout den meeting.

It was Saturday. The morning sun was shining. The boy felt the heat stroking his neck. Suddenly he spun around, a full circle. Then he ambled over to the flowers.

His mother watched him play from a kitchen window. His behavior puzzled her. She did not know that he pretended to have a cord plugged into his back. When the cord became twisted around his legs, he had to turn around to untwist it. When the game was on, he had to plan the routes he took, lest the cord become hopelessly wrapped around trees and telephone poles and houses. He was careful to retrace his steps home from school so that the cord could rewind freely behind him.

The zinnias drew the bees. Their perfume was pungent. Golden honeybees buzzed about the rich velvet petals, dipping into the flowers' organs, sipping syrupy nectar. Suddenly he saw it—a yellow jacket! The huge black and yellow bee hovered over the head of a scarlet zinnia. Its wings whirred, producing a delectable hum of vibration. Its movements ebbed and flowed over the flower's stigma, as if in slow motion.

The boy was drawn to it. He became aware of how easily he could grasp hold of the bee. He could close his hand gently around it to clasp it. He would feel the buzzing in the palm of his hand, a pleasurable, tingling sensation, and then let the bee go to pollinate the flowers. He stretched out his right hand; his fingers encircled the large insect.

The bee responded. Instinctively it reacted and jabbed its abdomen downward, a protective reflex. The hard sharp barb at the base of the abdomen pierced the skin in the palm of the hand. It stung the nerve endings and irritated the skin tissue so that the hand sprung open. The frightened bee fled.

The boy let out a howl and tried to bite back his tears. But the pain in his hand was intense, and the flesh around the wound was reddened and swelling.

His mother heard the wail. She approached him, wiping her hands on her apron. "What did you do to yourself now?" she prodded.

"I tried to hold it, but it stung me. I wasn't going to kill it," he added.

"You shouldn't have touched it," his mother chided, inspecting the wound. "Come inside. I have a tweezers and a tube of ointment in the bathroom cabinet."

Her touch was gentle, motherly. She had soft creamy skin and had done up her hair in a French roll. Her eyes, nut brown, were alive and alert. As she bandaged his hand, she hummed the tune of a recent hit, Pat Boone's "April Love." She sang the final verse: *And if you're the one, don't ever let it go away.*

Her look was distant, preoccupied. "Dad and I are going dancing tonight. Laura Birch is going to baby-sit; Ginger Mauch is busy." She started to say something more but stopped. "Frankie, I want you to go up to the store for me. Here's the list. I've already called and told them you're coming."

The boy headed outside, grocery list in hand. On his way he passed the old vacant house across the alley with its neighborhood ball diamond. The big boys could hit the ball over the alley into Pattersons' yard, a homerun; someday he would, too. Today the lot was empty. He continued on his journey south, past Pattersons'. The Stein boys lived across from the

Sawyers, and leery of Ray and Robbie, he slowed his pace and became watchful.

Sure enough, Robbie Stein was playing in the back yard. Frankie slowed his pace and tried to become invisible. It did not work.

"Come here, you little twerp," the older boy commanded. Instantly the younger boy recalled the gas can and the bag containing Barbie Rausch's cat. He looked to run, but his legs obeyed the command. Soon, he was within the older boy's range. Robbie's eyes widened and he grinned. "You see this?" He held up a knife handle and flicked open the blade.

Frankie looked questioningly.

"This is a switchblade" he proclaimed proudly. "We're going to play Cowboys and Indians. You're Roy Rogers and I'm Geronimo. I'm going to scalp you! What's that?" he asked, pointing at the paper in the smaller boy's hand. He leaped forward and seized hold of the grocery list. Robbie twirled it in his hand and then dropped it to the ground.

Frankie was petrified. *Fffluck*! The knife jabbed into the ground just inches from the sheet of paper. Frankie pounced on the grocery list and snatched it up. Then he ran for his life. Robbie made an attempt to tackle him, but the younger boy was quicker and wriggled free. Not looking back, he raced up the alley past Obers' and Koellers'.

He scampered into the grocery store, and the little bells above the door tinkled. He proceeded to the counter and offered the list to Susie, Ben's youngest daughter. Susie was slender, with brown puppy dog eyes. Her skin was tan from the sun, and her nose, freckled. She was chewing a wad of bubble gum. "We have your groceries ready," she announced, pulling a brown paper bag from underneath the counter. "Your mom called."

Without warning, she puckered her cheeks and blew an enormous bubble. When it popped, her eyes crossed. "Oops!" she laughed. She scraped the gum from her nose and lips with her tongue, and the wad disappeared inside her mouth.

The little bells above the grocery store door tinkled. Robbie Stein walked through the door and grinned.

That's when it happened. Overcome with emotion, the boy began to pee. He tried to stop it, but potty dribbled down his pants leg.

When Susie caught sight of the boy's pants, her eyes opened wide. "What are you doing?" she blurted.

It was Big Ben who saved him. Coming up from the butcher's counter, the man put a hairy arm on the boy's shoulder. He turned to Robbie. "Go home, Robbie; you're up to no good."

"I just want to scalp him" was Robbie's parting shot as he left. Once more the bells tinkled.

The man spun the boy around to face him and took hold of his shoulders. "Don't mind him," said Ben in his comforting voice. "He's a bag of wind, just talk. Don't you worry."

The boy stared at Big Ben's belly. His apron was stained with blood.

Big Ben let out a raucous laugh. "This is only cow's blood. It's what you eat in hamburger. Right, Susie?" She blew another bubble.

Ben reached into a box behind the counter and pulled out a small plastic package. "Here's some gum for you," he stated, "and a baseball card. Do you like baseball?" The boy nodded.

He opened the card and plopped the pink square of gum into his mouth. Chewing it settled him. Staring up at him was the face of a ballplayer, a New York Yankee, Mickey Mantle, 1956. He felt lucky; the Yankees were his favorite team. When he got home, he would deposit the card with his other stored cards in the orange shoe box that he kept tucked just inside the attic.

Grocery bag in hand, he left Tegelman's store, first peeking both ways for any sign of Robbie. But the coast was clear; the sidewalk was empty. He trudged west alongside the highway to avoid the Stein house.

Then he turned right and walked down 11th Avenue, past the Rausches' and Sawyers'. Across the street was the Birch residence. In their driveway sat a sports car convertible with the top down, an emerald Pontiac Catalina. A stout, burly lad of seventeen, clad only in shorts and a t-shirt, was busy polishing the car. Neil Birch was short and squat and muscle-bound. He had never said a word to Frankie in his life. He ignored the neighborhood boys.

As Frankie looked on, Mr. Birch emerged through the front door of the house. He was middle-aged and balding. An unlit cigar protruded from his mouth, and he carried a rolled up newspaper tucked under his arm. He was in a hurry and jumped into the convertible, punched the engine to life, and wheeled into the street. Before he left, he flipped a $5.00 bill to his son. "I can use the car tonight; can't I?" called out Neil hopefully. But the Catalina was already roaring away.

At the side of the house, sunbathing in a recliner, lay the oldest of three sisters, Laura Birch. She was relaxing before her baby-sitting job that night. She didn't know that across the street the young boy she would baby-sit was studying her closely.

It was past 6:00 when his father stepped through the doorway. Frankie was tucked into his customary spot in the corner up against the broom closet.

His father entered slowly, leaving his legs exposed. "Grrrr..." the cub growled as he leaped forward and attacked. His arms encircled, barely, the adult male's legs, and they squeezed tightly. He tried to hold on.

"What's this?" the father roared. "A lost young bear cub!" He grabbed the youngster with both hands under the armpits and heaved him skyward. Over the father's head the boy soared until his back touched the ceiling. He looked down at his dad's smile. On the man's face he saw the blue black stubble of a day's growth of whiskers, from which rose a lingering scent of Vitalis aftershave. On the man's breath he smelled gin.

The father set the boy down and enveloped his wife in his arms. They kissed. She stroked his cheek. "You need to shave after supper," she stated. "Laura Birch will be here at 7:30."

Then she hesitated. "You're late," she murmured, inquiring into his eyes.

"I stopped at the Wagon Wheel" was his reply.

She gave him an absent stare. "She's here again... in the living room."

"Grandma made Mom cry," blurted out the boy. "She checked the kettles when she came in the door. Mom ran into the bedroom."

"Nothing I make is good enough for her." Mom's lips were trembling; her voice was husky.

"What are we having?" asked Dad.

"Beef roast and mashed potatoes."

The boy winced. He was a finicky eater who cared little for beef roast.

His dad listened, but he stopped short of criticizing the woman in the other room. He had depended on her as a boy. They all had. And he could not—and would not—challenge her authority. He owed her that.

* * * * * * *

It was the spring of 1932. The children were dressed in their Sunday finest. The three girls were wearing sun dresses with sashes and shoes that buckled. Each had a flowered cap tied in a little bow under her chin. Both boys were clothed in black suits with black ties around their necks. The Great Depression had gripped the country for three long years, but Mary Frances Kucher would not let that reality keep her family from having the respect she craved.

The five children gathered around the flower bed in the front yard of the family farm east of Duelm, Minnesota, and posed for a picture. The occasion was the funeral and burial of their father.

"We're orphan children now," twelve-year-old Berneda told the next in line, her sister, Luella, who was two years younger. It was a perception that would last a lifetime.

"No, we're not!" the younger girl countered. Her bottom lip trembled pensively. "We still have Mother."

"One down, one to go," Berneda chimed.

Young Clifford, age eight, was thinking of his father. The man had been taken to a hospital in Minneapolis after an appendicitis attack. He was expected to stay a week and then come home. It never happened. Penicillin had been discovered by Alexander Fleming in 1929, but it would not be distributed for general use for ten more years. It would have saved him. His father's parting words to the boy had been a simple command: "Obey your mother."

With summer fast approaching, Mary Frances had made a decision. Only she knew that they would lose the farm to the bank. She would go to work: menial labor was available. She could cook and sew and wash clothes to earn a living.

She focused the camera. In the background of the framed picture was the rebuilt porch. The old one had burned down three years earlier when cleaning fluid caught fire in the kitchen. It was gasoline, used to clean men's suits. Only her quick thinking had saved the house. With her bare hands she had grabbed the scalding washtub and flung it through the doorway into the porch. For two critical hours a bucket brigade of neighbors worked feverishly to preserve the house, but in the end the porch was consumed by the flames.

She snapped the picture. Her little boy, Leonard, had been born in that house. Barely two and fatherless, he was busy picking the petals off a daisy in the flower garden. His sister, Lucille, only six-years-old, was trying to make him stop. But he was determined and persisted with the daisy until she pried it from his fingers. Lucille had been born in the old milk house next to the barn.

Mary Frances snapped a second picture. She had already asked her relatives to take the children. Clifford could go to her Uncle David's farm down the road. A summer wasn't such a long time. In the fall they would reunite and be a family again. They would move to St. Cloud. They would be poor, perhaps the poorest family in town, but they would survive as a family unit—together.

Within six months they had moved into East St. Cloud. Young Clifford, now nine, was the man of the house. His mother entrusted him with responsibilities.

While the weather was good, she had him ride his bicycle across the Division Street bridge over the mighty Mississippi River. His destination was the St. Cloud Hospital, specifically the back door facing the river. There the nuns would load food into the basket bolted to his handlebars: beef and chicken, spaghetti goulash, and tuna casseroles in glass containers, piping hot. It was supper for the day. Sister Sebastian and Sister Gabriel were good Christian women. They loaded his basket to overflowing. They also filled the rucksack that he carried on his back with vegetables and fruits: cabbage and sweet corn and turnips, apples and oranges and sun-dried figs.

"These came straight from Jerusalem," Sister Sebastian confided, revealing her gap-toothed grin. Berneda had told him that Sister Sebastian's gapped tooth was a sign that she was a child of Venus. She had whispered it to him like it was something dirty.

The two women wanted him to laugh and joke with them, and occasionally he told them a story about home. But he was on a serious mission. Their generosity had just as often rendered the boy speechless.

At home his mother waited. He deposited the sacks of food on the center of the kitchen table. My how she cooed! He observed her calloused hands and the lines from worry forming on her brow. He didn't like her to worry; the thought made him uncomfortable. When he was old enough to work, the money he earned would be placed on the center of that kitchen table—every penny.

Mary Frances relied on her children. They were loyal to her. The drama came one day, seven years later, when Berneda fell in love with a Lutheran, a Missouri Synod Lutheran backed up by a strong-willed Missouri Synod Lutheran family. A child was born. The resulting marriage amounted to rebellion.

The child must be baptized Catholic. Mary Frances, armed with her two sons, drove across the Mississippi and turned north into Sauk Rapids. Mary Frances, followed by Clifford and Leonard, exited their car and marched up to Berneda's front door. She peeked through the screen door to catch a glimpse of Baby Jane, and then she spoke her mind.

Berneda refused to open the door. "A Lutheran baptism is just as valid as a Catholic baptism," she argued.

To Mary Frances, that assertion was blasphemy. She did not want that baby, flesh of her flesh, to go to hell. Still, Berneda would not open the door.

Behind their mother, Clifford and Leonard squirmed. "This is an evil place," their mother proclaimed. "Lutherans are no different than heathens!"

At this, Berneda's resolve jelled. She must end this argument before her husband, Lawrence, came home. He would be as mad as a hornet when he found out what her mother had tried to do. She slammed the inside door shut and slid the deadbolt sideways. Then she slumped against the door, bracing it with her back.

"Don't you dare!" she heard the woman outside bawl. "I'm not finished."

Yes, you are, Berneda thought to herself. But she knew that the rift between them had widened and that a deep rift might never completely heal. The voice outside departed.

She watched her baby flailing her arms on the floor. Soon, she heard the tiny girl's cooing replaced with soft petulant cries. The young woman knelt down next to her child. She felt weary and burdened. "You need a diaper change, don't you? A Lutheran diaper change."

Shamed, Mary Frances retreated. This was not the end of it. She was not deterred that easily.

* * * * * * *

The man of the house placed his arms around his wife's shoulders. He looked deep into her face. She pulled back. He knew that she was annoyed by the gin and vermouth on his breath. Undeterred, he held her to him, and he shifted two big thumbs to smooth over her tear-stained cheeks.

That roast smells good," he stated. "Go wash for dinner, Frankie." He let his arms drop and side-stepped around her.

"Did you catch the market report, Mother?" His voice rang out as he entered the living room.

"I'm just watching it. The DOW jumped another twenty points," the woman in the room cackled. "Sit and rest your feet, Clifford." He complied.

As the woman in the kitchen set the table with plates and silverware, she could hear the chit chat from the living room, excited outbursts about stocks and bonds and mutual funds. A rising market was good for business.

She lifted the cover from the roast, and steam billowed from the pan. The meat looked gray; it was dry. It had simmered too long on the stove. She slammed the cover back down. This was her excitement in life. She fought back another round of tears, and then her face brightened. But not tonight. Tonight she and her husband were going dancing.

The potatoes boiling over brought her out of her reverie. She drained them and mashed them.

"This meat is overcooked," her mother-in-law chided, seated on the chair to the right of her son. "The carrots are good, though."

"You brought those, Grandma," stated the boy.

"Pass the carrots to Grandma," the father growled to his son. He avoided his wife's eyes.

"Did you see your name in the paper, Grandma?" the boy asked. He had seen her poring over the day's edition of The St. Cloud Times, searching for her name under the by-line: Bridge Winners Announced.

"Yes, I did!" answered the elder woman. Sadie Brandel and I were first on Monday, and we're playing again tonight. The boy loved to hear of his grandmother's exploits. He watched her gnaw on a beef bone as she retold the story of her first bridge game: how Alvina Leither had invited her and two other ladies over to play. "And I won first," Grandma stated matter-of-factly. Her face beamed at the memory.

On Monday a new player, a man, had congratulated Sadie on a good play. Grandma eyed him suspiciously. "I could have done that," she informed him. Her voice had an edge to it, as if she were issuing a challenge. Her grandson understood the older women's competitive drive. Obviously, compliments were not welcome, unless they were for her.

The time was approaching 7:00 o'clock. His mom leaped to clear the dishes. Grandma, with her coat on and a bandanna wrapped around her head and tied under her chin, exited for the bridge game. The boy stood inside the bathroom door and watched his father shaving. The man stood in his boxers and t-shirt. Still in a slightly alcoholic state, he leaned against the sink to steady himself. He pulled the razor across his skin slowly, face and neck. The eyes that reflected in the mirror peered back in dazed, deep thought.

Next, a comb parted the black strands on his father's head. The man began to whistle *I'm a Yankee Doodle Dandy*, an old drinking tune from his war days. At the end of the song, the whistling paused. "That's how it's done, Frankie. A man has to stay one step behind his wife but two steps ahead." He winked into the mirror and resumed his whistling.

Just then, there was a rap on the back door. Laura Birch stood nervously on the top step. The evening air had a chill to it.

She entered through the kitchen doorway, and in with her came a whiff of cigar. Suddenly the boy felt a fuzzy feeling. She was nine years older than he was, but he was mesmerized by her looks: creamy skin that was tanned, auburn hair that rippled in soft curls about her head, ample curves.

His mother spelled out her instructions and then turned sharply toward her brood. She looked directly, threateningly, at her eldest son. Her final words were "Be Good." Then his parents left.

The four children stared up at the pretty girl. "You're wearing lipstick," noted the boy. The two girls giggled.

"Red lipstick," observed his sister, Jeanne, who was next in age. From that moment on, the boy sought the adolescent girl's attention. It became his mission.

"Do you want to watch television?" Laura asked hopefully.

A chorus of "yeses" greeted her. "*Lassie*'s on," said Jeanne.

"*Lassie… Lassie…*" echoed young Mary and Dan.

Frankie objected. "I want *Gunsmoke*."

"They want *Lassie*; let's watch that" was Laura's decision. She turned on the television set and plopped down onto the couch. Immediately she buried her nose in a *Vogue* magazine that she had extracted from her purse. The three young faces of Jeanne, Mary, and Dan glued themselves to the tv screen, eager to watch their favorite canine in action, protecting Timmy.

Frankie was not satisfied. He was the alpha male. He would show his dominance. At the first commercial, he marched to the television set and turned the channel. He gripped the tuning knob fiercely while his sisters and brother mobbed him. They wrenched at his hands. It mattered not that they cried.

"Stop that!" ordered the girl on the couch. Only after she rose from it, did he relent. The baby-sitter snapped off the television and scowled. She deposited the magazine back into her purse. "Is it time for bed?" she questioned.

"No, not yet," answered the chorus.

"Not until eight forty-five o'clock," said Jeanne, ever helpful.

"Read us a story," stated Mary, eyes bright.

"Read us a story.... Read us a story...." the chorus chanted.

"Let me see your books," said Laura. She glanced through them and selected the thinnest. "Let's read this one. It's called 'The Pied Piper of Hamlin.'"

"About the rats," said Jeanne.

"Once upon a time…" began Laura. The three youngest children nestled in beside her. "Sit still," she ordered. "Don't squirm." Frankie watched her face. He liked to see the light from the lamp on the end table shine in her eyes while her lips moved and her voice modulated, creating the different characters. The fuzzy feeling had returned.

The story was finished in eight minutes. "Read 'Brer Rabbit and the Tar Baby' next," insisted Frankie, opening up his favorite book. He wanted to see her mouth move and hear her voice again.

"'The Tar Baby!'" exploded the chorus. "Read us 'The Tar Baby'!" their voices pleaded.

As she read, he was absorbed in her articulating red lips and in the feminine, high-pitched tone of her voice. He felt persistent. "Read 'Pecos Bill,'" he demanded.

"'Pecos Bill'... 'Pecos Bill'..." reverberated off the walls. "Pecos Bill, he lassos the wind," said Jeanne.

"Okay, but then you're all going to bed," the teenaged girl countered as compensation.

The older boy stared at her, and as he did, an idea came to him.

"Go brush your teeth," Laura ordered as she closed the book. She did not give them time to consider an alternative.

The children's beds were all upstairs. At bedtime Frankie sat on the bottom step and made the baby-sitter lift him, and drag him, up the stairs to his bed. Her arms cradled him, and he felt their warmth around his torso. Instantly he slid back down the stairs on his buttocks, giggling with pleasure as he forced her to hoist him back up the stairs. It tickled.

"Stay up here," she commanded. But he had no intention of obeying; her words only encouraged him more. He liked this game. He descended again.

"Come back, you little bugger!" she burst out. She was perturbed with him as she clambered down the stairs a third time. Agitated, this time she was no mere girl, but woman. His back was to her. She grabbed him in a stranglehold and squeezed.

Her hold pinched off his airway, but he didn't resist. He let his body slump, limp dead weight. "You bastard!" she hissed. He felt her arms release his head, slide under his armpits, and clasp his tummy. She pulled him upward. As she tugged, he could feel her perspiring through her blouse. Her breathing became labored. He felt keenly aware of the warm breath exhaled through her throat and nostrils. He was winning the game.

At long last, the night was over. His parents returned. The boy slipped down the stairs one last time and saw them sitting on the sofa, surrounded by the moon's light. Their voices sounded strained, irritated. And then he saw the slap, his mother's hand against his father's cheek. They both were stunned to silence, and then his mother rose quickly.

The boy leaped silently away, up the stairs to his bed. He lay on the mattress trembling, until finally the tremors of shock left his body and he succumbed to sleep.

When he came downstairs in the morning, his mother was spooning boiled eggs from a kettle into a bowl. His father, dressed in a blue suit, was sitting at the kitchen table reading the stock market quotations in the Minneapolis Tribune. He smelled of cologne and hair oil.

He looked at his son. His eyes were icy blue. "Laura Birch's mother called this morning. Laura wants more money. Do you know why?" He paused.

The fuzzy feeling in the boy evaporated. He felt nervous. He looked up at the light and squinted.

"Your mother told you to be good. But you weren't very good."

His mother approached, carrying a black cast iron frying pan with the handle wrapped in a dish towel. "No tv for you today!" she snapped. "No tv!"

His father sipped on his coffee while the boy's mother dished out potatoes.

CHAPTER FIVE

"Do you want to go fishing, son?" The beam of a flashlight licked his face. It was his dad. The clock on the nightstand read 4:00 a.m. Outside, all was darkness.

The boy rose and dressed in the dark: grass stained blue jeans, gray sweatshirt, white cotton socks, and tennis shoes blackened with grime. At the kitchen table he gulped down a bowl of cereal, Wheaties drenched in milk and sugar.

His father was outside, hooking the boat trailer onto the ball hitch of the truck. He latched the safety chain and returned to the kitchen for the lunch box of sandwiches and the thermos of nectar that were sitting on the stove. Goodbye, Pat," he volunteered and kissed the woman in the doorway on the lips. Her face was red from crying. "We'll be meeting Len at the lake." He turned quickly and left, followed by the boy.

Father and son drove in silence through St. Cloud on Division Street and crossed the Mississippi River. They exited onto Highway 23 and angled northeast toward Foley. The road was deserted. They passed Duelm a mile north of the farm where the man had spent his youth. A fleeting thought entered Frankie's mind: his father had once been a boy like him. A second thought replaced the first: his Uncle Len didn't like him.

The truck's motor purred, and the heater poured out a stream of warm air. The dashboard lights were aglow. In the light he could see his father's hands, big strong hands that gripped the steering wheel. They were covered with grease from working the chain.

Through Milaca, the halfway point to Mille Lacs Lake. Another half hour took them up and over a small hill, and then he saw it—a vast expanse of rolling water. The man cranked down his window to feel the morning air, and this brought in the sound of the waves crashing onto a rocky shore. The waves looked stately as they marched in unison, an unhurried procession. They undulated and then, in the throes of death, arched their backs and flung their crests forward. With the sound came the smell of rotting seaweed and decomposing fish. It filled the lad's nostrils.

In the light of the dawn, the boy gazed out his window at Mille Lacs Lake, a flat body that stretched to the horizon. Father and son drove along the western edge of the lake toward Wigwam Bay. Halfway there, they reached Indian Point. Here they stopped at Shorty's resort.

Uncle Len stepped forward to grasp his brother's arm. "Hi, Cliff. It's a west wind; the walleyes should be biting."

"We'll need minnows," said his brother, "mostly shiners and a few fatheads." They hurried into the bait shop, the boy tagging along.

They launched the boat by half-light, securing the drain plug in the bottom of the aluminum craft first. The cable on the trailer whirled in circles as gravity dragged the boat backward until it slid into the water. It floated gracefully and immediately began to veer sideways in the waves.

The boy's uncle in the boat caught hold of the end of the oar extended to him by his brother, and together they guided the nose of the boat to shore and pinned the side against a dock.

His father left to park the truck and trailer. During his absence, the boy sensed that his uncle was staring at him. He squirmed uncomfortably and squinted, then averted his eyes down to the shoreline. The watery rim was littered with scum, bubbly and stinky. He focused on a bloated perch, white with an orange belly. Its left eye was partially dislodged from its socket. A seagull was pecking at it, tugging at the eye with its beak. A second gull hovered just above them, looking for an opportunity to join the feast. He heard his uncle's voice. "That'll be you someday… when you die," said the man. And then the man laughed.

His father returned. It was obvious to the boy that his dad was anxious to be on the lake, moving. The life preservers, seat cushions, extra gas can, fishing rods, net, and minnow bucket had already been stowed between the seats. He handed the lunch box and gallon thermos jug to Len while his son crawled aboard. Then the father stepped from the dock over the side into the sixteen-foot Crestliner.

Three pumps on the gasoline can and three pulls of the engine's starter cord brought the outboard motor to life. It coughed several times and emitted a blue smoke that dissipated in the cool morning breeze.

Moments later the engine rumbled, and the fisherman shifted the gears into reverse. The propeller blades beneath the 10 horsepower Johnson did their work, and the fishing boat eased away from the shore. Frankie watched the resort recede.

His father shifted the gear box through neutral into forward and pulled the motor's steering handle sharply into his belly. Simultaneously, he twisted the throttle on the steering handle. The engine roared, and the boat sprang forward. He aimed the nose of the boat at Indian Point. "The big females should be finished spawning out there," he yelled into the wind. But the wind swallowed his voice so that neither Len nor Frankie heard him.

The son saw his father relax with his spirits buoyed. The youngster turned to face the open water ahead. In the bow of the boat, he grabbed hold of the anchor rope that was tied to the handle at the front and rode the waves. Over each crest he rose and leaped, only to have his bones jarred as the boat's hull plunged downward into the next trough. Again and again, he bounced over them.

He counted the waves. He noted their pattern. Every seventh wave seemed bigger than its brothers. In crossing over these giants, the boat's keel would pound into the base of the titanic waves. Fresh water sprayed upward, dowsing him, the beads of fresh water slapping his face. His rain jacket and hood could not save him. Yet, there was no time to let down his guard. He could see the next monster in the distance.

A small tree-lined island at the tip of a peninsula came into view. Indian Point, extending into Mille Lacs Lake, was a spawning ground for walleyes. Its tip was rocky, and where it ended, a ridge extended under the water. This submerged portion of the point dropped off from a shallow seven feet to thirty feet. Each spring females deposited their eggs along the ridge. Males would fertilize the eggs. Now, in May, the water was cold and crystal clear, transparent. But by summer the sun's heat and light would cause the bottom to grow weedy, offering a protective bed to the young walleyes that had hatched and survived. By July the water would be green and warm, thick and murky.

"There's a good walleye chop on the water," noted his dad, who had killed the motor and let the boat glide to a stop. Immediately it turned sideways in a swell and began to drift along the rocky ridge away from the shore. "Five dollars for the first fish," Dad stated. His eyes were bright and alive.

He swung the tip of his rod outward and opened the face of his reel to let the line stream out. The shiner minnow hooked at the end of the line was lowered into the water and sunk away, pulled down by the weight of a sinker twisted onto the line two feet from the hook. A swivel above the sinker allowed the minnow to right itself and swim freely until the hook through its jaw and head exhausted it or a fish grabbed hold.

When the weight touched bottom, the line went slack. Without thought the man turned the crank to stop the outpouring of line. Immediately he curled his right index finger around the line while the other three fingers and thumb clutched the cork handle of the rod. Then he reopened the reel's metal bail. Only his index finger held the line, eight-pound test, in check. If a fish bit, he could release the line on the spool instantly; the fish would feel no resistance.

Lifting the tip of the rod gently, he could feel the weight of the sinker lift off the bottom. As the fishing boat drifted in the wind, the sinker hovered just above the rocks with the minnow trailing behind. The father was a practiced fisherman. He took great care not to let the sinker snag in the rocks and perhaps break the line.

The boy baited his own hook. The minnows in the bucket squirmed in his fingers and wriggled free. Finally he extracted one and curved the hook into its lower jaw and out the top of its head. Suspended in the air, it flopped about, alive and active. The boy imitated his father's actions, and the minnow dived downward. The sun's rays were piercing sideways from the east; morning had broken. Two other boats, silver with red bottoms, bobbed among the waves.

The motor puttered at trolling speed. The father was adept at guiding the boat along the edge of the reef, just away from the dangerous rocks. At the end of the underwater point, they would wind in the bait and splash back to the starting point.

It was on the second pass, near the outer tip of the point, that the father felt two rapid tugs in quick succession. Instinctively he uncurled his right index finger and let the line go limp. The fish below the boat felt nothing. "One… two… three… four…" counted the dad. At "fifteen" he turned the crank forward half a turn. The bail clicked shut, gripping the line. He pointed the tip of the line lower toward the water. Near the back of the boat, the water's surface was covered in a light chromatic oil from the chugging motor.

When he felt the next tug, the man yanked the rod up and back. This action set the hook in the fish's mouth. The rod curved in a great arc, the thread of filament in its eyeholes pulled taut. The man concentrated on the task at hand. He cradled the rod in his hands, keeping constant tension on the line. The reel groaned under the strain, releasing line reluctantly when the fish dove downward. The man cranked it in slowly. Gradually the fish rose.

"He'll make a run for it soon," whispered the father. "Walleyes fight to stay deep." He knew that that moment was the fish's best chance to escape. If the drag on the reel was set too tight, it would break the line and be free. The man's job was to tire the fish out by keeping tension on the line, but not to pull on the fish when it dove.

The boy watched over the side of the boat as his father played the fish. He followed the line downward into the oily water. Then, four feet below the surface, he saw a black shadow. The fish saw the light above him. Energized, it dove for the safety of the rocks below. The line sizzled out of the reel for ten seconds, the drag doing its work. The reel had just enough tension to keep the hook secure, but not enough to break the line.

The zinging line stopped, and the father turned the reel's crank to take up any slack. He dragged the fish upward. His brother, Len, held the net in anticipation. The boy felt a yearning to net the fish, but his father considered him too young and too uncoordinated to net a big fish—not a walleye, not on Mille Lacs.

Swoop. The uncle, over-eager, lunged at the fish, his hands plunging the net down into the water. The splash alerted the fish, and it dove madly for the bottom. *Zing.* "God A'mighty!" Len swore.

Zing. Zing. Another ten seconds of line sizzled out from the reel. But the fish was tired and soon yielded. The mouth of the net surrounded it, and only too late did it thrash about as it was hoisted out of the water into the bottom of the boat.

"That's five dollars for me," chortled Dad. His eyes were aglow. "That's the first fish. It's a male." Catching the first fish was a sign of good luck to come. Catching one fish meant there would be a second and a third. They would not go home *skunked*. The father twisted the throttle and spun the boat back toward the shore to start another pass.

Halfway out along the ridge, Uncle Len felt a long slow tug on his line. It bent his rod to its limit so that he had to release the line. "I'm snagged," he growled, "on a rock." He was chagrined and angry at his own failure to keep the line free. His brother nodded and turned the boat around, and the uncle reeled in the slack. The older brother maneuvered the Crestliner so that it glided directly on top of the rock.

For a full minute Uncle Len yanked his rod this way and that, back and forth, trying to free the sinker. It seemed hopeless. He stood up and jerked the line viciously, mumbling invectives and curses, not caring any more whether or not he broke the line.

It was at the height of his fury when he felt the line give ground. Suddenly he felt a great heaviness in his hands and then a pulsation. The spool on his reel began to sizzle as the line flew out.

"It's a huge fish," observed Dad, exploding in excitement, "a big female!"

But the drag was set too tight. His uncle fumbled with it awkwardly. His knuckles were white from the cold. The strain on the line was tremendous, nearing the breaking point.

"Loosen the drag!" Dad shouted. "Move the net, Frankie," he heard his Dad command.

The boy grabbed the net to pull it out the way. In his haste the net bumped his uncle's fingers working the drag. "Get out of my way!" the man yelled.

The fish pulled downward, desperate to get away. Moment by moment, it was gaining ground. Four times, the tip of the pole broke the lake's surface. Equally desperate, the man in the boat tried one last resort. Uncle Len's free hand grabbed hold of the bail on his reel to release the line entirely. However, his hands, partially frozen and numb, did not work swiftly enough. Before he could loosen the bail, the line snapped.

The rod jerked straight and lifeless. Seconds ago, it had been quivering in his hands; now it was limp and still. The big fish was lost.

"The drag was set too tight," stated the older brother. The younger man knew this was true, but the knowledge did not appease him. He vented his disappointment.

"He hit my hand with the net," Leonard rationalized thickly. With a swipe of his hand, he grabbed the net away from his nephew, who sank into the bow of the boat. The lad could feel his uncle's penetrating gaze.

By 10:00 o'clock they had six fish, one limit. Twice Frankie had had to pee, and twice the outer pail of the minnow bucket had been passed to him. His father and uncle had no need of the bucket. They simply stood and sprayed outward over the side of the boat. Only once in his life had he ever seen his father really need the bucket. The man had produced a length of toilet paper from inside his shirt pocket. When finished, the contents of the bucket were dumped overboard and the bucket was rinsed in a wave.

At 10:30 the father opened the lunch box and unwrapped the sandwiches, summer sausage with mayonnaise and lettuce. The man grinned. He continued to fish, for he knew that when you are preoccupied is the time most likely for a fish to strike.

Sure enough, just as he bit down on a sandwich, a fish bit down on the minnow hooked at the end of his line. He held the bread and meat in his teeth while he let the line go slack. The boy watched him intently as he yanked the rod up and back and set the hook. The line sizzled as the drag gave way.

"I want to net it," said the boy. He felt the uncle's cold stare upon him. "Can I net it?" he pleaded.

The father felt the weight on the end of the line; it was not a massive fish, no trophy. He nodded to his son. The boy grabbed the net and shifted his feet toward the center of the boat. "Switch spots with Len," ordered the father.

The fish was swimming closer to the boat. In the dark water it pulled downward against the tip of the rod. "When the fish comes up, don't lunge at it," coached the fisherman. "Put the rim of the net into the water and then net it quickly. Be sure to get the net under the fish's body. Then lift it up out of the water."

The boy did as he was told. The father coaxed the fish to within two feet of the water's surface. "Now!" commanded the father's voice.

The boy responded. He held the net tightly in both hands and shoved it into the water beneath the dark, speckled fish. The fish, realizing the trap, flipped its tail in desperation. The boy saw the defiant, translucent eyes of the walleye as he heaved the net upward. The belly, dazzling white, sagged into the cords of the net. The boy could see the hook in the walleye's lip, with the dead minnow dangling outside its mouth and sharp-pointed teeth. With all his might he lifted the net over the side of the boat. He could not keep his eyes from the prize. His father reached over and tousled his hair.

"That's seven," the boy counted as he watched his uncle pull a stringer of six walleyes into the boat. The stringer was chained to an oar lock.

By noon they had ten fish. In the afternoon the fishing slowed. He was ready to go home, but he knew that his father would fish until dark. "Dawn to dusk," his father always said. The sun became warm and pelted down on them. His father removed his heavy coat and fished in his flannel shirt, always holding his rod carefully to keep the bait working, presentable to the next fish.

Frankie listened to the purring of the motor as it rumbled in the water. Occasionally it choked and coughed in a swell, but it always recovered its breath. In the middle of the afternoon, his father switched gas cans, unplugging the empty one in favor of the full spare.

The afternoon sun descended toward the west. The sky, full of cumulous clouds, became a patchwork of yellow and orange, turning as dusk approached to red and purple. The light was fading when his father hooked their final fish. He wound it in slowly, his satisfaction evident on his weather-beaten face.

Uncle Len lifted two stringers into the boat, eighteen walleyes, their limit. The Crestliner darted across the waves toward the dark outline of the shore. Seven miles of water. Theirs was the last boat to tie up to the dock. One old man with a lantern greeted them. He was short and stubby and looked down at the sparkling flesh in the bottom of the boat. He nodded.

"Indian Point?" he asked.

"No... the Mud Flats... out there," lied the father. He pointed to the middle of the vast lake.

They loaded the boat onto the trailer and dumped the minnow bucket into the weeds at the side of the road. Only a few shiners flopped in the dirt along with two dozen fatheads. These had been lucky enough not to be baited onto a hook, but now their luck had run out.

The three fishermen ate a late supper at Shorty's: grilled cheese sandwiches and potato chips. His father poured a huge mound of ketchup from a bottle labeled Heinz onto his sandwich.

"Why do you eat ketchup on grilled cheese?" asked the son, his nose wrinkled.

"Try it and see" was the man's cryptic reply. And so the boy did.

Before they left, they passed a case filled with fishing lures and various snacks: candy bars, gum, peanuts. The boy stopped to inspect the contents of the case. The father knew what the boy wanted. "One Nut Goodie, Shorty," he stated to the man behind the counter. He was the same old man who had greeted them at the dock.

"You have a good haul," said the resort owner. "So, Indian Point?" the old man asked.

"No, the Mud Flats," countered the father.

Shorty handed the Nut Goodie to the boy. "Indian Point?" he persisted.

"The Mud Flats," echoed the boy and caught his father's wink as they left the resort.

They sent six walleyes with Uncle Len and parted ways. Father and son rode home in the dark. The truck's heater made the cab warm and cozy. The boy unwrapped the Nut Goodie, his reward for venturing along.

Beside him, the father sat at the steering wheel. He was not tired. He could not afford to be tired; he still had a dozen fish to clean. He didn't mind the Nut Goodie. It was a small price to pay. With his son along he could bring home one extra limit, six more walleyes. It was important to keep the boy happy.

The boy's eyelids drooped, and he snuggled into the father's stomach, fast asleep. He did not feel his father place a hand on his shoulder. Nor did he fathom that one day he would become the prodigal son.

CHAPTER SIX

A week passed. It was Saturday again. The boy had planned plenty of activities. On this day school would not interrupt them. He had decided against watching Saturday morning cartoons and Westerns on television even though he had begged his mother to let him watch them. She had relented, of course. But he chose to be outside on this day. Mighty Mouse, Roy Rogers, and Sky King would have to wait. He zipped up his jacket and headed west.

Three blocks from his home lay the community park with its community shelter that housed both an outdoor pavilion and an indoor kitchen. On the Fourth of July and on Spas Tag Day, a beer garden was set up adjacent to the shelter, equidistant from both the picnic tables in the pavilion and the bathrooms beside the kitchen. In the winter the village's firemen flooded the rectangular parking lot just north of the shelter. When the water froze, the lot became the local skating rink. The north end of the enclosed portion of the building served as the warming house.

On this morning the community shelter was deserted. A small creek floated through the park along the back edge of the property. The young boy climbed upon a rock at the water's edge where the creek widened into a small oval, a pool. Floating in the water were young lily pads that had sprouted from the bottom of the creek. Then he saw what he was after—a big bullfrog atop a lily pad. The frog was sunning himself, totally unaware of the boy's presence.

He did not move until after the boy's fingers clamped down on him. His skin was slippery; his feet, webbed. The boy looked into the frog's eyes and squinted. A frog prince? Maybe. He let his imagination wander. Then he put the frog into the bucket he had brought along and closed the lid.

An hour later the bucket was hopping with frogs. Once, he had overturned the pail, and most of the frogs had sprung out. He had tried to catch them in mid-leap, but they had bounded into the safety of the water and hidden themselves in the undergrowth along the bottom of the pool. He had recaptured two, and now he had eight specimens in the bucket. He would take them to school, to Sister Mary Andrew for show and tell.

He spent the next hour tracing the creek back toward its source. The undergrowth became thick and matted and scratchy. The creek narrowed as it meandered back and forth behind the Little League baseball diamond. Here the bugs were alive and thick. A mosquito landed on his arm, and without a thought he swatted it dead. Flies were out in the morning sun, as were bugs that crawled. He saw caterpillars and centipedes on the leaves of plants.

Surveying the creek's watery surface, the boy detected a coveted species. Curled on a rotting log that floated in the water, a garter snake, perhaps fifteen inches long, lay sunning himself. It was within reach. The boy knelt down. Slowly, imperceptibly, he moved his arm, and then at the last second he swiped at the coiled body and grabbed it by the tail. He dearly wanted to add the snake to his collection in the bucket, but the reptile slipped from his grasp and escaped. It plopped into the water and slithered into the weeds behind the log. It was gone.

It was near the highway that the boy found what he was searching for, a pool of water four feet deep. The bottom of the pool was quicksand. If you fell into it, the muck at the bottom would suck you down, far into the bowels of the earth.

The boy had heard stories about it. It was a fine silt that would constrain your legs, tightening its vise-like hold the more you flailed to escape. Struggling made death a certainty. But so did inaction. If possible, you must grab hold of a young sapling and yell for help. The stories were warnings to be believed, to be taken seriously. His mind was alive with possibility.

With the morning waning, the boy retraced his steps. He followed the creek downstream toward its mouth. It left the community park and crossed behind the Moose Lodge. There it connected with the Sauk River, a muddy, not-so-mighty river that wound from west to east through the whole of Stearns County from Sauk Centre to St Cloud. Northeast at Sauk Rapids, it dumped itself into the Mississippi River, which was a mighty river that flowed south all the way to the Gulf of Mexico. But this was not yet part of the boy's world.

The previous summer he had gone on an all-day journey. His adventure had taken him two miles down river to where a small cement bridge crossed the Sauk. On the village side of the river, the bridge was connected to a small park. The park was situated on a shoulder of land that long ago had been an embarking spot for eager travelers to begin their trek across the open prairie to a new life beyond. A hundred years earlier, settlers in covered wagons had made a fresh start out onto Indian land in western Minnesota and the Dakotas. Many had started here. Most had never returned. A few were well-publicized victims of Sioux massacres. The majority, however, were unprepared for the harsh winters that made survival highly tentative.

They had come from Europe: Norwegians and Swedes, German Russians, Irish, French, a few Italians. The promise of the land had driven them on, and the land itself had tempered them. Men, women, and children: they were self-reliant souls. They had to be.

The small visitor had looked up at the large granite monument fully two times his height. He had felt the enormity of what it marked, the beginning of an era.

Engraved into the gray rock was a picture of a family of homesteaders on the move. A team of two oxen were yoked to a covered wagon. Driving the wagon was a man in a straw hat. Beside him sat a woman in a bonnet. They were heading west into the frontier. Some were escaping religious persecution. Others dreamed of owning their own land. Sodbusters, they would etch their lives into the prairie's soil. When need be, they would fertilize the ground with their own sweat and blood. All were looking for opportunity and a better life.

Under the cart were carved the words HENRY C. WAITE MEMORIAL in capital letters. Below them, an inscription entitled *Waite's Crossing*. The boy read it carefully.

This river crossing was the ford used in the 1850s by the Red River ox carts of the Hudson's Bay Company, an enterprise that was engaged in international shipping between central Canada and England by way of St. Cloud. Soon afterwards, homesteaders in covered wagons ventured forth across it, westward into the Dakota Territory and beyond.

The boy left the park and crossed the bridge. It was barely wide enough for two oxen pulling a cart. He walked into the afternoon sun.

As his feet padded over the dusty cement, he was keenly aware that thousands of men, women, and children had forded the Sauk River at this point, heading west. Even his own ancestors, his mother's family, had been among them. All had been restless.

Some had traveled a thousand miles to settle in the foothills of the Rocky Mountains. A few had even gone over those high, rugged peaks all the way to California's ocean. Lured by gold, these had died penniless.

Many had surged onto the Dakota grasslands. They homesteaded the territory under a Federal government land grant. They were willing to share the land with its native tenants, the Dakota.

In time, as more and more white men and women arrived, the Indians resisted. The pale skin of the white men's faces was foreign to their own native red. So were their customs and their ways. Particularly aggravating was their habit of building fences to lock in their farmland. These barriers created obstacles to the Indian way of life. The Indians were skilled horsemen and hunters. They were nomads. The tribes followed the buffalo, uprooting their tepees with the change in seasons. Their religion taught them to be one with the land, with its spirit. They were a respectful people, and trusting, at first.

The settlers from the east were intruders. They did not hunt the buffalo. They did not move and relocate. Instead, they dug into the earth and grabbed hold of the ground by the roots. They built permanent houses and barns that could withstand wind and rain and hail and sleet and snow. And they fenced it all in. The landscape was changing. The buffalo and their brothers and sisters, the Indians, could no longer roam the land freely, as they pleased.

The Indians learned much from these strangers. The white men made treaties with the Indians. And then, when convenient, they broke them. They were not men of their word; they could not be trusted. Instead of Dakota, meaning friend, they now called the red man Sioux, or enemy. And then they taught the Sioux how to scalp and showed the Sioux how to rape.

Despair set in. Fully human, the young warriors refused to listen to the wisdom of their fathers, who urged a policy of acceptance and cooperation. But young men are savages. They set upon the settlers by night, throwing torches through the windows of the houses, feasting on the women and young girls as they fled the flames.

Those homesteaders who escaped watched their possessions burn. And this bred a venom that no snake on earth could match. They went to war. With guns and knives as their fangs, they took revenge, Indian village after Indian village, and slew these red-skinned people who had become their mortal enemy.

Now, as the frontier shrank, the last remaining frontiersmen were solicited to hunt the Indian's source of sustenance, the buffalo. They slaughtered entire herds. Frequently they wasted all but the tongue, which they loaded onto riverboats for shipment to St. Louis and New Orleans, the gateways to civilization. When the Dakota saw this, it galled them. A great sadness ensued, mingled with hostility. Thus, the natives fought on for their way of life. White men and Indians would not co-exist for the next hundred years and then only after the Indian people were condemned to reservations, where their servitude ate at their pride. Large numbers of them looked for solace and found it in whiskey. At least it numbed their pain.

* * * * * * *

Johannes Otto and Elsie Eva Meierhoffer forded the Sauk River at Waite's Crossing and headed west. Elsie noted the splashing steps of their trusty oxen, Clover and Clarabelle, who pulled their covered wagon. In the bed of the wagon was everything they owned: a small table and four chairs, two bed frames and two lumpy tick mattresses, a small cook stove and a crate of pots and pans, dishes, and utensils, two lanterns and a can of kerosene. There was a large trunk, filled with clothes and personal items including two framed family photographs, very old, one from each family. Remembrance of the past was a necessity. The wagon contained farming equipment too: a sturdy plow to turn the ground, four precious gunny sacks of seed, a hammer and nails, and a rusty saw.

Sprawled among these treasures were two small children: a boy, Herman, and a girl, Sadie. These two were eyeing the supplies of food brought along, enough to last four months: flour to knead into bread, potatoes to boil into dumplings, carrots and onions to cook in soup, sugar and apples to bake in pies.

"No, Herman," admonished little Sadie, "put that apple back. We must save it for winter." But her brother, older and stronger, ignored her. "Mom!" she tried to tattle, but he clamped his open hand over her mouth. Then he sat back and munched steadily on the apple and found it comforting. At the fourth bite, Sadie took an apple, too.

Johannes settled deep into thought and let the reins go slack. He allowed the two oxen to do their work, pulling the cart along. He watched their wide rumps moving in unison as they marched step after step in the yoke. They would travel two miles an hour, twenty-five miles in a day. Further west, where the ground was flat, they might go thirty. Here in central Minnesota, the landscape was gently rolling hills.

The man's thoughts were good thoughts of fallow fields and barns filled with grain. He envisioned livestock in pens: cows and pigs and chickens for milk and meat and eggs, to ensure their survival and to be sold for profit at market. He would prosper. Johannes puffed lazily on his pipe. He did not think of dangers. If there were any, they lay far ahead.

To Elsie, the dangers were more vibrant. The previous night, encamped on a bank of the Sauk River, she and several women had talked about the strange-colored men who inhabited the plains. Wild, beastly, and unchristian, these virile red-skinned men were savages. She saw them in her dreams, whooping and hollering, waving tomahawks above their heads as they ambushed the settlers' farmsteads at night.

Her eyes drifted over to her husband. He was a man of courage who would fight to save her. His rifle and a box of bullets were tucked just inside the covered wagon, within easy reach. But they would not be enough to stem an Indian attack; she was sure of that.

The midday sun was high in the sky, directly overhead, when they stopped beside a small creek that flowed at the side of the trail. Johannes unhitched the two oxen to let them drink from the stream and rest. After several prolonged gulps, they ambled into the nearby meadow to partake of the thick grasses. Clover, aptly named, found the white-flowered clover particularly sweet.

Elsie spread out on the ground a red and white checkered tablecloth. She produced a woven basket that contained a picnic lunch: cold fried chicken and homemade biscuits. She watched her husband chew and swallow. She watched the determined lines on his forehead, which glistened with beads of sweat. He had removed his large straw hat, exposing a thick shock of hair. That, too, was damp, as were the chest and armpits of his shirt. The day was hot.

The two children, Herman and Sadie, looked at the new world they had entered, a vast arena of grassland that encircled them. They removed their shoes and waded barefoot into the shallow stream. A small bass jumped in front of them, splashed into the water, and streaked away at an angle. "Pa, did we bring my fishing pole?" called out Herman. Already he was taking a liking to this place and its new adventures.

"Aye, son, but they're all packed up," called back his father.

His sister wiggled her toes into the sandy bottom. Soon her feet disappeared, covered with sand. "Look, Herman, I have no feet," she giggled, and indeed it appeared so. Life in this new land could be illusory.

Elsie cleared the luncheon table cloth and repacked the woven basket. She washed her hands in the stream and then crawled up into the seat of the wagon beside her husband, who whistled for the oxen to pull. The wagon lurched and settled into the same steady gait as before lunch, two miles per hour.

By 4:00 o'clock they had traveled seventeen miles. The sun was now far ahead of them, reaching for the western horizon. It had taken on a yellow pallor, and its position in the sky, more directly in front of them, made the couple squint. Johannes had pulled the brim of his hat down to shield his eyes from the glare. Elsie was cupping one hand over her brow. Inside, the children dozed to escape the tedium. All four were dreaming.

"How many more days?" Johannes wondered. "How many more days until we find the land that will be ours?" Hundreds of miles of frontier stretched before them.

Caught in his reverie, he did not see the rock or the washout. Clover and Clarabelle were pulling the wagon in tandem when Clover stepped on a large rock that had been loosened by the spring rains.

The rock gave way and slid into a washout at the side of the trail. Clover lost his footing and slid with it, yanking the wagon suddenly to the right. The mighty ox gave a terrifying groan and then a weighty moan as he tumbled over. Johannes heard something snap, followed instantly by a thunderous crack. The animal tried to regain his feet, but the traces of the wagon restricted his movement. Finally he stood up and balanced gingerly on three legs. The right hind foot dangled awkwardly in the dust.

But something else was very wrong. The wagon itself sat tilted to the right. The pin holding the wheel in place had shattered during the ox's fall, and the wheel itself had come off. The jolt had broken the axle into two pieces.

"What will we do?" questioned Elsie.

"What *will* we do?" repeated Johannes, dumbfounded. He focused on the animals and shook his head.

"What's wrong?" came a small male voice from inside the wagon. "We're tipping."

"Shall we say a prayer?" came the accompanying small female voice.

"Yes, say a prayer," answered the mother's voice. "We may have to unload the wagon."

"Why?" the small male voice asked immediately.

Johannes was busy removing the traces that hitched Clover and Clarabelle to the wagon. He patted the oxen gently and spoke to them in their ears, like he had always done since their birth. They were brother and sister and had never been separated. He knew what must be done.

"Take Herman and Sadie on a walk," he ordered. He avoided his wife's eyes.

"Oh, Johann!" she lamented. "Must we?"

"We must," he answered. "It is God's will."

Elsie fought back her tears as she walked back along the trail, clutching her children's hands.

Fifteen minutes later, she heard the report of a rifle. When she returned, she found her husband sitting on the ground with the wagon wheel in his lap. The ceremonial whiskey jug had been removed from the wagon and opened.

"Prosit!" He raised the jug mouth toward her and then to his lips

"Johannes," she cried, a wild womanly shriek that brought him to his senses. "Can you fix the wheel?" Her voice cajoled him.

"The axle is broken," he muttered in despair.

But so often Misfortune is tied to its mirrored twin, Good Fortune. Just then a wagon approached, a buckboard pulled by two mules, driven by a man in a straw hat.

"Guten tag!" came a voice toward them. "Need any help?" The buckboard drew up beside them, and the driver surveyed the scene.

"Ya, we do need help," Johannes replied. His voice was defeated, humbled.

"Welcome to St. Anna," said the man.

"St. Anna?" Johannes asked.

"It's our settlement, just over the next hill. Would you mind staying with us tonight, the missus and me and the kids? Our farm is a quarter mile from here, that direction." He pointed to the northwest.

Herman's voice chimed in. "Did you say kids, mister?"

The man chuckled. "Yes, I did. There's three of 'em: a boy, Rudolf, about your size and his sister, Gertrude, like you." He nodded to Sadie. "And there's an older girl, Sophia. We'll bring along your ox now and fetch your wagon tomorrow. We'll have to replace that axle. I think my brother, Wilhelm, has one to spare. I'm Gunther Muellerhagen… Gunther Mueller. It's just Mueller now. We've recently shortened our name because… because we are American!"

Elsie could not believe her luck. She found Gunther and his wife, Myrtle, most gracious. That night she slept in a feather bed and dreamed of a new life for her family, safe from the attack of red-skinned savages who raped and scalped. Elsie's tears were tears of relief and of joy. Myrtle seemed to understand her fears.

The next morning they entered the budding settlement of St. Anna, and Wilhelm Mueller produced the necessary new axle. There was no shortage of help to lift the wagon and repair the axle. They were a community. These men of the prairie were hardy souls, tinkers in the new American tradition. They could make repairs using their ingenuity as craftsmen and builders. They could fix equipment that needed repair by fashioning spare parts out of wood and metal and rock.

Johannes knew that the loss of Clover meant a change in plans. With only one ox, they would never be able to travel far to the west into the Dakota Territory. That day Johannes and Elsie found a plot of land just west of Gunther Mueller's homestead. To their delight, the land possessed a small meandering creek that snaked its way through it, enough water for themselves and their livestock. Johannes knelt down and let the fertile soil trickle through his hands. "Praise the Lord!" he exclaimed. He was home.

That night Johannes and Elsie celebrated their new beginning at a wedding dance, held in Gunther's barn. Friedrich Muellerhagen, Wilhelm's son, married Sophia Mueller, Gunther's daughter. In time Herman Meier, formerly Meierhoffer, married Gertrude Mueller, and two years later Sadie Meier married Rudolf Mueller. The family had long ago dropped "hoffer" from their surname. Johannes and Elsie watched happily as their children marched up the aisle of newly erected St. Anna's Catholic Church, the most recent addition to Stearns County's growing body of architecture. Nearly two decades had passed since the day of their arrival in St. Anna, all of seventeen miles from Waite's Crossing at the western edge of St. Cloud, gateway to the frontier.

* * * * * * *

"The way they live and multiply is shameful," the boy's grandmother once chided. "It's sinful! Inbreeding!" she hissed. "It's the Stearns County Syndrome at its worst!" Her voice was scathing, and those at the dinner table lowered their heads in embarrassment. But she, herself, felt no chagrin.

"Then why do you go out there?" a boy's voice asked. It was her grandson.

"Because they invest," she stated unabashed. "That's business." She spat the words out.

Frankie followed the Sauk River back to Waite Park. He thought of his mother's family. They had ventured a full forty miles from St. Cloud to Sauk Centre before they put down roots.

Great Grandpa Promenshenkel had led them out into western Stearns County. He had been a farmer in the old country and would be a farmer his whole life. He had a love for the land; it was in his blood. A generation later, during the Great Depression to come, the land had saved them.

His six boys grew up to be farmers. When the time came, each, in turn, purchased a small farmstead with his father's help. His four girls married the sons of farmers. They, too, became farmers.

Young Alex Promenshenkel purchased 350 acres two miles southwest of Sauk Centre, just west of the Sauk River. He set to work on his first priority, building a barn. His whole life revolved around his livestock; they must be tended to first. Creature comforts for his young bride would have to wait. For two years they lived with his parents.

Theresa Promenshenkel, who called herself Tracy, was a patient woman. She understood her husband's needs. The one thing that could prod him into building a house for them was to start a family. She would conceive soon. She smiled at the thought. This she confided to her younger sisters. They, too, were still living at home, both engaged to be married the following spring.

The following year a baby boy, Julian, was born. Alex started to work on a two-story farmhouse. They moved in shortly before a second baby, Cecelia, was born. A well beneath the kitchen with a hand pump over the sink provided water. Alas, the only bathroom was an outhouse behind the house. Tracy would not be satisfied until the house had indoor plumbing. But it would be many years before her wish came true.

The farm thrived. Alex milked cows, black and white Holsteins, morning and evening. During the day he plowed the land into furrows, wave upon wave. Then he tilled the soil with a disk and planted it: plenty of alfalfa to feed the cows, corn for the pigs, oats and wheat for sale.

Nothing went to waste. Tracy was entrusted to raise the chickens. They pecked at the chaff that fell to the ground in the farmyard and scoured for seeds in the grass between the two big laundry poles that were set in concrete and strung with wire to dry the laundry. Tracy worked with great joy. She sang as she hung up her husband's work clothes.

Beside the barn lay a massive garden, producing enough potatoes and beans and sweet corn to feast on at table throughout the winter, enough carrots and lettuce for salads, enough beets and cucumbers for pickles. She insisted that her husband plant two apple trees beside the house. Each fall she baked delicious apple pies with sugar and cinnamon and nutmeg. In front of the big picture window in the living room, she planted one flowering crab apple tree, not so much for its fruit but for its beautiful white blossoms. The tree bloomed in spring, and Tracy watched as the petals dropped to the ground like snowflakes. In the evening she liked to walk on the carpet of petals, enchanted. It calmed the fluttering in her heart.

Her family grew: another boy, Alvin; another girl, Sylvia; and then four more boys in rapid succession: Alfred, Alex Jr., Vern, and Donnie. The last boy was the smartest of them all. The last child was a baby girl. The parents named her Theresa, after her mother. But the children clamored for Patty. "Patty! Patty!" they begged. And so the little girl came to be known.

She was Daddy's little girl and followed him out to the barn to milk the cows. She played alone, tracing her footsteps around the silo. She did not understand when her oldest brother, Julian, left them. Nor did she understand when her father left to bring Julian back, his body in a casket, the victim of a landslide in Wisconsin. She had listened to the story many times from her brother, Alfred. He had never seen his father and mother embrace like they did when Julian's body was brought back home.

Young Patty was nine when her closest sibling, Donnie, took ill with scarlet fever. A small room at the top of the stairs was prepared for him. Patty would spy into it when no one was looking. Her brother's cough bothered her. Within a year he succumbed to it. Donnie's death nearly killed his mother. Her heart was heavy; her soul, tormented. She no longer sang. Worry drained her energy.

In 1940, one year after Donnie died, her mother's heart gave out. It signaled to her children that it was time to leave home and get on with their lives. Within three years Patty's two older sisters married. Two of her older brothers, Alvin and Alfred, left for a Catholic seminary to become priests. Alfred would be there for over eighty years. Alex Jr. and Vern soon joined the navy to fight in WWII.

Little Patty was left home alone with her dad. She was still Daddy's little girl, and he let her get away with murder. The nuns at St. Paul's Elementary School just shook their heads. She would grow up to be a rebellious teen; they were sure of it.

The little girl blossomed into young womanhood, and the nuns nodded knowingly to one another that their predictions were coming true. She lacked discipline. Her father was too permissive. He allowed her to use the family car on Sunday afternoons to drive around and pick up a carload of her girlfriends. They would cruise main, and somebody once saw them drinking a six-pack of beer in the car. Patty and her friends liked the company of boys. That was dangerous. Her thoughts were too focused on this world's pursuits, not enough on those of the next, the after-life.

Finally Sister Felicity, the principal of the high school, had had enough. Young Patty needed to be taken down a peg or two. But rather than talk to Alex Sr., she opted to speak with Alex Jr., a rough and tumble lad on leave from the United States Navy. But before listening to Sister Felicity's objections to his little sister's behavior, he asked her a question: "Why are you talking to me and not to Dad?"

"Because it won't do any good talking to him," she answered crossly. "He won't do anything to discipline her."

Alex Jr. listened carefully to Sister's litany of complaints. "What's wrong with that?" he stated as sincerely as a twenty-one-year-old, man-of-the-world sailor boy could. The good sister found his response most disappointing.

Upon graduation, eighteen-year-old Patty left home for college at St. Benedict's in St. Joseph, Minnesota, five miles west of St. Cloud. After one year she took a more realistic view and transferred into nurses training at the St. Cloud Hospital. There she was sheltered by a group of young women who trained with her, who roomed with her, and who took her on an occasional night out on the town down the road to the Bloody Bucket to meet eligible young men.

The young boy glared into the surface of the Sauk River as he recalled his mother's stories of how she and his father had first met. Two weeks later, they met again at a dance at the Colosseum on the other side of town, just outside of Waite Park's village limits.

"There," she said, "his father spotted her and called out 'Hi!'" His father remembered the chance meeting quite differently— that she had seen him first and called out "Hi!" to him.

The boy's grin faded, and he focused on the river in front of him. Just out from shore, barely three feet from where he was standing, was a small island. It was oblong in shape, covered with grassy weeds, and he desperately wanted to be out on it. Three feet. He could hurdle that distance easily.

He crouched down, and his leg muscles tensed. Then he sprang outward, and through the air he flew. He jabbed both feet into the ground on the island.

He had been deceived. The island was entirely muck. His feet sank into watery weeds and plunged downward to the river bottom. The muck enveloped his whole body up to his chin. The spring water felt cold.

Immediately he scrambled to escape the clutches of the watery vegetation. He felt foolish. He looked to see that he was alone. The smell of rotting plant life in stagnant water was strong; his nostrils burned. He picked up his bucket of frogs and trudged the five blocks home to wash the decay from his body.

His mother, frying hamburgers on the stove for lunch, watched him as he entered through the back door. "What happened to you?" she questioned.

He could feel her soft brown eyes upon him. "I fell in the river" was all he told her.

CHAPTER SEVEN

Monday morning came. Sister Mary Andrew's classroom was alive with chirps and giggles and laughter. The First Graders were eager to show their wares.

None sat more excited than the young boy in the second row next to the windows. He cradled a gray metal minnow bucket in his arms and awaited his turn. His best friend, Terry Joe O'Brian, tried to pry the lid off the bucket. But the plaster cast on his left arm from wrist to elbow hindered his grip. The owner of the bucket resisted, holding the cover down tightly.

"What do you have in there?" Terry Joe asked.

"Nothing. You'll see," the boy replied, "when it's my turn."

"Is it a snake?" Terry Joe asked hopefully. And in that instant Frankie deeply regretted that it was not a snake. But that prize had escaped, this time anyway.

The first to show and tell was little Abigail Hoganson. A bit of a tomboy, she lived with her mom and dad and big brother out south of town by the stone quarries. These quarries produced granite. The miners dug down, foot by foot, and lifted out the precious chunks of stone with cranes. Cutters, grinders, and polishers, all skilled machine operators, worked together like a colony of ants to carve out useable slabs for sale worldwide.

Often they would dig deep into the earth, hundreds of feet down, ripping the granite out of the walls and floor. Eventually the cutters would gouge into a wall and breach it, causing a small spring to erupt. Then it was time to move on and start a new quarry. The spring would continue to flow and eventually fill the cavity. These became swimming holes for Waite Park's youth and lovers' lanes for teenage boys and girls with more that suntans and refreshing swims on their minds.

Abigail Hoganson pulled a precious rock from her pocket. "This is an agate," she explained. "It's from the quarry behind our house."

"How much is it worth?" Terry Joe blurted, suddenly deeply interested.

"A quarter," Abigail replied, "at the rock shop in St. Cloud." Terry Joe seemed impressed.

"Are there more of them?" he asked.

"Sure there are," answered Abigail, "but they're way down at the bottom where the water is filling the quarry in."

Frankie looked at the agate and then at the girl. She had her hair in two long blond braids. Her eyes were set wide apart, and she had a bit of a pug nose. For a girl, she was alright, never wearing dresses but always a hand-me-down flannel shirt tucked into a corduroy skirt.

Sister Andrew turned the class's attention to the back row. "John Lewis, what do you have in that box?" The box had been chirping for nearly a half hour.

A handsome young boy wearing an orange bow tie dislodged himself from his desk and carried a large box to the front of the room. There were a dozen holes in the sides of the box, and in two or three a head was sticking out. He set the box down on the teacher's desk.

"*Cheep*!" The contents of the box were no surprise, for John's family owned and operated the hatchery on the hill beyond the viaduct, just across Highway 52. Then he removed the cover.

The children surged forward for a closer look. Twenty-four plump yellow puff balls looked back at them. Each tiny chick was wearing an orange ribbon tied around its neck as a little bow tie. Obviously, Mrs. Lewis had an eye for coordinating colors.

"*Cheep*! *Cheep*!" The baby chicks banded together and sang in chorus. The girls found this irresistible and elbowed their way close to the box. They're like the ladies in our church choir," noted Irene Pressler.

"Yeah, they're all fat," giggled Gail Teigen.

"Jeanie Kovar looked at John Lewis's bow tie. A good singer herself, she asked, "Why don't you sing? Stretch your neck out, like this." She imitated the baby chicks, crossed her eyes at John, and cheeped. Then she broke into convulsive laughter. The other girls joined her.

Jerry Unger shook his head. "Birds of a feather flock together," he whispered to Frankie, borrowing one of his father's favorite lines.

"Can I pet one?" asked Abigail Hoganson, bolder than her peers. She picked up one that seemed to like her. "This one's hungry," she said, stroking its beak. It opened its mouth and swallowed.

"They're all hungry," tutored John. "They're always hungry, all of them."

"Ew!" shrieked one of the girls, Mary Ambrose. She wrinkled her nose. "Look at that one." She pointed her finger gingerly. All eyes bent forward, even Sister Andrew's.

In the corner lay a corpse-like skeleton covered in skin and feathers. It was pancake thin, not plump like the others. It looked more like a fried egg, sunny side up, than a live bird.

It's dead," stated Terry Joe. "I can smell it."

John Lewis reached a hand in and raised a squishy carcass up to his eyes. He identified the bird. "This one's Elvis. Chickens pick on one another. It's called a pecking order. The weakest ones never survive." Indeed, the other First Graders, too, could smell the rotting flesh, and some backed away.

Sister saw an opportunity to educate. The time was right. She spoke. "Children, life and death go hand in hand." They stared at the bird. "Death is the natural end of all of our lives. Before any of us can go to heaven, we have to die. It's God's plan. Even Jesus died for our sins."

Just then, the bird in John Lewis's hand defecated. Its bowels let loose, and a foot of slippery slime splattered onto the floor.

"It has the runs," announced Terry Joe. How can a dead bird do that?" he asked, seriously curious for once.

"Well…" hemmed Sister.

At that moment Elvis's torso shivered. Suddenly a wing flapped, and the bird's neck and head arched upward. It elevated its beak and opened it. "*Cheep*!" Both eyes bulged in their sockets.

"Elvis!" screamed Terry Joe, and half a dozen boys echoed the scream.

"Dad says Elvis is a slow starter," said the hatchery owner's son. He was relieved and grinning. "Here, feed him these seeds. He's hungry."

Jerry Unger plopped a pinch of wheat grain into the open beak.

Terry Joe O'Brian had been thinking, more than usual. The recent prolonged season of Lenten sacrifice and Easter was still fresh in his memory. "It's a Resurrection!" Full of astonishment, he looked at Sister Andrew.

"No, it isn't," corrected Sister Andrew.

"Elvis has come back from the dead. He's been reborn," the boy argued.

"No, he hasn't!" she chastised. But her words rang hollow and she stopped. The bulging eyes stared at her, the beak wide open.

Decorum was restored. Next up was Susanne Danbury. Frankie sat back in a disinterested pose and gritted his teeth. Susanne was the epitome of a girl—prissy and critical of what she did not like. "My mother and I baked cupcakes," she exclaimed, and she lifted a dish towel from a tray laden with twenty-four cupcakes. They were frosted white and decorated with little pink and blue flowers.

"Pink for girls and blue for boys," she commanded, setting the parameters for their distribution. Frankie licked the frosting first and then nibbled at his cupcake, preserving the blue flower for last. He could not stand the smile on Susanne's face. She seemed to be gleaming at him with her big round head and flashing white teeth.

Across the aisle, Terry Joe bit savagely into his cupcake and the whole frosted top, flower included, disappeared.

Just before recess it was Frankie's turn to show and tell. He set the bucket down on Sister Mary Andrew's desk. He opened the lid and reached in. The class leaned forward curiously.

The big bullfrog saw the light for the first time in two days. He was hungry and in no mood to dawdle. He leaped with all his might. Out of the bucket he sprang and landed on Sister Andrew's desk, smack dab on a pile of arithmetic papers that Sister had graded the night before and intended to return.

The papers scattered when the bullfrog leaped again, right into Susanne Danbury's lap. She screamed and several boys laughed. The bucket tipped onto its side, and this agitated the other frogs. They, too, saw the light and leaped out of the bucket. The class learned something about frogs that day: that they do not tarry when escaping and that they can leap, repeatedly, to all corners of the room and even down the hallway.

One frog, a youngster, sought refuge under Sister's habit, a long black garment that stretched to the top of her shoes. This frog was slippery. Its skin was covered with slime after forty-eight hours closed in a bucket with its brethren. When it jumped, Sister screamed. That one shout brought the room to attention and to amazed stillness. For a long moment the only activity in that room was the hopping of a dozen frogs, scattering to the winds.

For Sister, the recess bell was a relief. The girls were dismissed in unison. The boys were strongly encouraged to stay and help corral the frogs. Sister glared openly at the boy, Frankie. He felt its sting on the back of his neck. One by one, the frogs were recaptured and returned to the minnow bucket. The lid was closed.

Sister Mary Anthony, the principal, was summoned. "Who did this?" she scowled. And after a silence, "Who brought the frogs?"

Frankie raised his hand. Sister Anthony escorted him as he carried the pail to the janitor's room. The boy didn't look at her directly, but somehow he thought she was chuckling.

Down the hall fifty paces, the Third Graders were absorbed in a story from America's history. The storyteller was a diminutive nun, standing barely four feet and ten inches tall. Still, she exuded a passion that no other sister in the school could match. Sister Mary Agatha believed in the sanctity of the American Indian, and her classroom was a testament to that belief.

Mounted on all four walls of the room were gigantic framed pictures of Indian chiefs and squaws, men and women of courage and honor: not just famous warriors like Crazy Horse and Geronimo, but also wise leaders like Sitting Bull of the Sioux, Chief Joseph of the Nez Perce, and Crowfoot of the Blackfeet. Their frozen faces stared down from a height at the white children as the boys and girls studied. It was as if they were examining the souls of their conqueror's children. They were constant reminders of a past that was, unfortunately, slipping into oblivion and drunkenness on the reservation.

On a bookshelf beside the teacher's desk at the front of the room was a sculpted bust of Sakakaweja, the young Shoshone woman who had helped Lewis and Clark explore the Louisiana Purchase up the Missouri River. And standing in the corner of the room, opposite the door, was Sister Agatha's pride and joy: a full-sized teepee sewn from buffalo hides. Surrounding it was a scene of family life in a tribal camp during the late 1800s. Mannequins of a man and a woman and two children were dressed realistically in buckskin and fur. The woman held a small bundle in her arms, a black-haired "papoose," her baby.

The man was a hunter. He held a sharp spear in his right hand and a bow in his left. A quiver of arrows was laced to his back. A colorful bonnet of eagle feathers graced the man's head, and his face was painted red and black for war and death. His arms were ringed in bracelets made out of bone, and a small leather pouch hung from a belt at his waist. Rumor had it that the bag was full of scalps, taken in glorious battle. Even grown-ups who had been taught by Sister Agatha many years before believed this. Half-naked, the red man wore moccasins and leggings, leather thongs that crisscrossed his legs.

His wife sat by a fire. She had once been a beautiful woman, a chieftain's daughter, according to Sister Agatha. She was clothed in a supple dress, fashioned out of fur: mink and fox.

The children followed their parents' example. The boy was coming of age. Clad in buckskin shorts and bare-chested, he too wore a painted face and a single eagle feather in his hair. In his hand he cupped a tomahawk. The Indian boy's sister was little more than a child. She was draped in a shapeless deer hide dress, and her rich black hair was braided into two long strands. She cradled a doll in her arms, imitating her mother's maternal instincts.

On this morning the display caught the eye of one of the Third Grade pupils, Robbie Stein. Robbie felt in his pocket for the switchblade knife. It did not measure up well against the tomahawk.

A commotion in the hallway outside the First Grade room interrupted Sister Agatha's tale of Pocohontas helping Captain John Smith at Jamestown; and curious, and annoyed, she stepped outside her classroom to investigate. What she saw did not please her. A big bullfrog was hopping down the hallway toward her room. And little Terrance Joseph O'Brian was hopping along after it, not seeming to catch it and, in fact, losing ground.

She turned and retreated into the world of her classroom. All was hushed. Something was wrong. She sensed fear in the eyes of the children, all of them except one. Robbie Stein stood rather guiltily with the tomahawk in his hand. In the display something was terribly amiss. The head of the papoose no longer rested in the mother's arms. It lay in the fire, chopped off at the neck.

"I scalped it," Robbie grinned, but his mirth instantly disappeared amid Sister Agatha's wrathful shriek. It was in Ojibwe.

"Wanaadizi Sa! (He is damaged!) Agadendaagwad!! (It is shameful!!)" Robbie did not understand the tongue, but he knew the message full force.

Sister Mary Agatha, all four feet and ten inches of her, was proud of her Indian heritage. "Go!" she ordered, "outside. Not you, amik (young beaver)." She barred his escape and shut the door. "Dasoozo! (You are trapped, pinned down!)" she exclaimed. Her ferocity swelled. She latched hold of the tomahawk.

On her desk was a wooden chopping block, often used by Sister Agatha to cut food for her lunch: a melon or a sandwich or a piece of meat. She did not like knives. She much preferred the tomahawk. It spoke to her imagination. It appealed to the warrior in her blood. *Whap!* The chopping block felt her wrath. It quivered under the tomahawk's bulk. She felt its power inside her.

"Akawe! (Look!)" *Whap! Whap!* She struck the chopping block again. "Amiko-wiinzob. (You are a beaver gall bladder.) Angotoon! (I will reduce you to nothing!) Amiko-zhiigozhigan!! (To a beaver carcass scrap!!)"

Her eyes never left those of Robbie, and his were riveted on the tomahawk. The blade was razor-sharp. He thought he saw blood on it and perhaps dried flesh. Then he looked into Sister's eyes. There was no mercy in them.

For the first time that anyone could remember, Robbie Stein's eyes moistened with tears. *Whap!* The tears thickened and blurred his vision. He could hear the tomahawk plainly. It sounded closer and closer. The drops crawled down his cheeks in tiny streams.

"Zhazhiibitamowin! (Disobedience!) Zhaagode'evin! (Cowardice!) Zhishigoshkaw! (I will crush him under my foot!)" Sister Agatha's chanting in her ancient native language unnerved him. The chiefs and squaws were looking down on him in disgust. She fingered the knotted cord at her waist. Her hand closed around it. *Whap! Whap!* "Zhaagooji'! (Defeat him!)" Her voice had become low and hoarse, threatening.

Suddenly the boy felt a great need to escape. Knees shaking, he bolted for the door. He heard the swish of Sister's habit behind him. He threw open the door and emerged into the white man's civilized world.

Terry Joe O'Brian had finally caught his frog. He stared in disbelief as Robbie Stein sprinted past him for the lavatory. Others, too, watched in amazement. Sister Agatha, pint-sized, female, and religious, had made Robbie Stein cry. She was the only one ever to do so. From that day on, even when he was in jail, he refused to cry. But he never again threatened to scalp anyone.

Terry Joe, bullfrog in hand, peeked through a crack into Sister Agatha's room. The tomahawk had been restored to its rightful place in the Indian boy's hand.

She was kneeling down at the fire, like at a sacrificial altar. She was holding something in her hand. It was a baby doll's head, a little black-haired head with the eyes open. Sister Agatha rocked back and forth, crooning a song in a strange language. To Terry Joe, it was obviously a song of mourning.

The school day ended with a blast from the same bell that began it. The tone was identical, but oh what a difference! Children, having been dragged into the classroom in the morning, now bounded away from it with a bounce in their step. Armed with lunch boxes and school bags, they exited.

Accompanied by his best friend, Frankie carried his minnow bucket in both arms as he trudged home. He was thinking.

What are you going to do with 'em?" inquired Terry Joe.

Frankie sighed. "Dump 'em back in the swamp," he replied. "They should be let go, set free."

"Don't let Robbie Stein catch you with 'em. He'll drop 'em off the viaduct onto the tracks. He's mad as hell at Sister Agatha."

Instinctively the boy carrying the pail turned and looked behind him and quickened his pace.

Two blocks from home, they came to the alley behind Grandma O'Brian's house. There stood Timmy, a coffee can in his hand. He approached nonchalantly. "Hey, twerp, wanna play marbles?" he asked his neighbor boy. He looked closely at the minnow bucket. "What's in there?"

"Nothing. Just something for school, show and tell" was the reply. "Some frogs."

"Wanna play marbles?" the older boy asked again.

"I can't right now, but later. I'll go home and get my marbles."

"We'll play pot," stated Timmy, "right here in Grandma's alley. I'll dig the hole. Hurry up!"

Playing marbles was a child of spring. Every April on one of the first warm days, stashes of marbles would appear, magically, like the pots of gold leprechauns flaunt on St. Patrick's Day. Filled with marbles, cans and bags that had slept for a year in hibernation found their way onto the playgrounds and back alleys of the village. The schoolyard became a testing ground as boys vied to capture each other's marbles.

The majority played chase. The lead weapon was a shiny metal ball bearing, dubbed a steelie. Most were an inch in diameter. Taking turns, each boy tossed his steelie, trying to hit his opponent's steelie. When the shooter succeeded, he won a marble from the other boy.

In Waite Park the Great Northern Railway's car shops housed on storage shelves a vast assortment of ball bearings for trains. Boys coveted these "steelies." After sufficient begging by his sons, a father who worked for the railroad might give in to their wishes.

Timmy and Terry Joe O'Brian had pleaded and nagged for days on end until finally they got what they wanted. Bill O'Brian brought home a shoe box of steelies, an array that made his sons grin. The older boy spotted the treasure immediately. He reached into the corner of the box and extracted a huge ball bearing, two and a half inches in diameter. It was a great pearl, hiding in an oyster.

"These are from your Uncle Squeak," stated Bill O'Brian flatly.

Timmy extracted the prize gingerly and tested its weight. It was almost the size of a baseball. It would crush an average steelie. This whopper suited his personality, and he was eager to exploit it.

That day he had brought it to the schoolyard at lunch. The other boys were in awe—all except, strangely enough, little Johnny Fisch. "I'll play ya," Johnny volunteered. Timmy O'Brian's smile broadened into a sadistic grin.

The other games were uncharacteristically suspended while the boys settled in to watch the match. It would be a slaughter; they were sure.

Little Johnny Fisch's steelie was as diminutive as Timmy O'Brian's was huge. Barely half the size of a pea, it reflected little Johnny's masochistic temperament.

Plink. The little ball bearing glanced off its hefty cousin. Timmy gave little Johnny a marble. Johnny raised the small steelie to his eye and dropped it, bombardier fashion. *Plink.* Another hit, another marble in payment. The giant steelie was an easy target, a Goliath and no match for the pellet from David's sling shot. Timmy resorted to a new plan of attack. He tried to toss the massive orb and strike the tiny steelie a fatal blow, but his plan backfired. He missed and missed.

Plink. Plink. Little Johnny's throws had uncanny accuracy. Aware of the audience, he began to taunt the oversized steelie. He chided it at first, then mocked it. He spoke in the small steelie's voice, the helpless victim, urging the giant to hit him and end his misery. "Come on, hit me! Hit me!" His tone became whiny and suicidal. He was nearly crying.

The schoolyard fell silent, waiting for Timmy to explode. He, too, was aware that all eyes were on him. His coffee can was being depleted rapidly; it was now only a third full.

He knew that he must save his dignity. He thought of punching little Johnny, pummeling him into submission, and then taking his marbles as a spoil of war. He would make him shed real tears.

But one greater thought prevented that. Little Johnny could throw a rock farther and harder than any boy in Waite Park. He had been known to do so and once, in a fit of rage, had broken two of his older sister Josephine's front teeth. When his temper flared, he showed no restraint, no mercy.

The school bell rang. The boys shuffled into the schoolhouse, whispering that this game was far from over. And yet they knew it was over. Timmy and his great pearl had been beaten soundly. Still, there was a good chance that he would seek revenge. Secretly they hoped that the bigger boy would not let it go—that they would get to see Johnny Fisch's blood.

There was still a half hour until supper and two hours until dark. Timmy stood in the back alley behind his grandma's house. His modified plan was to replenish his can of marbles at the younger boy's expense. In the dirt he had dug a deep hole, stretching from fingertip to mid-forearm. "Come on, twerp. Put your ten marbles in." Then they marched back seven paces.

"Where's your big steelie?" Frankie asked innocently.

"Shut up and throw it" was Timmy's curt answer.

The younger boy's steelie stopped two inches in front of the hole. The older boy's steelie veered two inches to the right and stopped a foot beyond the hole. "Put two more marbles in," Timmy commanded, dropping in two more himself.

On the third roll Timmy struck pay dirt. His steelie glided to the rim of the hole and disappeared. He had won the pot; his luck had turned. He fished out a large, two-fisted handful of round solids, interspersed with coveted cats' eyes. These sparkled in the waning sunlight. He wanted more.

They split the next two pots, and then Timmy had an idea: "Let's put ten in after every miss."

Frankie hesitated, weighing cost versus reward.

"Come on, twerp! What's your problem?" This goading had the desired effect; the younger boy nodded.

As evening darkness settled in, the pot grew. Neither boy could find the range. Ten marbles at a time after each miss.

Once Frankie made a shot, his steelie falling just over the edge. He could hear the marbles in the hole clatter as the steelie cracked onto glass. But Timmy's luck held, and he rolled his steelie accurately. *Clack*! It dipped into the hole and smacked the younger boy's steelie a resounding blow. The pot began to fill.

After six more throws, the boys could see the topmost marbles in the hole, which now held two-hundred and twenty marbles. Frankie's cloth bag was half depleted; Timmy's can, nearly empty. Both boys were excited. The payout would be quite a day's wages for one of them.

They were taking turns shooting first. Timmy stepped to the line and heaved his steelie forward. It landed with a thud and rolled directly toward the hole and its mound of marbles. However, friction intervened and the steelie stopped just short of its goal. Frankie stepped forward and toed the mark. He squinted into the fading sunlight, and the sun's rays diffused into hazy vertical streaks.

"Come on, twerp, throw it," said the voice behind him.

The younger boy focused, swung his arm back and then forward in a pendulum motion. Lofted in an arc, the steelie spun through the air. It landed five feet from the pot and then rolled in the dirt. For a brief moment, it looked like it would strike

Timmy's steelie and knock it in. But the rolling ball bearing evaded the opposing sphere and plowed headlong into the pile of marbles, where it stopped dead. Both boys leaped forward. The winning orb lay there in the fading sunlight, basking in a sea of marbles.

Frankie sunk to his knees. He snapped up the losing steelie and flipped it away toward Timmy. Then he opened the drawstring his mother had sewn into the cloth pouch. The mouth of the sack opened wide to receive its repast.

Timmy lowered his head in defeat. He was disgusted and flung his tin coffee can into the distance. Then he glowered down at the boy who knelt before him.

It was his brother, Terry Joe, who retrieved the can. "Come on home," Terry Joe stated. His voice was anxious. "Mom wants you home now! Kevin's been burned in a fire."

CHAPTER EIGHT

The Friday before Memorial Day was the last day of the school year. Summer vacation would start on Monday, a prolonged three-month reprieve from the tedium of the classroom.

To celebrate, the principal of St. Joseph's Elementary, Sister Mary Anthony, ordered an afternoon picnic. The teachers did not disagree with her decision. It had, as always, been a long school year. They could use the rest. If anyone was against it, she did not express it.

That morning Frankie had been excited. He had gone to school and after mass received his report card. He saw one "A" in Religion and another "A" in Reading. He liked to read. According to the report card, he had earned a "B" in Science and another "B" in Arithmetic. Music, Art, and Handwriting were all "C." He would not realize until years later that every boy at St. Joseph's received a grade of "C" in Music, Art, and Handwriting—no matter what. Performance did not matter; gender did.

The boy knew that his parents would examine closely the second page of the report—Behavior. Any minuses would sound a grave alarm; fortunately there were none. Sister Mary Andrew was an experienced teacher who understood how the parents in Waite Park thought. She was not a vindictive nun.

He turned the card over. On the back he saw the three signatures his father had written, one after each of the first three quarters. They were identical and the cursive spoke of eloquence learned through the Palmer method of repetition when he had attended country school in Duelm.

The most important information was written beneath these signatures, and it was signed by the principal to make it official. It said that he was being promoted to the Second Grade.

At noon the boy raced home for lunch, a Friday fare of grilled cheese sandwiches and tomato soup. Only then did he notice the red dots on his arms. He raced into the bathroom and peered into the mirror. His face had them too—red spots that puffed out slightly with pus.

"You have the chicken pox," said his mother. "It's contagious," she added in her nurse's voice. It was absent of any alarm or dread.

Then realization dawned on him. "But Mom," he cried, "I have to go to the picnic!"

"You can't," she replied matter-of-factly.

"But I want to," he persisted.

"You can't go," she repeated and smiled sweetly. "You can stay home, and we'll bake chocolate chip cookies," she suggested. But he did not stay in the house to hear any more.

The venue for the picnic was the community park, seven blocks west of the school. At 1:00 o'clock the students assembled in their classrooms, where their final attendance for the year was taken and recorded. Then the children were released to walk to the park.

The older boys and girls intermingled and strolled in clusters of three and four. The boys wanted to impress the girls, and they clowned around, making nuisances of themselves. Several made suggestive remarks. A few of the bolder ones were crude. But the embarrassed tittering of the girls made them stop, or should have. Behind them, the younger kids clumped together as an entire class: boys to one side, girls to the other. A few marched in unison. It was a bright sunny day, and the warm weather was welcome.

The teachers, too, tended to clump together. Several parents, men and women, had been recruited to help chaperone and to serve snacks and beverages. Once at the park, a few would search out a private spot to smoke a cigarette.

Frankie and Kevin O'Brian sat on a picnic table in Scandan's back yard and watched the parade. Kevin was a year younger than his brother, Terry Joe. His left leg had been burned severely in Rex Luxmeir's garbage bin.

Rex had raked his yard and was burning the dead grass and leaves in an iron bin out back. He was also burning fallen branches and twigs from the elm trees he had trimmed. He went into the house for a minute, just for a minute, to get a beer.

Kevin was passing by and found the fire unattended. He threw sticks onto it to increase the size of the blaze. Satisfied with his work, he stepped closer and up onto a log for elevation to look into the burning bin. Without warning, the fire flared and Kevin's pants caught on fire. Half a minute passed before Rex heard the boy's shrieks of pain.

Thinking quickly, the man tore off his flannel shirt, wrapped it around Kevin's legs, and rolled the boy in the dirt to extinguish the flames. But it was almost too late. Rex could smell the stench of dying flesh. It reminded him of the war.

From right to left the children came. Frankie sat, elbows on his knees and hands under his chin, and watched. The laughter and banter of his schoolmates intensified his disappointment at being excluded.

They watched the Third Graders pass. Sister Mary Agatha's eyes, ever vigilant, were following her cherubs closely, especially that wayward, devilish Robbie Stein. She seemed to be clutching the rosary at her waist.

"Look at Sister Agatha. She's praying the rosary," observed Frankie.

"Like hell, she is!" countered Kevin. "She's gonna use it to whip Robbie Stein. Just watch. She's Irish," added Kevin, "and they're all mean." He concluded his assessment by dislodging a great wad of spit from his mouth and letting it drool between his legs to the ground.

When Timmy and the Fourth Grade class passed by, he ignored the two lads sitting on the picnic table in the neighbor's yard. Frankie watched him closely. The thought of the marbles he had won from the older boy gave him pleasure. It tickled his insides. He squinted. They were approximately the same size. Maybe next year he would find the gumption to stand his ground when Timmy challenged: "Come on, twerp, let's fight." Next year would be a new year. He decided to contemplate it further.

The parade was thinning. Frankie looked at Kevin's leg. It was heavily bandaged to protect it and keep it clean. "Can you show me your scar?"

"Don't touch it with your chicken pox!" Kevin ordered. He turned down the bandage for Frankie to see.

"Will they have to put maggots in there, to eat the rotten flesh?" Frankie inquired. He had heard stories from Terry Joe. "That would itch."

"No Way!" Kevin reacted. He nearly shouted the words. "That's what my brothers say." He pulled the bandage up into place. He looked glum.

When Sister Mary Andrew and the First Graders passed by, she was perspiring. Obviously, her long black habit and black veil did not shed the heat sufficiently. She waved at her pupil, the boy. He felt uncomfortable to be the center of her attention. He lifted his chin in response and waved his hand briefly from the hip.

"I hope you get over your chicken pox soon," she bawled toward him. At the words "chicken pox," the entire class reacted. Susanne Danbury rolled her eyes in her big head and shifted direction. She led the girls to the far side of the street; the boys followed them. They kept moving and quickened their pace. Only Terry Joe held his ground. "Hi, Kevin!" Hi, Frankie!" He waved.

Five minutes later, the street was deserted. "Let's play pitch and hit," suggested Kevin. "I'll bat first." He limped over to the driveway in front of his dad's garage, bat in hand.

Standing in the street, Frankie clutched a rubber ball. He wound up and threw it as hard as he could at the overhead garage door. Kevin swung and missed—a strike. Another pitch. Another swing and miss. Another strike.

Each time, the ball caromed fiercely off the wood paneling of the garage door. Both boys knew that Bill O'Brian would not have liked it, or condoned it, but he was not there.

On the fourth pitch Kevin swung and made contact. The ball sailed over Frankie's head. He turned to chase it, but it landed across the street beyond him—a home run!

Kevin's face beamed. He did not run any bases. In this game you didn't have to. Anyhow, with his leg burned he couldn't have run them if he had tried. He stood in his batter's stance and tapped the business end of the bat into the pavement. "Maggots… schmaggots…" he muttered under his breath. He wanted to forget what the doctor had told him.

SUMMER

CHAPTER NINE

As if on cue, a new season arrived. Memorial Day signaled the beginning of summer and freedom. The last days of May turned sultry. In the back yards the gardens were all planted. Seeds had germinated and become seedlings. The radishes were first, the vanguard of summer's plentiful bounty. Their tiny green shoots had pushed their way through the earth's topsoil crust and sprouted leaves. These were soaking up the sunlight. Next to them, rows of leafy lettuce had also nudged up through the dirt.

Memorial Day was a traditional day for the boy's family. It was his grandfather's birthday. Each May 30th the family loaded the car to drive to Sauk Centre at the western edge of Stearns County. There on the family homestead, they celebrated. It was the same farm where the boy's mother had been born, where she had her roots.

Frankie sat in the back seat and gazed out the side window, but his thoughts were elsewhere, distant. Grandpa was the family patriarch. Two of his sons, Alvin and Alfred, were in the priesthood at St. John's Abbey, situated half way between Sauk Centre and St. Cloud on the shores of Lake Sagatagan. Another two sons, Alex and Vern, were businessmen in Sauk Centre. For the sake of brevity, both had dropped the *shenkel* from their last name and were now simply *Promen*. Alex Sr. did not like the new ways. Still, he could not stop the march of time. The day came when he sold his farm to his daughter, Cecelia, and his son-in-law, John. For this, he was granted the right to live with them.

Occasionally he would drive his Studebaker forty miles to visit his daughters, Sylvia in St. Cloud and his youngest, Patty, in Waite Park. These visits were rare. To Patty, her father seemed uncomfortable, as if he felt obligated to visit. Perhaps it was that she had already given birth five times. Five children. He didn't resent them, but he saw them as symbols of his daughter's married life. She was no longer his little girl but some other man's wife, and this was hard for the man to accept. Yet, he performed his duty and came.

His visits were always in the mid-afternoon when his son-in-law was away on business. They would start awkwardly. The house was constantly busy, never at rest. He would stand outside, where he had lived most of his life milking cows and planting corn. He felt more comfortable outside, more at ease, but his daughter insisted that he come in.

Grandpa smoked a pipe. His grandson sat in an armchair across from him and watched the ritual. First, the elderly man would remove a pouch of tobacco from a side pocket in his coat, unfold it carefully, and extract a pinch. This he packed carefully into the bowl of the pipe. Then he would tear a match from its book and strike it upward on the cover. His was a practiced hand. He would light the tobacco, sucking in his breath in short bursts. The flame ignited the tobacco. Soon, the embers burned orange, and a warm smoke wafted upward. The boy stared at the pouch sitting open on an end table. On the front he could see the picture of a man's head wearing an odd, antiquated hat. He read the inscription underneath, *Prince Albert*. The brand had a pungent aroma.

Puffing on his pipe seemed to relax the grandfather. Then the man and his daughter would talk. The ritual and the conversation would end with the grandfather turning the pipe upside down and tapping the dottle into an ashtray.

The elderly man felt little comfort. Perhaps it was simply the passing of time or that she was no longer a farmer. "We're raising mink, Dad," she had told him on his last visit. He sat and gazed at her, his mind a vacuous haze, for he could only understand cows and pigs and horses, not mink. The man stared

into his daughter's soft brown eyes, so much like his beloved
Tracy's. She knew what he was thinking.

"You miss her, don't you, Dad?"

"I do," he acknowledged, and both became teary-eyed. Then
the soft words flowed between them, words of remembrance: of
tightly-curled ringlets and a delicious lock on a woman's brow
from under a bell-shaped cap. The man's visits never lasted long.
He was always anxious to return to his home in Sauk Centre.

When it was time to go, he would reach into his pocket
and extract five silver dollars, one for each child, tokens of his
affection. The children would clutch the coins and inspect them.
The money looked shiny and new, embossed with the picture of
a woman, Lady Liberty, on the front and a bald eagle clutching
an olive branch in its talons on the back. After his grandpa
departed, the boy would drop the silver coin into his piggybank
with the others.

The family drove west in the morning sunshine. The boy
watched his mother carefully. As she looked out the window,
reminiscing, the look on her face was exactly the same as
her father's.

Finally they drove down a rutted lane into the farmyard.
His father steered carefully and avoided the deeper grooves
and potholes. When they arrived, the birthday party was in full
swing. The boy loved these times. There would be a card game
in the house and a softball game in the yard, "kitten ball" his
Aunt Celia called it. The culmination would be a picnic dinner.
His father was opening the car's trunk and lifting out a large
cooler containing potato salad, his mother's contribution.

But first, the boy had to do something. He raced into the
house and through the kitchen. There his aunts, Celia and Katie
and Viola, were at their pre-assigned tasks, preparing to serve
the picnic foods.

In his haste, the boy weaved through them and their startled
expressions. He launched straight ahead into the dining room,
where the adults were playing cards, past his grandfather's gaze,
and turned left at the stairway. Up it he scampered to a landing
with a window facing the yard. From this vantage point, he
could see the pasture that was the ball field. His older cousins
were already throwing softballs back and forth. He liked to
show them how fast he could run the bases and how adept a

fielder he was. His cousins were good-natured, less competitive than he was, and they applauded his talents. This fed his ego.

Another turn brought him to the top of the stairway, where his pace slowed. He suddenly felt what he had long anticipated, a reverential awe. Hesitantly, step by step, he inched his way forward to the room at the end of the hallway. The door was open, and he peered over the threshold. And there it lay, a cast iron double bed—the very bed his mother had been born in—in the very room in which she had been born! It was a heady thought that gave his young brain a stir.

He held his breath and turned on the light switch. He squinted at the light glowing from the fixture dangling above the bed. He could hear his mother's first petulant cries, her tiny screams, now that life was hers. He could see the faces of his grandmother and grandfather, much younger then, smiling lovingly, sharing these first moments of birth together.

The wallpaper was the same as it had been thirty years before, blue and velvety. A dresser stood at attention along the far wall. He was drawn to it irresistibly. He snooped. The bottom drawers were empty, but in the top drawer he found a hat box containing a woman's hat. The hat was late Victorian, not modern. It was large, wide-brimmed, and feathery, with a sash around the stovepipe peak tied into a neat bow.

He reached in and removed it from the box. Under it he discovered the letters, more than a dozen, written on white stationery in the hand of his grandfather. The boy realized them for what they were, love letters from a young man to a young woman. He opened one and read:

June 9, 1909

My Dearest Tracy,

You shall never know the joy that lies in my heart when I see you. This day shall forever be mine—the day you said "Yes" to my proposal. (I must admit that I was shaking like a leaf.) I am most flattered! With God's guidance we will farm together and raise a family. As your husband I shall strive to serve you all the days of my life.

Ever faithfully yours,
Your future husband,
Alex

The boy stared into a picture. He envisioned his grandfather at home, sitting with his back against a tree, too excited to be inside the house. Pen in hand, he was composing a letter, committing himself to a promise that would never fade away. "Till death do us part" the marriage vows read. But he would never ever part from her, even after she died.

Frankie returned the box of letters, sheltered by the hat, to the top drawer and tiptoed backward from the room. A few paces down the hallway, he came to another room on his left. The door was shut and locked, but the key was in the keyhole. He was alone. His fingers turned the key and then the doorknob. A child's room came into view, a small bedroom with a single bed, a room that had been preserved just so since his Uncle Donnie had died there in 1939.

The boy was immersed. How often had his mother crept into this room to gaze at her dying older brother? What agony had she felt! Bewildered by the thought of death, he felt a sudden chill. A picture of Donnie in a white shirt and bow tie sat on top of the dresser. He had his arm draped around his little sister, Patty.

On the wall above the bed hung a family portrait, framed in gold with a glass front. All families have one, thought the boy. It's as if the people were frozen and preserved at that age forever. The pain in his grandmother's face was already evident. She had once been carefree and spirited, but of late her heart had been fluttering. Did she sense that her end was near? Woman's intuition can be a tormenting thing. This would be their last family portrait.

Frankie trudged down the steps. "Come over here," called his Aunt Sylvia. He entered into the sphere of the adults. "You play my cards. I have to help in the kitchen."

She left him, and he stared at the three coins sitting in front of him on the table. He felt self-conscious, out-of-place.

The menfolk sat around the table, drinks in hand. Three or four favored brandy sweet, a concoction of brandy and 7 Up. "Those quarters are your chips to play," said Uncle Vern. Grandpa was sitting to his immediate right, and this relaxed him.

They were playing skit. He felt lucky. Hand after hand, he either won or at least failed to lose. Then once he did lose, and he had to pay one quarter into the pot. But his good fortune

returned until finally all except him and his grandfather had
been eliminated. The men around the table watched as the boy
and the older man alternated drawing cards. Then, triumphantly,
the boy tabled his cards—a king, a queen, and an ace—skit! He
had won the game. The men whooped. "Hurray!" shouted his
Uncle Vern. A "Hurray!" for him. He felt overwhelmed.

"Go on, take them—they're all yours," his grandfather chuckled.

He scooped the quarters into his hands and charged off into
the kitchen. "Aunt Sylvia! Aunt Sylvia! Look what I won
for you." He tried to deposit the quarters into her lap, but she
pushed his hands away.

"No, they're yours, kiddo—all yours." She laughed at the boy's
puzzled look. "You won them," she explained, "fair and square."

"She wants you to have them," added her older sister, Aunt
Celia. "Now shoo! Out of the kitchen so we can serve lunch."
She picked up a large crystal bowl, full of cherry punch, and
carried it out to the table on the back porch where a buffet dinner
was being set up.

Outside, his uncles were reminiscing. "See that upstairs
window?" Alex Junior pointed above the porch. "That's the
window Vern and I climbed out of to go gallivanting about town."

"How I remember!" mused Vern. He grinned at the distant
memory and chuckled good-naturedly. "Do you remember that
time I was chasing you around the house, and Dad took after us?
Before I could get out the door, he grabbed me. I was the only
one he caught, and I got walloped for it!" He looked at his father
sitting in a lounge chair on the porch. "Right, Dad?"

Frankie looked at his grandfather. The only proof of
recognition that the man had heard his son was a larger puff
of smoke that billowed from his pipe. Uncle Alex joined his
brother in high-pitched, giddy laughter. "Vernie, I got off scot
free; you were in the wrong place at the wrong time. Here they
come; let's eat!"

Now the ball players showed up. It was as if the aroma of
baked ham, and beans baked in brown sugar, and potato salad, and
glorified rice in marshmallow cream and pineapple had infiltrated
the ball field and drawn them to the porch. Heads bowed, and his
mother's brother, Alfred, ordained Father Fintan, said grace.

"Dear Lord, we give thee thanks for your great bounty.
God bless Dad on his seventy-first birthday. Keep him in good

health. God bless our mother, Tracy, and our departed brothers, Julian and Donnie." The boy looked at his mother. Her eyes were closed and moist, and her lips moved silently in prayer.

The priest continued. "May they rest in eternal peace. Bless us all and hold us in the palm of your hand. Look with favor on us and on the food we are about to eat, this bountiful feast—Amen!"

"Amen!" the family echoed.

"Hey, Father," Sylvia's husband, Larry, chirped. "I bet you wouldn't eat this good at the abbey." He watched his brother-in-law load his plate to the gills.

"Not this well," admitted Father Fintan.

And then fate twisted. Uncle Larry, a bit tipsy, stepped toward the table and in a sudden instant tripped on a chair leg. He stumbled forward, off balance, and bumped awkwardly into the table. Plates and platters shook briefly but stood their ground—all except Aunt Celia's crystal punch bowl. It rocked off its base, and the liquid sloshing inside tipped it backward a half-turn. It rolled to the edge of the table and over the edge.

The crash was ear-splitting. The crystal bowl shattered, and shards of glass flew in every direction. Punch the color of blood flowed across the concrete floor.

Uncle Larry, red-faced, dropped to his knees. His hands were shaking, and the men, including the boy's Dad, tried to help him up. But he refused. He knelt, hands to his face. "I'm sorry," he apologized. "I'm so sorry."

"Don't worry about it," said Celia's husband, Uncle John. "Forget it," the host added, trying to console his brother-in-law.

But Uncle Larry could not be consoled. He rose to his feet and looked at those around the table. He was once again the black sheep of the clan. Woe flooded over him. He looked at his father-in-law's eyes. Before giving his daughter Sylvia's hand in marriage to Larry, Alex Promenshenkel had withheld his blessing for a year. The young man had had to work in the WPA to earn his father-in-law's respect. He had been forced to leave home and his fiancée, Sylvia, to do so. His father-in-law stared back at him now, his eyes full of pity.

Larry walked away. A crowd of on-lookers gazed after him as he moved off into the distance. He followed a cow path, parallel to a windrow of pine trees, due south.

By this time Aunt Celia had fetched a mop and bucket of water. She would not let this accident ruin her party. "Go fetch him, John," she pleaded. "The rest of you, eat!"

Her husband nodded, and the family watched Uncle John drive a tractor down the cow path. The gap between the tractor and Uncle Larry narrowed and then disappeared. Minutes elapsed.

And then the tractor turned around. It emitted two puffs of black smoke as it accelerated and chugged back up the cow path into the farm yard. Uncle Larry was aboard. He waved as he jumped down. Uncle John put his arm around him and ushered him to the table. The mess was gone. The floor had been cleaned of its red spill, and a new yellow bowl of punch sat in the center of the table. It was ceramic, not crystal, but that mattered little. The crisis was over; the family was whole again. Both men filled their plates. When the picnic lunch was over, the women cleaned up. The men and cousins retreated to the softball field and picked sides.

The day ended too soon. It always did. The boy never wanted to leave Sauk Centre when his parents did. "Poor Larry," stated the boy's dad as he drove homeward. "He was embarrassed."

"He had too many brandy sevens before dinner" was his mother's assessment.

"Now don't start on that," said the dad. "It was an accident. He tripped on a chair leg."

"The Determeier family has always had a bad reputation. This just adds to it," countered the mother.

"They're outsiders. He's not a farmer; that's why," explained the father. "I know how he feels."

At this his wife bristled. "We've always accepted you. And speaking of reputations, you're the one who's worried about his reputation. You don't like that I'm friends with Marilyn Wojcheski."

"You should keep your distance from her," Dad advised.

"Why?" asked Mom. She wanted him to say it.

"You know why—because she's divorced," stated her husband."

Marilyn and Tom Wojcheski were the only divorced couple in Waite Park. It was sinful and shameful, yet the boy's mom had befriended Marilyn. The divorcee had visited on occasion, riding her bike in a skimpy outfit: a halter top and shorts. His mother's eyes had caught him once staring at this sinful woman. His mother had not invited Marilyn inside the house, but instead they had chatted at length in the back yard near the garden. "I'll give him a haircut," he heard the visitor say, and his mother consented. And on an appointed day he had ridden his bike to a house in Oakdale. She had given him a haircut in her kitchen, but she seemed preoccupied. Her four children were noisy and rambunctious. Without her husband to help, she had her hands full.

"The Catholic Church does not condone divorce. It's a scandal. That woman is a Mary Magdalene." The boy's dad could not conceal the venom in his harsh words. He was obviously irritated by his wife's behavior.

She flared back at a perceived injustice. "She needs my support, and I'm giving it to her," his wife stated.

The man settled back into silence. His wife stared out the passenger window. She sighed. "I don't have any fun in my life," she offered.

"Didn't you have any fun today?" was her husband's response.

Another sigh. "I did today, but I don't at home. All I do is cook and clean and do laundry—and take care of five children while you go to the Wagon Wheel after work.

The man thought. He felt bad about criticizing his wife. Finally he put forth an idea. "I know: let's have a square dance at our house in the basement. I'll clean it up," he volunteered.

His wife's face brightened. "When?"

"This Friday night. We'll invite Ted and Kathy Fercho, Donny and Lil Trellwick, and Ed and Jeanette Banfield." The idea sunk in.

"And Val and Henry Latimer. They'll come from Sauk Centre," added Mom. She thought fondly of her old high school friends. "We'll dress up!" She was visualizing the scene.

"We'll be the perfect hosts," proclaimed her husband. "Let's do it."

CHAPTER TEN

Money was scarce in the village, so bartering became a way of life. Trading was easy, particularly if you had something the other person wanted.

On this day the boy was carrying home a large carton. It was nearly suppertime; the rush hour traffic on Highway 52 was heavy. He walked west over the viaduct and saw the neon lights of the Swan Café burst on. They flooded the parking lot and also the south yard and back steps of the Koeller house. The boy looked at the covered crate in his arms and slowed his pace.

Just then the eastbound 4:45 Great Northern Empire Builder thundered into sight and disappeared under the viaduct. Its rumbling shook the viaduct's supports and caused a slight vibration. Instantly the boy was reminded of an unfortunate cat.

Inside the carton was life itself, a dozen chicks. Also inside was his orange shoe box of baseball cards. He had visited Lewis's hatchery and traded young John one card for twelve chickens, his 1956 Mickey Mantle card that Big Ben Tegelman had given him. It was a good trade, for the card was a duplicate.

Little did he know that the chickens, all males, were scheduled for slaughter. John Lewis's dad had ordered his hired man to "drown them in a can. They're not worth the seed it takes to feed them."

"What will you feed them?" asked John. "I'll give you enough seed for a week. But it will cost you two more cards, Whitey Ford and Yogi Berra." The young visitor, turned entrepreneur, thought for a moment. Then he spit in the palm of his hand and extended it. His friend did the same, and the deal was consummated.

Careful to avoid Robbie Stein and his switchblade knife, he turned right immediately at the base of the viaduct and headed east for half a block.

"Whatcha got there?" He heard a siren's voice. He looked up and nearly dropped the carton. Looking down on him from her perch in a tree was Joyce Rader. Her crossed eyes had a twinkle in them. She dropped to the ground and reached for the carton. She lifted the cover. Squawking erupted from within.

"Can I have one?" she asked. Her hands reached in and extracted the biggest bird. She hugged it close to her bosom and stroked its head. Immediately the beak opened wide. Frankie recalled John Lewis's comment to Sister Mary Andrew's class: "They're always hungry."

"What will you feed it?" the boy inquired.

"Bugs and insects," she answered. "There's plenty of them around."

"Here, you'd better take some seed," he volunteered. "They're always hungry." He replaced the lid on the carton and shuffled off down the alley.

He passed Grandma O'Brian's and stepped across the marble pit, now filled in with sand. At the end of the block, he turned left. Tillie Kuchenmeister was standing on her porch, shaking rugs. Her husband, Harold, was sitting in a rocking chair, a bottle of beer within reach on the railing. His nose was buried in the evening edition of the St. Cloud Times.

Tillie spotted the boy and called out to him. "Tell that little squirt friend of yours that he owes me a new pair of leather shoes. I had to throw the other pair away. I couldn't wash the stink out of them." At that the newspaper just grunted.

He crossed 10th Avenue. The O'Brian yard was empty. They ate supper earlier than his family did. He crossed the alley. Parked across the street was his grandmother's car. By the time he entered the house, his excitement was building. So was his trepidation. He would have to be smart and convincing to keep his new pets. He set the carton on the counter next to the sink. It had holes in the sides to let in air.

"Oh, they smell," noted his sister, Jeanne, when the cardboard top was removed. The birds inside spread their tiny wings and fluttered up and down.

"We can't keep them," his mother stated flatly.

"I have birdseed for them," the boy countered, "enough for a week."

"Oh, listen to them squawk," observed his little sister, Mary.

"That's because they're hungry," the boy explained. His tone became pleading. "Can't we keep them, please?" he begged. "I'll take care of them. I'll keep them downstairs."

"Let's keep 'em," said Jeanne, jumping on the bandwagon.

"Yeah, let's keep 'em," added Mary. "They're so cute."

"Can I hold one?" Jeanne asked.

"Me too," stated Mary. Both girls reached for a plump young bird.

"No, we can't keep a dozen live chickens in the house" was their mother's retort. She tried to make it sound like an order.

"There are only eleven," the boy corrected.

It was his grandmother who was curiously silent. The boy didn't trust her completely, for she often kept her real motives hidden. He thought he saw her lick her chops. "Let's fatten 'em up!" said Grandma. And that swung the tide, at least for the time being.

"We'll ask your father" was all his mother would say. "Take them down to the basement, and for Pete's sake, keep the lid on tight."

Friday, the day of the square dance party, was soon at hand. The basement had undergone a transformation. It had been cleaned, and the carton of chicks had been relegated to the furnace room, where it was warm. Nestled next to the furnace, they liked the heat of that locale. They continued to gulp down birdseed by the handful, and they thrived. Frankie's main job was to clean the box, which was growing too small by the day.

Of course, the children had named them all: Humpty and Dumpty, Dr. Jeykll and Mr. Hyde, and the seven dwarfs. This had helped sway their father's vote. He and his wife, both, had grown up as farmers, and a love for animals was in their blood.

After looking through her wardrobe, Mom had settled on a Western theme. One room in the basement was suitable for entertaining. The boy's father had had the foresight to pour a cement floor that was green and polished, not too slippery, just right for dancing. The walls were painted cream with strips of red trim to create wainscoting. The door to this paradise was a matching red.

The boy's mother had been busy decorating for the party. The wash lines had been taken down. She had pinned a collection of snapshots to the wall, eight by ten pictures of Hank Williams Sr., Patsy Cline, Mel Tillis, Patti Page, and the singing cowboy himself, Gene Autry. These she had borrowed from their square dance clubroom in St. Cloud, home of the Swingers.

A new hi-fidelity record player sat atop the freezer with a pile of square dance albums, all 78s, stacked next to the player. She set up a card table in the corner by the piano for the hors'doeuvres: cheese and crackers, and ham sandwiches.

Her husband had been busy washing the floor and setting up the bar. By the morning of the dance, it was well stocked. Then he hung a twirling globe from the light fixture in the ceiling. Mom radiated her pleasure and hugged her husband. It would set the mood, be the perfect touch.

The children could not contain their excitement. They had been ordered into their pajamas early, and their faces and ears were washed long before the first guests arrived. A knock on the back door caught everyone by surprise, and the entire family froze for a moment. Then it leaped into action.

The Ferchos and the Banfields were the first to enter. Their costumes did not disappoint: the women wore swishing skirts with multiple layers of starched petticoats under them. Their blouses matched Mom's, pretty prints with musical notes and polka dots embroidered on them. The men were bedecked in tight-fitting jeans with calico vests and kerchiefs tied around their necks. They wore boots on their feet. To top off his costume, Ed Banfield displayed a large, ill-fitting cowboy hat.

The excitement grew with the arrival of the other couples. Everyone retired to the basement, mainly because that's where the refreshments were, and soon the dancing began. Their faces beamed as they listened to the patter of the caller.

Allemande left your partner and swing her do-si-do... Circle to the left... Circle to the right... The record player blared and the music thumped. Frankie and his sisters and brother squeezed down the steps, careful to remain unnoticed. The red door was open. The globe in the room's center rotated slowly, radiating its light in all directions, creating patterns of dots on the ceiling and walls. Through the doorway they saw their mother beam, twirled lightly back and forth in formation by her husband. The little girls giggled. She was having fun!

When the square dance ended, the dancers re-formed, and soon another number played. *Everyone face your corner... Everyone face your partner... Now take her by the hand... Promenade your partner... Now everybody swing*!

The circle of women skipped lightly: swinging right arm, left arm, right arm, left arm from man to man, finally interlocking arms with their original partner. The men stomped in time to the melody, their boot heels and soles clicking on the green cement.

The room was growing hot, and the young couples were perspiring. Beads of sweat streaked down Donny Trellwick's face, and he headed to the bar to cool off. He plopped himself down on a stool in the corner and ordered a gin and tonic from the male host, who was now mixing drinks.

The door to the ballroom stood open, and then the boy's mother caught four sets of eyes watching them. "Shoo, little flies! To bed you go," she commanded, and the children scampered up the basement steps. Lil Trellwick and Kathy Fercho laughed. It would have been no different at their house. The women drifted over to the cheese and crackers. The men had already consumed one platter of sandwiches. They were quenching their thirst at the bar.

All of the children obeyed, except for the oldest boy. He returned to the basement and stole into the furnace room. He uncovered the box of chicks, for it was very hot and he worried about them. They were growing. Nearly eight inches in height, they were not baby chicks but young roosters. John Lewis had told him that the hatchery preferred young hens, pullets, and that there was always a glut of young males. In their bartering he had whispered that these chicks would soon have their testicles removed, and this had helped seal the deal.

"You mean they cut off their balls?" asked Terry Joe when he had seen the brood. "But where are they?" he wondered, searching between one chicken's legs. "I don't see them." When the chicken squawked, he dropped it.

"Grandma calls them capons," Frankie lectured. When they're big enough for butchering, she'll ask Dad to do it. She's always hungry for chicken."

At this point, the dance music started up again. *All join hands and circle to the left... Now circle to the right...* He could hear the clatter as shoes and boots tapped in rhythm on the floor. The boy was about to replace the lid on the carton when he felt a sudden urge: he had to go to the bathroom—now! He scampered into the downstairs bathroom and locked the door.

Donny Trellwick sat perched on a stool with one arm on the bar. He clutched his glass in one hand and tapped his foot on the bar stool's bottom rung. He knew all the songs and was singing along as they played. Donny was a "good egg" because he was a good sport. He was likeable, and his friends ignored his speech impediment. He had particular trouble saying a hard "g." It always came out "d." "Div' me a gin and tonic, Cliff," he had requested. "But div' it to me in a dirty dlass," he had joked, imitating Bob Hope's comic line when he ordered milk instead of hard liquor in the 1952 Western comedy, *Son of Paleface.* Both men laughed, but for different reasons. The tall host, turned bartender, was amused by his friend's lyrical language.

Donny raised his glass to finish his drink, and through the bottom he saw an image that made him stutter. It was the head of a chicken that was not fully grown and was, perhaps, eight inches tall. The image was magnified in the thick glass surface. Its eyes bulged, and Donny rocked back on his chair. He let out a raucous roar. "Hey, Clifford, I didn't know we were having chicken and dravy," he bawled. Someone stopped the music. All eyes looked at Donny. Then they shifted to the top of the bar. There they saw a parade of little chicks, all eight inches high, investigating the top of the bar. Several had found the condiments: green olives and maraschino cherries. One had plopped down in the bowl of swizzle sticks, as if ready to take a long bath.

The boy emerged from the bathroom and peeked into the ballroom. It was curiously quiet. Then he saw a horrible sight, his brood of chicks up on the bar and everyone frozen. The birds must have fluttered up onto a chair and then onto the bar. But this was not the only horrible sight. It was the chagrin on his mother's face, the tears in her eyes streaming down her cheeks amid her whimpering.

Quietly he backed out of the room and closed the red door. He darted up the stairs and up a second set of stairs to his bedroom. There he pulled the covers over his head to hide. He was trembling. Downstairs, he could hear both the front and back doors slam shut. The party was breaking up early. He clutched the blanket and pulled it tight over his head. Then he heard a voice, that of his sister, Jeanne. "What happened?" she asked. But he did not answer.

In the morning the chickens were gone. There were only a few feathers in the bowl of swizzle sticks on the bar to commemorate the event. He wondered if his grandma would now have her wish.

CHAPTER ELEVEN

In summer baseball reigned. Most villagers spent Sunday afternoons at the ballpark. Every small town had an amateur men's team: St. Joseph, Cold Spring, St. Rosa, Paynesville, St. Martin. St. Anna always boasted a Mueller or a Meier who could whack the long ball out of the park regularly and frequently. The community followed the team, mostly spouses with young children at their feet and newborn babies on their laps. The grandstands were uncovered, sun-filled rows of wooden benches wide enough to accommodate the many baby strollers parked there on Sundays.

The local lineup was filled with Blommers and Thelens and Theisens and Christens and Schleichers and Litzingers and Kallas, names synonymous for generations with the village team. Sons followed fathers, and brothers followed brothers. The players were local boys. Their parents and siblings all watched them play, as did their friends with whom they would celebrate—or commiserate—over a pitcher of beer later on. These young men had grown up with a baseball in their hand. A leather glove and a wooden bat completed the list of equipment needed. Baseball was a source of pride, and winning equated with success and human dignity. It was what told you what kind of man you were.

Occasionally a team would bring in a ringer, a player from outside the town: a pitcher with a blazing fastball or a nasty curve, who could mow down the opposition's batters. Although not illegal, it smacked of unfairness and poor sportsmanship. It signaled that the other side wanted to win at all costs. Waite Park never brought in a ringer. When another team did, the locals took it as a challenge.

Alas, the Waite Park Parkers seemed to lose more than they won. In some years victories were few and far between. The effort was there, but the talent lay across the diamond in the opponent's dugout. Still, the fans in Waite Park would do what the popular song, "Take Me Out to the Ball Game,"urged them to do: *Root, Root, Root for the home team*.

Waite Park's "Big Town" ballpark was located on the southwest edge of the village, across Highway 52 and three blocks west of Frankie's house. It lay just north of the Crushers, a business that ground rock into small bits and piled it high. Several large mounds of pea rock of various sizes formed hills that rose above the third base skyline, too far away for foul balls to reach them.

Across Highway 52 to the north was the Little League diamond, the training ground for future prospects for the men's amateur team. Home runs to left field were seldom retrieved, for the quicksand pool lay just beyond the outfield fence.

Young Frankie was excited; this year he had joined a team. Local businesses and clubs sponsored the teams. Each year the sponsor bought the players uniforms, caps, and a few new baseballs and bats. They also paid the umpire fees. Five of the teams were old standbys: Plaza Park State Bank, the Moose Lodge, the American Legion, the Dairy Bar, and the Booster Club. The one new sponsor was Civil Defense. The sole financier of the Civil Defense team was the local police chief, Chester Gritt. He was also its manager. This ensured that his two sons, Joey and Ricky, would play every inning of every game.

It was to the Booster Club that Frankie was assigned. At practice he demonstrated his skill at catching ground balls and rifling his throw to first base. He could hit too, if the pitching wasn't blistering fast. Although he was the youngest player on the team, the manager, Larry Poindexter, named him the starting shortstop. The boy beamed with pride and vowed to himself not to let the team down.

On the evening of the first game, the ball field was packed with spectators. They lined the chain link fence, starting at the backstop and stretching down both the first and third base lines. They were a rowdy bunch, eager to hoot and holler at any spectacular plays, good or bad, but especially at miscues by the opposition. It was great fun to humiliate the boy who had erred, so they strove to do it. That was Waite Park's way.

The Booster Club was ready. The boys sat on the bench just outside the fence along the third base line. The young shortstop was more than nervous. He felt sick to his stomach. But not because of the game. Next to him sat his teammates, boys aged seven to twelve. He was still only six, and he had lied on the application. With the sun glaring in the western sky, he could feel its heat on his neck and back. But in his mind's eye, he kept seeing the application form that he had had his father sign. "*Are you between seven and twelve years old*?" it had asked. He had not filled in that blank until after his father had signed the document. He had lied. He would not turn seven until September 16th, after the season was over. He felt exposed and horrible.

He was sitting sullen on the bench, steeped in misery, when he heard the magic words, "Let's play ball!" The Booster Club, the home team, leaped from the bench and funneled through the narrow passageway in the fence. They surged onto the field, eight boys, tossing baseballs around. But no shortstop.

"Hey, where's your shortstop?" howled a voice from across the diamond. "You're not a chicken, are you? *Buc... buc... buc...*" clucked the voice. It was Howie Kappas. A few others chimed in: "*Buc... buc... buc...*" Then they let out an uproarious laugh. The season was under way—off to a fine start.

"Hey, Kucher, get out there!" Larry Poindexter barked. "What's wrong with you?"

The manager's voice brought the boy to his feet. He trotted sheepishly onto the diamond, keenly aware of many eyes staring at him. Terry Joe O'Brian at first base rolled a grounder to him. But he wasn't ready, and he booted it. More laughter from the first base line. He picked up the ball and snapped a throw back to Terry Joe. The crowd heard the smack in the glove and were stilled. His instincts were starting to take over. It was just baseball, just a game.

"That's a good throw, Frankie," called Terry Joe from across the diamond. "You show 'em." It was not the first time that his best friend's support had saved him. He would show them.

No one thought it odd that the umpire for this game was the visiting team's manager, Chester Gritt. Nor did anyone question his wearing sunglasses. They were accustomed to it. He wore them day and night. It helped a policeman if you couldn't see his eyes and read his thoughts.

Chet Gritt stood behind the pitcher's mound and fidgeted with the ball and strike clicker. He hated waiting. He checked his watch and then repeated his words, "Play ball!" He looked at his team on the first base side. He looked past them across the street. There stood his house, bathed in evening light. The sun's rays were glancing off the glass in his west windows. It would be hot inside, and his wife, Loretta, would be sitting at her knitting, fussing. Police chief or not, he could only ignore her complaining for so long. This summer he needed to put awnings on those west windows.

"Batter up!" he heard himself bray, and his son, Joey, helmeted and with batting gloves on, stepped up to the plate. Three pitches and three mighty swings later, Joey struck out. "Strike three!" bellowed the umpire, and Joey turned and retreated toward the bench to sit down.

"How can you call your own son out?" yelled a voice from behind the backstop. It was the batter's mother, Chester's wife. Unobserved, she had escaped the heat in the house. She was livid.

"But he swung and missed," explained Chet, his arms flailing at his sides. "I can't help him if he swings."

"Well, you don't have to be so nasty about it," she countered.

"Batter up!" he commanded.

But his team got the message. Joey's little brother, Ricky, dug himself into the batter's box. He bent his knees and scrunched down, way down, presenting as small a strike zone as possible. Four pitches later he had his walk. He trotted down to first base and jettisoned his batting helmet in favor of his cap with the Civil Defense logo sewn onto the front.

Before Ricky reached first base, Larry Poindexter was out to the pitcher's mound. His visit served two purposes. The first was a plea to his son, Paul, to "throw strikes." "Throw it right down the middle," he ordered.

His second reason for visiting was more subtle, to remind Chet Gritt that an umpire has an obligation to be neutral. "I know your sons have just batted, but now you have seven batters who are unrelated to you. "Let's see some impartiality, Chief." He turned and trudged back to the third base fence.

The next three batters walked and pushed home little Ricky for a run. The crowd along the first base line was elated; their counterparts along the third base line, somber. Their hopes were quickly being deflated, but Larry Poindexter seemed unperturbed, as if he had a managerial trick up his sleeve.

Two more runs scored and the bases were again loaded before Civil Defense was retired. In the bottom half of the inning, the Booster Club countered with two runs of its own to make the score respectable at 3 to 2.

When the second inning started, a new pitcher took the mound for the Booster Club, Abner Johnson, a gangly right-handed thrower who lived on a farm southeast of the village, just beyond the township. He kicked with his heel at the dirt in front of the pitching rubber while his manager implored him. "Throw the ball down the middle." That was all Larry Poindexter said by way of instruction. Then he ambled back to his station outside the third base fence by the backstop.

Once again, Chester Gritt's son, Joey, was the first batter. *Zip*... swing... miss. "Strike one" called his dad from behind the mound. *Zip*... swing... miss. "Strike two" called his dad. Joey pounded his bat onto home plate and cocked his arms to swing.

"Come on, Joey, don't swing!" urged his mother in the stands behind home plate. But her urging went unheeded. *Zip*... swing... miss. His father raised his right arm but said nothing. Joey threw his bat against the fence and his helmet over the fence into his mother's lap.

A wisp of a smile crossed Larry Poindexter's face. "Remember, Abner, fastballs—right down the middle—fastballs," he reminded his pitcher with a weighty glance at Chester Gritt. Two batters later, the side was retired in order.

The score stayed the same into the sixth inning. Both pitchers were dominating the game. The first two Booster Club hopefuls struck out. Terry Joe was up next. "Come on, Frankie," he grinned. "Let's show 'em. Let's be heroes!" His voice was full of the confidence that his best friend lacked.

Terry Joe strode into the batter's box and tapped the barrel of his bat on the plate. The baseball darted from the pitcher's hand into the catcher's mitt. "Strike one," bawled the umpire. Another pitch, a wicked curve. "Strike two," cried Chester Gritt with a similar cadence. The umpire was finding his rhythm. Frankie was on deck, awaiting a chance to bat. He closed his eyes and anticipated hearing the thud of the ball in the catcher's mitt. Instead, he heard the thwack of leather on wood. Miraculously, Terry Joe's bat had met the ball and slapped it in the face. Frankie opened his eyes and saw that the ball had caromed off the bat and was rolling into the hole between two infielders into left field. In baseball lingo, the ball had "seeing eyes" and evaded the two players. It rolled into left field, where it stopped in a clump of grass and lay still. Terry Joe now clung to first base. His teammates let out a raucous roar, and the Booster Club fans cheered like banshees. Their attention shifted to the next batter, the young shortstop in the on-deck circle. Several groaned in dismay.

It was the boy's turn to bat. His first time up, he had made an easy out. He had listened to the taunts from the opponent's fans. "Come on, chicken!" sang Howie Kappas. "Stand in there. Don't be afraid."

"*Buc ... buc ... buc ...*" warbled a chorus of hecklers. It made him mad and eager, and he swung recklessly and hard. The result had been a soft foul ball that rose straight up in the batter's box, a pop-up that the catcher, Joey Gritt, caught. The gleeful laughter of the Civil Defense fans turned to scorn and ridicule; his ears burned with shame. It made him all the more eager his second time at bat. "*Buc ... buc ... buc ...*" rang in his ears, and this distraction caused him to swing tentatively at the ball and tap it weakly to the pitcher. Another depressing out. The laughter from the crowd was a bitter pill to swallow.

Once again, "*Buc ... buc ... buc ...*" greeted him from the chorus of voices. This time, however, he ignored them and concentrated on his technique. He didn't wait. On the first pitch he connected—a liner into the gap in right centerfield that split the center fielder and the right fielder. The ball bounced twice and then slammed into the fence. The boy, fleet of foot, scampered around the bases. He was rounding second base and noticed Terry Joe, who was not as fast, just rounding third. That's when the right fielder, little Johnny Fisch, picked up the ball and launched a mighty heave toward home plate.

Larry Poindexter stood on his tiptoes and leaned over the fence, yelling, "Stop! Stop!" His arms were waving frantically.

Terry Joe, half way between third base and home plate, put on his brakes and skidded momentarily, trying to stop.

"Not you, Terry!" screamed the manager. "Him! Run, Terry!"

He shifted his focus. "Stop!" screamed Larry Poindexter, cupping his hands over his mouth and yelling at Frankie. But the runner rounded third base and kept running, full throttle.

Thrown by the strongest arm in Stearns County, the ball arched upward, reached its zenith, and then curved back to earth in a long, parabolic trajectory. It was on target, aimed directly at home plate. It was on a collision course with both the runner and the catcher. The play would be close, extremely close. Sensing desperation, the crowd held its collective breath.

Four feet from home plate the boy trying to score slid, leaning back, stretching his left big toe forward, curling his right leg under his left thigh. This sent a spray of dirt into the air and across the five-sided platter.

"*Smack*! The ball reached Joey Gritt's catcher's mitt belt high. The jaws of the mitt snapped at the ball to swallow it. The catcher dove to apply the tag.

"You're out!" screamed a voice from in the stands behind home plate. Joey's mother was standing on top of a seat in the metal bleachers.

"You're out!" echoed her husband who had moved in front of the pitcher's mound and taken off his sunglasses for a better look.

And then everyone saw what wife and husband had not seen. The baseball had squirmed out of the catcher's mitt and was squirting along the ground toward the backstop. Joey Gritt, upended by the slide, peered into his mitt. The ball was not there.

Larry Poindexter gasped. "He's safe! He's safe! There's the ball, Chief."

"He's out!" screamed the female voice from behind the plate. "He had it long enough."

"He didn't hold it," Larry Poindexter cried.

"He did," she yelled back, challenging his very manhood.

A silence erupted.

"I never had it, Mom," admitted the catcher. "He's safe." The umpire, his dad, never spoke a word. He just turned his back on them all and walked back to his post.

"The score is 4 to 3, isn't it, Chief?" declared Larry Poindexter. He was trying, delicately, to coax a confirmation from his counterpart. The umpire stared stoically through his sunglasses, refusing to confirm or deny the outcome of the play. "Batter up," he pronounced.

It was the top of the 7th inning. Three more outs, and the game would be over. Once again Abner Johnson took the mound and kicked with his heel at the dirt in front of the pitching rubber. He had performed this routine at the start of every inning.

Few noticed the lone figure that saddled up to the fence just beyond the third base bag. He looked strange in his overalls with suspenders and a red flannel shirt. He looked out of place in his thick work boots. Atop his head sat a weather-beaten cap advertising DeKalb seed corn. His face was dry and wrinkled, leathery after years in the sun. Obviously, he was a farmer and a simple man.

One person who did notice him was the boy who stood on the pitching mound. A brief glance gave way to a longer sidelong look and finally to a lengthy stare at the dirt between his shoes. He kicked harder and harder at the dirt, vehemently gouging it out, as if digging a trench all the way to China would satisfy him. But it wouldn't have.

His first pitch sailed high above the batter's head and clanked off an iron pipe supporting the backstop. His second pitch dove into the ground five feet in front of home plate and ricocheted off the catcher's glove into the fence to the left of the backstop.

"Throw it down the middle. Just throw it right down the middle," exhorted Manager Poindexter. The third pitch struck the batter squarely in the belt buckle as he tried to elude an inside fastball.

"Take your base," Chet Gritt ordered.

"Time!" called Larry Poindexter, and he goose-stepped toward the mound.

"I told you to 'throw it down the gall darn middle!' You couldn't hit the broad side of a barn!" Abner Johnson had resumed his kicking at the dirt with his heel. The hole in front of the pitching mound was growing considerably deeper. "What's wrong?" blurted the manager.

"Him!" The boy motioned with his glove.

Larry Poindexter searched the line of fans standing just beyond the third base fence. His eyes stopped and focused on the farmer in overalls. The man stood awkwardly, hands thrust deep into his pockets.

"That hayseed!" spat Abner.

"Who is he?" asked the manager. "Your Pa?" At this Abner stopped kicking the dirt and stood up straight. He faced the intruder, and their eyes met.

It was the father who spoke first. "Come with me."

"I ain't going," the boy replied. "Never!"

"At thirteen, you need to be helping me on the farm. This baseball is not for us. It's shit." With this pronouncement and to emphasize his words, he spat onto the ground. "Come with me," he reiterated.

This was a poignant moment. All eyes were staring at father and son locked in a monumental test of wills. All but a few sensed the enormity of the raging silence. It was of Biblical proportions. It was Abraham obeying God's command to sacrifice his son, Isaac. But here the son was resisting, not accepting death.

"He can't pitch. He can't play in this league!" Loretta Gritt's voice from behind the backstop was shrill and resounding. "He's thirteen. He's too old. You have to be twelve until July 1st."

This pronouncement rang in Frankie's ears. His knees almost buckled, and his stomach felt queasy. He stood stiff and tense, terrified by his own transgression.

"He lied on the application." The female voice continued to trill. "He cheated!"

"Aye, he's thirteen," asserted the father, oblivious to the seething look of the boy. "Born on the summer solstice, June 21st, 1945, nine months after I came home from the war.

"He ignored the few snickers from Howie Kappas and his friends; he gazed at his son.

"Can't he just finish this game?" Larry Poindexter whimpered. We're in the last inning."

Chet Gritt's mouth grinned. "Not if we score and tie it up. He's thirteen. He can't play. You'll have to bring in another pitcher. I'm going to speak to the other sponsors. You may have to forfeit this game." The final rays of the day's sunshine danced off his sunglasses. HE was the authority. HE knew the law. HE *was* the law.

With each passing word the boy at shortstop winced. Liar... cheater... forfeit the game... Each accusation against Abner Johnson stung him. It was doubly damning, and nobody but him and his best friend, Terry Joe, knew it.

"Come on, Abner," said Larry Poindexter. "You pitched a good game." He put his arm around the boy's shoulders and led him away from the mound.

"I'm not going home with him," Abner whispered under his breath. He had convinced himself of this before the inning started.

"But where will you go?" asked the manager.

"To Grandma's," he blurted. "At least she cares about me."

The manager looked across the fence near third base for Abner's dad. But the spot where he had stood was vacant. The man had disappeared.

"He's gone," whispered Abner.

When they crossed the third base line, Larry Poindexter turned and motioned to his younger son, Mark, at third base. "You're pitching." He called the left fielder in to play third base, switched the right fielder to left, and inserted his last position player, Punky Peet, into the game in right field. It was the best he could do. He would have to hope and pray that the ball was not hit to right field. If it was, they would lose.

Punky Peet was near-sighted, with thick Coke-bottle glasses. He could see nothing clearly beyond twelve feet away. At practice, on balls hit to right field, Terry Joe O'Brian at first base had to call out constantly to tell Punky where the ball was going. After Punky chased down the ball, Terry Joe had to keep talking, creating a homing signal for which Punky aimed his throw. It was everyone's job to field the throw. Terry Joe was actually quite good at this, and he felt a certain pride that he had this natural talent. This method of teamwork worked well enough in practice, but alas, it would never work in a tight, one-run game.

Umpire Chester Gritt sensed victory. He was in his comfort zone now. The batter's strike zone shrank in size, for all practical purposes into oblivion. The next two batters walked. The bases were loaded with nobody out.

Larry Poindexter was at wit's end. He chattered constantly. "Come on, Chief. Let's play it fair and square."

Chet Gritt merely laughed. "Don't pester me, Larry. He's thirteen. I'll bet you knew that." The crowd along the first base line listened carefully. They nodded knowingly. Victory was near at hand.

The ninth batter in the Civil Defense lineup was little Johnny Fisch. His throw from the fence in right field to home plate—on the fly—had been impressive. But it had been a moment too late to make him a hero. That dimwit, Joey Gritt, had dropped the stupid ball. Perhaps he could win the game with his bat.

The Civil Defense batters knew the routine by now. Don't swing. Their manager would call very few strikes, certainly not enough to strike anyone out.

Larry Poindexter felt defeated. It stung. After little Johnny Fisch, the top of the lineup would be up, Chet Gritt's two sons, Joey and Ricky. His fate was sealed.

"Throw the ball over the middle of the plate, Mark. Make him hit it."

"Ball one," pronounced the umpire. Mark Poindexter turned and stared into Chester Gritt's sunglasses.

"That pitch was right down the middle, Chief," stated Larry Poindexter softly.

"Ball two!" the umpire blared.

"That one was on the outside corner, Chief, above the knees, below the letters. You know, in the strike zone." He sounded depressed.

"Don't insult me," countered Chet, "or I'll have you ejected and fined."

"Come on, Chief," play fair," was Larry Poindexter's only comment. He said it more to himself than to the umpire.

But the fans along the third base line picked up the idea. "Play fair!" they chanted in unison. "Play fair!"

Larry Poindexter had one final request of his son. He begged. "Float one in there, Mark. Let him hit it."

It was at the next pitch that little Johnny Fisch swung. He did not want to merely walk to first base. Sure, that would force in the tying run, but someone else, that stupid dimwit, Joey Gritt, would drive in the winning run. He, not Johnny, would be the hero. And that was not acceptable.

During that second that the ball floated toward home plate, it looked to Johnny to be the size of a beach ball. He cocked his arms and swung with all his might. The power of his swing drove the baseball with a solid smack over the pitcher's head toward center field.

At the crack of the bat, both middle infielders for the Booster Club, the second baseman and the shortstop, reacted. Both took a series of rapid, hurried steps toward the point of the diamond marked by second base and lunged, parallel to the ground, glove outstretched.

The Civil Defense runners on the three bases were startled by the sharp report of the bat. They had not anticipated this unexpected development. Instinctively they leapt into motion and ran for the security of the next base. Like dominoes in procession, each felt pushed along by the runner behind him.

The ball just missed the second baseman's glove. He plowed, nose first, into the infield grass, lost his cap, and after a barrel roll, stopped on his hands and knees in horror; his glove was empty. The baseball surged on.

The shortstop, Frankie, was the last line of defense. The ball was spinning, making it tail slightly left, his way. It stayed aloft just long enough. The boy, fully horizontal and three feet off of the ground, felt the impact of the ball against the webbing of his glove. Somehow the ball stuck, half of it showing, visible, like half a scoop of vanilla ice cream protruding above the top of a cone.

In making the catch, he tumbled in a summersault over the second base bag. But he squeezed the fingers in his glove tightly and held on to the ball for dear life. His momentum propelled him to his feet.

He observed the action on the base paths. The two lead runners were charging forward toward the next base. Only the runner on first recognized that the baseball had been caught for out number one. He was reversing course to tag up, stumbling toward the first base bag.

The young shortstop had but a split second to react. He covered the distance to second base in three quick steps, planting his left foot on the base a moment before releasing the ball toward first base. That was out number two. The ball, thrown full force, burned into Terry Joe's mitt. The runner was out by an eyelash—a triple play!

The game was over. Terry Joe raced toward his friend near second base and swallowed him in a bear hug. "You showed 'em, Frankie. You're a hero!"

But the young hero felt none of the jubilation that surrounded him. "I have to quit," he murmured.

"Why?" questioned his friend.

"I lied on the application. I'm no better than Abner Johnson," he cried.

It was the manager himself, Larry Poindexter, who hugged the boy to his chest. "You did it. You won the game. A triple play!" That's all he could say before the boy's teammates hoisted him onto their shoulders and paraded to the third base fence, where the Booster Club's fans were cheering and cheering.

Across the diamond, little Johnny Fisch was surrounded by his teammates. He was the goat. "Why did you swing?" questioned Joey Gritt. "Dad would have walked you. We lost because of you. That was a stupid play, a dumb ass play," he concluded. Joey Gritt would not let it go.

"You're a dimwit," countered Johnny. You always want to be the hero."

Joey growled but said nothing because the younger boy had hit the nail on the head. Finally he spoke. He knew his words would hurt. "You'll never be a hero, never."

"Well, kill me then," cried Johnny, tears rolling down his cheeks.

"I will," boasted Joey. "I definitely will."

Chester Gritt placed a hand on his son's shoulder. "We haven't lost this game yet, boys. We'll see about it in the morning."

CHAPTER TWELVE

It became official at 10:00 o'clock the next morning. Civil Defense had won last evening's game by forfeit, 2 – 0.

During the night following the game, Frankie could not sleep. He tossed and turned in the bed, overcome with guilt. By the time he fell asleep, streaks of morning light were showing in the east. He pulled the covers over his head and slept late into the morning, missing breakfast.

He awoke to the sound of men's voices in the back yard. He peeked through the blinds, and what he saw froze him. There stood a man in sunglasses with a silver badge pinned to his shirt and a pistol in a holster at his hip. Chester Gritt was speaking to his father and pointing at the truck parked in the driveway in front of the garage.

His father was nodding, forcing a weak smile. The boy pulled the covers back over his head and did not reappear until noon. When he did go downstairs, he bolted out the back door before his mother could finish her sentence. He darted across the alley into O'Brians' yard.

"I quit," he rasped.

Terry Joe was holding a branch from an ash tree. He was busy with a sharp serrated knife, sharpening the stick to a point. "It's a spear," said Terry Joe. "I want to hunt squirrels and rabbits. Dad won't let me have a gun—not yet—not even a BB gun. So, I'm making this spear."

"Did you hear me?" repeated the boy. "I'm quitting."

"I heard you," said Terry Joe. "But why? You know, we lost the game last night. Because of Abner."

"I'm too young. I lied on the application," the boy cried. "Chester Gritt was over this morning, speaking to Dad."

"He was?" asked Terry Joe.

"I saw them talking out by the garage. You're the one who told me to sign up," challenged Frankie.

"So what?" replied his friend, defending himself.

"I shouldn't have listened to you," he shot back.

"I faked it on the form, too. I was born on July 1st. That's one day too late. I was born at 12:01 at night. Timmy told me to do it. He said I was half out and half in at midnight. 'That's close enough.'"

"Which half?" asked Frankie, suddenly curious about such matters. For the moment he forgot that he was angry.

"The right half, I suppose. I'm right-handed. I'd pull myself out with my right hand."

"Ah, that's a bunch of crap," asserted Frankie. "It's either head first or feet first. Dad's friend, Leo, told us kids. A mother mink poops 'em out."

Then he remembered his anger. "Why did you tell me to lie?" His voice was harsh and challenging.

Terry Joe shrugged and picked up his spear. He did not, however, have time to turn and protect himself from Frankie's blow. A hard right fist crashed into his left eye.

In return, Frankie felt a frantic blow on his own chin. His bottom lip began to bleed, and he tasted blood. He kept at his adversary and tackled him.

They grabbed at one another for advantage, yet neither gained the upper hand for they were evenly matched. Tears flowed. The boys pummeled one another, straining to rise to their feet.

It felt good to fight. Frankie felt no fear, only release. He swung his arms repeatedly, fists pounding his friend's midsection.

To counter the intensity of his foe's blows, Terry Joe grabbed Frankie in a headlock and held on with both arms. His tears were flowing freely; somehow the savagery of his friend's attack had struck a nerve.

And then Frankie heard the impossible. He could not see behind the screened kitchen window, but he heard a woman's voice, an Irish voice, cajoling him. "Come on, Frankie, get him. Get him. Get him." It was Lorraine O'Brian, Terry's mother.

In that moment the boy felt utterly ashamed. He knew that Terry Joe had heard it, too. He saw his friend's tears and felt his own. He broke free and leaped back. Terry Joe rolled over and grabbed his spear. He pointed it menacingly at the other boy.

The fight was over. But Frankie felt fright at Terry Joe's pain. He was perplexed and sad for his adversary and best friend. They had had one other fight, in Pattersons' yard the previous summer. They would not fight each other again. There were enough other battles in Waite Park to fight.

The kitchen window behind the green screen slammed shut. Deeply disturbed, he turned and fled back across the alley, more aware than he had ever been of why Terry Joe was the way he was.

Chester Gritt returned just after supper that night. Still in sunglasses, the police chief was an imposing sight. He stood outside under a maple tree until the boy's father joined him, and then they went into the garage.

They came out together. The boy tried to stay out of sight, but his sisters and brother were curious. It was not every day that the police chief visited their home. He was drawn outside, too, and advanced within earshot.

Chief Gritt was explaining. "We put the powder on the pamphlets this morning. Before supper I found a few boys and asked to see their hands. Their hands were white. "Mine are clean," said Jim Blommer, holding out his hands. "But you should see Butch Carter's. They're all purple, up to the elbows. He's worried that it's a disease and he's going to die."

"It is a disease," replied the chief. "It's called theft. He isn't going to die, but he's going to wish he were dead." The police chief knew how to scare the village toughs. It helped keep them in line.

"I spoke with Butch's parents. He won't be interested in your investment literature any more. But you'd better keep your shotgun shells in the house, not in your pickup, at least until hunting season." The boy's dad nodded.

As Chet Gritt spoke, his sunglasses spotted Frankie at the edge of the crowd of onlookers. He asked, "What happened to your lip?"

"Nothin' much," the boy answered.

"He got in a fight," his sister, Jeanne, confided.

"With Terry Joe O'Brian," added his little sister, Mary.

"Don't squeal!" their older brother exploded. But then he clamped his lips shut.

"Fighting's no good," the chief responded. "That was a good catch last night, a good play. But we won the game anyway."

"I'm quitting" was the boy's cryptic reply.

"He's thirteen-years-old, for Pete' sake!" argued the man. "A rule's a rule. A law's a law. Your teachers should be teaching you that."

"He's only going into Second Grade," said his father.

"It's never too early to learn that," Chief Gritt shot back.

The boy clamped his jaws together and squinted his eyes. Rays of light from the man's sunglasses showered him. They entranced him.

"I have to go," said the police chief, and the spell was broken.

"Thanks for your help," the boy heard his father say.

"It's all in a day's work" came the acknowledgment. "That's why I'm here."

"I quit," Frankie told Terry Joe the next morning. They were back on speaking terms. His lower lip was swollen.

"You'll have to play tee ball," his friend warned. Terry Joe's left eye was puffy and black.

"I told Larry Poindexter last night. Dad took me over to his house."

"Did you tell him you lied?" inquired Terry Joe.

"Yep, Dad made me tell. He says that now I have a sin to confess when I make my First Confession this year."

"What did Larry Poindexter say?" prodded Terry Joe.

"To sign up next year." The speaker breathed a deep sigh of relief. "Now I feel good. I'm sorry about punching you yesterday. My bottom lip is all swollen, and I bit my tongue."

A brief silence ensued. "Did you tell him about me?" Terry Joe pursued.

The younger boy shook his head sideways. "Naw, he'll find out soon enough—how you were half born."

"Mom says I shouldn't fight you any more." Terry Joe let out a heavy sigh.

Just then Timmy O'Brian approached the pair. "Come on, twerp, let's fight." He assumed a boxer's pose. The younger boy could not tell how serious he was. "You leave Terry Joe alone, or I'll beat the livin' crap out of you." He faked a punch and let go a swift kick. It rose upward and landed with a thump in his enemy's thigh, just missing the groin.

"That's the new way of fighting, twerp. I'll stomp on you." And Frankie shrank back, rubbing his leg. The other boy was older and spoke brashly, and that made a difference.

"Ah, get lost, Timmy." It was his friend, Terry Joe, his best friend, coming to his rescue once again. "If you fight him, you'll have to fight us both." Immediately he raised his spear into position and assumed a fighting stance.

Timmy gazed at the sharpened point. It looked nasty. The older brother thought better of it and backed out of his fighting posture. "Go to hell," he challenged to maintain his dignity. "Wait till I tell Dad. He'll take that away from you and burn it. Then watch out for me!"

But the two younger boys knew it was mostly bluster. Terry Joe maintained his stance and then faked a thrust with his weapon. The feigned blow made Timmy flinch, and that was enough. He was piping mad—boiling—spoiling for a fight. But not two against one. "I'll kick the piss out of you! I'll stomp on your heads!" he bellowed. The thought made him grin. Then he left.

But before he spun around to go, Frankie thought he heard a voice, a lilting Irish voice from behind the green screen in the kitchen window: "Get him, Terry Joe. Get him. Get him."

Terry Joe raised his spear above his head and flung it into the neighbor's yard. It struck the Krauses' elm tree and rattled to the ground. A squirrel, clinging to the tree's bark, bounded to safety high among the branches where it chattered in protest.

Bang! *Bang*! *Bang*! The boy heard the shotgun shell reports coming from his garage. His imagination was aflutter. He peeked around the corner. There he saw his father and his dad's boyhood pal, Leo, hammering together wooden boxes. His father said they were mink boxes for the breeding stock he would buy the coming week. The boy's fantasy faded. The two men had been pounding away for weeks. His father was on a mission, a man possessed.

Hitting a baseball off a tee was easy; the ball didn't move. Relieved of a guilty conscience, the boy felt relaxed and happy. His teammates were younger boys, many of whom had older brothers on Little League teams.

The games were played in the afternoon just after lunch. Most of the spectators were women, the boys' mothers, for the Dads were still at work. The young lad enjoyed hitting the ball and scampering around the bases. Rarely could they tag him out.

Several hot, muggy June weeks passed. One morning the boy was at the Little League diamond, practicing for the next day's game. He was standing in the on-deck circle, awaiting his turn to bat. He was surprised to see his father's truck stop in the road, and the boy waved. The driver's window was down, and an arm was dangling from the cab. The arm motioned him over. "Get in the truck," his father stated. He seemed to be in a hurry.

"But it's my turn to bat next," the boy protested.

"Go get your glove and get in the truck," his father reiterated. Puzzled, the boy complied. The man waved to Val Krause, the team's manager, and shifted the truck into gear.

They turned left onto Highway 52 and drove east, past Tegelman's Grocery and the Swan Café. The truck accelerated up the viaduct, past Lewis's Hatchery toward St. Cloud. The father steered the pickup with one arm; the other rested in the open window.

Their route took them through the city's south side and then across the 10th Street bridge, a thin two-lane crossing near the state college. Beneath them stretched the mighty expanse of the Mississippi River, still flowing full with the spring rains. The water, fresh and sparkling, swirled rapidly beneath them. In August the river would shrink in the summer's drought, exposing large rocks that now lay beneath the surface.

His father guided the truck out of town and headed south, parallel to the river. He drove at a constant speed for ten miles. He did not speak for he was deep in thought, calculating costs and return.

At last, the truck veered off the county road toward the river. This driveway was a gravel road bordered by a windrow of pine and deciduous trees on the left and a corn field on the right. Rows of ankle high young plants stood rooted in the soil. With enough rain, they would be knee high by the Fourth of July. Midway, the road curved in a letter "S." It cut through the grove, shifting the windrow of trees to the right and exposing another field to the left. But this one was empty of corn.

In it stood five wooden sheds with tin roofs, newly constructed, with a large rectangular fence surrounding them. Inside the fence was room for many more sheds. At his father's insistence, the land had been bulldozed before construction, shaped from north to south into long mounds separated by shallow gullies so that rainwater would drain down between the sheds. To build the first sheds, he had enlisted the services of a friend from his youth, Ted Fercho. A carpenter, Ted had provided a blueprint. But the boy's father would build the rest of the sheds himself. He believed that if you built it yourself, it would be better. It would certainly be cheaper. It was a mink ranch in its infancy. The man's eyes sparkled as he surveyed the scene, and his son sensed the father's pride.

They parked outside of a concrete building, also newly constructed. This contained the feed room with a twenty-ton walk-in freezer attached and a work room with a trap door leading to upstairs storage. Soon, another car, trailing a cloud of dust, barreled down the driveway and parked next to them. It belonged to Leo Fercho, Ted's younger brother. Sitting next to the driver was a boy who was Frankie's age. Obviously, both fathers believed in putting their sons to work. Earning a paycheck was one of life's good lessons.

"This is Billy," said Leo, jumping out of his car. He nudged his son forward. "Hi, Billy," said the other boy's father. "This is my son, Frankie. If you're here to work, there's plenty to do."

"Hey, Billy," said Frankie.

"Hey, Frankie," the other youth replied. It was the start of an instant friendship born of common labor.

"It's hot," stated their boss. "The mink need water." There was a strain of urgency in his voice.

"How much do I make?" asked Billy.

The boss's son opened his mouth to answer. "Seventy..."

But his father cut him off curtly. "Fifty cents an hour," he replied. He glared at his son, who stood biting his lip.

"But Dad," protested the other boy. "You said..."

It was Leo's turn to interrupt. "If you work hard, you'll get a raise. Right, Cliff?"

The boss stopped and looked at the boy. "That's right," he agreed, "if you work hard."

He stared after them as they went into the mink yard to turn on the water faucet. The mink rancher shook his head in disgust. "Just like his dad," he muttered to himself, "selfish and impolite."

The two boys spent the next hour dragging a garden hose around the three breeding sheds, filling over three hundred metal cups. The mink, all black, were in wire pens facing the outside. Each pen was divided from its neighbor on either side. A wooden box, lined with straw, hung on the side of each pen. In these the mink could curl up at night to sleep. They were also where the females had delivered their young.

Born in April and May, the young mink kits lived with their mothers for six weeks. The older ones were now being weaned. That was Leo's job. He was moving adult females into the two furring sheds.

Three weeks ago one mother mink had died, leaving behind a single kit too young to survive on its own. In desperation, the boy's father had transferred the baby mink to another mother, tagged Number 246. The man had listened to the baby mink, which was virtually blind, crying for its mother.

The mother inside Box 246, with four young kits of her own, had heard the whimpering. The man watched in hope.

The female stuck her nose outside the box into the pen and sniffed. The moment of decision was at hand. She might feel that her litter was threatened and kill the intruder on sight. Her teeth were razor sharp. Instead, she grasped the infant by the scruff of the neck and dragged it into the box. Acceptance. A human instinct. The man smiled.

The next morning he hurried down the third shed to the far end to check on the kit. He opened the cover of Box 246 and looked inside. What he saw was unforeseen and unwanted. A lone kit was nursing at one of the mother's nipples. Four little black carcasses lay dead in the doorway—all slaughtered. In the night the mother must have become confused and felt threatened. This climax illustrated the harshness of nature. The man felt downcast. His attempt to alter nature's way had failed.

The mink were nervous animals when they were thirsty. Their black fur absorbed the sun's heat, making them uncomfortable. Most lined the front edge of the pen, traversing it back and forth, back and forth in figure eights, anticipating the filling of their cups. As the cups were filled, they refreshed themselves by dunking their heads in the water.

"Mink on the loose!" the boys heard Leo cry. He had been catching the young females to move them into the furring sheds. One had slipped his grasp. He was wearing a pair of elk hide gloves to protect his hands. "Grab a pair of choppers and get the net," he yelled.

There was no fear of escape, just the excitement of the chase. Both boys slipped on a pair of thick gray gloves, and Frankie grabbed the fishing net that was stored at the end of the third shed. The mink scampered down the shed's aisle, the boys in hot pursuit. Keenly aware that its freedom was in jeopardy, the mink dashed out of the shed and raced for the fence. Instinctively it knew that its freedom lay beyond the boundary. It leapt onto the heavy chicken wire and climbed upward. But the metal guard at the top of the fence angled back into the yard, and the mink could not crawl upside down and over it. It was trapped. Billy's hand grabbed for its tail, but the mink leaped out and landed on the ground.

The net, however, closed over it, and it was caught. Leo had watched; he had let the boys have their fun and run off some energy. He grabbed the mink by the tail and untangled it from the net. Suddenly the mink curled up and latched onto the man's wrist. Its teeth were sharp. Excited from the chase, its adrenaline flowed, and it clamped its mouth tight.

"*Yeowwww!*" Leo let out a yowl and dropped the animal. Again the net swooped down over it and pinned it. This time Leo clamped a hand around the mink's neck. Its jaws opened and it hissed at him. It also sprayed a fine mist from its bottom outward into the man's face. This was the final straw. The human raised his free hand to cuff the culprit but stopped before he struck when he spied his friend and employer watching him.

The boy's father approached quickly. "Give her to me," he stated. His voice was calm and soothing. The rancher grasped the mink by the tail and let it play with the thumb of the other glove. The mink settled down to chew on the glove. Its fur shone blue black in the sunlight. "Isn't she a beauty?" the man exclaimed. "Look at the under-fur," he tutored. "It's so smooth." He appraised the animal. "She's a *three check* for sure." He loved everything wild.

"That s.o.b. bit me," Leo bawled. His wrist was bleeding profusely.

"Just put her in the pen, Leo," his friend ordered.

The mink saw Leo and hissed again.

Angrily, Leo turned and stomped into the third shed. He could see the other man watching him until he deposited the mink into its cage. "I'll have the last laugh on you," he stated flatly. He looked to see that the boss was no longer in sight. Then he took out a grease pen and reached up to the ledge where that mink's identification card was stapled. *Two check*, he scribbled on the card. "That will seal your fate. You'll be dead this fall."

"Scrape these wires," the boy's dad dictated. "Here's how you do it." He held a wire brush in both hands and drew it back and forth over the wire at the top of the cage. It was where the mink were fed, and dried feed from past feedings clung to the wire. He brushed five or six pens until the wire shined. Then he handed his son the brush. The boy looked down the long row of pens and frowned. But the boss had spoken.

It took two more hours to scrape the old feed from the wires. "Come with me," stated the boy's dad. He pointed to three piles of wire bottoms, each bottom the size of a pen's floor. They were crusted with piles of mink droppings compressed onto the quarter inch squares. Now that the young mink had grown sufficiently, the false bottoms were no longer needed.

Again, the boss took the brush and demonstrated how to clean the wire. It was a mammoth task that would take days, even weeks, to finish. Billy's sour expression brought his father over. "They need to have a little fun too, Cliff, not just work. Let them go down to the river and explore for a while. They'll work better after that."

"We didn't play when we were young, not when there was work to be done," the boy's father argued.

"Those false bottoms can wait," Leo countered. "They'll be here tomorrow and the next day."

The boy's father thought about his friend's advice. There was some wisdom in it. *All work and no play makes Jack a dull boy.* The children's adage ran through his mind. He did want his son to enjoy the ranch, not grow to hate it. He nodded his consent. "Take a break, boys. You might want to go down by the river," he suggested. He smiled. "Stay away from the poison ivy."

Both boys brightened. "Did you bring in my fishing pole?" Billy asked his father.

"It's in the car. Two of them."

Down the thirty-foot high river bank they crawled, toting fishing poles, sliding feet first to keep their balance. Billy carried a tackle box; and Frankie, an open can of corn for bait. Their spirits soared as they descended.

The path was barely visible, a jungle overgrown with vegetation. Frankie knew that the bulk of it was tri-leafed, poison ivy. But their downward momentum made them powerless to avoid it. Near the bottom the final ten feet dropped away over a sandy ridge. The boys sat down and slid feet first to the river basin.

A new and primordial world opened up to them. It was unfamiliar, primeval, luxuriant. The sound of rushing water greeted their ears. Having receded slightly after the spring flood, the water swirled around and over rocks, some below the surface, others with their tops exposed to wind and sky.

To the north, upstream, the river basin formed a canyon. Its lush shores were lined with rotted trees whose trunks stood twisted at the river's edge. The base and roots of many were submerged. Their limbs hung over the river: arms, hands, and fingers extending toward any boatman or canoeist drifting down the river's channel in a dreamy reverie. They stretched forth in this dreary forlorn chasm, like souls in purgatory beckoning for respite. The shadows along the watery edge under this canopy of trees were mesmerizing, the substance of Romance.

Logs, half-submerged and their pores clogged with water, protruded into the river, clinging to the shoreline by their roots. Many were a hundred years old and had toppled at last in a wind storm.

Across the river a lone tree stood dead, its trunk bleached white. Atop it sat a bald eagle, a solitary figure surveying the watery scene below.

Down river, closer to the mink ranch, the river canyon opened up, and the land across the way sprawled out. The shoreline beneath their feet was in that stage of erosion where many small stones had accumulated. Strewn among them, the boys found clam shells that had been deposited by the spring flow of water over the past decade. Most were broken open, exposing an empty, meatless cavity. The twin-sided shells had been vandalized by birds and animals, hungry creatures higher up the food chain.

The boys explored the beach. They found rocks, weathered smooth, baking in the summer sun. Some were flat. They skipped them across the water's surface. *Plunk. Plunk. Plunk. Plunk.* Four bounces.

At the water's edge shallow pools had formed and were collecting algae and debris. In this muck swam carp, mouths open at the surface, sucking intently, inhaling bugs and insects trapped in the muck. The carp were scavengers, bottom feeders, and they bobbed casually up and down.

The boys set about to fish. With several kernels of corn strung on a hook, Frankie dangled the bait in front of a carp's snout. It could not resist. The corn was pungent and sweet. The water swirled as the fish swallowed the juicy kernels. The boy set the hook.

Whizzzz! The line flew out. The carp was burly and strong. Annoyed by the resistance, it tugged fiercely against the line threaded into the eyes of the pole—great sport for the young fisherman. The youth pulled the fish onto the rocks, where he dislodged the hook from its mouth. The fish stared impassively back at him. Quickly the lad strung the hook with more corn and dangled it in front of another open mouth. *Whizzzz*! "I've got another one on my line," cried the youngster. "Can you eat carp?"

"Wind it in," yelled his new friend. "Dad will smoke 'em." They caught several more fish, those that were in the shallows near the shore.

"Let's see who can cast the farthest," challenged Billy. And he flung his line outward into the deeper part of the river.

Frankie followed suit. The current took hold of their lines, and the baited hooks drifted downstream, finally stopping a short distance out from the shoreline.

The fishing slowed, and the boys became bored. They piled up rocks around the handles of the rods to secure them so that, when left unattended, the poles could not be dragged into the river. The tips of the rods pointed skyward. If a fish struck, one of the boys would race to that rod and reel the fish in.

"Let's play baseball," suggested Billy. He had found a stick in the willows.

Frankie pitched a stone. It clunked off the stick and clattered to the carpet of rocks on the ground. Another pitch. Another *clunk… clatter clatter*.

Suddenly they heard a massive WHOOSH… WHOOSH… WHOOSH, the flaps of the eagle's wings. It had lifted off of the dead tree upriver and was surging down the canyon toward them, low, over the water's surface.

"Look," pointed Billy. Downstream were two hawks flying at treetop height, coming within range.

The eagle plunged ahead, directly at them to defend its territory.

The hawks heard the eagle's wings pounding, flapping powerfully across an expanse of seven feet. The lone bird's talons hung beneath its body. The intruders veered upward and soared high toward the clouds until they were safely out of range. The pounding stopped. The eagle returned to its perch and glared at the scene around it. Order had been restored.

The boys resumed their game of baseball. *Clunk... clatter clatter. Clunk... splash. Clunk... clatter clatter.* On the next hit, they heard a strange sound ring out. *Clunk... thud.* It stopped their play.

"What was that?" Billy asked. They walked over to the weeds to inspect.

Then the boys saw something huge rise up out of the earth. It was a heavy, corrugated shell, gray and dusty, rounded like the helmet of a soldier. The dome elevated on four legs, and a head protruded at the end of an elongated neck. It was a giant snapping turtle, aroused from its slumber by the batted stone. It did not like being disturbed. Its eyes were heavy-lidded and blinked sparingly, once they locked on the intruders. The ancient reptile's mouth opened and closed in snarls, intimidating threats intended to drive the enemy away. The hissing would have driven Frankie off, but not Billy.

"Grab a hold of its tail," Billy ordered. He held the end of the stick up to the behemoth's mouth. *Crunch.* The reptile clamped down on the stick. At this, the boy began to push.

But the other boy was wary and reluctant, fearful of unknown dangers. Eventually though, he did grab hold of the tail, and the boy holding the stick continued to push. The front end of the stick was disappearing into the entrails inside the shell. The turtle continued to bite the stick and hiss.

The work was laboriously slow. Billy grinned as he toiled, sweat dampening the underarm pits of his shirt. And then, finally, the front end of the stick reappeared, and the great beast was reduced to a piece of meat on a spit. It was skewered. The point of the stick was red and sticky from the impaling.

Each boy grabbed an end of the stick, and they carried their prize to the base of the hill. Up and up they clambered, dragging the carcass through the weeds, gouging the path. The turtle's enormous shell dug up the sandy loam as if it were a spade.

At last, nearly exhausted, they reached the top, and their emotion burst from them. They yelled like savages. "Ayeeee! Ayeeee! Ayeeeyah!" Their whoops were tribal outbursts.

Leo heard their call and hurried over to the river bank. He beamed at the sight. "Carry it into the feed room," he said. "I'll butcher it. Go get the carp," he ordered. "I'll smoke them tonight. And don't forget the fishing rods."

For the next hour he carved up the giant turtle into steaks and chops, like he had done as a boy. He whistled softly to himself, intent on his work. He looked at the bite on his wrist; it had swelled to fight infection. "Even better to do it on company time," he said to himself. He did not hesitate to include the hour on his time sheet before he left.

To end the work day, Leo's son helped the boss's son water the mink one more time. "Fifty cents an hour," Leo grumbled and shook his head in disgust.

June's days were the longest of the year. Frankie and his father rode home in garish sunlight. The sky's fiery disk loomed large and blared brightly through the driver's window, midway between its zenith and the western skyline.

"Do I still get seventy-five cents an hour?" the boy asked his dad innocently.

"Yes," his father nodded.

"How come I get more?" the boy inquired.

"You're family," answered his father. "This is a family business. I'll be expecting more work out of you" was his father's reasoned reply. "Someday you might even have your own mink."

The boy considered the possibility. He had found his father's bossy behavior uncomfortable. He recalled the man's genuine happiness at the female mink's beauty and his near despair at the death of the four young kits.

The boy squinted out the window into the light. This triggered his imagination. My father, the mink... he thought. He fed the notion briefly and pictured his father as a mink of human scale with human features. But it was not a comfortable thought, and he quickly suppressed it.

Back home in Waite Park, they heard the news from the boy's mother. Sylvester Sawyer, two doors to the south, had bought his daughter, Cheryl, a new car. She, having just turned sixteen, was now the proud owner of a red two-door convertible, a Chevrolet Corvette.

"He's out of his mind!" the boy's mother exclaimed. "He must be tetched, going senile, to buy her that."

"Syl loves his daughter," her husband countered. "She's his baby, and he has the money. What's wrong with that?"

"He inherited the money," his wife corrected, "from Trudy. He never made that much money on his own. He shouldn't squander it."

"It's still his money," the husband argued. "He can do with it what he wants."

"She barely has her license" came the instant retort. "When I was her age, my father loaned us his car for a few hours on Sunday. He didn't buy me a car. This will spoil Cherie."

"And your father didn't spoil you?" The man's words hung in the air. "You drove from farm to farm and picked up all your girlfriends. Each one had a bottle of beer stashed in her purse, her taxicab fare. You cruised Main Street, sipping on them until they were empty. No wonder Sinclair Lewis criticized the locals in his books."

"Who told you we did that?" the woman challenged.

"Henry Latimer... at our square dance."

"How would he know? He wasn't there."

"How do you think he'd know? From Val."

There was a brief, troubled silence, broken by the boy's mother. "She never did know how to keep quiet. It's in the past." She raised her eyes in alarm. "Clifford, I don't want you to tell our kids. It's hard enough to raise children nowadays."

He took her hands in his, leaned forward, and brushed her lips with a soft kiss. "Theresa Promenshenkel, your secret's safe with me."

The boy stood in his mother's garden among her flowers like a statue. He tried to remain as still as possible, holding his breath. If he could hold his breath and count to sixty, that would be a minute. He was practicing. He wanted to be able to hold his breath under water for a full minute, like a turtle or a frog. Then he could dive deep and approach other swimmers undetected and scare them. As he counted, he kept his eyes focused on the action on the other side of the street.

Across the street Cherie Sawyer's new red sports car was parked a few feet from the door of the garage, next to Nelson Birch's Catalina. In the passenger seat sat her best friend, Laura Birch.

"Isn't it lovely?" spoke Cherie, rubbing her hand along the white leather seat cushion. "Dad promised me he'd buy me any car I wanted when I turned sixteen, and he did. He kept his promise. I wanted this Corvette."

Laura scowled. "My dad never promises me anything. He's too cheap. Does the radio work?" She reached for the dials.

"Sure, it works. We'll take it for a joy ride in a minute—up to the gas station to show it off."

Instinctively Laura reached for her compact to touch up her makeup. The compact and her lipstick were in her purse on the floor beside her feet. As she reached for it, she glanced in the side mirror. There she spied the blond-headed boy in the flower garden across the street. He was entirely motionless as if stuck or planted there. And he was looking their way, at *her*. "You bastard," she cursed. "There's that little creep, that kid I baby-sat. He was nothing but a royal pain in the ass. I was so mad. They paid me extra the next day for all the trouble. I had Mom call them."

"They did? They paid you extra?" Cherie questioned. She knew that her friend, Laura, had a way of getting what she wanted.

"Let's go, Cherie," Laura urged.

The driver reached to shift the car into reverse.

Just then a car pulled up behind them, honking its horn. It was also a red convertible, a Chevy Impala, driven by Bertie Norton. He liked red cars. He nudged the front bumper of the Impala forward until it bumped the Corvette's rear end. "Checkmate!" he called out, laughing. His face behind dark-rimmed glasses was pockmarked and full of pimples. His hair was fire engine red, as were his ears.

"Move it, fatso," squealed Cherie. "You butthead!"

"Yeah, you creep, get lost," squeaked Laura.

But their hostile outbursts only encouraged him to resist. They didn't understand him; nobody did. He only wanted to play. He would have his fun. He would scare them, even if he had to bully them.

Bertie revved his engine, and a stream of white smoke billowed upward out of dual exhaust pipes. He eased the car into gear and bumped the smaller car again, pushing it until its front bumper touched the garage door. He laughed wickedly at his own joke and at the panic in the girls' faces. This time their screams were real.

His fun was interrupted when the front door of the house opened. Out stepped Neil Birch, Laura's brother.

The first things Bertie noticed were the muscles rippling in Neil's shirt. His chest was broad and his abdomen, chiseled. His arms were massive and powerful. He leaped to the ground from the top step.

Bertie tried to throw the Impala into reverse. Neil balled his hand into a fist and slammed it down onto the hood. "You have a dent in the hood, right here," Neil exclaimed, and when he removed his fist, there was, indeed, a dent in the hood.

The driver winced at the damage and then cried out in anguish.

"Back your car out of the driveway and beat it," the older boy admonished. Bertie whimpered and complied. Safely in the street, his bravado returned. "You'll hear about this from my dad and his lawyer," he warned.

"You were trespassing on our property," Neil replied.

"You're an asshole," Bertie called out as he shifted the Impala into first gear. "You're all assholes!" Then he raised his left hand above his head, palm turned inward, and stuck his middle finger up. The Impala, rumbling as the back tires spun and squealed, sped off.

"I'm late for my date," Neil Birch called to his sister. "Nice car, Cherie. Enjoy your ride." "He jumped into the Catalina and started the engine. His sister waved her thanks to him. Then he backed out of the driveway and accelerated toward the highway.

Laura spoke. "Let's go, Cherie. The boys are waiting at the gas station."

Her friend put the car into reverse. She was still upset by their encounter with Bertie Norton. She stepped on the gas, and the car responded, barreling out into the avenue. Wally Theen, sitting on the handle bars of his bicycle and riding backward, barely had time to evade the rushing automobile. Fortunately, he was a skilled rider. Deftly he shifted his balance and steered the bicycle to his left. His trusty Schwinn swerved just beyond the Corvette's left rear fender.

Catching sight of him, the driver slammed on her brakes. The young man on the bicycle continued to pedal, arms folded, with the same ease that he always displayed, and he tipped the bill of his cap to the girls and smiled as he continued on his way.

Cherie Sawyer waved back. "Isn't he a doll?" she sighed dreamily. He was such a contrast to that jerk, Bertie Norton.

"You almost ran him over," scolded Laura. Her hands were shaking like two leaves in the wind. "You could have killed him. Can we go?" she pleaded, and they drove hastily away.

Hiding in the bushes in front of the house, three little girls huddled together. They had watched the drama unfold and were now alone, to themselves. Jackie Birch, Laura's sister, pulled out a cigarette and showed it to the other girls, Janet Krueger and the girl from across the street, Jeanne Kucher. "It's my mom's," explained Jackie. "I stole it from her dresser." Somehow the act of theft made it seem more daring, more exciting. "My brother will clobber that big fat kid," she bragged.

"That fatso," stated Jeanne. She was intrigued by the terminology she had heard.

"That creep," added Jackie. "My sister calls your brother a creep. She won't baby-sit him any more."

"I know," said Jeanne. "Look at him over there. He's always pretending something."

"Let's light the cigarette," suggested Janet. When she struck a match, the boy across the street noticed the brief flare. But he was not the only witness. A shutter in the house bordering the Birches' house to the north flicked shut. A good neighbor needed to inform parents when their children were being naughty, and Marie Burkett was a good neighbor. She took the receiver off the phone and dialed seven numbers, the first of three calls.

At supper that night, the oldest boy broke a boyhood code: he tattled on his sister. "She was smoking in the bushes," he reported. Somehow, cigarettes were taboo in their household. Frankie did not know that his father had quit smoking the day his first child was born.

All eyes turned to his sister, Jeanne. "You're a creep," she blurted.

"Fatso," he retaliated. This stung her, and she responded by holding up her left hand in a fist, palm inward, with the middle finger extended.

Her mother gasped. She was the first to reach her daughter. She lifted the girl out of her chair with one hand and swatted her on the buttocks with the other. The blow was swift, and it stung. "Who taught you to do that? Jackie Birch? Janet Krueger?" She applied a second swat. "You're getting too big for your britches, young lady." She dragged the small girl toward the bathroom. "I'm going to wash your mouth out with soap. You'll have to apologize to your brother for calling him a creep."

"He called me a fatso," she yelled.

"Then I'll wash his mouth out with soap, too!" her mother vowed.

She was sent to bed immediately for her crime, where she cried bitter tears into her pillow. She was still awake when her brother tiptoed into her room. "Get out!" she commanded, but he just stood there, watching her. He squinted at the light and then turned off the switch. But he stayed in the room, protected by its darkness.

"Creep," she whispered.

"Fatso," he blurted.

"Butthead. Asshole." Hers were the final words, and if he could have seen her left hand in the darkness, he would have seen it stretched toward him, upraised in a small fist, palm inward, with the middle finger extended up.

CHAPTER THIRTEEN

The Fourth of July had long been a day of celebration throughout the land. It was particularly festive in the village of Waite Park, where people were pleased with their lives. The men had jobs that supported their families, and that was enough. The women had the support of the men in raising their families, and that, too, was enough. The children themselves had little say in what was said, but that little say was enough.

It was a day-long event, filled with tradition and pageantry, and the residents of the village anticipated it and prepared for it months ahead of time. Patriotism was the predominant theme. The people displayed a love of country. Many men had served during World War I or World War II in the United States armed forces. Their wives, some with children, had waited patiently at home for their return. Girlfriends with rings on their fingers had waited impatiently to start their new life.

The soldiers did return, most of them, and reunited with their loved ones. They had performed their duty as expected, with honor. Some had been called upon to show ardent valor. A few were heroes. Others like Frankie's father had supported those at the front lines by building ships or by repairing planes and keeping them airborne. Collectively, they had all fought bravely for their country to keep it independent and to keep its citizens free. Each year they took one day to commemorate the glory of the country and the sacrifices that had been made over generations to preserve it.

Sales of red, white, and blue streamers were brisk at Walt Unger's bicycle repair shop. Children of all ages would plug them into the handles of their bicycles as they rode in the annual parade. In a bin on the counter stood a supply of small flags with red and white stripes and white stars in a blue field. The latest flag had fifty stars to acknowledge the addition of the two newest states, Alaska and Hawaii. It was the symbol of the nation and a source of pride to the men who visited Walt's shop. Boys at heart, they liked to see his collection of photographs and miniature trains and, of course, Walt's life-sized model of himself, the engineer. It made the men dream.

The store contained other novelties such as cards to clip onto a bicycle fender's supporting frame with a clothespin. These "noisemakers" would draw attention as they flapped against the wheel's spokes. The shelves in the front counter contained many rolls of crepe paper to be threaded between the spokes of bicycles and doll buggies and to decorate the floats, which were the focal points of the parade. A host of businesses promoted themselves every year: Tegelman's Grocery, the Swan Café, Rocky's Shoe Shop, Luedtke's Cleaners, Elmer's Skelly, and Lornie's Liquors. Waite Park's service clubs: the American Legion, the VFW, and the Moose Lodge were also proud sponsors of floats.

Out of sight behind the front counter, Walt had on hand an assortment of fireworks, which he sold to a narrow range of customers. Bottle rockets sold well, as did firecrackers. These were popular with the teenage boys, who liked to set off whole strings of firecrackers at one time. The men warned their sons to "be careful," but their admonishments had little effect. The boys liked to light matches. They liked the ear-splitting reports, like gunshots. The longer and louder the firecrackers popped, the better. Loud "ka-booms" were heard frequently in every neighborhood.

The younger children were startled by the terrifying noises created by their older brothers and sisters. Dogs hid under porch steps. Babies in strollers cried. Because of this the youngsters preferred visual effects, sparklers that sizzled and chemical worms that, when burned, oozed silently onto the sidewalk.

The day's events started at 8:00 o'clock sharp with the annual soap box derby. To the men of Waite Park, this was a source of pride and a challenge. They were skilled craftsman. Almost all of them had a shop in their garage, where they tinkered. They were more than happy to build their sons a soap box for the derby. If asked, most agreed to construct one for their daughters, too. The trick was to design the most streamlined car, one that would travel down the slope the fastest.

The venue for the derby was the hill on 4th Street that descended due west from 10th Avenue to 13th Avenue, three blocks away. Just beyond the finish line was the community park, where the community picnic and games would be held that afternoon.

A ramp was constructed at the top of the hill to facilitate the start. Two cars would race at a time. It was fair because the boards preventing the cars from moving prematurely were released at the same moment. Then gravity took over, aided by design. At each intersection the street leveled off, and then the slope resumed. It was not a steep pitch, and not every car maintained enough speed to finish the course. The winners did.

The originator of the derby was Elmer Johnson, owner of Elmer's Skelly. He had built the first two soap boxes for his children. He was the honorary chairman and official starter. And he was a kind man. If a child showed up and wanted to race but had no soap box, he volunteered one of his own. They were not the fastest race cars, but the spectators nodded their appreciation. It gave the event a good feeling.

The soap boxes came in every size and shape imaginable. Almost always the winners were the Beckers. Roland Becker had worked as a tinsmith at the Great Northern Railway's car shops for over fifteen years. He was a wise builder, who understood the importance of aerodynamics. He constructed his sons' cars carefully, testing them for acceleration and wind resistance. Roland was always interested in improving the car's design. One year he welded together a chassis with a steering column, whereby the driver turned a steering wheel instead of pulling ropes attached to the front end, like on a sled. The next year he experimented with the conical shape of the car's front end, enclosing the nose of the car to create a slip screen that reduced the wind's drag. Tucked down into the cockpit, one of his sons would inevitably gain a slight advantage in speed, resulting in a precious few feet of separation, enough to win the competition for Roland. He was seldom denied victory.

Chief of Police Chester Gritt was troubled. He was not a mechanic by trade, so he did not possess the technical skills to shape metal with his hands. Men like Roland Becker did. For three years running, Chet had watched young Billy Becker's soap box car surge ahead in the final heat to win the derby. Chet's son, Joey, had finished second each time. This year would be different. The chief was privy to information that he should not have had. It would make his son a winner, so he would use it.

By chance, Chester Gritt had discovered Roland Becker's newest secret. In March he had visited Walt Unger's shop to investigate a report of a stolen bicycle. There on the counter he spied a cardboard box with an unusual postmark—Akron, Ohio.

The chief was curious. "What's in the box, Walt?" he pried.

"Wheels," Walt replied.

"For the derby?" Chet pressed. Walt was noticeably silent.

And then Chester saw a name scrawled on the box above Walter Unger's address—Roland Becker. It made his heart skip a beat.

"Let's see 'em," Chet ordered. Walter started to open the box but then checked himself. He sighed.

"I shouldn't show you," he whimpered. He stared into the chief's sunglasses.

"Open the box, Walt," the police chief repeated.

Inside the shipment were four wheels, but not of typical vintage and design. They were vastly different from the prototype eight-inch, hard rubber wheels with metal centers. These were inflatable tubeless tires on twelve-inch rims with spokes radiating from a hub.

"They're made in Akron, Ohio, the rubber capital of the world," Walt ventured, "at the Firestone plant."

"I see that," Chester Gritt acknowledged. Instantly his decision jelled. "Order me a set of these, four wheels," he stated. "And Walt, let's keep this our secret."

Chet Gritt grinned when he was excited, and he was grinning from ear to ear when he left the bike shop. He had intercepted his adversary's course of action, broken Roland Becker's enigma code, as it were. He had neutralized the builder's advantage and leveled the playing field. But he wanted to do more. He wanted to tilt the playing field in his favor. There must be something else. He looked for an edge.

The new wheels arrived three weeks later in April. Chester Gritt tested them on Joey's car. They rolled smoothly and with less friction than the standard wheels. That was the key. These wheels had bearings. Less friction equated with more rapid acceleration and more speed.

Chet found the answer in a magazine his wife, Loretta, had casually left open on the coffee table. It explained a new medical procedure she had had performed—breast implantation. She had wanted it badly. She had pouted and begged, said it would make her a new woman. Finally he had caved in. He gave it to her as a Christmas present. Chet read the article in its entirety. The latest development was a new synthetic material in the implants themselves, silicone. Two words stared up at him from the page, *friction free*. It set his mind to working.

That night Chet Gritt rolled over in bed. He put his hand under the covers and groped in the darkness until his fingers made contact. Loretta's eyes blinked awake. Sensing her husband's proximity, she grunted in disgust. "Not now, Chet. I have a headache."

"Lie still," he stated. "I want to check something." He felt around and patted her. He didn't feel much friction.

"What are you doing?" she asked. "We haven't done this in ages. Why now? Mother warned me; she told me this would happen."

Her husband continued to massage and squeeze.

Then unexpectedly her breathing quickened. "Oh, Chester!" She squirmed under his arm and emitted a soft moan.

Deep in thought, Chet ignored her and rolled onto his back. Suddenly he switched on his night lamp. The light was bright, so he put on his sunglasses. He picked up the magazine from his bedside table and searched for an address. Near the bottom he found it, a Dow Corning plant out in Midland, Michigan.

In the morning he ordered a tube of silicone lubricant to be shipped by express mail to an address in Waite Park, Minnesota. The order was on police department stationery, marked "Miscellaneous," and the bill was to be sent to the village clerk. The chief was sure there was enough in petty cash to cover it.

The soap box derby was an exciting affair. Frankie, himself, did not compete because he didn't have a soap box car. His father had been too busy building mink boxes to divert his time and energy for something so frivolous. And the boy was too shy to ask Elmer Johnson to loan him one. But he loved to watch the action.

His eyes shone fire when his best friend, Terry Joe, sat helmeted in a car at the top of the starting platform. "Come on, Terry Joe, you can do it!" he urged.

When the lever holding the cars in place was released, the boy raised his voice in a loud cheer. But after an even start, his friend's car fell behind and settled into a steady gait. The driver tried willing the car to move faster, but it was reluctant to do so, at first.

Then the little soap box car hit a bump and leaped into the air. It dove forward and began to sprint. Terry Joe tried to control the car, steering with two ropes tied to a connecting rod. But he was unfamiliar with the extra speed created by the bump. His car accelerated down the pavement and veered right almost across the road, and then it weaved back to the left. As he sped by, Terry Joe was screaming. Many spectators misinterpreted his determination as fear. They were seriously alarmed.

At the bottom of the first block, on the northeast corner of the intersection of 4th Street and 11th Avenue lived three elderly spinsters, the Hecht sisters. Their neighbors had nicknamed them the Bronte sisters. Newcomers assumed, naturally, that the name referred to the three 19th Century Victorian writers, Charlotte, Emily, and Anne. They nodded their approval, an impressive testament to Waite Park's literary acumen. The locals, however, knew a different truth: that Bronte stemmed from *brontosaurus*, so labeled because of the sisters' prehistoric attitudes and slow wits.

The three women airily disregarded this truth. They actually liked the notoriety and took to calling each other Charlotte, Emily and Anne. The names seemed so dignified, so aristocratic. They were much more polished and Classical—less frumpy—than Gertrude, Nora, and Irene. The neighbors joked about them, throwing up their hands: "Oh, what the Hecht!" or "Go to Hecht!" One neighbor across the street, Howard Kappas, was more blunt: he referred to them simply as Hecht's hags, the sisters of fate nobody wanted to live by. According to Howard, all they did was bring property values down.

Only Charlotte, alias Gertie, had ever come close to marriage. She had liked a boy once. But the brief romance had dried up, and that was as far as it had gone. Now the sisters sat on the front porch and made up for lost time, spinning lovelorn yarns of reveries imagined. Thus, they entertained themselves on a daily basis; there was nothing better than a captive audience.

The three sisters had one brother, Henry. He functioned as their servant: butler, chauffeur, and household repairman. Henry did manage to marry, and the sisters graciously accepted Henry's wife as their brother's assistant: cook, maid, and lady-in-waiting. She left after one year and disappeared, complaining to her husband that continual gossip was hard to take, especially when she was the subject. "A year is long enough," she proclaimed one evening, and the next morning she was gone. Six months later, rumors circulated that someone from Waite Park, Phil Schultz they suspected, had seen the woman in Las Vegas on the arm of a high stakes roller. She was gambling away his poker chips, having fun.

Today, as was customary on sun-swept Fourth of July mornings, the three women had ventured beyond their porch. They desired a closer look at the race. They were sitting on high-backed dining room chairs on the boulevard. Henry had been kind enough to set the chairs out and serve tea.

"Here they come...," observed Gertrude, "...finally. Look at that crazy one! He's swerving all over the road." She pointed up the hill.

Her two sisters leaned forward and searched the concrete roadway above them. "He's heading for us," gasped Nora with a feeling of dread. "He's going to crash into us!" She tried to lift herself out of her chair to escape the collision; but her movements were slow, and she could not stand up abruptly.

Irene could not watch. Involuntarily, she buried her eyes in her hands. Nora, anticipating a horrible crash, covered her ears. Gertrude's reaction was to squelch her scream. She clapped her hands over her mouth. Witnesses would say later in amusement that they were the mythical three monkeys who could see no evil, hear no evil, and speak no evil. But to the Hecht sisters, evil was lurking; Terry Joe seemed doomed.

Totally out of control, the race car tilted onto two wheels and then flopped back onto four. Men, many of whom hadn't run in years, and boys who ran everywhere chased after it and along side it, trying to stop its momentum. They were converging on the run-away vehicle. It was Tiny Rausch, Paul Rausch's eldest son, Junior, who took the final hit. His four hundred pounds was the immovable object; the small soap box car, the irresistible force. Tiny took the blow square on, just below the belt. *UUUFFFF!* The car took his legs out from under him. Terry Joe ducked, his head disappearing into the cockpit as Tiny's shadow flew over him. But the collision turned the soap box sideways, and it skidded with a jolt into the curb. The immovable object had prevailed. The crowd was relieved. Tiny smiled wanly and waved. He had a busted leg, but Terry Joe was unhurt.

Roland Becker was troubled. The final heat of the derby was at hand. Two cars stood poised on the starting ramp. And they looked identical. Both had steering wheels that aided precision. Both had conical noses to limit drag due to wind resistance. But most surprising—and disturbing—was that both had inflatable tubeless tires on twelve-inch rims with spokes radiating from a hub. It was too coincidental. The chief must have found out, somehow. He didn't play fair. He wanted his son to win, almost as much as Roland did. Something was rotten in Denmark. It smelled to high Heaven.

The crowd of onlookers shifted their gaze from one car to the other and back again. They were intrigued. The cars seemed to be spitting images of one another, evenly matched. They were curious who would gain the upper hand. Perhaps it would come down to the drivers. Both boys were experienced. It was impossible to predict who would win.

Roland Becker gazed at his rival across the street. The chief was standing still, calm and confident—too calm, too confident. Roland wondered what Chet Gritt had up his sleeve. Had he known that it was an ace, he would not have liked it.

When the starting lever was pulled, the plank holding the cars motionless was released. Both cars began to roll. They were in unison as they reached the bottom of the plank. The inflated tires spun. Instantly the crowd knew that these were by far the two fastest cars in the race. Ten feet down the road, the cars passed Roland Becker's position. The man frowned. His car had not gained one inch. In fact, it had lost an inch, a precious inch. And Roland knew that distance would magnify inches into feet and feet into yards. He cursed himself. "I should never have had my wheels sent to Walt Unger's shop." In despair he watched the race unfold.

The gap widened. When the cars passed the Hecht residence, young Billy Becker was three feet behind. Something was wrong; he couldn't match Joey Gritt's speed.

But the three sisters did not see it. They were safely back inside their house. They were once again the Bronte sisters, sitting on their dining room chairs, having a luxurious brunch. Henry was waiting table.

Chester Gritt peered down the slope through his sunglasses. The silicone was working: less friction equaled faster acceleration and greater speed. He laughed openly. The bearings of each wheel were packed with dabs of synthetic lubricant used in his wife's breast implants. She wouldn't like it if people knew. "Good for Joey," he thought. "Good for my son."

Joey Gritt's car crossed the finish line first and kept going. At 13th Avenue it turned right and glided another block, all the way to the Moose Lodge parking lot. Anticipating victory, Chester had insisted on patriotic colors: red, white and blue. He had defeated Roland Becker's orange and green Great Northern Empire Builder. Chet had used his ingenuity to advantage, and ingenuity was the fountainhead of enterprise. That was the American way, and Chester Gritt was proud to be an American.

A parade is a way for a mother to play dress up. She enters her children in the parade as characters from books or movies or television, from historical fiction or fairytales or cartoons. It is her way of living the story vicariously.

The boy's mother had been busy sewing for weeks on end. "Costumes," the boy observed, "cleaned and pressed and hung up on hangers for the big day." Throughout the village it was the same—mothers measuring, cutting, and stitching fabric. In every household the children had been scrubbed. They would be on public display, and no dirty faces or sticky fingers would be allowed.

The children were excited because the mother was excited. She had let them use their imaginations and choose their depictions. Little Dan, bow and arrow in hand, was Robin Hood, ready to haunt the woods of Sherwood Forest to steal from the rich and give to the poor. Little Mary, after the application of grease paint, was a happy-faced Bozo the Clown. Their big sister, Jeanne, posed as a Victorian mother. She had seen a Norman Rockwell illustration in *The Saturday Evening Post* of a woman in a long skirt with a pillow tucked just above her rump. Wearing a wig on her head under a hat and high-heeled shoes on her feet, the young girl pushed a doll buggy. For a week she had practiced around the house, using her baby brother, Chuck, as a live doll. But on the morning of the Fourth of July, she was overruled. It was decided that she had to use one of her dolls instead. Her older brother was dressed in a white sailor's outfit: crew pants, a t-shirt, and a round deck hat. Sporting a corn cob pipe and a can of spinach, he was Popeye the Sailor Man.

"If Dan gets tired, put him in the doll buggy" were their father's parting words.

The parade route was a long walk through the center of the village. It began at the pump house located at the east edge of town, as close to the Oakdale Addition as one could get without being in it. Once it was set in motion, the line paraded west in a continual procession to McKinley Elementary School, where it turned left for one block and then right onto 5th Street. It again proceeded west in a straight line all the way to 13th Avenue, the last block down a steep hill. Every year several entrants paused to gaze down the slope, thought better of it, and quit. But the majority ventured on.

"Everybody likes a parade; nobody likes a quitter," quipped Howard Kappas. Over the years it had become Waite Park's unofficial motto when they reached the final hill. It's where people gathered, just to see who was made of what. Occasionally they were rewarded when someone in the parade did falter and collapse, exhausted and dehydrated after the long walk.

Safely at the bottom, those still "on parade" took one final right turn and gathered steam for the final two blocks. They paraded alongside the community park to the Moose Lodge, where many had parked their cars, and disbanded, a happy lot. Those who were hungry walked back to the community shelter, where dinner could be purchased for three dollars and a beverage for two bits.

If the floats were the focal points of the parade, then the marching bands were the drawing cards. High school bands from Monticello, Princeton, and Royalton were annual entrants. Attired from head to toe in full dress uniforms with tall hats held on by chin straps, the youth from these towns braved the summer heat. They were disciplined, drilled to act as a single organism, and that impressed the people of Waite Park. The village had no high school and therefore no marching band. The teenaged boys and girls went to high school in St. Cloud, to Tech or Cathedral, whose bands disbanded in the summer. Those progressive schools in the big city had given up trying. Anyway, it was the subject of much debate whether or not Waite Park's children would have had the inclination—or the discipline—

to march in unison on a hot summer day down a hot roadway, dressed in wool suits, playing their musical instruments.

The drum majorette drew everyone's attention. She was dressed in a one-piece sleeveless outfit, much like a swimsuit with a tiny skirt that flowed about her hips. It was covered in sequins. Accenting the gown, she wore a stylish jacket that was open in front, trimmed in her school's colors. It highlighted her position as the leader of the band. Her long legs were exposed, and she wore white, Western-style leather boots that came up high just below her knees. Her long legs were pumping her knees high like pistons.

In her hand she carried a baton, thrusting it up and down in a constant tempo. The beat of the song was stirring. The ensemble passed the judges' viewing stand. As if on cue, she twirled her baton and suddenly flung it high into the air. With practiced ease and in one motion, she pirouetted and snatched the baton out of the air behind her back. The spectators clapped their approval, and she smiled.

Behind her, four girls, high-stepping with precision, carried their hometown school flag. The majorette did an about face but continued to march, backward. A whistle dangled from her lips; and when she blew into it, a shrill command sounded forth. The band members stopped moving forward, but they continued to march in place. They played their song with a robust energy. The notes wafted through the air as clarinets and flutes piped and trilled, and as horns blared: trumpets, trombones, and tubas angled skyward. All were in syncopation, timed by the percussionists' beating drums. The climax of the song was punctuated by the clanging of cymbals, and then the song ended with a flourish. In unison the marching feet stopped, and the band members froze in a silent salute. The stillness was swift and penetrating and moving.

Those along the parade route applauded politely. When the applause stopped, the drum majorette blew her whistle again, and the feet of seventy-five musicians started pulsating up and down, in unison, and then upon the command of another whistle resumed their march down the road. The drum majorette shuffle-stepped forward and then kicked a white boot high into the air. She pranced in time to the band's next song, her baton pounding out the beat.

Spaced between the marching bands were the floats. Susie Tegelman, smacking her gum and blowing bubbles, rode on top of her father's float, a huge grocery cart advertising ground beef, extremely lean, at 28 cents a pound. The cart was filled with oversized replicas of produce and exotic fruits: mostly pineapples, peaches, and bananas, which could not be grown locally because of Minnesota's early frost and frigid winter. Her brother, Butch, the driver inside the cart, was worried. He was trying to stay far ahead of Rocky. He wished he could see behind the float, but that was impossible.

Rocky's Shoe Shop sponsored a float that was a reenactment of the children's story, "The Old Woman Who Lived in a Shoe." The float was decorated with red, white, and blue shoe strings and laden with children. Tillie Kuchenmeister, herself, was waving from the top of the shoe as it passed by. True, the float had survived years of Fourth of July parades. But now the shoe was badly in need of repair. Only last year Rocky had started driving the float himself. But he hadn't known that the driver was restricted to looking through an eyehole of the shoe. It created a narrow tunnel of vision that Rocky had never experienced before. Deprived of his peripheral vision, he had crashed into the handle of Butch Tegelman's grocery cart and put a serious dent in the shoe. The toe was caved in, as if the shoe had kicked a huge can in disgust and smashed its toe.

Howie Kappas laughed aloud and joked to Tillie, who waved. "Why doesn't Rocky fix that shoe *before* he puts it in the parade?" His laughter turned raucous. "Hey, Rocky, are you inside there? Did you stub your toe?"

Inside the float, Rocky heard the laughter and gritted his teeth.

The boy and his three siblings were assigned to follow Rocky. They traipsed along, enamored with the stares of so many people. Every street was lined with spectators. Little Dan, overwhelmed by the throng, clung to his sisters.

At McKinley school, the parade turned left abruptly. When Dan saw the school, he knew where he was and he knew the way home. He broke into a trot and did not turn. He proceeded straight ahead, following the course he knew.

"Come back, Dan! It's this way!" shouted his sister, Jeanne. People turned to look.

"Dan, oh Dan," whimpered Mary. She began to cry.

But the young boy was on a mission. He did not turn back and kept on running. His sisters and brother, under strict orders to "keep an eye on him," had no recourse but to follow him. By the time they reached 10th Avenue, they had caught him. The troupe turned left and slowed their pace. They walked a long block. Up ahead they saw the parade, oozing its way from left to right. The four children reached the intersection and stopped.

"Aren't you supposed to be in the parade?" yelled Terry Joe O'Brian from across the street. The O'Brians were planted in lawn chairs on their boulevard.

The three youngest children looked at their older brother. He weighed the option. But there wasn't an immediate opening in the line-up. Besides, they had been instructed to follow Rocky's shoe. "We'll wait for Rocky," the boy decided. So the four of them stood on the curb and watched the parade.

The next float was approaching. Sitting on a wicker throne atop the float was Laura Birch, the village's Great Northern Empire Builder's Queen for 1958. She was dressed in a regal gown with long white gloves on her hands and a diamond-studded tiara on her head, tucked into her beehive hairdo. Her complexion was cream-colored, and she was wearing red lipstick. Frankie's pulse quickened, and he held his breath.

Laura was smiling, waving to both sides of the street. Her mother and dad would be at the next corner, watching for her with her sisters, Sandie and Jackie. At this moment she was proud, and it showed in her bearing.

Suddenly she saw the boy dressed in a sailor's suit looking at her, and it unnerved her. Her waving hand faltered. "You little creep," she shrieked. "Stop staring at me!" Only a few onlookers heard her before she caught hold of herself. But hearing her voice directed at him made the boy tingle.

The four children were tired and sat down on the curb. That's just when everyone else stood up. So, they stood back up. People around them began to cheer and clap. Along 5th Street was coming the entire Ryngsmuth clan—three generations—all on unicycles! Back and forth they pedaled, keeping their balance. Those who were more adept spun around in circles, waving to the crowd of onlookers. Frankie saw his schoolmate, John Ryngsmuth, streak by, followed by John's mother, who glided effortlessly in the saddle.

"Go June!" bystanders encouraged. She was obviously enjoying the day. Graciously she circled around in the street, putting on a show for her well-wishers. It kept her from getting too far ahead of her husband. Many of the women in the crowd felt her vibrancy. They admired her poise and charm. And after having six children, one only a month ago! Five of the six were on unicycles, even young Peter, a toddler who was riding on his older brother Paul's shoulders. Only the new baby was absent.

"Here comes Grandma!" shouted a voice from the crowd, and Johanna, the Ryngsmuth matriarch, came riding down the street on a unicycle, flanked by two of her granddaughters. She balanced herself comfortably and waved to those who cheered her on. She did not look to be sixty-years-old.

Then the hoots and hollers commenced. The mayor, Al Ryngsmuth, was approaching, bringing up the rear of the pack.

"Come on, Al, you can do it."

"Hey, Mayor, you're falling behind."

But he was concentrating, mouth clenched in a determined grin. Back and forth, right, left, twist, turn, he fought to keep his balance. Slowly but surely he made his way west, a few feet at a time.

That afternoon the mayor's family was the subject of much discussion over lunch at the community park. "Al will never lose an election with June on his arm," asserted Val Krause to Lorraine O'Brian over a plateful of baked chicken and potato salad.

"They can't eat until they learn to ride" was Howard Kappas's assessment. He was enjoying his meal, especially the heaping mound of chicken legs that he was working through. He liked the drumsticks best.

The parade was nearing its end. Frankie and his siblings sat back down. They watched the approach of a red fire truck in the distance, Waite Park's finest, driven by the fire chief, Guilford Bartholomay. His son, Boomer, was manning the pump, dousing any unsuspecting urchins with a sudden spray of water. The witnesses laughed. It was great sport, something for which the Waite Park parade was famous.

Up ahead one block, the children's mother was fretting. Her camera had been in her hands for an hour, at the ready. She was peering back up the street. "Have you seen them?" she asked her husband for the umpteenth time. "They were supposed to be after Rocky's float. But Rocky has already gone by." Her voice was grim and lines of worry were creasing her forehead. "Where are they?"

'I don't see them," her husband answered for the umpteenth time. He was trying to remain stoic in front of the neighbors, Dan and Marie Scandan, whose boulevard they were sharing. Marie was busy entertaining Baby Chuck, who was in his stroller under a shade tree. The youngster was keeping his eye on her.

"Will you go look?' the wife suggested. Her eyes pleaded with her spouse.

"They'll be along shortly," he stated. He wanted to keep her calm. "They can't be lost. There are two thousand people watching the parade."

She ignored his logic; real fear was rising within her. "Lost!" she wailed, envisioning the worst. The word sent a shiver through her body. "Go find them!" she commanded. She was totally exasperated.

Just then the Great Northern Empire Builder's float passed by. Laura Birch was sitting on her throne as if in a trance. She had stopped waving and was gripping the arm rests in both hands. She did not look at the young couple whose son had caused her fit. She stared straight ahead. All she could do was snarl.

Across the avenue, her family rose in unison to cheer the queen. Cherie Sawyer was with them. But alas, Her Majesty was exasperated; her moment in the limelight had been spoiled.

Her father sensed her foul mood. "What's wrong with Laura?" Nelson Birch asked his wife. "She looks disturbed."

"She looks normal," replied Laura's sister, Sandie.

"You shush!" ordered her mother. The woman kept her smile pasted on.

"Maybe it's that time of the month," suggested Sandie. "She's always bragging how she's having those periods now."

"I said 'shush' and I mean it," threatened the mother. "Keep waving. Keep smiling. We'll find out what's upset her later. Nellie!"

"Here comes the mayor and his family," cried the boy's father across the street. "Just look at them—a circus act!"

"Right out of vaudeville," mused Dan Scandan. He was old enough to have seen vaudeville acts firsthand when he was a boy. "Look at the mayor," he chuckled. "He won't give up."

"That's what we like about him," stated Frankie's dad. "He's tenacious, a bulldog. You'll make it, Al!" he sang out. The mayor tried to wave his hand to acknowledge that he had heard. But it almost cost him his balance. He grunted and turned, stopped and turned back, while his wife completed two circles around him and sped on.

"Watch yourself going down the hill," the boy's father warned.

"I'll be careful, Cliff," Al Ryngsmuth replied. "I've been thinking about it for the past four blocks."

In the distance to the east, the spectators saw the flashing lights of the village's newest acquisition, its fire truck. It was the last entrant in the parade.

"Here comes the end," yelled Terry Joe from across the street. "Get ready. He'll try to squirt us."

Guilford Bartholomay's fire truck crossed 10th Avenue, and he turned on his siren as a "hello" to all of the O'Brians. Bill O'Brian had risen and was folding up his lawn chair. Behind the parade, along 5th Street, everyone was doing the same.

Without warning, Boomer turned on the hose to splash them. Water shot out in a misty stream. But he was not prepared for the reprisal. En masse, the O'Brian clan flung a volley of water balloons at the young man in a surprise attack, a sortie that left him drenched. Like daring subversives in the Irish Republican Army, they raced into the street and lobbed the colorful bombs at him. Even Grandma O'Brian heaved one, but it misfired and smacked her son, Gene, in the back of the head. Her second toss landed three feet away in the gutter.

They pelted Boomer mercilessly, and a great roar of Irish laughter exploded from the curb. The victors stepped back, avoiding Boomer's retaliatory spray. In the cab Guilford Bartholomay chuckled at his son's plight. It would do the boy good, teach him to stay on his toes.

"What's that siren for?" asked the four children's mother a block ahead. "Are they hurt?" she cried in utter agony.

"There they are," stated Dan Scandan, pointing with his cane from his lawn chair.

Little Dan could wait no longer. At the alley he bolted across Dan Scandan's yard, through Marie Scandan's garden, and into his house. He had to go to the bathroom—bad.

His sister, Mary, chased after him, fulfilling her promise not to let him out of her sight. At the end of the block, their mother spotted the action. The woman felt an immense relief.

Here, take a picture," she ordered, thrusting the camera into her husband's hands. Then she rushed up the sidewalk to intercept her little Robin Hood and his escort, Bozo the Clown.

Frankie and his sister, Jeanne, did not go home. They were curious additions, tacked onto the end of the parade. The people still left on the parade route waved to the boy and girl, as they gathered their lawn chairs and blankets. They enjoyed seeing the children's commitment, their *stick-to-it-ive-ness*.

At the top of the final hill, the boy looked up. He suspected what was up in the trees. Hidden in the branches and leaves was a tree house belonging to its occupant, Jack Kertcher. He was two years older than Frankie and a whole lot meaner. Recently he had become more than a nuisance; he was now a nemesis. But that was to be expected. Boys and girls in Waite Park had to hold their own, a task made more difficult when you had no older brothers and sisters to look out for you. Jack Kertcher was a small boy with a swarthy complexion, but he had a sharp tongue and worldly ways.

He had built the tree house himself in an elm tree in his back yard with lumber he had stolen from the Rausches' woodpile. The hammer and nails had been stolen too, from a hardware store on 3rd Street in St. Cloud. The house was high enough in the tree to afford him the freedom to indulge in his emerging adolescence, to experiment with his budding manhood and escape detection. He was peering out of the doorway of his lodge; and when he saw the boy and his sister, he stiffened and leaned forward. Below, the boy saw him stare, a maniac's dislike in his expression.

Also peering out was Lucy Stephens, a girl with dirty blond hair and a sour reputation. Yet, curiously, at school she never showed shame. She lived across the street.

"Hey, Wiener," came a voice from on high, "I'm up here." It was the voice of Jackie Birch, aimed at his sister and her doll buggy. She was looking out over Jack Kertcher's shoulder.

Frankie looked at his sister. She was gazing up into their lair, her curiosity aflame. His spine steeled. He was the older brother. He would have to protect her from the devil. One day he would fight Jack Kertcher.

"Don't look up at them," he admonished. "They're up there smoking cigarettes and having sex."

He walked on, and ten steps later he heard his sister's voice behind him, "What's sex?"

He kept walking along. Sex was a vague concept. Once he had heard his dad and Leo talking about it, but he hadn't caught the details. They were laughing.

"It's good breeding," Frankie replied. It's at the mink farm… in March.

"But you said it was up in that tree."

The older brother didn't want to talk about it anymore. He kept walking ahead of his sister down the street.

Finally she spoke. "Okay, I'll ask Dad."

He turned abruptly and looked at her. "No," he told her, "ask Mom."

The celebration at the community park had a carnival atmosphere. The Ladies Guild of St. Joseph's Parish served the chicken dinner in the pavilion. The American Legion ran the beer stand next to it. Both were popular venues as Waite Park's citizens paused to relax and renew friendships. Families gathered to eat and to socialize. After dinner, many played BINGO. The elderly sat in the shade of the pavilion's canopy and enjoyed the sunshine just beyond.

Games had been set up. Most were children's contests. In pairs they ran three-legged races, one leg of each partner tied together. To win, they had to work in tandem. Then they hopped in gunny sacks, like Mexican jumping beans. The men and older boys gambled. In particular, they loved to play Beat-the-House.

By 4:00 o'clock, Clarence Bruns and Paul Rausch were at wit's end. The House was nearly broke. They had lost a considerable sum, nearly five hundred dollars, and they were considering shutting the game down.

Frankie watched the two men approach his father. The boy's dad was standing at the beer garden, enjoying an afternoon away from the mink farm. His pal and hired hand, Leo, had offered to feed and water the mink.

"We're losing our shirt," Clarence Bruns wailed. "The village council loaned us five hundred dollars seed money, and we're out. We'll have to shut the game down."

"Would you take over, Cliff?" Paul Rausch asked. His tone was pleading. "I'll give you one hundred dollars to get started. It's all I have on me."

The boy's father nodded, and he reached into his shirt pocket and extracted a pair of sunglasses. He put them on and stepped out into the afternoon daylight. The boy followed him to the gaming table.

The Beat-the-House table was crowded. Several bettors voiced "hurrays" that the game was being resumed. The boy's father tied on an apron and stuffed Paul Rausch's one hundred dollars into it, five twenty-dollar bills.

He asked someone to make change, and Tweet Thorsten complied. His father set the rules. "All bets will be fifty cents to two dollars."

"Can't I bet ten dollars?" asked Howie Kappas. "That's what I've been doing. I'm up a hundred. I want more."

"Fifty cents to two dollars" was all his father would say. He explained it to his son the next day: "You can't win all the small bets and then lose one or two big ones. It's better if all the bets are the same size. Remember, the House takes all ties. That's its edge. Of course, it helps to be a lucky shaker, and I was lucky yesterday."

The boy's dad took hold of the dice box and put the two dice into it. He shook the box for good measure. "Place your bets," he stated. And then he shook the box again and rolled the dice onto the green felt surface of the table. A nine. That was the point.

The boy watched the bettors shake the dice, trying to beat the nine. Only one did, and his father paid the man. It was Abner Johnson's father.

Another shake. A pair of ones. "Snake Eyes!" screamed Howie Kappas. Clarence Bruns winced and started to cry out, but he felt Paul Rausch's strong hand grip his wrist. "Let him be," whispered Paul. "He's a good man. I have faith in him."

To save time, his father paid out to everyone. He shook again. An eight, the new point. Again most lost, two tied, and only one won.

Another shake. A ten. The tide was gradually turning. Standing at his father's side, the boy found himself rooting for him, wanting success for him. He was no longer his boss; he was his dad. The boy could not see his father's eyes through the sunglasses. But he watched how he acted and learned from it.

His father, the seller of investments, was considered a white collar worker. The men and boys around the table were blue collar. They wanted to win from his father, but they respected him.

Twice the point was low—a three. The boy looked across the table and saw Robbie Stein push out fifty cents, belatedly, after he saw the point. His father ignored it and paid Robbie off. The son was mystified. He sensed that his father had seen the boy cheat. But no one else could tell, for they could not see the man's eyes. That and several beers had dulled their senses.

His dad rolled another point. A twelve. Box Cars! He took all of their coins and bills, including fifty cents from Robbie Stein, whose timing had slipped.

The game continued even as the sun marched toward the west. His father was a lucky shaker, indeed. By 6:00 o'clock, the House was no longer in the red. His father had made up the five hundred dollar deficit and was two hundred dollars in the black. Much relieved, Clarence Bruns went to the community shelter to eat supper.

Dusk settled in, and the game continued into the darkness. A light, a single bulb, was hung above the table. Only the serious shakers remained. The small fry had lost all of their money. Those still betting were trying to recover what they had lost.

"If only I had quit when I was ahead," mused Howie Kappas to Tweet Thorsten. "But now I'm behind, out one hundred dollars. He's a lucky s.o.b.," muttered Howie.

The man shaking the point said nothing. He remained stoic, steadily increasing the House's winnings. His son looked at the stash of coins piling up in front of them. His father's apron was stuffed with bills, mostly twenties, but some fifties and a few hundreds.

When the fireworks started at 9:30 p.m., the Beat-the-House game was still going strong. It was the only activity still going. His father kept shaking the point and gathering in coins and bills while fireworks exploded overhead—bright bursts of red, white, and blue that splayed out against the darkness and the stars. The burning gunpowder detonated above them, and the booms filled everyone's ears. The people of Waite Park huddled together on blankets and gazed skyward. What a great land! What a great country! At the dice table, the men continued to shake.

CHAPTER FOURTEEN

"You won a thousand and fifty-four dollars," the boy noted the next morning. He had watched his father count the money, separating it into piles. He had counted along.

"Paul Rausch and Clarence Bruns will be here soon to collect it," his father told him. "Paul will be glad to get his hundred back."

"Grandma thinks they should invest it," the boy added, squinting into the light.

His father shrugged. "It's not theirs to invest. It's just their responsibility." He stood up. He was anxious for the men to arrive.

The man looked directly into his son's eyes. "We have to go feed and water the mink. Leo won't be there today. I need your help."

The boy looked at the piles of money. The mink were his father's responsibility. And he was being asked to help. In that request he could feel the importance of family.

It was still early that morning when news of the accident surfaced. It swelled like a tidal wave and spread throughout the village. One boy was dead; three were injured. The deluge shook the community.

Four of Waite Park's youths had held their own Fourth of July celebration out at Dead Man's quarry. They had brought their own fireworks—dynamite. A forgotten cache had been stored in a shed at the bottom of the newest dig. They had taken a few sticks, just for kicks. The danger was intriguing. The blast would make an impression on their friends. "Fireworks are kid's stuff," declared Gordan Hoganson. Dynamite was more manly. A minute later its power was unleashed, and he was dead, his body lifeless, sliced to shreds. The explosion had rocked the granite quarry, scattering debris outward in a wicked blast.

If truth is a flood that drowns, then false rumor is a wildfire that burns. Over back fences gossip ignited and spread, a rampage fanned by the wind of exaggeration.

"There was a big party. Alcohol was consumed. *Tsk...Tsk...*"

"One boy's leg was blown off, severed at the hip."

"Another boy nearly drowned after the explosion, having been blown sideways by the blast into the stream at the bottom of the quarry."

How had it happened? Each new shred of discovery fueled the story with rumors of what had occurred. Few of them were true.

"Boys will be boys," Howard Kappas was heard to say. But his tone was subdued. When asked to explain, his voice fell mute.

"Who was it?" the boy asked his friend, Terry Joe. "What happened?"

"It was Gordon Hoganson, Abigail's big brother," his friend informed him. They live out at the quarries. He's dead, blown to bits. Rodney Koeller blew off his foot. He'll have to use a cane.

Terry Joe paused, not quite knowing how to phrase his next statement. Gary Kukoluck lost his manhood." Terry Joe's voice was hushed. He waited a moment to let the image sink in.

"His manhood?" questioned the other boy, squinting into the morning sun. "What do you mean?"

"His you know what," Terry Joe asserted. "You know, his dink. It was cut off in the blast. Now he'll talk with a high, squeaky voice." The listener stopped to picture the details.

"He won't be saying much," said Terry Joe.

"Why did they do it?" asked Frankie.

"They were having a party out at the quarries," stated Terry Joe. "My brother, Tom, was going to go, but he didn't. After the party four of them stayed out there." He paused again for dramatic effect.

"Why?" asked his friend.

Terry Joe had his own theory. "Remember that agate? The one Abigail brought to show and tell? They blew up the dynamite to loosen more agates. They're worth a quarter apiece at the rock shop in St. Cloud." The storyteller sat staring into space, imagining the fortune that lay at the bottom of the quarry.

By the end of the day, the real story solidified. Abigail Hoganson's brother was indeed dead. Rodney Koeller did not lose his foot, but he hurt his heel in the blast and would walk with a limp for the rest of his life. No one had been blown into the stream and nearly drowned. There was no stream in that quarry as of yet. And no one had lost his manhood.

The funeral for Gordan Hoganson was set for 11:00 o'clock the following Wednesday. Frankie thought about the accident. Poor Abigail! To lose her big brother. Death was painful, so permanent; it could never be reversed. The more he thought about it, the more his heart ached.

On Wednesday morning he heard the bells summoning the congregation to church. Ray Schaffner, the caretaker of the church and the school's janitor, rang the church bells himself by pulling a rope strung to a combination of pulleys high in the bell tower above the south entry. Ray lived just across the street in a house conveniently located close to his work. Every day at noon and every evening at 6:00 o'clock, he rang the bells, a reminder to the faithful to pray before meals. The boy thought nothing out of the ordinary. It was customary for Catholics to pray; his family said the Angelus before every supper.

Frankie walked to St. Joseph's Catholic Church while the funeral was in progress. He crossed through the nun's yard just west of the church and drifted into the rectory yard to the northeast, between the church and Pinor's Market. The school stood just across the street. There in the priests' yard, he hovered behind a tree.

When the funeral mass was over, the church emptied into the waiting cars. The bells peeled overhead, announcing the time: 12:00 noon. The burial would be in the cemetery out toward the quarries south of the village. The burial ceremony would precede the funeral luncheon.

Father Kent Thiel, the assistant pastor, exited the church and looked about. Another sad day for the parish amid such a beautiful setting! The rose bushes he had planted in the rectory yard were thriving, full of richly-colored flowers: pink and red and creamy white. God had a way of juxtaposing death and beauty. The irony was not lost on him.

The priest did not suspect that a visitor was hiding in his yard behind one of his trees. The boy watched intently. The casket was lowered down the front steps by six youths, the dead boy's friends. Gordon Hoganson's parents and sister followed closely behind. The boy in hiding could see the women weeping. They followed Mr. Daniels, the funeral home director. The pallbearers set the black burial box on top of a gurney with wheels. A gold crucifix adorned the cover.

It struck the boy that Abigail was clothed in a dress. He was accustomed to her tomboy attire. He studied her carefully. She placed a hand on her brother's casket; she could no longer touch him.

And then the casket was turned around. The priest, Father Thiel, stepped forward to pray for the salvation of the boy's soul and to bless him. The pallbearers lifted the casket and shoved it into the hearse to send Gordon Hoganson's body on its final journey.

In this poignant moment the boy in hiding realized that life is fragile. He kept his focus on the deceased boy's sister. He felt sad for Abigail. He imagined what it would be like if he were dead and how terrible his sisters and brothers would feel—just terrible. Death was indeed harder on the living. They had to press on. Their lives would be different, and there was nothing they could do about it.

The boy's eyes were riveted on the girl. He was sorry for her, so so sorry, so sorry that he fell in love—his first love. Puppy love, they called it, a boyhood crush. But it was real.

That night he dreamed. He was older and more mature. He lifted Abigail Hoganson and held her tightly in his arms. He twirled her. They were in a rose garden in Munsinger Park in St. Cloud, and she was happy. The moonlight shone brightly upon them, and the flowers smelled of perfume. He made her forget the loss of her brother. Overwhelmed by her acceptance of him, he felt ecstatic. They were lovers. He held her tight and spun. The night sky was full of milky stars. He looked up, and his heart sang. Then he looked into her face. What he saw shocked him. He was holding and caressing a girl with a big round head and flashing white teeth, Susanne Danbury. Her face was full of wonder. She clutched him tightly and would not let him go.

In desperation, he tried to croak his disapproval. But his voice was silent. She grinned, accepting his advance. Her response was honest, but she could not have known the truth.

He awoke suddenly in a cold sweat. The horror of the dream broke over him. It was a nightmare. He vowed to himself: *never again would he dream*. He tried to forget Susanne, to think only of Abigail. But the attempt was futile. He could sleep no more. He lay awake until daylight dawned. Then he arose, dressed, and slipped downstairs into the kitchen, where his mother was frying bacon. He did not want to be alone.

The Friday meeting of the Knights of the Round Table commenced, as it always did, with a round of beers delivered by Fat Frannie. She was a large, fleshy woman but attractive in her own way. Perhaps she was thirty-five, perhaps forty. No more. She was adept at her work, sumptuous, able to snuggle delectably close to each customer as she placed a bottle in front of him, positioning herself just so to show off her best features. She was careful to expose enough skin to force them to look, and she relished the attention she received. A pinch here and there was to be expected. It increased the size of those patrons' tips.

It had been only a week since the Fourth of July, and the villagers still had not gotten over the death of the Hoganson boy. Celebration juxtaposed with regret was difficult to reconcile.

"Ah, Sir Lancelot, a tragedy it is," exclaimed Sir Gawain. Cortney Johanson, in character, looked sad and shook his head. "A young squire met a gruesome fate out by the granite quarries."

"That's true," agreed Sir Pellinore. "The granite quarries have long been places where young people experiment. Don't you recall our own youth?" Herman Braun, grinning at the memories, was struggling to stay in character.

Howard Kappas, alias Sir Lancelot, spoke to them matter-of-factly. "You have to be careful when you play with dynamite." His next comment was cryptic. "We, too, must be careful; we must always be on our guard."

"What do you mean, Howie?" asked Cortney, his lifelong friend.

"We must never take anything for granted." Howard sensed that they were puzzled, and troubled, by his comment.

"What do you mean?" asked Herman, rather gruffly. He was annoyed.

Howard continued. "The King Arthur legend is based on one fact: we are humans, and our lives are flawed. I won three hundred dollars at the Beat the House game on the Fourth of

July. I felt invincible—that I couldn't lose. I thought I'd win a thousand bucks. Then I became greedy. I should have quit when I was ahead. But I couldn't quit playing. I lost it all, the three hundred dollars and another five hundred of my own money—five hundred smackers! Cliff Kucher stood there in his sunglasses and robbed me blind. But it was my own fault."

"It all went to the American Legion," Herman rationalized. "At least it went for a good cause." He held out his glass toward them and raised it. "To the service of our country!"

"To the service of our country!" they all repeated and clinked their glasses together.

Cortney spoke next in a voice that was subdued but earnest. "We are the Knights of The Round Table. We long for battle. It's been too long. We're growing rusty during this long period of inaction, and we've become irritable. Sir Lancelot, do you know of anything that we can do?"

Howard shifted his gaze around the room. For a time he trained his eyes on Fat Frannie to make sure she was not eavesdropping. Then he leaned forward toward the center of the table. The other two also leaned forward expectantly.

"King Arthur needs us," whispered Howard. Gawain and Pellinore stared at him, their eyes narrowing.

"When?" asked Gawain.

"Tomorrow night," answered Sir Lancelot. "Meet as usual in the parking lot of the Moose Lodge at 10:00 o'clock, and we will proceed together into Camelot." The three men smiled knowingly, and then their smiles broadened.

"To good fortune!" toasted Herman, and he raised his glass like a sword.

"To good fortune!" echoed the other two knights.

"Remember, we must always be on our guard," Howard reminded them.

"Do you know of any threat to our plans?" asked Herman.

Howard fiddled with the empty glass in his hands. He could see that these two men had courage in their veins. He took his time to answer. "None that I'm aware of," said Sir Lancelot.

"Then there's no need to sound a false alarm," responded Herman. "I'm not afraid of my own shadow, Howie."

"We'll be careful," added Cortney with a laugh. It's been a long time between battles. We can all use a few extra ounces of gold." With that, he sat back and caught Fat Frannie's attention. He motioned for her to bring them a second round. Frannie leaned over them seductively, her eyes flirting openly as she set the bottles in front of them. She wiggled her hips as she walked away.

Cortney followed her movements. Then he lifted the mouth of his beer bottle to his lips, sipped at length, and swallowed. "Who is our King Arthur anyway?" he asked, and he took another swig.

"I don't know," Howie lied. "And you had better not ask. We're on a need-to-know basis, just like in the Marines. The less we know, the better."

Sir Gawine and Sir Pellinore looked skeptical.

"I don't know who it is; I just call a phone number," explained Howard. "I don't want to know."

"You could find out from the telephone company who the number belongs to," suggested Cortney. His reasoning made sense to Herman.

Howard shook his head sideways, rejecting the idea, and answered emphatically, *"That would be suicide."*

July days were hot, but August days were hotter. The produce in the garden was ready to be harvested. Frankie's mother expected his help. Piles of beans, yellow and green, needed to be snipped. Dumped onto newspapers, they covered the table entirely, and the boy and his sisters spent hours breaking off the ends, stem and flower. Their mother washed the beans, cut them up, and blanched them. She parceled them out into plastic storage bags, and the boy hauled them down to the deep freezer.

The sweet corn met a similar fate. The stalks of corn at the end of the garden near the alley, three rows, were stripped. The yellow ears, sweet and juicy, lay wrapped in their sheaths. These were husked and boiled, and then the mother, wielding her knife, cut the kernels from the cobs. She bagged the golden kernels in plastic bags, and her son deposited them in the freezer, also.

Ripe, red tomatoes—the garden's main produce, according to his father—were dipped in boiling water, de-skinned, and canned in quart jars, which were heated in a water bath in a large blue kettle on the stove until the lids, stamped Kerr, sealed. Throughout the winter this fruit would serve as the main ingredient in spaghetti hot dishes and casseroles.

Canning was a never-ending job. It seemed to the boy that his mother was canning constantly. With her children's help she dug up beets and pickled them in glass jars. Then she would buy a box of peaches and can them, cutting each peach in half to remove its seed and pouring sugar into the jars along with sticks of cinnamon.

The center of the garden always contained several patches. One was a patch of cucumbers, picked and eaten throughout the summer in fresh salads or in a creamy dressing. She canned the smaller ones, soaking them in brine and home-grown dill. Gradually they were transformed into pickles to be used on hamburgers cooked on a charcoal grill.

Finally, like she did every summer, his mother canned the lug of cherries that her husband purchased from the Piggly Wiggly grocery in St. Cloud. These were sweet and juicy. More than once, the boy stole into the basement and devoured an entire jarful. He was not guilt free, but the canned fruit was irresistible, reminiscent of the forbidden apples picked from the Tree of Knowledge of Good and Evil in the Garden of Eden. Without knowing the theology, he shared in Adam and Eve's original sin.

Lakes abounded around the village. One hot August evening the boy's dad suggested they go for a swim. The children voiced their approval, and their mother consented. They packed into the family truck: parents and Baby Chuck in the cab, children in the back. Dressed in his swimsuit and t-shirt, Frankie sat upon a wheel well. He wanted to be the first into the water.

They drove the six miles to Beaver Lake in St. Joe. Instantly the boy leaped to the ground and darted into the water. It was warm. He liked that it was absent of chlorine, a foul chemical that permeated the municipal pool in St. Cloud. Here, swimming was more natural. He filled his lungs with a gulp of air and dove deep into the water and detected a patch of sunfish weeds that covered the sandy bottom of the lake.

His sisters and brothers joined him, Baby Chuck splashing water into his sister Mary's face. His parents nudged their bodies into the water slowly. He could see his father's farmer tan: white skin covering his torso and sunburn covering his face, neck, and arms. The man was only an occasional swimmer, and he settled into an easy sidestroke. His wife, sporting a blue bathing cap and a black one-piece suit, followed him out into the lake after she was fully immersed.

A raft floated lazily in the distance. It was tied to an anchor, and sitting on it were three young men and three young women, obviously couples. The boy saw them. They were drinking out of bottles and kissing. He saw his father take notice, a wrinkled expression on his brow.

Then the boy heard them speak. "She's his slut," one boy uttered.

"How do you know she's a whore?" asked one of the girls.

The answer was brazen. "Her nipples are stiff—like yours." The laughter from the raft could not be ignored.

"They're probably nigger lovers," another young man proposed.

The boy's father sensed that his children were listening. He chose to speak. "You should watch what you say," he advised. "There are children present."

One boy stood up. Drink had made him bold. "You had better clear out before we beat the piss out of you!" he challenged.

The boy's father could see that the young man meant it. He thought for several moments. "Let's go home," he called out.

"You had damn well better go" came the voice from the raft. "And take your slut with you." His friends on the raft laughed, but the situation had turned ugly. In silence the father turned and swam to shore.

The family collected their belongings and loaded the truck. The father turned the key in the ignition, shifted into gear, and backed up. As he drove away, he thought of the shotgun in his gun cabinet. He thought of his years in the Marines. "Those kids have no respect," he stated. They need a stint in basic training. Sergeant King would do it. He'd teach those juvenile delinquents with their foul language to have some manners." As he thought about it, his mouth creased in a wicked grin.

I'm glad we left," stated his wife. "They could have hurt the children. Why don't they go swim in the quarries? At least there are no children there."

But the man's blood was boiling. He'd been challenged. "They need to be taught a lesson," continued her husband. "They're just a bunch of punks! This is America. Everyone needs to be respected."

His wife looked at him. "What about Marilyn Wojcheski?"

"That's different," he argued. "That poor husband of hers, Tom. Why can't she learn to obey him?"

"It's not her fault," the boy's mom retorted. It's him!"

The cab fell silent. Finally the man asked, "Why do you care about her so much?"

"Because she needs me," his wife replied. "And I need her."

The following Tuesday the telephone rang. The woman answered. "It's Father Thiel," she whispered to her husband, clutching the receiver to her chest. She sounded perplexed.

"I'll be in the garage if you need me," he announced and departed quickly.

It was not polite to eavesdrop, but the boy listened anyway. He heard only one side of the conversation, his mother's.

"Yes, this is she."

"Hello, Father. I'm fine."

"No, Father, I'm not busy. Now is fine."

"Yes, Father, I am friends with Marilyn. Why are you calling, Father?"

"Yes, I know that you and Father Schumacher are the caretakers of the parish."

"Yes, I like being a member of this parish."

"Yes, Father, I know she's divorced."

"Yes, Father, I believe in the sanctity of marriage."

"No, Father, I will not divorce myself from her."

"Father Thiel, you sound like my husband."

"Has he been talking to you, Father?"

"I thought so, Father."

"No, Father, don't come over. There's no need."

"Goodbye, Father."

She slammed the phone receiver down into its carriage. The nerve of that man!

Of them both! All three!

She would show them what it meant to be a Christian. The church was a sanctuary, was it not? Even sinners were welcome. In that moment she made up her mind. She would take Marilyn Wojcheski to church with her one Sunday. Her friend would see that their God was a forgiving God.

The doorbell rang. It was the boy's grandma. She had a crate in the car that she wanted hauled in. In it were eleven chickens, all males, ready for decapitation.

"Clifford's in the garage," his mother informed the older woman. You can tell him from me that *his* neck is on the chopping block."

CHAPTER FIFTEEN

The dog days of August were fast approaching.

Uncle Charley drove into town with three boys in the back seat of his Cadillac.

A fourth boy, little Roy, was nestled in the front seat between Charley and Dad's sister, Aunt Lucille. The entire family had anticipated their arrival for days. This year they would all be going to Pickeral Lake on vacation.

They were coming to the Midwest from New Jersey, and the boys were anxious to see the vestiges of the Old West. These cousins were city slickers, boys who were intrigued by the Western heroes they saw on television: *Roy Rogers*, *Gene Autry*, and *The Lone Ranger*. Recently they had graduated to the hour-long drama, *Gunsmoke*; it was more lethal. The lure of wide open spaces had cast a spell on them.

They were intelligent kids, future engineers like their father, used to the advantages of city life. Their cousin, Frankie, sensed that they believed in the superiority of the East. They were accustomed to their life along the eastern seaboard. They had never been west of the Alleghenies, so they were naïve about life in Minnesota.

For several months before their arrival, the boy had primed the pump. He told them in his letters that the well beneath their hand pump in the kitchen was running dry, but that a water tower was being built and they would soon have running water piped to them. "It's a slight stretch," he told his dad who scanned the letter.

"It's a big fat lie," Dad corrected.

"Just a skinny little lie," he argued.

"We did have a pump in the back entry when I was a boy," mused the man. He looked at his wife.

"Our pump was above the kitchen sink," stated the boy's mother. "You've seen it at your Aunt Celia's farm in Sauk Centre."

Dad continued reading. "What's this about a new outhouse, made from knotty pine?"

"It's a two-holer, Dad. It gets really cold on your tush in winter."

Mom blushed. "Your imagination is out of control, young man. Erase that."

"But Mom, it's fun! They'll believe it! That's the best part. They'll see soon enough when they get here."

"Don't be a *spoil sport*, Pat," said her husband. He was warming up to this practical joke. She bristled at his insinuation; he looked away and laughed into his sleeve.

"Perhaps Lucille will tell them the truth," Mom speculated.

Dad considered this. "I think she'll play along. I know Charley will."

"Let me see that letter," Mom held out her hand. She read it. "Indians!" she blurted out. "Since when are there Indians in Waite Park, Minnesota? Teepees... buffaloes... the cries of Indians on the warpath... a recent scalping outside of St. Joseph's Catholic Church?"

Suddenly Dad whooped. He howled like a banshee. His mischievous side had surfaced.

Mom set the letter down on the table. "Yes, they will believe it. Those boys are gullible."

Uncle Charley and Aunt Lucille did play along. As the sleek black sedan glided to a halt beneath the basketball hoop, three sets of eyes were glued to the back seat windows. Their young hosts, a warrior chief and two ferocious squaws, came running out to greet them, dressed in full Sioux regalia: buckskin shirts, feathered headdresses, war paint, and bows and arrows—last year's Christmas presents from Santa. The fourth attacker was Robin Hood. They screamed at the top of their lungs as they circled the Cadillac in mock attack. "Oooo Wooo Wooo Wooo! Oooo Wooo Wooo Wooo!" They thumped their flattened hands against their mouths and danced the Ghost Dance. When they loaded their arrows onto the bows and took aim, the boys in the back seat ducked. Uncle Charley stepped out directly into the line of fire.

"Don't hit my car," he commanded. "I just had it washed and waxed in Monticello." The locals stopped their charade. "Hey, Uncle Charley. Hi, Aunt Lucille."

"Come on out here," said Uncle Charley to no one in the back seat. "Come meet your cousins from Minnesota."

Aunt Lucille, the boy's godmother, looked right through his war paint. "Give me a hug," she beckoned. "I've come a long way for this."

Uncle Charley was quite a character. In summer he liked to drink beer. Every year he provoked his mother-in-law, the boy's grandmother, by hauling a case of Grain Belt Premium into her house. She was convinced her daughter could have done better. According to Grandma, Charley had only one redeeming quality: he played his cards well. During his visit they drove over to the Labor Temple in St. Cloud for an evening of bridge. Frankie never remembered them not finishing in first or second place.

After supper Dad and Uncle Charley sat in the living room, sharing stories and trading jokes. The boy plopped down onto the couch, next to his uncle, and listened. He had fetched two beers for them from the refrigerator, and they were sipping on them, savoring them.

His father liked to tell jokes. On the road selling investments in mutual funds, he would stop at a farmhouse and step out of his blue Cadillac in his blue suit and walk through the mud to the house. Once inside, he would "talk farming" with a husband and wife. He would tell them about his growing up on a farm and about raising mink. The farmers trusted him; he was one of them. Then he would tell a joke or two. They liked that he always laughed so hard at his own jokes, sometimes starting to laugh before he finished the punch line. "It reassures them," he told Grandma.

"Just make sure you close the sale," his mother admonished.

As always, he heeded her advice.

Sitting in his rocking chair, the boy's father leaned forward for effect. "Charley, I had a hunting dog once, a Black Lab, and I lost him. So, I put up a sign offering a reward. It said:

Lost: Hunting Dog.
Only 3 legs. Tail broken.
Blind in left eye. Recently neutered.
Answers to the name of *Lucky*.

"Ha! Ha!" Both men roared with laughter. They were as thick as thieves.

"How's that one?" Dad asked.

"Funny!" Uncle Charley answered.

The visitor from New Jersey looked up and surveyed the far wall. "That's a huge walleye, Clifford."

Dad's blue eyes stared at the mounted fish. "I hope I catch a bigger one...," he replied, "...this trip."

The drive to Pickeral Lake took three hours. The final stretch of road was a sandy path that twisted through birch and pine trees until it opened up to a narrow expanse of water in a bay. Beyond the bay lay a larger body of water, shaped like a boot, with fishing holes for walleyes and crappies and sunfish.

The families arrived in mid-afternoon. The setting was woodsy. Six cabins, all identical, all painted white with red trim, lined the shore. The boy's father had rented two of the cabins. The water in the small bay shimmered in the sunlight, and the surface danced in a light breeze. Six boats with identical engravings, SUNSET RESORT, were tied up to three docks at the water's edge. They rocked gently against old tires hung on the dock's posts.

The boys and girls scampered out of the cars into the cabins. Tired of being bottled up, they sought to explore their new surroundings. Immediately it became an adventure.

Frankie led the way. His sister, Jeanne, followed close behind. He quickly surveyed the scene. The entrance to the cabin opened up to the kitchen with its rectangular table made of birch. Adjacent to this was a large living room, paneled with knotty pine. One wall contained a big picture window that faced the lake. The focal point of the room was its large heater that burned wood and provided warmth. A pile of kindling was stacked in a corner of the room. The explorers turned down a hallway, and they found two bedrooms at the back of the cottage. The boy looked about. Here, there was, in fact, no bathroom, only an outhouse outside. They would be "roughing it."

They reversed course. Then Frankie saw the stairway to the attic and bolted for it. His sister was at his heels. Up he clambered. The attic was dark; the only light was from the kitchen below. He must explore every corner. He let his imagination roam and pretended it was spooky. "Watch out!" he cautioned his sister. "Or the boogeyman will get you." He stepped across a two-by-four into the darkness beyond.

Below, his father had just entered the cabin. His arms were loaded down with groceries and suitcases full of enough clothes to last a week. He was just in time to see a foot plunge through the ceiling, a small foot in a tennis shoe attached to a long leg in blue jeans. He heard the muffled scream from above, welcoming him to Pickeral Lake.

The father drove to town to buy a hammer and nails. He was gone an hour. The boy sat in a chair in the corner of the kitchen, facing the wall. Looking up, he noted that there was already an L-shaped line of nails in a ceiling panel. From this he took a modest amount of comfort. Someone else's child, also, had been foolish enough to explore the attic.

The next day Dad and Charley rose early to go fishing. Dad took his oldest son along. To catch their limit: six walleyes, fifteen crappies, and thirty sunfish each, he would fish from sun-up to sun-down if need be. The boy looked at his dad and saw a man's man. He was an outdoorsman: a fisherman and a hunter.

Pickeral Lake was a relatively small lake, no Mille Lacs, and on this morning there was only a wisp of wind. Still, the young lad enjoyed sitting in the bow of his dad's sixteen-foot Crestliner, bounding over the flat surface as the 10 horsepower Johnson motor pushed them along.

Two islands, one large and one small, lay a mile out, their rocky reefs and underwater sandbars a safe haven for young walleyes and other small fish. Tucked into the lake's natural structure, they could escape larger predators.

His father guided them out to the middle of the lake to the bigger island. Arriving there, the man twisted the handle of the motor to close the throttle. When the boat stopped, it rocked gently in the swells caused by the boat's wake.

They fished with shiners and fathead minnows and leeches and big worms called night crawlers. Occasionally his Dad tried a jig. They trolled for walleyes or drifted if the wind was right. Later on, they tried casting into a crappie hole and a sunfish weed bed.

In the evenings that followed, his father took the younger children out to those weed beds to fish "sunnies." The children fished using long cane poles with bobbers shaped like ink pens. When the bobber submerged and disappeared, the boy or girl lifted the tip of the pole into the air. The cane pole would bend in a great arc as the fish *zig-zagged*, cutting through the water. The fisherman simply lifted the tip of the pole skyward; there was no need to reel the fish in. The reward was a bluegill or a pumpkinseed, wiggling on the hook.

More than once, his father had been slapped in the face by a slab of sunfish dangling at the end of a line. "Can you take it off for me, Daddy?" The man was kept busy removing the hooks from the fishes' mouths and re-baiting the hooks. On a busy night, he barely found time to drop his own line into the water. But he never complained.

On this first morning, when the boy grew tired of fishing, he stared at the iridescent blue water and the walleyes on the stringer at the side of the boat. He insisted that he net the fish the others caught; it was the most exciting part of fishing.

The weather was cool. There was a light breeze stirring, freshening the morning air. As the day brightened, the temperature rose.

For a while the fish stopped biting. Finally his father felt a nibble on his line. He let the line go slack immediately and waited patiently... ten... fifteen... twenty-five seconds. Then he turned the crank on the reel one half turn so that the line tightened. Just a moment before the fish could feel him, he yanked the rod upward at a 90 degree angle. It set the hook.

The rod bent in a great curving arc. *Zzzzz... Zzzzz...* The eight-pound test line streamed from the reel. Only the drag, set lightly, kept some pressure on the fish. As the fish expended its energy, the line slackened slightly. So, his dad reeled in the slack. This happened again and again, his dad always forcing the fish to fight the hook in its mouth. But this was a fish of great strength.

Uncle Charley watched with keen interest. His brother-in-law was relentless, holding the fish in check and reeling in any slack line. The scene brought to mind Ernest Hemingway's *The Old Man and the Sea*. Clifford, like Santiago, felt a close bond to the beautiful fish he would kill.

"It must be massive," muttered Charley, looking into the inky water.

"It's a big fish," said Dad. "Get the net."

His son reached for the net, but Uncle Charley put his hand on the boy's hand. "I had better net this one," he stated. He was serious for once. He took hold of the net and shifted into position, eyes focused on the blue-black water. He watched his brother-in-law continue to crank the reel ever-so-slowly, ever-so-patiently.

The boy's dad loved catching walleyes because they always fought deep. Catching one this size was a struggle he reveled in, every fisherman's dream. He loved the exertion.

The sun was now bright, and the day was growing hot. His dad's armpits were damp with sweat. After fifteen minutes the fish neared the boat. The rod was bent into a half circle, the rod tip quivering near the water's surface. Then suddenly the boy saw a flash of gold in the far depths. He gasped and took a quick breath. It was a creature of the deep!

The fisherman lifted the fish upward, but suddenly it dove for the bottom of the lake. The surface was not where it wanted to be. *Zzzz… Zzzz…* The line zipped out, but not for long. The fish's strength was waning. Dad reeled it upward again. The fish never gave up the fight. It swam back and forth, trying to spit the hook out. But it could not dislodge it.

The walleye was well over thirty inches long, thick-bodied, monstrous in size. Dad reeled it to within a foot of the water's surface. "Wait, Charley!" he ordered, but it was too late. The uncle was lunging toward the water to shove the net under the fish.

He managed to do so and lifted it. The fish came out of the water. Charley heaved it toward the boat.

But the fish was not in the net! It was so long that it lay cross-ways on the net's circular rim. The force of Uncle Charley's heave threw the walleye high into the air and over Dad's shoulder. It landed in the water behind the boat, and the line went limp. The fish had broken the line and escaped. Uncle Charley slumped into the boat. Dad stared into the oily water behind the boat's motor.

"That was a big fish," Dad repeated. "But it got away." It was vivid in his memory.

"I'm sorry, Clifford" was all Uncle Charley could say.

Paul Rausch and his sons: Tiny, Jimmy, Roger, Joe, and Frannie, followed the Crestliner down the alley. From across the alley came the O'Brians, Bill and his sons: Tom, Tim, Terry Joe, and Kevin. They converged on the boy's father, who sensed the purpose of their visit.

"So, how was fishing?" asked Paul Rausch innocently. Your coolers look heavy, full of fish."

The man who had caught them was hemmed in. It was customary to display the catch, to open oneself to the accolades of admiring neighbors. He was expected to feel pride. He opened a cooler, exposing the fillets on ice. The men and boys leaned forward, and secretly their mouths watered.

"So, where did you go on vacation?" Terry Joe asked his friend, Frankie. It was a harmless question. The boy who was questioned did not realize until later that the entire line of questioning had been rehearsed, part of a neighborhood performance.

"Pickeral Lake," he answered. "We were gone for four days." He saw his father's grimace of disappointment and realized his mistake.

"That's up by Detroit Lakes, isn't it?" asked Jimmy Rausch.

"Yes, I know where it is," acknowledged Bill O'Brian, his face broadening into a toothy grin.

The boy tried to cover up his mistake. "We caught them at Indian Point…no, the Mud Flats," corrected the boy. But it was too late.

"What? No, Indian Point is on Mille Lacs Lake; that's only walleyes," clarified Tom O'Brian. "Look at all those crappie and sunfish fillets."

Frankie looked into the open cooler. The crappies were as white as ivory. Speckled yellow and black and pumpkinseed orange, the sunfish still had the skin on, the way his father liked them. His mother would dip them in flour and fry them in butter. His father refused to spoil them with tartar sauce.

"It's a nice catch, Cliff," Paul Rausch complimented. He had played his role in the conspiracy. But his tone was sincere.

Two days later, the boy's father awoke early to the sound of activity across the alley. Bill O'Brian and his sons were loading gas cans and minnow buckets into a boat that was on a trailer hitched to Bill's pick-up. Their fishing tackle was stored inside the truck's topper. Bill's cigarette glowed in the darkness as he worked. It was still the dead of night when they pulled out.

Ten minutes later, two more rigs, loaded down with fishing gear, rumbled down the alley. The boy's father could see the faces of fishermen inside, Paul Rausch and his sons. The man shook his head; his spirit was deflated. Now that the word was out, his neighbors and their relatives, and *their* friends and *their* relatives, would fish the lake out in two years. He had fallen into their trap, an orchestrated conspiracy, and they had left him no escape.

"All's fair…" he muttered to himself. But it didn't seem neighborly to use children to fool children.

AUTUMN

CHAPTER SIXTEEN

School started on Tuesday morning, the day after Labor Day. St. Joseph's Elementary was bustling with activity. In the hallways the Catholic children of Waite Park, seraphim and cherubim, created a heavenly choir. Each year the first day of school was a day of hope: hope for the children that they would not be bored to tears and hope for the teachers that they would not be utterly frustrated.

The principal, Sister Mary Anthony, stood at the front door welcoming the children back. It was her sixth year at the helm. She greeted those parents who came with the children and assured them that all would be well—that the school was in God's good hands. She noted that the parents of the older students did not come to the door as much. They tended to drive off in a hurry, speeding away to work or to enjoy a few hours of freedom.

This school year was already starting off on the wrong foot, literally. One of the Second Grade teachers, Sister Mary Bede, would be a week late, due to a fall. She had slipped while turning cartwheels on a diving board at a family reunion in July and broken a bone in her left foot. The foot was immobilized in a cast. Sister Mary Anthony had wished her a speedy recovery, by Labor Day if at all possible, but the cumulative prayers of the Franciscans at the convent hadn't worked fast enough.

Mrs. Mabel Kuffeld, a Fourth Grade teacher and one of two lay people on the faculty, knew a cherub from a fallen angel. She would not take Robbie Stein. She threatened to retire. "Lad wants me to quit," she stated flatly when she saw Robbie's name on her class list. "He's been wanting me to retire for two years now. I think it's time."

Sister Anthony knew it was a ploy. "Robbie Stein will be transferred," the principal promised, "to Sister Mary Samuel's Fourth Grade class." Sister Samuel was a young, first-year teacher. She was naïve but would learn quickly. "But the paperwork will take two days. We have to contact his parents first. You could fill in for Sister Bede in Second Grade this week," Sister Anthony proposed hopefully.

Mabel Kuffeld sighed. "I wouldn't feel comfortable in Second Grade," she confided. "I tried it once; they're awfully energetic. Lad thinks I should retire." The principal's hopes were being dashed.

It was at this juncture in the conversation that the elderly schoolmarm brightened. "What about asking Mrs. Willow to teach Second Grade for a week? I could teach her Seventh Grade—until Robbie Stein is transferred."

Sister Anthony, herself, sighed. Her hands were tied. She knew that she would be pressed into service teaching Fourth Grade for a week, and she knew from past experience that even two days in the same room with Robbie Stein would be purgatory—if not a living hell.

Mrs. Winifred Willow greeted the Second Grade children as they entered her room. She was a shapely woman, rather buxom, and the children took notice for they were only used to having nuns teach them. This boisterous woman was not a sister robed in a shapeless black habit with a white bib around her neck and a white headdress with a black veil on her head. Mrs. Willow wore nylon stockings, a girdle with garters, and an oversized brassiere.

Winifred Willow was an English teacher at heart. She loved all facets of English: reading, writing, speaking, grammar, and spelling. "Good morning, children," she greeted them. I have a story to tell you. Instantly the class became silent and attentive. Did any of you go fishing this summer?" In response, most of the students raised a hand. She proceeded with her story. "This is called 'The One That Got Away.'"

"Once upon a time," she began, "there was a young fish who wanted to go fishing. He complained to his mother: 'How come the humans fish us, but we can't fish them? It isn't fair.'

His mother was wise and told him, 'Just stay away from them.' But he did not like her answer, and he was not good at obeying.

The next morning he was swimming, diving up and down in the sky blue water, when lo and behold he found a fishing pole at the bottom of the lake. There was a hook tied to the end of the line. He decided to disobey his mother.

'What can I use for bait?' he wondered. And he asked himself, 'What would a young human boy want most?'

The bottom of the lake was sandy. There, hidden in a patch of weeds, was the answer, a golden starfish. It had died many years earlier, but its brittle cover was still shiny. So, he strung one arm of the starfish onto the hook and tossed the line up onto the shore.

Sure enough, a boy was playing there. He spied the starfish but did not see the line or the hook. And then it moved! The boy stepped closer to inspect it, and it moved again, closer to the water at the edge of the shore. He wanted the starfish, so he picked it up. Its skin was crusted over and hard.

Just then the fish below felt a tug on his line. He jerked the rod to set the hook, and he managed to snag the boy's finger. He reeled frantically to catch the boy.

The boy was caught off guard and off balance. He tumbled into the water, pulled by the line that was tied to the hook caught in his finger. He tried to stand up, but he was being pulled head first into the lake.

Soon, the water covered his body. Below, the fish kept reeling in the line. He saw the boy in the water, an enormous catch. He would have to use the net he had found.

Alas, the boy grabbed a hold of the line and yanked it hard. The fish tried to tug it back, but the rod and reel slipped from his fins. You can't grasp a pole very well if you only have fins." Several boys in the classroom looked at their own hands. They nodded in agreement.

"The boy pulled the line hand over hand, and then he saw the tip of the rod. He pulled it from the water. It was fairly new, much better than the one he had. He yelled with glee. Sure, he was sopping wet and he had a sore finger, but he had a new rod and reel; it was a fair exchange."

At the end of the story, Mrs. Willow laughed, and her whole body shook. Her laughter was joyful and contagious, disarming.

Frankie sat in his chair next to the windows and contemplated. He liked the story because it was different and creative, and he liked Mrs. Willow because she was natural and happy. Across the room his nemesis, Susanne Danbury, was wrinkling her nose. She wasn't sure that she approved of the story. She would reserve judgment on Mrs. Winifred Willow until the end of the week.

Next, Mrs. Willow opened up her Seventh Grade lesson plan for that day. "Now I'm going to read the class a poem," she announced, "just the first stanza." It's titled *A Book*. It's by a woman named Emily Dickinson, who lived a long time ago.

There is no frigate like a book
To take us lands away,
Nor any coursers like a page
Of prancing poetry.

It had a beat when she read it. "Hear the rhythm? A poem doesn't have to rhyme," she instructed. "But it has to have a rhythm." The teacher wrote the two words on the blackboard in big printed letters. She explained the difference.

Without meaning to, she digressed. "There's a poet named e. e. cummings, who I just can't stand. His capitalization and punctuation are atrocious, and so is his spelling. Hearing this, the Second Grade children felt an immediate dislike for this off-beat poet.

"What's a frigate?" asked Terry Joe, who also was sitting by the windows just in front of his best friend.

"It's a ship," she answered. Emily Dickinson lived before airplanes were invented. You had to travel on a frigate to go across the ocean. But a book is better because it can take you anywhere in the world—even back in time!" The children paused to consider this marvel. "A book lets you use your imagination."

"What are coursers?" was Terry Joe's second question.

"They're horses that prance to a certain rhythm." You can ride away on them to distant lands. Remember, rhythm is the beat; rhyming is when words at the end of two lines have the same vowel sound: a, e, i, o, u. The children, mystified by the explanation, stared at the teacher. Perhaps when they reached Seventh Grade, it would all become clear.

"Emily Dickinson was a woman who never traveled. She only read books."

"Did e. e. cummings ever travel?" asked Terry Joe.

"I'm sure he did" was Mrs. Willow's curt reply.

It was time to give an assignment. I want you to write a short poem for tomorrow," the teacher stated.

"But we don't know how to write," protested Susanne Danbury, "only print." She could be a stickler.

"Well, amen! So be it. Print it then." Mrs. Willow amended her instructions with another chuckle. "'We'll read them out loud," she added.

Now Susanne Danbury's eyes brightened. She liked showing off. All of the boys, however, except John Lewis in his orange bow tie, gulped. They did not feel comfortable reading in front of the class, especially reading their own work. Their minds were busy searching for a way out of this unexpected predicament.

Mrs. Willow shifted gears. "This year in the spring you will be making your First Holy Communion. It will be on Easter Sunday! But before you can receive your First Holy Communion, you have to make your First Confession. You have to have a clean soul to receive the body and blood of Christ. You will have to tell your sins to Father Schumacher or Father Thiel in the confessional. The priest will listen and absolve you of them. Your sins will disappear, and you will have a clean soul, filled with grace. Father Schumacher will be here tomorrow to explain. He'll be teaching you religion on Wednesdays.

Near the windows Frankie was daydreaming, thinking about those three little rooms at the back of the church. He had opened the door of one once and peeked inside, but it had been dark and he could see nothing. He had thought about the air inside. It must be full of sins others had confessed, so he had closed the door quickly, lest they float out the door and escape into the church's nave. He had felt guilty for snooping. Already he was forming a conscience. Perhaps it was true what his mother had told him: he had reached the age of reason.

The next morning the school day began, as it always did, with the class standing and reciting the Pledge of Allegiance to the Flag. After that, the students plopped back down into their desks. Immediately Mrs. Willow clapped her hands together and announced, "It's time to read our poems." She was obviously excited.

The girls had centered theirs on top of their desks; the boys had hidden theirs in their tablets. "Who's first?" Mrs. Willow asked. Her gaze settled on the freckled, red-haired tomboy in the front row. "Come to the front please when you read."

Abigail Hoganson stepped to the front of the room and turned. Her eyes were puffy.

> I had a brother.
> I miss him at night.
> He killed himself
> With dynamite.

Utter silence followed. The air thickened. "That's very good, Abigail, very heartfelt," the teacher noted. Frankie could see that Abigail was crying. His heart ached for her.

Mrs. Willow quickly shifted her gaze to a boy by the windows. "Terrance O'Brian," she blurted. "Come forward and read your poem." Terry Joe drifted to the front of the room.

> I shot an arrow
> Into the air.
> It fell to Earth;
> I do know where.
>
> I flung my spear;
> It hit a tree.
> My dad took it
> Away from me.

The teacher let the poem pass without comment or critique. It spoke for itself.

John Lewis, the good-looking boy in the orange bow tie, glided forward. The girls in his path, Mary Ambrose and Gail Teigen, giggled.

Cockle Doodle Do
Go the Roosters.

Buc Buc Buc
Go the Hens

Cheep Cheep Cheep
Go the Chicks

Every Day
And All Night Long.

"Thank you, John. Chickens make a constant clatter" was Mrs. Willow's assessment.

"Yes, ma'am," he replied. "That's all they do is chatter and eat."

"And poop," blurted Gail Teigen. This observation drew a chorus of laughs, but not, the boy noticed, from Susanne Danbury. Mouth open, feigning shock, she was aghast at this callous, uncouth remark. The teacher, however, remained smiling.

"Jean Kovar, it's your turn." The pretty, dark-haired girl waltzed to the front of the room. The other children envied her confidence.

She sings so sweetly
Soft and low.
Her voice is tender,
Her eyes aglow.

The men stare up.
They listen to her.
They cannot stop
Their beating hearts.

Frankie noted that Jean Kovar's voice was low and husky, like the singer in her poem. She was more mature than her friends. But the poem was about love, so he ignored it.

The teacher called on Jerry Unger. He was a large, gangly boy, somewhat awkward as he lumbered to the front of the room.

My Dad, the Engineer

My dad was an engineer
On the Great Northern's trains.

He crossed the prairies;
He crossed the plains.

He drove up a mountain;
He drove it back down.

It whistled in the valleys
And stopped in the towns.

"You're obviously proud of your Dad," noted Mrs. Willow.

"His name's Walter," replied the boy. Unger is German. He's retired. Now he fixes bikes."

"All work is honorable," quoted the teacher. "Fixing bicycles has merit, too."

"Not to my dad," stated Jerry. "He still wishes he was a train engineer." His voice contained a sadness that filtered through the room.

Mrs. Willow scanned the class, and her gaze settled on a slight girl with dishwater blond hair and a dirty face. She noted a greasy paper on top of the girl's desk, not the standard 8½ by 11 piece of tablet paper, but a smaller sheet of yellow stationery. "Lucy Stephens, how about you?"

The girl meandered forward, clasping her sheet of paper.

He sits in a tree
Just waiting for me.
I climb the limbs
To be with him.

Mrs. Willow complimented her. "That's very good, Lucy. The tone sounds genuine. I like that. Who else has a poem to read?"

Several boys raised their hands. Curiously, each had heard a limerick and decided to write one. Jimmy Holston jumped up. He prefaced his reading with an explanation. "Limericks are Irish poems. My dad told me one, but he made me promise not to say it in public or at school. Here's mine."

> There once was a man on the street
> Whose life just wasn't so sweet.
> He said to his wife as she toyed with a knife,
> "Cut me off a hunk of that meat."

"We're Irish," proclaimed Terry Joe O'Brian. "That poem sounds like the ones my Uncle Squeak tells."

"It's a limerick," instructed the teacher. "It's a poem with a certain style of rhythm, a certain beat. It also has a patterned rhyme." Her pupils were lost again.

"I want to hear some more of those," said Terry Joe. His wish was soon granted.

"Who else has a limerick?" asked Mrs. Willow. A handful of boys marched forward in succession. Most of their poems were about a man from somewhere who there once was.

"I have one, but it's not a limerick," spoke a boy with a soft voice.

"Who are you, young man?" asked Mrs. Willow politely.

"Jonas Duane."

"Well, Mr. Jonas Duane, come forward and read us your poem."

"It's a parody. That's what my mother calls it." He was a sensitive boy, not eager to read out loud in front of his classmates, especially in front of the girls. Yet, somehow they found his shy nature attractive and inviting.

"Read it, Jonas," said Irene Pressler. "We won't laugh."

> There is no book like a frigate
> To take us far away;
> Nor any prancing poetry
> Like coursers eating hay.

The girls did laugh. Jonas's cheeks flushed, and his ears turned red.

"That's just an imitation of Emily Dickinson's poem from yesterday," stated Gail Teigen. Her assessment sounded harsh and disappointed.

"Leave him be," came a voice from the back of the room. Lucy Stephens was standing. "Just leave him be."

Soon, there were only two students who hadn't read, Susanne Danbury and Frankie. Mrs. Willow settled on Susanne. "Please step forward and read your poem, Susanne." The girl rose from her desk and skipped to the front of the room, her large head bobbing in anticipation. Her eyes were bright. In her hands she clasped a folded sheet of paper.

She turned and addressed the teacher. "This is a parody, too." She waved the paper in front of her. "My sister, Mary Ellen, had you last year in Seventh Grade. She said that you like Joyce Kilmer.

"Who's she?" blurted Terry Joe.

Susanne turned abruptly to face the questioner. "Joyce Kilmer was a man!" she snapped. Mrs. Willow rocked back in her chair, somewhat amused.

The girl continued. "He was born Alfred Joyce Kilmer in 1886, and he was killed by a sniper's bullet in 1918 at the end of World War I. He was only thirty-one. Winifred Willow stopped rocking and leaned forward, sincerely impressed. Obviously, the girl had done her research.

At the back of the room, Jerry Unger shook his head in disgust. "She wants brownie points," he muttered to no one in particular.

Susanne Danbury turned back to her primary audience, her teacher. The young girl continued. My sister told me that you met Joyce Kilmer once. But that was a long time ago."

The girls in the class snickered. "Oh, not that long ago," Susanne corrected herself nervously. Mrs. Willow sat bolt upright and bit her bottom lip to keep her composure.

"I did meet him when I was a little girl," she confirmed. She had no reason to feel flustered. In fact, she was proud to have met him, a real war hero. "Read your poem, your parody, Susanne. I'll bet I know which poem you imitated. It's his most famous one."

"The poem I imitated is called *Trees*. Mine is called *Bees*. As she read, she tried to make her voice sound expressive, even dramatic.

I think that I shall never see
A poem lovely as a bee.

A bee whose honey mouth is prest
Against the Earth's sweet flowering breast.

A bee that looks at God all day
And flaps her buzzing wings to pray.

A bee that may in summer sting
A flock of blue jays as they wing.

Upon whose abdomen sleet has fallen
Who ultimately transfers pollen

Poems are made by fools like thee,
But only God can make a bee.

A hush fell over the Second Graders; they did not know how to respond. The poem sounded silly, but they dared not criticize it. Susanne was an intelligent girl who was easily hurt—and angered—if someone showed disapproval or a lack of understanding. They would keep silent and follow Mrs. Willow's lead.

"Joyce Kilmer was a Catholic poet," Mrs. Willow stated. "He saw God's handiwork in the beauty of nature, whether it was a tree or a bee."

"Who's the fool?" asked Terry Joe, tempting fate.

"You are!" replied Susanne. "Anyone who can't make a bee." Terry Joe shrugged. She was still her annoying self. She walked to her seat, her large head still bobbing.

The teacher looked at her watch. "I think we have time before recess for one more, the last one. She motioned to the young boy, Frankie, sitting by the windows. He was not at all sure that there was enough time. He was squinting at the clock on the wall when his adversary spoke up.

The girl with the large head spoke sarcastically. "He doesn't like to read because he can't read very well. He doesn't want to try."

"That's enough, Susanne!" The teacher asserted her authority. "Don't gloat; it's not lady-like." But the damage was done, intentionally inflicted. She had goaded him, and his temper flared. How dare she criticize him! He would show her just how expressive he could be.

He trudged to the front of the room, turned to the class, and paused. When he had their undivided attention, he spoke. "My poem is about fishing. We went with my Uncle Charley and Aunt Lucille and our cousins to Pickeral Lake last week. That's by Detroit Lakes in northern Minnesota. It was our first vacation ever! My foot fell through the ceiling. And my Uncle Charley threw Dad's big walleye over the motor, and the line broke. And we caught two coolers full of sunfish! He glowered at the girl with the bright eyes. She was staring at him, her face flushed with mirth.

Sunfish

Kerplup
Nibble nibble…
Kerplup
Nibble nibble…
Gulp!

Zing zing
Zig zag zig zag…
Tug tug
Twist turn twist turn…
Whee!

Leap up
Wriggle Wriggle…
Leap up
Spin spin… spit!
Splash!

Dive down
Bubble bubble…
Look look
Nibble nibble…
Kerplup!

He had never heard his voice so vibrant, so full of action. He pretended to be the haughty little fish, who is unafraid of the hook in his mouth—and only exerts himself wildly to be free. Then, when the danger has passed, he once again becomes curious, fascinated by the tantalizing bait on the hook. For him, it's a game he plays.

The boy finished and took his seat. He was trembling, still mad at his tormentor with her big mouth in her big head. Yet, for some unknown reason he felt elated with how he had read his poem.

"That was an impressive interpretation, young man!" The teacher praised him, and coming from Mrs. Willow, it felt good.

The Reverend Cornelius J. Schumacher, O.S.F. was a prayerful man. If he had had his druthers, he would have preferred a life of solitude, kneeling before the Lord, his God, in private conversation with his maker. Unfortunately, however, as a parish priest and the pastor of St. Joseph's Catholic Church in Waite Park, he had other administrative responsibilities.

He now stood in front of Mrs. Willow's Second Graders with one overriding concern: he needed more altar boys to serve at mass, especially at the 6:30 a.m. daily mass.

The good priest had not anticipated this year's exodus. The most recent crop had stayed faithful into August, until after the annual altar boy picnic at Pearl Lake.

The day was fun-filled: grilling hot dogs and hamburgers and drinking pop, swimming and diving off a raft and waterskiing, playing softball between the trees. In the evening they consumed ice cream and roasted marshmallows over a crackling fire that blazed in the woods. Their faces and naked chests were illuminated by the flickering flames. Away from the fire in the shadows, boys conversed and told stories.

It was a day of reward for a year of service. Both parish priests relished the day. It was a day when they, too, could be boys, free from the daily routine. Father Thiel pitched softball; Father Schumacher drove the speedboat. The picnic was the carrot on a stick in front of the donkey's nose. As long as the picnic was in sight, the altar boys plodded along, licking their lips in anticipation.

Of course, once they caught the carrot and ate it, the pastor's hold on them was gone. Several boys had quit the day after the picnic. The Davies twins, Derwood and Delbert, had quit after serving Sunday mass, no less. Father shook his head. They hadn't even had the decency to wait until Monday morning. They gave no notice. Neither of them would be at Monday morning mass, ever again. The two brothers had decided that, on balance, sleeping in before school was preferable to rising in the middle of the night. It was better to quit now when the weather was warm. In the darkness of winter, it would be worse.

It happened every year, just not to this extent. Father Schumacher could not recall a year when so many boys had abandoned ship. It had become an epidemic. Perhaps his hold on the parish families was slipping. He needed to recruit new blood and do so quickly.

The priest had a practiced eye for likely candidates. He searched the fresh faces before him. Some of the boys had older brothers who had served at mass, like the O'Brian boy. He suspected that this specimen was sleepy like his brothers and lacked staying power.

"You are all God's children," spoke the Reverend Father. "And you need to listen to God's call. He needs you to serve him by serving his church. One way to be a good Catholic is to serve at mass. You will be close to the altar and closer to God. For your service he will give you grace, and that will help you get to heaven.

He raised his voice to effect compliance. "Who wants to be an altar boy?" It sounded like a cheer or a call to arms.

Several hands shot up, followed by more hands. They included the O'Brian boy's hand and that of the boy behind him.

"Come to the church at 8:00 o'clock in the morning on Friday for practice. Holy mass will be at 8:30 for the school children. It's First Friday. Come to the sacristy through the back door."

That night Frankie looked at his homework. He was puzzled. Father Schumacher had told them to memorize a specific passage of praise spoken during mass. It began: "Per Ipsum, et cum Ipso, et in Ipso... Through Him and with Him and in Him…" He stared at the page in his missal. The prayer was written twice, in Latin and in English, side by side. He did not remember which one the priest had specified. Masses were in Latin. He decided to memorize the Latin; it was safer.

CHAPTER SEVENTEEN

The recruits knew that something was terribly amiss when they saw Robbie Stein in the sacristy, dressed in a black cassock and white surplice. Father Schumacher had made a mistake. He had been overzealous in recruiting new altar boys to make up for the shortage. Father's description of the picnic's pleasures had been too convincing, too alluring. It had enticed Robbie to "come see for himself." On top of that, Father was late.

Robbie Stein's angelic face was scrubbed clean, and his hair was slicked back, the perfect disguise for what lay underneath. He primped in front of the mirror, admiring himself. "Let's get this show on the road," he suggested. "Where is he?" He inspected father's closet. The vestments were hanging on coat hangers, clean and pressed: green, red, purple, white, and gold. "How would I look in this?" the boy asked, grinning. He held up the purple vestment Father wore on Good Friday.

"It's too long," answered Terry Joe.

"Well, then I'll cut it off," the older boy retorted. His right hand disappeared underneath his gown, and from his pocket he withdrew his switchblade and flicked it open. He laughed at his own daring.

Then he snooped in the cupboards. There he spied the hosts. The circular wafers lay in a box on the bottom shelf, unconsecrated. "Yum, bread!" He extracted a handful and munched on them.

"Hey, these taste like shit," he complained. "They don't have any taste at all." He seemed genuinely disappointed.

"Hey, twerp," he addressed his young neighbor, "where do they keep the wine?"

All eyes shifted to the cupboard beneath the counter. "In there," said the boy. He pointed at the door. "But it's locked."

"Where's the key?" asked Robbie, seriously interested.

"I don't know," said the boy. "Father has it."

Robbie's instincts told him otherwise. "It's hiding in here. Let's find it, twerp."

But the younger boy stood rigid. Despite his fear of retaliation, he said nothing.

Robbie Stein peeked out into the church. Beyond the sanctuary the pews were filling up with school children as the classes were escorted over. Mass would begin soon. The candles on the altar were burning.

Robbie's decision jelled quickly. He was too much of a non-conformist. This setting was not for him. But he would not simply slip out the back door; he would make a glorious exit. Just as Father Schumacher was climbing the back stairs to the sacristy, Robbie Stein appeared in the sanctuary, grinning. He was on stage, and he had the stage to himself. The lights were bright, spotlighted on him. It was the moment all actors dream of; he had center stage and everyone's attention.

He glided over the polished marble floor in front of the altar and disrobed. He took off the white surplice and dropped it to the floor. Then he unbuttoned the black cassock, held it up in the light, and dropped it with dramatic effect. He spread his arms wide and raised his face upward. His audience in the pews was spellbound. He felt an actor's delight as he manipulated the scene. His grin broadened. He was indeed an angel—if not a god! This was his moment of triumph. Far away in the back pew, it crossed Mrs. Willow's mind that the poet who wrote *Paradise Lost*, John Milton himself, could not have scripted it any better.

At the peak of his performance, Robbie saw something in the front pew moving. It was the diminutive figure of Sister Agatha in black. Instantly his feelings mixed inside him—fear of her hostility toward him and of her sharp Indian ways, but also anger that she felt no fear of him. She had shamed him once. Now he would stand up to her and defy her.

Sister chose the direct path through the center opening in the communion rail. The gates were open. Robbie Stein was perched on the altar steps above her. Other nuns used their belt, a white cord with knots, as a disciplinary tool. Sister Agatha was swinging her rosary. She swung it round and round in circles, much like David must have swung his sling shot at Goliath. The crucifix at the end of the rosary's chain was metal and heavy. *Thud*! It hit Robbie under the chin—squarely. It drew blood.

"Ow!" he cried, as the crucifix struck again. That morning Robbie learned two new words from Sister Mary Agatha, one in English, one in Ojibwe—sacrilege and maji-maridoo (devil). "You can't fight Jesus and win," she wailed. "Hay' angwaakizo. (You will go to hell, where you will burn completely.) Glory be to God!"

The principal, Sister Mary Anthony, stepped forward. She looked undecided whether or not she should rescue Robbie from Sister Agatha. She led him to the back of the church and sat him in a confessional.

"That bitch hit me," he complained. He rubbed his chin. "I'm telling my dad," he warned.

"Father Thiel has already called him," Sister replied. "He's on his way over."

"No!" Robbie gasped. "Keep him away from here."

Sister fought to suppress a chuckle. She looked deeply concerned. "Think about where you are, Robbie."

"In the church," he replied, somewhat puzzled. Suddenly his face brightened. "Hey, I can have protection in the sanctuary. Dad can't get me there." He leaped to his feet.

"Sit down, Robbie," said Sister. He sat. "I mean think of this little room you are in now. Do you know what this is—what happens here? It's a confessional where you confess your sins and are forgiven."

"Okay, I'll hide in here," he stated.

"Think about it for a few minutes." She shut the door. Mass was starting. Father Schumacher, bedecked in a red vestment, had entered the sanctuary and climbed the steps to the altar.

It was dark in the confessional and curiously silent. Robbie heard Sister lock the door. He tried to open the door latch, to no avail. He felt the door and its casing. They were made of thick timbers. He banged on them. "Let me out! Let—me—out!" he rasped. He couldn't breathe. In the cavity of the church's nave, the congregation could hear his screams of belligerence turn into terror.

Holy mass stopped. Father Schumacher turned and nodded. Sister Anthony let out a big sigh and unlocked the door. It swung open, and Robbie Stein bolted out the front door of the church and raced into the street. He could breathe again. His dad found him two hours later at Pinor's, shooting pool.

Sister Mary Bede returned to work Monday morning. Her foot, still in a cast, was a curiosity piece. Pulling her habit up to her knees, she let the children sign the cast with an ink pen. Her toenails were painted red, and the girls wondered openly if this was a common practice among the Franciscans. They doubted it. Sister just smiled.

The discussion turned to health and medicine. Sister Bede had a scientific bent, more so than Mrs. Willow had. She did not care a lick for poetry.

"How long will you have your foot in a cast?" asked Terry Joe.

"Two more weeks," she replied.

"How did it happen?" questioned Gail Teigen.

"I was goofing off on a diving board at my parents' lake cabin. I used to be a gymnast in college, but I guess I'm too old for that now. I'm no spring chicken any more."

"How old are you?" asked Irene Pressler.

"Twenty-three," Sister revealed. The children nodded. She was old.

"How many of you have ever had a cast?" asked Sister.

One hand shot up. "I broke my arm, my ulna, in two places, here and here, riding my bike," said Terry Joe, "last spring." I rode down a hill in Mrs. Beebehauser's alley and hit a car in the door.

His explanation brought back painful memories and a feeling of guilt to Frankie. It could easily have been his ulna that was broken if he hadn't insisted that his best friend go first. But Terry Joe was grinning from ear to ear. He wore his war wound proudly.

Attention shifted to an average-looking boy in the middle desk of the middle row. Sister Bede stared at him. Soon, he felt the need to speak. "I've never had a cast," said Curtis Benton, but I've had crutches. Sister Bede looked at the boy's legs and shuddered. One was missing below the knee, replaced by an artificial limb.

"I'm so sorry," Sister apologized.

"Don't be, Sister," said Curtis, trying to comfort the woman. "I lost it jumping onto a train into a boxcar. But my foot slipped."

The room fell silent, so Curtis kept explaining. "I tried to hold on, but I fell under the wheels. Dad says, 'Don't let it get you down.' I can't run very fast, but I can still do everything." He set his lip in a determined pose. Undaunted, Sister walked over to him and patted him on the shoulder. Then she returned to the front of the classroom.

"Who's been sick?" asked Sister, turning the discussion. Everyone raised a hand. Frankie thought of his chicken pox, untimely contracted, that had prevented him from going on the school picnic.

The class discussion turned lively. Everyone had had the flu and diarrhea. Most had had the measles or the mumps or both. Some had had whooping cough, including Frankie. For these Second Graders the rarer the disease, the better. It would impress Sister Bede and give them bragging rights. Jimmy Holston had had a tapeworm once. Ricky Shenker had had a fungus on his athlete's foot.

"I get a bad cold every year," declared Susanne Danbury. "My Mom says I have allergies. My eyes water and I sneeze a lot."

Sister Bede had an idea. "I want each of you to write a report on a disease. You can bring it to class on Friday, and we'll share them."

"Do we have to read them to the class?" asked Jimmy Holston. His voice did not sound hopeful.

"Of course, you do," replied Sister Bede. "One page is long enough. Don't print too big," she admonished. She was experienced enough to know their tactics. She cut them off at the pass. "Write at least ten sentences." The boys slumped in their chairs; it was going to be a long year.

By mid-afternoon the class had studied a wide array of subjects. In Arithmetic, Sister demonstrated the commutative property of addition by adding two quarters to five dimes and then re-adding five dimes to two quarters. A brush up on subtraction would have to wait until the second semester. Multiplication would be introduced to them in Third Grade; and division, known to the school's children as *goes intas*, would be introduced in whatever year that teacher saw fit. In Geography, Sister Bede told them about her home town in Acapulco, Mexico. Yes, she had been born there. "No, Terry Joe, Mexico is not a United State west of California; it's a foreign country." That explained her suntan that refused to go away, even after Christmas. In Religion, Sister read them a story from the Bible about Jonah living inside the belly of a whale. "How could he breathe under water?" the children wondered. "Wouldn't he have been crushed by all that blubber? Wouldn't he have been choked by the whale's stomach muscles and intestines? Or wouldn't he have been dissolved in the whale's digestive juices? That's acid, you know."

"The Lord God was protecting him" was Sister's cryptic answer. "God can work any miracle he wants. And he wanted Jonah to stay alive."

When the recess bell rang, they went outside. The boys forgot about Jonah and played kickball; the girls climbed the monkey bars or sat on the swings and gabbed. Gossip was an art; it had to be learned early on and cultivated through practice.

Refreshed, the children returned to the classroom. Before eating lunch, they had Music. They sang songs. Frankie particularly liked "The Happy Wanderer." Sitting by the window, he forgot his shyness and sang robustly. *Valdereeeee… valderahhhhh… Valdereeeee… valderah ha ha ha ha ha ha… Valdereeeee… valderahhhhh… Come join my happy song*! He tempered his volume only when out of the corner of his eye he spotted Susanne Danbury and her big head smiling at him. He scowled back at her.

After lunch the afternoon started with Art class. The boys and girls colored a picture of Leonardo da Vinci's *The Last Supper*. "These are the Twelve Apostles," Sister explained. They are Jesus's friends, except for one—Judas Iscariot. He will betray Jesus with a kiss. Can you pick him out?" The children stared at Judas.

"Why would he kiss another man?" Jerry Unger wondered out loud to himself. All of the boys were thinking the same thing.

"Jesus is breaking bread with them and consecrating it and the wine. It's now his own body and blood. He tells them to eat it. We do the same thing at mass. Father is like Jesus. This year in the spring, you will make your First Holy Communion when you eat Jesus's body. At the altar the priest will also drink his blood."

Susanne Danbury in the front desk was looking a little peaked. "Does it taste like blood?" she asked quietly, somewhat disturbed.

"No," Sister responded, "but it really is his blood."

"It's time for English." Sister's voice broke the silence. For English, they had penmanship. They traced letters, and she stretched their brains by showing them the letters A, B, and C, capital and small, in cursive. "Writing neatly is next to cleanliness, and cleanliness is next to Godliness," she declared. There was a hint of warning in her words.

Without any warning, the principal, Sister Mary Anthony, appeared in the doorway. Her face looked stern. She did not enter the room. "Russell Stein, Terrance O'Brian, and Frank Kucher, come with me." She motioned to them, wiggling her index finger inward. "Now!" she commanded.

Frankie jumped when his name was called. He did not expect it. The three boys slid from their desks and exited into the hallway. She glowered down upon them as they stepped across her path. The boy wondered why his name had been called. He suspected nothing, but he was worried. He followed Russell Stein and Terry Joe down the hallway toward the principal's office. Behind him Sister Anthony's heavy black shoes pounded on the wooden floor. Their clattering sounded ominous. Each footstep made him more and more nervous.

They entered her office, by-passing the secretary's desk. Mrs. Virginia Schwartz looked up, but she refused to smile. Trouble was brewing; it hung in the air.

Frankie had never been in the principal's office. A large picture of Jesus and his sacred heart hung behind her desk. "Sit down," Sister Anthony ordered. She looked at Russell Stein. Her interrogation began. "You're Robbie Stein's brother, aren't you?" she asked.

"Yes, Sister," came the reply. The boy did not sound nearly as brash and troublesome as his wayward brother.

"And you are Timothy O'Brian's brother?" She looked at Terry Joe questioningly. The boy nodded his head.

"Yes, Sister." He, too, seemed more reasonable and more likeable than his older brother.

"And you." She turned her attention to the blond boy in the third chair. His heart skipped a beat. "You're the boy who collects bullfrogs." The boy blinked hard and nodded. She did not see him gulping in air or his pulse quickening. She did, however, observe him squinting awkwardly into the lights above him.

"You have been bad boys," Sister stated flatly. I received calls from three mothers last Friday. They told me that you like to hide behind a bush and then jump out and scare the First

Grade girls. Their daughters came home crying and are afraid to go to school. Is this true?" Her tone of voice was matter-of-fact, as if she already knew the answer. Frankie looked down at the floor in front of him.

Her accusation was true. It could not be refuted. The boys had had great fun the previous week, preying upon the young girls, scaring them, sending them home on the run. They had laughed excitedly at their boldness and at their power. Now it was all crashing down. The boy's frazzled nerves were making him shiver. His hands were shaking. He stared hard at his shoes.

Sister's voice hardened. "I will not condone intimidation— of any kind!" She spoke sternly, without compassion. It was obvious that she meant business.

"What bush?" asked Terry Joe. It was a feeble attempt to put her off track.

Sister Anthony smiled wickedly. "Don't try that ploy on me, mister. You know what bush—the one Father Thiel planted in the front yard of the convent by the sidewalk, the one big enough for three witless boys to hide behind, boys that like to frighten little girls."

"What's intimidation?" asked Terry Joe innocently.

"Scaring people!" came the reply. "You will cease and desist that activity from this moment on—Or Else!"

Immediately Frankie was reminded of the sign in Rocky's Shoe Shop's window. None of the three boys dared ask "Or Else What?" The boy who collected frogs began to sniffle. He was on the verge of tears. The nun relaxed. She offered him a tissue from the box on her desk. The other two boys were trying to remain stoic.

Sister did not smile, but her voice once again became matter-of-fact. "Gentlemen do not frighten young girls. Do you gentlemen have any questions?" For ten seconds the boys were silent.

"Anything?" asked Terry Joe. His voice sounded inquisitive and sincere.

Sister hesitated. "Anything… within reason."

"Do you have hair?"

Her answer surprised them. Without a word, she removed her veil and headdress. Bright red locks of hair were pinned to her scalp with the bulk rolled neatly into a bun at the back.

"That's a pretty red," said Terry Joe.

"Thank you, Terrance. I'm Irish, like you." The boy blushed. "Franciscans have pretty hair." Sister was not afraid to show her vanity. "I went to school with your mother, Lorraine Sullivan. My name was McManus, Shannon McManus." She put the headdress and veil back in place on her head.

Terry Joe raised his hand. Sister nodded that he had permission to speak.

"Do you wear clothes under there?" he asked sheepishly.

It was Sister's turn to remain stoic. "No, of course not," she answered. "That would be too hot."

"Are you wearing underwear?" came the next question out of the blue.

Instantly Sister tensed. She felt the heaviness of Catholic virtue on her shoulders. It was not a question a gentleman would ask. But a curious young boy might. "Yes, of course I am," she volunteered. "That would be too cold." She stood up. The audience was at its end. "It's time for you to go back to your classroom. Sister Bede will be worried." She picked up the receiver of the telephone with one hand and a sheet of paper with the other. "I have to call these mothers. Now scoot!"

CHAPTER EIGHTEEN

On Friday the Second Grade children assembled as usual. Sister Mary Bede was busy taking attendance and verifying the lunch count. When the bell rang, they all stood and recited the Pledge of Allegiance to the Flag. Then they sat down. It was a routine that never varied.

Sister was about to present the day's arithmetic lesson on adding two two-digit numbers when she noticed something out of the ordinary: Terry Joe O'Brian had raised his hand. "Yes?" she inquired.

"Sister, how come you nuns all have men's names?" It was an unusual question that no one had ever asked her.

She paused briefly to reflect. "Well, the apostles were all men. It's an honor to have one of their names. We still call ourselves Sister Mary to keep our femininity, our girlishness."

"But Bede wasn't an apostle," countered the boy. Was he a she?"

"No, he was a man," corrected Sister. He lived in the 7th Century AD. That's over six hundred years after Jesus.

"Why did you pick his name?" asked Irene Pressler.

Sister hemmed and hawed briefly. "I didn't actually pick it," she stated.

"You mean somebody picked it for you?" asked Gail Teigen in disbelief.

"Yes," Sister replied. One vow we nuns take is to be obedient. Letting the Mother Superior give us our name—and accepting it—is a way to practice obedience."

Mary Ambrose spoke up to challenge this assertion. "What about Sister Carmita and Sister Carmela? They have women's names." The class quickly broke into chaotic discussion of this fact.

"Let's be quiet please," Sister reminded them. "Only one person should be speaking at a time. The rest of you need to listen. That works best." She considered her response carefully. "Times are changing. Some of the younger nuns have been allowed to request their names. It's more prevalent now. It helps with recruitment and retention."

The faces in front of her looked puzzled. She clarified her point. "More young women will join the convent and stay nuns if they have more say."

"You mean they don't want to obey?" asked Gail Teigen.

"Not without some say," Sister admitted. She was being uncommonly truthful, but that was the way she was. Most other nuns tended to hide behind the order's rules and traditions. In the convent strict secrecy was a way of life. Authority was from the top down.

The girl wearing a flannel shirt tucked into her skirt spoke up. "Why didn't you ask to pick your own name?" asked Abigail Hoganson. She had said very little to anyone since the death of her brother.

Sister spoke to her. "Because I like Bede; I like the man he was. He was a historian and I love history. He wrote a book called *Caedmon's Song* about a poor man who worked in the stables. Caedmon did not like speaking in public because he stuttered badly, but he could translate Biblical passages that he saw in his dreams. He played a harp and sang the translations clearly, without stuttering. He sang them to Hilda, the Abbess of Whitby Abbey, where he lived. She was a nun who became a saint. Bede was a Father of the Church. In the history books he's called *venerable*; that means *holy*. I want to keep his name."

"I wouldn't," said Gail Teigen. "I would want a woman's name. But it doesn't matter because I'm going to get married when I grow up."

Sister looked at the clock on the wall. "It's time to read our science reports," she said. "Do I have any volunteers?"

There were three. Three boys had decided that it was better to read their reports first and get them out of the way. They would have to sweat it out if they waited. All three reports were about poison ivy. You caught it in the woods when you crawled through the brush, usually while hunting squirrels. You could also catch it if you fell from a tree.

"Does anyone have anything else?" asked Sister, "something that doesn't itch?"

Her eyes settled on a boy near the window. "What disease do you have?"

"Diphtheria," he answered.

"That's good," stated Sister. He interpreted her subsequent silence to mean that he should stand up and read his report. Frankie trudged to the front of the room.

"1848 – War!" His voice resonated dramatically, like he had practiced. His father had told him that all reports needed a good attention-getter. "Revolution erupts inside the Austrian Empire!" He made it sound urgent, like a news reel special report.

"In 1852 a Bohemian family, Joseph and Anna Kucera and twelve of their thirteen children, left Plzen, Bohemia (That's in western Czechoslovakia.) for America. Plzen is where they make beer.

In 1852 the Kucera family boarded a ship for a four-month voyage across the Atlantic Ocean. They were escaping from war-torn Eastern Europe, searching for a new homeland. They left their oldest boy behind. George Kucera stood on the pier, waving up at the ship's lower deck. His mother waved back, a tearful goodbye to her firstborn son. She knew she would never see him again. George did not die of diphtheria.

During that four-month voyage tragedy struck. Diphtheria broke out on board.

Otto Kucera died of diphtheria and was buried at sea.
Ludwig Kucera died of diphtheria and was buried at sea.
Adolf Kucera died of diphtheria and was buried at sea.
Rudolf Kucera died of diphtheria and was buried at sea.
Hans Kucera, a twin, died of diphtheria and was buried at sea.
Franz Kucera, the other twin, died of diphtheria and was buried at sea.
Johann Kucera died of diphtheria and was buried at sea.
Martin Kucera died of diphtheria and was buried at sea.
Wolfgang Kucera died of diphtheria and was buried at sea.

How their mother must have cried herself to sleep! The father, mother, one little boy and two little girls survived. They disembarked at Ellis Island in New York and changed their name to Kucher. After that they made their way west to St. Nazianz, Wisconsin. There they farmed the land.

In 1853 my dad's grandfather, Joseph Kucher, was born. He did not die of diphtheria. He was hit by a train in broad daylight and killed. This is my report on diphtheria."

Sister Bede asked the following question as tactfully as she could. "Did your father help you with your report?"

"A little," the boy admitted.

"Did you explain anything about diphtheria itself? How the disease works?"

The boy looked at her oddly. "Yes, Sister. You die from it."

The school day ended without further fanfare. The children scampered home. Tonight was the school carnival. They anticipated fun and games galore.

Frankie walked back to school with his best friend, Terry Joe O'Brian. The O'Brians did not have as much spending money lying around as his family did. Bill O'Brian worked at Franklin Refrigeration; he received an hourly wage. Once in the O'Brian back yard, the boys had quarreled over their parents' earnings. Mr. O'Brian happened to be in the yard. The boy from across the alley bragged. "Well, my father sells investments. He makes over 80,000 dollars a day!" This sounded so definitive that it ended the argument. Bill O'Brian listened and then stomped into his house.

The carnival was held in the gymnasium-auditorium-lunchroom. It was a room full of color, decorated by the moms and dads in the Parent-Teacher Organization. Red, white and blue streamers, purchased at a discount from Walter Unger, hung from the ceiling. Balloons, filled with helium and tethered to weights on the tables, floated upward. Chips and pop were available for a nickel each. Games were set up and run by the parents. To play the games required a ticket, purchased from Tillie Kuchenmeister at a table just inside the front door—ten cents a ticket, twelve for a dollar.

The fish pond was a favorite activity of the little tykes. It cost two tickets. The children would swing a long cane pole with a basket tied to the end of the line over a backdrop "into the lake." Soon, there would be a tug on the line, and the fisherman would lift the basket out of the water and over the backdrop "into the boat." In it there was always a prize. The boy's two sisters, Jeanne and Mary, were busy fishing. They had their brother Dan in tow. From their haul of prizes, it seemed like they had caught their limit. But they wanted more. He was sure they were almost out of money. He avoided them on principle. He had warned them before they left home to *stay away from him*.

Next to the fish pond was the duck pond. Hundreds of yellow baby ducklings floated in two large laundry tubs. For one ticket, you could pluck the duck of your choice from the water. On the underside was a number which told you the category of the prize you had won. Of course, you could store up your winnings and claim a bigger prize.

The older children preferred games of skill. The ring toss was popular. You won a bottle of pop if you managed to land a ring around the bottle's neck. So was the bean bag toss, where you aimed at the mouth of a happy clown, his face painted on a sheet of three-quarter inch plywood. Naturally, the boys tried to show off their prowess in front of the girls.

At the far end of the floor, away from the stage, the older children shot basketballs. Val Krause was conducting her annual free throw contest, two divisions: boys and girls, and the winners received a new Spaulding basketball. Frankie noticed that one had Bob Cousy's signature on it and the other, Bill Russell's. Both men were stars for the Boston Celtics. Both men were champions. He would have liked the Cousy ball.

Val Krause was donating the Cousy ball, the one her daughter, Norma, had won the previous year. Norma was an avid fan of the hometown Minneapolis Lakers and refused absolutely to play with a Celtic ball. It was silly. Val was glad she had kept the carton intact.

Between the duck pond and the ring toss stood a long sturdy table, used to serve salads at school lunch. It was loaded with glass figurines. The two boys were drawn to it. Mrs. Merrow, his Cub Scout den mother, had ordered the glass pieces as a fundraiser. She suspected that they would be popular items at the carnival. The figurines were replicas of animals, fish, and birds. These novelties might become gifts that a child would give to his or her mother, wrapped up for her birthday or for

Christmas, whichever came first. Clarence Bruns was busy manning the display.

Both boys made a purchase. It cost them five tickets apiece. Frankie selected a black panther, long and lithe, pacing through the jungle, ready to pounce. It had a shiny coat with yellow eyes and a red mouth and whiskers painted on its face. Terry Joe bought a glass angel fish, its fins delicately poised like wings to balance the body as it swam, suspended in the water. "You're lucky. This is the last one of these," Clarence Bruns informed him. Terry Joe could not take his eyes off it. He cradled it softly in both hands.

The two boys wandered over to the stage, where several of their classmates were congregated. Too late. Propped on the edge of the stage was Susanne Danbury and her friend, Doris Kurtz. Susanne's large head swiveled on her neck as she led a discussion on allergies. When she saw the two new boys enter her circle, her eyes brightened. Immediately she spotted the glass fish that Terry Joe was sheltering in his hands.

"Oh, can I hold it?" she pleaded. She reached for the ornament, but Terry Joe shielded it from her grasp. "Please let me hold it," she begged. "I'll be careful."

Terry Joe was apprehensive, unwilling to let go of the piece. Then he remembered Sister Mary Anthony's words: he was now a gentleman. Reluctantly he let the girl take the figurine from his hands. She held it up. It was translucent, pink and then fuchsia and then violet as she turned it in the light. She was mesmerized by its beauty. She let her imagination flow. "It's a lovely little fish that swims in the sea." Her voice was soft and faint, wishful.

She lifted the tiny fish to eye level and pinched it between thumb and forefinger to look underneath it. In that moment the figurine slipped from her grasp. It fell to the floor and landed with a crack. "Oh no," she wailed with a quick intake of breath.

Terry Joe dropped to his knees. His fingers caressed his beautiful little angel. One wing was broken off. The fin had shattered. He stood up holding the splintered pieces. His eyes were moist with tears. "My mother's birthday is next week," he stated. This fish was for her."

Susanne Danbury sat glumly on the stage. "I'm so sorry," she whispered. Her bottom lip was quivering. "I'm so… so…

sorry." She reached for her coin purse in the pocket of her sweater. She opened the latch and took out three copper pennies. It was all she had. "I'll buy you another one," she said.

"This was the last one," Terry Joe informed her. He put the remains of the fish into his pocket.

Frankie stood next to his companion and seethed. He looked at the culprit angrily, his feelings bordering on rage. But what could be done? He saw the pain in his friend's eyes, turned away, and formulated a plan.

The two boys moseyed back along the gym floor to the table holding the figurines. Clarence Bruns was busy showing his wares. He nodded to the boys to acknowledge their visit.

Frankie was nervous. Three times he reached out his hand. Three times he pulled it back, fearful that Clarence Bruns would see him.

On the fourth try he succeeded. He snatched the closest ornament and stuffed it into his jacket pocket. He was sure he had been seen, but he heard no outcries. No one intervened. It took several minutes for his breathing to calm down.

"Here, take this." He pulled the glass piece from his pocket and placed it in Terry Joe's hand. It was a chicken with white scallops for feathers on its breast and a yellow beak and a red comb.

"Where did you get this?" his best friend asked.

"I took it" was the boy's reply. "You can give it to your mother."

The two boys stared at each other knowingly. It would be their secret, at least until next spring when they made their First Confession. Now Frankie had five sins to confess: lying about his age to play Little League, making the babysitter ask for more money, frightening young girls and not being a gentleman, stealing a glass chicken for his best friend, and hating Susanne Danbury. He was not so sure that hating Susanne Danbury was a sin. He was sure that Jesus would see how the girl tormented him, how she was driving him to the point of exasperation, how his feelings against her were really *her fault!*

CHAPTER NINETEEN

It was Sunday morning, the boy's first time serving Sunday mass. Father Schumacher, pastor of St. Joseph's, was bent over his kneeler just inside the sacristy, saying his morning prayers. This was his custom. Dutiful prayer made the man seem saintly, and the two altar servers tiptoed around the room lest they disturb him. It behooved the altar boys to be quiet; the pastor tolerated whispers only.

As he lit the candles on the altar, Frankie was keenly aware of the four children and two women in the front pew. The heads of his three oldest siblings, two girls and a boy, were perched atop the pew's railing, their chins resting on the oaken trim in front of the kneeler. Their faces were staring at him. His sister, Jeanne, waved, but he did not respond. He kept his focus on the candle lighter, tilting the wick just so, lest the flame become extinguished. He had learned to push enough of the wick out of the brass tube to keep the fire burning brightly, but not too much to waste the wick. At the foot of the altar, he genuflected. He knew he was under the watchful eye of Father Schumacher.

His mother sat in the pew, wearing a dress, a pastel mink stole, and a stylish fur hat. Her husband liked when she advertised the business. She was holding Baby Chuck, and her eyes roamed around the pew at her children, who were standing on the kneeler.

For the moment the baby was content, preoccupied with the toy rattle his mother had brought along. The woman sighed. She would have liked to have had her husband here with her. He was, of course, out at his ranch, feeding mink. She knew that in reality he had escaped and was avoiding any showdown.

Next to her sat a tall woman with rather angular features, a sharp-cut nose, and glasses. She possessed clear blue eyes that were penetrating. She wore no hat, just a large blonde beehive hairdo, held in place with bobby pins and a tortoise shell clip. Her friend had told her about the friendliness and openness of the Church. Catholics were tolerant. St. Joseph's was a place where she would be welcome. Marilyn Wojcheski was a woman who had come to see for herself. She had no expectations. She had been ridiculed enough to know better.

Holy mass started with a hymn from the choir standing in the loft at the back of the church. Ten women and five men sang three versus of "Ave Maria," a tribute to the Blessed Virgin Mary, Mother of God and Queen of the Universe. October was one of three months designated by the Church to honor her.

The singers were accompanied by the church's pipe organ; the organist, none other than the mayor himself, Alcuin Ryngsmuth. Mostly elderly, the women warbled and the men croaked. The high tenor voice of Andy Virden could be heard the loudest. Andy had lived in the village since birth and, by everyone's admission, was the brightest man in town. He was a very learned man, and there was no subject with which he was not familiar. Extremely pleasant and polite, he was also blind. He was a striking fellow with deep dark sockets where his eyes would have been, rather rotund, but always impeccably dressed in a handsome suit and a bow tie. He carried a cane to help him maneuver the streets. People found it inspirational that he did not let his blindness hold him down.

The priest ascended the three steps to the altar. For the duration of the mass, except for the reading of the Epistle and the Gospel, the preaching of the sermon, and the distributing of Holy Communion, he would have his back to the congregation. The customs and rituals of nearly 2000 years did not change overnight.

"In nominee Patriis, et Filii, et Spiritus Sancti, Amen," the priest chanted. Behind him the people touched their right hand to their forehead, stomach, left shoulder, and right shoulder, making the Sign of the Cross. "Introibo ad altare Dei," proclaimed the celebrant. I will go to the altar of God, thought Frankie. He had studied the translations and memorized them.

The boy was kneeling. Now he bent low to the floor, nearly prostrate, his nose almost touching the tiles of the first step. It was his turn to speak. "Ad Deum qui laetificat juventutem meam." To God, the joy of my youth, he translated to himself.

To his left, Jonas Duane mimicked the boy's words. Together, the two acolytes rattled off the prayers. Because they could recite them in Latin, he and Jonas had been chosen by Father as the first boys in their class to serve mass. It was a privilege and an honor. But the foreign words had no meaning to them, no relevance.

The dialogue between priest and servers continued. It was mechanical, rote. The boy's mind drifted to his other duties. He would ring the bell seven times: once when Father extended his hands forward over the offering, three times when the priest raised the consecrated host, and three more times when the celebrant raised the chalice filled with Jesus's precious blood. During his first mass early one morning, he had forgotten to ring the offertory bell. Soon, he caught Father's sidelong glance to the right and a brief, biting pause. He felt chagrin. The regulars at daily mass had noticed and smiled. He would not forget again.

"Confiteor Deo omnipotenti..." I confess to Almighty God... he translated silently, "...quia peccavi nimis cogitatione, verbo, et opere...." that I have sinned exceedingly in thought, word, and deed.... he interpreted.

At this point, he and Jonas beat their breasts three times. "Mea culpa, mea culpa, mea maxima culpa..." Through my fault, through my fault, through my most grievous fault... The boy remembered the school carnival two days earlier. It was not his fault, grievous or otherwise. It was her fault, that girl with the big head and the bright eyes, Susanne Danbury. She had forced him to steal a chicken. Of course, he felt remorse for breaking the Seventh Commandment, *Thou Shalt Not Steal*, but his feeling of guilt had been overshadowed by the pain in his best friend's face. She was to blame. His sin was really the girl's fault.

The boys sat back in two chairs allotted to them at the side of the sanctuary. Father Schumacher ascended the podium and faced his congregation. He was the shepherd; they were his flock.

He read the Epistle from St. Paul's letter to the Corinthians. Paul, the great persecutor of the Christians, had been converted on the road to Damascus, having been struck from his horse. Paul, the great ambassador to the gentiles, now became the Church's greatest defender, its champion. He converted the Greeks and the Romans, those superior to the lowly Jews except in their faith.

The Jews had killed Jesus, the Christ, and nailed him to a cross, and Paul never let them forget that. It was a sin they would be destined to carry forever, even to their graves, unless they repented and converted.

In the first pew Baby Chuck had grown tired of his rattle and began to fuss. His mother searched a bag loaded with diapers and toys and located a bottle of warm milk. The baby knew what it was and reached for it and stuck the nipple between his gums. The other children had settled back in the pew and were examining their shoes. They nudged one another. How shiny they were!

In the Catholic Church, October was a month dedicated to the Virgin Mary, the Mother of Jesus. Frankie remembered one time when Terry Joe had asked Sister Mary Bede, "How could Mary be both a virgin and a mother?" He had been listening to a conversation among the older men and boys in his clan, including his Uncle Squeak. The question had frozen the children in the class. It was something the girls had wondered about and been afraid to ask.

Sister's response had been icy. She gave Terry Joe a cold stare that made him wither. "It's a miracle," stated Sister, selecting her words carefully. "God had her conceive his child in his own way, not in the customary way. It's called the Immaculate Conception. Immaculate means pure." Sister relaxed. She seemed satisfied.

Terry Joe's brow wrinkled heavily. "Weren't we conceived in a pure way?" he asked.

"I should say not," growled Sister. "That's why we all have Original Sin. But the Blessed Virgin Mary was free from Original Sin. She never had it."

Father Schumacher finished reading the Gospel, exonerating Holy Mary, the Mother of God, once again. His flock seemed satisfied. They sat down to listen to Father explain God's word. A few checked their watches. In ten minutes, seven if they were lucky, they would have moved on to the Liturgy of the Eucharist: the offertory, consecration, and Holy Communion. A few fingered in their pockets, searching for an envelope to deposit in the collection basket.

The Reverend Cornelius J. Schumacher was a tall and stately man. He was a devout servant of the Lord, who prayed frequently. He prayed for guidance that he might lead his flock to verdant pastures, where they would dine in grassy meadows and then find repose. He was about to embellish today's Gospel about Mary, the Blessed Mother, when for the first time his eye caught sight of the visiting woman in the front pew. He stopped in mid-sentence and stared at her. He saw her blouse, low cut, below the limit of modesty. She wore no hat. She sat stiffly, tilted forward away from the back rest, and her bearing was one of defiance. She would listen and then challenge his assertions. It was the look in her eye that was the most disconcerting. She was a divorcee and perhaps an adulteress.

Father Schumacher, defender of his faith, turned against her. He picked up several sheets of foolscap in his hand and crumbled them. He let them fall to the floor. It was a symbolic gesture. A hush settled over the church. Thus, he began:

"In the beginning God created Adam and Eve, man and woman. But man was first. The woman was formed from the man's rib. She was part of him. Together, they lived in the Garden of Eden as man and wife. They lived in perfect bliss, partaking freely of the fruits of Paradise. They were instructed that all was theirs except for the fruit from the tree in the center of the garden, the Tree of Knowledge of Good and Evil.

One day the serpent, his heart full of guile, entered the garden and spoke to Eve. He saw her weak nature and tempted her to eat from the forbidden tree. She would not be merely a human, but a goddess! And so, she disobeyed God's command. She ate an apple and then gave it to her husband to eat. In that instant they looked at each other and saw that they were naked. They realized that they had sinned and were no longer welcome in the garden.

Why did the serpent approach the woman? Why did he tempt her first? He did so because he knew that she would be susceptible to temptation, to his false promises. Would Adam have succumbed to temptation from the serpent? From the devil himself? We will never know. We do know that he was influenced by his wife's sin. When she asked him to join her in sinning against God, he complied. So strong was the influence of this wayward woman!

God banished them into the world, and we are paying for it now. We are born with their Original Sin, and only through Christ's death on the cross and his resurrection have we been granted new life. Hopefully, we have learned our lesson. The Church is God's bride. We must obey our husband's command and love one another.

Recall Lot. He was told by God to leave Sodom and Gomorrah, sinful cities that God would soon destroy by fire. God told Lot and his wife to walk away from their home and not look back. But look what happened! Lot's wife disobeyed. She could not resist the temptation to turn around and see God's wrath, his vengeance. Instantly she was turned into a pillar of salt. She lacked the willpower to resist temptation. Her husband was powerless to prevent it."

The pastor continued. "You have heard the story of Samson, a strong Jewish man betrayed by Delilah, the woman he trusted. She cut off his hair when he was asleep and left him powerless against the Philistines. She was a wicked woman, who was self-serving. Samson should never have put his faith in her, but he was gullible. She plied him with drink and then took advantage of him while he slumbered. She connived with the enemy to capture him, and only in the end, when his hair grew back, was he able to pull down the pagan temple and destroy the Philistines. But he, too, was crushed to death."

At this moment the side door of the church suddenly opened. Four teenaged boys entered and, rather puzzled, sat down in the back pew. Father paused to let this interruption play out its course. Two of the boys checked their watches. They couldn't be that early. They had finished their pool game at Pinor's as usual and expected the mass to be further along—nearly to Holy Communion, of which they would happily partake.

Rather sheepishly, they hung their heads and awaited further developments. The parishioners in the congregation took little notice of them. It was a compromise that worked well most Sundays.

"Look above you." Father Schumacher resumed, and he pointed to a beam high above the communion rail. There stood a depiction of the crucifixion of Christ. They were life-sized statues.

Jesus hung dead on the cross with nails in his hands and feet and a wound made by a Roman soldier's spear in his side, from whence poured blood and water. At one side of the cross stood Mary, his mother. At the other side, Mary Magdalene. "Read the inscription below the scene," Father instructed. "Greater Love Than This No Man Hath." Frankie had read it many times, but never with the conviction expressed in Father Schumacher's voice.

Father's focus seemed to shift. He was no longer speaking to the entire congregation but directly to the woman in the front pew. His voice narrowed. Mary Magdalene was a sinner. She was a wayward woman of ill-repute. When she met Jesus, she was renowned as a sinner who led men astray. No respectable Jewish man would be seen with her. And yet, Jesus saw fit to forgive her. She became obedient to him and gave up her sinful ways. She washed Jesus's feet with perfume and wiped them dry with her hair. Only because of her love for him—and her obedience to him—did she save her immortal soul."

The four newcomers in the back pews rechecked their watches. Poor Father Schumacher! They had never heard such a rant from him before.

"Remember, the Pharisees tried to trap Jesus. They asked him if it was right for a woman to divorce her husband. The Law of Moses stated that if she did, she was an adulteress. But Jesus did not believe in divorce. He refused to condemn these women, and so we follow his example here today. Men are to love their wives, and wives are to be obedient to their husbands. That's the natural law. That is God's command. Woman, obey your husband, and he will love you."

It was at this moment that Marilyn Wojcheski stood up. Her face was a mixture of regret and anger. She stepped into the middle aisle and paraded, with her head up, toward the back of the church.

Father Schumacher watched her and shook his head in disgust. She was wearing a skirt that barely covered her thighs. She did not look repentant. She was anything but a Mary Magdalene. Her high heals clip-clopped as she made her departure.

The boy, sitting in a chair at the side of the altar, saw a second woman rise, his mother. She followed her friend out the door. In her arms Baby Chuck gaped at the many faces that were staring at them.

"Oh, Marilyn," the woman wailed as she scuttled down the front steps. "I'm so sorry! He's not like that really."

"Neither was Jesus" was the woman's retort. Her skepticism was apparent. She seemed more like an outsider, a stranger, than ever before. Her laugh was replete with sarcasm. "He's such a kind man, so full of decency, and so loving. I think I'll go home and obey my husband," she suggested. "Tom will be thrilled." Then she shuddered. "He won't even be there!" she wailed, more to herself than to the other woman.

"Oh, Marilyn," her friend cried. "Please don't blame me."

"I don't blame you," spat Marilyn. "It's the men of this world and their attitudes. I blame them. Your Father Schumacher is no different from the rest of them. He's just another man, that's all. He's no saint. He's not Jesus. He's just another crummy man, like all the rest of them. And you can have them. Take them all, Pat. By the way, why doesn't he speak to those boys who came in late? Do they do that every week? Now there's hypocrisy for you—tolerating that malarkey. What's he afraid of? That they'll desert the Church?"

She stopped abruptly. Her friend was in tears. She was clutching her baby to her bosom, rocking him. "What's wrong, Pat? It's my problem. Why are you crying?"

The boy's mother looked at her. "I'm pregnant," she blurted. "I'm due next spring in May."

"Dear Lord!" her friend exclaimed. She put her arms around the other woman's shoulders. Her bottom lip was trembling. "You poor thing! May Heaven help you." Her eyes blurred, and she turned and departed.

Twenty-five minutes later the church bells clanged, announcing that the mass was ended. The followers of Jesus exited the church. They avoided the woman on the corner holding her baby. They felt sorry for her. The other woman was nowhere in sight. Thank goodness!

Down the steps clumped the other three children. They surrounded her with questions: "Where did you go, Mom? Why did you go? Are we going to the school to get the bouja?"

Two minutes later her oldest son arrived. "Did Father Schumacher say anything to you?" she asked.

"No," he lied. "He just looked at me for a long time. He looked sad." The boy was unable—and unwilling—to tell her just what the priest had said to him.

"Can you go get the bouja?" she asked. "I think I'll sit in the car. I'll drive up."

They had left their five-quart kettle on a table in the cafeteria before mass. She had pre-paid, $2.75, the amount scrawled on the cover with a grease pen. By the end of mass, all of the kettles had been filled with chunky soup, laden with chicken, beef, and vegetables: carrots, potatoes, onions, and celery, cut up the day before by the Ladies Guild. The men of the Knights of Columbus had cooked the soup in four large, black, fifty-gallon kettles over an open fire. They had begun at 4:00 a.m. and let the broth simmer for six hours until the juices had married together. The key to the flavor was pickling spice. It created a thick tangy soup that drew customers from far and wide to the village on the first Sunday of each month throughout the fall.

The four children found their kettle, and Frankie picked it up. Clarence Bruns nodded to him as he carried it out the door. "Nice job of serving mass. Your Latin sounds good. Maybe someday you'll become a priest."

But the boy did not reply. He felt a twinge of guilt about stealing that chicken for his best friend, Terry Joe. He would feel guilty until he made his First Confession. But what if it was to Father Schmacher? After today, he would try to go to Father Thiel instead.

One thought disturbed him most. After mass Father Schumacher had, in fact, spoken to him. "She's another Salome," the priest had uttered. "She wants my head on a platter." His comment was a direct reference to the Bible, the boy was sure. But he was unsure exactly what the Man of God meant.

"So, that's what he thinks!" the boy's mother exclaimed. She made it sound like an indictment. She found out from her husband who had found out from their son. "He's equating himself with John the Baptist. He thinks he's a prophet. You should have been there, Clifford. It was one accusation after another. Poor Marilyn! She took all she could take."

"I wish I had been there," her husband acknowledged.

She looked at him skeptically. "Don't lie to me. You had no intention of going with us, no desire. You don't want to be seen with us, not if we're with Marilyn Wojcheski." Her words sounded harsh, but they were true. "You've made your views known to us quite clearly—how you support her husband, Tom.

Father Schumacher was ugly to her. He was anything but Christian, comparing her to Eve, Lot's wife, Delilah, and Mary Magdalene. It was a horrible litany. And then to tell our son that she is another Salome!"

"Who's Salome?" asked the boy, who, curious, was listening. He looked at his father and then at his mother. The woman looked into her husband's eyes. The man saw her frustration and then looked at his son. His son's innocence was disappearing, and this disturbed him. It was the boy's mother who answered.

"Salome was the daughter of Herodias and a niece of Herod, King of the Jews. Herodias hated John the Baptist because he was critical of her marriage. Do you know who John the Baptist was?" she asked.

"Jesus' cousin," replied the boy. "He lived in the desert on dead birds and insects."

"He also baptized people and prepared the way for Jesus," instructed his mother. "He announced that Jesus, the Savior of the World, was coming.

Herodias had a plan. She arranged for Salome to dance before Herod. The king was so pleased with the girl's dancing that he promised to give her any *one* thing she wanted. Her wish was for John the Baptist's head on a platter."

"Should you be telling him all this?" the boy's father asked. He looked deeply troubled.

"He needs to know," his wife answered. "He's reached the age of reason. Her voice was full of conviction. "He'll be making his First Confession in a few months. He needs to know just what kind of man Father Schumacher is.

Salome and her mother caused the death of John the Baptist. I've been looking at a painting of it by Titian in the art book my sister, Sylvia, gave me. She's a teacher, you know, at St. Paul's in St. Cloud."

Again the boy's father growled. But his wife persisted. "Herodias and Salome were vindictive women. The book says that Herod never wanted to put John the Baptist to death. He had heard stories about him, and he feared John's reputation—that he had even risen from the dead. But the king granted Salome's request anyway." The boy's mother shuddered. "Those women were horrible and hateful.

And that's how Father Schumacher sees Marilyn Wojcheski. He thinks he's a voice in the wilderness, and he's willing to be a martyr for the cause of Catholicism." Her voice had risen in pitch and was full of anguish bordering on rage.

She stopped and studied her son. "You told me Father Schumacher didn't say anything to you after mass. Why did you lie to me?"

The boy shrugged.

"What's in that kettle?" her husband asked. He pointed toward the stove.

"Bouja," his wife answered. Marilyn left her kettle at school. I had to go back and get it after the next mass." She eyed her husband. "Would you take it over to her?" The man looked down at his feet, averting his eyes. "I thought so," his wife concluded. "Then would you at least drive me over there, and I'll take it in?"

"I'll do that with you," responded her husband. He looked relieved.

"I told her I'm pregnant," she added. "She just said 'Oh dear' and called me a 'poor thing.' Her whole body was shaking. She has four little children."

"Don't be mad at Father Schumacher," stated her husband, taking a new tack.

"Don't tell me not to be mad at him!" she flared back at him. Her voice was full of challenge. "And after I told Marilyn how decent Catholics are, how kind and accepting Father would be. I was so embarrassed."

"It's not Christian to hold a grudge, especially against the parish priest," the man persisted. "Perhaps you need to talk with him in confession," he suggested. He said it softly, not wanting to pressure her. He put his arms around her shoulders in a mild embrace. It was his way of comforting her, of showing he cared. It was also his way of detecting her mood. He could feel her resolve weakening.

She submitted to the man's strong arms and took a slow, deep breath. "Perhaps I do," she agreed. "I can't even go to Holy Communion feeling like this. He needs to know how I feel."

"How's the baby?" her husband asked. The question jolted her.

She stepped out of his arms and reached to pick up the kettle of bouja. But her husband intercepted it. They left the house together and left their oldest son in charge. They would not be gone long.

The other children were upstairs, playing house. Still dressed in their Sunday clothes, his sisters were serving tea to their brother, Dan, and a bottle of milk to Baby Chuck. The boy in charge turned on the television to watch football. His favorite team, the Green Bay Packers, had just scored a touchdown against the Lions of Detroit and were leading 10 to 6. He did not mind that the broadcast was in black and white, not in color. He had never known differently. He was intrigued by these behemoths. He speculated. Perhaps one day he would play in the National Football League.

CHAPTER TWENTY

The October chill brought hunting season with it. Frankie seldom saw his father so joyous and energetic.

"Let's jump this pothole," the man told his son one Saturday on the way to the mink ranch. "There might be a few ducks in there." He stopped the truck and turned off the engine and the headlights. It was early morning; dawn was just breaking.

Sure enough, there were four mallards in the slough: two greenhead males and two females with brown plumage, their mates. They were feeding on the heads of wild rice that grew at the edge of the pond. Father and son crawled up on them through the tall cattails, and then the man stood up, shot twice, and hit two of the birds. They plummeted earthward and splashed into the watery surface. Instinctively the man's dog whimpered. He wore no leash. But he did not plunge into the water without being commanded to do so.

The dog was a Black Labrador. The man had trained him well to retrieve, using a floatation pad to simulate a duck that had been shot. The dog was intelligent with a keen sense of smell. He could flush pheasants and locate a wounded bird in the thick underbrush. He had won two trophies for his master, and that had made the man proud. He had named the dog Jet.

Once the previous year, the boy recalled, several hunters had downed a pheasant. It was hiding in the thick prairie grass that grew in west central Minnesota. The men had watched their three dogs fail. The canines could not dislodge the bird.

The boy's father had been standing off to the side, observing. He didn't know the men. Jet sat at the man's right side, face upturned, watching for his master's signal. The men saw the stranger. They asked if he would like his dog to try. His father nodded.

He stepped forward and barked a single word—"Heel!" The dog complied. The man positioned the dog toward the underbrush. He stretched out his hand as if to shake hands with someone in front of him, and the dog knew that this was the track he must follow. Then the boy's dad uttered a second word—"Fetch!"

The hunting dog burst forward, lunging into the dense weeds. Back and forth he leaped, searching for the scent of the pheasant. His path covered the patch systematically. He covered every inch of ground. The men watching were impressed with the dog's endurance.

Then the lab found the scent. He jumped forward into the thickest patch of grass and disappeared. A minute elapsed, and then the dog reappeared, holding a rooster pheasant in his mouth. It was a brilliant rust color with a green head and a red comb. Its black eyes, outlined in yellow and black, shone fire. Jet did not clamp his teeth into the bird, but held it tightly in his jaws, unharmed. The dog's mouth was frothy. He padded up to his master's right side and sat, awaiting the command to give the bird up.

The men cheered mightily at this success. They nodded to each other. These men knew their sport. They understood. It had been their good fortune to see this display, and they appreciated what they had just witnessed.

The master grabbed the bird by both feet and commanded that the dog relinquish it. "Give!" Jet let go, and the pheasant fluttered its wings mightily to escape. The boy's father held the bird out to the hunter who had asked for help.

The man smiled. "No, you keep it. I've never seen a dog work like that." He looked down at the dog, who was still looking up at his master, awaiting the next command. "Can I buy him?" The boy saw that the man was serious. He could not take his eyes off of Jet. "Name your price!"

His father shook his head. "He's not for sale." The master reached down and patted the dog behind the ears. The boy felt a keen sense of relief.

"Thank you for the bird," his father said. With that he grabbed the pheasant's head and cranked the body in a vicious circle, snapping the neck. The wings stopped flapping, and the father stuffed the dead rooster into an inner pocket of his jacket.

Besides waterfowl and game birds, the man hunted squirrels and rabbits. He loved the taste of wild game. He had even eaten bear meat once. "It's sweet," he told his mother. Grandma shared his taste for this cuisine. Together, they ate liver and heart and pickled tongue. On Sunday mornings his father devoured head cheese made from pig's brains.

"We're having hasenpfeffer tonight," the boy's sister, Jeanne, informed him one afternoon. "Mom's cooking it in a pot."

"It's a rabbit," explained his sister, Mary.

The boy squirmed. He was a finicky eater at best. He even did not like chicken or roast beef or fish. He found his father's culinary tastes unappetizing. But the man remained undaunted and ignored his son's complaints.

In the first week of November, his father hunted deer. He put aside his Browning twelve-gauge shotgun and traded it in for his 30.06 rifle. The gun was powerful. Left unchecked, its bullets could travel well over a mile. But his Dad felt comfortable with it in his hands. He was a marksman and had been awarded a sharpshooter medal in the Marines.

Last year he had hunted with his chum, Leo, and with Dick Kuypers, the son of Ma, who owned the local bar on 3rd Street across from the Great Northern's yard. They had hunted up by Camp Ripley, an army camp near Little Falls.

It had been a cold day, frosty with two inches of new snow on the ground. His father told the story of how he had sat in a tree stand for two hours before daylight, his fingers freezing but clutching his rifle.

Just then a huge buck followed by two does sauntered through the woods and stopped to take stock. The man in the tree aimed his rifle. In that instant the stag detected movement. Alarmed, he leaped high into the air. *Bang!* The first bullet pierced the buck's heart, and he crumbled in a heap. *Bang! Bang!* The hunter pulled the trigger two more times. The two does, trying to bound forward, also fell to the ground dead with bullet holes in their chest cavities filling their lungs with blood. The hunt was over. The other two men never fired a shot. Not only was the boy's dad a marksman, but he was also quick on the draw.

Within seconds the three men had their quota—three deer: a buck and two does. That morning they drove back home thirty miles and hung the three deer from the swing set in the back yard. The animals' black noses nearly touched the top bar, and their hind feet hung just above the ground. The animals were gutted, their chest cavities propped open with stout sticks of lumber.

The boy and his siblings peered into the opening. They saw the dried blood and the meat on the rib bones. Venison. The boy looked up at the deer's faces. Their tongues were hanging out of their mouths. It played upon his imagination. It made their expressions seem ludicrous, as if they were laughing at their fate.

The men posed for a picture in their hunting gear. They wore red jackets and red caps. The hunters held their rifles at-the-ready. Dick Kuypers knelt on one knee beside the three deer; the other two men stood. The boy noted the look of success and pride on his father's face. He had shot all three deer. *Bam*! *Bam*! *Bam*! Inside of five seconds. The other two hunters did not look nearly as proud.

Shooting three deer only whetted his father's appetite. The following month his dad was gone for five days. He and a mink rancher named George Ruhrland and two of George's friends had driven to Kenora, Ontario, in Canada, to hunt moose. They had rented a ski plane, a four-seat Cessna 172, and landed on the Lake of the Woods, 120 miles east of Winnipeg.

The weather was unusually frigid, and the ice on the lake was already thick. Both men made their kill. The trick had been to lift the Cessna off the ice and become airborne, carrying three men and four quarters of moose meat weighing 700 pounds. Most of that was *extra* weight.

The pilot had already made three trips. The boy's father and George Ruhrland were on the last flight out. It was nearing dusk. Bad weather was setting in, and the pilot was nervous. They were loaded to the gills, too heavy. The pilot spun the plane around and accelerated. Across the ice they flew, gaining speed, albeit slowly. He pushed the engine to its maximum capacity and at the last moment deployed the flaps downward and lifted off.

They were rapidly approaching the end of the lake, and a thick forest of pine trees lay directly in their path. His father blinked hard. George Ruhrland laughed. The pilot was an old-timer. He had flown in hunters to Canada for years. He pulled up on the joystick with both hands, straining for every ounce of lift, every inch of altitude. But with the Cessna loaded to capacity, he could only reach the desired height so fast. The pilot screamed at his machine to coax it higher.

The boy's father held his breath. He heard branches snap underneath the plane's skis. With only inches to spare, the aircraft rose upward and propelled itself into the airy sky.

The pilot relaxed. George Ruhrland grinned and extracted a bottle from his jacket. "Care for a bump, Cliff?" he asked. "You'll have a freezer full of moose meat," stated his dad's friend.

It was the end of a long day. The boy's father felt relieved. He sipped on the bottle. Brandy had never tasted so good.

"What are we going to do with all that moose meat?" his wife cried. "We don't have room in the freezer as it is."

"I'll buy another freezer, a larger one," was the man's response. "Most of it will be moose sausage," he stated, "mixed with some pork." He bought the second freezer that afternoon. Even now, a year later, it was still filled to capacity with wild game: mostly moose roasts, steaks, chops, and red sausage. His wife had been right. Only Grandma did not complain.

But it had been worth it. The excitement of the plane lifting off the ice and barely clearing the forest of jack pines had been the thrill of a lifetime. He could still see the huge moose charging toward him. Firing three bullets, he had shot and killed it. His only regret was that they had had to leave the beast's rack behind on the ice. The trophy could not be transported. But it would have made a dandy showpiece on the living room wall.

Jet, the Hunting Dog

My Dad has a hunting dog. Yep! Jet, the Hunting Dog. He's a Black Lab. We also have another dog, Spike. He's a Golden Retriever. They live together in the dog kennel in our back yard. The kennel is a cage made of wire, and it has a slanted roof. Sometimes my friend, Terry Joe, and I climb up there to sit and look down. There's a dog house at the end, where the dogs can go when it rains or gets cold. It has yellow straw in it for bedding. Spike likes to sleep in the dog house, so Jet has to sleep outside in the kennel on the cement.

We feed them dog food from a white bag Mom keeps in the closet and table scraps left over from breakfast, lunch, and supper. We keep the scraps in a bowl inside the refrigerator. I bring the dog dishes out to the kennel, and I fill up their water bowls. That's my job.

Jet always eats first. He gobbles down his food like there's no tomorrow. He licks his dish clean with his tongue. Then he eats some of Spike's food, too.

Yesterday evening Spike got mad. He jumped onto Jet's neck and bit him on the head. Jet tried to break away. He jumped out of the kennel because I had left the door open. Spike jumped out, too. They wrestled in the yard, rolling around on the grass. They kept fighting until my dad came out of the house and broke it up. Spike tore Jet's ear off. It was his right ear. The vet had to sew it back on. He did a good job.

My Dad is going to get rid of Spike. He won't tell my brothers and sisters because it would make them cry. But he told me. He said he's going to have the dog "put down." That's his story. But I know the real truth. He's going to take the dog out into the country on his way to the mink ranch. Dad will have his gun, and they'll go hunting. But Spike won't be coming back. Dad will shoot him behind the ear lobe like he did our other dog, Ringo, who got too old. Dad just came home whistling softly, but I knew he felt sad. I saw it in his eyes. You can't keep sadness out of your eyes.

Dad is keeping Jet because he's the best hunting dog. When Dad shoots a duck, Jet whimpers and looks at him with those big brown eyes. He's saying, "Let me go fetch it now, please!!!" He's always eager to retrieve the ducks that Dad shoots. He's a good swimmer.

And he can flush pheasants with the best of them. Dad says that Jet has a good nose for smelling fowl. (That means birds.) He has won two trophies for being a good hunting dog. Yep! Jet, the Hunting Dog. That's the end of my report.

In Minnesota, October was the month to prepare for winter. The boy's parents were busy "buttoning up" the house and yard.

To attain maximum efficiency, they settled on a division of labor. Each was in charge of a portion of the work. The children were their work force.

During August and September their mother had plucked vegetables and fruits from the garden. Mounds of beans had been snipped, washed, cut, blanched, and frozen. Bags of sweet corn kernels had been frozen, too. Tomatoes that weren't eaten fresh off the vine had been stuffed into glass jars and now lined on shelves in the basement. Beets, dill pickles, peaches, and cherries sat beside them.

But now, with the first hard frost approaching, the garden must be "picked clean." The last of the lettuce had been cut down long ago. What remained tasted woody and was inedible. Beside it, however, were rows of carrots that had been left in the ground until the end of the growing season. The woman and the children dug them up and shook them by their green tops to free them from the clumps of dirt that clung to their orange roots. They were stored in boxes in the basement, where they would keep the whole winter long. Onions from the garden were stored beside them.

Next, they dug up the potatoes and loaded them into gunny sacks, which Frankie and his dad hauled down to the cellar. These tubers were the staple of the family's diet. Most of the time, his mother boiled and mashed them, serving them with butter and gravy along with the meat she had cooked. On Sunday morning she cut them up and fried them in butter. Her husband and children liked the thin wedges with ketchup. She always grew enough potatoes. They had eyes, which she would use as the seeds for the next year's crop.

The patches in the center of the garden grew thick, a sprawl of vines that twisted into a tangled labyrinth beneath the plants' leaves. These harbored squash, gourds, and a few watermelons. Pumpkins too. By early October the pumpkins were plump and heavy. The children each picked their favorite to carve for Halloween. With a candle implanted inside, the pumpkin became a jack-o'-lantern that fed the imagination.

Each year the woman watched wistfully as her flowers drooped and died. It signaled the end of summer. By the middle of October, the garden was empty and bare. The mother turned her attention to other tasks. On a given Saturday she washed the windows inside the house. This year, of course, because she was pregnant, she must be more careful and watch her step. Her husband had admonished her to stay off the ladder. "Don't stand on any chairs!" But she did not obey him. She chose not to heed his warning. She was not that far along.

Doing the laundry was a Herculean task. Mountains of summer clothes had to be cleaned and stored. Winter clothes, including long underwear and sweaters, had to be unpacked. Coats and scarves and caps had to be brought upstairs from the basement and hung in the closets. Boots had to be extracted from the cellar and tried on. Every year several new pairs had to be purchased because the old ones no longer fit. The children's feet seemed to grow faster than the weeds in the garden.

The boy's father took responsibility for the outside tasks, washing the outside windows and repainting the trim on the garage. He had already trimmed the trees during the summer months: maple and birch, elm and ash and oak. But now in October, they shed their leaves. Together, the man and his children piled the leaves high in the garden. The man paused and, leaning on a rake, watched his children jump into the pile. At night he lit a fire and burned the leaves. Throughout the village across the neighborhoods, fires flared.

The children watched the pile ignite and burst into flames. The leaves crackled and snapped. Plumes of gray smoke wafted upward and then drifted sideways into the adjacent yards. The scent of burning leaves was intoxicating.

The children saw their father's face illuminated by the roaring fire. They watched him, rake in hand, control the fire, sweeping the loose debris at the edge of the pile into the fiery center. Occasionally a spark would fly toward them and even hit them, leaving a small hole in their sweatshirt or jacket.

Invariably the mother joined them. She took her husband's arm, and they stood together in the garden, their faces brightly lit, their bodies and those of their children casting long shadows into the darkness beyond. They were a family.

Gradually the fire died. The flames succumbed to the lack of fuel. Only burning embers, red and glowing, remained inside the belly of the pile. The rest was a great heap of ashes. What became of them would be determined in the next few days. If the wind blew, the ashes would scatter. If the rains came first, they would sink into the soil. Either way, they would disappear.

The next morning the boy looked out an upstairs window. The pile in the garden was gray and cold in the sunlight. Ashes to ashes and dust to dust. The same thing happened to people, the boy supposed. It's what Father preached at church—that only the spirit lived on. It made him think about the bodies in graves in the cemetery, about Abigail Hoganson's brother, about decay. The same thing would eventually happen to him. But it was no use thinking about it any more. If it happened, it happened. He wouldn't feel a thing.

CHAPTER TWENTY-ONE

The room was abuzz, for the children were excited. On a long table in front of them was a large display of prizes. Attached to each was a card bearing a number from one through five. The boy next to the windows could see that the better prizes had larger values.

A man stood at the front of the classroom beside the table. He wore a suit and tie, dark-rimmed glasses, and a crew cut. His shoes were polished shiny black. Sister Mary Bede had introduced him as a salesman. She explained that helping him would help the school.

The man reiterated this point. "I'm giving you an opportunity" is how he put it. "I'm asking you to sell magazine subscriptions. St. Joseph's school will receive one half of the profit on anything you sell—one half! I suggest you start in your neighborhood. Those people know you. They'll be inclined to help you. Call your grandpas and grandmas and your aunts and uncles. Be sure to tell them it's for the school." Frankie wondered if his grandma even read magazines. He doubted it.

"And don't forget your parents. They have the biggest reason to support the school—you! They have a vested interest. Your teachers know how valuable money for education is. Right, Sister?"

He paused and looked at Sister Bede, who was seated on a stool at the back of the room. Sister had pulled up her habit and was busy examining her toenails beneath her cast. She was distracted, and his question caught her off guard. "Right what?" she inquired. She pulled her habit back down over her legs.

The man frowned. He did not understand modern Catholicism. He focused on the students in front of him. "Show the people how eager you are to sell. That's the best way to make a sale." He held up a brochure that unfolded into three sections. "There are over two hundred magazines to choose from: *Time*, *Newsweek*, *Look Magazine*, *Life Magazine*, *The Saturday Evening Post*. There's *Sports Illustrated* for the men who like sports and *Outdoor Life* for hunters and fisherman. *Fix-It* is for those who are Do-It-Yourselfers." The children nodded in unison. Most of their fathers fit into this category; they had a shop in the garage. "Here's *Hot Rod*," the man stated, "for the younger men.

For the women, we have *The Ladies Home Journal*. It's filled with tips for the modern-day housewife—how to decorate your home." Frankie thought of his own mother at home. She was always hinting that she wanted new drapes in the living room. Perhaps she would buy a magazine subscription to help her convince his dad to buy them.

"Young women will like *Glamour*. It's a beauty magazine with the latest tips on makeup and lipstick. There's also *Movie Stars Parade*, about Hollywood and all the newest stars."

"It's filled with gossip," Gail Teigen interjected, "juicy gossip!" She laughed knowingly, and her friends laughed with her, although most of them did not know as much.

The salesman had primed the pump sufficiently. He settled down to the business details. "Don't collect any money," he cautioned. "The subscriber will be billed later. Have the subscribers fill in their name and address. Remember, each subscription must be signed. You can sell them after school. Tonight at seven o'clock I will be down in the pavilion at the community park to collect your subscriptions. You will receive your prizes then." He turned to face the table. "Just look at what you will receive." The children followed his gaze. They looked at the display again, drooling over what they wanted most.

Frankie stared at the prizes with desire. They were not simply trinkets that might be won at the County Fair. These were expensive items that a maturing boy or girl could use. Some

FRANK KNIER

were toys: a cap gun, tiny racing cars, a bow and arrow set, and Barbie dolls. Others were electronic gadgets: a transistor radio, head phones, and a walkie talkie two-way radio with batteries included. There was a fishing rod and a View-Master with disks and a camera.

The man began to close up shop. He took down the display with practiced ease and piled the prizes on a cart that he had parked just inside the door. "Now, if two or three of you strong lads could carry the table for me down to the next room… let's see… Room 105, Sister Mary Agatha, I'd appreciate it. Thank you, Sister. Remember, you're doing this for the school." He departed, pushing his cart down the hallway, followed by his table.

The school bell clanged, signaling the end of the school day. On this occasion the school emptied more quickly than usual. The students hurried to start selling subscriptions.

"Do you want to buy a magazine?" the boy asked his mother. "It's for the school."

His mother looked skeptical. She was sitting at the kitchen table, darning stockings. "What magazines do you have?" she inquired.

"A whole bunch," he answered. "There's over 200 different magazines you can buy. There's one called *The Ladies' Home Journal*. It's about drapes," he informed her.

She deferred the decision. "I'll see what Dad has to say about it." Her son was surprised that she remained noncommittal. He felt a twinge of disappointment.

"It's for the school," he repeated. "They get half of what we sell."

"I know," she replied.

He exited the house, carrying a handful of blank subscription forms. He tucked a pen inside his pants pocket. In the alley he met Timmy O'Brian, who was also carrying a handful of blank subscription forms. "Wanna go selling together?" Timmy asked.

Frankie thought it a good idea. They would go from door to door, alternating houses. His anticipation level was high.

"Remember to tell them that it's for St. Joseph's School," Timmy reminded him. "That will make them feel that they have to buy one."

"What if they're not Catholic?" the other boy asked.

"If they're Methodist or Lutheran, tell them that it's for McKinley School."

"But what if they know I go to St. Joseph's?"

"Just tell them," Timmy blurted. He was starting to sound exasperated.

Frankie struck pay dirt across the highway at the Park Motel. The proprietor thought he needed a travel magazine in the lobby of the motel. *Get Away!* contained exotic pictures and photographs of Caribbean beaches and Amazon rainforests and mountains in Nepal. It also pictured young women and young men, scantily clad, posing in those far away places. The magazine would show those registered in the motel where they should be, far from the monotonous prairie land of Waite Park. So, he filled out a subscription form and signed it.

The boy grinned as he rejoined Timmy outside. "I got one," · he informed the older boy.

"Let's go down 11th Avenue," Timmy suggested. "The Hecht sisters live down there. They'll buy one."

The two boys made their way down the avenue as planned. What was not planned was their lack of sales. An hour had gone by, and they hadn't sold another thing. Both were disappointed. Their hopes of earning prizes were being dashed. Even the Hecht sisters had refused. Six children had approached them already.

Irene tried to "shoo" them away.

"Stay away from here," Nora scolded.

"Go home and eat supper," Gertie Hecht suggested.

"I've already missed supper," stated Timmy. "We eat at five o'clock when Dad gets home."

Two doors beyond the Hecht residence, the boys laid down on the sidewalk. Frustrated, they began to laugh. It is said that laughter and tears go hand in hand. Comedy and tragedy are drama's twin masks. And then an idea struck them.

Timmy O'Brian took his pen out of his pocket and began to write. ZEKE JONES, he printed on a subscription form. He looked up at the house in front of him. A house number stared back at him, 328. He wrote 328 11th AVENUE on the line marked address. He scribbled a signature in the appropriated blank. "That's one," he stated and looked at the younger boy. "Your turn."

Frankie took out his own pen. JOHNSON, he printed. And then he thought. ZEKE, he wrote in front of the last name. He looked at the house next door, 324. He wrote 324 11th AVENUE on the form. And he, too, scribbled a signature. The boys looked at each other. "That's two," stated the younger boy.

They giggled. This was easier, more satisfying. Soon, they each had eight subscriptions, more than enough for one of the big prizes. Only a half hour had elapsed. They had been careful to select addresses from a variety of streets and avenues in several neighborhoods. The two boys were giddy with excitement. At 7:00 o'clock they would claim their prizes. They walked home.

Supper was in progress when the boy entered through the back door. "I'm not hungry," he told his mother. He looked at the table. Moose steaks, he observed. Then he quickly scampered up the stairs before she could order him to sit and eat.

The two boys walked together to the community park. Each carried his eight subscriptions in the back pocket of his blue jeans.

A large crowd had assembled. Most were the school children who had been asked to sell. Mixed in were many parents who had come to watch the prizes be distributed. Some held babies in their arms. Others had small children on their shoulders so that the youngsters could see the action.

The children were summoned in random order, girls first mainly. The two boys stood back in the center of crowd and waited their turn. The excitement of the afternoon returned as the children were rewarded for their sales.

The man in the suit and tie with the dark-rimmed glasses and shiny black shoes and a crew cut presented each prize with much aplomb. He thanked the seller and reminded that boy or girl just how much they were helping their school. His voice was sincere; the look on his face behind his glasses, believable.

The villagers were happy. The adults were happy to see their children happy. They "*oohed*" and "*ahhed*" as a son or daughter thrust a prize in their face. It was like Christmas, two months early.

A few children remained to turn in their subscription forms. The crowd had thinned slightly as some spectators departed. The morning would come early for those who worked. But most stayed to watch. It was Frankie and Timmy O'Brian's turn. They climbed up the steps onto the raised platform, where the man in the dark-rimmed glasses stood. They handed their subscription forms to him.

The crowd stood by and observed. Eight forms each. That was the most of anyone. Frankie sensed that his classmates were eyeing him expectantly, perhaps with a touch of envy. He spotted his nemesis, Susanne Danbury, in a corner of the crowd.

He was pointing to the transistor radio, a five-point item, when he heard a male voice resonate in front of him. It sounded distorted and surreal, like a call from far away or the hollow whisper of a ghost. "These aren't real," he heard the voice say, and then the sound crystallized and became audible and clear. It was real enough. He felt the eyes of everyone staring at the back of his head. But what he saw in front of him made him shudder. The man's eyes, behind the dark-rimmed glasses, were like those of an eagle. They were piercing and condemning. They didn't blink. "These aren't real," the man's voice repeated. The eagle's talons were sharply embedded in him, and its beak was picking at his flesh. It showed no compassion, no forgiveness. "These signatures are forgeries!"

The boy felt the sting of embarrassment throughout his whole body. The shock immobilized him. It left him virtually catatonic.

It was Timmy who rescued him. "The kids signed them," Timmy lied.

The eagle looked down at him in disbelief, but his intensity eased. He spoke to the crowd, instructing them. "The subscriptions must be signed by an adult." The crowd nodded. They listened and agreed. But everyone knew the truth. It was etched into the boy's face.

Suddenly he spoke up to the man in charge. "But this one's real." He pointed to the subscription from the Park Motel. The salesman inspected the form. "That's right," he agreed. "You have a prize coming, one worth one point. Pick something."

The boy chose a small camera. He accepted the prize and descended down the steps, averting his eyes. He knew his classmates were all staring at him. They parted to let him through. His friends would feel sorry for him. It was a lesson from which they could all learn. He knew that Susanne Danbury would be smirking, shaking her big head, chastising him in front of her friend, Doris. But he soon forgot about them. It was another woman, older than them, who he worried about most—his mother.

When he reached the road, he began to run. He ran up the hill on 5th Street, not bothering to look up at Jack Kertcher's tree house. He raced the next block, past Kuffelds', and crossed 11th Avenue at Dan and Marie Scandans', angling toward his house.

Out of breath he entered the house. He called to her. His mother was alone in the living room. She sensed his alarm, his panic. She looked into his eyes, and instinctively she knew something terrible had happened. A mother's instinct is seldom wrong.

"Oh, Mom," he wailed. "I cheated and they caught me. Down at the park. I filled in the subscription forms with fake names and addresses. Everyone was watching me. Timmy told the man that the kids signed the subscriptions. But they all know the truth. And I know they know!"

He agonized. Bound by guilt, he was in misery. He felt the need to be comforted. "I'm sorry, Momma!" the boy cried. "I'll never do it again." And then he felt real tears in his eyes, bitter tears that stung.

His mother said nothing. She just sagged into her rocking chair. She was crying, and that hurt the boy the most. She had nothing to say with her voice, but it was her body language that told him her story. She was disappointed in him, so terribly disappointed. He regretted that. It was something a son should never have to feel.

When he trudged upstairs, he noticed that the camera was still in his hand. Quickly he hid it in a drawer underneath his socks and underwear. He could never use the camera, knowing how he had obtained it. Little did he know that in the days to come, it would be a constant reminder of his transgression, of the sixth sin he had to confess. It taught him a lesson. Now he understood why there was a need to go to confession: he wanted desperately to feel forgiven.

The woman knelt and prayed a long time before she entered the confessional. Ever since her childhood in Sauk Centre, the church had been a place of comfort to her. When she had lost her brother, Donnie, and then her mother, she had gone to St. Paul's to find out why. She had prayed for the answer. Her father was a prayerful man. She had knelt at his side, hands folded, and talked to Jesus. "Speak to your Father," she had told him, "and tell me why they had to die."

God had not told her why directly, but indirectly in little revelations and insights. She came to realize that when a loved one dies, it challenges the living to accept God's plan, his design. She had come to believe that God had a purpose for her—to marry and bring forth children into the world. Her pregnancies had given her solace. Each child was precious.

Now she found herself questioning her role in God's design. That was sinful. Her friend, Marilyn Wojcheski, had called her a "poor thing." She had listened and heard. Her husband's sixth child was in her womb. Did she resent that? The thought made her tremble. She hoped not. That could not be. Was she beginning to resent her marriage? Had her husband sensed in her a change of heart? She didn't know.

She disapproved of her husband's habits: too much fishing, too much hunting, too much stopping at the Wagon Wheel for a drink on his way home. She viewed him as selfish, and she had ridiculed him for that. Nagging was its own sin.

Her husband was a good man, better than most, and a good provider. But he didn't see eye to eye with her when it came to Marilyn Wojcheski. He had avoided them when the two were together. He did not support her. He was not envious, but he was condescending. He considered them to be above her friend's lowly station.

His wife sensed a deeper truth. He would not accept a divorced woman because he was fearful of his church. The Catholic religion held archaic beliefs, but her husband would not probe inside them. Instead, he hid behind them. He was but one sheep in the flock, and he followed his shepherd. Then, too, he was a man in a man's world.

She continued with the examination of her conscience. She reviewed the Ten Commandments, searching for her sins. Yes, she had been short-tempered with her children: she had been bossy to a fault. But these were venial sins because she had quickly apologized to them.

She disliked her mother-in-law. But this was also a small matter because she tried to be kind and pleasant and understanding. She accepted Grandma's idiosyncrasies and crass behavior as an old lady's quirks. Oddly enough, Grandma viewed her daughter-in-law's politeness as retaliation.

As the woman concluded her preparation for the sacrament of confession, one sin predominated. It stood out above the rest, and it was a serious sin, perhaps even a mortal one. She was angry. Ever since the mass that Sunday, she had held a grudge against Father Schumacher. She had shared in her friend's shame. Her temper had raged, and her heart had hardened against him. Here in the confessional, she knew that she must confess this. She must repent and be forgiven. As she thought of the Act of Contrition she would recite, she knew that she must be truly penitent. Otherwise, her sin could not be forgiven.

"I absolve you of your sins," the priest would say, "in the name of the Father, and of the Son, and of the Holy Spirit, Amen." He was Jesus's representative here on Earth, acting on his behalf, administering the sacraments.

But she must not sulk in silence either. Her visit to the confessional, this time, had a dual purpose. She wanted Father to know how she felt, that he had overstepped his priestly bounds in condemning Marilyn Wojcheski. Marilyn was no Eve; she was no Wife of Lot or Delilah or Mary Magdalene. And she certainly was not Salome, daughter of Herodias, dancing seductively to bring about the death of John the Baptist. Yet, Father had painted this picture of her in front of the whole congregation. The man had sinned, too. He must know that. She wanted him to admit it.

She pondered. She knew what she must do. The question was how to do it. The woman entered the confessional with much on her mind. She knelt in the darkness and fidgeted with her skirt. In a minute she would be talking with Father Schumacher face-to-face, with only a thin screen between them. It was an intimate setting, and she was well aware that the pastor's position of authority in the Church gave him a distinct advantage over her. He was the spiritual leader of St. Joseph's parish and a figurehead in the community. Who was she to challenge him? That, and the fact that he was a man, made her nervous.

The window in front of her slid open. She spoke.

"Bless us, Father, for we have sinned. My last confession was four weeks ago Friday." She stopped when she heard a male voice.

"What do you mean by 'we'?" asked the confessor.

"You and me, Father, we have both sinned and need to be forgiven."

The other side of the screen was still. She could see nothing. "Please explain," said the voice.

She hesitated, not sure what to say. "I'm pregnant, Father."

The priest responded. "Being impregnated by your husband is not a sin."

She bristled. "Of course, it was by my husband!" Her outburst surprised her.

At this, he remained silent and waited for her to continue. The woman in the confessional tried to calm herself.

"I brought Marilyn Wojcheski to mass last Sunday. I told her that she would be welcome. I told her that the Catholic Church is for everyone and would accept her—as she is. That's what Catholic means, doesn't it, Father?"

"We would accept her, but not as she is," replied the priest. "She has divorced her husband and is living outside the boundaries of the Church. That is sinful."

"She is not Eve or Lot's Wife or Delilah or Mary Magdalene. You called her Salome!"

"I did not."

"Yes, you did. You said it to my son after mass. He was an altar server."

"That was private. I said it to myself."

"My son heard you."

The man reflected on Sunday's mass. "Did you see how she was dressed?" he asked. "It was indecent. And in the middle of my sermon, she waltzed up the aisle, wiggling her hips at me."

"At whom?"

"At *me*," he asserted. His voice had grown stern. "She was dressed immodestly. Her blouse was low cut and revealing. Her skirt didn't even come down to her knees. It barely covered her bottom! You shouldn't have brought her here looking like that. I am a defender of our faith. I am the shepherd. I am here to guard the flock against anyone who threatens it. That woman's whole demeanor was offensive."

"Whom did she offend?" Pat Kucher's voice was full of challenge. "Did she offend the four boys who came in late? They come in halfway through mass every week, and you say nothing."

"I am the pastor of this parish. I must uphold our Catholic beliefs. Like Elijah, the Prophet, I must rise up against those who put themselves before God and even above God. That's idolatry. I stand firmly against those who challenge God's authority."

"Father Schumacher, I feel hate. Since last Sunday, I have felt hatred in my heart for how you treated her. It's weighing heavily on me. I cannot go to Holy Communion feeling this way. It's affecting how I act, how I treat my family. These feelings are strong. Because of them, I have been sharp with my children. I don't listen to them. I can't take care of their needs.

I am also becoming resentful toward my husband. I find myself putting my needs before his, at least my emotional needs. At times, I have distanced myself from him. Then I feel guilty. I am feeling what Marilyn Wojcheski must feel every day—that she has been judged unfairly under a law of the Church that is severe. The penalty is harsh—alienation. She's being forced to live in isolation. She's a leper in our midst."

The confessor's reply was heartfelt, but critical. "Marilyn Wojcheski has made little effort to mend her ways. And you are lending her support. Mrs. Kucher, do you know the damage you are doing? That woman has a family, four little children. They need their parents, both a mother and a father. I have talked to the men in this parish. They've told me that Tom Wojcheski is a good man. Your own husband has told me that. He sees how your friendship with this woman is driving a wedge between him and you. Mrs. Kucher, think of the consequences for your own family before it's too late."

The woman replied, "Do you know that Tom Wojcheski has beaten her up?"

"That's because of the stress she's causing. A divorce is never pretty."

"If Clifford hit me with his fists, I'd leave him, too."

"He would never do that…" The priest's voice trailed off.

"Unless I provoked him. Unless I drove him to it." She finished his sentence for him.

"I am not excusing everything the man has done. But a marriage succeeds only when a wife submits to her husband. The Bible, in Ephesians 5:22, tells her to obey her husband, and he will love her for it. Putting yourself first is putting yourself before God. You become a believer in a false god. Jezebel tried that in the Old Testament. Read the First Book of Kings. She worshipped the pagan god, Baal. Elijah rode his chariot, preaching against her, chastising her. He prophesied her doom. Elijah predicted that she would die a horrible death, and it came to pass just as he had predicted." The priest in the confessional lowered his voice and aimed it at the woman behind the screen. "Mrs. Kucher, I want you to listen carefully."

She listened in horror to her confessor's story of Jezebel's death. When he finished, he advised her: "Take note! Take heed!"

He cautioned her. "You must repent. You cannot have hatred in your heart and save your eternal soul. Are you sorry?"

"I want to be," she replied. She tried to sound contrite.

"But are you really sorry for your sins?" He did not sound like he believed her. "Will you refrain from condoning that woman's divorce?" He paused. "You can still be friends."

She did not accept his compromise. "I am not sorry that I am her friend. I am not sorry that she turns to me when her husband hits her and she has nowhere else to go. I am not sorry that I brought her to church last Sunday. I am sorry that you did not act more like Jesus Christ. You rejected her, Father. You showed her no compassion. You sinned."

"Then I cannot absolve you of your sins. I'm sorry for you, Mrs. Kucher." The small wooden window slid shut.

When she stood up, her knees ached. She felt a stiffness in her legs. She left the confessional and stepped into the darkened church. She did not feel comfortable. In fact, she felt sick to her stomach. She exited through the main door into the street and found it deserted. She slipped into her car and drove the five blocks home.

The boy's mother had learned long ago that when she felt troubled, she should confide in her husband. As she entered the house, the man saw the look on her face. She was upset, nearly hysterical. Their son, sitting quietly on a chair in the corner, saw it too. They both knew that something had gone awry. She told her husband about her meeting with Father Schumacher, including the fact that the priest had refused to give her absolution. This bothered him.

She explained what had happened. "Now he's calling Marilyn a Jezebel. He told me the entire story. Jezebel committed idolatry. She loved herself more than God, and she worshipped a false god, Baal. She was killing off the Lord's prophets.

The prophet, Elijah, predicted how she would die a frightful death, and it all came true. She was thrown from a tower by her eunuchs. These servants betrayed her. And then she was eaten by a pack of wild dogs. Only her skull, feet, and hands remained."

The wife searched for an insight into the priest's behavior. "He was trying to scare me," she concluded.

"And he succeeded," her husband agreed.

"He wanted me to submit. The nerve of that man! To call Marilyn Wojcheski a Jezebel, an idolater. He needs to go to confession."

Her husband stared at her. He was deeply troubled. She stopped and stared back at him. His voice was sympathetic. "He's not calling Marilyn Wojcheski a Jezebel."

"He's not?" she asked in disbelief.

"No, he's speaking about you."

A brief silence followed. "Good Lord, how can I not hate him?" asked the boy's mother.

"You need to go to confession to another priest," the man stated, "perhaps to Father Thiel or someone in St. Cloud. Go to one at the Newman Center at the college; they're more liberal…" She looked at him askance. He winced. "…more understanding. Or go to the priest in Clearwater. I like him. He says mass on Sunday in seventeen minutes."

The next day on their way to school, Frankie told Terry Joe about his mother's confession. He told him about Father Schumacher's story about Jezebel.

"What's a eunuch?" Frankie asked his friend.

Terry Joe's eyes glassed over behind his glasses. He looked up at the clouds in the sky as if they held the answer. "I don't know."

His best friend looked up with him. "Are you looking for Heaven?" he asked.

"No," the other boy answered. He shrugged. "I'll ask my Uncle Squeak. He knows all that stuff."

But by the next morning they still did not know the answer although several theories had been put forth. Terry Joe reported on his visit to his Uncle Squeak. "He said that it's a man who doesn't like women."

The other boy, Frankie, looked at his friend hard. "Is Crazy Milo a eunuch? He doesn't like woman."

"He doesn't like anybody," stated Terry Joe. He was still confused. He had an idea. "I'll look it up in the dictionary," said Terry Joe, "that big fat one that's always open on Mrs. O'Leery's book stand."

That morning Sister Mary Bede heard the strangest request she had ever heard in her life as a teacher. Terry Joe O'Brian raised his hand.

"Yes?" she asked guardedly.

"Can I stay in from recess today, Sister? I want to go to the library." She had looked at him quizzically and finally nodded, granting his request. It was an unusual request. She would look into the library later and check with Mrs. O'Leery about what had transpired. She was curious. What did the boy want?

The Second Grade boys huddled around Terry Joe when he came out onto the school's playground. Recess was almost over. He was grinning from ear to ear.

"What did you find out?" Frankie asked him.

"I found it," he answered. He pushed a sheet of paper under his friend's nose. "It's not under 'y.'" Several words starting with 'y' had been crossed out: younick, younic, younik, yunych. "It's under 'u.' I finally found it: *unique*." He had copied the definition down verbatim. "It's a French word, meaning 'being without a like or equal; very rare or uncommon; very unusual; strange.

I wonder what makes a *unique* uncommon," asked Terry Joe. No one in the huddle knew the answer to that question.

"What's that little *adj.* mean?" asked Jimmy Holston. He had been staring at the paper containing the definition. No one knew that either.

"Let's ask Sister Bede," suggested Terry Joe. "She'll tell us if she knows."

"Let's ask Mrs. Willow," suggested Ricky Shenker. "She'll know." The boys in the huddle agreed. Mrs. Willow loved English; she loved words. She wanted them *to have a way with words*. She would know.

Across the playground Susanne Danbury sat on the steps. She was bothered. The boys had huddled in secret. That was unusual, totally out of character. For the entire recess they had left their football on the ground, untouched. Why had Terrance O'Brian gone to the library? That made her deeply suspicious. She had broken his fish. It was an accident and she had apologized. She had volunteered to pay for it. But he had been terribly upset. He had planned to give it as a present to his mother. Today was her birthday. She was sure they were discussing her. That irritating boy, Frankie, had seen her looking their way. He had scowled at her. That confirmed it. They were discussing her, plotting some revenge.

"No," Mrs. Willow explained, *unique* is not a person; it's an adjective describing a person. There is no such thing as a *unique*."

"Well, then what is a eunuch?" asked Terry Joe, point blank. He showed her his paper from the library. The woman roared with laughter until her eyes watered over.

"Why do you want to know?" she responded, still laughing. "I'll tell you this much," she volunteered. "It's a man who has been found wanting."

"Was he lost?" Terry Joe inquired.

She let loose with another laugh. The second bell rang. She nudged them toward the door, and they shuffled off to class.

"How can that be true?" Terry Joe whispered to the boy behind him. "I asked my Uncle Squeak again last night. He told me that a eunuch doesn't even want anything. That's just the opposite of what Mrs. Willow told us. She said that it's a man who does want it. One of them is lying. I think it's Mrs. Willow. Did you see how hard she laughed?"

The next day at recess the boys huddled again. Once again, the football lay in the dirt, unused. Susanne Danbury, on her steps, was in a tizzy. That boy, Frankie, had scowled at her again. She felt inclined to report him to Sister Anthony before anything happened.

The young girl's report of impending violence against her brought Frankie to Sister Anthony's office once again. He was accompanied by his friend, Terry Joe O'Brian. Sister sized the boys up with a quick glance. They seemed harmless. The boy who collected bullfrogs in the swamp seemed on the verge of tears once again. She looked at the tissues on her desk. They would be handy if needed.

"So, why are you congregating on the school yard in a huddle during recess?" she inquired, coming to the point relatively quickly. She directed the question to her girlhood friend's son, Terry Joe.

"Because we're wondering" was the boy's cryptic reply.

"And what are you wondering about?" was her next question.

"About the meaning of a word," he answered.

"Okay, I'll bite," she stated. "What word?"

"Eunuch." He showed her his paper from the library.

She did not laugh quite as hard as Mrs. Willow had, but her

eyes became moist. This time, it was she who needed a tissue. She helped herself to one.

"Sister, just what is a eunuch?" Terry Joe's question had that same sincere quality in it that she had sensed in him before.

Suddenly, however, she reminded herself that she was a good friend of the boy's mother, Lorraine Sullivan. This complicated the situation. Lorraine and her husband, Bill, might not like Sister educating their son on such a personal topic. The young boy was not afraid to ask questions. It might open a whole can of worms. In a Catholic community the birds and the bees, and all things related, were typically delegated solely to the parents. This was a delicate matter. She had best defer.

"I'll tell you this much," stated Sister Anthony. She considered the proper phrasing. "A eunuch is one without two." She smiled. She, too, could be cryptic when she had to be. "I'll leave you boys to figure out the rest. It's time to leave. I'm busy. Oh, yes, and you," she pointed her finger at Frankie, "stay away from Susanne Danbury."

That would be easy, thought the boy. He had no intention of being near that girl with the big head and the big mouth, ever. He turned his attention back to Sister Anthony's definition of eunuch. But why had she laughed. It's a riddle, he concluded as he returned to the Second Grade classroom. Why do adults always speak to children in riddles?

The next day's huddle convened, and several boys had new information. Out of frustration and some desire to return to playing football at recess, they had asked their fathers what a eunuch was.

"My dad says it's a human capon," said John Lewis.

"What's a capon?" asked Terry Joe.

"It's a chicken," replied the hatchery owner's son.

"How can a chicken not like women?" countered Terry Joe. "That doesn't make any sense. A chicken is not a man." The other boys could not refute his logic.

Jerry Unger spoke up. "My dad says it's a locomotive engine that has run out of steam. It can't make it up the hill. But I don't know if I believe that. Dad is always talking about train engines. That's all he ever talks about, unless he's fixing a bike. And he was laughing, sort of. He chuckles a lot at his own jokes."

It was then that Frankie spoke up. He told the boys what Sister Anthony had told him and Terry Joe. "It's got to be something holy, something in the Bible," the boy reasoned. Father Schumacher said it to my mother in confession. Sister said it was "one without two."

Jimmy Holston spoke up. He sounded skeptical. "One minus two is arithmetic."

"It's not arithmetic," argued Frankie. Those are cubits, like Sister had us add up when we measured Noah's ark. This is religion. Sister said "one without two."

Chester Benton stared down at his wooden leg. "I'm one without one," he muttered. "Maybe a eunuch has no legs."

"It's the Trinity." The words came from a meek voice at the back of the huddle. It belonged to Jonas Duane. "There are three persons in one God. 'One without two' must mean when they are alone. The Father, the Son, and the Holy Spirit are eunuchs when they're alone."

Jimmy Holston did not sound convinced. "The Holy Spirit is a pigeon. It's a bird. It can't be a person. It's not a human being."

"It's not a pigeon; it's a dove," corrected Jonas.

"It's still a bird," argued Jimmy Holston.

"A chicken is a bird," added John Lewis, still defending his father's definition. "And a capon is a chicken."

"I think Jonas is right!" stated Terry Joe, suddenly excited. "Sister told us that the Dove is just a picture of the Holy Spirit. He's not really a bird. She said that there are three persons in one God. The Holy Spirit is one of those persons. When they're together, they're the Trinity. When they're by themselves, they're eunuchs." He was satisfied with his assessment.

It sounded plausible. But the Bible was a mysterious book. Frankie walked home that afternoon, still puzzled. He didn't know what to believe.

He received a far different explanation that Saturday when he drove out with his father to the mink ranch. While watering mink, he asked his friend, Billy Fercho, what a eunuch was. He tried to sound casual.

Billy didn't know; the Ferchos weren't Catholics anymore. So, Billy asked his dad, Leo.

Leo roared with laughter so hard that he almost choked. "Hey, Cliff," he yelled. "Come here and listen to this."

Much to the boy's chagrin, his own father entered the room. The man looked at his son. "What's the problem?" asked the man. "Did you finish watering the mink?"

The boy nodded. Leo spoke.

"These boys want to know what a eunuch is." The boy's father held his gaze steady and continued to look his son in the eye.

"Well, tell them," said his father.

"It's a man who doesn't have any balls."

"You mean he's a fraidy cat? A coward?" asked the boy.

"NO!" roared Leo. "He's had his nuts cut off. That way he won't go after women. He'll never want to. He'll have no libido for the rest of his life."

"But why would they cut them off... er... do that to a man in the Bible? Jezebel had eunuchs who threw her off a tower, and wild dogs ate her.

It was his father who answered. "Castrating slaves was a common practice back then. It made them focus on their work better. Without their testicles, they had no testosterone. They lost their desire. So, they no longer cared to chase women. They stuck to the business at hand." He looked at his watch. "Which is what I want you to do. It's time to brush the old feed off the wires. Next month we'll be pelting our first crop. The mink are looking good. They'll start furring out just after Thanksgiving." He looked at his pal, Leo. "We have to be ready. Get going, boys."

As Frankie brushed the wires, it made perfect sense. He was glad he had not told his father about the Trinity. The man might still be guffawing. He might even tell the boy's mother. Maybe even his grandmother.

The boy would have to tell his classmates. They had been suckers. He hoped the girls would never find out. Gail Teigen and Irene Pressler and Jeanie Kovar would eventually stop laughing, but they would never forget. He pictured Susanne Danbury with her big head and sarcastic smile. He shuddered at the thought. That would be awful. That would be something he could never live down.

CHAPTER TWENTY-TWO

"Cat licker!"

"Pot licker!"

"We used to stand across the street from each other in Sauk Centre and hurl insults," the boy's mother related. "Of course, we were only children, so it was on a smaller scale. But the fact that it was on a smaller scale didn't decrease the intensity of our outbursts. The Protestants did not like us very much, and we didn't like them at all. That was back in the late 1930s and early '40s. I guess much hasn't changed."

The information was in response to a guarded question, "Mom, why are some kids so mean?" The inquiry had come not from the boy but from his sister, Jeanne. The question had caught the boy's ear, though.

The children's mother had thought about her answer and taken her time to respond. "For us, it was a matter of religion. No Catholic liked any Protestant, and vice versa. My dad wouldn't even let me date a Lutheran boy when I wanted to once. And you know how Grandma Kucher feels about Uncle Larry. She wanted Jane baptized Catholic. She was afraid that the baby would die and go to hell, or at least to purgatory.

Grandma has changed her tune, but not entirely. The Reeders are Missouri Synod Lutherans; they're hard core believers. They can't stand Catholics. I'm sure Aunt Berneda has had a hard time.

It's still the same way in Ireland. Look at Northern Ireland. That's Protestant, the color orange. The rest of Ireland is Catholic, green. They still hate each other after centuries."

"But we're not Irish," protested the boy. "We're German and Bohemian."

"Not Grandma Kucher. She's half Irish, on her mother's side."

"The nationality doesn't matter as much any more anyway; the religion does. Look at our country. We haven't had a Catholic president yet—all Protestants. They're scared of us. They're afraid the pope will take over America."

His sister, Jeanne, had a second question: "Why do some kids pick on other kids?"

"Who's mean?" asked her mother. "Has someone been picking on you?"

"Jackie Birch. She likes to climb up to that tree house down there." She pointed toward the west. "She'll only be my friend if I climb up there." Her brother felt a grave alarm at this news. "She called me a 'fatso'."

"Stay away from her for a while," the mother advised. "She'll come back to being your friend. If it gets too bad, I'll speak to Florence."

"Not her mother!" cried Jeanne. "Jackie wouldn't like that."

"Precisely," her mother replied.

Every boy in Waite Park knew that it was only a matter of time before Bertie Norton would call one too many people an "asshole" and flick his middle finger at someone one too many times. They hoped that justice would come to him swiftly, sooner rather than later.

When Bertie saw Curtis Benton limping after a soccer ball on the public school playground at McKinley Elementary, he laughed. Then he snarled. "Hey kid," he called to Curtis, "you're an asshole. You're a Catholic asshole. That's worse. What are you doing over here on our playground?" To emphasize his message, Bertie began to hobble, limping heavily on one leg, mimicking the younger boy.

It had been a long time since Curtis Benton had cried. Now he fought back his tears, tears of hate.

The game stopped. The players formed a half circle around Curtis. These were younger boys, no threat to him, thought Bertie. He laughed indifferently.

But someone else was watching. Across the street in his house, a man stood at his living room window. He could not hear what was being said, but he could see the facial expressions. Then he saw the older, red-haired boy raise his fist, palm inward, with the middle finger extended up.

Roland Becker gritted his teeth. He felt indignant. He was a good Catholic man, but he knew how to feel wrath. And now he felt a righteous hostility toward the red-haired bully. The boy was a fat pig with no respect and no manners. "That boy needs to be taught a lesson," Roland stated. He was passing judgment.

With Roland Becker was his oldest son, Marty. He heard his father's wish. In effect, it was a command. He rose to his feet. "I'll take care of it, Dad," the boy said. He was nearly a young man: well-built, lithe, and strong. He left the house via the back door and catapulted down the steps. Inside, his father continued to watch.

Outside, the neighborhood children were congregating. Bertie Norton continued to bully them. "Damn Catholics!" He was turning aggressive. He pushed Curtis, and the younger boy, caught off guard, lost his balance and fell.

Immediately the crippled boy jumped up. "You're a big dumb ass," he yelled. True to his breed, he was defiant.

The red-haired boy clipped him across the jaw with his fist. "You'll eat those words," he howled. And grabbing Curtis by the arm, he tripped his good leg out from under him and pushed the smaller boy's head into the dirt.

The bully looked up just in time. He turned to sidestep a blow. Marty Becker had sprinted across the playground and swung mightily at Bertie Norton's jaw. It was only a glancing blow, but it had enough impact to send the red-haired boy back two steps. Bertie raised his arms, fists cocked, to defend himself.

"Get him, Marty. Get him for me." It was Curtis's voice. He was sitting up, trying to stand. His fists were clenched.

The people of the village knew that there was one family from whom they should keep their distance, the Beckers. It was a family that could be traced back to Waite Park's earliest days. It was a large family, fighters all. They stuck up for one another. When there was a lull, they fought among themselves. The other youths in the village knew to give them a wide berth. If you befriended one, you befriended them all. If you became an enemy of one, you became an enemy of all. It was why Frankie sometimes wished he had an older brother—for protection. His father had labeled the Becker family a "*nest*."

Marty Becker circled his opponent. Like his father, he was crafty. He calculated speed and distance, and knew that the bigger boy was slower. He decided to attack the boy's midsection. It was mostly flab.

He struck Bertie twice in the belly and then a third time. He side-stepped the retaliatory blow and connected again. The large red-haired boy's head was rocked back.

His eye glasses lay twisted across his forehead, and one of the lenses was broken. His nose was bleeding. Bertie took hold of his glasses and flung them to the ground. They landed next to Curtis Benton, who stooped and picked them up.

The crowd of younger boys cheered Marty Becker on. "Come on, Marty. Hit him."

"Beat him to a pulp."

"Kill that asshole."

"Cut off his balls. Make him a eunuch!"

Behind the living room window across the street, Roland Becker continued to stare. It brought back memories of fights he had had when he was a teenager. One, perhaps the most vicious, had been with his best friend, Carl, Curtis Benton's dad. Roland had broken the boy's nose with a decisive blow to the face.

The crowd swirled around the combatants. "You're an asshole," Bertie said to Marty Becker, and the crowd's hero attacked again. He was relentless. He punched the fat boy in the face, knocking a tooth loose.

Bertie shook his boar's head. He spat out a mouthful of blood, and the tooth fell to the ground. He remained obstinate and determined, resolute. But there was no reprieve, no escape.

Then Marty hit him in the guts, hard, with all his remaining might. It doubled his adversary over, but the red-haired boy would not go down. "Go down!" Marty shouted.

But Bertie Norton staggered and then regained his balance. He was still standing. His nostrils flared as he tried to breathe. But he was bleeding profusely from his nose, and this inhibited his intake of breath. He sucked in air through his mouth. He wavered and wobbled on two feet, a beast ready to be slaughtered.

"Go down, or I'll kill you!" the stronger boy commanded. He struck another savage blow to his foe's chin. But even that failed to knock the other boy off his feet. He would not give up.

Frankie stood at the back of the crowd. He felt sick to his stomach. He had been bullied by Bertie Norton more than once, but he did not hate him. Bertie would not submit. He had taken the punishment that Marty Becker had inflicted, but he stayed standing. The other boys sensed something, too, and they were hushed.

And then they heard one terrible outcry as Bertie Norton sank to his knees and covered his face with his hands. "Where are my glasses?" he bellowed. "My glasses! I can't see without them."

Marty Becker was sweating profusely. He gulped great drafts of air. Suddenly he had had enough. He spat, turned, and headed home.

The crowd of boys stepped back and slipped away, leaving Bertie kneeling alone, dead meat. The red-haired boy was helpless. He pitched forward and fumbled blindly on the ground, searching for his glasses. But he would never find them. Curtis Benton had taken them. At the edge of the playground, Frankie saw Curtis drop them on the sidewalk and grind them under his heel, the heel of his wooden leg.

As Frankie plodded home, he was deeply disturbed. Bertie Norton would not submit. Even after a merciless pummeling, he had refused to give in. Not once had he threatened to tell his dad or mentioned his dad's lawyer. He had refused to give up of his own will, even though he was overmatched. He knew it. Yet, he had taken a severe beating. That was a lesson in character: to stand your ground, win or lose.

Submit. Wasn't that the word his mother had used? Father Schumacher had wanted her to submit, but she had refused. She, too, had stood her ground. It was a strange connection, and it gave the boy an awkward feeling.

In Waite Park one had to fight to survive. It came with the territory. It was a test of a boy's manhood. His day would come. Eventually he would have to brace himself and stand his ground. He cut across O'Brians' yard and crossed the alley. His father's truck was already in the driveway. He was late. They were eating supper without him.

In summer and fall the children of Waite Park chased one another. "Tag, you're it!" evolved into a variety of games, some more sophisticated than others. *Fox Lost His Trail* was popular in most neighborhoods. It was a game of search and discovery. Of course, the children knew the best places to hide. In Frankie's neighborhood, they had free rein of the city block to roam, but not beyond.

The foxes hid; the hunters and their hounds had to find them. Once found and tagged, the fox turned into a hound. That was the thrill of the game for the boy. Eventually all of the children would be chasing him. He felt the surge brought on by fear as the pack of hounds closed in. It pushed him to run harder.

In the northeast corner of the village, the Ryngsmuths and their neighbors played *Capture the Flag*. They created two armies that opposed one another and vied for advantage. To win, the boys and girls had to be bold and shun safe refuge. They had to cross the middle border, a "no man's land," and dart into opposing territory. If they were lucky enough to grab the enemy's flag, they had to sprint back to their side for victory. It required strategy and teamwork to mount a successful campaign. Each side took turns coordinating a series of attempts, some feigned, to lure the defending army out and render it vulnerable. And then, suddenly, the real thing! A lightning strike that was not anticipated.

The game taught a lesson about life. The mayor's children were learning that they must take calculated risks. It was a quality that their father possessed. As Al Ryngsmuth sat with his wife on his porch and watched the game unfold, he knew that it would serve them in good stead when they were older.

All across Waite Park in the neighborhoods, children played.

> *Starlight, moonlight, hope to see a ghost tonight.*
> *If I may, if I might, have the wish I make tonight.*
> *Ready or not, here I come!*

They played the game at night, when the darkness stirred the imagination. It was an atmosphere that instilled fear, the fear of being caught.

On Frankie's block the pursuit would commence. The team who was 'it' would tag the other children. These unlucky ones were taken to "jail" on the Krauses' steps. It gave the boy great satisfaction to sweep in, evading tags, and free his teammates. Once freed, they would scamper away, only to be pursued again. And so the game continued.

The boy loved to run, full speed, exerting himself. The night sky was clear. Looking up, he saw the stars twinkling brightly in the heavens. He squinted at them and their light diffused into vertical streaks. He knew the constellations. Foremost was the Little Dipper, anchored by its handle's outermost star, Polaris, the North Star. He had read the stories, the seafarer's lore. They used the North Star to guide them, to help gauge their location on the sea. The star never varied its position in the sky, never wavered. It was a fixture, a constant that could be relied on. The Big Dipper was aligned to it: the two stars on the front pointed directly at the North Star. Above him, he recognized Cassiopeia, shaped like a large "W," and the three stars in Orion's belt.

The autumn moon was a pumpkin moon, round and orange in a cloudless sky. Farmers called it a harvest moon. As he ran, the boy watched his breath. The air was cool, and the sweat from his body evaporated quickly. He wanted to be the last one caught. There was a thrill to the chase. He envisioned himself to be a wild horse, a mustang who could not be roped and tamed. A stallion. But there were other horses in hot pursuit. Some were fillies. The fastest was his neighbor from across the street, Jackie Birch.

Across 10th Avenue on Tillie Kuchenmeister's boulevard, three O'Brian boys and Johnny Fisch were playing a far different game.

"Lie down and pretend you were hit by a car," Timmy ordered. Johnny Fisch complied. His torso lay on the lawn; his head and arms dangled in the street. The other boys retreated to their own yard and hid behind a clump of evergreens. They waited patiently.

Soon, a car's headlights emerged from the highway. A sedan sped down the avenue and then suddenly screeched to a halt. The headlights illuminated Johnny Fisch's body. A worried man exited from the driver's side and raced toward the injured boy. The man's wife, in the passenger seat, rolled down her window. "Is it serious, Henry?" she inquired.

"I don't know," the man replied. He knelt down next to the boy. "Are you hurt, son?" he asked. Johnny Fisch moaned.

"How bad is it?" He stooped down to pick up the lad and carry him out of the street. He reached down under the head and lifted it gingerly.

It was the unexpected moment Johnny Fisch needed to make his escape. He leaped to his feet.

"No, son. Lie still."

But Johnny Fisch ran into the street and across it, toward the O'Brian's yard. He was laughing.

"Don't come this way," Timmy growled. But it was too late. The man saw them hiding. The four boys ran across 5th Street away into the night.

The man pursued them but only briefly. He roared in anger. "How dare you!" he yelled. "You little shits! You scared me!" He stopped his chase and returned to his car, glad to be done with them.

"Can you believe it?" he asked his wife. She had rolled up her window. He was shaking. "He scared me."

"You were a good Samaritan, Henry."

"And this is what I get," he muttered. He shifted the car into first gear, pulled away from the curb, and punched the accelerator to the floor.

The four boys crossed the alley. They cut across Grandma Tegelman's yard and ran past a second house and a third. Eleventh Avenue was empty of traffic. They slowed their pace and stopped when they reached Johnny Fisch's house. It was a basement house.

"He's not following us," Terry Joe said. He was puffing. They crawled up onto the Fisches' roof and sat down behind the chimney, out of sight from the street.

"Why did you run our way?" Timmy scolded. "He could've caught us. Next time, run the other way."

Johnny Fisch felt rejection. "Well, kill me then!" he screamed.

The older boy lightened his tone. "It was a good joke," Timmy chuckled. "Did you see his face?" He peered into the darkness, looking for any pursuers. The coast was clear. "Let's go home. Kevin, you jump down first."

In the light of the pumpkin moon, Johnny Fisch sat on his rooftop, crying. He so wanted to be accepted. He did not feel loved. People said that he looked like his mother. But she did not love him either. The moon was full, an omen. Winter was fast approaching, and he had no real friends.

The knock on the door came a few minutes before 5:00 o'clock in the evening. The boy's father got up to answer the door. Before him stood a young female pirate, holding a cloth sack in her hands. "Trick or treat," she said. She stuck the bag out toward him.

"Come in," he stated in welcome. "We're all in here."

She followed him into the living room, where five people were kneeling, a woman and four children. She recognized them all. One was in her class at school, Sister Bede's Second Grade.

It was October 31ˢᵗ, 1958, Halloween. Norma Krause, a neighbor from across the alley, had decided to get an early start trick-or-treating. She was bedecked accordingly, in costume. She wore a loose-fitting blouse and a skirt with a ragged hem that swished about her calves. She wore black, ankle-length boots on her feet and a red kerchief on her head, tied in a knot at the back. On top of her head perched a pirate's hat with a skull and crossbones sewn on the front and a plume in back.

Accessories accented the costume. Large, circular earrings dangled from Norma's ears. They matched the gold bracelets she wore on her wrists. Those matched the rings on her fingers, all ten digits, gold bands set with large rubies and emeralds and diamonds and topaz. She wore a pearl necklace around her neck and, at her insistence, a pink carnation stuffed into the blouse, tucked into the tiny crease in her bosom. She was wearing make-up: eye-liner and eye-shadow and red lipstick, and her fingernails were painted red. Fortunately, Val Krause had been visiting garage sales recently and had come across a large store of costume jewelry for sale at Tillie Kuchenmeister's. She had bought the entire lot.

But the costume was still not complete. She was fully bedecked only when she covered her left eye with a black patch and strapped a scabbard with its cutlass around her waist.

The boy's father presented her to the others. He took a long second look, himself. She fit the part perfectly, every bit a salty wench belonging to Long John Silver, Robert Louis Stevenson's hero in *Treasure Island* or to Blackbeard, the swarthy English sea captain of the *Queen Anne's Revenge.*

"Shiver me timbers, Cap'n!" the man pretended. He envisioned a pirate ship, berthed in a port on Barbados in the Caribbean. By golly, it was enough to suggest a pirate's song. *Yo Ho Ho and a bottle of rum...* He chuckled to himself.

But she was early. The boy's father looked at his hands. They held a rosary. After all, October was the Month of the Most Holy Rosary. "Kneel down here," the man stated. "Take this rosary. We're just starting the second decade." He returned to his place by the window and knelt down. He pulled another rosary from his pocket.

The children were dumbstruck, fascinated by Norma's attire. "She's a pirate," Mary whispered to her sister, Jeanne.

"I know," her older sister whispered back.

Their brother, Dan, just stared. "That's Norma... Norma Krause... Norma from across the alley," Mary informed him. She pointed toward the alley. "She's a pirate."

But the young boy continued to stare. One thing bothered him: Why does she have only one eye?

His older brother did not look at the visitor. He, too, was bothered, but perplexed by something completely different: Why does she have rings on her *thumbs*?

Norma Krause didn't want to kneel. She didn't want a rosary; she wanted candy. She wanted to be out the door and on her way. But she knelt down anyway.

"Hail Mary, full of grace, the Lord is with thee," the man's voice articulated. "Blessed art thou among women, and blessed is the fruit of thy womb, Jesus." He stopped.

His wife and children responded. "Holy Mary, the Mother of God, pray for us sinners now and at the hour of our death. Amen." They stopped.

Norma watched. The father, the mother, Frankie, and his sisters and brother all moved their fingers to the next bead. So, she did the same.

"Hail Mary, full of grace, the Lord is with thee," the man began again. When he finished, the family responded again. Again, they moved one bead forward, in unison. So, Norma moved her fingers to the next bead.

As they prayed, Norma felt a growing dislike for Frankie. She bristled. She was Anne Bonny, the pirate, a woman with luscious red locks and a dangerous temper. She was not the 'hailed Mary.' She didn't even want to be 'full of grace.' That wasn't what a modern girl wanted. She had been told by Laura Birch, "If you want to know what women of today like, read a magazine." Norma had.

After ten Hail Mary's the prayer changed. "Our Father, who art in Heaven, hallowed be thy name..." the man prayed.

"Give us this day our daily bread..." the chorus responded.

If the pirate wench was antsy, she never showed it. She kept advancing her fingers to the next bead, each time counting how many more were left. She mouthed the final twenty Hail Mary's and the last two Glory Be's. By then, they had become ingrained in her. She had memorized the Catholic prayers once, a long time ago. But they had faded from her memory. The Krauses did not pray the rosary.

Finally the man made the sign of the cross. He and his family kissed the crucifix on the end of the rosary's chain and stood up. Norma was the first one to her feet. Frankie thought she looked ready to flee. She headed for the back door as if bent on a mission.

"Aren't you forgetting something?" the boy's father reminded her.

She turned and checked for her sword. He held up a bowl of candy.

"Oh, trick or treat," she stated. It was a perfunctory statement. She reached into the bowl with a hand covered in rings. Inside, she felt miniature candy bars.

"Take just one," her host instructed her as she started to withdraw her hand. "We need to have enough for everyone."

She let the other candy bars drop and took one.

"They're Mounds and Almond Joys," stated Jeanne. It was an Almond Joy.

The pirate lass made her escape quickly. She leaped down the steps and did not look back. It had been a full twenty minutes: forty Hail Mary's, four Our Father's, and four Glory Be's. She was behind schedule.

Frankie did not give Norma Krause's departure another thought. He had his own plans. By 6:05 he had gulped down supper, two sunfish fillets and a plate of baked beans. It was Friday, a day no meat was allowed. A minute later he bolted outside through the back doorway. He nearly tripped over the jack-o'-lanterns, now lit from within, that his mother was displaying on the back steps.

There were four of them. Each child, except Baby Chuck, had helped carve one. The top of each pumpkin had been cut open so that the seeds could be scooped out with a spoon. The top then became a lid that opened so a candle could be placed inside the pumpkin.

Each had a face with triangular eyes, a triangular nose, and square teeth. Most of the teeth were missing. The jack-o'-lanterns smiled broadly, and their missing teeth gave them a haunting appearance.

The neighbors' houses and yards were decorated to create a bewitching atmosphere. Ghosts in white sheets and goblins hung from the ceilings of the porches, where they rustled in the night breeze. Occasionally a gust of wind would make them flutter and fly. Skeletons, the bones of the dead, rattled, twisting slowly back and forth as if the living body had been hung by the neck. The skulls were hollow and when a youngster stared at the empty eye sockets, they stared back!

Cobwebs hung in the trees. If a child looked closely, he or she would see a spider in the web, awaiting the unsuspecting fly. The houses themselves were haunted. Bats flew overhead on strings. Warty toads whose eyes bulged and throaty frogs whose voices croaked guarded the doors.

Eerie noises, laughs and cackles, emanated from some of the houses, perhaps from a phonograph buried subtly within. These abodes were spookier, for sounds enveloped in darkness were enchanted and preyed upon one's sanity, especially the sanity of children.

Many people in the village of Waite Park, themselves, dressed in costume: witches and cadavers and vampires, even Count Dracula himself. Beware the footman with the haunted eyes! Beware the butler's gracious bow! "Come in, my child." It seemed so real. Occasionally a young trick-or-treater, overcome with anxiety, would run home to his mother, crying.

"Trick or treat!" the children shouted. And their threats were heeded. They collected candy and gum and caramel apples and homemade popcorn balls wrapped in cellophane, and they stuffed the treats into a pillow case. They would inspect their haul later. Some would splurge immediately, gulping down enough to give them a tummy ache. They would eat until their cache was gone. Others, however, rationed their hoard after counting all of the pieces and categorizing them, separating them into piles. They parceled them out over time, allotting themselves only so many pieces per day. Woe to the child who stole from them!

The boy left his yard and crossed 11th Avenue to the Birches'. Laura Birch was at the door, passing out candy. Immediately he felt the fuzzy feeling return. He did not speak. He just stood on the front stoop and stared at her. When she realized who the cowboy standing in front of her was, she slammed the door and flicked off the lights. He could hear her shriek of horror behind the door. It was an inauspicious start.

The next day when Norma Krause saw her neighbor, Frankie, at school, she ignored him. The boy looked puzzled. He thought she liked him. They were friends. But he understood that the ways of girls were mysterious. They were moody creatures. It was often best to leave them alone.

In class, she refused to look at him. Outside of class, she wouldn't speak to him. Her dander was still up. She was still in a huff, still stewing. She would never go trick-or-treating at his house again. It had been a complete waste of time.

It was quite obvious to her now. Whatever possibility there had been of a future romance with him was now defunct, dead, irrevocably doomed. She would teach him a lesson with her silence.

Norma had complained to her mother, and Val Krause had just laughed. "That's Cliff Kucher for you," said the girl's mother. I thought you might be a bit early. They don't eat until six."

"I hate him," her daughter proclaimed.

"Who?" the mother asked, "Mr. Kucher or his son?"

"That Frankie," the girl replied and skipped away.

Val Krause shook her head in disbelief. Her daughter had said it without any trace of emotion. She had suddenly become distant and detached, as cool as a cucumber.

WINTER

CHAPTER TWENTY-THREE

The advent of winter in the village was always marked, unofficially, by the first snowfall. Although winter would not arrive officially until the calendar said four days before Christmas in December, the villagers made the transition when the skies above chose to pour down their white, flaky powder. Typically, that was in November.

For an entire month the sky had threatened. The temperature had hovered around the freezing mark. Dawn was delayed a few minutes more each day. The children of the village woke up sleepy-eyed and looked out their bedroom windows, anticipating the earth to be blanketed in shining white. Instead, the November mornings were gray and sunless.

The first weekend in November the boy's father left the house to hunt deer. He returned home late Sunday night, empty-handed. The boy had peered out his bedroom window into the back yard, expecting to see a deer hanging from the swing set. That was typically how it went. He listened carefully as his father told Bill O'Brian and Liege Kylie from across the alley how a huge buck had escaped him. That was not typical, for his father was a crack shot.

Early Saturday morning at 4:00 a.m., before the first light, he had climbed an oak tree in the woods near Camp Ripley.

The army camp was an hour's drive north and west of St. Cloud, just outside of Little Falls. He had shot deer there before. He perched in a deer stand, fifteen feet off the ground. He had found this spot and erected the deer stand the day before in the afternoon. It stood just a short distance from a shallow gully from which a deer path emerged. Experience told him that this tree might give him a good vantage point. A deer coming up from the gully would not see him until it was too late.

It was a bitterly cold morning. High humidity during the night had created a layer of frost that covered every branch, every twig. His discomfort was compounded by a stiff breeze out of the northwest that penetrated his flannel shirt and even his thermal underwear and chilled him to the bone.

He could see nothing. The sky was dark, pitch black like tar, with no moon and not a star to light his way. His eyes were useless. After climbing up to his stand, he had put his flashlight into his pocket. He dared not use it, for a deer could spot its shine from a great distance away.

And so the man waited quietly… ever so quietly… patiently… ever so patiently… frozen in stillness and clutching his gun, a Remington 30.06. He could do nothing to mute the cold. The tips of his fingers went numb within the first hour. Even though he was wearing buckskin choppers lined with sheep's wool, the gloves were too thin to insulate his extremities.

The hunter needed his fingers to work, especially those of his right hand that must depress the safety button and squeeze the rifle's trigger in a moment, without delay.

Bill O'Brian and Liege Kylie listened intently to their neighbor's story, as did the man's son. They remained quiet and attentive, not interrupting the narrative as it unfolded.

The hunter forgot about his left hand completely. The most he could do was rub the fingers of his right hand against his belly to try to keep the blood in them circulating. Unconsciously he massaged the tips, kneading them into the belly fat inside his coat. He wished they had more feeling in them.

Another hour passed. Still no light. He stared straight ahead, trying to see the gully that he knew was out here. He listened for the breaking of branches on the path. The man smiled; he could see nothing. He, himself, was reduced by the darkness to a state of blindness. He was being forced to rely on his other senses. Yet, he was not an animal of prey; he was a predator relying on his hunting instincts. And his instincts told him that he would have his chance to strike if he could be patient long enough to out-wait his quarry. He must not move a muscle. He must remain motionless and quiet in the dense darkness.

As the morning approached, anticipation stirred in him. He fought to remain still... absolutely still... a part of the landscape. He even stopped massaging his fingers. Inside the glove he could feel them sting.

A few soft streaks of dawn's first light arose over the gully to the east. They exposed a shadowy world separating sky from land, heaven from earth. The light grew stronger. Now he could see the path used by deer to cross from the ravine to the higher ground. But he, too, could now be seen. The budding daylight exposed the tree in which he sat, nestled into the branches close to the trunk. He had taken care to carve an opening in them, enough to aim his rifle and fire it.

The man fought to regain his bearings, to remember the topography of the land beneath him between the tree and the gully. He searched for the opening where a deer climbing out of the gully would first appear. That would be his best chance, before the deer could observe him. The wind was favorable, directly into his face. His human scent would disappear behind him and never reach the deer's nostrils. Slowly he moved his gun into place and aimed it at the opening in the path.

Then he spotted movement. He saw the horns first, moving from right to left in the distance. The air seemed to clear before his eyes. He breathed rhythmically, exhaling slowly before the next breath to minimize the steam that was being expelled from his lungs. This method of calculated breathing helped calm him and alleviate the excitement building within him.

The deer continued to walk, stepping guardedly out of the gully. The man saw the beast's breath, brought on by exertion, rising in a steamy cloud in the morning half-light. The man heard the animal grunt as it climbed the side hill, its shoulder muscles surging. Then he saw the animal emerge from the gully. It was a mature buck with a huge symmetrical rack extending from its head. At each step it inspected the land carefully, quizzically, with deep suspicion, for at the top of the gully the land spread out before him. Instinctively he felt less confined, less protected.

The animal's head sat upon a long, beautifully curved neck. Its eyes were jet black. The head swiveled, and the eyes adjusted to the waxing daylight. They searched the landscape for movement. The great buck tensed, ready to spring away into the brush if it detected any threat.

The hunter had repositioned himself just in time. He was sitting on a narrow board. His left arm formed a "V" with the elbow pointing down. His left hand was cupped under the barrel of the rifle, supporting it. The barrel stretched forward horizontally, and the butt of the stock was wedged tightly into the man's right shoulder. This configuration allowed him to look through the rifle's scope, which magnified a field of sight. In the growing light the image became clearer with each passing second.

The man had removed the glove from his right hand. His hand cradled the neck of the gun's stock with his index finger inside the trigger guard, resting gently on the trigger itself. Moments earlier, that same finger had pushed the safety button off. The man was ready. He would remain stationary, immobile, until it was time to pull the trigger. Then all parts of the hunter would work together to keep the gun steady, aim, and fire: eyes, arms, hands, and hopefully his fingers would work in unison to expel a bullet from the 30.06's firing chamber and propel it through the barrel, through space, and then into the deer's neck. He did not question their ability to execute. They had worked together successfully many times in the past. But this was a trophy buck; he did not want to miss.

Step by step, the huge deer moved into view. It was within range, fifty yards away. The image of the deer appeared in the gun's scope, and the man moved the rifle ever so slightly to train the cross hairs on the deer's neck. Then he saw the enormity of his quarry, a once-in-a-lifetime chance. Shooting for the neck was dicey. He decided to shoot into the beast's heart. He moved the cross hairs down and back, just behind the front shoulder.

The large buck lumbered to the top of the gully. It turned its head, almost facing the man. "It's as if he knew I was there but could not see me," explained the boy's father. "I could see the tremendous span of the rack on his head. His breath rose like a chimney from his nostrils. I think he saw my breath, too, because he snorted.

I couldn't wait a second longer. I squeezed the trigger. *Cliiiick.* It was so slow, an eternity. The firing pin refused to snap forward." It lacked the momentum and power needed to ignite the powder in the shell. It didn't explode and drive the bullet forward."

Although slight, the gun had made a sound. It was audible to the quarry. Alarmed, the deer leaped high to avoid any danger. Then he turned and dove into the brush that guarded the gully. He bounded down the embankment and up the far side, his legs churning in flight.

"I should have ejected the shell immediately and shot again," the man concluded. "The firing pin had frozen."

The three men and the boy stood quietly beside Liege Kylie's fence. "So, are you going after him again?" Liege asked. It was the question on all three of the listeners' minds.

"The season is still open this weekend," the storyteller responded. "But I doubt that I'll get a second chance at him." His son, however, could see from the look in his father's eyes that the hunter would try.

His father did not tell the neighbors the second tale of the weekend hunt—how his brother, Leonard, had become lost in the woods and how he had found him. It came out midweek after supper when Grandma asked about it.

On Saturday afternoon the boy's father and uncle had gone back out into the woods to hunt. They walked a half mile to Uncle Len's deer stand, positioned beside a small clearing. A deer path crossed the clearing, and they detected deer sign. The two men squatted down to inspect it. "It's fresh," the older brother whispered. "This is a good spot."

The younger brother nodded and slung the strap of his gun over his shoulder. He climbed the tree, ascending the make-shift rungs he had nailed to the trunk the day before.

"Wait here," said the older brother. "My stand is beyond the next ridge over there." He pointed further into the woods. "It's one o'clock. I'll come back in three hours. It'll be dark by five. We'll have to be out of here by then." The young man in the tree nodded and watched his brother depart.

Uncle Len sat for an hour and a half, waiting. The time was 2:30. He had not seen a deer. They are elusive, he thought. They know how to evade the hunters. Still, on this first day of the season, the hunters had the deer on the run. The animals were scared out of their hiding places. He wondered if they felt the same fear humans felt, or love for their mate, or grief when one of them was struck down and fell dead. One thing was certain: the animals could not be as cautious as they wanted to be.

Just then he heard a volley of three shots in the distance, and his senses became alert. Three minutes passed. And then he saw them bounding down the path from left to right, a buck in the lead followed by two does.

Uncle Len was left-handed, and he had situated himself so that the tree's trunk would not be in his way and impede his shot. He pushed the butt of the rifle's stock tightly into his shoulder, and his left hand surrounded the neck. He pushed the safety button off. He was at-the-ready, poised to shoot.

The man stared into the scope of the rifle and searched along the path. When the deer reached the clearing, they accelerated: the buck's strides lengthening, the does that were chasing him, straining to keep up.

The hunter aimed just in front of the leader. He squeezed the trigger. A loud report echoed through the woods, and he felt a sudden sense of joy. The deer had stumbled in its tracks and fallen to the ground. It was hit! The two does avoided the fallen buck and continued on. But just as suddenly, the male scrambled to its feet and tried to bound off in pursuit of the females.

The man in the tree saw that the deer was slower and less sure-footed than it had been. He saw the bright red stain on the animal's side near the stomach. The buck hobbled along the trail and stumbled a second time. Again, it rose to its feet and limped away. Soon, it was out of sight.

The hunter scrambled down the tree trunk, clutching his gun. He, too, fell when he reached the bottom. Something fell from his pocket. But he did not take the time to retrieve it. Whatever it was, he could get it when he took down his deer stand the next day. He quickly recovered and rose to his feet. He had no time to lose. He must chase the deer and track it, if necessary. He turned his face skyward at the sun shining above him. Then he looked at his watch—2:35. He had plenty of time.

The deer was bleeding. At the spot on the path where he had shot it, the man saw blood. The grass was matted down where the deer had fallen, and the leaves were painted red.

As he followed the trail of blood, he left the clearing behind. Then he saw that the buck had turned left off the path and veered into the woods. He saw three sets of cloven hooves in the dirt. Evidently, the does had panicked and altered course. Their mate was trying to follow them.

His quarry must not get away. The man thought of how proud his brother would be when he congratulated him on this kill. The hunter left the path and followed the wounded animal. They called it game, and indeed it was a game of sorts, he thought. "Better to be the hunter than the hunted," he said to himself. And only the cold breeze from the north heard his words.

He could still see the blood trail clearly. He was in the woods now, surrounded by trees. Amid them he pictured a fallen deer, bleeding profusely on one side, in the throes of death. His feet—and his emotion—carried him to the top of a hill. He took a moment and surveyed the landscape around him to get his bearings. Then he plunged down the slope on the far side, eager to find the stricken deer.

At 3:00 o'clock he came upon the buck's corpse. It lay at the bottom of a hill from which it had tumbled when its lungs finally filled with blood and burst. The hunter screamed in jubilation. He scrambled down the embankment and nudged the deer's head with his foot. It did not move. He felt the deer's throat. The jugular vein refused to pulsate. The life was gone; the animal was dead.

He knelt down and took his knife out of its sheath on his belt. He cut a deep vertical incision in the deer's belly. He pulled out the animal's guts, cutting where need be, careful not to lacerate the intestines or the stomach. An error, even a small nick, would result in an awful stench, and it could ruin the surrounding meat. He felt a deep satisfaction in carving through skin and flesh.

When the job was finished, his hands were bloodstained. He wiped them on fallen oak leaves and put away his knife. The young man looked up from his work. Above him, the sky was noticeably darker. The shadows of evening were peeking in early. The daylight was receding swiftly, giving way to the oncoming night. The buck was heavy. It would take two men to drag the deer's carcass up the hill and out of the woods. He must seek his brother's help.

He stood up and looked about him. Although leafless, the trees seemed to swirl about him. He twisted about. More trees…

and an eerie silence… He was to meet his brother at 4:00. The time was now past 3:30. If he could find him, they would exit the woods together. There was safety in numbers, and comfort. But he was alone.

He remembered his brother's words of caution: "Travel due north, and you will find the road." He reached into his pocket for his compass. It was gone! "That's what fell out by the tree stand," he said aloud in disbelief. One thought dawned on him— he was lost. The thought spurred him into action. He scrambled up the hill and broke into a trot, back the way he had come. He abandoned the deer and left it lay at the base of the hill. They would search for it in the morning. Perhaps they would find it.

The trees and bushes surrounded him. They mocked his helplessness. He plunged through the brush, eager to find a trail. But the woods stretched out ahead of him, vast and endless. Their canopy of branches and twigs closed over him. He tried to remember his brother's instructions: "Head north and you will intersect a road." But with no compass to guide him, he was as lost as a rudderless ship at sea, spinning out of control with nothing to point out the way. Fear rose within him. He fought to control it and keep his wits about him.

But it was becoming pervasive. Danger lurked. The biting wind told him just how cold the night would be. To spend the night outside in these elements was treacherous. He would have to hunker down to survive. "I'll build a fire," he announced.

Then he heard a fierce howl from somewhere close behind him. Coyotes! They traveled in a pack. They would not test a human during the daytime unless they were starving. But at night…

The man slapped the side of his face. His mind was playing tricks on him, exacerbating his fear. Still, before moving on, he lifted the strap of the rifle off of his shoulder and clutched the gun in his hands. One thought only comforted him: his brother would come for him. His brother was at home in the woods. He would come searching and would find him.

At 4:00 o'clock the older brother returned to the designated meeting point, his brother's tree stand. He was surprised to see it empty. He surveyed the scene. Looking down, he caught a glimpse of a metallic glint shining up at him from the base of the oak tree. A compass. He picked it up. The initials LFK were etched into the back of it. This raised an alarm inside him. He checked his watch. Darkness would descend upon them in an hour. He pocketed the compass and moved down to the deer trail. He found the bloodied grass, and what had transpired there became crystal clear. His brother had wounded a deer and was tracking it. But how far away was he? "Len!" he called out. "Len! Can you hear me?" But his shouts only reverberated in the woods and echoed back to him. Their emptiness worried him.

He followed the blood trail down the path. Soon, he reached the spot where the deer and the hunter had veered away, off the path. "Oh no!" thought the man. He did not consider the situation for long. His kid brother was out there—somewhere—without a compass, alone and discouraged. The young man's one hope would be that his big brother was searching for him. He would do so into the night, if need be. Without further consideration, the older brother turned left into the woods and followed the blood trail. He would follow it until the sunlight faded away.

The younger brother continued to trudge through the woods. Every few minutes he stopped briefly to get his bearings. But he had little sense of direction. Where the light was fading must be west. But the woods was one big sea. For all he knew, he was walking in a gigantic circle. He knew his mind was playing tricks on him. At each stop he drank water from his canteen. Somehow, this comforted him. Now the canteen was nearly empty.

The light was diminishing to a glow on the horizon. The air was chilly, colder than before, and the wind was rising steadily, gusting, and becoming more intense.

In a recess of his mind, he remembered a conversation he had had with his older brother. It was speculation. What should they do if they became separated and lost? He tried to recreate his brother's instructions: "Climb to high ground on a hill, if possible, and fire one shot every two minutes. The sound will travel farther if it comes from high up. If you shoot from in a gully or in the woods, the sound will be muffled. It won't radiate as far. I will fire a return shot if I hear you. Stay put! I will move in the direction of your shot."

Len was tired. His feelings of hopelessness were draining him. At twenty-seven, he was a strong young man, but now he felt exhausted and defeated. He crawled up a nearby hill and sat at the base of a tree that was situated at the edge of a small clearing. He took his flashlight out of his belt and looked at his wrist watch. Every two minutes he was to fire a shot. He looked at his ammunition belt and counted the shells. It contained twenty-four cartridges. He had five bullets left in the magazine in the gun, one more in the chamber. Thirty shells total, enough for one hour. But if he used them all, he would have none left for the coyotes. He would be defenseless, at their mercy if they came.

He aimed his rifle skyward and pulled the trigger, firing the first shot. Then he looked at the watch on his wrist. He followed the second hand as it marked the time passing, the outer point revolving around its pivot point clockwise at a constant speed. After one minute, the second hand plunged downward again and, upon reaching the bottom of its descent, once again began to climb. Finally it reached its zenith, and the man elevated his gun and fired a second shot. "Number Two," he counted. And then he grinned. His brother would hear it. His brother would save him. He always had.

As he pushed along through the woods, the older brother marshaled his thoughts. Unfortunately, this was more than a reconnaissance mission; it was one of search and rescue. The imminent threat was the impending darkness that would permeate the landscape and impede his footing. If the rescue was delayed, a second more palpable threat loomed—bitter cold. He wondered if Len knew to conserve his water supply. Did he have any food with him? Dehydration and lack of sustenance would increase fatigue and rob a man of his faculties and his common sense.

He took out his flashlight. Soon, he would no longer be able to see the blood stains. Here and there, he thought he detected signs of footprints and a path. But he knew that the mind plays tricks, especially when one is desperate and wants something to be so.

He fought to keep his senses alert. Hearing now trumped vision. As he trudged through gullies and up hills, he wondered about his brother's condition and his state of mind. How clear-headed was he? Would he recall their conversation of a year ago? Would he crawl up a hill and shoot off one shell every two minutes? That was rapidly becoming their only hope.

Fifteen minutes passed, and then he heard something—or thought he heard it. Was it the report of a rifle? He couldn't tell.

He stopped and took out his brother's compass. The sound had come from far to the south. He released the safety on his rifle and fired a bullet skyward. Then he moved off in a southerly direction, quickening his pace. He kept one eye on the second hand of his watch. After two minutes, he paused to listen. He heard the sound again. The excitement in him roared to life. He fired a second shot and a third, and raced on.

Two minutes later, he heard another muffled thud. It buoyed his confidence that he was heading in the right direction. Len's compass told him that his course was due south. "Keep moving," he told himself. "Just put one foot in front of the other. You'll get there." His doggedness was tenacious. This demonstrated one trait that he had inherited from his mother—resolve. Like her, he was determined to succeed and would let no obstacle stand in his way.

Two more minutes passed, and the next shot rang out. This one was more distinct, and it had a sharper sound. He kept his legs working, insisting that they move at his command. Two more shots followed, each as clear and distinct as a bell.

Time sped by, punctuated by more reports, equally spaced. Forty-four minutes had elapsed since he had heard the first shot.

Another report of a rifle cracked the air. He let his mind wander. He had once been invited to a raccoon hunt at night. He had listened to the baying of the hounds. The hunters stood still in the woods while their dogs chased the quarry. The men with rifles moved off in pursuit only when the barking changed pitch to indicate that the dogs had cornered the raccoon up a tree. The canines sang out for their masters to come. His mind wandered back. These shots were equally persistent, calling him.

Twenty-three shots; forty-six minutes. He pleaded into the dark night air. "Don't stop now, Leonard. I'm almost there." And then a new fear surfaced. "Don't run out of shells," he warned.

Deep down, he believed that he was close. But it was difficult to assess exactly how close. There was no way to be sure, not in total darkness. The woods were dense. The trees and shrubs absorbed sound, making it difficult to figure out the exact point from which the shots were being fired.

He looked ahead. The ground was rising; he must be climbing a hill. He crossed his fingers in hope as he reached the top. Alas, his hopes were dashed; it was not the right hill. Two more shots had been fired, to no avail. His brother was nowhere in sight.

The younger brother sat atop a hill. He looked at his dwindling supply of ammunition. He had five shells left, all that remained of his initial cache. Still, he kept his eyes trained on his watch. His stint in the navy had trained him to be disciplined. He would fire one shell every two minutes without fail until his supply was gone. Then it would be time to look for concealing cover, to gird himself against the wintry chill. He would have to brace himself for a long night of siege in the cold. He was out of water and had no food. It would be a test of his endurance. And then there were the coyotes to be reckoned with. He hoped they would not come.

"Fire another shell," he ordered himself.

"Do your duty, sailor."

"Yes, sir, Lieutenant," he replied. Then he fired off another round, his twenty-sixth shell. Fifty-two minutes, he thought. Only eight more to go.

There was no two ways about it. If you were lucky enough to be an American, you owed your country. "I am a patriot!" he proclaimed. His voice was strong. And he began to sing: *Anchors Aweigh, my boys, Anchors Aweigh!*

In the family living room, the storyteller paused and looked at the faces of his audience. Their eyes were riveted on him. He looked at his wife and children. They knew how the story ended, but they wanted to hear it from him again. He turned and looked at his mother. She was nervous and uncomfortable, and she shifted in her seat. Her back was ramrod stiff. She stared at her son, and he saw that her eyes were moist. She could not force a smile. The storyteller proceeded on to the climax of his story.

The boy's father, the older brother, was startled when he heard the twenty-ninth shot. It made him jump and nearly knocked him off his feet. A projectile had rocketed in his direction and whipped by him, full force. The report and its shock wave had stunned his ears. A brief silence followed..., and then he heard a voice, a tenor voice: *Over hill, over dale As we hit the dusty trail, And the caissons go rolling along....*

The melody wafted through the air toward him and consumed him. In the distance he saw a shadow leaning up against a tree. The music was his welcome. He replied in kind with his own song, sung in baritone: *From the Halls of Montezuma to the Shores of Tripoli; We will fight our country's battles In the air, on land, and sea....*

The shadow stood up and turned. It sprinted toward his position. Brother met brother, and they flung their arms around each other, slapping each other's back.

"You came for me, Cliff. I never lost faith in you—thanks!"

"How many shells do you have left?" the older brother asked.

"Just one" his brother replied.

"Save it for tomorrow, Len."

"I shot a buck, Cliff. But I panicked and left it behind."

"We'll search for it tomorrow. Now we need to get out of here. Let's go. Here take this; it's yours." He took an object, engraved with the initials LFK, out of his pocket and handed it to his kid brother. He said nothing more about it, and nothing more needed to be said.

"A good soldier guards his gear and stows it away," the younger man stated. "I learned that lesson today, the hard way." It was his way of apologizing.

But his older brother was already walking off into the distance, heading north. He was not his brother's confessor.

They found the road an hour and a half later. An observer, had one been present, would have found it amusing, perhaps, to hear a strange chorus of one tenor and one bass exit the woods in utter darkness on a cold November night in 1958, far away from civilization in the middle of Minnesota: *Off we go into the wild blue yonder, Climbing high into the sun: Here they come zooming to meet our thunder: At 'em boys, Give 'er the gun!* They sang lustily, a rousing rendition.

Their spirits soared, but physically they were exhausted. They clambered up onto the roadway and set down their packs on the shoulder. It was a paved road and frequently traveled, an artery leading from the military base into Little Falls. The two brothers had parked their truck along the roadside a half mile outside of town.

Two headlights appeared in the distance. They belonged to a military truck owned by the US army. The truck slowed, and the two hunters waved for it to stop. The driver rolled down his window. "Are you having trouble?" asked the man, a young buck private, who looked to be Len's age.

"Yes, we are," replied the younger brother. "I got lost in the woods and my brother brought me out. I'm in the navy," he added, "the reserves. My brother, Clifford, was a marine—a long time ago. He fought on Guam in the Pacific. We sure would appreciate a lift to town. Our truck is parked a half mile out, this side."

The young army recruit stared at the young navy enlistee. "You're lucky he found you. It's a big woods out there." And then after a pause, "The army is always glad to be of service. Strictly speaking, it's against regulations. But hop in."

"GIs have to stick up for one another," the army lad stated as the two hunters exited the truck's cab. He waved to them and saluted as he put the truck in gear and drove off.

In the living room the family breathed a collective sigh of relief. They had listened intently to the father's story. "So, you may have saved Len's life," the boy's mother stated. She looked at her husband and felt admiration for him swell within her.

"Brothers have to protect brothers," asserted Grandma. "It's how the family survives." Her voice resonated with feeling. "It's how I raised them," she added. No one challenged her for taking credit. Uncle Len was her baby boy. He was less than two years old when her husband died of appendicitis, leaving her to raise their family without him. Somehow she had coped.

"What happened to Uncle Len's deer?" asked the oldest boy.

His father finished his story. "The next day we went looking for it. We tracked it to the base of the hill where Uncle Len had gutted it. Coyotes had eaten it. They tore it apart with their fangs and chewed it with their razor-sharp teeth. They ate all the meat. They must have been hungry because they devoured the whole deer."

Grandma, sitting in a rocker, sucked in her breath. The boy's sisters sat in awe, envisioning the sight. "They could have eaten Uncle Len," said Mary. Her face was horrified, and she began to cry.

"Devoured him," stated her older sister, Jeanne. Distraught, she, too, began to cry. Little Dan began to cry. If his sisters were crying, he should be crying, also.

"Don't talk like that!" snapped Grandma. She flung the words at them. She looked at them with pain and disgust. "Shame on all of you!" Her rebuke was harsh. Frankie saw tears in the woman's eyes that he seldom saw. She was livid with anger, and she continued to scold them. "Your father rescued him. He's a protector. He protects all of you... all of us." Her bottom lip was quivering. "Oh, Clifford," she cried, "the family has to stick together!"

Her two granddaughters sobbed even more deeply, but the older woman's tears were drying up. She took out her handkerchief and wiped her eyes. "You don't appreciate him enough." She directed her criticism more at the children's mother than at the children.

At this, the children's mother crossed over to the couch and sat between her daughters. She put her arms around them to comfort them, to protect them and to be protected. Her husband picked up young Dan and set the boy upon his knees. He bounced the youngster up and down gently until the boy giggled. He sang their favorite ditty:

> Pony boy, Pony boy, won't you be my Pony boy?
> Off we go, don't say no, over the fields of snow.
> Giddy up, Giddy up, Giddy up... Whoaaaaaaa...
> My Pony boy.

On *Whoaaaaaaa*, the man straightened his legs and let his small son slide down them. It was great fun for both father and son. It stopped Dan's whimpering.

The oldest son was thinking, remembering another story his father had told. He spoke up loudly to gain their attention. "It's like when you and Uncle Len were lost on Mille Lacs Lake." The boy recalled his dad's words vividly. "You were out in the middle of the lake over the Mud Flats when a dense fog set in. You and Uncle Len were fishing so hard that you didn't notice that all the other boats had left. Then a strong wind came up and made huge waves that rocked the boat. A storm was brewing."

The father was listening to the boy's account. "That's right," said the father. "That's the way it happened. Suddenly we lost our sense of direction."

"You didn't know which way to go," continued the boy. "Then you spotted the marker buoy that you had thrown out when you caught the first walleye." His father nodded.

"Then you saw another marker that someone had left. It was a miracle!" The boy repeated his Dad's words exactly as he had heard them.

"'We have to go that way!' you yelled to Uncle Len. You pointed in the direction of the shore because you remembered how the two buoys were lined up. You pulled the cord and started the motor and turned the boat so it was pointing in the right direction. Then you twisted the handle and opened the throttle full bore." The boy was envisioning the scene. He had watched his father start the engine and steer the boat many times.

His father looked at the young storyteller and smiled. "You have a good memory," the man stated. His son's eyes were ablaze.

"You couldn't see your hand in front of your face in the fog. Still, you kept the motor going, full speed. It was six miles to shore. Fifteen minutes later, you saw the shoreline on the horizon. You made it home safely!"

That's right," added his father.

"If you hadn't been going in the right direction, you would have run out of gas."

"That, also, is right," his father agreed. "We were lucky."

"No," the boy corrected. "You saw the buoys. You knew the direction they pointed, like an arrow points. It wasn't luck."

His father posed a question: "But what if I hadn't seen the second buoy?" Then he posed a second question: "What if the other boat had taken their buoy?"

The seven-year-old son had no answer for this.

"Did you bring your buoy home?" asked his sister, Jeanne.

"We were too afraid to wait and find it. After we saw it, we lost it again in the fog."

"But you remembered the direction!" argued the boy.

"That's true," agreed his father, accepting his son's argument. "But part of our making it to shore was still dumb luck."

"It wasn't dumb," countered the boy. "It was smart."

"I'll take that as a compliment," said the father. They stood up, and the father tussled his son's hair. "It's time to get ready for bed."

The boy left the room and went upstairs. After he put on his pajamas, he looked out his bedroom window. A silhouette hung from the crosspiece of the swing set, a doe.

His father had shot two deer on Sunday afternoon and given one, a young buck, to Uncle Len, who had pinned his license tag on its hind leg between the shin bone and the supporting tendons. His dad had pinned his own tag on the doe.

Perhaps Grandma had said it best to the boy's mother. "Clifford is not only the provider for this family, but he is also its protector. Every day you should get down on your knees and thank God for that."

CHAPTER TWENTY-FOUR

"Gimme back my cap!" The young boy's face flushed with anger and a twinge of dread. His voice had an unusual determination in it. The other boy sensed the change, and his own face broke into a grin. The young boy repeated his demand. He was speaking to his neighbor, Timmy O'Brian.

Frankie, Terry Joe, and Timmy were playing in the O'Brian front yard. The weather was cold, but the boys still preferred playing outside to playing inside under the surveillance of their mothers. Baseball caps had given way to stocking caps.

They were wrestling in fun, testing their strength and grappling technique. Timmy lay on his back in his brother's grasp and giggled as Terry Joe tried to pin his shoulders to the ground. Above him, he saw the branches of three conifers, pine trees extending high up into the clouds. It gave him an idea.

In time he broke his brother's hold and escaped. He stood up and looked at his brother curiously; Terry Joe's nose was bleeding. "Hey, Terry Joe, your nose is bleeding like hell. You've got blood all over your jacket." Timmy knew this would irritate his kid brother and prompt another attack.

The younger brother lunged at him again, low to the ground. He was attempting to tackle Timmy, but the older boy pushed him aside. They circled one another, and then in a calculated move, Timmy slipped close to the third boy, who did not expect what happened next.

Timmy grabbed the neighbor boy's cap, a black stocking cap. "This is my trophy," he proclaimed. He did not expect that he would have to defend taking it.

"That's my cap," said the boy. "Give it back to me." He sounded worried. Clearly, it was a plea.

Timmy had tormented the younger boy many times in the past. He did not expect that his challenger would sustain the challenge. He decided to see just how far the younger boy was willing to go. "Hey, twerp, it's just a cap. You'll have to come over here and get it."

Frankie made a move to do so. He took a step toward the older boy. "If you do, I'll beat the piss out of you. I'll kick your head in," vowed Timmy. He sounded like he meant it.

"Give me back my cap," the other boy demanded fiercely. Clearly this was an open challenge. For the first time in his life, he knew that he would stand his ground against this older boy. He felt a strange calm come over him.

"You won't fight," Timmy prodded. "You're a chicken shit!" He was a master at provocation. He grinned. This teasing was great sport. What fun!

He was somewhat surprised when the younger boy approached him. Timmy backed up. Playfully he held the cap away from the cap's owner and danced away from him. "You can't have it," he boasted; "it's mine." Then he snarled.

But for once the younger boy was determined to act. He reached out and grabbed the sleeve of Timmy's jacket, the sleeve of the free arm with which he was deflecting his opponent away. Frankie reached under his adversary's extended arm and around his torso and tried to grab the cap.

At this, Timmy realized that to fend off the other boy, he must let go of the cap. In the nick of time, he freed his right arm and flung the cap upward. It lodged high up in the branch of an evergreen tree. "Get your hands off me, twerp." He swung his fist to smash it into the intruder's jaw.

In a flash, Frankie responded. He leaped upon Timmy and threw him to the ground. With great agility he plopped down on the older boy and pinned his head to the ground. He felt a sudden strength, bred of indignation. His whole body was energized.

"Get off me," shouted the older boy, his mouth spattered with dirt. But the other boy would not release him.

"Give me back my cap," demanded the younger boy.

"GET OFF ME NOW!" the older boy demanded back. "I'll kill you if you don't."

"But the neighbor boy did not loosen his hold on Timmy's head. Instead he tightened his grip and increased his leverage so that the boy beneath him could not get away. He continued to push the older boy's ear into the ground.

Timmy's anger was mushrooming. He wriggled to extract his head from Frankie's tight hold, but he could not budge him. They were similar in size. Although Timmy was slightly heavier, he was not any stronger.

Terry Joe was watching the action. He had been curious at first about the outcome. Now he was amused. "Keep him down," he ordered. He was busy wiping his nostrils on his sleeve. The nose was swollen.

Timmy was fuming. "I'll kick the snot out of you, too, Terry Joe..., when I get up. So, you had better shut up!"

"You can't get up," Terry Joe replied. There was something about his comment that made him chuckle. "You're the twerp, Timothy!" He laughed hard as he dabbed at his nose with the jacket sleeve. He liked seeing his brother pinned to the ground, helpless.

"You'd better not call me that, Terrance," the older boy threatened.

"Give me back my cap!" Frankie stated. It was all he could think of to say. This was new territory he was exploring. He didn't know what would happen if he let Timmy up. The boy on the ground was trapped. But Frankie couldn't hold him down forever. When he did let go, he would have to jump up and keep his distance. "Give me back my cap," he repeated.

Struggling was useless, the boy on the ground concluded. He must try a different tack. He decided to use a new ploy. "I can't get your cap if you keep holding me down. It's up in that tree." Timmy had changed his tone. His voice sounded much more conciliatory, even friendly.

"Don't let him up," advised Terry Joe. "He's a liar."

Timmy ignored him. "I'll get your hat down; I promise." He tried to sound sincere.

Frankie considered the two alternatives. His body was still shaking from both his exertion and his daring. He had never fought an older boy before. He had struck in the spur of the moment, an involuntary reaction. Now that he had crossed the line, there was no going back; the future was uncertain. His confidence was shaken. He felt a gloom.

"Don't let him up," Terry Joe repeated.

But maybe everything would be all right, Frankie thought. It was more a hope than anything else. "Will you get my cap if I let you up?" he asked the boy below him.

"Sure thing," the boy responded.

At that, the younger boy released his hold and stood up. He leaped away, just in time to miss Timmy's counterattack. The older boy flailed his arms, trying to punch his rival. He had been humiliated. The boy was three years younger. Timmy tried to kick him. But the punches and kicks failed to land more than a glancing blow. "I'll kill you!" he threatened. And when he could not land a solid blow on the neighbor boy, he turned on Terry Joe.

"I'll kick the crap out of you, too," he declared. And he lunged at his brother. Terry Joe twisted to avoid contact, but one of Timmy's fists landed squarely on the swollen nose.

He would have struck again, except for the reaction of the neighbor boy. How often had Terry Joe come to his defense? Now it was his turn. He stepped quickly between the two brothers, fists cocked. It made Timmy step back warily.

Frankie was shaking like a leaf at his daring. He stared at his opponent silently, trying to think of something to say. Finally he asked, "Are you going to get my cap out of the tree?" He could think of nothing else.

"Go eat a turd," the older boy suggested, and then he turned and walked away. They heard the storm door slam as he mounted the front steps and disappeared into the house.

"Booger Breath!" Terry Joe yelled after him.

"He likes being a bad ass," Terry Joe muttered. "You're lucky you don't have an older brother like him. He's a bully. He's mad because you threw him down and sat on top of him. You'd better watch out for him. One day I'm going to beat him up myself."

He was massaging his nose gingerly. "Mom won't let him get away with this. She'll have Dad whip him with his belt when he gets home." The thought brought a smile to the younger brother's face. "Let's go get a cane pole. We'll get your cap down. There's one in the garage."

The weather in November continued to be bleak. The air was bitterly cold; the skies, threatening. One morning the boy's father sat at the breakfast table and looked up from his paper, the early edition of the Minneapolis Tribune. He addressed the boy's mother who was at the stove, stirring oatmeal. "A ship sank yesterday on Lake Michigan, the *Carl D. Bradley*. There was a blizzard with sixty miles per hour winds. Thirty-three men died." He slurped his coffee as he sipped from the mug. "The same thing could happen on Lake Superior. That's an even bigger lake and more treacherous."

"It's a waste of human life," responded the boy's mother. He could see that she was sad. "Those men left wives and children behind."

"Some people die and others are born," the father replied. "It balances everything out."

"It's still a tragedy," argued the mother. "Don't be so callous."

"I'm not callous," countered her husband. "That's just the way it is." He pointed at her tummy, now protruding slightly inside her pajama top. How's the new baby doing?"

When she refrained from answering, he returned to his paper. He sipped from his coffee cup and stared at the article. Then he turned the page to the financial section. "The market's up again," he noted, but she did not acknowledge him.

SNOW! The first snowfall finally arrived two-and-a-half weeks before Thanksgiving. The children woke up to a bright white world.

"Did you see it snowed?" his sister, Jeanne, asked him. She had entered his room because she wanted to be the first to tell everyone the news. Her announcement brought the boy to his feet. He rolled out of bed and peered out the window. A light fluffy layer of flakes blanketed the ground. It had been much longed for, a toy with which the children played. As of yet, the snowfall in the yard was untrampled and pristine.

It was a Sunday morning, and the children of the village busied themselves with the snow. After 9:00 o'clock mass, the boy's two sisters changed into snow suits with hoods that tied under their chins. Each girl wrapped a scarf tightly around her neck. Thus garbed, they stomped through the snow, delighting in the footprints their boots made. In unison, they flopped onto their backs in the front yard. They flapped their arms like wings and spread their legs apart and snapped them together, making snow angels.

Soon, the whole yard was a heavenly cloud of seraphim and cherubim. They did not leave one square of earth untouched. The girls giggled as they played while their mother watched them from the windows. She couldn't help but smile. What pure joy to be a child! she thought. Our adult troubles are mere trifles in their lives.

Across the alley in O'Brians' screen house, four boys worked feverishly. Their task was to make snowballs, ammunition for surprise ambushes on unsuspecting neighborhood children. Frankie, Terry Joe, Kevin, and little Johnny Fisch spent hours compacting snow into baseball-size spheres. These they stored in the screen house under a canvass tarp.

Little Johnny Fisch had an idea. The final batch of snowballs would be specially made. Kevin exited into the house and returned with his mother's sprinkler can, which she used in summer to water geraniums along the side of the house. It was filled with water, and little Johnny carefully sprinkled the water onto the snowballs that lay in rows on a tray. His eyes gleamed as he poured. The water soaked into each snowball. The freezing air would harden them into ice balls.

Every winter the boys of the village challenged each other. Snowball fights were common; they came with the territory. Inevitably, there would be an all-out war against Timmy and his band of thugs. This year the younger boys would be ready. The ice balls would be their surprise weapon. They would sting mercilessly and give the four boys an edge. So, they worked diligently to prepare them.

Little Johnny Fisch's laugh was ghoulish. He could throw the hardest of any boy in the village. The thought of inflicting pain on those who tormented him was appealing. Woe to the boy who stood in his way! He would not show mercy. He would guard the door. When an attacker came into range and tried to enter, he would pelt the boy. A direct hit would discourage further attacks.

The boys hid the ice balls behind a sheet of plywood that stood against the far wall. Easy access was mandatory, especially in the heat of battle. The screen house was their fortress, to be defended against attack by Timmy's goons.

Bill O'Brian had lashed sheets of protective plywood over the screens to keep out the snow. Unbeknownst to him, the four boys had removed both the plywood and the screens from the east side and the north side next to the door. They had hidden the screens in the garage and then replaced the plywood. When the war started, they would unlatch the plywood, and the windows would be clear for them to counterattack. Two sides open; two protected. And a generous supply of snowballs at the ready. And the stash of ice balls in reserve. When the boys finished, they grinned at one another. It was their secret.

By nightfall, snow forts dotted the landscape in every neighborhood. By the end of the week, most would be destroyed by bands of marauders. It was reminiscent of when Attila the Hun's brutal barbarians attacked the Roman Empire during the early years of the Dark Ages or when the dreaded Norsemen ravaged England's coastal towns in the 8th, 9th, and 10th Centuries A.D. It was a re-creation of the Middle Ages, when Mongol hordes led by Genghis Khan invaded Europe. Some of Waite Park's children built; others destroyed. But always they fought to defend their territory or to take it by force.

After the snow forts were constructed, the children began to dig. Snow plows in the street pushed mounds of snow onto the boulevard, forming a ridge. As boys and girls walked to school on top of this ridge, their boots wore a path.

Wherever a mound of snow grew big enough, the youths used shovels to carve out a cavern. They had read in school about igloos built by Eskimos in Alaska. The cave grew in size, large enough to house three or four youngsters. Industrious builders borrowed candles from their mother's hutch to give the room light. It was cozy and, fatigued by their exertion, they rested inside. They imagined that they were in hiding. No one knew their whereabouts. They sat cross-legged or lay on their sides curled up in their new den, snug, protected from winter's elements.

Only those who had ever been ice-fishing knew this feeling—how the wind could howl outside and swirl about them while they sat warm and protected inside their make-shift home.

On Monday after school, Frankie and his best friend, Terry Joe, waited behind a bush in Vaneks' yard, kitty corner from the

O'Brian house. They watched as the city bus approached from the east on 5th Street. It paused, and the door opened to collect Tillie Kuchenmeister, who was going into downtown St. Cloud for her weekly hair appointment. The door closed.

"Now," said Terry Joe. He leaped from behind the bush, followed closely by his best friend. They latched their mittens onto the back bumper of the bus and "oohed" with delight as it turned north onto 10th Avenue.

The bus accelerated. What great fun to hook the bus and catch a ride down the block! Their black boots, buckled to their feet and ankles, slid through the soft snow like skis. The roads were never plowed clean.

Halfway down the block the bus hit a bump, and the boys were lifted upward and then dropped back down with a thump. Terry Joe lost his balance and his grip on the bumper and fell. Going twenty-five miles per hour, his head pitched forward and he tumbled along the street. His friend looked back over his shoulder. Terry Joe stood up; he was grinning. But then he had to dive out of the way onto the boulevard, for a car, a red Chevy Impala driven by Bertie Norton, was barreling down on him.

Frankie clung tightly to the bumper of the bus. He repositioned his grip and, knees bent, retained his crouch behind the bus. Exhaust fumes poured out of the tailpipe into his lungs. But he held on. The Impala closed the distance and followed closely behind. The boy could hear Bertie Norton's voice chuckling through an open window.

At the end of the block, the bus stopped. Another passenger perhaps, thought the boy. But it stopped too long. Suddenly, the red Chevy swerved around the bus to the boy's left and accelerated. Frankie could see the right arm extended toward him with the palm of the hand facing inward and the middle finger flipped up.

He heard the door of the bus open, and then his instincts sounded a grave alarm. He heard footsteps, crunchy in the snow, coming toward him. And then he ran, back in the direction from which he had come. Boomer Bartholomay arrived a moment too late to take a swipe at him. "Stay away from the bus, you little fart. It's a crime to hook the bus. You're the Kucher kid, aren't you? And O'Brian," he yelled, "that goes for you, too! I'll have Chet Gritt arrest you. He's a friend of mine."

But the boy kept running. Halfway down the block he joined Terry Joe, and they both sped back to the friendly confines of their neighborhood. The two boys crawled into the cave they had dug out in Frankie's front yard. They had been wise to construct it beyond the garden near the Pattersons' front yard, where it was sheltered by three pines. It was not easily detectable unless you knew it was there. Timmy and his friends seldom traveled this route. This was the two boys' private haunt. In it they felt safe and protected. Now they sat inside, breathing hard.

They recounted their deed. And then they began to laugh at their own daring. "That Bertie Norton is a jerk," said Terry Joe. He thrust his hand out and extended the middle finger up. His friend stared at it and nodded. "He's going to get that finger cut off," Terry Joe added. "The Beckers aren't done with him yet. And Curtis Benton's still hopping mad. He thinks he's been insulted. Just wait. You'll see."

Two days later, Timmy destroyed their cave. The snowball fight occurred much sooner than anticipated. On Saturday morning Terry Joe retaliated for the wrecked cave by spitting in his brother's bowl of cereal. The older boy did not notice until it was too late. He wondered why his younger brothers and sisters were staring at him.

It was young Kathy who ratted on Terry Joe. A chase around the table ensued, and then Lorraine O'Brian, awakened by the furor, shooed them outside, barefoot and in their pajamas. She locked the door.

"I know where she hides the spare key," Terry Joe stated, "in the front porch under the rug." He tiptoed gingerly through the snow to the porch. There he fished under the rug for the key, and as he bent down, Timmy kicked him in the ribs viciously. "That's for spitting in my Rice Krispies," he growled. "We'll get you today," he vowed. "We're taking over your fort! You can't stop us." And he laughed.

Terry Joe inserted the key into the lock and turned it. He stepped inside quickly, and while Timmy laughed, he shut the door and locked it. He had to be quiet, for his mother had gone back to bed. You can stand out there in your underwear and freeze, he thought. His brother began to pound on the door. "Open up! or I'll kill you!" he demanded. Then he began to holler. "Mom! Terry Joe won't let me in."

The four young warriors removed the sheets of plywood from the east and north sides of the screen house. They would have a clear view of their enemy's approach. Their stash of snowballs lay undisturbed under the tarp.

Little Johnny Fisch patted an ice ball. It was his weapon of choice. Then they saw them, a band of five, led by a pudgy boy of Irish descent. Douglas Lauerman pulled a sled behind him. A cardboard box sat on the sled, and in it the four boys in the screen house could see a pile of snowballs heaped up.

Whap! The first snowball hit the screen house, followed by two more. Then the attackers found their mark, and several snowballs flew through the windows and penetrated the defenders' lair. Kevin was hit squarely in the chest, and he cursed his older brother, Timmy.

The boys inside the screen house fired back. Five minutes passed with snowballs whistling through the air past their ears. Some connected, mostly glancing blows. Fiercely, they exerted themselves. Before long, all of the boys were sweating profusely, and their mouths were frothing.

The younger boys cheered lustily when Frankie took aim and threw a strike, hitting Freddy Schultz in the back. Then they cheered some more when Terry Joe's aim found his brother, a bullet in the chest. "You got him, Terry Joe!" Kevin exclaimed. His eyes were bright with fire. The leader had been hit.

The result of this blow was an intensified attack. Now determined to conquer, Timothy O'Brian gave the order for an all out assault. No more siege. They would swarm the fortress en masse and take revenge on the occupants. Inside, the four defenders sensed an onslaught and switched weapons—from snowballs to ice balls.

The attackers charged, yelling and screaming to build up their courage. The boys in the screen house were younger lads, they concluded, no match for them. They would have their revenge and exact retribution. They would punish them by stuffing a snowball down the throat of each. If possible, they wanted to draw blood. Nothing could be better. The thought of it was thrilling, intoxicating.

It was Douglas Lauerman who entered the screen house first. He was a big boy whose frame filled the doorway. Inside, little Johnny Fisch had been waiting for his chance. Now the moment came. His arm reared back, and he flung the projectile forward with all his might. The ice ball found its mark, Douglas Lauerman's left cheek. It cracked the bone.

The impact stopped the boy in his tracks. He rocked back two steps and moaned in great agony. Then he fell down in a heap. He continued to moan, and a huge lump formed on his face. The swelling extended and the skin turned a fierce red and his left eye blackened. The fighting stopped, and an eerie silence penetrated the frosty air. The magnitude of the blow was evident to all of the combatants.

The attackers backed off. They looked in horror at little Johnny Fisch. Timmy, their leader, picked up the ice ball and stared at it. Repulsed, he dropped it to the ground and kicked it away in disgust. He knelt down beside his fallen comrade. "It's okay, Doug. You'll be okay." And in that moment Douglas Lauerman blacked out.

Timmy put his hand under the boy's head. It was heavy, dead weight. He turned to the screen house. "Kevin, go get Mom."

That afternoon a light, powdery snow fell from the sky. By nightfall it had covered the earth in another half foot of snow. The surrounding air had been warm during the snowfall, above freezing. This had caused the snow on the roads to melt and the road surface to become slushy.

But then the temperature plummeted. The layer of slush turned into ice. More snowflakes fell on top of it, and a soft second layer accumulated. It concealed the slick surface beneath it.

Cherie Sawyer was a young driver, new to snow. She lacked experience. On this evening she was running late. The dance at the Avon Ballroom would start at 9:00. She was in a hurry; her friends were waiting. To make up time, she punched the accelerator to the floor. The engine responded to her wish, and the red Corvette sprang forward, accelerating west down Highway 52. The snow was still falling. Ribbons of sleet bombarded the windshield, like darts. *Splat*! Momentarily, they blurred her vision. The car streaked along. She steered into the passing lane.

And then a semitruck pulled out in front of her into the left-hand lane. It was intent on passing a slow-moving sedan.

The young girl's right foot slammed on the brake pedal. But to her surprise, the car did not respond. She turned the steering wheel abruptly to the right. The nose of the car turned forty-five degrees to the right, but the vehicle itself did not change direction. It slid sideways, and its momentum threw it forward. Frantically the girl pumped the brakes like her father had taught her to do. But the car refused to slow down, and the young driver screamed.

The red Corvette slammed sideways into the back of the semitruck's trailer. The impact caused a jolt that spun the car in circles, and it caromed off the trailer into the center median. It hit a guard rail. The car, twisted metal, skidded back to the right across the highway and into the ditch, where it turned upside down and then settled into a deep snow drift. The young girl lay inside, pinned in the driver's seat, squashed by the twisted metal. She was dead.

Frankie attended the funeral with his mother. At Father Schumacher's request, he served as an altar boy at the funeral mass. The young girl's body was buried in the Waite Park cemetery, and the red convertible was disposed of in a junkyard in St. Cloud.

"Yes, I'll speak to him about it." The boy's father put down the phone. He looked at his son. "That was Chester Gritt. Have you been hanging onto the back of the city bus? The boy was silent. That constituted an admission of guilt.

"He said Boomer Bartholomay called him and gave him your name. Was Terry Joe in on this?"

His son nodded. The father frowned. "I want you to stop it. It's dangerous. You could be run over. Besides, it's against the law."

The boy looked up from the floor and squinted into the light. He was nervous. Then he looked at his Dad. "Joey Gritt has the record," stated the boy.

"What record?" asked the dad.

"He's hooked the bus the farthest so far. Two days ago, he was pulled all the way to the pump house on 2nd Avenue, where the parade starts.

"Chet Gritt's son?"

The boy continued to explain: "He was mad because he was going to have to walk all the way back. But his dad saw him and gave him a ride home in the squad car."

The boy's father smiled. He contemplated this news for a moment. His scolding softened. "Well, we have to do what the police chief tells us to do. He was good to us when Butch Carter stole my shotgun shells out of the truck and my investment pamphlets out of the garage. I want you to quit hooking the bus."

"Before or after I break the record?" the boy asked.

His father patted the boy's head. "Before," he mused. "We have to obey the law. Forget about breaking the record this time." And then he laughed. "Chet Gritt needs to keep his own house in order."

"He has a double standard," his wife stated when told about it. "Most men do."

"What's wrong now?" her husband asked. "You're not still upset about Marilyn Wojcheski and Father Schumacher; are you?"

"The nerve of that man!" She was still riled. "Advent is coming up. I'll have to go to confession. But not to him."

"Are you keeping track of your sins?" She looked squarely at her son. He lowered his gaze and squinted. "The new year is just around the corner, and you'll be making your First Confession this spring."

"Is hooking the bus a sin?" the boy asked her. He was sincere and wanted to know.

"Your father's right. It's against the law *because* it's dangerous. Stay away from the bus."

"But it's fun," the boy protested. "I'll be careful."

She looked down at him. She knew he was susceptible to a guilty conscience. "You've been warned. If you disobey, you'll have to add it to your list."

CHAPTER TWENTY-FIVE

The Knights of the Round Table convened on Friday, and merriment flowed freely. The three men were happy and celebrated their success with raised glasses and shouts of approval. They toasted themselves. These were good times.

"Ah, Sir Lancelot," asked Sir Gawain, his friend Cortney, "is this not better than being merely the foreman of a railroad crew? We have no one to please but ourselves. I ask you, 'Is this not better?'"

The question was meant to inflame Sir Lancelot, to rankle him. Verbal jousting had ever been their fare. There was great sport in it.

"To Paul Rausch!" toasted Sir Pellinore, their friend Herman. He winked slyly at Gawain. He and Cortney clinked their glasses together, but their friend Howard, Sir Lancelot, would not join in. This added fuel to the fire.

"Bastard," muttered Howie. "I'll never drink to him. He stole my promotion." Their teasing had struck a nerve. "But I'll get even." At that, he stopped talking. It was his custom when he was riled.

"And how will you manage that?" pried Cortney. "If I can be of service, I shall do so."

"Perhaps you do need our help," chided Herman. Paul

Rausch is a bigger man than you." He paused and both men looked at Howie.

"He's a big slob!" croaked Howie. "And a thief."

Cortney grunted. "Aren't we all?" Then Howie relaxed and smiled. Their banter was a fine diversion from what he was feeling.

Repartee must flow both ways. Not to be outdone in this exchange, he slapped Herman on the back. "Next time I'm going to ask that you, Sir Pellinore, and you, Sir Gawain…," here, he tipped his glass to Cortney "…receive the same share of the treasure that I get. I will ask King Arthur personally."

"You mean we don't receive the same share?" asked Herman. He stared in disbelief, and his voice had an edge—a sternness— to it. "But we do the same work as you do."

Howard's stubborn silence served to curdle his blood. "Did you know this, Cortney?" the Knight asked in anger.

"I thought you knew, Sir Pellinore," Cortney replied.

Howie suppressed a smile. Brilliant! How good of Cortney to play along. The worm had turned. Together, they would make a fool of poor Pellinore. Herman began to rant.

"I will not be left in your dust. I must be paid the same share as you. I'll take no less. I will complain to King Arthur himself. Bastards!"

"Arthur is a bastard King," Howie informed him. You insult him by calling him this. It's an old wound. He won't be pleased."

"You're the bastards," corrected Herman.

"Those who do more receive more," needled Cortney, "as well they should. I thought you knew."

"You're joking," Herman growled. He tried to laugh, but his face betrayed that he was not amused.

"I'm afraid it's true," corrected Sir Lancelot. "Don't complain, Herman. It's not like a knight to complain. We must accept our lot. Accept your lot." Inwardly Howard chuckled to himself. He would have the last laugh—on both of them.

"The Knights of the Round Table knew that the greatest quality a knight in the kingdom of Camelot could have was truth. I'm speaking the truth now. My take is more than yours. I receive a fatter share of the profits than you do because I'm second in command."

Now it was Sir Gawain's turn to bluster. "But we do more than you do!" he cried. He looked genuinely perturbed. "We do all the work. We do all the heavy lifting... on both ends of the job. You just sit and give us orders. You don't lift a bloody finger. You don't give a fairy's fart that we..." And then he stopped in mid-sentence. He looked glum. "You *are* the biggest bastard, Howie," Corky pronounced. He said it as if it were a crude anointing.

That's when Howard let out a raucous laugh that shook the entire barroom. He rocked back in his chair and flung his head back and roared. Fat Frannie and the other patrons turned their heads to see what had prompted the outburst. Even Hank at the sink was startled enough to stop washing glasses. Howard whooped! He had won the joust. He had bested them both.

By their third beer the three men were friends again, lost in previous exploits. Their ventures, quests they called them, had always been successes, never failures. Sir Lancelot looked about the room and then leaned forward. "I have a message from King Arthur himself. He needs us in battle." His two companions nearly leaped for joy.

"When?"

"Tomorrow."

"Good old Arthur, whoever he is," stated Herman. "Fill us in on the details please, Sir Lancelot. We've been waiting for this day. It comes none too soon, for we are impatient men."

In a sotto voice Howard explained the task to be undertaken and the role they would play. Tomorrow night at 9:30 sharp, they would meet south of the Sauk River at the west end of the Moose Lodge parking lot. There were no street lights at that end. Long ago, the flood light that illuminated that end of the parking lot had been conveniently shot out with a .22 caliber rifle. The bulb had never been replaced.

At exactly 9:35 two pickup trucks, one driven by Corky and the other by Herman, would pass through the west gate of the Great Northern's car shops using a "borrowed" key. The keys were Howard's responsibility. He would let no one else handle them. Howard would produce the key and also see that the gate was re-latched firmly and re-locked.

Then with their headlights doused, the two trucks would drive between the central plant and the administration building to the rear of the central plant. A second key would open the outside door. There, inside the back entrance they would find a stash of tools, newly purchased to replace those that had worn out and to update the inventory.

The railroad's bosses knew the value of good tools. Superintendent Steichel, himself, had once told them in a speech: "A man is no better than the tools he carries on the job." He knew from personal experience. He had worked his way to the top, starting at the bottom. Long ago, before being promoted, he had worked outside in the yard. He was proud that he was a self-made man.

The tools to be heisted were stacked in crates along the far wall. They had already been counted into the inventory, and Cortney and Herman wondered why they would not be missed. How this occurred, however, was not part of their job. This mission, as all of them had been previously, was strictly on a need-to-know basis. A good soldier did not question why to jump. A good soldier asked only "How far?" And they were good soldiers. They were marines. They were the best.

Once loaded onto the beds of the trucks, the crates of tools would be covered with tarps. Howard would secure the door to the building. The trucks would retrace their route back between the two buildings and through the west gate. The entire operation inside the Great Northern's fence would take less than fifteen minutes.

Then they would drive to their planned drop off point, far north of town along the Sauk River, to the park where stood the monument dedicated to the founder of the village, Henry Chester Waite. Little did he know that at his feet would lay a small fortune of stolen tools. Within ten minutes they would be gone, picked up and delivered to another destination. But this was not the concern of the Knights of the Round Table. They were commissioned only to deliver the packages to the shrine.

As they unloaded the two pickups, the men would hear the rustle of water flowing in the river bed. It was still November, and the river had not yet frozen solid. Long ago, oxen had pulled carts across the river here, where the river was shallow and the river bed flat enough to be forded. Beyond the park stood a wooden bridge. It had been constructed by the WPA during the Depression to replace the original bridge. In the moonlight it would stand deserted, a skeleton of the past.

The men would work in silence, listening for intruders. They were confident there would be none. King Arthur assured them that they would not be bothered by the police. That was part of his role as the mastermind. "There won't be a glitch," Howard informed them.

The men nodded. They trusted what he said. There never had been a glitch. All would proceed as planned, without a hitch.

Once again, they raised their glasses in a toast: "To Arthur, the King!"

"Look at him," Herman stated. He pointed with his chin toward a table at the far side of the room. "Poor devil," he added.

"He's not a devil; he's a saint," chimed in Cortney. "With a wife like that," he exclaimed.

"The man has suffered greatly," spoke Howard. "She's the devil. King Arthur calls her a witch… like Morgana," he added. "She was a sorcerer like Merlin the Magician, and she was also Arthur's sister and the mother of his son."

"Mordred, the Black Prince," stated Corky somberly.

At the far table sat the subject of their discussion, Tom Wojcheski. He was quietly downing his fourth whisky and called for more by tilting his glass toward Fat Frannie.

He seemed not to notice her advances as she brought him another glass, and this miffed her. She "harrumphed! She was not used to being ignored.

Suddenly he realized that the men across the room were watching him, and he lifted his glass to them in a silent salute. His face was grim and had not changed expression. He tried to force a smile, and they saluted back.

Then he settled back into his own thoughts, arms resting on the table. When Frannie approached him for the fifth time, she nuzzled close to him, letting her weight rest upon his shoulder. But he would not be comforted.

"Even the priests at St. Joseph's know that she's a wayward woman," stated Cortney. "Father Schumacher scolded her in front of the whole church a few Sundays ago."

"Oh, she's a loose woman," asserted Herman. "No doubt about it. I've heard the stories."

"She's misguided," stated Howard, using a softer label.

"She's a bad influence," added Cortney. "She's been stirring up trouble with Pat Kucher. Cliff and I talked about it when we went fishing on Mille Lacs last summer. He's worried. He says Marilyn Wojcheski could break up his marriage."

"He'd better put a stop to it right now," suggested Herman, "before it's too late."

"I told him that he'd better put his wife in her place," stated Cortney.

"Poor sap! Look at him. She's driven him to drink." Herman spoke in a soft, low voice under his breath. "He's really pouring 'em down."

"He's not even noticing Frannie," observed Cortney. "Look at her work him over. Doesn't he see the skin she's showing off? And those ripe, juicy pears?" He was salivating.

"No," answered Herman, "he doesn't even see them. Let's invite him over," he suggested. "We'll cheer him up. He needs a good laugh."

"He needs companions," stated Cortney. "Being by yourself is just no damn good."

The annual Firemen's Sweetheart Ball would be held for the second time that year at the Moose Lodge. The ball had originally been scheduled for Valentine's Day in February of the following year, but several large donors had requested that it be moved into the 1958 calendar year. They needed the tax write-off.

"But we already had one Sweetheart Ball this past February" had been the premise behind the opposition's complaint. Amos Borg, on behalf of his wife, Crystal—Crystal Clear, they called her—had brought up the motion at the previous council meeting.

"This isn't the place for that motion, Amos," argued Al Ryngsmuth. "It's a decision of the Firemen's Association. We have no jurisdiction over it."

"They're paid by the village, aren't they?" countered Amos. "That brings them under our wing, so to speak." The mayor simply shrugged.

With the mayor opposed to the motion, it would not pass. So, Amos withdrew the motion. Instead, he took it upon himself to telephone one of the major donors, Homer Hegge. "Can't you deduct the donation you made last February?" he inquired. "That's still in the calendar year."

"Don't state the obvious, Amos. That's insulting," Homer chastised. "Two is better than one; twice is better than once."

It sounded like a line lifted from the pages of a book. "You're not reading George Orwell's *Animal Farm*, are you, Homer?" Amos resorted to sarcasm when he was beaten.

"Huh? What's that? No, I'm not," said the donor and he hung up.

And so, the Firemen's Sweetheart Ball for 1959 was rescheduled for the Saturday before Thanksgiving in November, 1958. The planners had tried to hold it in December, but the Moose Lodge was booked solid into the new year. No one seemed to mind except Crystal Clear Borg.

Unfortunately, the speaker that had been reserved for February was not available in November. The committee chosen by the Firemen's Association had been forced to scramble. They turned to a fellow civil servant, Chester Gritt.

"I'm the police chief, not the fire chief" was his initial response.

"The speaker we wanted has a schedule conflict," stated the fire chief, Guilford Bartholomay.

"Why don't you offer to pay him more?" Chester suggested.

"We tried that," replied Guilford. "I wish we could get him. He tells a good story. But he's booked."

The chief of police dug in his heels. "Why don't *you* do it?"

"I'm already the emcee," the fire chief answered.

Chet Gritt was feeling cornered. "I can't do it. I have to make my nightly rounds at ten o'clock," he argued.

"You'll be home by nine," the fire chief responded. "They don't want a long speech."

"Well, then I'll give them one!" Chet threatened.

"If it goes past twenty minutes, you'll be fired," his mentor warned.

The police chief looked discouraged. "I'm not much of a speaker. I have nothing to talk about."

"You'll do just fine," Guilford Bartholomay replied.

"You're trying to boost my confidence, Guilford," Chester Gritt whined, "and I don't like it."

"You'll do just fine. Just talk about what you know."

"Like what?" asked Chester. "I don't know anything."

"Talk about crime. Talk about danger. Talk about misery. People like that sort of thing."

"Like when I pull someone over and give them a ticket? They look miserable when I do that."

"Not that," stated the fire chief. "That would hit too close to home. Talk about murders and burglaries and how you solve the crime."

"We haven't had many of those lately," responded the police chief.

The fire chief sighed. "Talk about how we help each other. Talk about the harmony between the police force and the firemen. That would be an appropriate topic, you being the liaison between them."

"Liaison hell! I'm the only cop in town. I *am* the police force. You've got me cornered in a pen, Bartholomay!"

The police chief stood silently, biting his lower lip. Guilford Bartholomay could not see the man's eyes behind his sunglasses. Were they moist or dry? Dry as a bone, he guessed. Chet Gritt never cried, even when he had something to cry about.

Guilford Bartholomay stood up. "Well, you'll think of something, Chester. You have two weeks to become inspired. Good luck. I've got to run—And thanks!"

For the next fourteen days Chester Gritt did think hard about his topic. He decided to start with a few jokes to lighten up the atmosphere. And then he'd tell a gentle story or two about the cooperation between the police and fire departments. That's what Guilford Bartholomay wanted.

The Saturday night before Thanksgiving finally arrived. By 7:30 the Moose Lodge was filled to capacity, standing room only. Roland Becker sat at a table with his wife, Mavis. He was chatting comfortably with Bill O'Brian and Paul Rausch, who with their wives were seated with them. The men were talking fishing, gesticulating with their hands to indicate how they set the hook and the size of the catch. Their wives sat impatiently, waiting for the music to begin. They were bored. But the music wouldn't begin until after the keynote speaker's speech.

Lorraine O'Brian could see that her husband was in the middle of a lengthy, tedious fish story. She had heard them all before, in order. This was the one about Pickeral Lake. She was not interested at all. "Let's go take a peek at the silent auction," she whispered to Ione Rausch.

Ione saw a chance to escape. "Let's get away from here," she whispered back. "The dance won't start for an hour. Let's mingle." The two women pushed their chairs back and stood up.

"Roland Becker looked at his wife. "Go with them," he commanded, and a trifle flustered, she, too, stood up.

Across the room Howard sat with Cortney Johanson and Herman Braun. Their wives were busy bidding at the silent auction. The parking lot outside was full. No one had paid attention to the two pickup trucks parked side by side in the shadows at the far end of the lot.

Howard was keeping an eye on Roland Becker. How dare he sit with Paul Rausch! How could he join with the enemy? But then Howard nodded, a tell-tale nod that revealed nothing. No one in the room suspected what he was thinking, not even Cortney and Herman.

Roland Becker, their King Arthur, was clever. Roland knew that sometimes the safest place to hide was in the midst of the enemy, where no one would suspect you. How shrewd! At close range Roland could keep an eye on the proceedings. He would stay on top of the mission, watching and listening for unseen developments, for signs that something had gone awry. Of course, once the mission started, there would be no way to abort it; Roland would have no way of contacting his knights. Yet, if he sensed that something was about to go wrong, he might be able to alter the course of the action and snatch success from failure— and save them all! He would certainly try. Howard Kappas stared across the room. Roland Becker looked relaxed and calm.

Howard let his mind go over the details of the plan one more time. The three knights would exit from the lodge separately at 9:30. The dance would be in full swing, so no one would notice their departure. Their wives would stay behind. People knew that the women would never leave with the silent auction ready to close. At 10:00 o'clock it would be over, and the winners would be announced. Howard grinned. Wild horses—or bored husbands—could not drag them away. Everyone understood this distinction between the sexes. No one would think twice if the men left without their wives. No one would question the reason for their departure. No one would suspect the truth.

As Roland Becker listened to Bill O'Brian's fish stories, he looked like he was enjoying himself. But he was only half-listening. He watched his wife proceed to the silent auction tables and join Lorraine O'Brian and Ione Rausch. Their reactions were those of typical village wives shopping for bargains.

By 10:00 o'clock the heist would be nearly completed. Howard and the boys would lift the goods, nearly $4,000 worth, by 9:50. Half of that sum was profit for Roland, himself. By 10:00 o'clock the booty would be unloaded in the park up north along the Sauk River under the statue of Henry C. Waite. The park would be deserted, Roland was sure. Ten minutes later his son, Marty, the Black Prince, along with a trusted accomplice would have the tools loaded onto Roland's truck. They would drive to a warehouse in St. Cloud, to HAMMER TOOLS on 3rd Street near the Labor Temple.

The labor hands were Roland's friends. They were union men like himself. Best of all, they were loyal and knew how to keep their mouths shut. The stolen tools would disappear onto the racks of shelves in the tool company's warehouse. When the time was right, they would be summoned to reappear.

Roland Becker had long been employed by the Great Northern Railway as a bookkeeper. He had always had a head for numbers. Still, he too had been denied a promotion. He had applied to be the new bursar and been turned down. When he suggested that he had been "overlooked," Superintendent Steichel told him that he was too valuable where he was. "We need you as a bookkeeper to ensure efficiency. You're a resource the railroad relies on, Roland. You're in charge of accounts receivable and accounts payable. That's enough. You're a trusted employee." The boss had smiled and considered the request denied, the case closed.

Roland didn't complain; he didn't get angry; he would get even. The superintendent underestimated how good a bookkeeper Roland Becker was—how resourceful he could be. Roland formulated a plan. He would put his genius and his accounting skills to work.

It had been easy for Roland to enlist the aid of his boyhood chum, Howard Kappas. Howard, too, felt resentment. He disliked Paul Rausch, and not unreasonably. Paul had been awarded the job Howard desperately wanted—and deserved. Roland was a good judge of character. He knew the ill-feelings, the grudge, that Howard harbored.

At Roland's suggestion, Howard volunteered to help Paul Rausch inventory the car shops' tools on a regular basis. Paul had not denied him this consolation. The foreman would not have been so agreeable had he known that Howard was altering the numbers.

Roland authorized payment of the bills, but he also modified the numbers before he verified them. With Howard's help some tools were not accounted for on the inventory ledger. Those tools disappeared. Roland Becker was a patient man. He was not greedy. He only skimmed off the top, never in a quantity large enough to be noticed by the plant foremen or to trigger an audit.

He was a man who planned carefully. Many months might go by before he moved again. Always he sought an advantage over his foe. He would not act unless he was certain that the time was right, that nothing could be detected, that nothing could go wrong. He insisted that he have an edge.

The coup de grace was what happened later in the aftermath. The Great Northern Railway constantly needed good tools. Roland saw to it that these were ordered from HAMMER TOOLS. The supplier's location in St. Cloud was convenient. Roland signed the purchase orders, and the tools were put in boxes and delivered. Many were the same tools that had been stolen and disappeared. When the time was right, hammers, wrenches, drills, and saws all reappeared; they were resurrected.

Roland laughed to himself. He thought it a good joke. The Great Northern Railway was purchasing the same tools it already owned. And it was paying for them again. The irony was not lost on Roland. It was only fitting after the disservice they had done to him.

Of course, HAMMER paid Roland handsomely. His trusted friend, Johnny Morris, the bookkeeper at the company, saw to that. The two men had long been friends, back to their playing days on Waite Park's baseball diamond when Roland had been the pitcher and Johnny his catcher for the Parkers. They had been in scraps together before, standing shoulder to shoulder, fighting fiercely, protecting one another's back side. The two men saw eye to eye. They always had.

As the Firemen's Sweetheart Ball got into full swing, Roland kept his eye on Chester Gritt. The police chief was the one man in the room who could prove to be his undoing. Roland watched as Chester circled about the room. People were shaking his hand and wishing him well on his speech. In a tuxedo accented by his sunglasses, he looked rather sporting.

The dirty bugger, thought Roland. He cheated me out of victory in the soap box derby. I should never have let Walt Unger order those wheels.

"It was a walleye twenty-eight inches long," Bill O'Brian stated. "Really!" He spread his arms apart to indicate the size of the trophy fish.

"That's a huge fish," agreed Paul Rausch, "like the one Cliff Kucher caught last spring."

"Bigger!" asserted Bill.

Roland's gaze returned to the men at the table with him. They looked his way. He merely grunted. He could not be coaxed into commenting, so they let him be.

Just after 8:00 p.m. the program commenced. Guilford Bartholomay climbed the stairs to the podium and addressed the crowd:

"Ladies and gentlemen, I want to welcome you all to this year's…er…next year's Firemen's Sweetheart Ball. The dancing will commence in twenty minutes." He glanced at Chester Gritt, who was sitting alone at the head table near the podium, waiting to be introduced. Chet's wife, Loretta, was at the silent auction tables, protecting her interests.

"Tonight we have with us one of Waite Park's most respected men. He has given our village twelve years of dedicated service, protecting our community and keeping us safe. When I spoke to him recently and asked him to be our keynote speaker, he jumped at the chance. He told me personally that he wants to tell you how the police department and the fire department cooperate to serve you, the public who supports us. He called it an 'opportunity.'

Waite Park is a small, tightly-knit village. It's a good place to live and to raise our children. There isn't much crime here. You can rest assured that if there was, our keynote speaker would know about it—and solve it. He's determined to keep it that way. With him on the job, you can sleep well, knowing that you and your loved ones are protected.

And so it is with great pleasure that I introduce to you a man who cares deeply about you and about Waite Park. He's not just the police chief; he's a good friend to us all! Please welcome Chester Gritt.

As he mounted the steps to the podium, Chet Gritt heard scattered applause. "Keep it short, Chief!" Larry Poindexter's voice could be heard above the din. Several similar cries echoed throughout the room.

Uff! Larry gasped when his wife, Donna, elbowed him in the ribs. "That's not funny, Larry, and you know it."

The crowd settled back in their chairs. They wondered how long they would have to remain seated. Guilford had *promised* them twenty minutes. Alright, they could sit that long. They wondered what the police chief would have to say: something of interest, they hoped—something unusual, out of the ordinary. Standing up there in his tuxedo and sunglasses, he looked like he was capable of giving a good speech.

"I'm honored to be here as your keynote speaker," Chester Gritt stated. Immediately interest in the speech began to wane. Behind his sunglasses Chester looked puzzled. Guilford Bartholomay had assured him that this type of audience would like hearing this from him. "Flattery goes a long way in a mixed crowd," Guilford had advised. Now the police chief did not feel so sure.

Chester looked at the sea of faces out there in front of him. The women looked pleased; the men looked grim. They all wanted blood.

"It's important to get off on the right foot," Guilford had admonished him. Chet decided to pass the buck. "The fire chief has asked me to speak about the cooperation between our departments." Chester noted instantly that interest in the speech was continuing to fade. "Cooperation is very important in a growing community like Waite Park. But we have had our disagreements." He paused momentarily. For the first time Chet detected a flickering interest in the speech.

The police department and the fire department each have a separate office in Village Hall. However, we share a break room down the hallway. Our main disagreement concerns the coffee pot. Who will make the coffee? Should we take turns? Should we alternate by days or by weeks? Should the firemen make it on Monday, Tuesday, and Wednesday, and the police make it on Thursday and Friday. When I proposed this to them, they answered 'No.' They complained strongly that they would have an extra day. I told them, 'There's half a dozen of you and only one of me.'

'But not all at the same time,' they responded. 'We work in two shifts of three.'" Again, the speaker looked into the sea of faces; interest was still flickering.

"A bigger problem is that they make the coffee weaker than I do. I'm a strong man. I like my coffee strong. Guilford likes his weak.

They disputed the logic. They argued that since there are more of them, they should decide how the coffee is made. After all, I'm only one man. 'It's better to please three people instead of just one.'

I disagreed vehemently with this. The police department of the Village of Waite Park will not be dictated to! So, we were locked in a stalemate.

I'm pleased to report that both disputes have been resolved; the disagreement has been settled." He paused for effect. "The village clerk, Henrietta Clayborne, who works farther down the hall, has agreed to make the coffee the five days of the week she is there, every week. She makes the coffee weaker on Mondays, Wednesdays, and Fridays, and stronger on Tuesdays and Thursdays." He gestured. "The police department is still getting the short end of the stick, only two days to their three. But they do have three firemen on duty at a time, and I am only one man. We're putting the issue to rest because we know how important it is that we cooperate."

Here the police chief paused. He didn't know what to expect from the sea of faces in the audience. He was delighted to hear himself drowned in a chorus of laughter. Even the men didn't look so glum; they were applauding.

Chet Gritt raised his arms to quiet them. The chorus quickly shushed. "The second area where we cooperate," he continued, "is in the area of recreation management.

Saturday night, once a month, is poker night. Chief Guilford and I play poker together with Amos Borg and Father Thiel. But on which Saturday of the month do we play? And at whose house? Do we take turns and rotate? Guilford's house has better lighting than mine. In my house the refrigerator is closer; his is in his utility room, farther away. When it's Father's turn, do we play in the rectory? Would we disturb Father Schumacher? Remember, Father Thiel is only the assistant to the pastor. He says it's worse than being married. Would it spoil our fun if we had to play in the church? In God's house? Think about it. There the lighting is always dim.

We never go over to Amos Borg's house. The one time we did, Crystal insisted on staying in the room. She wanted to talk to us."

At this, the crowd whooped! They let loose again; they approved of the speech's content. The ovation was premature, but genuine, and a few of the woman stood up to applaud. Their mouths were filled with laughter, and their eyes were filled with tears, especially the eyes of those who knew Crystal.

This time Chester let the laughter go on. He waited for the applause to settle down. "We've worked the problem out through cooperation between the police department and the fire department. We only play poker at my house or at Guilford's, never at the rectory or at Amos's. We let Father decide on which Saturday to play, depending on his schedule for confession. Guilford and I don't allow ourselves to drink coffee, lest it bring up an old wound, our old feud."

"Why don't you play at Village Hall, Chief?" Larry Poindexter yelled. "It's never busy there. Henrietta could come over and make you a pot." More titter from the audience filtered forward toward the podium, and Chester Gritt raised his hands as if he was under arrest.

"Of course, Guilford and I also cooperate to win. We have to work together if we want to collect any money from Amos. We decided this months ago, and it's been working ever since."

"Cheaters!" arose a cry from the front of the room. It was Amos Borg. He was standing. "Is Father Thiel in on this? He's been winning more than his share, too."

"No," said the keynote speaker, "he's not involved in our partnership. Sit down, Amos, and relax. I'm sure Father Thiel relies on prayer."

"He's a helluva bluffer," Amos admitted and sat down.

The crowd roared their approval of the speech. Chet Gritt checked his watch. "So far, so good," he mused. Ten minutes had elapsed.

"Seriously though," he stated, "we do cooperate with each other. In our line of work, we have to." Chester noted that once again the faces of the men in the audience had turned grim. Interest was fleeting; it could disappear in a moment.

"We have had our tragedies, even this year, out at the granite quarries and on the highway." He looked at a table along the wall to his left and caught the gaze of Syl Sawyer. The police chief nodded toward him. Rodney Koeller's parents were sitting with Syl; the Hogansons were nowhere in sight. "These are tragedies that have taken the lives of our young people, our children." A hush fell over the room. Faces turned toward the table at the side of the room.

"I was there shortly after the dynamite exploded at Dead Man's quarry. So was Guilford Bartholomay and the rescue team. I saw the work those men did, lifting the pieces of a dead boy's body into an ambulance. As gut-wrenching as it was, they had to do it.

I was out on Highway 52 on a snowy night recently between Waite Park and St. Joseph, where a car rolled over. So was Guiford Bartholomay and his fire crew. We had to use crow bars to pry the twisted metal apart to extract the body of a lifeless young girl." All eyes rested on Syl Sawyer and the Koellers; the eyes were filled with pity.

The crowd was hushed. Chester Gritt wondered if they were holding their breath. He was convinced. They wanted to hear about tragedy, about sadness and pain, other people's pain.

"We live *vicariously*—he had looked the word up in the dictionary—through our children. They bring us joy and sadness. I'm a father myself. I don't know what I'd do without my two boys, Joey and Ricky."

"And I'm a mother! Did you have to use that purple powder on my boy?" The voice came from a table in the back of the room, and it was filled with frustration. It belonged to Marge Carter. Heads turned toward her, and then they shifted toward Cliff Kucher, who was sitting, glass in hand, in the middle of the room. Cliff hung his head and fumbled with his drink. He did not like the limelight. His wife, Pat, who was sitting next to him, placed her hand on his knee under the table to calm him. His knees were shaking.

The police chief stiffened. "He was stealing, Marge. Theft is serious business. A thief is the worst of the lot, the lowest of the low. We have to teach our children when they're young that taking property from someone else is wrong. They should be teaching that in school, but they're not... not enough anyway. If our children don't learn to be honest at a young age, they may go on to bigger things later on." He sounded stern.

Marge Carter shuddered. "Did you have to use that purple powder?" she wailed. "It still hasn't all washed off. It's shameful. Everyone who sees him knows."

Chester Gritt looked out at the woman. She was quivering with anger. "We use it when we have to, to catch the criminal. I know it's hard to wash off. It has to wear off, just like the impulse to steal has to wear off. I'm sorry."

"They're just little boys," Marge shouted back at him, "not criminals! You treated my son like a common thief. Chief Gritt, I resent that!" Her criticism was fierce, bordering on rage.

"But he was stealing shotgun shells out of a pickup truck. In a child's hands, gun shells can be as dangerous as dynamite." The comparison was not lost on the audience. Many nodded in agreement.

"You play favorites. You picked on us." It was an accusation. She was yelling.

"I don't do that," replied the chief.

Marge Carter screamed at him in hate. "You're a liar! You picked on us because of who we are. How often do you use that purple powder?"

Chet Gritt leaned forward, accepting her challenge, and took off his sunglasses. He looked her squarely in the eyes. "All the time."

Marge Carter burst out in tears. If the police chief had been near her, she would have spit in his face, right between his eyes. As it was, her husband, Pete, escorted her from the room, all the while looking daggers at Chester Gritt.

The keynote speaker put his sunglasses back on. He checked his watch. "Is there a question? I can take two. I have to make my nightly rounds soon, at ten."

Larry Poindexter raised his hand. "Are you going to umpire Little League again this year, Chief?" It was an easy question.

"I plan to," Chet Gritt answered. "Baseball is a way to keep kids off the streets and out of mischief. Perhaps the fire chief will cooperate with me and help sponsor my Civil Defense team. We could split the costs fifty-fifty. Eh, Guilford?"

Guilford Bartholomay simply smiled.

"I asked you if you are going to *umpire* the games," Larry Poindexter tried to clarify.

Chet Gritt ignored him. "Last question?"

"Have you stopped the boys from hooking the bus?" The inquiry came from Tillie Kuchenmeister. "I ride the bus to the beauty parlor every week. That O'Brian boy and that Kucher boy are hooking the bus. I guess boys will always be boys. But it's getting out of hand."

This time when he heard his name mentioned, Cliff Kucher leaned forward and smiled. His knees were no longer shaking.

Chief Gritt chuckled good-naturedly. He shrugged his shoulders. "Boys *will* be boys," he agreed. But hooking the bus is dangerous. Their hands can slip off the bumper, and they could be run over by a car. I've spoken to the parents of all the boys who do it. They've agreed to put a stop to it."

"Even Joey?" Cliff Kucher was surprised to hear the question come from the woman seated beside him, his wife, Pat. A silence stiffened the room.

For a moment Chet Gritt was caught off guard. Looking sheepish, he did not have to feign embarrassment. But he recovered handsomely.

"I've spoken to his mother," he acknowledged confidentially. "She has agreed to speak to her son about it." The humor worked its magic. "Thanks!"

The twenty minutes were up. The speaker waved his hand and stepped aside from the podium. The music started as if on cue. The men and women stood up and stretched their legs. They were ready to dance the night away.

Chester Gritt descended down the steps. Guilford Bartholomay was the first to greet him. "Congratulations, Chief! Well done!" He shook Chet Grit's hand. "You gave them what they wanted, Chet. You were a huge success."

Chester Grit floated about the room for an hour. People wanted to shake his hand. They had not heard such an entertaining speech in years, and he accepted their compliments graciously.

Roland Becker watched the police chief carefully. He knew that the man was unpredictable, prone to impulsiveness. Roland didn't know how he would react to the stress of giving his speech. Roland couldn't know that. Marge Carter had been tough on the chief, challenging him. Now the pressure was off. He had weathered the storm. But how would he react?

So..., Chester Gritt played poker. But so did Roland. And he had a card up his sleeve. Roland's ace in the hole was Loretta Gritt, Chester's wife. She would never leave the ball before ten. She had bid on too many items. And she wanted them badly.

She had even sat at a silent auction table during her husband's speech. Roland was a good judge of character. He knew that Chester would have trouble telling his wife "no." She was the only person in the world Chester felt obligated to listen to.

Howard Kappas was antsy. This new music agitated him. The Night Owls, known locally to be a good band, had altered their style. For the first hour they had played good old-fashioned swing, tunes like Glenn Miller's "Moonlight Serenade" and "In the Mood" and Tommy Dorsey's "I'll Never Smile Again."

But the band members wanted to prove their versatility and appeal to the younger generation, too. When the second set began, the Night Owls switched from swing to rock and roll. They played the songs of Elvis Presley, and their singer gyrated and the music thumped. It pounded in Howard's ears. He tried to ignore it, but he couldn't.

At 9:20 he left the table to get his coat. He stepped outside into the cold night air. The music inside the Moose Lodge was still throbbing, and the dancers were still pulsating with it.

Outside was better. He could relax and concentrate on the task at hand. He drifted down toward the west end of the parking lot.

Two minutes later, he was joined by Cortney Johanson. "Jump in," said Cortney, zipping up his jacket.

Herman Braun arrived a minute later. He checked his watch. "We're five minutes early," he noted.

"So what?" croaked Howie. "It's five minutes saved. Why waste time? Let's go."

Cortney started his truck's engine and drove off slowly, turning right onto 3rd Street. He proceeded at normal speed east toward the west gate of the Great Northern Railway's yard. A hundred yards behind, Herman followed him.

The final countdown began at 9:30. Roland Becker had watched the three knights leave the Moose Lodge between 9:20 and 9:25. Would they stick to the time schedule? He didn't know. Howard Kappas had always been a renegade. He was persuasive; the other two would comply with his wishes.

The ticking clock was Roland's beating heart. Time moved at a constant speed. *Tick. Tick. Tick.* It's steady pace was inexorably slow.

9:31… 9:32… Roland kept his eyes trained on Chester Gritt, who was seated with Syl Sawyer. Roland watched them. Syl's face was red; he'd been crying. Chester leaned over and said something into Syl's ear.

Roland's internal clock continued to beat. *Tick. Tick. Tick.* 9:33… Had they entered the car shops by now? Fifteen minutes inside the place would mean exiting at 9:48, comfortably before Chet Gritt made his 10:00 o'clock rounds. Or, had they waited as instructed. Those extra two minutes could be life-saving. Failure to improvise could spell their doom.

Roland focused on Waite Park's chief of police, his eyes riveted on the man's face. You could tell everything about a man by the look on his face. Often, this insight gave you a few minutes to react. 9:34… 9:35…

Something was afoot. The police chief suddenly stood up. He patted Syl Sawyer on the shoulder. Immediately several well-wishers flocked to Chester's side, but he extended his arms sideways, palms out, as if to push them away. He was shaking his head and backing away from them. Roland watched Guilford Bartholomay approach the chief. 9:36… 9:37…

Chet Gritt had had enough attention. He didn't care if he never again shook a well-wisher's hand or heard the word *Congratulations!* He told them, "I can't talk. I have to go. I must go and make my rounds."

"But it's not ten o'clock yet," Amos Borg informed him.

"That makes no difference," the chief replied.

"Have one more drink," Amos coaxed. "Let's talk."

"I haven't had *any* drinks tonight. I don't want to talk. I have to go—*now.*

Excuse me. No, I can't shake your hand. I'm leaving. Move out of my way. Guilford, would you tell these people to leave me alone?"

"Tell them goodbye, Chester. They mean well… and smile. Congratulations again on your speech."

Chester Gritt winced. The wince turned into a grimace. He turned to go. And then he remembered to smile. His face burst into a forced grin, but he continued to keep his feet moving toward the front door. Clear of interference, he lengthened his stride and quickened his pace.

Chief Gritt's path took him in the direction of Roland Becker's table. Suddenly Roland stood up and stepped into the chief's path. "Congratulations on the speech, Chief. You were a big hit."

"I have to go," Chet replied. He tried to sidestep Roland.

"Even though the speech was silly." Roland stood his ground, blocking the other man's way.

Chet Gritt frowned. "What do you mean by silly?" he asked, annoyed. "Those were jokes at the beginning to lighten everyone's mood. They worked. People have been coming up to me for an hour, telling me they liked it."

Inside Roland's chest, the clock was ticking. 9:38... 9:39...

"They're fools," Roland stated. They wanted to hear about the deaths of the Sawyer girl and the Hoganson kid, and you gave it to them."

"You're not that interested in kids, are you, Roland? Except your own. You took care of Bertie Norton, didn't you? Do you know that Art Norton wants to sue you? Don't be surprised if he does."

"That Norton kid is a pig... like his father. They all are. He had it coming. He started it. He was beating up Curtis. I watched it from my living room. Marty was protecting Curtis after the Norton kid pushed him down. I saw the whole thing. He's a bully." Roland Becker was growing livid. Still, he kept his composure. "It's not a crime to protect a cripple."

"It is a crime to mangle a boy's face." Chester Gritt was disgusted. "Look, Roland, I have to make my rounds. Get out of my way."

"Where did you get those wheels?" Roland changed the subject.

"You know where I got those wheels. The same place you did—from the Firestone plant in Akron, Ohio. Now move! I'm going."

"So there you are! You're not leaving yet. It's still twenty minutes to ten." Loretta Gritt bounced into the conversation.

Chet glanced at his watch. "It's 9:41... 9:42... I have to go—now!"

But the silent auction ends in eighteen minutes," Loretta protested. "We can't go yet. I have to be here in case someone tries to outbid me at the last minute." She put her arms around her husband's midsection and squeezed. "Please, Chester!"

Roland spoke. "What did you put in those wheels to make them go an inch faster in ten feet? I want to know."

Chester Gritt relaxed. "That's a trade secret," he answered. He put his arm around his wife's shoulders.

"Come on, Chester, be fair. Let's keep the playing field even—on the level."

Chet Gritt laughed out loud. He enjoyed seeing his rival squirm.

"Oh, go ahead and tell him, Chester," Loretta urged. "I don't mind."

"Okay." Chester told his secret. "Silicone."

"Silicone?" exclaimed Bill O'Brian in disbelief. "Don't they use that in breast thingamajigs?" He gestured with both hands chest high.

"They use it in a lot of things," Chester acknowledged. I guess breast implants is one of them. He squeezed his wife's shoulders. Bill's eyes roamed downward to Loretta's chest area and stopped. He saw the broad expanse of cleavage she was displaying in her bosom. He stared at it, somewhat amused, until he thought of his own wife's lackluster breasts.

"Where do you get it?" Roland Becker persisted. 9:43...

"Somewhere in Michigan." Chet's answer was terse, succinct. "I'm going now." He let go of his wife.

"But how will I get home?" she pleaded.

"Her husband looked around the table. "Roland can take you home," he blurted and moved off.

Loretta Gritt looked after her husband as he departed. "He's in such a hurry. I wonder what's bothering him. Are you going to take me home, Roland?" She turned in his direction. But Roland was gone.

Outside in the hallway, Roland spoke harshly to Tweet Thorsten, who was using the pay phone. "I have to use the phone, Tweet. It's urgent. Get off."

Tweet looked over his shoulder at Roland. "But I just got connected."

Roland reached over and pushed down the lever that ended the call. "Now!"

Roland Becker dialed a number. "Answer, Marty," he pleaded. "Answer the phone." He heard the numbers clicking on the other end of the line. "Come on, Marty, answer the damn phone!" The other end of the line did not respond; there was no one there.

9:45... Not enough time had elapsed! His desperation bordered on panic. The timing was all wrong. He was sure of it. Chester Gritt would drive down 3rd Street and intercept the caravan of two, two trucks emerging from the west gate of the Great Northern's car shops. When their headlights suddenly came on, he would spot them. He had watched the police chief exit in a hurry, on the run.

Self-preservation is said to be the strongest instinct, but to Roland Becker preservation of his family was paramount. He must save his son. "Abort!" Roland screamed into the receiver. "Marty, abort! Abort the mission! MARTIN!"

In anger he yanked the phone cord hard and tore it from the wall. Roland fled the scene. When Tweet Thorsten returned to use the phone, he found it on the floor, unusable, dead.

Chester Gritt left the Moose Lodge behind and nearly sprinted toward his patrol car. He was glad to be free of it all, finally. He unlocked the front door and settled into the driver's seat. Chet was thinking about the last five minutes. The more he reflected, the more suspicious he became.

Roland Becker was an annoying bastard. He had acted strangely. Why had he stood up? That was out of character for Roland. Roland was a proud man; he rarely stood up for anybody. How curious! Then he had blocked Chester's way; he had refused to step aside. Why?

Chester was annoyed with himself. "Why did I tell him about the silicone?" He cussed himself. That secret was my advantage, my edge, Joey's edge.

Then he recalled Roland's last question: "Where do you get the silicone?"

Roland didn't need to ask. He ordered items for the railroad all the time. He could easily have looked it up himself. That was his line of work, his expertise. Why did he ask? It was all very strange. In Chester Gritt's mind it became a puzzle that Waite Park's police chief wanted put together.

He turned the key, and the car's engine sprang to life. He turned on his headlights and shifted the car into gear. 9:46... He turned right onto 3rd Street and accelerated. His rounds through the village would take him a little more than an hour. By 11:00 o'clock he would park the patrol car in his driveway down on 13th Avenue across from the Little League ballpark.

Loretta would be home, waiting to show him the results of the silent auction, her purchases. The town would be quiet. Most of the townsfolk were still at the Firemen's Sweetheart Ball. A few of the men had left; they always did.

As he approached 10th Avenue, the police chief slowed down. He stopped at the stop sign and looked to his left. Far in the distance he could see two sets of tail lights, red lights rounding a bend on their way toward the park bordering the Sauk River to the north.

It is a quiet town... *his* town, he thought. His right foot stepped off the brake and pushed down on the accelerator. The police car responded. It continued straight on 3rd Street.

Chester Gritt passed the Great Northern Railway's car shops. The yard was empty, and the gates were locked. He proceeded slowly down the street, past Ma's Bar. Frannie had already dimmed the lights and was ready to close early.

A lone straggler stepped out of the bar and staggered to his car. He was a bit tipsy, and he glared into the patrol car's headlights as it approached. When the man saw the lights on top of the car, he backed away. He decided against driving the four blocks home, and he wobbled away up the avenue.

Far to the north on 10th Avenue, the two pickup trucks driven by Cortney Johanson and Herman Braun turned into the park that was nestled alongside the Sauk River. They turned off their headlights and drove to the statue in the center of the park. The time was 9:48. Quietly they unloaded six large boxes of tools from the bed of the two trucks and covered the boxes with two tarps. The boxes were heavy, and Howard Kappas smiled. "We're early," he announced. "They'll have to sit here unguarded for a little longer than usual, but I don't think Henry Waite will mind."

"He can guard them," Herman joked. And then he climbed back into his truck.

Harvey sat beside Cortney. "Don't speed," he ordered. "Chet Gritt will be making his ten o'clock rounds." They didn't know that by the time they reached the intersection of 10th Avenue and 3rd Street, the police chief would be a mile to the east in the Oakdale Addition, already well into his rounds.

Howard was satisfied. The plan had gone smoothly. The loot was theirs. His share would come in handy in the coming days. It was almost Christmas, and he would use the extra cash to buy gifts. Maybe, just maybe, he would surprise his wife, Kitty, with a new mink jacket like the one Cliff Kucher had bought for his wife. Kitty wanted something warm.

Not until the days that followed did the men realize how close they had come to disaster. Two minutes had separated the foxes from the hound. The Knights of the Round Table congratulated Howard on his shrewd decision to leave the Firemen's Sweetheart Ball five minutes early. He applauded them for agreeing to his decision.

Howard had born the brunt of Roland Becker's wrath. Howard had listened to Roland rant over the phone. "I insulted him. I had to," Roland complained. "And I argued with him. But then I had to kiss his ass. Do you know how that makes me feel, Howard?"

Roland had cursed a blue streak. The chief's unpredictable exit had rattled him. Tweet Thorsten had witnessed his vehemence and his violent reaction. Perhaps others had too.

But King Arthur had saved the day. His gambit had been ambitious, and in the end it had paid off. His tactics and obtuse behavior had delayed Chester Gritt's departure by five minutes. Those had been five precious minutes.

Roland had sworn into the phone. "I will be more careful in the future. Damn it! I must be certain."

But the mission was a success. They split the $4,000 and celebrated. Fat Frannie brought over three brown bottles.

"Sir Lancelot, here's to you!" Cortney proclaimed.

"And Sir Gawain, here's to you!" Herman declared.

"And Sir Pellinore, here's to you!" Howard exclaimed, completing the trio of toasts.

Then he raised his glass high. "To the Knights of the Round Table" proposed Howard, "and to their quest for the Holy Grail!"

Fat Frannie looked in their direction and shook her head. How silly these men were, grown men playing their little game of fantasy! But sometimes they took it so seriously. She wondered why. Oh well, their patronage paid the bills. She liked to see them happy. They tipped better when they were in a good mood.

CHAPTER TWENTY-SIX

"Children, do you see that painting of Grandma and the turkey?" Sister Mary Bede pointed up to the wall above their heads. The Second Graders, all seated at tables in the library, gazed upward, following the direction of her outstretched arm and finger.

"Do you mean the grandma and the grandpa?" inquired Terry Joe.

"That's her husband," asserted Gail Teigen. "The turkey's on the platter. Don't play dumb, Terrance Joseph," she admonished. The teacher let the reprimand pass.

Mrs. O'Leery, sitting at her librarian's desk, merely grunted. She was tuned in to Sister's lesson.

On the wall above the children's heads hung four large prints, forty-six by thirty-six, of Norman Rockwell's famous paintings: *The Four Freedoms*. They had been commissioned by President Franklin D. Roosevelt himself in 1943 to help sell war bonds.

Horace Rugemeyer was one of Waite Park's most respected citizens. He had served in World War I and been wounded in France. He walked with a limp, a daily reminder of his service to his country and the price he had paid. Now he heard his president's call, loud and clear, to support the war effort. Like many other veterans, he was overcome with patriotic feeling.

He promptly bought war bonds and also purchased a set of prints of the four paintings and hung them in his living room.

"They're too large," Mildred Rugemeyer had argued, but it was only after the war ended that her husband agreed to take them down. He stored them in the attic to keep them dry. Then one Sunday old Horace died, and Mildred decided it was time to clean house. She found the paintings stored away and bequeathed them to the church.

Young Father Schumacher, too, noticed how large the paintings were, and he wondered if they had any monetary value. Father Denery, the former pastor, said "No." The new pastor thought about refusing the gift but then thought better of it.

He would heed Father Denery's reminder that Horace Rugemeyer had been a sturdy supporter of Catholicism in Waite Park. He had been a long-standing trustee on the church council, the school board's president, and a stalwart financial contributor to St. Joseph's parish. A financial gift from Mildred might be forthcoming, an endowment perhaps, and it could be rather substantial. Father Schumacher was very gracious in his acceptance of Horace's set of four large paintings.

The following Monday he paid a visit to Sister Isidore, the principal of St. Joseph's Elementary in 1946. He informed her of Mildred Rugemeyer's gift to St. Joseph's. "They're educational," Father stated. "They belong in a school where children can see them and understand what it means to be an American."

"Oh, for Pete's sake, Father," countered Sister. "Millie's had those paintings in storage for over a year, since the atomic bombs exploded over Japan. Now that Horace has died, she's cleaning house. She wants to get rid of them. She doesn't care if they're on display or not."

Father's silence was stoic. Although his upper incisors were busy biting his lower lip, his gaze at her was steadfast and unyielding.

"But they're so large. Where will we put them?" she said in exasperation.

"Hang them in the library," Father answered. "That way all the children can see them and learn about America's freedoms. They were painted by Norman Rockwell, you know," Father explained, "the illustrator who does the covers of *The Saturday Evening Post*."

"I know," said Sister. She was feeling cornered and helpless.

The four pictures were duly transferred from the priests' rectory to the school's library across the street. Mrs. O'Leery, in her first year as the school's librarian, was in no position to say "no" to her boss. "They're so large," she observed.

"I suggest you hang them over there, high up, above the magazine rack," advised the principal. "You'll get used to them. By the way, do we subscribe to *The Saturday Evening Post*?" Mrs. O'Leery shook her head sideways in the negative.

The prints had hung on the north wall above the magazine rack for twelve years. Frequently they looked a bit time-worn and hazy. Mounted up high as they were, they were hard to dust.

The boys and girls looked at the four pictures. Sister Bede had talked about them collectively before:

Freedom of Speech—a common man, wearing a leather jacket, standing to speak up at a town meeting.

Freedom of Religion—the heads of a diverse mixture of people bowed or uplifted in silent prayer.

Freedom from Fear—a mother and father tucking their sleeping child into bed.

Freedom from Want—a grandmother and grandfather, a generation older, serving a turkey on a platter to their hungry children and grandchildren. Everyone looks joyous.

"What holiday is it in two days?" Sister Bede continued. Every hand shot up.

"Thanksgiving!" her pupils answered in unison.

"We get off school, don't we?" asked Ricky Shenker.

"Sure, we do," responded Jimmy Holston. "We get to watch football on television."

"What do we eat on Thanksgiving?" Sister inquired.

"Turkey!" the class sang out, a chorus of voices. Many of the students were smiling.

"Why are so many of you smiling?" Sister persisted.

"Because it's a happy day," Terry Joe trilled. "Because we get to eat cranberries!" He nearly shouted.

"Why do we eat turkey and cranberries?" Sister prodded. She was pushing them to their limit and beyond.

"We have sweet potatoes too," stated Susanne Danbury, her big eyes in her big head burning bright. "With marshmallows on top," she added, flashing her teeth.

At the counter, Mrs. O'Leery continued to stamp new books. She had learned this lesson before, many times. It seemed that every new teacher was infatuated with the story of the Pilgrims landing at Plymouth Rock and being rescued by the Indians who taught them how to survive.

All except Sister Agatha. She resented how the white intruders from Europe had taken advantage of the red-skinned men, women, and children—her ancestors. "Savages!" That's what the White Man had called them. It was unchristian, but secretly she wished that the Indians hadn't been so neighborly to the first white men and had let the bitter winter take its toll.

Mrs. O'Leery remembered Sister Agatha's lecture to her class about Thanksgiving. She had used a harsher tone than the one normally used by the nuns at St. Joseph's. Mrs. O'Leery had been shocked, and then somewhat amused, by Sister Agatha's interpretation of American history. The diminutive nun preached a vision for America that was far different from the usual.

"So why are they eating these foods?" Sister's question seemed to stump the children. Momentarily their minds ground to a halt. Then the current in their brains surged from synapse to synapse, searching for the answer.

Because they taste good," replied Terry Joe. It was the obvious answer. Sister's silence and pasted-on smile told him that this answer was incorrect.

"These are American foods," Sister informed them, "first grown and raised in the Western Hemisphere, North and South America. There were no turkeys, cranberries, or sweet potatoes in Europe, the old world across the Atlantic Ocean." Sister's next fact was a bombshell. "There were no cacao plants either— hence, no chocolate." She paused to let the horror of it sink in.

"No chocolate?" they whispered in disbelief.

"That would be terrible," stated Irene Pressler. "My grandma would have a fit. She loves chocolate and has it hidden all over her house."

"Even in the bathroom?" questioned Ricky Shenker, snickering.

"Especially in the bathroom," asserted Irene. It shut Ricky up.

Sister continued her story. "The Indians were the original Americans, having lived here for generations. Over the centuries they learned to survive. When the strangers with white skin landed from their ships, the Indians treated them kindly. It was November, 1620. That first winter was bleak and extremely cold." The children sat in silence, imaginations aflutter, visualizing the scene. Waite Park's children knew all about winter.

"The natives traded with the visitors and gave them gifts, mostly animal skins for clothing and blankets to keep them warm." Instantly Frankie thought of his father's mink and of his father's excitement. The first crop of ranch mink would soon be pelted for their precious fur. His father had given the boy's mother a mink jacket the previous Christmas. To him, wearing mink was a sign of prestige. She liked that the jacket was warm.

Sister continued teaching. "The Indians gave the Europeans food to cook over a fire. They gave them maize to eat."

"I've been in a maze before, out in that cornfield by St. Augusta," said Terry Joe. "They always have it at Halloween. We got lost in the field because the corn was over our heads... over everyone's head!" he clarified. "Dad said that the farmer had made the trails so that they crisscrossed each other and all of them, except one, led back into the middle. They charged us a dollar to go in. My Aunt Hildegard started screaming, so they had to come in and get her."

"The word maize might be related to the word maze," explained Sister. "But it's not the same thing." Terry Joe looked puzzled, as did all of the boys and most of the girls. "A maze, spelled m – a – z – e, is a labyrinth, like your cornfield. If you're lost in one, you're confused and don't know the way out."

"My aunt was in a daze," Terry Joe interjected. "So, they took her out." Sister ignored the interruption.

She persisted. "Maize, spelled m - a - i – z –e, is corn. It's a food you eat, often right on the cob after you roast it over a roaring campfire." Suddenly Sister's face was lost in some distant memory and a far away longing.

"We cook it on the stove in a kettle of water," said Terry Joe. He was grinning.

Sister returned from her reverie to her senses. "The Indians taught the Pilgrims how to raise corn. You dig a hole and put a fish in it with a seed. That fish is the fertilizer for the corn plant."

"Why didn't they just eat the fish?" asked Terry Joe, now puzzled once again by this account of history. "A fish is too much to trade off for an ear of corn."

"Perhaps they did," agreed Sister Bede. "Fish guts would have worked just as well as the whole fish." Sister's shocking language didn't shock her students, except for Susanne Danbury, who clamped her hands over her ears. Evidently, the word "guts" was too common for her delicate ears. Her classmates stared knowingly in her direction.

Jerry Unger leaned over to Frankie, seated next to him. "Prissy," he whispered in the boy's ear and nodded in Susanne's direction.

Sister waited for her Second Graders to settle down. Then she posed this question: "Have you heard the saying, 'If you give a man a fish, he will eat for one day; but if you teach a man to fish, he will eat every day'?"

"That sounds like my Uncle Squeak," said Terry Joe. "He taught me to fish. My dad doesn't like to give his fish away... to anyone. He'd rather eat them himself. Frankie's dad doesn't like to tell where he catches his fish. But we found out anyway." Once again, the boy was grinning. Behind him, his friend winced.

"The point I'm making," said Sister, coming directly to the crux of her lesson, "is that the Indians were very helpful. They were instrumental in saving the lives of the Pilgrims. Without the Indians' help, the white men, women, and children would have starved."

"They should have starved!" had been Sister Agatha's assessment. Mrs. O'Leery remembered the nun's words precisely. The white men had been anything but kind to her people.

After accepting gifts from the Indians, they wanted more. They always wanted more. They were never satisfied. They traded useless trinkets and beads for valuable furs and food, even land. They tricked the natives. In 1626 they purchased the whole of Manhattan, New York, for a measly $24 in beads, baubles, and trinkets—a paltry sum.

True, her people had been gullible. But the white men were liars and cheats. They were devils, full of deceit. Sister had nearly screamed in agony and wrath. Then her voice became barely a whisper. "Rape. Broken promises. Theft of our land. Killing the buffalo. More Rape. More Broken Promises. More theft of our land. Killing *all* the buffalo. The white man's government made treaties with the Indian chiefs and then broke them when it was convenient to do so. "Wayaabishkiiwed wiinaange." The white men were vultures, turkey buzzards hovering over a dying people. "We were outnumbered," Sister rasped. "We could not fight them all."

Sister Mary Bede redirected the children's attention to the picture. "Why are the people at the table so happy and excited?" she asked.

"Because they have enough to eat," said Jimmy Holston. "Look at how big that turkey is!"

"And the whole family is together." The voice, rather muffled, came from an unexpected corner. It was that of Abigail Hoganson. The other children looked in her direction. They were startled because they had not heard her speak much since the new school year began.

And then another thin voice with a quaver in it spoke up. "At least they have a whole family. I don't, not anymore." Lucy Stephens held her head in her hands and fought back her tears. Everyone knew the Stephens' saga, how four years ago her sister, Lana, had run away from home with a drifter and disappeared. The other children felt sorry for her.

It was Ricky Shenker who brightened everyone's spirits. "That family is happy because it's Thanksgiving!" postulated Ricky, obviously pleased with his assessment. "They're in the mood!"

"They're happy and giving thanks for all they have to give," added Terry Joe. "Look at the grandfather's face. That's how my grandfather looked when he was still alive."

"No, they're thankful for what they've been given," stated a shy, soft voice at the back of the room, correcting him. It belonged to Jonas Duane. "It's gratitude. Thanksgiving means gratitude."

Terry Joe shrugged. Suddenly he frowned. "Sister, why is the painting called *Freedom from Want*? Shouldn't it be called *Freedom to Want*?"

Sister thought for a moment. "A want is when you need something you don't have."

"I want my spear back, but my mom says I don't need it, so I don't get it. I want my spear, so if a want is a need, then I should get it back. I need my spear back."

"The word *want* has several meanings," stated the teacher. "Here, it doesn't mean anything about a stick... or a spear."

"But I want my spear back," argued Terry Joe. "I should have the freedom not to have to want it." He pointed to the caption at the bottom of the picture high above his head.

The bell sounded. Sister Bede was grateful. It was time to return to class, to normality.

Mrs. O'Leery sighed. No wonder education was in such a pitiful state. Traditional facts were being challenged by children who knew next to nothing. That O'Brian boy was a prime example. It was up to their teachers to set them straight. But it depended upon what teacher you had. She was glad her children had already graduated and were making their way in the world.

Once, long ago, she had visited Sister Agatha's classroom and asked her about her display of Indian artifacts. The smallish woman, bedecked in her nun's habit, had confided to her.

As the next class entered the library, the words of Sister Agatha rang in the librarian's ears: "My mother was raped. My great aunts sat around a fire in the Chippewa Forest near Mille Lacs Lake and told me about it. How my mother screamed! I am not thankful for that. My spirit was wounded, but they could see I was a fighter. Like my mother, I would not give in.

People called me a half-breed. I could not live on the reservation any longer, so my great aunts took me to the Crosier seminary in Onamia. The priests told them to take me to the Franciscan convent in Little Falls. I learned to be a Catholic. That's how I ended up here. They tried to bury my heart, but I will never give up my Indian ways, my Ojibwe birthright. It is who I am."

Mrs. O'Leery could feel the defiance.

At home Frankie's sister, Jeanne, was displaying her art project, made that day in kindergarten. She had constructed a turkey using her own hands, literally.

Seated at the kitchen table, she was repeating her project's design. Her younger sister, Mary, seated next to her, was imitating her. They were tracing their hands on large sheets of pastel brown construction paper. The two hands, lying flat, were mirror images of each other. The fingers, spread apart, were the turkey's feathers. The thumbs would become the head and the neck. "Leave room at the bottom for the legs," Jeanne admonished, and this prompted a slight erasure and alteration in her sister's drawing.

At the sink their mother peeled potatoes. They were having mashed potatoes and gravy again that night, a staple in the family's diet. The roast beef was in the oven, smothered in onions and carrots with the cover on. The time was quarter to five. Fifteen minutes earlier, she had lowered the temperature to 275 degrees so that this time the meat would not dry out. Grandma was coming over. The children's grandmother and their father had been selling investments together that day, up Highway 52 to farmers who lived near Freeport. Mother and son were on the road together and would be home in an hour. The family would eat promptly at 6:00 o'clock.

The mother watched her girls, young innocent girls nowhere near womanhood. She liked to see them playing together, the younger sister following her sister's lead. Mary was lonely during the day when Jeanne was at school, even though it was only half a day. She wanted to be like her big sister and do what Jeanne did when she was away. Almost every day they played "school" together, with Jeanne *teaching* Mary what she had done that day.

Thanksgiving was only two days away. The two girls traced outlines around their fingers. "Now color the feathers," Jeanne instructed. "Bright colors, but not red. Red is for the head. Leave the body brown." And thus the turkeys took shape. "Be careful to color the same finger on both hands the same color. They are two sides of the same feather.

"Oops!" cried Mary. "Now what should I do?" She took the eraser in hand.

"No, don't erase it," ordered her sister. "It will smear. Just color over it. You'll have the same color, just a darker shade on one side. Nobody will know because they'll forget by the time they look at the other side."

At the sink the mother smiled. Just like when we went to school, she thought. We did the same project.

"Now take a pencil and draw the legs and the face." Two straight lines became stick legs, with two stick feet pointing outward attached to them. Each foot had three stick toes.

"Be careful with the face," Jeanne warned. She inspected her sister's drawing. "Draw just one eye," she instructed. "The other eye is on the other thumb—over there on the other hand." Again, the younger girl erased her mistake.

The mother peeked over at the table. Then, potato and potato peeler in her hands, she walked over to the table to inspect. She peered at the two drawings. "They're taking shape," she proclaimed. She wanted to encourage them. "They look like turkeys ready to be baked and eaten."

"First, the feathers have to be plucked," stated Mary.

"And they have to be killed," added her older sister. "First, you chop the head off. Then you can pluck them." She continued to color the tom's head and neck. "Don't forget the beak," she reminded her sister.

The woman pretended not to look surprised. "They're a couple of gobblers, all right. Nice and fat," added the mother, undaunted.

"That's because our hands are fat," laughed Mary. She stared at her hands and then at Jeanne's. "Your turkey is bigger." Her sister ignored her observation.

"Your hands aren't fat," spoke the mother. "They're just pudgy. All young girls have pudgy hands."

The older girl changed the subject. "You should see John Holston's turkey. It has one feather missing, where John cut his finger off under the lawnmower. Sister Carmita said he should trace a different finger twice to have a whole turkey, but he didn't want to. So, his turkey is missing half a feather. She looked down at her turkey, avoiding eye contact with her mother. It's the middle feather."

Perhaps she isn't so innocent and naïve after all, concluded the mother. That Jackie Birch... and that Krueger girl... I'll have to speak to Florence Birch.

The two girls finished their artwork before supper. They cut out the two turkeys, following the pencil line they had made by tracing around their fingers. The girls were amazed how splendidly the two halves of each bird matched. They giggled with pride. Several dabs of Elmer's glue bonded the two sheets of construction paper together.

"Put them on the table, and you can show them to Dad," the mother stated. "Here, prop them up against this centerpiece," she added. "I won't be lighting the candle today, not until Thanksgiving Day."

"What's this?" their father stated when he entered the room? Both girls had taken him by a hand and led him to the kitchen table." Close your eyes," they had requested.

"Don't look," stated Mary.

"Now, open them," Jeanne commanded.

"Turkeys!" the Dad cried, one big one and one small one." He smiled broadly. "Look at how colorful the feathers are, Mother?"

"Oooooh," trilled Grandma. "They're nice and fat. But you can't eat paper. I'm hungry! Is supper ready?" Her son's wife nodded. "Then let's eat."

The people of Waite Park celebrated Thanksgiving in the Norman Rockwell tradition. Families celebrated together. Youngsters in college came home for a home-cooked meal and to be with friends. Their younger siblings looked at them strangely, wondering if they were the same as when they had left in the fall. Or had college changed them.

Turkeys were consumed. Dinner was long and leisurely as the family members told stories of the year gone by. The adults spoke and the children listened. Occasionally an older child, a visitor who was home from college or perhaps on leave from military service, would be asked to relate something about his or her new life away from Waite Park. Uncles and aunts were eager to tell stories about their own children, whether their offspring were present or not.

Before long, the children grew antsy and asked to be excused. They were eager to play children's games, either inside or outside, depending upon the weather.

"Anyone want to play Monopoly?"

"Sure, I want to."

"Me too."

"Not me. I'm going skating down at the park. They have a rink and a warming house."

"That sounds like fun! I brought my skates."

"Let's go outside. I'll show you my new snow fort."

"I'm staying in to watch football."

"Let's go outside and *play* football."

"In the snow? Are you crazy?"

"Let's go outside. It's fun. You slide around and don't get hurt."

"For real?"

"That's how we do it here."

The men and older boys retreated to the living room to watch football, the NFL. They watched the action and listened to the announcers describe the heroics of Frank Gifford of the New

York Giants and Jim Brown of Cleveland. It was best to pick a side to root for. The boy's father booed when Johnny Unitas of Baltimore passed to Raymond Berry for a touchdown. Father and son shared a favorite team, the Green Bay Packers. Located in neighboring Wisconsin, this team was the closest one to home. They cheered lustily when the Packer quarterback, Bart Starr, passed the football to Max McGee to tie the score. The boy had a secret favorite player, a running back, Paul Hornung. He was nicknamed *The Golden Boy*.

The women continued to chat, long into the afternoon. Finally, when there was a lull in the conversation, they sighed and stood up. They gathered in the kitchen and resigned themselves to washing and drying the dishes. For this occasion the good dishes had been used: Noritake china and Fostoria stemware, received as wedding gifts, and Oneida silverware that had been handed down to them by their mothers. The hostess counted the pieces: forks, knives, and spoons, before storing them away. That was customary. Before the guests left, a second meal, a light supper, would be served on the inexpensive dishes that the family used daily.

The villagers were a humble people who acknowledged that *they had much to be thankful for*. The men worked hard to provide an income for their wives and children. The women worked equally hard to obtain the necessities their husbands and children needed. And thus, from their parents' example, the children came to understand that work itself was a necessity. This was one of life's lessons.

The Great Northern Railway was the primary source of employment in the village. The community rallied around the railroad's car shops, and the workers took pride in their role in the operation. If necessary, they would protect their jobs. They were fiercely appreciative, genuinely thankful. On this day they took the time to express their gratitude openly. Throughout the village before the people ate, they bowed their heads and prayed.

CHAPTER TWENTY-SEVEN

On Thanksgiving Day one man in Waite Park was not celebrating. He was busy counting. He had been at it steadily at the kitchen table for two hours after supper. The man's brow furrowed. He leaned back and placed his hands, palms down with the fingers spread wide apart, on the paper in front of him. Unlike the neighbor girls three doors down, he did not trace the outline of his hands. He stared at them.

They were calloused and aged from work. There were cracks in the skin that no longer healed, and the knuckles were red and bruised like those of a prize fighter. The nails were jagged, trimmed unevenly, and the left thumbnail was black and purple from a hammer blow that had gone awry. They were not good at figuring.

Paul Rausch was worried. Perhaps he had made a mistake. His eyes drifted from his hands to the paper beneath them. The sheet was a piece of yellow foolscap, rather grimy at the edges, upon which he had kept track of the railroad's inventory of tools. This was his private list. He had started keeping it as a matter of routine when he had been named foreman of a work detail.

The figures on the sheet of paper stared up at him. They did not add up. He had added them three times, using a stubby black pencil that he kept in a kitchen drawer. He was confused. He did not work well at night. Somewhere in his calculations he had made a mistake. He would tally the numbers again tomorrow, and then yet again—to be sure.

Three doors to the north, his neighbor was excited. The pelting season had arrived. For the past month the boy's father had watched his mink carefully. It started at the tip of the tail—a thick, bushy winter coat of fur. In the days that followed, it progressed up the tail to the hips and back legs and then up the mink's torso. Eventually the shoulders and front legs were covered in a dense under-fur and winter coat. Finally the new coat covered the head.

The rancher would hold a mink by the tail and head and wrap the body around his elk hide glove. Blowing softly into the fur exposed the bluish under-fur to the sunlight. The man's eyes danced. The buyers would like the quality of his pelts. The fur was jet black, perhaps not quite the desired sleek texture of the mink raised by Clarence and Kenneth Kroeschel, his friends in Hinkley, Minnesota, but next year he would buy breeding stock that would match any in Minnesota. He would even spend the money necessary to purchase high-priced Blackglama mink from the Atkin's ranch in Utah.

Now that the mink was completely furred out, the entire pelt glistened in the sun's rays. The man released the head of the animal, and the mink splayed out to escape the human's grasp. But the man held the tail securely. He smiled at the mink's muscular agility and its beauty.

If the animals sensed the changing season, they did not show it. They refused to be bothered by the cold air and the brisk wind. Their rich new coat protected them from the winter chill. Little did they know the fate that awaited them—how their new shiny coat would be both a blessing and a curse.

The mink rancher was intent on expansion. Over half of the females would be kept as breeding stock. Most of the males would be pelted. Only one male in four was needed because mink are polygamous breeders.

The boy's father returned the mink to its pen and snapped the door latch shut. Inside the cage the mink was inquisitive. He stood up expectantly against the front of the cage, associating the man's presence with food. He wove around the front of the cage in anticipation, back and forth, his head bobbing in figure eights. But the performance went unheeded. When the food did not come, he took a sip of water from his cup and leaped up into the loft above the wire cage. He nestled into the hay, snug and warm. The young mink, barely seven months old, closed his eyes and slept.

The mink rancher spent Thanksgiving Day with his family, eating turkey and watching football. He dozed in his favorite chair, resting up for the work that would start tomorrow. He dreamed of the task ahead. They would be busy, for the mink had to be killed in their prime before the winter coat lost its luster. The pelts, minus the carcasses, would be stored in the big twenty-ton walk-in freezer until all the mink selected to be pelted were killed and skinned. Next week the workers would unthaw the pelts and flesh them, removing the layers of fat and stretching the pelts onto boards to dry. When dry, the pelts would be inside out, with the leather outside and the precious fur inside. Only then would they be ready for shipping to the Hudson's Bay Company in New York, still in business after two centuries.

The rancher intended to fly to New York to watch the proceedings. He was keeping it a secret for now; he wanted to surprise his wife. He would ask her to join him on a well-deserved and much-needed vacation. They both had earned it. He had already asked Mrs. Pfappenstein to watch the children. The thought of success and a fat paycheck was intensely pleasurable. It woke the man up.

He could not contain his excitement. "I've hired two men to help with the skinning and the fleshing," the boy's father informed his wife. "Two brothers, Frank and Tony Czenk. They're from Sauk Rapids. They've worked in the mink business before. They're Bohemian, like me!"

"How much will you have to pay them?" asked the boy's mother.

"Three dollars an hour each" was the reply. "But I'll learn how to do it. And then next year I'll teach Leo, and we'll be able to pelt the mink ourselves. In a way I'm hiring them to teach me. It'll save money in the long run." He sounded satisfied with his decision. To his wife, he sounded smug. She didn't like it when he was so self-assured. Men spoke that way. It was an attribute most women lacked, a strength she did not have.

On Friday, the day after Thanksgiving, the boy's father came home late. He looked tired but elated after a long day of work. "We pelted one hundred and fifty mink today. It's work. But Frank and Tony know what they're doing. Thank God, Leo is taking a week's vacation from the fire hall. The four of us will manage." He grasped his wife around the waist and pulled her in. He kissed her gently. "We're going to make it."

She accepted his caress. She listened to him in silence, choosing not to tell him about her day. "Phew, you need a shower," she said belatedly, extracting herself from his arms. "Supper is ready. The kids have eaten. I waited for you."

In the evenings of early December, the boy's mother made a point of looking out the kitchen window. The moon was full, and it shed a strong light on the neighborhood. Up the alley she saw a man standing forlorn. In his back yard Syl Sawyer stood in the snow and stared south, past the highway toward the cemetery. "He's trying to forgive himself," she told her husband. "You can see his regret for buying her that car."

Her husband was silent. He had nearly had an accident himself that day, and he was an experienced driver. Snowy roads can be treacherous, he thought. He looked at his five children and at his wife's tummy—one child on the way. Life was chancy. You never knew when it would be your turn. Poor Syl Sawyer! What he wouldn't give for a second chance. But that wasn't the way life was.

Each day, rain or shine, the man stood in his back yard and stared toward the cemetery. And his neighbor watched him. She felt his pain at the loss of his child while inside her womb her baby grew. For her, it was an uncomfortable juxtaposition of death and life, two opposite ends of the spectrum, causing regret and joy.

At the end of the block, Paul Rausch slumped back in his kitchen chair. Every day for a week he had counted, checking and rechecking his figures. The results were always the same. The figures on the yellow foolscap did not match the most recent inventory.

His suspicions had surfaced soon after his promotion, but nothing of this magnitude. Now the figures in front of him generated an alarm. They were short. He added the totals in the right hand column one last time—$18,000. My God! he thought. The Great Northern Railway is short $18,000—and on my watch. Someone is stealing. But who?

Sitting in his kitchen with darkness all around him outside, Paul Rausch made a decision. Of course, he would have to ask for Ione's permission, her blessing. She would understand. He hoped she would support him; she always had. But it would exhaust their life's savings. They would once again be poor, like they had been when they were first married.

His determination jelled. He was due to retire in the spring, but he would not leave the railroad in a shambles. Oversight of the tools was his responsibility. He accepted it. He would replace the stolen property out of his own assets. That's the type of man he was, a faithful servant.

Paul was proud of his record of service. It's what had driven him. It's what had made him get up each morning and go to work. It's what had guided his decisions. Now that he was on the verge of fulfillment, he would never let his reputation be tarnished—not ever.

"We've been robbed! They're gone," his father blurted. The man's face was ashen. "Somebody stole the mink pelts, over 300 of them," he cried out. He nearly stumbled as he staggered to a kitchen chair, sat, and buried his face in his hands.

Frankie did not remember if he had ever seen his father cry. Fathers didn't cry; mothers did. Fathers were strong and unyielding. Mothers were weak and relied on their husbands for support.

His mother put her arm around his father's neck to comfort him. "We have insurance," she whispered. "We'll manage."

"That's not the point," he countered. She could see that he was wounded.

"It's not right... after I worked so hard. Someone has cheated us." He was sorting through his feelings. "We've been violated!" He looked into his wife's eyes, searching for support.

"What will you do?" she asked.

He stood up and walked, more steadily now, down the steps into the basement. When he returned, he was carrying a gun case. He laid it down on the kitchen table and unzipped it. In it was his shotgun, a 12-gauge Browning. He examined the gun closely. It was cleaned and oiled, a custom the man had practiced since he was a boy.

"Must you?" inquired the woman at his side.

"I'm going to protect what's ours," he asserted. Now his voice was calm, heavy with conviction. "Would you pack a bag for me, Pat?"

"Have some lunch first," she pleaded. "And say goodbye to the children."

He nodded. "The sheriff has already been out," he stated. "He thinks he knows who did it."

"Who?" she asked.

"The Czenk brothers, Frank and Tony."

"No!" the boy's mother gasped.

"He says they have long criminal records." The man shook his head. "The trouble is proving it." The boy's dad was wringing his hands in anguish. "And I trusted them!" He almost spat the words out. "They *are* Bohemians!" he cursed. "They're gypsies... lawless gypsies! I should have known better; it's in their blood."

"But aren't we Bohemians?" Frankie asked.

The man squelched a denial. He paused before he spoke. "We are," agreed his father. "But we aren't of the same ilk that they are. We're not dishonest!"

The boy gulped at this assertion. For a moment it made him recall his list of sins to be confessed.

His father set the shotgun on the table and stood up. "I have to get some shells," he said more to himself than to anyone else. And he made a second trip down the basement steps.

"Won't Daddy be staying with us?" The question belonged to the boy's sister, Jeanne, who with Mary and Dan had wandered into the kitchen.

"Not tonight," answered her mother.

"What about tomorrow?" asked Mary.

"Not tomorrow either," added the mother. "Something bad has happened."

"Someone stole the mink," the boy clarified. "The two Czenk brothers, Frank and Tony. They're crooks."

"We don't know that for sure," the mother corrected. And then the girls and their younger brother spotted the gun on the table.

"Is Daddy going to shoot them?" asked Mary, her fears rising.

"No, he's only taking the gun with him to the mink ranch," replied the mother.

"They've already stolen all the pelts," stated the older brother.

"Not all the pelts, but over 300. I'm going to protect the rest. We still have 600 mink to pelt." Their father's voice sounded strong and committed.

"We'll manage," the mother added. She wanted to assure them. "We'll be okay; don't worry. We have insurance."

"What's that?" asked Mary. And she began to cry. This alarmed her younger brother, Dan. He, too, began to whimper.

"Don't cry, not now," their mother directed. "I'll explain it after lunch. Let's eat. Go give Dad a hug. He needs one. We all need one."

"Before he left, the man held his wife in an embrace. "Will you be okay with the children?" he asked. "I hate to leave them alone with you. I'm going to hire a new man, Dick Berg. He owns Sportsman's Kennels, where I bought Jet. Keep your fingers crossed."

"He's not Bohemian, is he?" she probed. She forced a smile.

"No, he's not Bohemian," her husband answered. He did not smile. "With any luck we'll be finished with the fleshing by Christmas." He felt the small bulge between her stomach and abdomen. He looked down at it. "You're starting to show. Stay off your feet. The kids can help you more. "If you need me to come in, call me."

"I'll manage," she whispered. But her cheeks were moist as she fought back her tears. She looked into his eyes. "If you need me to come out, call me. I'll come."

He kissed her. She looked beyond his shoulder and through the kitchen window, up the block. Two houses away stood a man in a light jacket, smoking a cigarette. He was looking south across the highway toward the cemetery in the distance. "I feel sorry for Syl," she blurted. "So, so sorry…"

"How do you kill a mink?" asked Terry Joe. He was holding his spear in both hands, making jabs into the air.

"How'd you get your spear back?" asked Frankie, his friend from across the alley.

"I found it in the boat, tucked under an oar," he related. "Dad didn't hide it very good. Now I'll hide it from him." He jabbed it forward viciously, pretending to stab his brother, Timmy, in the guts.

"So, how *do* you kill a mink?"

"Not with that. A spear would poke a hole in the pelt and ruin the fur. You break its neck. He demonstrated by pretending to hold a mink by the neck with the head inside his right hand. Then he flipped the imaginary body onto its back and secured his left hand around the animal's neck. Suddenly he twisted his right hand around the head, exposing the front of the neck. He positioned the mink's body between his thighs, and slid his hands powerfully in opposite directions, the right one down, the left one up. He grunted heavily as he demonstrated how the neck would be broken. "*Snap!*" he pronounced emphatically. A long pause followed, both boys deep in thought. The forcefulness of the blow was evident. "You hear tiny crunches as the vertebrae crack," said Frankie. "That's what Leo says."

"It's a crummy way to die," acknowledged Terry Joe, deeply awed.

"It's quick," countered his friend. "It's how we do it."

Another pause. Finally the mink rancher's son spoke. "Some ranchers are switching how they do it. They're asphyxiating the mink with the feed cart," explained Frankie.

"Ass-what?" asked Terry Joe.

"It kills them with the gas fumes from the engine's motor, carbon monoxide. You put them into the feed cart with a cover on the top. Then you stick in a hose that forces the exhaust from the engine into the tub of the cart. Dad says that mink have such a fast heart rate that it kills them by the time you drive up to the shop. He's thinking of switching. People say it's not as brutal, more humane."

"It still kills them," said Terry Joe.

"It does the job," replied his friend.

"Leo wants him to switch. He says it'd be easier on their arms and hands.

Dad says, 'That's not the way the Kroeschels do it up in Hinkley.' He doesn't always want to take the easier way. Leo does."

Terry Joe resumed jabbing his stick into the air. But for some reason, his jabs were less vicious. "What if the mink aren't dead, but only unconscience?" he asked.

"You mean *unconscious*," his friend corrected. "I've thought of that, too. When you break the necks, they're dead for good. They curl up and clamp their teeth together, sometimes biting their tongue. The men kill twenty-five at a time and then go up to the shop to skin them. If they were only unconscious, the skinning would kill them before they woke up. So, it doesn't really matter."

Terry Joe stopped thrusting his stick forward into empty space. "How do you skin a mink?" he inquired.

"There's a machine that goes up and down, a heavy machine," explained Frankie. "You sit at it and work a lever with your knee. First, you cut off the front feet. Then you push the lever to the right. It pulls the carcass up, and you peel the hide down."

"Like a banana?" asked Terry Joe.

"No, it's different," replied the speaker.

"The fur's on the inside. You have to cut around the head with a knife so that the hide and fur don't tear. Then you push the lever to the left, and the carcass comes back down. You throw it away into a big drum and start on the next mink."

The boy enhanced his explanation with gestures as he acted out how the deed was done. "Leo says, 'It's slicker than snot.'"

"Is it bloody?" wondered Terry Joe.

"No, most of the blood stays in the carcass."

"What do they do with the carcasses?" asked Terry Joe.

"They're sold to a rendering plant where they use the mink oil to make lotions and ladies' perfumes. Dad says he's just glad to get rid of the waste. He sells it to them cheap."

CHAPTER TWENTY-EIGHT

"How can you do this to us?" Ione Rausch faced her husband. Her jaw was set, but her lips were trembling. The corners of her mouth twitched like that of a singed cat. She was feline and wounded.

Paul Rausch sat back in his chair with his arms folded. He had anticipated his wife's argument, an argument arising out of fear. Her motherly instincts were strong. She would fight to protect the children. "It's something I have to do," he replied. "I've failed the railroad, and I have to make it right. I owe it to them." There was a despondency in his voice and a sense of urgency.

"You don't owe the railroad when somebody else steals," she challenged. "You're not responsible for everybody else, just for yourself." Her nostrils flared in anger. "Can't you see? You're only punishing yourself—and us! We're the ones who will suffer!" Her words were scorching, blistering. Then she uttered the words she did not intend to say. "Don't be a fool!"

That stung him. "I was in charge," he countered. "It was *my* responsibility. They stole those tools from right under my nose," he wailed. "How could I not see it?" Now he was fired up.

She sensed the agony in him. She must back off for the moment. He was a good man, better than most, a man of deep convictions. And he was hurting. She was sitting across the table from him and leaned forward. "Do you know who did it?"

He stared at her and then down at his hands. "No, I don't know."

Her eyes stared at him; they did not waver. "You must not do this, Paul."

"We have the money in the bank," he replied. "And a little left over. I'll still get my pension." His voice did not falter. He stopped. In the silence that followed, she detected a note of finality.

She knew now that she must try to shame him. "Our family needs the money, Paul." She spoke softly. "The children will need help to go to school. Junior and Jimmy and Roger are young men. They'll go to work. But not the others. Frannie and Vickie want to go to college. We won't have enough money to help them. How can you do this to our children?" It was a helpless cry. She was pleading with him, if not begging him.

Paul Rausch looked up and across the table at his wife's face. She had never asked for much—and seldom anything for herself. But she would stand up for her children.

My, she had aged! Her face was wrinkled. Her hair showed streaks of gray—a winter's gray. My God! She had whiskers, a smattering of an aging woman's hair lining her upper lip and a few straggly strands under her chin. How had he not noticed this before?

They had lived together for half a lifetime. When they had married, she had vowed to be his lifelong companion. That was a commitment he cherished; he felt honored. It had made him want to kneel before God with her and then stand by her side. She had been loyal to him, even in the most difficult times. Now he was asking her to do the impossible for him. Oh, how he loved her!

Paul had wanted to give the world to her. Together, they had dreamed of his retirement, of traveling in the car to California to visit her sister, Irene, in San Diego. That would require money for gas and for motels, money they would no longer have. They had speculated. Perhaps instead of journeying by car, they would ride the Great Northern Empire Builder itself as passengers in first class. What fun that would be! Or they might fly in an airplane to New York City and then embark on a grand steamship for a voyage across the Atlantic Ocean. There were lands beyond the horizon that the railroad, grounded to the earth, could never touch. They would visit those far away lands where, as a young man, Paul had fought in the great world war, four decades ago. He wanted to show Ione those places, France and Germany.

These were desires they shared. Now he was asking her to give up their dreams.

How could he do this? How could deny her these longings? Deprive her of her wishes? How could he be so selfish? What kind of monster was he?

He leaned forward, closer to her face. His eyes became moist, and she saw it. The weight of guilt was taking its toll. "There's someone I must talk to first," he stated.

"Paul, don't do this to yourself," she whispered.

He began to breathe heavily, gasping deep breaths. His body shook.

Instinctively she leaped to his side and sat beside him. She turned toward him, and he slumped against her, his head resting on her shoulders and on her breasts. She felt him shiver, and she felt the spasms brought on by fatigue. "Forgive me, dear," he begged. "Please forgive me." And then he could say no more.

She, too, wept. She tried to console him, to comfort him. She placed her arms around his shoulders and pulled his body into hers. And she began to rock him, back and forth, back and forth.

"Bless me, Father, for I have sinned." The small chamber was dark, and only when the window slid open did a tiny light from the priest's cubicle filter through the screen. It illuminated but a meager portion of the confessional.

Paul Rausch had waited patiently for his confessor to finish absolving the sinner on the other side of the confessional box. He had prayed for guidance and been denied. Perhaps he had not prayed long enough or hard enough. He had been taught from a young age on that the Lord God Almighty listened to every prayer and answered some of them.

The man confessing continued. "My last confession was six months ago, before Easter. Father Schumacher, I have sinned. And I am sorry, deeply sorry. I'm here to ask for your forgiveness and God's forgiveness. I can't go on without it." He stopped.

"Tell me about it, Paul," spoke the voice on the other side of the screen. "God is listening." And then the voice grew silent.

In the grim darkness Paul Rausch spoke through the wire screen toward the little light that radiated from within. He told his story. He knew that a man was listening. He believed that his God was hearing it, too. His faith led him to believe that there existed a supernatural being who was greater than himself. This being could forgive his sins and heal him.

He told about his promotion to foreman of the railroad crew and about the misgivings he had felt in accepting the job. He told about his initial suspicions when he saw his fellow workers whispering to each other behind his back and then falling silent when he approached.

He told about his sense of duty and about his pride. "I should not have felt so proud, Father. That was sinful. I'm sure the men resented it. I was the chosen one. Some of them had been passed over. I gloated and flaunted my good fortune." He felt bothered by the money his friends had displayed—an excess they could not afford. "I wondered how they could buy new cars, new boats, expensive toys, and gifts for their wives and children. Such extravagance! It worried me. I checked into their salaries. Their pay from the railroad did not permit such spending."

Then he told about the yellow sheets of foolscap—how the numbers did not add up. In dismay he told about his suspicions being confirmed.

"Do you know who stole the tools?" asked the confessor.

"No, I don't, Father... not now... not yet. I may never know. I only know that I am responsible and I must pay it all back. It's on my conscience always, Father. I can't sleep at night."

The man paused to hear the priest's response. For a time he heard nothing. The silence on the other side of the screen was troubling.

"I do not agree that you are responsible for the behavior of these other men, Paul. You are not to blame. Men are weak. They are greedy and selfish. That's human nature. It's part of our original sin from Eve and Adam.

A man can be jealous of another's good fortune. That, too, is a sin. You were chosen to be the foreman of your crew for a reason. You are honest and trustworthy. You are capable. The people in charge know your character, Paul. They have seen how you lead the men in your charge. You know how to lead, how to give orders and see that the work gets done. But you are also capable of showing compassion. I see that now. You wouldn't be here if you didn't care about your fellow man.

Friends can be fickle, Paul. You must be careful not to let them destroy your life. You feel betrayed and abandoned, but you are not to blame. You have not sinned in this, Paul."

"I have sinned, Father. I need to be forgiven."

He told about the size of the sum, $18,000 worth of tools, that was missing from the inventory. He heard a muffled gasp behind the screen. "I plan to give the money back—to make it right."

"But where will you get it?" asked the priest.

"From my savings, Father. I don't want anyone to know but you."

"Does Ione know?"

"She knows."

"And does she agree?"

"Yes, Father, she agrees. But she doesn't want to agree."

"What did she say?"

"She said, 'Do what you must do.' She's a brave woman.

But I'm hurting her, and I'm hurting our children. This will use up most of our savings. Our dreams for retirement will disappear. She's suffering because of me; she's heartbroken because of my stubborn pride. This is a grave sin." He paused again, seeking a reply.

"Paul, you do not need to make this restitution." The pastor's voice was sharp and to the point.

"But I must, Father, don't you see?"

"I see that you feel an obligation. You feel a sense of duty. But your duty is to your family, Paul. You must turn in the guilty. You must ferret them out."

"But Father, vengeance is its own sin. I must turn the other cheek, like Jesus did. That's what I was taught as a young boy. That's how I've lived my life."

"Paul, I sit here before you as God's representative. Confession is a sacrament, a holy sacrament instituted by Jesus to give us grace. It stands beside the other sacraments. In conjunction with them, it gives us the strength to live a good and decent life, a holy life.

Listen to me, Paul. There are seven sacraments:

When you were born, you were *baptized*. You were cleansed of original sin. That means you now have the ability to be a good man, to gain entrance into Heaven when you die.

As a youth you made your *First Holy Communion*, probably right here in this church."

"Yes, Father."

"You were given the privilege of consuming the body of our Lord, Jesus Christ! That is an aspect of the holy mass that strengthens you each time against the temptations of the devil.

Then you were *confirmed*. As a young man you became a soldier of Christ, ready to lay down your life for him if ever called to do so. You willfully made a serious commitment.

In *matrimony* you committed yourself to a woman who loves you. Together, you and Ione have been open to children. You should revere both your wife and your children, Paul. Do not cast them aside.

We priests have a different calling. We have taken a special vow of *Holy Orders*, to lead the Catholic Church as Jesus's successors. I'm speaking to you as Jesus would have. I feel very strongly about this, Paul. I urge you to do the right thing for your family and for yourself, as well.

And finally, when we are about to die, we receive the sacrament of *Extreme Unction*. That is a Latin word that means the Anointing of the Sick. It protects a man on his deathbed. If necessary, it gives him the strength to die with dignity and in peace.

Father Schumacher paused momentarily and then raised his voice to speak with emphasis. But of all the sacraments, Paul, *confession* is the most important. It allows you to save your soul, again and again. Humans are weak; we have our faults. We continue to falter, to turn against God—on purpose! We choose to disobey. Can you believe it? Without confession, our souls would be lost forever to damnation and eternal fire. Heed this advice, Paul. Please heed what I have said."

The pastor of St. Joseph's parish concluded with a final plea. It echoed a passage in the New Testament scriptures that Jesus himself had spoken the night before his death: "Let this cup pass from you, Paul."

"I can't, Father."

"Then may the Lord have mercy on your soul."

Paul Rausch knelt in the darkened church and prayed. Dutifully, he said his penance: three *Our Father's*, three *Hail Mary's*, and three *Glory Be's*. He did not feel good. Although forgiven, his soul was not at rest. He thought about the crime and what he had decided to do. Was there more he could do? He didn't know.

The lights in the church were dim. High above him he saw the figure of Jesus of Nazareth stretched out on the cross, dead, surrounded on either side by his mother, Mary, and by Mary Magdalene. "Greater Love Than This No Man Hath" proclaimed the words on the beam beneath the scene. They spoke of sacrifice.

Among the shadows he wandered up the side aisle on the left to the statue of Mary, the Lord's mother. He reached into his pocket and found a dime. He deposited it into the slot in the collection can. Then he lit a candle. It burned brightly in its red holder along with the other candles that had been lit by others. He looked up at the statue's face. It startled him. There he saw Ione's face, calm and serene, looking down at him. He saw what love is.

His guilt returned. How could he just "turn the other cheek"? Perhaps there was something more he could do. But it would be a disagreeable task. He decided to think about it. "Sleep on it," his father had always told him. He would know in the morning.

In the confessional Father Cornelius J. Schumacher paused to reflect. He thought about what had transpired. He believed he had spoken strongly enough and convincingly. Hopefully, Paul would come to his senses and change his mind.

Ione Rausch was a saint. She was the epitome of what a wife should be. She would support her husband through thick and thin, right or wrong. He admired her courage. Paul Rausch was a lucky man. If only Marilyn Wojcheski could see this woman and learn from her example—her dutiful obedience to her husband. Instead, she flaunts her body and wiggles her hips at me. Salome! She tried to tempt me. Father's face scrunched up in disgust.

He snarled. And she has poisoned Clifford Kucher's wife against him. Pat Kucher—that Jezebel! She has turned against me and against the Church."

In the morning Paul Rausch knew. A cold clarity had come to him during the night. He had dreamed, and he had listened to the voices in the dream. He recognized them all.

Paul spent the morning filling out the paperwork, order forms mostly, for new tools for the car shops. He would buy only the best: DEWALT power tools, a supply that cost a pretty penny.

When tallied, the bill came to just over $18,000. He smiled craftily. He would have the bill sent to his home address on 11th

Avenue. No one must know of this gift or of his sacrifice, lest they feel sorry for him and Ione. Complete secrecy was important.

He wanted no pity, just respect. When he walked out the door into the sunlight of retirement, he would be free and unencumbered, with no burden of regret on his shoulders.

The confirmation letter arrived eight days later in a brown envelope mailed from Lancaster, Pennsylvania, to his home address. The tools would be shipped from DEWALT to HAMMER TOOLS ten days before Christmas. They were scheduled to be delivered to the Great Northern Railway's car shops on Friday, December 19th. The timing was perfect for a Christmas surprise, a Christmas present.

The following week the entire railroad facility would close down during the Christmas holiday. The workers would be given a week's paid vacation. It was a bonus, given annually for their hard work, authorized by the railroad's president himself, Jimmy J. Hill. It acknowledged his appreciation. The men could stay home with their families and relish the fruits of their labor. They could bask in the Great Northern's success. It had been another year of tidy profit.

When the railroad's yard whistle blew at precisely 4:30 p.m. on Friday, the 19th day of December, Waite Park's car shops would be shut down for nine days. North of 3rd Street, all along the railroad's property, the gates would be locked. The entire premises would lie deserted until the gates reopened.

CHAPTER TWENTY-NINE

The weekly convocation of the Knights of the Round Table had an unexpected visitor. No one had invited him, so he had invited himself. It was December 12th, less than two weeks before Christmas, and Paul Rausch was in a slightly alcoholic state. He was celebrating.

"Frannie!" he called out. "Bring another round of beers for my boys." She waved from behind the bar and set out on a tray on the counter four bottles of Hamm's.

"The time has come," he announced, "for me to retire. This spring. It's finally been approved. I was in to see Superintendent Steichel this morning. He wished me well. *Bon Voyage*, he said."

"Will you and Ione be traveling?" Cortney asked.

"We will," Paul answered. "To California to visit Ione's sister, Irene." His voice was loud. He grinned. He took a swig of beer and then gulped it down. Soon, the bottle was empty.

The next round of beers arrived. Frannie nuzzled close to Paul, sending out her siren's signal. He was feeling intoxicated and gaped at her. He reached for Frannie's middle and settled for her wide rump. Clutching it, he pulled her close to him and looked up into her face. He patted her back side gently. Howard looked on, wondering when he had last seen Paul drunk.

"I'm retiring, Frannie. I'll be free to come in and see you every day." He slapped her bottom crisply. He giggled, and then he burped.

She scrunched her face. "That's crude!" she rasped and wriggled free from his grasp. She collected the empty tray and walked back behind the bar.

Paul belched again, a long satisfying drone. "Excuuuse me," he blurted, looking in Frannie's direction. Then he turned back to the men at the table.

"Did you see that we're getting new tools?" He took another gulp of his beer. "Power tools," he confided. "DEWALT stuff, the best. Power saws and power sanders, power spray painters and cordless power drills, the works. You name it. Jimmy J. Hill, himself, authorized them. Roy Steichel said that his boss in St. Paul wants to upgrade our inventory, bring us into the modern world. The superintendent was down in the Twin Cities this week for a meeting. Jimmy J. Hill told him personally that it's a Christmas present to reward us for the good years we've had."

"That's good news, Paul," Herman acknowledged.

"It is!" Paul agreed. He raised his voice. "Anudder beer... Frannie!"

Cortney laughed. He was not used to hearing Paul Rausch slur his words.

Frannie brought the beer, but this time she did not brush against the customer. She held it out at arm's length. He tried to grope for her and nearly fell off of his chair. "Come here, Frannie old girl," he beckoned. "What's wrong?"

"You're drunk, Paul," she stated flatly and turned on her heels.

"No..." he guffawed, "I'm not in...inebri...briated, am I?" He took a long drink, guzzling down the contents of the bottle. And then he wiped his mouth on his shirt sleeve.

Cortney Johanson looked at Herman Braun. Their eyes were alight with curiosity. "When will the tools be in, Paul?" Cortney asked.

"They're already... ordered," Paul replied. His voice was loud. "They're being shipped... hic... on Monday..., and they'll be delivered... hic... here... on Friday..., the day... of the Chri... hic... Christmas... hic... party.... hic... hic... I... have... hic... the hiccups.... hic..."

Cortney and Herman looked at each other knowingly. They relaxed and sipped slowly on their beers.

"It's been a long time since you were here, Paul," Howard stated. He looked steadily at the large man across from him. To Howard, he was an unwelcome visitor.

Paul looked at him and tapped both hands on the table in front of him. "The Round Table... I remember.... hic..." He raised his empty beer bottle. "To my good friends,... hic... the Knights of the Round Table!" Instinctively he put the mouth of the bottle to his lips and tried to suck down a draft. The bottle was dry.

"You were Sir Ector," Herman informed him.

"I was Sir Ector," Paul Rausch acknowledged. "hic..."

"Before you were promoted to foreman of the crew," Cortney added.

Paul shook his head knowingly. "It's lonely... at the top... But someone... hic... has to be there...."

Paul looked directly into Howard's eyes. He could see the man's resentment. "No hard... hic... feelings, Howie," he blurted. He waited for a reply. When none was forthcoming, he continued. "Besides..., I'm retiring... hic... in the spring.... Perhaps... hic... you'll get the job next..., Howie."

Paul laughed a hearty laugh and slapped Cortney on the back. "Drink up, boys.... hic... Let's celebrate! Four months from now..., I'll be driving with my sweetheart... hic... to Californy.... She's a good girl..., my Ione.... wants to see her sister.... hic... hasn't seen her in years.... Here's to us!"

He tried to take another swig from the brown bottle and, holding it upside down, realized it was empty. He yelled out, "Brrring me anudder one, Frannie!" She ignored his request.

When Paul Rausch finally stood up to leave, he tottered, rocking back and forth on his feet from toe to heel. When he ambled to the door, he could not walk in a straight line. He zigzagged hesitantly and nearly stumbled. He walked, holding onto the backs of chairs as he crossed the room. He caught himself on the door casing and flung the door open. He turned in the doorway and faced Fat Frannie. "Strumpet!" he blared. And he blew her a kiss.

Paul staggered outside and let the door slam shut behind him. A slight breeze had picked up, and the air was cool against his face. It had begun to snow. He wrapped his coat about him tightly and tugged at the bill of his cap. He hobbled a few steps past Ma's window with a Gluek beer sign hanging in it.

Once he cleared the window's view, he steadied his gait and quickened his pace. He trudged swiftly in the light snow, his balding head angled into the wind. He was no longer inebriated.

Paul smiled to himself as he walked along. Frannie had called him a drunk. He had belched in her face. His behavior had been crude, far from Christian. He would have to make it up to her and apologize someday... someday when it was all over.

Paul wished that Howard did not hate him. Howard had looked skeptical; he always did. But Cortney and Herman had looked pleased and eager.

Anyway, the sting was set up. The tools, $18,000 worth, a fortune bought with his own money, would arrive on Friday. They would sit in boxes, unopened, over the Christmas holiday. He and Howard would not inventory them until the Monday they returned to work.

As he plodded homeward, the man thought of his wife, Ione. She would have already fed the children, and she would be making a late supper for him. He had told her that he would be late, that he was stopping off at Ma's for a beer after work.

Paul grunted. She was a loyal woman. She understood him. She understood his needs and the sacrifices he was asking her to make for him. He loved her more than she would ever know.

Yes, the hook was baited. Now he would have to wait, to see if the fish would take the bait and swallow the hook, where it would lodge deep in its gullet—or maybe just in the thin corner of its mouth.

"hic... hic..." Now he really did have the hiccups.

Inside Ma's Bar the three men argued.

"It's a fortune, ripe for the taking," Cortney stated.

"Power tools," Herman noted. His friends could see that he was salivating.

"I could use the money," Cortney added. "It's almost Christmas." He stared at Howard, who remained silent. "What's wrong, Howie? This is the Holy Grail. For Pete's sake, don't chicken out now."

"I'm not chickening out," Howie replied. "Why did Paul Rausch come here today?"

"To celebrate his retirement," voiced Herman. "He just found out the good news this morning. It's official. I'd celebrate too."

"Maybe," said Howie.

"Did you see how drunk he was?" Cortney chortled. He had been amused to see his foreman so tipsy. He chuckled. "He gave Frannie all she wanted. He couldn't keep his hands off her."

Herman chimed in. "He acted like a randy old boar. He wanted to give her the *what for!*"

"Boorish!" Cortney concurred.

"Maybe," said Howie again.

"Power tools," repeated Herman wistfully. "You're going to call King Arthur, aren't you?"

"Maybe," stated Howie.

"We have all Christmas off. He can pick the time of his own choosing," added Cortney. "It's the perfect setup."

"Maybe... maybe not..." replied Sir Lancelot. He was still bothered by Paul Rausch's sudden appearance in the bar.

Howard argued with himself. He considered both sides of the argument. Paul had consumed a dozen beers in a short time. The drinks had loosened his tongue. Of course, alcohol could do that to a man, even a large man like Paul Rausch, especially on an empty stomach.

Would Paul ever cheat on Ione? That did not ring true. Paul Rausch loved his wife. He cared about her.

Of course, most men did care about their wives. That didn't mean that they wouldn't look elsewhere for comfort. In the pasture the grass was always greener on the other side of the fence. Howard remembered. And Frannie was an eyeful. She was a good-looking young woman. She was a woman of the flesh. Even Paul Rausch might not be able to resist.

Cortney and Herman were adamant, like children at a counter in a grocery store looking at candy behind the glass. They were insistent. "Call him, Howie," urged his friend, Cortney. Let's hear what he has to say."

"Talk him into it," ordered Herman. If you won't, we will," he threatened. Howard knew it was an empty threat. Neither of them knew the number to call. Neither of them even knew who King Arthur was.

But that night Howard Kappas did make the call. "Roland? This is Howard."

"Don't say my real name," the voice on the other end commanded. "Just speak to me."

Howard explained Paul Rausch's unusual visit. Roland

Becker did not express surprise or concern. His lack of reaction felt strange to the caller.

"So, have you heard about this shipment?" Howard asked.

"I was notified of the order myself by HAMMER TOOLS," answered the voice on the other end of the line. "It's for $18,000 worth of DEWALT power tools out of Lancaster, Pennsylvania."

Roland toyed with his accomplice, forcing him to speculate. "Why do you think the shipment is being delivered on Friday, the 19th?" He paused, waiting for an answer. Howard's silence annoyed him. "Because it's the day before Christmas vacation, damn it! The party will be in full swing. Nobody will want to work, so the shipment won't be inventoried for over a week.

Dummy packing slips with *corrected* totals have already been fabricated. My friend has seen to that. The crates will be numbered. When you open a crate, substitute the dummy slip for the real one. The dummy packing slips will be delivered to you. I'll handle the invoices myself when they arrive and authorize *full payment* to HAMMER TOOLS. That's the way it's always worked, and it's worked smoothly.

This time it's different. There's a wrinkle. These tools have never been inventoried by the railroad. With no inventory yet, you will need to leave all the crates. Are you listening to me, Howard?"

"Yeah, sure, I'm listening," Howard managed to say.

"There will be eighteen crates. You have to leave the crates where they are. Someone must have counted them by now. Open them carefully. Every tool has a tag. Remove only those tools with the red tags. They are not included on the *revised* packing slips. Then close the crate. Do you understand?"

"I understand," Howard told him. "I wonder about Paul Rausch," he informed the mastermind. "He was drunk, totally smashed. He made a fool out of himself with Fat Frannie. It was hilarious. It's been a long time since I've seen Paul drink that way—or act that way. He had no shame."

King Arthur's ears perked up. "Tell me about it." And he listened as Howard explained the details of Paul's antics.

The phone was silent for an extended time. Finally Roland spoke. He was chuckling. "When a Rausch drinks, he drinks hard. I've known them all my life. After all, he was celebrating his retirement." He paused briefly. "There's no need to be jealous any more. Just let him be."

Howard bit his tongue. But he hasn't retired yet, not until spring, thought Howard. He was still skeptical, but he did not voice his opinion. He let the subject die.

Roland Becker insisted that he alone make the decision; he would have it no other way. He weighed the pros and cons; this time the pros seemed to outweigh the cons. He considered all sides and all angles as he talked into the mouthpiece. "The timing is right. We may never get another shipment in like this. It's an opportunity." He stopped. The pause was lengthy.

"This is the Holy Grail," Howard whispered. Another lengthy pause. And then he heard the man on the other end of the line sigh. "Alright, we'll do it. This will be our final quest."

"When?" asked Sir Lancelot. "Next Saturday?"

"No, wait until after Christmas," the other voice directed. "I have to line it up with the others."

"Gawain and Pellinore will be happy," Sir Lancelot stated. "They're your loyal subjects."

"And you?" asked the man on the other end of the line.

"You're the king," answered his most trusted knight.

"Somehow I don't trust you, Howard. I want to, but I don't." Sir Lancelot's end of the line went dead silent. "Don't you dare cross me."

What would you do? Howard thought.

Roland Becker read the thought. "Don't tempt me, Howard. You don't want to know."

Roland Becker hung up the phone. He stood in his living room and looked out the window into the darkness. He laughed. It was like taking candy from a baby. He began to think through a plan, the final plan. Within an hour, though, worry crept in. It was easy, too easy. He was troubled. Not by Paul Rausch, but by his old nemesis, Chester Gritt. The police chief was wily. Could he orchestrate a sting? Roland decided that he could. Was he setting a trap? That was a possibility. Two hours later, he was convinced that it was a certainty.

Roland was aware of the risk, but he also knew the table stakes. Chester might raise the ante, but Roland thought that his own hand was the winning hand. He considered calling Johnny Morris and canceling the mission. That would be throwing in his cards. He thought about the rewards. The power tools were worth a fortune, but more important to him was his pride.

He did not want Chester Gritt to win again. Roland Becker decided to play his hand.

He picked up the telephone receiver and dialed a number. When the connection came to life, he spluttered into the mouthpiece. "I've thought about canceling the mission."

"But why?" sounded the voice on the other end. "I've already told the others about the plan. This is the Holy Grail!"

"Tell them I've decided to go ahead with it," stated King Arthur. "That's my decision." He heard Howard's audible gasp of relief mixed with a budding excitement.

"But I want to take out some insurance. Howard, here's what I want you to do...."

The new tools arrived on schedule. They were delivered by HAMMER TOOLS on the Friday morning before Christmas as planned and immediately set aside. The inventory could wait ten days, until the Monday after Christmas. Something far more important—a Christmas party!—was in progress on this day.

The Christmas setting inside the car shops' central plant was festive. A spruce tree had been set up in the corner of the break room, and it had been decorated with colored lights and bulbs and tinsel. A miniature train set, a Great Northern Empire Builder, circled the base of the tree again and again. Its colors, orange and green, reminded everyone of the larger models they worked on daily. Musical accompaniment played in the background, featuring the Christmas songs of Fred Waring and his Pennsylvanians. The voices of Eddie Fisher, Perry Como, Bing Crosby, and Eartha Kitt filtered throughout the room.

Tables in the center of the room, draped in red and green table cloths, were loaded down with goodies: fruit cakes and cookies and candies and nuts and eggnog! Coffee was served. It was rich and flavorful, most welcome on this cold morning. Small pitchers of cream and bowls of sugar were generously in place beside the coffee urn. If desired, they accented the black brew. On the center table sat a large glass bowl, filled with a fruity punch of orange juice and pineapple juice and Seven-up, spiked with champagne. This was tradition. Serving liquor on railroad property, especially during work hours, was against company policy. But on this one day of the year, company policy was overlooked.

The workers relaxed. They would go on paid vacation tomorrow. The outside crews were encouraged to "come inside out of the cold" and celebrate with the managers. Superintendent Steichel, himself, waited on table. His apron, displaying Christmas scenes from Charles Dickens' *A Christmas Carol*, brought joy to the masses of men.

Tiny Tim, and Bob and Mrs. Cratchit, and old Scrooge himself all were vestiges of a distant past, of that time in the mid-19th Century when the Industrial Revolution had brought turmoil to the landscape. Certainly, the influence of the machine had evolved. The train itself was a symbol of the new age. In Dickens' time, class distinction had been more pronounced, the lines more unequivocally drawn.

Times had changed. Yes, indeed, times had changed. Superintendent Steichel was *serving them*. The treats and refreshments on the table were for everyone, great and small alike. It was meant to show that the Great Northern Railway was one family. That was the spirit of the Christmas season in this modern age in Waite Park, Minnesota, in the year of our Lord, 1958.

Paul Rausch and his crew, Howard Kappas and Cortney Johanson and Herman Braun, accepted Superintendent's Steichel's open invitation to "come inside out of the cold." They were in high spirits, for they always looked forward to this day.

As they crossed through the central plant, they noticed the large wooden crates stacked in a corner of the room. The crates were labeled, the number of each marked clearly on the front. Johnny Morris, the bookkeeper at HAMMER TOOLS, had seen to that. Howard noticed that they all had the HAMMER TOOLS' logo, a hammer and tongs, stamped on the side.

Three of the men looked longingly at the crates. They knew what was inside them and the value of the contents. The power tools were valuable and would bring a hefty price. Each man had figured privately what his share of the profit might be.

The men were desirous, wishful. But they were also disappointed, for they knew that this mission would be the last one. King Arthur had spoken. He had delivered his decree with an ultimatum. Only Howard knew what that ultimatum was. A quest should never be the final one. When it was over, these men would still feel a longing inside them. No more battles would be a tragic loss.

"What a haul!" Herman muttered. His eyes drifted over the stacks of crates.

"It's a massive treasure for us," Cortney growled, "worth a fortune."

"It's right here in our grasp," noted Herman. "All we need to do is *touch* it."

Harvey listened to their yearnings.

"There are the new tools... DEWALT power tools," Paul Rausch stated. He pointed toward the wooden crates in the corner. "Let's go have a look."

Howard shrugged, and they followed their foreman. What three of the men did not know was that the fourth man had purchased the tools, all of them, with his own money, money needed to drive his wife to California when he retired. Now the money was gone, spent. It was being used elsewhere to buy replacement tools for those that had disappeared during the fourth man's watch.

"I see the crates are all numbered," noted Paul. "That will make it easier for us to inventory them on Monday, Howie." Paul Rausch's voice sang throughout the room: "I'm the foreman! I have the best crew. And now we have the best tools!" He nearly danced on his toes in delight.

That comment stuck in Howard's craw. It began to work on him, and by the time Superintendent Steichel served him a glass of punch, he was feeling downcast.

He watched the superintendent step around the table to greet his friend, Paul Rausch. They shook hands. "Hi, Paul. Merry Christmas!" he said, and his voice was warm and full of feeling. "Say hello to Ione for me. You know, you stole her from me."

Paul Rausch caught his boss in a big bear hug and lifted him off his feet. "I'll give her your regards, Roy," he replied, just as warmly. "Merry Christmas to you and Sally, too!" Paul set the man down gently; both were smiling.

"You'll be retiring soon," the superintendent stated. "We'll miss you. I'll have to fill your position, hire a new foreman." Roy Steichel's eyes fell on Howard Kappas.

Howard forced a smile.

"Howie's available," Paul Rausch stated. "He's a good man."

"I'm glad to hear that testimonial," the boss replied.

Now resentment swelled inside of Howard. While Cortney and Herman ate fruitcake and cookies and drank spiked punch, he sulked. His friends could not entice him to tell them the reason for his melancholy mood, so they left him alone *to stew in his own juices*. It was Christmas, for Pete's sake, a time to be jolly!

Howard Kappas's friends did not know what he was thinking. He had an idea. He was devising a plan. At first, it seemed preposterous; but the more he thought about it, the more it pleased him. It brightened his mood. Perhaps this would be *his* final quest. Cortney and Herman would join him. Of course, he would have to defy Roland Becker, but it was a chance he was willing to take. "A man has to do what he has to do," Howard said to himself. He sipped on his glass of punch, deep in thought. *I will have my revenge.*

CHAPTER THIRTY

"Mrs. Pfaffenstein! Mrs. Pfaffenstein!" The younger children stomped around the kitchen table, repeating the same words over and over.

"Is she coming here tonight?" the boy's sister, Mary, questioned.

"Yes, tonight," replied their mother, confirming it.

"Mrs. Pfaffenstein! Mrs. Pfaffenstein!" Mary began the chant anew. Her younger brother, Dan, joined her, shuffling around the table. Even Baby Chuck clapped his hands together and watched the children parade.

"When is she coming?" asked their older sister, Jeanne.

"After supper," the mother answered. "And then I'm leaving."

"When will the baby be born?" Mary asked.

"Tonight," Jeanne replied.

"How long will you be in the hospital?" was the younger girl's next question. They always associated the arrival of Mrs. Pfappenstein to baby-sit them with their mother's delivery of a new baby.

"Not tonight," the mother laughed. The baby won't be born until May. That's after the snow melts. The girls looked at her, puzzled.

"I want the snow to melt! I want the snow to melt!" Mary began to chant, and then her sister, Jeanne, and her brother, Dan, joined the chorus. Another parade around the table ensued. The children were excited.

"Tonight I'm just going out to the mink farm to be with Dad. He's lonely. I'll come home tomorrow morning."

"Tomorrow morning! Tomorrow morning!" Mary began another exuberant chant.

"Mrs. Pfappenstein will only be here tonight. You'll have fun with her." The oldest boy, silent up to now, was not so sure. Georgianna Pfappenstein had thirteen children of her own. One boy, Keithy, was in his grade in school. She doesn't always listen to me enough, he thought to himself. She was a cheerful soul with a continually pleasant smile, and the boy did not like that either.

When she read a book to them, she read one of the books she had brought: a science story about Ben Franklin and the mouse, Amos, discovering electricity; the Wright brothers and their first flight at Kitty Hawk, South Carolina; Madame Curie and her husband, Pierre, discovering radioactive isotopes. Mrs. Pfappenstein was long on education. These stories bored the boy; he'd heard them in school. He wanted adventure.

She ignored the games he tried to play, especially the ones where he tried to make her mad. She thought them silly. Why should he bend to her whims? She was there to entertain him; was she not? These thoughts flooded the boy's mind, and then he heard a knock at the back door.

Georgianna Pfappenstein filled the doorway when she entered. She was a plump woman with a plain face, who wore her hair up in a bun. She did not make him feel tingly like Laura Birch did.

"Mrs. Pfaffenstein! Mrs. Pfaffenstein!" the three middle children shouted. Their boisterous grins were disarming.

"I'll be back in the morning early," the mother reassured her children. "Wash your faces and brush your teeth." She grabbed her overnight bag and headed toward the back door. Then she turned to her oldest son, her firstborn. "Be good or Mrs. Pfappenstein won't come back here any more. That goes for all of you. Thank you, Georgianna. I'll be home by nine tomorrow morning."

Frankie watched her go. Only that day he had had a confrontation with her. He had disobeyed her, and she had tried to spank him with a stick.

For nearly a year he had enjoyed his bow and arrow set, a gift from Santa Claus last Christmas. Now that the feathers had rubbed off the arrows, however, his mother had started using the arrows as spanking sticks. The sticks were long and thin. They whipped. A whap across the buttocks stung. Now he rued that bow and arrow set.

Today he had refused to vacuum the living room couch and chairs. That was his job each week, worth twenty-five cents most weeks. His refusal angered her. When she tried to spank him, he instinctively grabbed her wrists to ward off the blow. He succeeded partially in deflecting the stick. He was growing stronger, harder for his mother to handle. Good thing his father was sleeping at night out at the mink ranch. He would not have been so tolerant of his son's resistance.

The younger children were aghast. "Be good" were their mother's parting words, "or Mrs. Pfappenstein won't come back here."

Mary whispered to her sister, Jeanne, her eyes filling with tears. "If Mrs. Pfaffenstein doesn't come back here, there won't be a new baby."

"We have to be good," Jeanne whispered back.

"Be good, Dan," Mary cautioned, looking into the young boy's eyes, "or there won't be a new baby. Mrs. Pfaffenstein won't come back."

Dan stared at her in recognition, mouth open. "Be good," he stated. All of their eyes turned toward their oldest brother, Frankie.

"Who wants to read a book?" Mrs. Pfappenstein asked. Three hands went up. "Not you, Frankie?" she questioned. "Then you can sit over there."

The first book was about Henry Ford and the invention of the motor car. The babysitter laughed at the early models that failed. "My grandpa had a car like this," she informed them. "He used to give us rides out in the country." Frankie sat in the distance in an armchair, listening.

"Mrs. Pfaffenstein, who watches all your children when you're gone over here baby-sitting us?" Jeanne asked the question.

"The dog," the mother of thirteen children answered. The children looked mystified.

Georgianna Pfappenstein laughed exuberantly. "My husband, Alf, helps the dog. Together, they manage."

"What's the dog's name?" Jeanne asked.

"Arf" was the short reply. "Arf Arf, really."

"We keep our dog, Jet, outside in the kennel," Mary volunteered.

I don't like her, thought the boy in the arm chair across the room. He wondered if Mrs. Pfappenstein would be up for a challenge.

It was almost bedtime. The children filled the bathroom sink full of warm water and took turns scrubbing their faces with a washcloth. Then they brushed their teeth.

"Time for bed," the sitter snapped, and the children scampered up the stairs. All except the oldest. He sat on the bottom step, waiting to be dragged upstairs so he could let his weight fall dead against her. He thought of Laura Birch and the warm fuzzy feeling.

"Aren't you coming up?" asked the adult woman from up high in the girls' bedroom. He did not answer.

Mrs. Pfappenstein took a long time putting the other children to bed. He could hear them all giggling upstairs. He bided his time on the bottom step. He would outwait her.

Finally he heard her voice above him. "Come upstairs, Frankie," she called, "and I'll tuck you in." He did not budge.

Then he heard movement and the sound of Mrs. Pfappenstein's weighty shoes clomping down the stairway. She tried to get by him, stepping past him with one leg and over him with the other. But she misstepped, and her shoe planted itself on top of the boy's hand.

"Owwww!" he cried. But she continued on, pushing past him and down the final step.

"Good night, kiddies!" she called up the stairs.

"Good night, Mrs. Pfaffenstein, came the immediate reply. And then she switched off the light and shut the door.

The stairway was dark and his hand hurt, and he was feeling a strong dislike for Keithy's mother.

Suddenly the hallway light switched on. Above him were three faces staring at him.

"Be good, Frankie," his sister, Jeanne, scowled, "or Mrs. Pfaffenstein won't come back here." He could see that she was angry at him.

"Yeah, be good, Frankie," his sister, Mary, pleaded. She was almost in tears. "Or Mom won't have a new baby."

He watched his brother, Dan, four years younger, descend the steps until they were eye to eye. Dan's face was full of concern and worry. He stared speechless at his older brother; he could not speak. "Be good," his eyes implored. And then he retreated up the stairs, and Jeanne switched off the light.

The children's mother returned home at 9:00 o'clock the next morning. "How did it go?" she asked.

"Well enough," the baby-sitter reported. "The girls and little Danny were delightful. And Baby Chuck is a happy baby."

"How was Frankie? I had trouble with him yesterday."

The mother of thirteen children laughed. "That's the kind I let Alf and Arf handle. You know, 'Give a dog a bone…'"

The boy's mother looked perplexed.

"You know, Pat, if you ignore his naughty behavior and don't feed him, he'll be happy when you finally give him a bone." She chuckled. "And he'll obey." Georgianna Pfappenstein collected her overnight bag. "Get some rest. I'll see you in five months." A car horn honked. "That's Alf," she stated, and she disappeared into the morning light.

When they heard their mother's voice in the back entry, the younger children crowded around her. Jeanne expressed what they all were thinking. Her face was angry, in a mood to tattle. "Mom, Frankie didn't be good. He wasn't *being—haeve*!"

The woman's eyes were bright, and her belly was full of the new life inside her. "Don't worry," she assured them. "Dad will be home tomorrow night."

"He's home! He's home!" the children sang. Perched behind a window, they had watched impatiently for their father's arrival for over an hour. For nearly a month they had anticipated his return. Their vigil ended when they saw a truck drive slowly down the alley and pull into their driveway. "Daddy's home!" they exploded. "Daddy's home!" And they danced around the kitchen table excitedly.

The man entered through the back door and stopped. His face was grizzled after a month of hard work and loneliness. He was seeking comfort. As they raced to greet him, he saw the excitement on his children's faces. They gathered around him and hugged his legs. He crouched down to look at them at eye level. "I'm home," the man announced.

"But are you staying home?" Mary asked. She hugged his neck tightly.

"Yes, I'm staying home," he assured her.

"But are you staying home *for ever and ever amen*?" she inquired. Her blue eyes looked searchingly into his face; they were not those of her mother.

Her father nodded. "Until next year," he assured her. His face was beaming brightly. He hugged them and kissed each of them, all but one, the oldest boy who pulled away from him. It was evident that his son felt he was growing too big to be hugged and kissed.

"You smell," the younger girl announced, wrinkling her nose.

"That's the mink smell," her sister, Jeanne, explained.

"I'm a mink farmer," their father announced.

"Then I'm a mink farmer's daughter!" the younger girl proclaimed.

Their mother stepped between them. "Go shower and I'll wash those clothes," the man's wife urged. "There's time before supper."

The husband pulled his wife to him and brushed her lips with his. "We finished," he stated. The pelts were shipped to New York this afternoon." He looked into his wife's eyes. They were troubled, searching his eyes for signs of change.

"It's almost Christmas," she stated. "I'm glad you're home. The children need their father. They missed you, especially Mary and Dan. They wore a path in the linoleum marching around that table."

He winked at her. The wink told her that his month in isolation had not changed him. I'll be heading out early tomorrow morning," he whispered, "to shop." He squeezed her to him and then looked down at the pouch forming inside her tummy. She let him place his hand on the bump. He touched it gingerly, caressing it.

The children watched them, and the girls giggled. Their father was home, home to stay—to be with them. They were a family.

That night the man stayed home and was their dad. He played house with his daughters, letting them serve him tea in a miniature teacup and then dinner on a doll's plate. Mary poured the tea.

"Here's mashed potatoes and gravy and a moose steak for your supper," stated Jeanne, and she handed him a plate heaped with boiled macaroni. The girls had already set the table with silverware and a napkin. He ate it all.

"And here's a big piece of banana cake for dessert... with ice cream," Mary stated, offering him a bowl with two chocolate chip cookies in it. He ate them too. It was all make-believe, of course, the father acknowledged, except for the look of happiness on their faces. That was real, something to be cherished. It had been a long month, and he had waited for this night.

After supper the man bounced young Dan and even Baby Chuck on his knees, playing *Ponyboy*. They laughed and whooped and hung on as best they could, sliding down his legs when the horse stopped on "*Whoaaaaaaa!*"

"Again! Again!" the three-year old pleaded, compelling the horse to bounce him repeatedly.

His older brother had something else on his mind. "Santa Claus comes tomorrow night," Frankie stated, "and I'm going to catch him."

"You are?" asked his father. "But won't you be asleep?"

"I'll stay awake," the son asserted, "all night long. I'll catch him."

"I hope you do," his father responded. "But if you do, he may not leave any presents."

It was a warning, but the boy didn't care. He would still continue to make his preparations. Somehow, however, he was bothered by the knowing smile on his father's face as the man turned his attention back to the two little boys, and he wondered about it.

The house was decorated for Christmas. The boy surveyed the scene. The Christmas tree, a balsam fir with prickly needles, stood in the corner of the room. It was richly laden with strings of colored lights and bulbs, both handmade and bought, and silver tinsel, which hung from every branch.

A star balanced on the topmost tip, reflecting the lights around it. His mother had told him that it was the Star of Bethlehem that had guided the three kings from afar in their search for the new King of the Jews. Those kings from the Orient, the gentiles, were already marching toward Bethlehem. The boy could see them on display on his mother's sewing machine table across the living room, still miles away. They were bringing along a camel that was loaded down with gifts of gold, frankincense, and myrrh. They would arrive on Epiphany.

Surrounding the star at the tree's top, gathered on the branches nearby, was a host of angels. Some were blowing trumpets, proclaiming the season's good news. All were rejoicing.

Beneath the tree were stacks of presents. One was a heavy gift-wrapped box from his godparents, Uncle Charley and Aunt Lucille, mailed all the way from Rockaway, New Jersey, on December 10th. The lad eyed the package longingly. It would be something electronic and interesting.

At the base of the tree lay a Nativity scene, positioned prominently front and center. A wooden stable rested on a layer of white cotton batting, snow on a chilly night.

"Was there snow in Bethlehem?" his sister, Jeanne, asked skeptically. She had seen pictures in a magazine. "It looks too hot in the desert."

"I would like them to have snow there," her mother answered. The manger scene is how we, over here, picture the first Christmas. We have snow."

"Oh," Jeanne stated, but she did not sound convinced of her mother's logic.

The children's father had built the stable himself, using the bark of an oak tree as shingles. A light bulb mounted inside at the back illuminated the manger and guided the way for strangers.

Above the crib an angel hovered, guarding the precious bundle that lay within. Just outside, shepherds and their sheep stood by, watching in wonder.

The stable was home to an ox and an ass, animals that lounged on straw and fed on hay. The bulky mass and steamy breath of these creatures provided a measure of warmth.

A woman and a man knelt in the stable around a manger full of straw. And in that manger lay a baby, newly born. They were statues, of course, but to the family the manger scene was a reminder of the dual nature of Christmas—secular in its festive array of lights and bulbs that bedecked the Christmas tree, but also religious in its commemoration of the birth of a child whom they believed to be both God and man. It's what their grandparents had taught their parents and what their parents had taught them. This dual message had been passed down from generation to generation and been preserved.

The children's father was gone most of the next day, and he came home in the late afternoon. It was Christmas Eve and the family celebrated. Grandma came over for supper. She had dropped off two chickens the day before, and the boy wondered if they were capons. He suspected that they were two of the small flock he had brought home and taken to the basement.

The smell in the kitchen was savory, a combination of fried chicken and boiled potatoes to be mashed and tangy gravy and corn. The children hung about the kitchen. They crowded close to the oven, for in it were two cherry pies their mother had baked, bubbling with sugar and spice. The aromas wafted throughout the house and whetted their appetites.

Grandma was awarded the neck and the schwanz of a chicken. She gnawed on each down to the bone, and then she wiped her mouth on her napkin. All the while she chirruped about investments and about bridge. The children learned that she was a big believer in the stock market, especially the American Funds. "Don't try to time the market," she advised. "Just put your money in!"

"You like selling stocks, don't you, Grandma," her granddaughter, Jeanne, noted.

"It pays the bills," the older woman replied curtly. "But I don't sell stocks, just mutual funds."

The children could see a proud woman who believed in herself and her abilities. But Frankie knew that her passion was playing bridge. "I won first again last night," she beamed, "down at the club."

"I know," said her grandson. "I saw it in the newspaper this afternoon."

On this night Grandma was in the mood to tell stories. This was unusual for she was a secretive woman who seldom revealed much about her past.

It was Christmas Eve night, so she told them about Christmases long ago during the Great Depression, when there had been no money for presents. She and her husband and their five children had huddled together in a candle-lit room while a blizzard raged outside. The "storm of '31" she called it, and she described how they had tied a rope from the house to the barn to guide them during the snowstorm. All had been white: the landscape, the sky, the air they breathed—opaque and frosty.

"We lost a cow and two dozen chickens," she explained. "The cow would not go into the barn. She was petrified with fear. She stood in the corral, facing into the wind and refusing to move, even when Dad whipped her with a switch. Finally she fell over and died of exposure and dehydration. The chickens suffocated. The coop was filled with snow, and it smothered them in their nests. We found a few eggs; they were frozen and as hard as rocks."

While she talked, her son sat in a living room chair, nodding peacefully at the memories of his childhood.

And then she told about her husband becoming sick, a man they depended on. She related how his appendix had burst and he had not returned from the hospital in Minneapolis. Without him, they had to move off the farm into East St. Cloud. Those were turbulent years, and Christmas soon took on a very different meaning for them.

The man in the living room chair listened to his mother speak. His son, Frankie, watched him. The boy could not tell how his father felt. His Dad was a stoic man, not given to outbursts of emotion. It was how the men of Waite Park were. It was Christmas Eve, 1958. And his grandmother was telling stories about the distant past. His father remembered them but would not dwell in the past.

"Let's open our presents," he suggested.

"Yes, let's," his wife agreed.

"Presents! Presents!" the children cheered, and they leaped for the stacks beneath the tree.

The man watched them from his chair. He was the provider. The sound of their excited voices warmed his heart on this cold night.

That night Frankie lay in bed awake. He dared not close his eyes. The moon outside his bedroom window was shining, a waxing moon nearly full. Patches of clouds drifted in the sky. Occasionally one crossed in front of the moon, and the boy looked to see if it was Santa's sleigh. The night was still, and he listened intently for the clatter of hooves on the rooftop.

He tried to stay awake. *Silent night... holy night... all is calm... all is bright...* Outside his window a chorus of carolers gathered under the porch light in Scandans' front yard. Dressed in long coats and scarves and gloves, Victorian top hats and bonnets, they sang cheerily. The words of the hymn reflected the stillness outside.

He must keep his eyes open. He had a plan. From the box he had brought upstairs in secret, he took two toothpicks and slid them underneath his eyelids. He lay in bed, trying not to blink. A minute passed. His eyes became irritated, and they began to water profusely. And then he blinked. Owwww! Sharp pain shot through both eyes. He removed the toothpicks and blinked hard, massaging his eyeballs with his knuckles.

The alternative plan was to use duck tape. He had borrowed one of Bill O'Brian's rolls from Terry Joe. He stole down to the bathroom and stood in front of the mirror, taping his eyelids open. He pasted two strips of tape onto his eyelids and up onto his eyebrows and forehead. But the urge to blink was strong; the tape did not hold. So, he cut a long length of tape and wrapped it over his eyebrows just above eye level and then around his entire head. It held! He scampered up the stairs and crawled into bed. He lay under the covers and tried not to think about the tape.

Unfortunately the more he tried to ignore the tape, the more he thought about it. Soon, his eyes felt bone dry. He tried to ignore the discomfort. "Mind over matter," Sister Bede had taught them. But he could not hold up. He could not bear the agony. Defeated, he unwound the tape from his head. He whimpered when he tried to peel it off his eyelids. It was sticky; the skin wanted to come with it. Once again, he rubbed his eyeballs with his knuckles.

Finally he was forced to resort to advice Terry Joe and heard from Timmy—"Bite your finger."

That worked... for a while. At first, he listened to his brother, Dan, snoring softly in the bed beside him. But eventually his eyelids grew heavy, and his mind began to drift into slumber. He tried to ward off sleep.

For a time he focused on his other senses: he listened for bells jingling and reindeer prancing across the lawn; he smelled the soot from the chimney as a jolly fat elf descended down it and plopped into the fireplace. Santa unloaded gifts from his bag, and then laying his finger aside of his nose, disappeared in a flash up the chimney. "Ho! Ho! Ho!" cried the elf in a lusty voice as his reindeer spirited him away. The boy was feeling the magic of childhood beliefs.

But despite his efforts, he could not resist the heaviness of his eyes. He grew weary and his eyelids drooped. He thought he heard his father coming home from midnight mass. And then he dozed.

He must have dreamed for time flew by. The boy awoke with a start and sat upright in bed. The small night light in the hallway guided his footsteps. He descended down the stairs into the half-light of Christmas morning. It was not yet dawn.

Only the lights on the Christmas tree were aglow; they shimmered in a myriad of colors. Beneath them lay the presents they had opened the evening before. Suddenly Frankie spied a new set of treasures. Santa had come! He had brought the children gifts during the night while they slept.

They were real. Two new bicycles, both red, rested upright on their kickstands. The boy read the name, Schwinn, on the frames. One bike was larger than the other, he noted. It was a boy's bike with a round brace running forward from just below the seat to just under the handlebars. He scanned the room. Underneath the tree, he caught the glimmer of ice skates, two pairs of white figure skates. They looked like they would fit his sisters' feet. And then he spotted the prize.

At the far side of the tree lay a sheet of plywood, four-foot by eight-foot, with a miniature track nailed to it. The track was oval, and on it rested a tiny train. Its engine stood poised to pull the two cars and a caboose connected to it. The boy knelt at the side of the track and inspected it closely.

"Do you want to try it?" asked a voice from across the room. It was his father's voice. He looked up and saw his dad standing in the doorway, clad only in a t-shirt and boxer shorts. "Push the switch on the engine," the man instructed.

The boy complied. He pushed the switch, and the little train began to move. It circled the track again and again, the engine pulling the two cars and the caboose.

"Do you see the colors?" asked the dad. "Orange and green."

"It's a Great Northern Empire Builder. There's the goat climbing the mountain!" his son cried gleefully, pointing to the logo on the side of the engine.

"Santa must know that we live in Waite Park," the man replied. "Turn it off and let's go back to bed. I have to feed and water the mink tomorrow morning, early. You have to serve mass at seven-thirty. You'd better get some sleep. And be quiet. Don't wake them up." The man looked at his son. "Why are your eyes all red?"

The boy turned away. "It's nothing," he replied.

When the boy awoke in the morning, his father's truck was gone. It was still dark outside when he trudged the five blocks to church, but the sun was peeking out in the east when he trudged home.

"Hey, Terry Joe!" He met his friend, who was plodding the other way toward the church. "Want to play with my new football game? It's from my Uncle Charley and Aunt Lucille. It plugs in, and when the field shakes, the players move until the play is over."

"Sounds fun," his friend nodded. "But I can't play until this afternoon. I have to go to church until 11:30. Us O'Brians go to church twice on Christmas. Dad says that's what Grandma made him do. So, he makes us do it, too. Then we have to eat dinner over at Grandma's and talk to our uncles and aunts. Then I can play."

"See ya, around," the O'Brian boy added. "I'd better get going. Grandma will be there. She'll be lookin' for me."

Frankie watched his best friend shuffle off down 5th Street toward St. Joseph's Catholic Church.

That day the boy's mother and father had a surprise for the children. "We're going on a sleigh ride," their mother announced, "with the Ferchos and the Banfields and the Trellwicks, tomorrow afternoon."

"A sleigh ride! A sleigh ride!" the younger children chanted.

"Out in the country," their mother announced.

"Out in the country! Out in the country!" the children repeated.

The next afternoon they drove to a farm where a farmer, Mr. Irman, stood on top of a hayrack that was mounted on skis. Two large draft horses were in harness at the front, ready to pull the dray.

"Hello, Glenn! We're all here," Ed Banfield announced. "I'm glad you're at the helm." At that, the driver released the brake and jiggled the reins. "Nckk... nckk..." he clucked, and the horses stirred.

"Nckk... nckk..." repeated Jeanne and Mary, imitating Mr. Irman. They knelt on a bale of straw next to him as the sleigh moved over the snow and gained speed. They headed for the woods, following the tracks grooved into the trail during previous rides.

For the horses it was easy pulling. The two horses tugged in unison. *Clomp... Clomp... Clomp... Clomp...* The hips of each animal moved up and down like two pistons, separated down the middle by its vertebrae. Steam rose from their sides as they exerted themselves. Their breath was visible.

"Faster! Faster!" the children urged, and Mr. Irman cracked a small whip in the air over the horses' buttocks. "Nckk... nckk... Nckk... nckk..." he called. At his beckoning, the animals increased their pace slightly.

"Nckk... nckk... Nckk... nckk..." the children mimicked.

The riders sat on straw bales and watched the empty fields pass by. When the snow melted, Glenn Irman would plow the fields and seed them with corn. But for now they were vast empty spaces filled with sunlight. The rural air was crisp and fresh and clean, good for the lungs, and the sleigh's riders breathed deeply. They were cheered by the pungent farm aroma coming from warm straw and the sweating horses. When the animals exhaled, the riders could see their breath.

Donny Trellwick began to sing lustily in a throaty voice.

> *Over the river and through the woods,*
> *to drandmother's house we go...*

He was joined immediately by the other adults and by the children, too.

> *The horse knows the way to carry the sleigh,*
> *through the white and drifted snow ohhh!*
> *Over the river and through the woods,*
> *Oh, how the wind does blow!*
> *It stings the toes and bites the nose,*
> *as over the ground we go ohhh!*

It was a rousing rendition.

"Hurray!" shouted Ed Banfield. "It's almost 1959!" He raised an imaginary glass.

"Hurray!" Ted Fercho echoed him. He raised his glass to

complete the toast: "To the new year!" They were feeling the spirit of the season.

Dashing through the snow... in a one horse open sleigh...

Frankie recognized the woman's voice. It was his mother changing the tune. The chorus chimed in, singing the popular Christmas melody.

*Over the fields we go... laughing all the way....
HA! HA! HA!*

Soon the children, led by her two daughters, took the lead.

*Bells on bob tails ring... making spirits bright....
What fun it is to laugh and sing a sleighing song tonight....
Ohhh, Jingle Bells... Jingle Bells... Jingle all the way....
Oh, what fun it is to ride in a one horse open sleigh ehhh!*

The two draft horses continued to clomp along. Their gait was steady with the two halves of their rumps rising and falling in a consistent rhythm. These beasts of burden pulled the hayrack along at a constant speed, without variation in tempo. They were in no apparent hurry.

They entered the woods, and the atmosphere darkened. Even without their leaves the trees created a canopy that blocked out most of the light. The horses surged through the brush, between trees, and around fallen logs, following the path. The mood changed. Husbands put their arms around the shoulders of their wives and pulled them close. Together, they listened to the sound of the skis rushing over the snow. The landscape was frozen, but the crisp motion of the sleigh energized them and made them feel alive. It heightened their spirits.

Frankie stood on the hayrack, arms crossed, displaying his sense of balance. He was intrigued by a young girl sitting on the back of the sleigh. Twice, he caught her looking over her shoulder to inspect him. He felt the fuzzy feeling return. Twice, he jumped off the sleigh and ran behind it, following its tracks. Once, he stumbled in a deep footprint made by one of the horses. Embarrassed, he jumped up quickly. His face was full of snow, and he noticed that she laughed freely, despite herself.

When he reached the back of the hayrack, she reached out her hand to him. Running madly, he grabbed onto the hand and pulled himself up. He plopped down beside her, breathing hard.

At last, they exited the woods and saw the farmyard in the distance. The ride was almost over. The boy stood up and moved to the front of the sleigh. He saw his dad lean over to his mother and whisper in her ear. She looked startled and gave a little muffled cry and then kissed her husband on the lips.

"What is it?" asked Lil Trellwick, ever curious. The other adults had seen it, too. "Why so passionate? What's the surprise?"

"We're going to New York!" the boy's mother cried. "Clifford is taking me to New York City this month. He just told me the secret. It's his Christmas present to me. We're going to the mink sale."

"Donny Trellwick, are you taking me to New York?" Lil Trellwick's voice rose above the din. But her husband had moved to the end of the sleigh and was clinging to a pole attached to the corner of the hayrack. Instead of responding, he began to sing. *Sailing... sailing... over the ocean blue...*

"Donny! Donny Trellwick! Are you listening to me? Donny! Sweetheart! Take me to New York!" Lil Trellwick's pleading with her husband was to no avail. He took off his cap and waved it in the air, brushing aside her requests as if they were house flies. *Sailing... sailing... over the ocean blue...*

The young girl from the back of the hayrack had moved up front and stood beside the boy. "That's my dad. She pointed to the man dangling from the pole at the back of the sleigh. And that's my mom. I'm Donna Trellwick. What's your name?"

"Frankie," he answered. "And that's my dad and mom over there on the straw bale."

"My mom is your dad's cousin," the girl informed him, "his first cousin. That makes us second cousins."

The boy was silent. He pondered this information. Suddenly he recalled a lesson Father Schumacher had given them in religion class. "You can't marry someone closer than a third cousin," Father had asserted. "To do so is a mortal sin. It invites incest. Your children will be deformed." He had left it at that in the Second Grade version of his lecture. In the classes with older children, Fifth Grade and above, he accepted questions. But only questions he approved of.

"You can't marry someone closer than a third cousin," Terry Joe had told Frankie on their way home. "Unless you live out by St. Anna. Then it's okay."

"I know," his friend, Frankie, had answered. "My grandma told me about it, but she doesn't like it. People out there have a syndrome. But they invest their money."

Terry Joe grinned as he walked along. "Susan Danbury isn't your cousin, is she?" he inquired.

"No, she's not!" his friend blared in anger.

Terry Joe chuckled. He was in his glory. "Then you *can* marry her and still be in the Catholic Church. Right?"

"If you say that again, I'm going to punch you in the nose," Frankie threatened.

"I'm just asking. I only wanted to know."

Just then, the horses broke into a trot. They saw the barn ahead and knew that a healthy ration of oats lay in a feed trough for them. Their mission would soon be accomplished. The sleigh gave a jolt and slipped into a higher gear. Donny Trellwick was nearly thrown overboard from his mast aft.

"Hold on there, Donny," Ed Banfield yelled.

"It's a bit treacherous out here on the poop deck," Donny shouted back. "All hands to stations," he ordered. And then, waving his cap, he resumed bellowing out his song. *Sailing... sailing... over the ocean blue...*

"That's my dad," Donna Trellwick whispered. She was smiling. He takes a bit of getting used to. "I'm more like my mom."

Her male companion looked at her. He liked how she was: how natural, how genuinely at ease. He felt disarmed. Now that he knew they could never marry, he decided that they could become friends.

"Hey, Clifford, are you ddoe-ing to dine out in New York?" Donny Trellwick's voice pierced the momentary solitude. "Are you ddoe-ing to eat chicken and dravy?" He laughed vigorously, and so did everyone else on board the wagon, including Mr. Irman. It seemed to the boy that even the horses were laughing.

Donny Trellwick didn't mind. When they laughed at him, he laughed with them. Thus, they were laughing with him. "Ddive him another smooch, Pat. It's not every day you ddet a chicken and dravy dinner in New York." And so, the woman on the hay bale kissed the man beside her, her husband.

As if on cue, the horse on the driver's side lifted its tail. "Look at that!" Jeanne pointed in alarm. The massive equine let go a turd the size of a softball. And then another... and a third. *Plop... Plop... Plop...* The round nuggets fell to the ground and disappeared under the sleigh.

The boy, Frankie, blushed. His discomfort was made worse when the girl beside him whooped without shame.

"Oh no!" cried Mary. "The poor horse... Is she sick?"

"No, Mr. Irman laughed. "*He's* not sick. But he knows he's going to eat soon, so he's making room."

The horse made no break in his stride. The steam continued to rise from his sides because of his exertion, and his hips continued to bob like pistons, matching those of the mare beside him.

"They're married," Mr. Irman informed the children. "So, they're not squeamish about pooping in front of each other."

"Don't tell them stories," Lil Trellwick laughed. "Or they won't sleep a wink tonight."

"Just having my fun," the driver replied. "Just having my fun."

Hanging on to the back of the sleigh, Donny Trellwick continued to wave his cap and sing. *Sailing... sailing... over the ocean blue...*

CHAPTER THIRTY-ONE

Paul Rausch was doubtful. Every day for seven days he had walked from his house to the Great Northern Railway's car shops to see if a fish had swallowed the bait. Thus far, he had had no bites, nary a nibble. As he walked along on this, the eighth, morning, he let his mind drift. He recalled one of Father Schumacher's sermons. The first apostles had been fishermen. Jesus had made them fishers of men. Now he, too, was fishing for men. How odd!

For seven straight days he had used a key borrowed from Roy Steichel to unlock the front gate. He had walked behind the central plant to the north entry and opened the door. He didn't know what to expect. He half-expected to see the tools gone—stolen. He half-hoped that they would still be there in the shop, accounted for. These were men he had grown to trust. They were his friends. He didn't like that he was doing a *dirty deed*. It made him feel miserable inside.

As the days had slipped by, he had grown more doubtful. Perhaps his unexpected appearance at Ma's Bar had sounded an alarm. Perhaps his little drinking charade had scared them off. But there was still the lure of the tools. He knew from experience that hungry fish wanted the bait. Yet, to date, no fish had shown any interest.

On this morning, as on the previous seven mornings, nothing had changed. The crates were all there, just as they had been stacked, and there was no sign of entry. Nothing had been touched. On this Saturday, the 27th of December, Paul closed and locked the door. Of the original twelve apostles, he was the doubting Thomas.

As he walked back up the sidewalk on 11th Avenue toward home, Paul considered the possibilities. Time was running out. In two days, on Monday, the car shops would reopen. The ruse would be over; the opportunity to steal the tools, lost. He and Howard would inventory the new power tools and catalogue them. If the fish was going to bite, it would have to be soon. As he approached his house up near the highway, he hoped it would be tonight.

In the back entryway he took off his cap and jacket and hung them on a hook. He stood in the doorway and looked at his wife, Ione. She stopped her housework to ask an unspoken question: "Anything new?"

He shrugged, like he had for the seven days before this one. Instantly it told her the news: "No change, nothing, nothing was amiss."

On Saturday evening, two pickup trucks met at the west end of the Moose Lodge in a darkened parking lot. The time was 9:00 o'clock. The two drivers doused their headlights while they waited for a third man to join them. He arrived soon after they did. He had walked a short distance from his home to the rendezvous point. The strap of a satchel was slung over his shoulder. In his arms he was carrying an object he had purchased the day before.

"What's that, Howie?" Cortney Johanson asked as his accomplice crawled into the passenger's seat.

"An insurance policy," Howie answered. "Let's get going."

"What's in the satchel?" Cortney pursued.

"The dummy packing slips," Howie replied. And then he fell silent.

Cortney Johanson looked briefly at the contraption in the rider's hands and shrugged. Then he motioned to the driver in the other vehicle and shifted his truck into first gear. He switched on his headlights and exited the parking lot, turning right onto 3rd Street. His friend and partner, Herman Braun, followed closely behind.

"Why are we going to put on rain suits?" Cortney asked. "It's a damned nuisance if you ask me."

"Do you have the plastic tarps?" Howie asked.

"In the back" came the reply. They're big ones, the size you wanted, sixteen by twenty. But why do we need a tarp that big?" Cortney asked. "And why two of them?" Howard Kappas could see that his fellow knight was frustrated.

"It's on a need to know basis," Howie responded. "Semper fi."

"So why rain suits?" Cortney persisted. "And ski masks and boots and gloves? Even goggles. I don't get it. We don't need them. It's overkill."

"Perhaps" was Howie's one-word answer, and that made it even more frustrating.

Cortney looked at the device Howie was holding in his hands. It looked like a scope of some kind with a battery pack attached to it. "What is that thing?" Cortney asked. He nodded toward Howard's lap. "Some sort of machine?"

"I'll show you when we get there." Howie replied, and he patted the instrument.

The two trucks turned into the car shops and stopped at the west gate. The drivers turned off their headlights. Howard jumped out and set his mysterious device on the front seat. He searched his pocket for a ring of keys and used one to open the lock. It clicked, and he pulled the gate open. The two pickups leaped through the opening into the yard. Howie re-locked the gate and climbed back in. He settled into the seat, clutching his device.

With the moon nearly full, there was no need to turn on the headlights. They drove between the administrative building and the central plant to the north side and stopped. Cortney turned his truck around and backed up to the loading dock. The bed of the truck was exposed so that it could be loaded easily. Herman parked his truck and stepped out of it.

They knew the routine well, but for some unknown reason, Howard altered it. He pointed to Cortney's vehicle. "Spread out the tarps in the truck bed," he ordered, "one on top of the other. Cover all four sides." The two knights complied.

"Remember," admonished Howie, "when we go in, don't touch a thing until I give the all-clear." The other two nodded.

Howard unlocked the door, and the three men entered. Herman switched on a flashlight. Before them stood the six stacks of crates, piled three high. The Holy Grail was within their grasp. Herman reached a hand out.

"Don't touch them," Howie commanded. His voice was insistent, full of authority. He flipped the switch on the scope, and it came to life in a flash of purplish ultraviolet light. Howard shined it on the top box, and then he swore. "Damn it!" he cursed. "Damn Chester Gritt! Damn Superintendent Steichel! Damn them all!"

Caught in the purple light was a purple powder. It was a layer of dust that spread across the top of one of the crates, the nearest box. The men looked at the purple film and then at one another. It was a trap, a setup.

Only Howard Kappas knew the protocol to be followed. King Arthur had instructed him to take along a black light, an insurance policy. That was now evident to Cortney and Herman. What they didn't know was that Roland Becker had issued a direct order, a very explicit direct order, in no uncertain terms: If a purple powder was discovered, they must abort the mission. "Do you understand this, Howard? You must abort the mission. You *must* abort it!" Howard had never heard Roland sound so stern. King Arthur was demanding that he obey. It was more than a command; it was a threat.

"What do we do now, Howie?" Cortney asked. He was at a loss.

Howard Kappas felt a burning hate in his chest and a desire to punish. Lancelot, the greatest knight, was seething with anger. He made his decision. "To hell with Roland Becker," he muttered under his breath, and he spoke to them.

"The hounds are onto our scent. But I have a plan that will put them off our track." He explained the details of his plan. "Are you with me?" he asked.

Cortney Johanson and Herman Braun looked at one another. "But there's nothing in it for us," Herman criticized. "This is the Holy Grail!"

"It's tainted," Howie replied. "They suspect us." He watched their faces darken. "Who knows *what* they already know? This will shift the blame. We'll be in the clear."

"But what will King Arthur say?" Cortney asked. "He may not like it. Did he say anything to you?"

Sir Lancelot shook his head sideways. "Not a thing."

Sir Gawain and Sir Pellinore nodded their consent.

"Put on these rain suits," Howie stated. He pulled them out of a large plastic garbage bag he had brought in. He watched the men put them on. "Now the overshoes... and these ski masks and goggles... and these gloves."

When they were ready, Howard inspected them carefully. He was satisfied. "Now you're protected. The dust can't penetrate the suits. But be careful... be very careful."

Howard stood aside and watched the other two men lift the crate with the purple powder on it. Gingerly they set it down on the plastic tarp on the bed of Cortney's truck. Then they lifted two more crates and loaded them into the pickup also. Cortney and Herman wrapped the top tarp around the three crates so that nothing was exposed. They tied a length of rope around the tarp to secure it. The purple powder was contained within.

Howard closed the double doors of the central plant and locked the entrance. While he did so, his accomplices removed their protective clothing.

"Start with the gloves," Howie instructed. "Change gloves now and after every item you discard." He indicated a box of plastic gloves he had set on the loading dock. He switched on the black light and aimed it at them. Purple dust sparkled on their clothing in the beam. They looked at one another. Most of the powder lay on their gloves and on the rain suits. The black light also detected small smudges of dust on their rubber boots with several spots on their ski masks and even a few pinpricks on the bulbs of their goggles. The evidence made an impression; it reinforced the need to exercise caution.

"Don't rush," Howie stated. "Don't make a mistake." He kept the black light trained on them.

The other two men worked together, methodically removing the gear from head to toe: goggles... new gloves... ski mask... new gloves... rain jacket... new gloves... rain pants... new gloves... overshoes... new gloves. Each item was deposited into the large plastic bag. When the job was completed, that bag was tied shut with rope and stuffed into another large plastic sack.

"Leave the top open," Howie advised.

"Why?" growled Herman, somewhat surprised.

"You'll see why later," Howie replied. "Scout's honor." Not quite satisfied, Herman hoisted the sack into the back of his vehicle. Then he and Cortney donned a second set of protective rain gear and rubber overshoes. They would put on new masks, goggles, and gloves at the destination site.

While the men worked, their breathing was ragged: shallow breaths and long slow exhalations. This stemmed not from any undue exertion, but from the recognition of the danger of their mission. The mind caused the body to strain. "Mind over matter," they had been taught. It had been drilled into them by old Sergeant Barker before they went into combat in the Philippines. They were trained marines. They had been in tight situations before, and they knew how to react under pressure. The two men performed their duty and changed clothes in silence, not speaking a word.

"Drive slowly," Howie cautioned. "Chester Gritt may be out and about on patrol. We don't want to arouse any suspicion. Go up 11th Street; it's not as busy as 10th," Howard dictated. "And then turn left into the Wagon Wheel parking lot and stop. I want to take a look. Herman, leave your truck in the parking lot. When the coast is clear, Cortney, pull into the alley and turn off your headlights. Paul lives in the first house. A row of high hedges at the back of Schwan Ober's yard will protect you from view across the alley."

They drove the three blocks south, crossing 4th Street a block west of the start of the soap box derby, just where Henry Hecht had set out high-backed dining room chairs for his three sisters and served them tea.

The two pickup trucks stopped as directed. The men inside inspected the house. The light above the back steps was off, and the house lights were dim. It was late. Paul and Ione were in bed asleep. So were the girls. No cars were in sight. The boys were out on dates.

The garage was unlocked, as were most of the garage doors in the village. Paul Rausch didn't even have a key anymore. The garage door, itself, was open. It was hinged to the door jamb of an old wooden garage made out of car shop lumber, and the door did not close completely. So, it was always left wide open. Someone had propped it open with a stick.

Howard signaled Cortney to drive ahead. The three men exited from the trucks. Howard watched for intruders as his companions put on their masks and goggles and gloves. Cortney and Herman worked in unison, carefully but quickly.

They unloaded the truck, placing the three crates far in the back of Paul Rausch's garage, out of sight. After the crates were safely inside the garage, they folded up the top tarp to contain the residue of purple powder within it. They manipulated the tarp carefully. Nothing must touch their skin or the truck. Finally, to secure it, they bound the tarp with rope. "It looks like a gigantic Christmas present," Cortney joked, "wrapped in ribbon."

The bottom tarp was a further precaution. At the disposal site it would be folded around the other tarp and tied with rope, creating a package within a package.

Next, they helped each other remove their protective outfits. Howard decided that it was worth the risk of detection to switch on the black light. The purple dust danced to life. It was pervasive, but not invasive; the powder had spread onto their clothing, but not into it. The need to change gloves after every item became evident.

They removed their goggles, ski masks, rain jackets, rain pants, boots, and gloves, one item at a time, and deposited them into a third plastic bag. They accomplished their mission without mishap.

Then they stripped down to their skivvies. Shirts and pants, belts, socks and shoes, all went into the large plastic bag. Howard had forewarned them not to wear anything valuable or nostalgic.

"Underwear too," Howie reminded them, and he chuckled at the sight of two naked men in the alley, shivering as they changed into blue jeans and sweatshirts and jackets.

"My feet are freezing," Cortney grumbled. "It's cold."

Herman just grunted. He twisted the top of the bag and tied it with rope. This he stuffed into a fourth sack and looked at Howard.

"Leave it untied," the leader ordered. "Put it in Cortney's truck. Go get the other sack out of your truck and transfer it into this one. We'll drive together." Howard surveyed the scene. "There aren't enough cars in the Wagon Wheel parking lot. The police chief may spot your truck. Drive home and we'll pick you up. We need to dump this stuff."

They drove the two trucks north down the alley past the Kuchers' house and turned right onto 5th Street. Herman lived in that direction, three blocks from the Catholic church. He parked his truck in the garage and closed the door. Then he crawled into Cortney's truck next to Howard.

"Are we going out to Granite City?" was his initial question. "Is that where we'll dump the gear?" He remembered the quarries fondly from his days as a youth. Those days had been carefree and fun-filled. He had taken his first girlfriend swimming there, Virginia Bruns, Clarence Bruns' sister, a young brunette whom he eventually married a month into her first pregnancy.

"No," Howie countered, "the quarries are all frozen over with three feet of ice, at least."

Cortney frowned. "What about the Sauk River down by the monument? It's running water."

"But it's too shallow," Howie replied. "I've checked. It's completely frozen over." He was being patient.

"Where then?" asked Herman, somewhat miffed. "The quicksand pool?"

"No," Howie explained. "We'll have to dump it in the Mississippi, down by Sportsman's Island. It never freezes over completely down there. I drove over there yesterday. It's wide open along the shore."

"I see why you have cement blocks and the rope," Cortney commented. "You've planned this whole thing out."

"What will happen when Paul Rausch finds the tools?" Herman wondered aloud.

"We'll have to wait and see," Howie stated. He did not speculate.

They drove into St. Cloud, past the state teachers college, down to the Mississippi River. The shoreline along Sportsman's Island was an isolated spot. Cortney and Herman each put on a new pair of gloves, and they placed a cement block inside both of the large sacks.

"Now tie the tops," Howie commanded. Then he nodded toward the river.

Together, his two fellow knights heaved the two bundles into the water. They splashed and then floated momentarily. The current, though not strong, took hold of them and twirled them in circles as they sank to the bottom.

"Fold the bottom tarp around the package and tie a rope around it," Howie instructed. "Knot the rope, but leave the ends long so you can tie the last cement block to the package. Snug it up tight."

The men responded as marines; they were quick and efficient.

"Now," continued Howie, "fling it out there as far as you can. But don't touch the tarp. That purple powder won't wash off your skin, and once it hits the water, it'll turn into ink, indelible ink that takes a month to peel off." He had seen the purple stain on Butch Carter's hands and arms.

Sir Gawain and Sir Pellinore grabbed the cement block in both hands and swung it back and forth between them. On the count of three, they let go, and the weighty block pulled the two tarps out over the water. It was the final act of their final quest.

The package landed six feet from shore and sank. It settled in the mud below in eight feet of water. Even if found, it could never be traced. Any fingerprints or any stain attached to the contents would be wiped clean.

"Throw the gloves in too," Howie reminded them. "They'll drift downstream and sink. Nobody will be the wiser."

He flipped the switch on the black light and inspected the bed of the truck. It was devoid of purple dust. He shined the light on Cortney and then on Herman. He saw no trace of purple powder, no evidence. He grinned. "You're both clean," he informed them, and their faces broke into broad grins.

On the way home, Cortney and Herman chattered. Alas, the final quest of the Knights of the Round Table was over. They had found the Holy Grail! But they would never partake in the loot. They regretted that. Covetous, they speculated what the power tools would be worth. At least the law would be off their trail. That was some consolation. For now, they felt a sense of relief and could relax their guard.

Howard Kappas sat in silence. His mission was accomplished. He had exacted his revenge. Paul Rausch had stolen his promotion, and now Paul would pay for that theft. Howard smiled wryly to himself. He would wait and see what tomorrow would bring.

"Hey, Dad, come out here and see what I found." Jimmy Rausch entered the kitchen and spoke to his dad, who was seated at the table, eating breakfast. Paul had just returned from Sunday morning mass. "It's in the garage," Jimmy announced.

"What is it?" Paul asked. He set aside his paper and looked at his son, a young man of twenty.

"There are three crates about this long." He opened his arms to approximate the dimensions. They say HAMMER TOOLS on the side.

Paul Rausch pushed back his chair and rose to his feet. He steadied himself with his hands, pressing the palms into the table. "Did you touch them?" he asked.

"I opened one crate," his son answered. "Dad, they're power tools... DEWALT power tools. Where did you get them? Why are they in the garage?"

Paul Rausch looked at his son's hands. He noticed a purplish cast. "Go wash your hands," the father directed. "But do it in the basement. Wash them in the laundry sink. And then come back here. Jimmy, we need to talk."

Perplexed, the young man clomped down the basement steps. Fifteen seconds later, Paul Rausch heard a desperate cry. "Dad!" his son's voice called sharply. "Dad, come quick! I'm bleeding! I'm bleeding! The blood is purple!" The voice rose in intensity. "Dad! It won't wash off! Dad!"

His father stepped down the stairs and into the laundry room. "Calm down. It's not blood," Paul Rausch informed him. "It's ink. There's a purple powder on the crates. It's almost invisible, especially in a dark place. The purple powder contains a dye. When it touches water, the water activates the dye and turns it into purple ink. It won't hurt you, but it doesn't wash off. It has to wear off." He looked at his son's troubled face. "Don't worry. It will wear off eventually... in four or five weeks."

"Four or five weeks?" The young man looked alarmed. "So, why is there powder on the crates? Who put it there?"

"Chester Gritt put it there. He uses it to catch criminals."

"But I'm not a criminal!"

"Jimmy, it's time I tell you about a crime that's been going on at the car shops—a theft of tools. His son looked up in disbelief, shocked.

"No, not me," his father smiled, "someone else. And I've gone fishing for him."

"But why did you let it get on me? My hands and arms are covered with purple stain. Why didn't you tell me?" Jimmy blurted.

"Chet suggested not to. The tools have lured the crooks out." His Dad turned his palms up and gestured with open hands. "I couldn't let them suspect the truth. I'm sorry, Jimmy, but I had to do it."

The young man continued to scrub his arms with a bar of soap. Not satisfied, he took hold of a wire brush.

"It doesn't wash off," Paul explained. "Using that brush won't help either. It'll just scrape into your skin. Don't do it. You could catch blood poisoning."

"Whose tools are they?" the son asked.

Paul Rausch thought about the question. "In a way, they're mine," he answered. Jimmy looked confused. "And your mother's," the man added. "They're ours." He paused. "They also belong to the railroad." Puzzled, his son stared at him long and hard. It did not make sense.

Paul looked at the young man's arms and hands and then eyed his face. "You're going to have to be understanding in this. You can start by throwing those clothes away. Change in the garage; Mom will bring you clean clothes. I'll buy you new ones."

"Does Mom know about this?"

"She knows. I couldn't keep something like this from her. I couldn't and I wouldn't."

Paul Rausch left his son, who continued to scrub his arms with the wire brush. He climbed the stairs. Paul chuckled at his son's persistence. "He's as stubborn as I am."

His wife met him in the kitchen doorway. "Call Chester Gritt," Paul stated.

"But it's Sunday," she replied. "Chester sleeps late on Sunday morning. He's still in bed."

"Wake him up," Paul ordered. Ione picked up the telephone receiver; the party line was clear.

"What's Jimmy doing down there?" she asked.

"He's taking a bath in the sink. He touched the purple powder, and it's left a stain all over his hands and arms."

Loretta Gritt's voice came on the line. She sounded sleepy. Ione spoke. "Loretta, this is Ione Rausch. Put Chester on…. I know he's sleeping, but Paul wants to talk to him…. Wake him up. Paul needs to talk to him *now*."

The line went dormant, and she handed the phone to her husband. Paul clasped it tightly in both hands.

"Chester? This is Paul Rausch. We have a fish on the line. It swallowed the bait: hook, line, and sinker…. last night… three boxes… in my garage… Jimmy found them…. Yes, he opened one box…. They're purple from his fingertips to his elbows…."

Yes, I know. Four to five weeks. I told him, but he'll have to learn that for himself. Right now he doesn't believe it....

Yes, I'll sit tight while you check them for the purple powder.... Chet, call me back when you've made the arrests.... Yes, of course. I'll keep him under wraps today until we have our proof. I'll wait for your call."

Paul Rausch hung up the phone receiver. His spirits sagged. Not only had the men stolen from the railroad again, but this time they had tried to frame *him*. How did the saying go? *With friends like that, who needs enemies?* They were being vindictive. Still, he did not like the thought of their going to jail, even if it meant recovering the money.

His wife looked at him. She read his thoughts. "You had to do it, Paul, for the sake of the children. It's going to be over. Chester Gritt will put them in jail, where they belong. They'll have to make restitution for their crimes, and we'll get our money back, enough to go visit Irene in California. Your part's over, Paul. It's over."

Paul was sitting at the kitchen table when he received the phone call from Chester Gritt at 2:30 that afternoon. "Not a thing," the police chief stated, "not a damned thing." Paul Rausch's brow furrowed. As Chester Gritt talked, Paul detected worry in the other man's voice. It was an unexpected development.

"I've been all over Waite Park," Chet explained, "to all of them... and more. Not one person has a trace of ink on his arms or hands. No one has skipped town. It's like the culprits have just vanished into thin air." He stopped to let the news sink in.

"So, what do we do now?" Paul asked.

There was another brief silence on the other end of the line. Finally Chet spoke into Paul's ear. "I have an idea. But Roy Steichel doesn't like it. He wants to see you tomorrow morning to discuss the situation."

"What's your idea?"

"Roy will try to talk you out of it?"

"Just tell me what it is! Let me decide if I'll do it."

As the police chief spoke into the telephone receiver, Paul Rausch listened carefully. Across from him sat his son, Jimmy, his arms stained with purple ink. Ione was sitting next to Jimmy, listening to Paul's end of the conversation. When Paul's eyes narrowed, she put a hand on her son's arm.

Paul saw his wife's action. He stared at his son. He saw the purple ink. Yes, it could work. It must work. There were risks, but he was willing to take them.

"I'll do it," Paul spoke into the telephone. You're right; the timing of the arrest is critical. We can't wait until tomorrow. If we're going to go through with it, we have to do it today, right now. We have to make it seem believable."

As he spoke, he saw his wife's hand squeeze Jimmy's hand. Her lips were pressed tightly together. She knew what he was thinking. She shook her head "no."

Paul ignored her reaction. He listened to the police chief's instructions. "Yes, I know what to do.... Alright, Chet, I'll see you in twenty minutes."

Paul Rausch hung up the phone. "Ione, I have to do this." The words hung in the air between them.

She squeezed her son's hand and released it. "I know."

Paul turned to his son. "Jimmy, I hate to ask you to do this. It's none of your business. But I need your help. I need you to be my accomplice. We stole those tools. They're our tools, but we stole them. We stole them from the railroad even though we gave them to the railroad. We paid for them, but we stole them. Chester Gritt is on his way over here to arrest us. We'll be spending the night in jail."

At this, Ione Rausch gave a sudden involuntary yelp. Paul looked at her and winced. "Does it have to be this way?" she asked.

Paul looked deep into her eyes. "I don't want to hurt you or Jimmy. But, yes, it has to be this way. Someone has tried to frame me. Now I want to know who it is. I've hooked a fish and I intend to net it. Will you help me, son?"

Jimmy Rausch stared at his father and nodded. "I'll do what you ask me to do, Dad, no matter what it is. Get ready. It's almost time to go."

Paul Rausch seldom cried, but on this occasion he felt tears in his eyes. He wiped them away with his sleeve. He stood up and walked around the table to his wife. He kissed her forehead gently. "Thank you, dear. How could a man be so lucky?" His spirits were bolstered. He was almost giddy as he put on his cap and jacket. He hated to ruin them, but he had to make it look good. They would have to be thrown away into the garbage can.

"Where are you going?" Ione asked him.

"To the garage," Paul replied. "Now it's my turn. I'll be needing that wire brush, Jimmy."

Ione stepped close to him. "Do you have to do this, Paul? I'm worried." He wrapped his arms around her and held her body tightly to his.

"Don't bring your clothes into the house," she told him.

"I have to," Paul disagreed. "It's what any thief would have done, any *unsuspecting* thief. I'll wash up in the basement and change clothes in the garage, but I have to come into the house and hang up my cap and jacket. And I have to come into the kitchen and sit at the table to take off my shoes." He squeezed his wife's hands. "It has to seem real. Remember, sweetheart, we're in this together. It's our money, our life!"

He opened the back door and skipped down the steps into the back yard. He angled toward the garage, to bathe his hands and arms in purple blood. He would be ready when Chester Gritt's police car pulled into the driveway.

Roland Becker knew when he received the phone call that the mission had been aborted. The call came from his son, Marty, the Black Prince.

There had been no crates delivered to the pickup point. He and a partner from the union had waited an additional fifteen minutes and then left. Roland notified his friend, Johnny Morris, at HAMMER TOOLS immediately.

"That's too bad," Johnny told him. "This was the mother lode. It would have been a great haul and a huge profit. What happened?"

"I don't know," Roland replied guardedly. "I'll have to talk to Howard."

By the time he hung up the phone, he knew something was wrong. He slammed down the receiver. He knew Chester Gritt was at the bottom of it. That bastard! He had meddled in Roland's affairs long enough. It was wearing on his nerves. But what could be done about it? What could *he* do about it? "But first, I have to find out just what happened," he said to himself. He picked up the telephone and dialed a number.

"Howard? Roland. What the hell happened?" There was a momentary pause. "Tell it to me now, Howard, and you'd better tell it to me straight."

As he listened, he clutched the phone tightly. The longer he listened, the tighter his fingers gripped it. He wanted to choke it and strangle it if he could. At first, Roland's face turned pale, then ashen, and finally it became flushed and turned red. He was furious.

"You disobeyed me, Howard," he snapped. "You shouldn't have done that. We'll have to sit tight and see. Don't panic, Howard. Sit tight and keep your mouth shut. It's all up to you now. If anything goes wrong, it'll be on your head. And if it does go wrong, Howard, I wouldn't want to be you."

Roland hung up the phone. He knew that what lay ahead would be a test of wills—his versus Chet Gritt's. He also knew it would be a battle of nerves. He could rely on Cortney and Herman. They were true marines, always faithful to the marine code of honor.

Roland Becker despised weakness in men. He couldn't trust Howard Kappas. That was his measure of the man. "Howard will break," he concluded.

His son entered the room.

"Marty?"

"Yes, Dad?"

"I want you to get a few supplies together for me."

"Sure, Dad."

"Here's what I want."

CHAPTER THIRTY-TWO

Paul Rausch did not show up for work on Monday morning. His absence was noticed by his fellow workers because Paul was never absent. If memory served them correctly, they could not recall when he had ever missed a day.

Inside the main plant, Al Seagar was busy vacuuming the crates of tools that had arrived before the Christmas vacation. He didn't know why. But he had been told by Superintendent Steichel himself to do so.

"Wear plastic gloves and put on this protective suit and these boots," the boss had advised. "And don't touch anything with your hands. Look for a purple dust. See? Right there. Like that. Don't let it come in contact with your skin. When you finish, throw everything into the trash." Then the boss had retreated into the office and shut the door tight. He had not reappeared.

Al Seagar obeyed the boss. He always did. He looked closely at the crates. He did see a purple dust on some of them, mostly along the edges. Al worked slowly and carefully. It was painstaking work. But the industrial model vacuum cleaner did its job. *Whoosh… Whoosh…* It suctioned up the dust, leaving the crates clean.

He did not touch any of them. He dared not. He didn't know what the purple dust was, but he suspected that it was contaminated. He didn't want to catch the disease.

Other men were coming into the building. They were curious. "Hey, Cigar, what's going on?" they asked, using his nickname. Al "shooed" them away, like the boss had told him to do. When he was finished with the job, he was supposed to inform the superintendent. Those were his orders.

"Ours is not to reason why. Ours is just to do and die," Al said to himself. Once again, his old military instincts were kicking in. He talked to himself often, repeating tidbits of wisdom he had learned overseas in the army. He remembered many little nuggets. But others seldom heard him. He liked that. He preferred that.

Outside, Paul's crew worked on a locomotive engine that had been damaged in a derailment. They knew what to do, even without the direction of their foreman.

Howard sat on top of the engine, removing part of a torn metal casing. He liked it up there. It was open to the wind and the sky, and it made him feel free. He enjoyed watching the hawks soar on high, up in the stiff winter breeze, gliding in circles overhead. Sometimes they chose not to make headway, but just tipped into the wind and floated, hovering over one spot. Perhaps they had detected a rabbit below them, a ball of fur with a white cotton tail, and were waiting for an opportune time to strike.

Howard looked out over the village. Waite Park had come into existence because of the railroad. The two were interconnected, two parts of the same entity: the heart that pumped the life blood through the arteries and veins and the body it nourished. It had a soul of its own. He liked the life there. It was his home.

Below, Cortney and Herman worked underneath the engine to repair damage to a wheel truck and bolster. The men were disassembling what was broken, piece by piece. Cortney was using a blow torch to cut through several twisted connecting rods. Eventually, the entire engine would be moved inside the main plant, where new replacement parts would be attached by the welders and sheet metal workers. "We take it off; they put it on," Herman said to no one in particular. Cortney was not listening.

"I wonder where Paul is. I wonder what's happening?" Herman stated.

"I don't know. I'm sure we'll find out," Cortney responded. The blow torch continued to make its deep cuts.

Howard Kappas spotted the patrol car first, coming from the west. From his vantage point on top of the disabled engine, he saw the flashing red lights blinking in the morning light. The patrol car was approaching at a rapid pace along 3rd Street.

"Hey, look at this," he called down to the men below. Cortney and Herman stopped their work to observe.

The blinking red lights zipped by, and then they turned left into the main entrance. The patrol car stopped in front of the administration building. Men throughout the yard watched the interruption. They stared impassively as Chester Gritt, shielding his eyes behind his sunglasses, opened the driver's door and exited. He slipped around the rear of the patrol car and opened the passenger door.

Paul Rausch stepped out of the vehicle. He was handcuffed, his wrists bound in front of him. He was wearing neither cap nor coat, only gray work pants and a flannel shirt with the sleeves rolled up. High above Paul, Howard noticed the deep purple stains on Paul's hands and forearms. He wondered how Paul had reacted when he realized the trap. He would have protested his innocence; that was certain. But who would believe him? The purple powder had done its job well. The stains on Paul's arms were irrefutable. The evidence was damning.

"He can burn in hell, for all I care," Howard muttered. He stared at the patrol car and sensed the irony. He could have been the one Chester Gritt was arresting. How the worm had turned!

For several moments, Paul Rausch looked around and surveyed the railroad's yard. His balding head pivoted atop his thick neck. His gaze stopped where his crew was working, and he caught sight of Howard. Paul dipped his head in a slight nod. Chet Gritt slammed the door shut and took hold of Paul's shoulder. He nudged him forward and guided him toward the administration building.

Inside Superintendent Steichel's office, Paul Rausch sat in a chair. The superintendent was feeling uneasy.

"Get those things off him," he ordered. Chester Gritt took a key out of his pocket and unlocked the handcuffs.

"Do they hurt?" the railroad boss asked. "I'm sorry, Paul, about this whole mess. I'm sorry."

Chet spoke up. "It's the way he wanted it. It was his idea to use the handcuffs and to turn on the flashers." Chester chuckled.

"He even wanted me to turn on the siren. But I told him 'no.' That's not what I would do when a man is already in custody. That would draw too much attention. It wouldn't seem real."

Paul Rausch agreed. "You're right, Chet. But I want you to make it look good. Don't be too gentle with me. Play the bad cop. Show a hostile attitude. Be callous. You don't like criminals."

"That's true," Chet replied. "I don't."

Roy Steichel stepped around his desk toward Paul Rausch and took off his glasses. From his back pocket he extracted a handkerchief and began to polish the lenses. "We've been friends a long time, Paul, our whole lives. We trust each other."

In that moment he looked at Paul squarely. "I don't want you to do this. There's too much danger involved... for you and for your family, both. Think of Ione. Think of Jimmy. Think of the rest of your children. What would they do if something happened to you... something bad? It's going to get ugly. What will happen when the workers find out that you are the enemy? That you've stolen from the railroad? When a man fears for his job, he becomes an animal. He's inclined to irrational behavior.

I don't know if I could live with myself for permitting it to happen. I can't let you do it, Paul. I can't let you do it to Ione." The superintendent paused and put his hanky away. He put his glasses back on.

Chester Gritt spoke up. "But what's the alternative, Roy? What else can we do?"

"We have an alternative!" Roy Steichel thundered. He turned to face the police chief. "We can *tell the truth*. That's our alternative. This was a sting; the crates of tools were a setup. But they failed to lure the thieves out; the fish didn't take the bait. We failed. But we tried!"

Chester Gritt spoke with concern; his voice was strained. "No, Roy, that would let them escape for good. Remember, they've stolen $18,000 worth of tools. What will happen to Paul's $18,000? It will be lost and never recovered. This is our one chance to get it back, our only hope."

The superintendent stiffened in his chair. His voice steeled. "Paul and Ione will never lose a single penny as long as I am superintendent of this railroad! The Great Northern Railway has insurance. We will file a claim for it. The insurance company will absorb the loss."

"But Mr. Hill won't like it," Paul responded. "He may take it out on us… on you."

There was a pause. "He doesn't like it," Roy Steichel admitted. "I spoke with him yesterday."

"Then let's go ahead with the plan," the foreman advised. "It can't hurt. Keep the hook baited. We may net a fish or two from it yet. If it fails, it fails. But I don't think it will. They're going to make a mistake. It's just my hunch."

The superintendent looked into his friend's eyes. He was deeply troubled. "But you can be hurt, Paul. And no one in Waite Park will like that you involved your own son in your crime. I disagree with this plan. I'm going to tell them the truth. They're good people. They'll understand why you did it."

"I don't want that, Roy! I don't want their sympathy. Don't you see? I want to retire with my dignity intact and my head up. I'm asking you to understand."

This time Chester Gritt was more subdued. "It's not right that the thieves get away with their crime. That will leave a bad taste in everyone's mouth."

Roy Steichel sat down at his desk and twiddled with his pen while the other two men stared at him. After some time he began to tap the end of the pen into his desk's top. "I don't want them to get away with it, either," he said finally. His anger was spent.

"So, where do we go from here?" he asked.

"To jail," Paul answered. "How much will the bail be, Chet?"

"Fifteen hundred dollars," the police chief stated. "A thousand for you and five hundred for Jimmy."

Paul thought a moment. "I'll have to have Ione withdraw it from the bank."

"No, you don't," his boss disagreed. "I'm covering it—personally."

A brief silence set in.

"No," Paul explained, "that wouldn't be real either. You work for the railroad. I've stolen tools out from under your nose. I've committed a crime, broken the law. You have to be on the side of the law, Roy. You can't condone a criminal, even if we were once friends. Now you have to be against me. Turn against me. I have to stand alone, even against the whole village if it comes to that."

Roy Steichel's eyes looked distant, far away. He was an educated man. "Just like in *An Enemy of the People*," the superintendent mused. Chief Gritt looked befuddled.

"It's a Norwegian drama by Henrik Ibsen," he explained. "In it, the town's doctor discovers that the water supply is poisoned. If the word gets out, it will ruin the whole economy. The people are afraid and turn against him. They shun him."

"Never heard of it." Chester shrugged, scratching his head.

The superintendent continued to look off into the distance. An idea formed. He stared at Paul. "We have to draw the real criminals out. This may do it. I'll call the men together at the beginning of work tomorrow morning. I'll inform them of what has happened and the impact it may have *on them*."

He paused. "It could get pretty rough, Paul. Are you sure you want to go through with it? We can still call it off and say that the fish didn't bite. I'll shoulder the blame."

Chester Gritt moved forward to the edge of his chair. He looked uncomfortable and concerned. He started to protest, but Paul Rausch cut him off.

"No, Roy, that would let them escape for good. Remember, they've stolen $18,000 worth of tools, Ione's money." He grinned at his friend.

Disarmed, Roy Steichel relaxed and smiled. "Watch out for yourself. You'll be on your own, alone. The world will turn against you."

"I have Ione and my kids."

"It will be rough for them, too. Do you want that?"

Paul Rausch thought for several moments, and then his face broke into a broad smile. "Rausches are a strong breed. We stick together. We'll manage."

Superintendent Steichel's lower lip was trembling. He stood up and walked around his desk and stuck out his hand. Paul stood up. The two men shook hands. "Good luck, Paul," the boss urged.

"I'll need it," Paul replied. The foreman clasped his friend's hand in both of his. The two large paws swallowed the superintendent's hand. Roy Steichel placed his free hand on Paul's forearm.

"You're not afraid your hands will turn purple?" Paul asked. He was still smiling. Then he let go.

Paul turned and folded his hands together as if in prayer. He held them out to be handcuffed. Chester Gritt stood up. "Make it look good, Chet. Snug them tight. Make it look real. It has to look real."

As the two men departed, Superintendent Steichel paced the floor, thinking deeply, preparing a short speech, deciding just what to say to his workers tomorrow morning.

On Tuesday morning at 9:00 a.m., Superintendent Roy Steichel stepped in front of a microphone to address his employees. They had assembled at his request in the central plant. He would deliver a speech to them. This was highly unusual and unorthodox, a break in the car shops' routine.

The content of his speech was unknown. But what had prompted the speech was well known. It had been bandied about since the previous day in whispers and in open discussions. Now the men in the room spoke in hushed voices, some with confidence and others with a hint of dread. All were curious. They eagerly awaited the details.

They gazed at Superintendent Steichel. He looked disturbed, like a man who had been forsaken. He spoke to them:

"I have called you all here this morning because I view us as a family. We have worked together, you and I, for many years. I started with the Great Northern Railway when I was a young man just out of high school. I'm not a young man anymore. This company has been part of me all of my adult life.

The railroad has flourished. I'm proud to say that I have been part of the Great Northern's success. So have you. And we have been compensated fairly for that success. Our reward is financial. But it's also the intangible satisfaction that comes from knowing that we have worked hard and done our jobs well. That feeling is what Waite Park was built on.

We are a family built on trust. For years we have worked side by side, trusting one another to perform the tasks necessary to repair the broken train cars and to build new ones. It's a mammoth task. Without a spirit of cooperation, we could not succeed. I have told you before that a man is only as good as the tools he carries. Now I add a corollary to that: You are only as good as the man standing next to you. It's critical that we respect the worker at our side, that we trust in his abilities and his judgment. It's vital that we get along."

Here, the superintendent paused. He surveyed the crowded room. So many lives before him depended on the railroad, over 450 men, and their wives and their children at home. What he was about to say would affect their futures. These men were depending on him to lead them, to ensure the prosperity they had come to know. He saw a deep concern on their faces. Their eyes stared up at him, curious about his message. They were loyal to him and to the company. They stood shoulder to shoulder, listening patiently to his words, absorbing them, assessing their impact and what it meant for them.

But what about Paul Rausch? The speaker's mind wandered briefly. He recalled his friend's warmth, his massive handshake, the sacrifice he had made for the railroad to preserve his honor.

Paul was a decent man. Roy Steichel's stomach turned in revulsion and knotted. It was difficult to think about what he must say next. How could he condemn betrayal among friends and then betray a friend himself? It was an irony, a cruel twist of fate. He didn't want to utter the words. But somewhere in a crevasse in his memory, he remembered Paul's plea: "Make it seem real, Roy. Make them believe you."

He heard his own voice speaking: "Something has happened to disrupt our family's harmony—something serious, something grave.

You may be aware that eleven days ago we received a shipment of new tools from HAMMER TOOLS—DEWALT power tools, the top of the line. You may have noticed the crates sitting here on the plant floor." Roy Steichel gestured to where they had been stacked.

"Three of the crates have disappeared. They were stolen last Saturday night." A sudden gasp arose from the crowd of listeners. This was shocking news. It was followed quickly by a buzz of disbelief that circulated throughout the room.

The speaker continued. "We suspected that this might happen. For several months now, management has been reviewing the record of our inventories and our payments. They don't match. Tools are missing. There can be only one explanation—theft. We believe that in the past two years over $18,000 worth of tools has been taken. That's a sizeable sum." Another gasp of surprise burst forth from the workers in the room.

"Yesterday, the thief was apprehended. Paul Rausch was caught red-handed."

"Purple-handed!" a voice interjected. This brought forth a twitter. The men shuffled nervously on their feet.

Superintendent Steichel ignored the interruption. "He had three crates in his garage. Chester Gritt arrested him before he could unload the tools. We believe he may have been selling them on the black market or perhaps to a supplier. That will be looked into upon further investigation." The crowd continued to stir. The superintendent listened to the reaction of the onlookers. He saw in their faces a brooding resentment and a twinge of anger.

"Under the direction of Waite Park's police chief, we devised an operation, a sting, to catch the criminal. On the Friday before the Christmas holiday, the chief spread a purple dust on top of the crates. The dust is powdery, nearly invisible to the naked eye. It does not wash off. In fact, just the opposite occurs. The dust contains a purple dye that turns into ink when it touches water, indelible ink. It stains anything it comes in contact with, including human skin and clothing. The stain will not wash off. It will only wear off in four to five weeks.

On Sunday morning Paul Rausch's arms and hands were smeared with purple ink. Obviously worried, he called Chester Gritt himself. When the chief questioned him, Paul protested his innocence. He still denies his guilt, but the evidence against him is overwhelming. No one else has come forward; no one else has the purple powder on his arms. Only Paul... and his son, Jimmy." The superintendent heard another wave of disbelief roll toward him.

"He, too, is under arrest. His arms and hands are covered with purple dye. It's evident that Jimmy Rausch was Paul's accomplice." Another gasp. The men in the room were shocked. How could a father drag his son into a crime?" The anger in the room was more pronounced, bordering on outrage.

"These are the facts as we know them. I'm sure more will come to light soon, after Paul and his son are questioned." The angry reaction was continuing to fester.

Superintendent Steichel paused. He let the conversations in the crowd play out until finally they died out, and he remained silent. He waited. The men, too, waited in silence. They could see that what he was about to reveal next was difficult to say.

"Paul Rausch was once my friend." Roy Steichel's voice was low and soft. "We were schoolmates here at St. Joseph's

Elementary and then in high school at St. Cloud Tech. It's painful to see our friendship dissolve. I don't understand his actions. I feel betrayed.

In America, our system of justice says that a man is innocent until proven guilty. Paul Rausch will have a fair trial. He has already posted bail and is out of jail, a free man. He has paid a thousand dollars bail for himself and another five hundred dollars for his son. I can't help but think that this money may have been gained unlawfully from the sale of stolen tools. I don't know for sure.

I am deeply disappointed by my former friend's actions. He has broken the trust I showed in him when I made him foreman of a work crew. I showed confidence in him and rewarded him for his years of service to the railroad. Paul's actions, deliberately chosen, have destroyed that confidence.

What I find most appalling is that he has brought his own son into his crime as an accomplice. Massive purple stains were found on Jimmy Rausch's arms, too. He helped his Dad lift the crates. This is a sinful deed. For a father to involve his son in such a dirty business goes against the Laws of Nature. The Fourth Commandment says that children are to 'Honor thy Father and thy Mother.' Paul's actions have brought dishonor upon himself.

I know the Rausch family well. I have known them all my life. I knew his parents. What would they think of his criminal acts? They would be heartbroken. What a painful, pitiable plight Paul has brought upon his family. How is his wife, Ione, taking this news? I'm sure she feels ashamed of her husband. I haven't spoken to her yet. But I wonder how she will cope when her husband and son are indicted, convicted, and sent to prison. This saddens me!"

Here, Roy Steichel stopped his speech and took off his glasses. He took out his handkerchief and wiped his eyes with it. Then he unfolded it and blew his nose. When he put the handkerchief back into his pocket, his eyes were dry. When he continued, he spoke more forcibly. Resignation had turned into resolution and determination.

"I am the superintendent of these car shops. I am a loyal servant of the Great Northern Railway. It is my duty to protect this plant and to safeguard it. Rest assured, I will do my duty.

I will not shirk my responsibilities, even if it means hurting a former friend. Paul Rausch will be prosecuted to the full extent of the law. I told you earlier that I feel betrayed. Perhaps you do also. After all, we are a family. We are in this together.

Yesterday, I spoke with Jimmy J. Hill on the telephone. He was not happy to hear the news. In fact, he was annoyed by my report. We spoke for twenty minutes. I told him that our reputation should not be blemished by the actions of one man. I told him that it's over. He did not reply immediately. At last, he stated that he would maintain his confidence in Waite Park's car shops and continue to support it. But obviously, that confidence has been shaken. I don't know. In this business there are no guarantees. I tried my best to persuade him. I asked him to treat us fairly.

Thanks to Officer Gritt, the stolen tools have been recovered. They were inventoried yesterday. But not by Paul Rausch! He has been in charge of the tool inventories for over two years. We figure that's when the thefts began."

At this point in his speech, Superintendent Steichel held up four sheets of yellow foolscap. "We found these in Paul's home. They contain lists of tools inventoried over the past two years. They don't match the inventories he submitted for payment. Paul Rausch is the one man who had the perfect opportunity to alter the inventories after the tools were delivered and before the railroad paid for them. So far, he is refusing to admit to his crime. I can see why: he's scared.

This shipment of DEWALT power tools was too lucrative to ignore. They had yet to be inventoried. Paul, himself, would have done that yesterday had he not been caught. How convenient it would have been for him! The tools would have been unpacked and put on the shelves, and no one would be the wiser. No one but Paul would know the exact count.

As of yesterday, I have relieved Paul Rausch of his duties— without pay. If he is convicted, his job will be terminated immediately. Until then, he is no longer welcome on these premises. I will not allow him in our midst. I expect that the court will require him to pay back the full amount he has stolen. Hopefully, he has the funds to do so.

In time, he will become an example of a man who has fallen from grace. He will be known as a tragic figure who let himself fall victim to greed. I ask you to bear with me and support me in this accusation. I will not let you down. We are a family. We must stick together to ride out this storm."

He looked out over the sea of faces. "Gentlemen, it's time to go back to work."

The speaker ended his oration with a wave of dismissal and stepped away from the microphone. He didn't know fully what impact his speech would have, but he could hear a low drone behind him as he walked away. The crowd of men stood looking at him as their leader. He was sure some were surprised by his words against Paul Rausch, not only by the words themselves but by the tenor of his voice. But the majority would understand it. He was the company representative charged with overseeing all operations. He had been stabbed in the back by a trusted friend. He could no longer call that man his friend. Paul Rausch was now the enemy of them all, and that included Roy Steichel. The superintendent was still their leader. They would rally around him and against Paul Rausch.

Of greater concern was what the superintendent had said about Jimmy J. Hill. In the discussions that followed throughout the day, the workers heard an alarm sounding. What might Jimmy J. Hill do? Close the car shops? That would be unthinkable—unpardonable! Their discussions were laced with anxiety and worry. They fretted.

As the day wore on, their anger brewed. If something so unthinkable happened, they could neither forget nor forgive. By the time the 4:30 whistle blew, their anger had mushroomed in scope and become full-blown. It was not without malice.

Streams of workers exited through the wire gates into 3rd Street. Several clusters formed as men grouped together and converged on Ma's Bar. They were not interested in drinking, but in talking the day's business out. Their exchanges grew heated. A few left in anger, but most stayed. By the time the others left the bar, a contingent of them had decided on a plan.

CHAPTER THIRTY-THREE

On the last Tuesday night of each month, Paul Rausch made a habit of going to confession. It was his custom to walk the six blocks to St. Joseph's rather than drive the car. The fresh air cleared his lungs, and the walk gave him time to think. It revitalized him.

This night was cold and clear. He had confessed his sins to Father Schumacher in good faith and said an Act of Contrition. In return, the priest had absolved him of the sins. Dutifully he had said his penance and then left the church quietly.

As he walked along 5th Street, Paul felt renewed. He was immersed in his thoughts, not quite attentive to the world around him. He did not see the headlights until it was too late.

Half a block west of the nun's convent, three cars stopped along the curb. A volley of men jumped out of the vehicles. They were wearing white hoods.

Paul felt the first blow hit him, a tire iron that struck the top of his head and carved a deep gash in his skull. He could feel blood, warm and moist, flow over his brow and into his eyes.

What followed was a Southern ritual that Paul Rausch had only seen in the movies. A dozen men attacked him. They grabbed his arms and threw him to the ground. He absorbed a multitude of kicks and punches, and he tried to cover his face.

He sought to catch a glimpse of his attackers. But this was impossible. They were dressed as Klansmen in white sheets. He could see only their hands; they were white.

Again, the tire iron descended upon his head. The blow made him feel woozy. "Thank God, I'm thick-headed," he mused to himself. It was grisly humor, and he covered his head with his arms to protect it.

This exposed his chest cavity. A sudden blow from a man's fist doubled him over. And then a torrent of blows rained down on his body. He fell to his knees and curled up on the boulevard, moaning in pain. Blood filled his mouth and throat. He could not swallow. The liquid flowed back into his lungs, and he began to gurgle.

One last boot dug into his cheek, and then the pointed toe of the same boot struck him in the ribs again and again. That was all Paul remembered, for as the boot sunk into his flesh the final time, he passed out.

Paul did not feel the soft touch of the woman. Sister Mary Bede found his body. She had been out on her evening walk and was going home. She knelt beside him and placed her ear next to his mouth. She detected shallow breathing and a faint wheezing. He was alive! She laid her head on the man's chest and felt his heart beating.

Sister rose to her feet and raced to the convent. "Call an ambulance," she shrieked. "A man's been hurt. He looks like he's been beaten up. He's lying unconscious out on the boulevard across the street. He may be dying."

Sister Anthony stood up. She raised the receiver on the phone to her ear and dialed the operator. "Delores? This is Sister Anthony. Call the St. Cloud Hospital," she ordered. "We need an ambulance." And then on second thought, she changed her mind. "No! Call the Waite Park Fire Department. Get a hold of Guilford Bartholomay personally. Do it NOW! Then call Chester Gritt. A man has been beaten to a pulp. He may already be dead."

She put down the phone. "Sister, do you know who the man is? Sister Bede?" She raised her voice. "Sister Bede?"

But Sister Bede was gone, back down the street, carrying an armful of towels and a blanket in her arms. When she reached the spot where the victim lay, she knelt down hurriedly.

Something was wrong! She cupped her ear over the man's mouth. He was no longer breathing.

"Oh God!" she exclaimed. "Please, dear Lord, don't let him die." *I must keep my wits about me* was all she could think of. As a member of her college gymnastics team, she had been required to take a course in basic first aid. But the training had been minimal. She tried to remain calm. What had they taught her? One... Two... Three... A... B... C... CPR, Cardio-Pulmonary Resuscitation. It was a new technique. *Breathe into the man.... Breathe for the man.... I must save his life if I can.*

Airway. She tilted the man's head back and took hold of his lower jaw. She pulled it open with her thumb pressed into his tongue.

Breathing. She took a deep gulp of air and filled her lungs. Then she placed her mouth over the man's mouth and blew her air into his lungs. She saw his chest rise slightly. "Harder," she told herself. She breathed again into his lungs. His chest rose further.

Circulation. She placed her hands on the man's chest and rocked forward over the spot. "Compress the chest," she told herself. "Harder. Thirty times." She counted fast. One... two... three... four... When she reached thirty, she took a deep breath and then exhaled into the man's mouth. She looked for the chest to rise. She took another breath and exhaled into him again. More compressions. One... two... three... four...

And then as she worked, she began to pray: *Our Father, who art in Heaven, hallowed be thy name. Thy kingdom come... Thy will be done...*

She was still praying in earnest when she heard the sirens. Their modulating sounds were coming her way. "Please Lord... please... please... don't let him die. I beg you!"

It was on the final breath she exhaled into the man's lungs that her prayers were answered. With a jolt, he gasped and he breathed. His chest rose and fell sporadically, and the man coughed and then vomited. Blood poured sideways from his mouth, but expelling the unwanted fluids gave his lungs room to take in air. She smelled the stench of the vomit. She didn't care. His chest began to rise and fall on its own. It was the most welcome sight she had ever witnessed in her life. The man was alive!

"It's Paul Rausch," Guilford Bartholomay told Sister Bede. He took hold of her hands; they were shaking. "You just saved his life. I was in church when I heard the call." He looked at her rather sheepishly. "I was in the confessional."

The young nun responded: "I prayed. I prayed that he might live. I prayed for his soul—and for mine. I have never prayed so hard in all my life."

Sister Anthony, the mother superior of the Franciscan convent in Waite Park, came up to her. "Sister Mary Bede, you are a brave woman. St. Francis would have done no more than you did. He was a man who helped those in need. She took hold of Sister Bede's shoulders; they were still shaking. She looked the young nun in the eyes. "And he became a saint!" She smiled. "Thank the Lord you were here."

The boy's father sat at the breakfast table, sipping coffee and reading the morning edition of the Minneapolis Tribune. As he read it, he liked to discuss the news with his wife. Frankie often listened to them in silence. Events in the world kindled his interest. Today a brief article describing the attack on Paul Rausch had been hastily prepared and included in the paper.

"They beat him up pretty badly last night when he was coming home from confession," the man related. He shook his head. "They were wearing white sheets and white hoods like the Ku Klux Klan. Paul was unconscious. They left him there, practically dead. One of the nuns found him."

"Which one?" asked the boy's mother.

"Sister Mary Bede." The boy's ears perked up. "Isn't that your teacher?" the father questioned. The boy nodded.

Today was New Year's Eve, another day of vacation from school. Frankie met his friend, Terry Joe, at the screen house. Long ago, they had destroyed its contents of ice balls. The boys had replaced the screens and pledged to Bill O'Brian that they would not take them off again.

Terry Joe pushed the argument of Paul Rausch's guilt. "My dad says that he's as guilty as hell. He says they caught him red-handed. His arms were covered in that purple powder. Three crates that he stole were in his garage. Jimmy Rausch was in on it, too." Terry Joe presented the evidence as facts.

His friend from across the alley countered these claims. "My dad says that Paul Rausch swears he's innocent. He believes Paul. He says that Paul is as honest as the day is long. He's known him since he and Mom moved here and built the house. Dad says Paul's a good Catholic. He doesn't think Paul would steal or lie. Besides, he had just gone to confession."

Terry Joe mulled this over. "If *he* didn't steal the tools, then *who* did?"

"I asked him that," Frankie replied. The boy looked up and squinted into the morning sun's light.

"What did he say?" Terry Joe asked.

"'Someone with a key.' He looked kind of suspicious when he said it."

Howard Kappas sat in the back pew awaiting his turn. He was having second thoughts. Should he go in or not? Perhaps he should leave while there was still time, before he regretted it, before he made a fool of himself.

His old preconceptions had returned the moment he set foot in the church. He remembered the darkness and the flickering of votive candles under the statue of Mary. Small red candle holders, perhaps two dozen or more, glowed beneath her feet.

Howard had debated with himself, long and hard. He was bothered by the direction the situation had turned. Paul Rausch had been beaten within an inch of his life. After four days, he was still only semiconscious. The men in white robes had knocked him senseless. He might even die. Thankfully, a sister from the convent had found him and had kept him alive long enough to be taken to the emergency room in the hospital.

Howard detested violence. He preferred to use sarcasm and wit to deliver a blow, not his fists and his boots. Somehow he felt responsible, and his conscience was bothering him.

Chester Gritt had been over to talk to him. "What can you tell me about Paul Rausch?" the police chief had asked. "What do you think of him?"

What did he *think* of him? That question from the chief had raised an alarm. What was behind the question? What did the man behind those sunglasses already know? Howard had nearly panicked. Roland Becker told him not to be alarmed, to stay calm. "Chester Gritt is just fishing, trolling the waters."

Recently, however, Howard had felt a change. People were looking at him strangely. Their comments were snide. They wondered about his new boat and how much it had cost. He felt their suspicions. It was only a matter of time before he would be caught and arrested. He was sure of it. This thought made him feel sick to his stomach.

A penitent, an old woman, exited the confessional, and another took her place. He was next in line. He felt nervous.

He looked up and saw the statue of Jesus hanging on the cross, surrounded on either side by his Mother Mary and by Mary Magdalene. *Greater Love Than This No Man Hath* said the words beneath their feet.

It had been a long time since Howard had stepped into the church. He was no longer practicing. But as he thought of the recent turn of events, he decided that there was no harm in playing both sides against the middle. A good gambler knew when to hedge his bets. His confession would remove any sin from his soul, if there was any sin, if, in fact, he even had a soul.

Father Thiel would understand. He was a card player. Howard knew him from the baseball diamond. Father Thiel seemed to be a level-headed man.

One thing Howard did remember from his time spent in the Catholic faith: the confessional was sacred ground. The priest was duty-bound to respect the sanctity of the sacrament. What was said in the confessional was private. It was secret. It could never be divulged. That thought comforted Howard Kappas as he rose from his seat and advanced toward the confessional. The woman ahead of him had exited and knelt in a pew to say her penance.

He almost changed his mind. He stopped in the center aisle that spanned the length of the church from the altar in front to the high double doors in the vestibule in back. The doors to the street stood to his right, securely closed. He eyed them. But then he proceeded on and opened the door to the confessional. He stepped inside and knelt down in front of a small rectangular window. Howard folded his hands. Moments later, the window slid back, and through a mesh screen Howard could see a small light shining within the priest's chamber.

He took a deep breath. "Bless me, Father Thiel, for they know I have sinned."

"Harvey heard an unexpected voice. "This is not Father Thiel. This is Father Schumacher."

"Where's Father Thiel?" Howard gasped. "He's supposed to be here. It's Saturday evening."

"We switched times," said the priest. "What are you doing here, Howard? You haven't been to church in years. You're not even a Catholic any more."

"Does that matter to God?" Howard challenged.

On the other side of the screen, the priest paused. "No, it doesn't, not really. Go ahead. Make your confession."

Harvey swallowed hard. "Bless me, Father, for they are going to catch me, and I'm sorry. I fear their wrath."

"But what about God's wrath?" came the voice from inside the priest's cubicle.

"Him too!" blurted Howard. His folded hands were shaking uncontrollably.

"Who might catch you?" spoke the voice behind the screen.

"Chester Gritt," Howard blubbered.

"What have you done, Howard?" the voice continued. It was now calm and probing.

"We've stolen some tools... tools from the railroad," the man admitted. He lowered his voice to a whisper. "I did it because I hated Paul Rausch." He almost choked on the words. "But I didn't want him beaten senseless. I never wanted him beaten up. Now I feel guilty because we're the ones who framed him. We set him up."

Father Schumacher paused. Then he spoke. "This is confidential, so don't be afraid. But you must tell me everything. God will forgive you if you are honest. He is a merciful father. He has his ways." The confessional fell silent.

"Stealing is a sin, Howard. It goes against the Seventh Commandment. You will need to make restitution—give back what you stole."

"Do I?" asked Howard.

"Yes, it's part of being contrite. Are you sorry for what you've done? To be forgiven, you must be sorry, truly sorry."

"I am sorry!" Howard exclaimed. "I told you that. But I don't want anyone to know."

"You must stop hating Paul Rausch. Jealousy and hatred go hand in hand. You have also broken the Fifth Commandment."

"I didn't kill anyone," Howard protested.

"But you have wished that he were dead; haven't you?" Howard was again silent.

"And you have borne false witness against him—letting him take the rap for your crime. That goes against the Eighth Commandment. Those men beat him up because you let him be the scapegoat. Are you sorry for doing this to him? You were the perpetrator." The priest paused again. When he resumed, he tried to sound encouraging. "If you are truly sorry, God will forgive you."

"I'm sorry that he was beaten up and is in the hospital," Howard replied.

"But are you sorry that you helped put him there?"

Howard Kappas considered this briefly and made up his mind. "I'm sorry," he declared. He tried to sound sincere. He was being truthful—to a point. He wasn't really lying, he told himself. A truth was a truth, even if it was only half a truth. "You can't fool God," he admitted to himself. "He knows what I have done." It was fair play to rationalize.

"I'm sorry," he repeated.

"Now say the Act of Contrition," the priest stated.

Howard had memorized the words on a card at the end of the pew. *"Oh, my God, I am heartily sorry for having offended you. And I detest all my sins because of..."* To Howard, they were just words, words to be rattled off, like they always had been.

When he concluded, the priest responded, *"Then I absolve you of your sins in the name of the Father, and of the Son, and of the Holy Spirit, Amen.* Go in peace."

Howard Kappas stood up. It was done. He stepped out into the nave of the church. The old women were gone. He knelt down in the back pew and raced through his penance. According to Church doctrine, that sealed it. He grinned. He had done it. His guilt was erased; he felt clean. When he left the church, he skipped down the steps, two at a time.

It was Saturday night. The five Rausch boys sat around the kitchen table. Their mother was gone to St. Cloud to visit their father in the hospital. She had sat by his side every day since late Tuesday night when he had recovered consciousness.

"Dad's been in the hospital for four days," Roger Rausch, a raw-boned youth, age nineteen, noted. "He even had to spend New Year's there. It isn't fair."

"No, it's not fair," his oldest brother, Tiny, agreed. "They hurt him; they hurt him bad."

"They could have killed him," young Frannie stated. He was a sensitive fourteen-year-old, whose feelings took after those of his mother.

"Dad's tough," his fifteen-year-old brother, Joe, grunted. He had his father's toughness.

"Mom comes home crying every night," said Jimmy Rausch. His arms were still marred with purple stain. "I can't stand it! She's suffering." He, like Frannie, was a sensitive young man.

Jimmy was the leader. He thumped his purple fists on the table, and the boards rattled. A strange light came into his eyes. "So, what are we going to do about it?" he thundered. "We can't let them get away with it." He scowled, and his hands clenched into blood-thirsty fists.

"No, we can't," his brother, Roger, agreed. He opened and closed his hands, and they, too, became bony weapons.

The two younger boys nodded.

"I'll drive," Tiny volunteered. He stood up. "Let's go now before Mom comes home."

"Who did it?" asked Frannie.

"His friends," stated Jimmy. His voice was filled with sarcasm.

"His friends?" questioned the youngest boy. "Who do you mean?"

"His friends at the railroad," Roger answered.

"He has no friends," Jimmy snarled. "He has no friends at the railroad. He has no friends in Waite Park. Only us. We're the only ones who believe him."

"What about Roy Steichel and Chester Gritt?" asked Frannie. "Weren't they supposed to protect him?"

"They didn't do it," Jimmy scoffed. "I don't believe they ever intended to." He glared at his brothers, full of hate for those railroad men who were cowardly enough to wear white hoods when they beat up his father. "But there will be hell to pay. Their sons will pay the price!" He struck the table another blow.

"It's Saturday night. They'll be over at Elmer's or at Pinor's or at the Colosseum or in St. Anna. *Wherever* and *whenever!* When we find one, we'll make him pay."

"KRISTALLNACHT!" read the headline on the second page of the Sunday edition of the St. Cloud Times. It was a reference to the Nazi raids of November 9th and 10th, 1938, upon the

Jews in Germany. The headline was designed to capture the reader's imagination.

Beneath the headline and the by-line was a small column reporting the previous night's attacks on juvenile males in Waite Park. Although there was nothing ethnic or anti-Semitic in the assaults on the village's youth, the writer intended to draw that parallel. The attacks did not seem to follow a pattern. There was no rhyme or reason to them, just wanton violence. Six boys had been taken to the St. Cloud Hospital. Two had been treated for cuts and bruises and then been released. The others had suffered broken bones: two had broken noses; one, a fractured cheek bone; one, a broken jaw.

No arrests had been made as of yet, but the chief of police, Chester Gritt, was investigating the incidents.

The boy's father looked up from his paper. "Kristallnacht!" he informed his wife. He could not help but notice a parallel. No, it wasn't ethnic, but it was an act of retaliation—in a war of revenge.

CHAPTER THIRTY-FOUR

It was now 1959. At St. Joseph's Elementary School the bell to start the new year's classes would ring in five minutes. Already, Sister Mary Bede's Second Grade classroom was buzzing. The children swarmed around her desk, encircling her. The girls in particular crowded next to her, anxious to hear her version of the incident. Curious, they did not want to miss a thing.

"Did you kiss him?" Gail Teigen inquired. She was their ringleader and self-appointed spokeswoman.

"No, I did not," answered Sister Bede. She knew what was on their minds. "I breathed for him until he could breathe for himself."

"How did you do that?" asked Gail. Collectively, the girls held their breath.

Sister smiled. "I put my mouth over his and breathed into it."

"Did your lips touch his?" the young questioner persisted. "Did you *press* your lips against his?"

"They did touch" was Sister's simple answer. "They had to."

"So, then you did kiss him!" the ringleader announced. Gail Teigen was bright-eyed, victorious.

Her friends gasped. As was often the case, they heard only what they wanted to hear. On the opposite side of the circle, Susanne Danbury clamped her hands over her mouth.

"No, I didn't," stated Sister. Her voice was uninspired, matter-of-fact. "I'm sorry to disappoint you. After I blew air into his lungs, I watched to see if his chest rose. Then I pushed down on his chest thirty times to pump blood into his heart and through his arteries." She demonstrated by placing one hand on top of the other and straightening her arms. Then she rocked forward.

"Did his chest rise?" questioned Irene Pressler.

"It did," said Sister.

"What would you have done if it hadn't?" the same young questioner wondered.

The teacher shrugged her shoulders. "I don't know" was her honest answer. "I would have prayed harder."

"The newspaper said you saved his life," stated a quiet female voice from the outer rim of the circle. It belonged to Abigail Hoganson. She had been speaking more often in class lately after finally coming to terms with her brother's death.

Sister Bede was pleased. "I had to try, Abigail," said the woman. "It was a Christian act."

"My grandma said she wouldn't have done it," stated Irene Pressler.

"I know a lot of Christians who wouldn't have done it," pronounced Gail Teigen. "And I'm one of them. Yuk! He's an old man."

"What did it feel like?" asked Mary Ambrose. "Did his whiskers rub against your chin?"

"I didn't feel any whiskers," answered the young nun. "I was just hoping and praying that he was still alive. And he was! Thank God. It was a life and death situation. You don't care about how it feels or how it looks. You just do it. I wanted him to live so very much. I prayed hard to our Lord, and it worked."

"Was it a miracle?" asked Terry Joe O'Brian.

"In a way it was," Sister admitted. She smiled at him.

"Sister, who were those men?" The question was asked by Jeanie Kovar. "Why did they hit him? And why were they wearing white sheets with white hoods and white masks? I've seen pictures of men like that in Mom's old magazines."

"They're men from the car shops," a young male voice from outside the circle interjected. It was that of Jonas Duane. "My dad tried to stop them before they did it, but they wouldn't listen to him."

"Which men?" asked Terry Joe.

Jonas spoke in earnest. "He knows, but he's not telling. He said that the men were worried about their jobs. He told Mom and me that they were 'protecting their livelihoods'."

"But how could they be doing that when they were hitting him again and again?" asked Terry Joe. "They almost killed him. That's murder!" He turned to face Sister Bede. "How could they do that, Sister?"

The young teacher shook her head. "I don't know" was all she could say.

The Friday afternoon meeting of the Knights of the Round Table was less than festive. Even Fat Frannie's voluptuous frame did not help. She tried. She wiggled seductively as she approached their table. "Hello, boys!" she greeted them. "What'll ya have... besides me?" That line usually brought about a big laugh, but on this day it failed her. They merely nodded to her and grinned half-heartedly, their teeth clenched together.

She brought a round of beers. When she bent over and set the bottles on the table in front of them, she nudged each man generously with her bosom. She paused just long enough to encourage the usual response. She would have played along and let them pat her for a moment, had they been so inclined. On this day they lacked the urge. "Something is wrong," she concluded. "Something is definitely wrong."

As she walked away, she exaggerated the sway of her hips. All for naught. Much as she tried, she could not coax the three men out of the doldrums.

"I'm not losing my touch, am I?" she wondered aloud to herself behind the bar. She looked at Herman Braun, his eyes tracking the movements of her rounded features. She smiled at him. "Don't be silly," she scolded herself. "I'm a curvaceous woman, and men who frequent Ma's Bar like that. It's good for business."

Of course, it had been a rough week at the car shops. Everyone knew about Paul Rausch. And everyone in Waite Park was tied to the railroad somehow.

Once the three knights were alone, the conversation turned immediately to the attack on Paul Rausch. "Paul's out of the hospital," Cortney informed them. "They sent him home yesterday."

"Did *you* beat him up?" Howard asked.

His two friends looked at each other and then down at their beers. "We had to, Howie. We had to join them to keep them off our backs," argued Cortney.

"That was a bad idea," Howard replied. He stared at Cortney and then at Herman. "Those Klan outfits make it look like the 1800s. That's why the North and the South fought the Civil War. Your little escapade is drawing attention across the state. It's bound to go national. It brings back memories of racial tension. The country is still going through that now. New laws are coming. Soon, everyone will eat in the same restaurant; everyone will drink from the same water fountain; everyone will piss in the same damn toilet. But it's mainly in the South. We don't need that attention up here—not in Waite Park.

What if you had killed him?" Howard continued.

"You can't kill him," Herman objected. "That head is as hard as a rock."

Howard ignored the objection and stared hard at Herman. "Then you'd have a full-blown investigation. Is that what you want? Big shot lawyers from Minneapolis would descend on us like flies on shit."

The speaker maintained his intensity. "It's escalating. Now the Rausch boys have gone on the warpath. They beat up over a dozen kids the other night."

"I know," said Cortney. "The guys on Tommy Stanton's crew had three of their sons beaten up. One has a broken jaw. Tommy's mad as a hornet. He says he's going to get even with the Rausches for breaking his boy's jawbone. Teddy never saw it coming. They jumped him out in the parking lot at the dance in St. Anna."

"Tommy was the leader of the attack, wasn't he?" Howard asked. Cortney Johanson just nodded.

Herman chimed in. "The newspaper said that Chester Gritt is investigating the incidents. I don't know about that; he seems to be dragging his heels. I told my oldest boy, Eddie, to watch out for them and stay out of their way. Six boys ended up in the hospital. If they do anything to him, I'll kill those Rausch boys myself."

"You see, it's escalating," stated Howard.

"Chester Gritt is suspicious," stated Cortney. "He was around last Monday night after work, looking at my truck.

He had a black light and shined it in the back and then in the cab. He didn't find anything."

"Mine too," added Herman. "He's a suspicious bastard."

"Good thing you had us wear those monkey suits," noted Cortney. Howard nodded at the compliment.

Then Howard shifted gears. "King Arthur is angry at me. I disobeyed him and defied his ultimatum. He's livid. He's threatening to hurt me if anything bad happens—if we're caught." Howard Kappas's voice dropped to a whisper. "It's making me jittery. He's a man who always keeps his word." Howard began to whimper.

"Who is he?" asked Cortney. "We should know in case he decides to come after us. Who is King Arthur?"

"If he decides to come after you, you won't escape him," protested Howard.

"That's more reason why we should know who he is," argued Cortney. He looked into his friend's eyes; he could see his friend's fear.

"Let us be the judge of that," Herman argued. He was perplexed by Howard's stubborn refusal to tell them. "We can take care of ourselves."

"No, you can't!" Sir Lancelot cried. He was distraught.

"Tell us, Howie," Cortney asked. His voice was mild and gentle. Ten seconds elapsed. "Is it Roland Becker?"

Howard's eyes filled with terror. "How did you know?" he blurted.

"I didn't know," said Cortney. "I just guessed."

By the time Howard Kappas stepped out of Ma's Bar, it was dark. He spotted his Buick parked a short distance away, facing east on 3rd Street. He fumbled in his pocket for the keys and extracted them. Several steps down the sidewalk, he passed under a street light in front of the building, its yellow rays casting a diffused light around him. He looked down as he walked. In the light's glow near the corner of the building, he spotted something at the sidewalk's edge. There, on the icy pavement lay a ten-dollar bill.

Howard chirruped. "It's my lucky day." For some odd reason, this thought bolstered his spirits and brightened his mood. Suddenly he felt gleeful. He bent over and reached a hand down to pounce on the stray bill, lest in a sudden gust of wind it blow away and disappear. He took it in his fingers.

At that precise moment a boot stepped down on the hand. It was a black boot with a pointed toe and a hard sole. The force of the boot had a man's weight on top of it, and in an instant the boot crushed a small bone in the little finger.

"Owwww!" Howard exclaimed. He tried to free his hand, but it was pinned down. His eyes saw a man in uniform: brown trousers with a black stripe up the sides. The man was wearing a heavy leather jacket. Pinned to the jacket was a silver badge. Howard looked up into the intruder's face. His eyes were met by the steely gaze of a man wearing sunglasses.

The officer of the law spoke: "You're busted, Howie." He lifted his foot off the hand.

"You busted my finger," Howie wailed. The tip of the finger hung sideways at an odd angle. "Look at it!"

"You were stealing the ten I dropped," the police officer countered.

Howie disagreed. "Stealing? No, I found it on the sidewalk."

The police chief persisted. "It's my ten. Let's have it."

"You dropped it on purpose," Howie complained, holding the injured hand in his free hand.

Chet Gritt grinned. He picked the bill from Howard's fingers.

"You're a dirty cop," Howard exclaimed.

"You don't need that finger to throw a curve ball. Of course, you never could throw much of a curve ball," responded the chief. "Maybe this will help."

"You're a son-of-a-bitch, Chester." When the policeman heard this, his grin widened from ear to ear, exposing his teeth.

The officer issued an order: "Let's go. Get in my car. We're going for a ride, a very short ride. We could walk, but we'll drive. There's someone who wants to see you."

Chet Gritt opened the back door of the patrol car and pushed Howard into the seat. "I won't handcuff you, Howie. It's such a short distance. But don't try anything silly. I'd have to shoot you."

They drove two hundred feet and turned left into the Great Northern Railway's yard. The gates were open. The police chief nudged the car into a parking spot in front of the administration building and stopped. He stepped around the car and opened the door. "Get out," he ordered. "The superintendent's been waiting for you for three hours."

"I'm expected?" asked Howard.

But Chester Gritt did not reply. He took hold of Howard's crushed hand and squeezed the fingers.

"Owwww!" Howard screamed in pain.

The chief tugged on the hand and yanked the man out. "Let's go. We don't have all night." He ushered Howard into the building.

Roy Steichel's office was at the end of a hallway. He was sitting comfortably at his desk when the office door opened. A second man was seated in a padded chair across the room.

When the two men entered, the superintendent motioned for Howard to sit in the chair to the right of the desk. It faced across the room. Chester Gritt took a seat near the door.

The room was dimly lit with only a small lamp in the corner illuminating it. Howard noticed the man across the room and winced. It was his foreman, Paul Rausch. It was the first time in eleven days that he had seen him.

Paul looked to be in tough shape. Howard stared at the man's face. Both of his eyes were still blackened, and his cheeks were bruised and discolored. His nose was swollen and dislocated, which forced him to breathe through his mouth. When Paul opened his mouth to breathe, Howard could see that several front teeth were missing. His lips, too, were puffy.

His large head was wrapped in a bandage that covered his forehead. His body sagged into the padded chair, protecting three broken ribs, and his left arm was in a cast that was held horizontal by a sling. Paul was holding a walking cane in his hand, resting it across one leg. He looked like a man who had been beaten by a vengeful mob, like a man who had been close to death.

"Well... well..." the superintendent articulated, "look who we have here." Howard was holding his bruised hand. "Did something happen to your pinky finger?"

Howard tipped his head in the police chief's direction and squeaked, "He crushed it under his boot."

"*Tsk...Tsk...* Now isn't that a shame," Roy Steichel commiserated. "Accidents happen all the time." He sounded sympathetic.

Howard stared at the man across the room from him. "Hello, Howie," Paul greeted him. "I've been waiting to see you for quite a while."

"What are you doing here? I thought you weren't welcome on railroad property." The speaker glanced at Superintendent Steichel.

"I'm fishing," Paul replied. "And I've hooked a fish. Now I'm going to net it and flay it and fry it in a pan of hot grease."

"I thought you were fired."

"No, Howie, I wasn't fired. I will be retiring, but not yet. This spring. I still have some unfinished business to attend to. He paused for a moment. "I believe you have some money that doesn't belong to you, a sizeable sum, $18,000."

"I have no money," Howard stated. He had anticipated this conversation long in advance. He was trying to sound calm and not waver. But his throat was dry, and it made his voice crack. His denial rang hollow.

"You see," Paul continued, "it's Ione's money, and she wants it back—all of it. You know how women are."

Howard Kappas gulped; he looked perplexed.

Paul saw the man's distress. "Let's just say she loaned it to the railroad."

"I don't have her money," Howard protested. He was trying to stall and buy time. He needed to think.

"That's too bad," the foreman replied. "I wish that weren't the case. I hope it's not true—for your sake."

Howard bristled. "What are you talking about?" he snapped. He must remain strong and convincing. "Do you think I stole those tools? Don't try to pin it on me."

"Oh, you had help," Paul continued, "your friends on our crew, Cortney and Herman. They, too, will be brought to justice."

"I don't know a thing about it," Howard protested. "Where's your proof? Where's your evidence? In court you need evidence to convict someone. You're just trying to trap me." The other three men were silent.

Superintendent Steichel spoke up. "Paul was in on the sting from the beginning. In fact, it was his idea. His and Chester's."

Howard listened. Now it all made sense. The more he thought about it, the more he recognized the signs of Paul's involvement in the sting: his excitement over the new power tools, his drunken charade at Ma's Bar, the fueling of Howard's own jealousy of him at the Christmas party, the flashing lights on the patrol car and the handcuffs when he was under arrest, the purple powder on his own hands and arms and on those of his son, Jimmy, his accomplice. Then there was Superintendent Steichel's speech, designed to turn the entire community against him. It led to his severe beating at the hands of an angry mob. Did he foresee that? Why had he risked it?

But his thoughts did not stop there. Had he really given Ione's money to the railroad? Their retirement money? $18,000? Impossible! This interrogation was all part of the setup. It was designed to make him confess. "Stay firm," he told himself.

Emboldened, Howard snarled with contempt. "I hope you fry for this, Paul, not in a pan of hot grease but in hellfire!"

Superintendent Steichel was stunned. He was a man who valued refinement and decorum. "*Tsk...Tsk...*" he uttered. "You will regret that wish. It's shameful. It not only goes against Christian charity, but it also goes against common decency. Heed this advice, Howard. You should learn to love your fellow man, not hate him."

"I'm innocent!" Howard asserted. His tone was becoming belligerent. "Are you going to arrest me? If not, I'm leaving. I'm through here!" He stood up. So did Chester Gritt.

"Sit down, Howard!" Superintendent Steichel ordered. His voice was stern. "*We're* not through with you yet." Howard sat down. His confidence was shaken by the authority in the man's voice. What was he hiding?

It was the superintendent's turn to state his opinion. He had waited three long hours for the opportunity. He spoke plainly. "Paul is sure that you're guilty. Look at him, Howard. Look at what you've done to him."

"I didn't beat him up," Howard defended himself.

"No, but you are responsible for it. You planted those crates in Paul's garage. You knew about the purple powder."

"Did you find any purple powder on me?" Howard interrupted.

"No, we didn't. You were careful, Howard. You're being careful now. But we know you stole those tools."

"How do you know?" Howard challenged. "Because Paul Rausch says I did? That's not good enough. That's not proof. It's his word against mine."

"Your word is no good."

"Ah, you're just fishing, trolling the waters, and you've come up empty." He repeated King Arthur's words. His swagger had returned.

"You stole those tools," the boss repeated. "We know it."

The four men paused, at a standstill. They had reached an impasse. The superintendent looked at Howard with disgust. "And to think I was going to make you the new foreman of Paul's crew because Paul vouched for your character.

Let's not waste any more time." Superintendent Steichel turned to Chester Gritt. "Bring him in."

The door to the inner office opened. A man stepped through the doorway into the room. He blinked hard several times to adjust his eyes to the dim lighting. Tall and stately, he was dressed in clerical garb. The man was wearing a long, black cassock that extended down to his shoe tops. Around his neck was a white collar, signifying that he was a Roman Catholic priest. The collar was a symbol, a sign of submission to God that had been passed down for centuries. He wore a crucifix on a chain around his neck. It hung down and lay upon his chest. In his hands he carried a rosary. While waiting to be called, he had prayed.

"Hello, Father," Roy Steichel said in greeting. "We're glad you decided to come. Sit down, Father, over here." He motioned to the chair to the left of his desk. It, too, faced across the room.

"Father Schumacher, I think you know these two men."

"Hello, Paul. Hello, Howard." His voice was thick and husky.

"What are you doing here, Father?" Howard Kappas asked. The look of fear in his eyes betrayed the terror he felt.

"I'm sorry, Howard," the priest admitted. "I don't want to be here, but I can't live with myself if I let this pass."

"But Father...," Howard rasped in disbelief, and then he fell silent.

"Tell us what you know, Father," stated the superintendent.

"It's difficult," replied the reverend.

"Just tell us what you told us," stated Chester Gritt. "We'll take it from there."

"You told them?" Howard Kappas rose from his chair. He pointed his index finger at his accuser. "You can't do this. You're a priest. The confessional is a holy place. Confessions are private between the priest and his people. The priest is the shepherd who guards his flock. He doesn't slaughter his own sheep. You used to preach that often; I'll bet you still do."

Father Schumacher sighed deeply. "I've thought it over, long and hard, Howard. I've considered all that you just said.

Believe me, it's true. I've prayed about it for nearly a week. When you left the confessional, I hoped you'd repent of your own free will. I expected you to come clean and turn yourself in.

I waited and I waited for six days. But you never spoke up. You never confessed, except to me. I can't, in good conscience, let you punish an innocent man with lies and deceit and your own foul hatred. I think you made a bad confession. I think you lied to me. I think you're still lying to yourself."

Howard Kappas turned his back on his confessor and faced the wall. That, too, was a symbolic act—of rejection and defiance.

Chet Gritt stood up. "Sit down, Howard, and look at the man."

But Howard Kappas did not sit down. When he turned back to face the priest, his face was full of anger. He spoke with indignation. "You can't do this to me, Father. It's against the Church's teaching. Confession is a holy sacrament. When you were ordained, you took a sacred vow to keep confessions sealed. Didn't you? Now you're forsaking that, Father. You made a promise to God, and now you're breaking your solemn promise. You lied to God!" Howard smiled wickedly.

Father Schumacher slumped in his chair. He held the rosary beads tightly, wrapped around his hands. No cross-examination could be more chilling, more damning.

"What will Bishop Hughes say when he finds out?"

"I've already told him," the priest answered. He looked tired. "I went to him and made my confession."

"And what did he say?" asked Howard.

"I'm being relieved. I'm no longer the pastor here at St. Joseph's."

Howard Kappas whooped. "That's a pity!" He spoke in a voice filled with sarcasm. For a long time he stared down at the man, and then he leaned forward. He intensified his accusations. He spoke with conviction and a determination to destroy the man before him. "You were baptized Catholic. Now you've abandoned your faith, the faith your parents gave you. You've broken a trust."

Father Schumacher sank lower in his chair, his spirit shattered. "I know," he said. "I've been the pastor here in Waite Park for over thirteen years, since the war ended."

Howard pressed his advantage. "If you go through with this, you'll be ex-communicated. Have you considered that?

435

The Catholic Church will sever its ties with you completely. You'll be cast out, like Judas Iscariot. The pope and the bishop will damn you to hell. They'll want to send a message to all sinful priests.

And what will the people here say? All your good work in the village will be wasted. You teach religion to the kids in the school; don't you? What will they think?" Howard looked at him as if he were a bug ready to be squished.

The priest raised his head to meet Howard's glare. "I know this, Howard. It's all true, every word of it. But I can't let you ruin a man's life. It's the choice I'm making."

Howard Kappas took two steps toward the priest and lowered his voice. "Who will ever go to confession to you again?" Father Schumacher cupped his hands under his chin and stared down at the floor. The crucifix of the rosary dangled between his knees. Howard drove home his final dagger. "The bigger question is "How will you live with yourself?"

"Leave him alone, Howard." Paul Rausch spoke. "He knows all that."

"But now *I know* he knows!" exclaimed Howard.

Chester Gritt stepped forward to intervene. "Sit down, Howard; you've said enough."

Pleased with himself, Howard sat down. How strange that he was both the accused and the accuser!

Chester Gritt took charge. "For the record, Father, what did Howard tell you in the confessional?"

Father Cornelius J. Schumacher raised his head and sat up straight. He looked at Paul Rausch and saw the pain in the man's face, not physical pain, but agony over what had just transpired.

Paul addressed the priest. "You don't have to tell us if you don't want to, Father. It will remain our secret." There was a pause. "We've agreed on this, Father. You can back out. Roy will call your bishop himself."

At this, Howard Kappas stared at the confessor in hope. Father Schumacher stared back; then he looked at each of the others.

"Howard told me last Saturday that he and some friends have been stealing tools from the railroad. He also told me that he placed three crates from HAMMER TOOLS in Paul Rausch's garage to frame him. He did this to shift suspicion away from himself and his accomplices. He also told me that he hated Paul

Rausch and was jealous of his promotion to crew foreman. He did say, however, that he was sorry that Paul was beaten up. He admitted these things to me freely and without coercion or solicitation. I simply listened.

I'm willing to testify to this, and I will do so in court. I know my duty to God's church, but I have a responsibility to God's people as well. They seldom conflict. I have had to make a choice, a difficult choice, a most difficult decision." He shook his head back and forth as he said it. "And I made it."

As he heard the words, Howard Kappas's jaw dropped, and he slumped deep into his chair. He fidgeted with his hands and began to whimper. He was a broken man.

He envisioned the worst and cried out in a high-pitched tone. "What can I do?" he bawled. "I have a family to feed. Where will I go?" He buried his face in his hands and cried openly, blubbering like a baby. His tears were real.

Howard lifted his head and looked at his foreman. "What made you suspect me?"

Paul Rausch took his time to answer. "Your spending. Waite Park is a small village. The people noticed things you bought— that Buick two years ago and a new boat last year. It didn't add up, buying fancy vehicles on a railroad man's salary."

Chester Gritt took over the floor. "We checked your bank account. I asked Florian Eickhoff to give us your statements for the past two years."

Howard's nostrils flared. "He can't do that. That information is confidential!"

"It's all there," Chester stated, "in black and white. That's evidence. That's proof," declared the police chief. "That's the proof you asked for." He held up several sheets of yellow foolscap. "Paul has the correct inventories right here."

Howard Kappas had nothing more to say.

Roy Steichel looked at the broken man. He felt no pity for him. Howard had attacked both Paul Rausch and Father Schumacher mercilessly and yet felt no shame. Roy's friend could take it. Despite his broken bones, he was a strong man. He was lucky. He still had his family to go home to, Ione and the kids.

The superintendent was not so sure about the priest. He was not so lucky. He had dishonored his religion and lost his parish family. He would become an outcast. Of greater importance was his spiritual well-being. Perhaps he was feeling that he had even sacrificed his soul and would be eternally damned. That belief could destroy the poor man's psyche.

"Howard Kappas, this evening in here you have demonstrated just who you are... and what you are worth to this company. Believe me, you have chosen a poor way to confess your guilt, attacking both your immediate superior and your spiritual father. No son could have chosen less wisely. If I were Paul Rausch, I would let you suffer and then rot in hell.

The Great Northern Railway intends to prosecute you to the full extent of the law. I spoke with Jimmy J. Hill personally on this matter. He agrees and has offered me the services of his own firm of lawyers." Howard Kappas's head sank to his chest.

Roy Steichel took off his spectacles and rubbed them with his handkerchief. When he finished polishing the lenses, he returned the hanky to his back pocket and put the glasses back on. Then he spoke casually. "Of course, no tools that belong to the railroad are actually missing." He stopped and rapped his knuckles on the desk. When Howard lifted his head and looked at him, he continued. "Paul has paid for them. He's out $18,000; the railroad is out nothing, zero.

Howard stared at him. "That's right!" He turned toward Paul and again saw the blackened eyes, the fractured cheek, the dislocated nose, the puffy lips, and the missing teeth. He cringed at the sight of the bandaged head, the broken ribs, the arm in a cast supported by a sling, and the walking cane in his lap. "I'm sorry, Paul."

They all heard the yelp. Father Schumacher laughed outright. He spoke. "It's true, Howard. We have to forgive our fellow man. It's a tenet of the Catholic Church. The Baltimore Catechism of 1941 teaches us that. But first, we must ask for forgiveness for ourselves. Saying you're sorry is only half of it." The room fell silent.

"And that goes for our fellow woman too, Father," Paul Rausch chided gently.

The priest looked into Paul's eyes. His bottom lip began to quiver. "That reminds me," he stated, "there's something I must do before I leave—someone I must talk to."

"Mary Magdalene was a good woman," Paul asserted. "She was ever faithful to Jesus."

"So is Marilyn Wojcheski, Paul. Don't fear. I will tell her so and ask for her forgiveness."

Superintendent Steichel took the floor. "As far as the railroad is concerned, we're not out *one penny*. Our insurance carrier has never been contacted. Paul and Ione have covered everything.

What about it, Chester?" Superintendent Steichel asked. All eyes turned to the chief of police. "You've spoken to Judge Frerick, I assume."

"I have," replied Chester Gritt. "I told him your idea. He has agreed to it in principle." The chief paused. "He will let Paul make the final decision. Paul, he's leaving Howard's fate in your hands."

Howard Kappas gulped and swallowed hard. He looked at his judge. His eyes pleaded for forgiveness. But his mouth was terribly parched, and he could not utter a word.

This time, Father Schumacher's laugh filled the room. It was the crazed laugh of a man who saw the irony of the situation. In the heated exchanges Howard had insulted Paul so viciously that it was doubtful that Paul would ever forgive him. How could he? Why should he? He had lost his life's savings. He and Ione would never travel. She would not see her sister, perhaps ever again. Strangest of all, Howard had no one else to blame; he had brought it all upon himself. Father Schumacher did not want to admit to himself what he was feeling: he wanted to see the criminal humbled, made to grovel and beg for mercy.

Paul Rausch took his time. He already knew about this turn of events. His friend, Roy Steichel, had let him know about it several hours earlier.

"Howie," this might just be your lucky day. I'm going to give you a chance to redeem yourself." Howard Kappas nearly jumped out of his chair. He dared not speak, but his eyes were alight. He leaned forward in anticipation.

"But you have to cooperate completely, or else Chief Gritt will have his wish and take you to jail and then directly to Judge Frerick. I'm sure the judge will not be amused to see you.

You see, Howie, I want to catch a bigger fish."

Howard Kappas's knees began to shake; his legs were restless, bouncing up and down on his toes. He wiped the palms of his hands back and forth on his thighs and squeezed them to try to stop the shaking.

"I want you to make a telephone call."

Suddenly Paul stood up. He pressed the end of his cane into the carpeted floor and hobbled slowly until he stood in front of Howard. Paul handed him a folded sheet of yellow foolscap.

Howard unfolded the paper. When he saw the number, he blanched. He looked up at Paul. "But he's going to kill me."

"Dial the number, Howie. Here's what I want you to say."

Howard dialed the number. A man's voice on the other end of the line answered. "Who is this?"

"It's Lancelot."

"Where are you?"

"I'm at home." He paused. "I'm alone. Kitty and the kids are gone to visit her mother."

"What do you want?"

"They've caught me."

"Who?"

"Chester Gritt."

"How did he catch you?"

"He has my bank records."

"He'll never find *my* bank records."

Howard began to cry. Paul smiled. That's a good acting job, he thought… if he *is* acting.

"Remember," he had instructed Howard, "make Roland drag the information out of you, one piece at a time. Frustrate him. Make him angry. I want you to make him sweat. He won't do it when he's on the phone, but he'll do it when he thinks about it tonight in bed."

"They're threatening me with five years in prison, unless I make a deal."

"What kind of deal?" Roland Becker was livid. He fought to keep his composure.

"They want me to tell them your name."

Howard could hear Roland gasp. The man on the other end of the line sucked in a mouthful of air and released it slowly.

"They say I'll have to testify against you."

Another gasp was followed by another slow release of air. "Are you willing to do that?" Roland Becker questioned sternly. "I've read that King Arthur expected loyalty from a trusted knight. So do I."

"But it's *five years*! Kitty and the kids need me. I can't be away from them for five years. That's forever. I won't do it."

"We're in this together, Howard. Don't tell them anything! It's all bluff. Do you hear me, Howard?"

Silence…

"Do you hear me, Howard?"

Silence…

"You're the only one who can point a finger at me."

"And if I do?"

"Don't tempt me!"

"What will you do?"

Silence…

"What will you do, Roland?"

"I'll kill you."

The line was silent.

Howard spoke. "I've taken out insurance. I guess I'll have to cash it in."

"That won't help you."

"I'm not talking about a life insurance policy."

"No? What then?"

"*Dummy packing slips.*"

The other end of the line went dead. Howard hung up the phone. "He says he's going to kill me." He looked at Chester Gritt. "I need you to protect me—and my family."

Silence…

"I need police protection!"

"I need those packing slips," said Chester.

"Not unless I have police protection. *They're my insurance.*"

Silence…

He looked from Chester Gritt to Superintendent Steichel to Paul Rausch. "Help me, Paul. Please help me!"

CHAPTER THIRTY-FIVE

"Let's go ice skating! Let's go ice skating!" The two little girls could not contain their enthusiasm.

"Dress warmly," their mother had urged.

The boy's two sisters, Jeanne and Mary, had dressed in layers. They had started at the bottom with warm woolen socks and long underwear. Then they had pulled on corduroy pants and snow pants. A cotton t-shirt covered the upper torso. It was covered by a warm pullover with long sleeves. They took turns zipping each other's jacket. To complete the outfit, each donned a woolen cap that tied under her chin.

Their mother inspected them. "Here, wrap these scarves around your necks. It's cold outside."

"Mom, help me put on my boots. I can't reach down that far," said Jeanne.

"Mine too," echoed Mary. "Oh oh... I have to go potty."

"Then go," her mother told her. The woman waited patiently. She was full of advice on this chilly night. "You'll have to take your jackets off in the warming house to put on your skates. Ask someone to help you. Lace the skates up tight! That will help keep your ankles strong and the skates upright. It's best if the blades are straight up and down. You don't want them to cave in." She demonstrated with her hands.

"Can we go?" Jeanne pleaded.

"Yeah, can we go?" her sister echoed.

"Follow your brother down there," said the mother. "I don't want you to get lost."

"How will we know when we get there?" asked Mary.

"You'll see it," said the mother.

"The fire!" Jeanne answered. Her eyes were bright in anticipation of the night.

"Follow me," said her older brother, "but not too close. I don't want you tagging along behind me."

"Dad and I will bring the boys along in a little while," their mother informed them. "Dad is outside, loading the tree into the truck."

"Don't forget these." She handed each of her daughters a pair of woolen mittens. "Put them on; they're warm." Both girls pulled them up to their wrists with their teeth.

The three children shuffled out the door into the night. They walked in single file. As they walked, they could see their breath, frosty under the street lights. The warm air from their lungs rose into the pitch black sky. The star-filled nights of the Christmas season were gone.

There's only a slip of a moon, noted the boy. It was a thin crescent in the western sky, and it reflected only a meager light from the sun. "The close end of the rink will be dark," he told his sisters, "dark and spooky."

The children walked past Jack Kertcher's house. It was dark and empty, as were most of the houses along the way. High up in the elm tree in the back yard sat a tree house. It, too, was cold and deserted. The boy noticed his sister, Jeanne, looking up at it as they passed by.

It was Saturday night, the 10th of January in the New Year, 1959, and the people of Waite Park descended on the community park. It was a long-standing tradition, once a year, and it served a dual purpose.

The primary objective was to dispose of Christmas trees. Each January the fireman built a huge bonfire at the west end of the community park's skating rink. Families brought their Christmas trees to the park. In return, each family member received a bottle of pop and a Dixie Cup of ice cream, free of charge. Everyone looked forward to the event.

The firemen heaped the trees twenty or thirty high before they lit the bottom layer. It ignited, and gusts of air fueled the flames, which shot upward in a riveting display. Blue spruces and pines and balsam firs crackled as they were devoured by the hungry flames. Their ashes floated skyward.

The second purpose of the festivity was to skate as a community. Guilford Bartholomay, the fire chief, was proud of his idea. Years ago, he had petitioned the village council to build a skating rink on the parking lot during winter.

"Let me construct it," he had offered.

The council members consented.

Since it had been his idea, it became his responsibility each year. He didn't mind, for it brought the people of the village together. Now he sat contentedly in the cab of Waite Park's new fire truck. He watched the fire burn. His son, Boomer, was afoot, organizing the feeding of the fire. Under the watchful eye of his father, the young man was being careful not to let it get out of hand. He circled the blaze, using a rake to sweep stray embers back into the fire.

Guilford had more than enough help. Whenever there was a need, the people of Waite Park worked together. Inside the warming house, volunteers handed out bottles of Orange Crush and Nehi Grape. They passed out the Dixie Cups of vanilla ice cream, which were provided by the local creamery, to every man, woman, and child. The people ate the ice cream, scooping it out with a wooden stick. The refreshments were complimentary, *funded* by the village through donations. That, too, had been Guilford Bartholomay's idea.

Mothers and fathers took turns supervising the warming house and helping small children tie their skates. They were also of service to hastily unzip jackets and remove layers of clothing when it became evident that the skater had to use the bathroom *in a hurry*.

The bonfire was a magnet that drew the people of the village to it. To some, it signaled the end of the Christmas season. But it was only a brief, nostalgic loss. The burning embers and furious flames energized them and propelled them forward into the new year. It encouraged them to start anew and to keep, perhaps, any New Year's resolutions they had made.

For many, skating was a release of that energy. People of all ages skated: sliders and gliders, steppers and slashers. They all swirled around the rink, sharing room on the ice.

Music blared from speakers attached to the warming house wall. They were lively tunes. Experienced couples skipped counterclockwise to the songs of the day. Still, an old tune, *The Skaters Waltz*, was always their favorite. The man took the inside position and cradled the woman's waist in his right arm; his left hand held her left hand, guiding it forward. They danced light-heartedly and stepped in unison as they pushed off until they could glide. They swept across the ice. At the end of the rink, they curved in a smooth arc until the turn was completed. Then, together, they sprinted a few steps and resumed the dance. The young couples held hands.

Children dashed about everywhere. The boys chased each other, and some of those who had not yet learned how to stop fell face-first into a snow bank at the end of the rink. Soon, they charged back the other way, playing tag. Later, when the rink was less crowded, they would play crack-the-whip.

The girls held hands and skated in pairs. They helped each other balance. Slowly one pulled the other along, often stopping to guide her partner in a two-legged turn. Both girls were waiting to be asked by a boy to skate. But that might not happen until later—when the fire burned low—if it happened at all.

"There it is!" screamed little Mary, pointing with her mitten. A great ball of fire rose into the sky. A strong light from the fire illuminated the west end of the rink. The east end lay in shadows.

"That's how the sun looks; only it's hotter," said her brother. "Hurry up! It's started."

When the three children entered the warming house, Tillie Kuchenmeister and Clarence Bruns were busy serving the refreshments. "Let's go skating before we drink our pop," said Jeanne. Otherwise, we'll have to stop right away and go to the bathroom." Her sister nodded.

The boy left them. He sat in a corner against the far wall and laced up his skates, black figure skates with a row of notches in the toe of each blade.

"Want a pop?" Clarence Bruns asked.

"Grape," answered the boy. The bottle cap was already removed. He chugged it down in two gulps.

"Want an ice cream?" Tillie Kuchenmeister inquired. "You only get one." He looked up at her. Always a woman of fashion, she was wearing her husband Harold's Russian Trooper beaver hat.

It looked like a furry dome on top of her head. "I haven't seen that little squirt friend of yours," she added. She was trying to make small talk.

"He'll be here," the boy answered, and he stood up and wobbled forward. His ankles weren't strong enough to hold his weight upright. He plopped down on the bench and re-tied the skates, pulling the laces as tight as he could.

He exited into the night. He looked at the bonfire. Thirty feet high and still roaring, it dominated the scene. A crowd of onlookers formed a ring around it. Perched at the edge of the fire, they watched as more trees were fed into its greedy mouth.

The warming house was situated at the southwest corner of the skating rink. A wooden ramp connected its metal door to the sheet of ice. The boy held the hand railing, pulling himself hand over hand as he worked his way down the ramp to the ice. When he stepped onto the frozen surface, he glided forward tentatively a few feet.

The rink was crowded. Small urchins on skates zipped by him, and one bumped squarely into him, nearly knocking him down. He pulled his mittens on tighter with his teeth.

Frankie looked for his friends. He spotted a group of his classmates huddled at the far end of the rink, and he skated toward them. At first, he skated slowly, gliding forward and testing his balance. Then he increased his speed. When he reached the group of boys, he grabbed a hold of Jerry Unger. He was not adept at stopping.

Just then Gail Teigen and Irene Pressler swished by. Good skaters, they turned the corner, stepping lightly with one leg crossing over the other. They were smooth and graceful. Irene waved to the boys as they passed by; Gail ignored them. The group of boys watched them, wishing they could skate.

"She's too good for us," Jerry Unger announced, and the other five boys nodded in agreement.

The two girls sailed by a second time, and a third. The boys watched. The fourth time that Gail Teigen came by, she was escorted by Freddy Schultz, one of Timmy O'Brian's disciples. He was three years older than the pretty girl. They were holding hands as they swept around the rink in unison. This time, she did not ignore them. She flashed her bright-eyed smile at them and curved sweetly around the turn.

Freddy Schultz did not mind. His friends were standing along the far side of the rink in the direction of the Moose Lodge. They whistled like wolves and called like cats. "Hey, Freddy, what's up?" they teased as the couple swooped by. Only a little embarrassed, Gail smiled broadly at them. Freddy Schultz grinned, and they continued on. At that moment she was his prize.

Frankie saw his two sisters emerge from the warming house. Hand in hand, they clumped down the ramp onto the ice. They skated together, clinging to each other as they moved slowly toward the shadowy end. His sister, Mary, caught sight of him and waved. "Hi, Frankie!" she cried. "Look at me. We're wearing our new skates. Whee!" Her sister pulled her along, and Mary kept her legs straight. Their brother gritted his teeth.

"There's your sisters," Jerry Unger stated. "One of them said 'Hi.'" And then the girls fell. They picked themselves up, laughing.

Next came Irene Pressler and Jeanie Kovar. Irene waved again. They glided smoothly around the turn and disappeared down the rink.

"Show-offs!" growled Jerry Unger. The next time he saw them, they, too, were being escorted by older boys.

The evening progressed. "There's my dad," said Frankie. "I'm going to watch them burn our tree." He left the group and shuffled gingerly along the ice. He navigated the crossing without falling. At the edge of the rink, he stepped into the snow and walked several paces toward the fire. Now he could feel its heat. The boy observed that the inside of the fire glowed red, rather than orange or yellow. It was hotter in the middle.

"Stay back," a voice told him; it was Boomer Bartholomay's. The boy took two steps back. But when Boomer moved on, the boy stepped forward.

The crowd of onlookers was still gathered around the fire. They watched in wonderment as the flickering flames shot upward and spluttered and popped. Some bystanders spoke to each other; most looked on in silence, entranced.

His father approached, carrying their balsam fir. For some reason, the boy felt uncomfortable watching it being thrown into the flames. It caught on fire and burned: the needles, then the branches, and finally the trunk. All were engulfed. He saw a message in the flames: it was time to move on.

"Let's play crack-the-whip!" Jimmy Holston yelled. It woke up the boys' interest. They grasped hands and dashed ahead in a line, each boy pulling the boy beside him.

The line of bodies rippled until suddenly Jimmy stopped and planted himself at the hub of a circle. He held on tightly. So did each boy in succession along the line. This created a centrifugal force, which accelerated the tail end of the line as it followed the trajectory of the circle's rim. The whip cracked! The line snapped as the boy next to last let go.

Frankie was the last skater in line. The force flung him forward at a great speed, away from the circle's circumference at an angle. In that instant he saw the huge bonfire ahead of him. It was as if he were shooting out of orbit into outer space toward the sun! But he could not control the acceleration. He spun out of control and crashed, landing with a thud and spinning on the ice.

"Yea!" shouted the others. It was great sport. The boy jumped up. "That was fun," he cried.

"My turn," said Jimmy Holston. "Your turn to lead, Frankie." And so the game progressed.

"That's little kids' stuff," taunted a boy in the distance. "Get out of our way." It was Jack Kertcher, skating hand in hand with the boy's neighbor, Jackie Birch. He was older but smaller, a pesky boy who liked to bully. Frankie didn't trust him. He looked quickly for his two sisters and spotted them at the other end of the rink. They now had their brother, Dan, in tow between them. Young Dan was trying to stand up on his twin-bladed skates while his sisters pulled him along.

"Where's Jeannie?" Jackie Birch called. "Where's Fatso?" She grinned at him over her shoulder as Jack Kertcher led her into the turn.

"She's a pig!" Jack Kertcher announced on the way back, and he looked her brother squarely in the eyes. Laughing, the pair skated off.

Frankie seethed in anger. "One of these times…" he said to himself, "one of these times I'm going to knock his block off, even if he is older."

He turned away in disgust. In the shadows at the edge of the rink, he noticed a young girl. He skated toward her and saw her turn away from him. It was Lucy Stephens. "What's wrong?" he asked her, but she did not respond. When she glanced at him, he saw that she was crying. He knew why.

"Forget about him," the boy urged. "He's no good. He's a bully."

"No, he's not," she cried out. She turned completely away from him.

"He's mean," the boy stated. "He always tries to push people around, especially people bigger than him."

"Just shut up," she retaliated. "And leave me alone."

The boy left her. In the distance he saw a large round head. Susanne Danbury was inching toward him. She was wobbling on her skates and barely moving. It was obvious that she was afraid of falling.

He saw her before she saw him, and he watched her slow progress. Her friend, Doris Kurtz, was pulling her along by the arm a few steps at a time and then releasing her.

Susanne slipped. She swung her arms wildly, rotating them like a windmill to try to keep her balance. First, they swung backward as she leaned too far forward onto the tips of her skates. Then, she overcompensated and had to rotate them forward quickly to keep herself from falling backward. In a panic, she reached out for Doris's arm and safety.

They drew near. Susanne saw him. She smiled, flashing her big white teeth at him. Suddenly she lost her balance again and stretched out her hand in his direction. She grabbed onto the boy's arm and steadied herself.

He pulled his arm away from her. "Sister says I have to stay away from you," he blurted. He looked at her meanly.

Feeling rejected, she pursed her lips and stared down at the ice, intent on avoiding his gaze. He saw tears in her eyes as she moved away over the ice. Doggedly, she allowed herself to be dragged by Doris around the ice rink, completing the circle.

The fire was shrinking. It had burned brightly for nearly two hours, but it had begun to starve itself. It had burned rapidly— feast or famine. It had not paced itself. Perhaps that was the world's way. Greedy consumption, satisfying its appetite. And then extinction.

That was just the opposite of what his mother preached. "Slow down.... Just a little at a time.... Save some for later.... Leave some for others.... Avoid excesses.... 'Don't drink so much... and so often,'" she had told her husband. Her son had looked up her word, *temperance*, in the big dictionary in the school's library. "Gluttony is bad.... So is sloth.... Get out of bed....

Don't waste time...." He had been studying these at school. In less than three months he would make his First Confession.

"The first shall be last, and the last shall be first," Sister Bede had told them. Jesus had preached self-sacrifice. But who did that in the modern world? The nuns, perhaps. Sister Bede, probably.

He watched the young girls skate in circles with the older boys. He wondered why they chose to do so.

It was time to quit skating; his ankles were tired. He found his sisters in the warming house, staring at Tillie Kuchenmeister's hat. "Let's go," he ordered. "And quit sucking on your mittens. They smell bad."

When they got home, they put their wet clothing in the bathtub. Their mother had dry clothes, underwear and pajamas, laid out for them.

"The girls in my class skate with the older boys," the boy informed his mother, out of the blue. She stopped hanging up their jackets and looked at him closely.

"I suppose they're experimenting," she acknowledged.

"Why?" he asked.

She saw that her son was bothered. "Girls mature faster," she replied. "Look at Dad. He's five years older than I am. It's nothing to worry about; you'll catch up."

Just then he pictured a girl with a big round head and flashing white teeth smiling at him. The image made him shudder. "I was just wondering. I'm not *worried* about it at all," he lied.

Frankie stood on the curb that was in front of Mr. Vanek's shrubs, kitty corner from Terry Joe O'Brian's house. He held two thin books in his hands. It was Tuesday afternoon, and school had been out for an hour.

His best friend saw him and strolled across the street, spear in hand. "Whatcha doin'?" Terry Joe asked.

"Waiting to catch the bus," his friend replied.

"I thought we can't do that any more. You promised your dad we wouldn't hook the city bus."

"I'm not going to hook it. I'm going to *ride* it. I have to go into St. Cloud every Tuesday after school."

"Why?" questioned Terry Joe.

His friend showed him the books. "Piano lessons," he muttered.

"What are those dots on the cover?"

"Notes of music. See that at the bottom?"

"Yeah."

"It's a keyboard. That letter 'G' with the shepherd's crook through it is the treble clef. It's for the high notes on the right side of the keyboard. You play those with your right hand. This backwards 'C' is the base clef. It's for the low notes on the left side. You play them with your left hand, mostly. I have to memorize the notes:

Every—Good—Boy—Does—Fine: E—G—B—D—F for the treble clef; Good—Boys—Do—Fine—Always: G—B—D—F—A for the base clef."

Terry Joe looked confused.

"E—G—B—D—F starting here two notes above Middle C. You go left to right.

G—B—D—F—A starting way down here, three notes and one octave below Middle C. You still go left to right.

"I don't get it," said Terry Joe. "Why are the two hands different?"

"I don't know," said the musician. "The problem is I can't read the notes fast enough. Every time I play E, I think Every. Every time I play G, I think Good. I wish I could just play the letters, but the words are stuck in my head."

"What's an octave?"

"Eight notes... eight white keys. Every eight white keys is an octave: A to A, B to B, C to C. The notes repeat."

"How high do they go?"

"To G. Count the letters to eight: A—B—C—D—E—F—G—A again.

"I *still* don't get it," said Terry Joe, scratching his head. "Why not just use the numbers, one through eight? Eight can be one."

"I don't know. That's not how they did it in the old days—Wolfgang Mozart and Ludwig von Beethoven and Johann Sebastian Bach."

Terry Joe grinned. "Funny names! *Wooolf-gang*... Lewd-wig... Yo-Han... Ha!" He chuckled.

"Hey, they're the names of the Kuceras in my diphtheria report. I guess they were common back then."

"Why do they have black keys?"

"They're the sharps and flats."

"Why are there two and then three?"

"I don't know."

"I'm *never* going to get it," said Terry Joe. He was starting to fiddle with his spear.

"Neither am I," said the musician.

"I hate going to Mrs. Neri's house. She's a friend of Grandma's. I have to give her six dollars each time and then ride the bus home; it's dark when I get back. I hate piano lessons. I hate Tuesdays; they're my worst days."

"Any guy who takes piano lessons is a fag." Jack Kertcher, haughty as always, marched up to the two boys. He looked at the piano books and suddenly knocked them out of Frankie's hands. He laughed maliciously. "You're a queer, Kucher."

The musician scrambled to pick up his books. The bus was approaching from the east. His nemesis reached to knock the books out of his hands again.

In an instant the younger boy reacted. It was a spontaneous movement that he did not think about. With a sudden burst of energy, he grabbed his enemy by the throat and flung him to the ground. He leaped onto him and pinned the boy's head to the ice in the street.

"Get off me," the smaller boy roared. But in that moment, the younger boy realized his own power. His mastery of his foe had been so rapid, so quick and easy.

The bus drew close, and the boy released his hold. He scampered to retrieve his books. The other boy stood up and rubbed the side of his head where it had hit the ice.

His bravado returned. "I'll fight you next Monday," he challenged, "at five o'clock. Come to my house. You know, next year I'll be bigger," he boasted. "You'd better watch out for me then, fag!"

The doors of the bus swung open, and Frankie jumped in. "Don't you know enough not to play in the middle of the street," Boomer Bartholomay scolded.

The boy reached into his pants pocket for fifteen cents change. Finding it, he deposited it in the metal box that registered paid fares.

"Next time, have your money ready," warned the driver, "or you won't be riding this bus any more." He wound the door shut. "Hurry up and sit down. You're making us late."

As the boy sat down, he looked out the window into the street. It was empty. He felt the isolation of the long half-hour ride into St. Cloud.

His emotions were mixed. He felt himself shaking like a leaf in the wind. He didn't like fights. But he had just learned something about himself. He would never again be afraid of Jack Kertcher, even if he was older. His victory had been so sudden and so complete. He now knew that Jack Kertcher's intimidation was just a cover up, a false bravado.

The date and time were set—next Monday at 5:00 o'clock. He balled his free hand up into a tight fist and gritted his teeth. He would keep that appointment. He would be ready to fight.

He sat in silence thinking as the bus started and stopped, picking up passengers and dropping them off. A cloudy thought suddenly cleared: he'll be bigger next year, but so will I! This realization bolstered his spirits.

The boy turned his attention to the upcoming piano lesson. He tried once again to memorize just the letters. But the words interrupted his thoughts:

E—G—B—D—F: Every—Good—Boy—Does—Fight.

G—B—D—F—A: Good—Boys—Do—Fight—Always.

He altered the words to fit the occasion. Still, he wished he could remember the notes without the words. Beneath his feet the motor of the bus hummed as it headed east along 3rd Street into St. Cloud.

The rest of the week passed. Monday arrived. All day the boy was nervous, checking the clock every few minutes. He could not concentrate on schoolwork. Sister Bede caught him day-dreaming. "Is something bothering you?" she asked.

"No," he told her. He would be glad when this day was over.

He spent an hour in the basement, breathing deeply and making fists of his hands. He practiced hitting the punching bag that his father had put up. He felt the power in his arms.

At ten to five, he blurted to his mother, "I have to go somewhere," and he leapt down the back steps. The temperature was mild, and he left his coat unzipped. He wore his black stocking cap but no gloves or mittens.

As he trudged the block and a half to his destination, he thought about his sister, Jeanne. He must be her protector, he decided. Once and for all, he would put an end to Jack Kertcher's insults. He would turn the tables and make the bully fear him.

Even Jackie Birch would see what kind of boy Jack Kertcher was. "Fatso..." Jackie would live to regret that word.

He arrived a little before 5:00 o'clock and stood on the boulevard across the street in front of Lucy Stephens' house. The Kertcher residence showed no signs of life.

The minutes passed, but no one emerged. Five o'clock came and went. The boy waited expectantly. Five-o-five passed and so did five-ten. He stood still, waiting patiently. But he began to wonder.

Five minutes later, the Kertcher's front door opened, and Jack stepped out. He bounced down the steps, and then he saw the boy across the street. If he felt any sense of alarm, he didn't show it. He swaggered to the edge of the yard and stopped, eyeing his adversary.

Frankie stepped into the street. His fists were clenched. He didn't speak a word, but his eyes were on fire. He felt utterly determined and strangely calm.

Jack Kertcher looked at the clenched fists briefly and chattered fluidly. "I can't fight you now. I'm going to a party and a dance. "Another time," he said smoothly with a flip of his head.

His opponent did not move a muscle. He stood there, still and stiff and ready.

The other boy stepped into the street. He turned away and walked jauntily up 12th Avenue toward the highway. Frankie watched him go. Finally he relaxed and unclenched his hands.

It was over. As he walked home, he breathed deeply several times to catch his breath. He grinned. It had not been a bloody fight, but he felt that it was a victory. The other boy had kept his cool, but he had backed out—*chickened out*.

The younger boy was proud of himself. He had stood his ground and showed courage. No one else had seen it, but inside he knew. *And Jack Kertcher knew*. If the bully ever again called his sister a pig, he would punch him immediately. He would crack him in the jaw with his knuckles. From this day forward, he was in control. He need never feel threatened by Jack Kertcher again.

When he reached his yard, he ran up the sidewalk to the back door. He entered the house and took off his jacket and cap. The kitchen was steamy, with a meatloaf baking in the oven and gravy simmering in a kettle on the stove. His mother was mashing potatoes. Her smile greeted him. He was just in time for supper.

CHAPTER THIRTY-SIX

Chester Gritt was the law. When he looked at Howard Kappas, he saw a desperate man. Howard was scared and for good reason. The police chief had lived in Waite Park long enough to gauge its people. That was a requirement of his job, and he was good at it. Behind his sunglasses Chet Gritt was a good cop.

He did not underestimate Roland Becker. He knew from experience that Roland was a man of his word. He had said to Howard over the phone, "I'm going to kill you." The policeman did not take it lightly, as an empty threat. Chester Gritt knew that Roland meant every word.

Chester understood the impact Howard's *insurance* would have. The dummy packing slips were lethal. With them, the case against Roland Becker and his friends would be sealed— lock, stock, and barrel. It was evidence that was incriminating and irrefutable.

The ring of thieves would crumble from within. No doubt, HAMMER TOOLS was involved. The packing slips would lead investigators to the inside source. He was sure that the ringleader at HAMMER would *sing like a bird*. He would be willing to make a deal. They always did.

Howard Kappas was walking on a tightrope, on a very thin line. The packing slips were his death warrant. Still, he dared not give up his insurance. Once the slips were out of his possession, he would be at the mercy of both Roland Becker and Chester Gritt. The two men wanted those packing slips badly.

Roland Becker, King Arthur, was the mastermind. He had that type of personality. Now that he was a wanted man, Roland would devise a plan. The police chief didn't trust him. He wouldn't put anything past him, and he expected the worst. As he left the railroad yard that fateful Friday night, Chet Gritt was sure Roland would try to keep Howard from testifying. His job was to prevent that from happening.

Thus began the longest journey of Chester Gritt's professional life. He had Paul Rausch at his side. Paul had volunteered to go with him and spell him when he became exhausted, when he could not continue on.

Chester Gritt was not present at the Christmas tree bonfire for long. He had stayed just long enough to drop off his tree. His nightly vigil had already started.

He knew that the hardest part of any vigil was the endless waiting. "In a way it's like fishing," Paul told him. "The fish is most likely to bite when you aren't tending to business, when you become discouraged and let your guard down. If you're not ready, it'll *spit the hook out*." Together, they hoped to catch the biggest fish of their lives.

So, they waited… and waited… for the fish to strike.

Every night, one of them watched Howard Kappas's house. Chester stood vigil the first night. After darkness enveloped the village and he made his nightly rounds, he drove home and parked the patrol car. Then he drove Loretta's old Ford Mainline sedan over to Howard Kappas's house on 11th Avenue. He had already arranged to park the car inconspicuously, four houses away in Henry Hecht's driveway on the corner.

Loretta had packed a knapsack for him with enough food to tide him over until morning. Each night, his first task was to inspect the goodies in the pack: sandwiches and fruit and cookies. He ate a ham sandwich. Then he poured himself a cup of coffee from the thermos she had sent along. It brightened his spirits on a cold night. He looked up at the moon, shining brightly down upon him. It would be full in four days. He hoped to catch his fish by then.

Chester stood vigil the first six nights. They were uneventful. He saw nothing more than a couple of lovers pausing for a goodnight kiss on the front stoop, Janelle Krueger and Wally Theen. Chet Gritt made a mental note. He would have to speak to Carl Krueger about is daughter.

It became a test of endurance. Despite the policeman's treating himself to a quick cat nap in the afternoon, fatigue set in. Paul Rausch sensed a growing weariness in Chester behind the sunglasses. He pushed to relieve him.

"I'll take the weekend shifts, starting tonight," Paul told him. "You can't go on this way, Chester; you need to rest."

The chief mulled it over. Finally he relented. "Don't try to take him by yourself, Paul, under any circumstances. Promise me that. If you see him, call me. I'll talk to Henry about using his phone. I'll tell him to leave the garage door unlocked so you can get into the house. The phone is in the kitchen."

The two men looked at each other. "He's a dangerous man, Paul. I wouldn't put anything past him. Be on your guard."

That night, Friday, January 16th, Paul Rausch sat and watched. He had stood on guard duty in the army, long ago during the war to end all wars. He knew that the mind played tricks, especially when a man was tired or bored. Ione had sent along his lunch box and a thermos containing his favorite drink, hot chocolate. To pass the time, he sipped on a cup of piping hot liquid and thought about fishing.

He loved to sit in the boat, rocking in the early morning waves. The *putt putt* of the motor, a 10 horse Johnson outboard, created a rhythm as it pushed the boat at trolling speed into the waves. It spluttered and gurgled as it labored to suck in water to cool the engine and then expel it through a slot in the shaft. The propeller twirled, pushing the craft along. Behind the boat he saw a small oil slick from the motor, diffusing the morning light in a prism of colors. Soon, Paul felt the sun's heat on his back, and he began to perspire. His flannel shirt soaked up the moisture.

The fishing line angled down into the murky water. The sinker, three feet from the hook at the end of the line, had taken the bait, a fathead minnow, to the bottom. The minnow wriggled on the hook and swam as it was pulled along. Eventually it tired and died of the wounds the hook had made. Sometimes, the minnow was lucky and had a quicker death when a walleye's teeth clamped down on it.

Paul Rausch waited patiently, sipping on his hot chocolate. It kept him warm on this January night. He sat with a warm woolen blanket over his shoulders and lap, his trusted old army blanket. Every two hours, he would start the car for ten minutes to warm the interior, four times a night: at ten, twelve, two, and four. At 6:00 o'clock his shift would end. After that, it wouldn't be long before the sun's rays peeked over the eastern horizon, up the hill where the soap box derby started. Of course, he was stationed down the hill, so it would take a few extra minutes for the dawn to break. He didn't mind; it was only a matter of time. He was retiring in four months. Then he'd have plenty of time on his hands.

He thought of Ione. What a woman! She was his faithful wife. He wanted to take her to visit Irene in California. She would like that. He owed it to her. He felt warm inside when he thought of her. Paul held the thought as long as he could. Then he turned off the car's engine and returned to his daydreaming, waiting for the fish to bite.

Nothing happened. The fish did not take the bait. Throughout the long night Paul Rausch sat in his car, fighting to stay awake. His cup was dry; the thermos of hot chocolate, empty. He dozed. When the sun awakened him, he drove home and went to bed.

Another day passed. He was on duty. He saw no sign of Roland Becker.

On Sunday night Chester Gritt relieved him, with the same result. The fish was not biting.

On Monday morning the police chief made a decision. He spoke with Superintendent Steichel. "Call Howard," stated Chester. "We have to turn up the heat on Roland. Tell Howard he's retiring early. Tell him to put the sign out in his yard."

When the superintendent of the Great Northern Railway called him, Howard was surprised. He had expected to be fired, but the news still came as a shock. He obeyed his boss and placed a metal sign in his front yard, pounding it into the ground with a hammer.

FOR SALE BY OWNER
CALL *BLACKBURN 2-3806*

Two days later, he attached another word to the upper corner: SOLD!

A second uneventful week passed. The temperature had dropped to ten degrees below zero. Chester Gritt sat huddled in his wife's car in a parka and an aviator cap, shivering. He had no idea how much longer he would have to wait or how long he could hold up. Perhaps another week... perhaps two... The sheriff's department from St. Cloud was helping him cover routine duties. But they would not agree to do this forever. He considered his options. Another week, perhaps... maybe two...

On Friday night Paul Rausch again took over the watch. Chester Gritt drove home exhausted and crawled into bed. He didn't even take off his boots. He was sound asleep before Loretta could pull them off, and he slept until the middle of the afternoon.

Howard Kappas had convinced his wife to pull the children out of school and go live with her mother in Fargo, North Dakota. He sounded desperate; she did not want to go. Finally he had broken down and told her the whole story. It was a bitter pill to swallow.

She broke down in disappointment. "Howard, how could you?" she cried. She wept, her tears flowing freely down her cheeks. Suddenly she screamed at him in anger. She could not help herself. "I want a divorce!" Then, just as suddenly, she crumpled to the floor, embarrassed. She could not look him in the face.

But soon, she lifted her head and gasped. She, too, knew Roland Becker and the vengeance he was capable of. "Oh, Howard," she blurted, "what will Roland do? I'm so sorry." She was afraid for him and fearful for the children. She agreed to leave. When she drove away, he didn't know if she would ever come back.

Inside the Kappas home, it was dark. Chester Gritt knew that Howard was holed up in his house, like a rat in a trap. He would be nervous, waiting for the cat to pounce. One afternoon Howard saw Roland's truck drive by. For a week he did not come out.

The neighbors wondered where the family had gone. And why? At work his co-workers became alarmed. "What's happened to Howard?" they wondered among themselves. "Why has he quit?" Rumors spread rapidly.

"What's wrong with Howie?" Herman Braun asked his companion, Cortney Johanson.

"I don't know," replied his friend. "I think the police are onto him." Cortney looked at Herman. "Has Chester Gritt talked to you?"

Herman Braun lowered his gaze and nodded. "He has. He wants me to make a deal."

"Me, too," Cortney responded. "I think we should take it."

Herman nodded again. "Have you seen Roland Becker?" Herman asked.

"No, he stays locked up in his office." Cortney looked hard at his friend. "Have you?"

Herman narrowed his eyes. "I have. He just stares at me." Herman fell silent. His words were disturbing.

Cortney Johanson lowered his voice. "Keep your eye on him," he advised. "Don't turn your back on him. Once he gets Howie, he's going to come after us."

On Saturday, January 24th, Clifford Kucher took his wife, Pat, on a jet to New York City. It was her 30th birthday. They were thrilled and full of high expectations. They were looking forward to a week of fun and frolic in the *Big Apple*.

Of course, the man was excited. Despite the stolen pelts, he had enough mink to sell at auction. He wanted to see the Hudson's Bay Company for himself. It was an old establishment with a history. In the fur business it was the pinnacle. He was curious to see his mink on display, to talk to the buyers as they inspected the pelts, to glean from their opinions suggestions on how he could improve his herd. He wanted to hear the auctioneer's voice rising to a higher pitch as the bidding escalated. He hoped for high prices. If the sale went well, he would have enough money to pay off his loan from the Production Credit Association and still have a handsome profit left over. He had waited a full year to see his first paycheck.

The sale would take three days. His mink would be auctioned off in twenty minutes. While it was going on, his wife would take in several Broadway shows. In particular, she planned to see two musicals: *The Music Man*, starring Robert Preston, and *West Side Story*, featuring the musical score of Leonard Bernstein. She had told her friend, Lil Trellwick, all about them.

She was curious to see 5th Avenue and its expensive shops. Later in the week, they would window shop together, arm in arm, like young newlyweds, and then make their way to their hotel, the Waldorf Astoria, to dine by candlelight and to talk about their dreams.

Wife and husband would try to forget about their children. The five of them would be at home, tucked into bed, under the watchful eye of Georgianna Pfappenstein. If she decided to use her *Give a dog a bone...* method of discipline on their oldest son, that was her prerogative.

Chester Gritt had not shaved in three days. He looked at his grizzled appearance in the mirror. With his sunglasses, it was almost comical; without them, it was. The third week was passing without incident.

On Friday morning, the 30th day of January, he went home to sleep. Paul Rausch would be on duty that night. Good old Paul! What would he do without him?

Chester Gritt had made up his mind. During the afternoon he called Roy Steichel. "This is the last weekend. This is it. If he doesn't make his move soon, I'm going to put Howard in protective custody in the jail in St. Cloud. He'll have to stay there until his trial."

"Howard won't like that," the superintendent noted. "He may burn those dummy packing slips before you arrest him."

"I know that," stated Chester. "It's a chance I'll have to take."

"He's living in that house like a wild animal. At least Kitty and the kids are gone."

"No one's safe over there. I feel it in my bones." The policeman hung up the phone and then picked the receiver back up. He dialed a familiar number. "Paul?"

"Yes, Chet?"

"If the fish doesn't bite by Monday morning, I'm going to arrest Howard—for his own safety." The police chief sounded pessimistic.

Paul Rausch was more optimistic. "He's going to swallow the bait," Paul insisted. "I'm certain of it."

Paul Rausch began his watch on Friday night at the usual time, 10:00 o'clock. He checked his watch frequently. Time passed by slowly. He fought to stay awake.

By 1:00 o'clock the late night traffic had thinned. Before long, the streets were empty, and the avenue outside of Howard

Kappas's home was deserted. Paul could not keep his eyes open. Even thoughts of fishing did not keep him awake.

He thought about his crew: Howard and Cortney and Herman. How proud he had been of them—until now. Good workers all. What was it about human nature that made a man steal? Love of Money? Was it really the root of all evil? Did it always have to turn his head?

He thought about his injuries: the blackened eyes, a broken nose and jawbone, a fractured cheek, three broken ribs and a broken forearm. Now he limped with a cane.

But he would recover. "Heal thyself," the priest had preached to him from the pulpit. But he was tired. He must find renewed strength to stay awake.

Paul did not see the sun rise. He was awakened by a sharp rap on the driver's seat window by Henry Hecht.

Wake up, Paul!" Henry called to him. He continued to tap on the glass.

Paul Rausch opened his eyes. The sun was already high in a blue sky.

"Gertie wants to go to church," he explained. He gestured with his hands as he spoke. "Her car's in the garage. You've got her blocked in."

Paul turned the key in the ignition and backed into the street. He still saw no signs of life on the avenue. Today was the last day of the month. He was weary. "One more day," he said to himself, "just one more day."

That evening Paul planned to go on duty early. He ate supper, a hearty portion of meatloaf and fried potatoes and then an oversized piece of banana cream pie. It filled him up. Ione would send a second piece of pie with him in his lunch box.

He lay down on the bed for a short nap and pulled the covers over him. They were warm. He felt cozy as he snuggled under them and drifted off to sleep. He set no alarm. He had instructed Ione to wake him up at 9:00 o'clock; he was trusting her to do so. He closed his eyes, and within minutes he began to snore. A few seconds later, he was sleeping deeply, peacefully.

Ione Rausch came into the bedroom at precisely 9:00 o'clock. She was about to sing out when she looked down at her husband. She stole to his bedside. The poor man! My loving husband...

She looked at his broken body and assessed his injuries. They were pitiful. How could they do this to him? It was an unpardonable act. He had chosen to *go fishing*, as he put it, to bring the guilty to justice. And he had paid for it dearly.

She heard him snoring softly. He was sleeping soundly for the first time in weeks. She would let him sleep a little longer, until 9:30. Then she would wake him.

"I'll lie down beside him," Ione said to herself, and she crawled into the bed, next to him. "He's my husband, and Lord, I do love him."

Soon, she too was fast asleep.

It's mere speculation what would have happened had Lillian McManus not had insomnia. Lillian and her sister, Luella, had grown up in Waite Park. They were identical twins, who had married local Irish boys.

Lillian and Michael McManus had produced and raised three sons and one daughter. The sons were typical lads, good-hearted but rather ordinary. It was the girl, Shannon, who brought life into their household. *Oh, but she was a lively Irish lass!* What her father was most proud of was that his daughter had been blessed with fiery red hair. That and her ability to tell a good Irish joke had endeared her to him. She was quick-witted. Michael McManus doted on her. Shannon had him wrapped around her little finger.

She had graduated from high school at the top of her class. The boys chased after her. The world lay at her feet. Still, she found herself called in a different direction. One day, she announced that she was joining a Catholic convent, the Franciscans out of Little Falls. Her parents were overjoyed; they were as proud as peacocks. The name she was given was Sister Mary Anthony. Her father wished it were more Irish. She was a school teacher by trade, newly-assigned to St. Joseph's Elementary in Waite Park. She came home! After five years in the classroom, Father Schumacher induced the school board to name her the school's principal.

Lillian's sister, Luella, had married Timothy Mayberry, the son of the local barber. She had been swayed by his beautiful tenor voice. And he loved to dance. They had but one child. Luella had given birth to a wee baby girl. They had christened her Loretta. By the time she was one, she too had a shock of red hair. Her parents sent her to St. Joseph's to be schooled. But the girl did not listen well and tended to be wayward. She had no intention of joining a Catholic convent, like her cousin did.

So, her parents were not surprised when she left them one day and hitchhiked to St. Paul. She wanted to try a fast-paced life. There, at a party, she met the man of her dreams.

The party goers were noisy and raucous. They disturbed the neighbors. Someone called the police. When the police arrived, Loretta Mayberry found herself under arrest. A girlfriend had handed her a bottle of beer. She was underage. She had not cared at the time.

She stared up at the young arresting officer. He was wearing sunglasses. "You can't arrest me," she stated. "I was being quiet... and orderly... and..."

"And what?" he asked.

"And my dad's the son of an Irish barber." Suddenly the room blurred, and she melted into his arms. "My, you're a big strong man!"

He arrested her anyway. But he liked her shock of red hair. And he liked how she had talked to him with her ridiculous sense of humor. And he liked how she had fallen into his arms.

Six months later, he asked her to marry him. They became engaged. Aunt Lillian found them a house, a rambler down on 13th Avenue across from the Little League ballpark.

"Now find him a job," her sister told her.

"What does he do?"

"He's a cop."

Neither Chester nor Loretta knew it, but Lillian McManus had been the deciding factor in his securing employment as Waite Park's chief of police. She had put pressure on her husband, Mike, who was a member of the village council. He, in turn, had pressured Amos Borg.

Amos Borg had been against it. Amos would never change his mind voluntarily. But Crystal Borg could change it. She had been *crystal clear* in her decision. "Let him have the job," she had ordered. "*Or Else!*"

He had not asked her "*Or Else What?*"

"And I mean it!"

He knew she meant it. So, he had relented. "But he always wears those damn sunglasses," Amos had objected. "I like to see a man's eyes."

"You mean the *whites* of his eyes," she corrected, "before you shoot."

Loretta had inadvertently spilled the beans. She told her mother, and her mother told Lillian. "Keep an eye out for anything suspicious," Luella had whispered to Lillian in secret. If you see anything, call."

"I don't go out of the house much, not in winter, but I'll try," her sister had promised. The only house she could keep an eye on was the house next door. Her picture window faced north. Usually she kept the drapes closed.

For years since Mike's death, Lillian had avoided sleeping in their bedroom. It had too many painful memories of him. She had taken to lying down on the sofa in the living room. She stored a blanket and a pillow in the closet. She seldom slept; she mostly rested.

On Saturday, January 31st, the last day of the month, Lillian McManus lay dozing on her sofa, half-asleep. It was a quiet night with half of a waning moon showing. The sky was filled with stars. She wanted to see them, so she had left her drapes open and only drawn the blinds part way.

She couldn't sleep. The boys next door had returned just after midnight. Their cars were parked in the street. Through the blinds she saw the lights come on in the house. An hour later, they blinked off.

Lillian was lying on her sofa, thinking of her daughter, Shannon. The little girl was playing on her father's lap, trying to remove his wedding ring from his finger. She was leaning forward, her red locks falling forward into her face as she worked; but she could not dislodge the ring. Her father laughed at her frustration. "Come on, Daddy, let me have it," she had begged. So, Mike McManus had twisted the gold band from his finger and given her the ring.

Lillian recalled the scene fondly. She was trying to remember just what had happened to the ring when she saw lights flash along her living room wall. They were patterned after the blinds in the window, and they moved along the wall above the sofa from left to right. The lights vanished.

Lillian sat up. She stole to the picture window and stared outside into the night. She looked toward the street and saw a truck at the end of the driveway backing into the street. There it paused momentarily as it shifted gears from reverse into forward. Then the truck lurched and disappeared from sight.

At that moment her big grandfather clock sounded. Its chimes startled her. "Three o'clock."

She peered out the window. Next door, all was dark and quiet once again. In the meager light of the moon, she saw that the garage door was closed. She considered what to do. She would chance it! She would snoop.

Lillian put on her robe and then her slippers. Quietly she opened her kitchen door in back and slipped into the night. She trembled at her boldness.

Several steps brought her to the neighbor's garage. It was locked. She decided to try the service door. As quiet as a church mouse, she tiptoed along the side of the garage to the door. It was unlocked. She pushed it open, just far enough to see inside. The garage was empty!

Lillian pulled the door shut and retraced her steps. Safely back in her kitchen, she took hold of the phone and dialed a number. Her hands were shaking with excitement and trepidation. She took a deep breath to calm herself. Shannon and Mike would be proud of her.

"Luella? This is Lillian. I've just seen something I think you should know about."

Loretta Gritt was sound asleep when she heard the telephone ring. She managed to pick up the receiver on the third ring. "Mother, why are you calling at this hour? It's after three a.m."

Her husband stirred beside her. "It's Mother."

"Hang up the phone."

Then she stopped and sat up. "What?" she exclaimed. "Are you sure?"

"It's Mother. She says she just received a call from Lillian. Roland Becker's truck has just been driven out of the garage." She switched on the nightlight.

Chester Gritt sat bolt upright in bed in an instant. Hastily he threw on his uniform: sunglasses first, then trousers and a shirt. He disregarded his stockings and pulled his boots onto his bare feet. By the time he buckled his belt, he was moving toward the back door. He grabbed his jacket from a hook in the hallway and disappeared into the night.

Loretta heard the engine start and the gears grind as he threw the patrol car into reverse. He pushed the accelerator to the floor. The car raced backwards, and Chester jammed on the brakes.

He flipped on his headlights, punched the accelerator down, and headed north.

Halfway down the block, Chester reached sideways into his glove box and pulled out a gun's holster. Strapped inside it was a police handgun, a .45 caliber revolver. "Just in case," he said to himself, "just in case I need it."

"Don't do anything, Paul," he said to himself. "Don't do anything until I get there."

Inside the house, Loretta Gritt watched her husband go, tearing away down the avenue. She picked up the phone and dialed a number.

Two blocks away, Ione Rausch woke up. She heard the phone ringing. She looked at their bedside clock. "My God, it's three o'clock. Who could be calling at this hour?"

And then she saw Paul's body asleep beside her. Oh My God! He's missed his shift.

"Paul!" she yelled. "Paul! Wake up!"

She picked up the phone. "Who is this? ... Loretta? What's wrong? What's happened?

Oh My God! ... No, he's not there. He's still here."

Paul Rausch rolled out of bed and stood up. He was wide awake and roaring. "What's wrong? What's happening?" He looked at the clock.

"It's after three o'clock," he bellowed. "Where's Chet Gritt?" His concern showed on his face.

Ione answered him. "He's gone—down to Howard Kappas's. He's gone to make an arrest."

Paul Rausch did not need time to dress. He was still in his clothes from the evening before. He reached down alongside the bed for his shoes, found them, and put them on. He would have to tie the laces later. He grabbed his jacket and lumbered out the door to the garage.

He started the car and backed out. "Three o'clock," he muttered, as he stepped on the gas and headed north. "And a fish is on the line."

He drove to the end of the block and turned right onto 5th Street, and then one block later turned left onto 10th Avenue. When the vigil began, the police chief had advised him to use this alternative route to avoid detection.

After one more block Paul turned left again and coasted down the hill. He stopped half a block away from the Hecht sisters' residence and doused his headlights. Chet Gritt's patrol car was nowhere in sight.

Paul exited from the car and hobbled down the alley. He could move only slowly with his cane. Four houses in, he veered left across Albert and Alma Mauch's back yard. Paul inched closer to their house and squatted behind an evergreen bush. Safely hidden, he peeped between the branches.

From this vantage point, he could not see Roland's truck. He knew that it must be tucked out of sight in the alley behind Howard's garage. One man was standing in the shadows in Howard's front yard. The other, a young man, was carrying a five gallon can. He was busy working, pouring a liquid from the can onto the siding of the house just above the foundation. Paul watched him disappear briefly around the side of the house. The older man waited. He stood in silence beside an elm tree, surveying the scene, on the lookout for signs of trouble. He was wearing a heavy leather bomber jacket but no cap.

Soon, the young man returned from around the far side of the house, holding an empty can. He nodded to his partner that all was ready. The stage was set. All that was needed was one final act.

Paul Rausch tensed as Roland Becker took a pack of cigarettes out of a pocket in his jacket. Roland tapped the bottom of the pack, and several cigarettes popped forward. He extracted one and put an end into his mouth, holding it between his lips. Then he reached back into his pants pocket and found a box of stick matches. He took out one of the matches and turned the box on its side, preparing to strike the match on the box.

Paul Rausch blinked hard. He knew what was about to happen. He knew that he must act. As Paul Rausch rose to his feet, he saw Chester Gritt emerge from the dark shadows of a neighboring porch.

Roland lit the match and touched it to his cigarette, sucking strongly in quick bursts until the cigarette lighted. He puffed several times, and then he inhaled the smoke deep into his lungs before letting it pour out through his nostrils. All the while, the stick match burned brightly in his hand. He took another puff and raised the match....

"It's over, Roland," Chet Gritt stated. "Blow the match out." The police chief paused. Then he spoke again. "The penalty for attempted arson is less than the penalty for arson and murder."

Roland Becker looked at Chester Gritt. He reached casually into his pocket. Then he saw the handgun in the police chief's grasp, pointed at his chest, and he heard the hammer click. He blew the match out and tossed it into the snow away from the house. He looked across the street at a man hobbling with a cane toward him. Roland snarled. The man, Paul Rausch, was holding a shotgun. "Don't tempt me, Roland. Please don't tempt me. I hate it when I have to go to confession."

"Where did you come from?" asked Roland.

"I've been on a fishing trip," stated the former knight. "And I've caught a big fish. I'm afraid, though, that it's only a bullhead, a slimy old bottom feeder! I won't eat that."

He continued to speak. "You asked me where I came from. I'll tell you where I'm going. You see, Roland, now I'm ready to retire... this spring. I'm going to take Ione to California to see her sister. He smiled, revealing several missing teeth. "And you're going to help me pay for it."

Just then the front door of Howard Kappas's house opened, and a man emerged. "I see you caught him," Howard stated. "But why did you wait so long? You almost let him burn down my house!"

"We had to let him swim all the way to the boat before we netted him," Paul Rausch explained. We needed hard evidence, incriminating evidence. Now we have it."

"Why don't you use his bank records?" Howard asked. He addressed the chief of police.

"Oh, that would be inadmissible in court," replied Chester Gritt. "Bank records are private; they're protected by law."

"But you have my bank records," Howard protested. "You asked Florian Eickhoff for them!"

Chet Gritt grinned. "We did. And he refused to give them to us, refused absolutely. He told us that they are confidential, even more confidential than what you tell a priest in the confessional."

He turned to his soap box derby foe. "Come on, Roland, let's go. You're under arrest. But first, I'll take that gun that's in your pocket." The mastermind stared at the police officer and grunted. Finally he withdrew his hand from his jacket pocket and complied.

Chester Gritt acknowledged the receipt of the gun. "Thank you; that was wise. To be honest, I was expecting a different ending. I've been reading about the legend of King Arthur and the Black Prince. They didn't get along."

Waite Park's chief of police, Chester Gritt, handcuffed Roland Becker and his son. "You stay here, Paul, and keep Howard company. Howard, get those dummy packing slips for me—now! If you don't, the deal's off. I'll release King Arthur here and the Black Prince. My guess is that you won't live until morning."

Roland Becker snarled again, this time more savagely.

Howard began to shake. "You can't do that," he protested.

"Try me. I may even give him back his gun." Howard shuddered.

"He's bluffing," said Roland, "but I'm not. Believe me, I will kill you. I'm a man of my word." His voice was full of arrogance and disdain. "You betrayed me, Howard."

"I'll get them," stated Howard.

"I'll wait for them," replied the chief. "Go with him, Paul. Keep an eye on him. *And don't light any matches*."

Howard returned with a satchel. He had hidden his insurance slips in the chimney of the fireplace, where they could be burned at a moment's notice.

Chester Gritt and his two prisoners walked to the patrol car, parked one block to the west. When they reached the car, he pushed them into the back seat. He shut the door and climbed into the driver's seat. He placed his gun conspicuously on the dashboard. "I still know how to use this," he admonished them. "Only fools don't heed warnings."

Having said this, he started the engine and let it warm up for a minute.

Finally Roland spoke. His voice was resigned but betrayed a morbid curiosity. "How did you know we were here, Chief? Every other night, you or Paul were parked in Henry Hecht's driveway. Why not tonight? Why did you suddenly show up at three in the morning?"

Chester Gritt gasped in disbelief. "So, you knew we were there all the time."

"Of course, we knew," Roland Becker hissed. "We were one step ahead of you—until tonight. Howard didn't sell his house. Come on, Chief, you're not playing ball with an amateur."

Chet Gritt grinned beneath his sunglasses. "Neither are you," he answered. "Let's just say you were done in by *The Snoop*."

On that note, he switched on the patrol car's flashing lights, and then he flipped on the siren. The time was 4:00 o'clock, time for the villagers to rise and shine.

Roland winced, showing his annoyance. "Do you have to do that?" he growled.

Chet's grin broadened. "For you, Roland, it's a pleasure."

He put the car in gear and drove back to Howard's house.

Slowly he passed by it. The house was empty, deserted. He didn't know that Paul Rausch had invited his old crew member home, where he could watch over him and calm his fears.

Chester Gritt drove the patrol car up 11th Avenue with the siren blaring, announcing the most recent news. Lights along the avenue switched on in its wake. The patrol car surged up the hill, crossed 4th Street, and continued up the next hill to 5th Street, which intersected it one block before the highway.

As the car crossed 5th Street, it woke up a couple who had just flown in that day on a jet from New York. Frankie's mother and father awakened at the wailing of the siren.

"What's he doing that for?" asked the wife. "It's four o'clock in the morning."

"I don't know," shrugged her husband. He was tired and had to get up early.

"He shouldn't be using the siren," his wife persisted. "It'll wake everybody up." She raised herself up and looked out the window as the patrol car flashed by. She craned her neck to see it. "It looks like it's stopping at the Rausches. I wonder why."

"Go back to bed, Pat," he urged her. "We'll find out in the morning."

The following Tuesday morning Chester Gritt and Paul Rausch met with Roy Steichel in the railroad superintendent's office. "The word has gotten out," stated the superintendent. "Your siren has spread it far and wide." Chester merely nodded behind his sunglasses.

In the post-mortem, the railroad boss posed a question: "How did Roland Becker know about your nightly vigil? I wondered about that all day Sunday and yesterday."

Chet Gritt had the answer for him. "Nora Hecht. She couldn't sleep with a strange car parked in the driveway. She went to her doctor, Dr. James O'Keefe, and told him about it."

"Sounds Irish," said the superintendent.

"He is," stated Chet. "He's friendly. Likes to tell stories. Likes to talk. When he heard the symptoms, he prescribed a laxative, his standard treatment for hypochondria. It worked like a charm. She's been sleeping like a baby ever since.

Here's the fascinating part. It just so happens that James O'Keefe is also Roland Becker's doctor. Nora met Roland in the waiting room. He was very cordial to her and eager to listen to her complaint."

"Where did you hear this?" asked Roy Steichel.

"From Henry Hecht. He likes to talk, too."

The police chief continued with his report. Much had happened since Sunday morning. He ticked through the latest developments:

"Bail for Roland Becker and his son, Marty, has been denied. They're being held in custody in the St. Cloud jail.

The preliminary hearings for Howard Kappas, Cortney Johanson, and Herman Braun are scheduled for next Tuesday. Judge Frerick expects he will honor their plea bargains. He wants to expedite their trials to save face for the railroad and the village.

Howard's insurance, the dummy packing slips, has been a gold mine. It's led to a bust-up at HAMMER TOOLS and the arrest of Johnny Morris, Roland's counterpart at HAMMER. They were boyhood friends. Some of the men at HAMMER will likely escape prosecution. They're union men and extremely loyal to each other and tight-lipped. All that "*Semper Fi*" mumbo jumbo. The same with Cortney and Herman. Without their deals, I don't think they would have talked.

Howard Kappas is selling his house! Kitty and the kids are moving to Fargo. He hopes to join them when he's freed from jail in a year, if she'll take him back."

Paul interrupted. "We had a long talk Saturday night. We're on speaking terms."

"I hope so," Roy Steichel interjected. "I think maybe he's starting to see the good in you. Although it's possible that he's just kissing your behind because you still hold sway with the judge. You're holding all the cards."

"It's possible," agreed Paul.

Paul had something else on his mind. "Say, Chester, I've been wondering where you were hiding. I was behind a bush right across the street, and I never saw you until you came out of hiding. Suddenly you just appeared."

Chester Gritt sat back in his chair and put his hands behind his head. "Stan Kovar and I built a little duck blind on his porch. We nailed it together, and I put dabs of silicone on the hinges so they wouldn't squeak. Now I'm almost out of silicone; I'll have to order some more. It pays to plan ahead and be prepared."

Paul Rausch laughed. "I didn't know you were such a handyman. I could use a good man like you on my crew. There are a few openings at present."

"No thanks," said Chester, holding his hands up with the palms out. "I'll stick with the job I have. Besides, I'm afraid of heights."

"How much additional time will having a gun in his pocket cost Roland?"

"Another year. Now he's looking at five years; his son, two. It's going to hurt him."

"I know," said Paul. "We all have sons."

Chester Gritt looked at his watch and stood up. "I've have to go," he stated, heading toward the door. He left.

Paul Rausch and Roy Steichel stood up and looked at each other. "Paul, I have some news to share with you." Roy paused and took off his glasses. "I'll be retiring with you this spring."

Paul looked at him in shock. His friend's lower lip was trembling.

"Jimmy J. Hill is closing the car shops here in Waite Park." He paused and rubbed a tear from his eye with his fingers. "Keep it under your hat, will you? I know you will. Thanks. You're my good friend, Paul. I'll hate saying goodbye to you. I'll miss you."

CHAPTER THIRTY-SEVEN

The recent trip to New York with his wife had awakened the man's primordial urges. Early on Saturday morning, a week after their return, he nudged her in the ribs to wake her up. "I'm going fishing… to Mille Lacs. I'm meeting Len at Shorty's at eight. I wonder if Frankie wants to come along." He obviously was thinking of increasing the size of his limit.

"Did you ask him?" his wife asked.

"I'll do it now," he answered. He rolled out of bed and stepped into his pants. He left the light off so she could sleep. "Leo's feeding the mink today."

The frozen lake was vast, stretching for miles to the north, east, and south. Large windswept patches of snow covered its surface. They formed patterns and formations that changed constantly when the wind blew and more snowflakes fell. By 8:00 in the morning, the early risers were already gone, out on the lake. They followed paths that had been plowed through the snow drifts by the resort owners to the fishing holes. Some areas were popular, and *tent cities* of fish houses dotted the bays along the shore and out over the Mud Flats in the middle of the lake. That's where the man and his son and the man's brother were heading on this day.

Shorty's was already busy with fishermen buying minnows, shiners and fatheads that were stored in large aerated tanks. Others used night crawlers, long worms that surfaced on Minnesota lawns after a rain. Of course, it was still too cold to collect them now, so these anglers had to buy them. Some preferred leeches or wax worms threaded onto small hooks, as bait.

Most of the early-morning fishermen already had enough fishing gear. But a few of the sportsmen new to angling purchased new equipment. They bought short wooden poles with an ice pick lodged in one end. Jabbing it into the ice kept the fishing pole upright. Shorty sold them spools of line on which they tied swivels and leader line, and he sold them sinkers and bobbers that they twisted onto the line. Multiple-colored lures and hooks and bobbers hung on the back wall of the shop, enticing the customers to buy.

The boy's father bought four dozen fatheads. They were hardier and lasted longer than the shiners. The boy and his uncle waited in the truck.

Frankie's father drove onto the ice. They followed the road that had been plowed by Shorty's sons, and six miles later they saw a small village of ice houses. By now, the sun was gleaming in the sky. The driver stepped out of the cab and zipped up his coveralls. He looked up into the morning sky and nodded to himself. It promised to be a clear, sunny day.

They unloaded the back of the truck. The father busied himself, untying the straps that held the fish house closed, while his brother shoveled a patch of ice to clear it of snow. The house was collapsible with two sides, the front and back, made of plywood. A door with a small window denoted the front. The adjoining sides and the top were made of canvass.

Before moving the house into position, the boy's dad drilled two holes. The Kluge ice auger was powered by gasoline, and its blade, twirling clockwise, spiraled downward and cut through two feet of ice. *Whoosh*! When the man lifted the auger up, a fountain of water gushed up with it.

His son peered down into the hole; it was black. "That one's mine," the father said. He drilled a second hole. *Whoosh*! "That one's Len's," he stated. Then he moved off into the distance and drilled a third hole into the ice. *Whoosh*! "That one's yours." The boy could see that it was outside the boundaries of the fish house.

The fish house had skis bolted to the back side. The two men and the boy slid the fish house into position. Then they tilted it upright. Frankie's father opened the door and stepped inside. He lowered into place a wooden floor that was hinged inside to the base of the back wall. It covered the ice completely except for a pair of two-foot by two-foot holes in opposite corners. Then the father braced the wooden walls with two-by-two lumber, up high, to stabilize the structure. He had performed this task many times, and he worked quickly. He trusted the construction, for he had built the fish house.

The boy peeked inside the fish house and looked down into a hole. The absence of outside light altered what he saw under the ice. The world below had suddenly changed color, to a lime green. It was no longer a murky black, but clear, and he could see several feet down into the water.

His father installed a kerosene heater in the middle of the house with a pipe venting upward through the ceiling. It hissed as it sprang to life and immediately gave off a measure of heat. The man placed his hands next to the heater and rubbed them together, for the air was nippy.

The two brothers unfolded padded chairs and sat on them. The boy sat next to his father on a five-gallon can that he had turned over. He sat on a cushion that his father had set on the makeshift stool. Soon, both men busied themselves with their fishing poles. He watched his father scoop out the fishing hole to remove a thin layer of ice that had formed on the top.

The interior of the fish house was dark, except for the meager glow from the kerosene heater. It was just enough to illuminate his father's face. On it the boy detected beads of sweat from the man's exertion. The kerosene heater continued to hiss.

The first time the boy's father dropped his line into the water, he didn't bait the hook. Instead, he clamped a weight onto it. He wanted to check the lake's depth. "Twenty-five feet," he said to his brother. He removed the clamp from the hook and looked at the length of the line from his sinker to his bobber. "I think we have to fish deeper."

"How deep?" asked his brother.

"I'll fish at twenty-two feet; you fish at eighteen. If one of us hooks a fish, we'll know how deep they are." They moved their bobbers farther up the line.

His father used a small net to scoop out a fathead. It wiggled on his knee as he hooked it just under its dorsal fin. He dropped his line back into the water, and the minnow on the hook sank. They had begun to fish.

The boy's father stuck his pole into the ice to secure it. The bobber on the line was white and green with red rings around the top. Shaped like a pencil, it floated on the watery surface in the hole. Five minutes passed. "Want a sandwich?" the father asked his son. "Fish bite better when you're eating. Then we'll get your pole rigged up outside."

"Where are the sandwiches?" the son asked.

"In the cooler, behind Len," his father replied.

"I can wait," the boy decided. He did not feel comfortable disturbing his uncle.

He stared down into the green water. The kerosene heater continued its hissing.

A minute later, the bobber in his father's fishing hole began to move. It bobbed up and down quickly three times, and then it steadied. A fish was nibbling at the bait.

Twenty seconds later, the bobber sank ten inches and then stood still. His father slid off his chair and knelt in front of the hole, fingered the line, giving the fish latitude. And then the bobber moved again, sinking down at a steady rate.

Immediately his father yanked hard on the line and pulled it upward hand over hand. "I feel it," he announced, grinning. "It's heavy." He continued to pull the line up and not give the fish any slack.

Six feet down they saw the walleye. The father pulled the fish into the hole and with a practiced hand inserted his fingers into the fish's gills. He lifted the fish out of the water. It's a male," he said under his breath, "a two-and-a-half-pound walleye." He looked over at his brother. "Twenty-two feet, Len." Immediately the boy's uncle pulled his line in and adjusted the depth of his hook.

"I want to fish," said the boy.

"Get your pole," said the father.

They went outside. It was colder than in the fish house, and the top of the hole was already freezing over. "You'll have to clean it out often," advised the man. He let his son drop the line into the water. The boy had observed how his father did it, and he watched the minnow disappear, pulled down by the sinker above the hook. "How deep am I fishing?" he asked his father.

"Twenty-two feet. That's the depth I caught mine. Come in when you get cold."

The boy stayed outside for fifteen minutes. By then, his father had caught another fish, smaller in size, but a keeper. His uncle looked antsy. "You're next," said his older brother. "This is a good spot."

It proved to be a good spot. By noon, they had twelve fish, two limits. The boy had caught two outside, but he had missed several others when he was inside the fish house, warming up. When he pulled up his hook to inspect it, the minnow was missing.

They were in good spirits. They unpacked their lunch cooler and ate: the summer sausage sandwiches, loaded down with mayonnaise and lettuce, were tangy. They ate apples and cookies for dessert and washed them down with nectar.

The fishing slowed in the afternoon. But his father would not leave the ice without their limit, six more fish. The boy became bored. He was tired of fishing and would have liked to go home.

"Go check your line one more time," his father told him. "Then you can take a break." So, the boy trudged through the snow to the hole. He was just in time to see the bobber disappear beneath the ice. The extra line he had left in the hole was gone, and the pole itself began to wobble, to and fro.

He threw his gloves to the ice and grabbed the line just in time. The top of the hole had frozen over, a thin icy layer, and he kicked the ice with his foot to open the hole up. Then he began to pull the line up, hand over hand, like his father had done. The fish tugged back.

He watched for the bobber and saw it return. He pulled on the line at a constant rate, careful, like his father had been, not to give the fish any slack. He didn't want it to spit the hook out. He hoisted the fish toward the surface.

In the daylight outside, the water did not look green and clear, but black and murky. Because of this, the boy did not see the walleye until it was just below the ice. When he finally saw it, he panicked. "It's a walleye, Dad! It's too big! It's too big! It won't fit in the hole!"

His father heard his cries and leaped out the door and raced toward him. "Keep the line tight!" the Dad yelled. "Keep the line tight!"

His father knew what he had to do. The son watched as his father unzipped his jacket and threw it onto the ice. Then, the man fell flat next to the hole and plunged his right arm down into the water.

"Keep the line tight!" he ordered. His head was flattened sideways against the ice so that his ear was in the water. As was his habit, he stuck his tongue between his teeth while he labored.

Uncle Len appeared in the doorway of the fish house, staring at them. When he realized what was happening, he ran toward the hole.

Slowly the boy's father pushed himself up with his free hand onto his left elbow. And then he rolled onto his left side. He worked to pull his right hand up. In it was a heavy weight. Again, he pushed into the ice with his free hand, and this time he rocked back onto his knees. He hoisted the weighty mass out of the water, a huge walleye. The man's middle finger was stuck deep in the fish's eye socket. His hand was bloody, for the right thumb was buried in the fish's mouth. Its teeth were pointed and razor-sharp.

His brother reached to help.

"Don't!" the older brother yelled. "My thumb is caught on the hook. The barb is lodged in my thumb."

The boy's father sat and cradled the fish. "Get the needle nose out of my tackle box," he stated. "We're going to need a pliers to free my thumb. Hurry! It hurts." And then he turned to his son. "Find the first aid kit in the truck. I'm going to need the disinfectant and the bandages."

He looked at the boy. He was starting to shiver, but his eyes were gleaming. "It's a lunker! And you caught it in your hole." He looked down at the mammoth fish and then at his swollen thumb. "I think it's time to go home."

It took Uncle Len fifteen minutes to extract his brother's thumb from the fish's mouth. He had to pinch the hook in the pliers and tear it from the walleye's flesh. The boy's father gritted his teeth, but he did not cry out in pain. He sat in the truck, nursing his injured thumb, while Uncle Len and the boy took down the fish house and loaded it into the back of the truck. The boy's uncle drove the six miles to shore.

Shorty was there to greet them. "That's a whopper!" stated Shorty, eyeing the fish. "Mind if I weigh it?"

"Go ahead," said the boy's father.

"It's nine pounds, three ounces, Dad. Shorty says his scale is 'right on'."

His father smiled weakly. "I'll have to drive home. Len, you keep the other fish. I can't clean them with this." He held up his hand. "We'll take this one home."

Shorty rubbed the whiskers on his chin. "Where did you catch it?" he asked hopefully. He looked at the man whose thumb was in a bandage. "A big fish like that... People will want to know. Indian Point?"

"No, over the Mud Flats," the man answered.

"Don't you mean Indian Point?" Shorty winked at the boy.

"No, the Mud Flats," the boy's father repeated.

"It *was* the Mud Flats," the boy insisted. "It really was." His father tousled his hair.

"Get him a Nut Goodie, Shorty. Then we have to go."

When they turned into the Wagon Wheel parking lot, it was after 5:00 o'clock. Paul Rausch was standing by his garage, talking with Syl Sawyer. Their neighbor slowed his truck and stopped.

"Been fishing, Cliff?"

"I have," his neighbor responded.

"What happened to your hand?"

"I got it caught in a fish's mouth."

Paul assessed the damaged thumb. "It must have been a big fish," he stated.

"It was."

"A walleye?"

"Yeah?"

"On Mille Lacs?"

"Yeah... Indian Point. Here, I'll show it to you." The fisherman climbed out of his truck and opened the cooler in back.

Paul Rausch's eyes brightened. "My, that's a keeper, a trophy fish. You're going to mount it on your wall, aren't you?"

"Maybe. But Frankie, here, caught it. It's his fish."

"Such a big fish..." Paul stated.

"Not as big as the one you caught last week," said the boy's father.

"No," Paul Rausch paused and shook his head, "that one was a lunker."

That Tuesday Judge Earl Frerick accepted the plea bargains of Howard Kappas, Cortney Johanson, and Herman Braun, with a stipulation. They were required to make restitution for the money they had stolen. "You're going to spend a year in jail," said the judge. Paul is going lightly on you for your crime. However, there is one condition: you must each pay $3,600. That's $18,000, divided five ways: you three, Roland Becker, and his son.

"But, Judge," Herman complained, "I didn't get as much as Roland and Howard did. I shouldn't have to pay as much."

Judge Frerick laughed openly. "Mister Braun, you were a Knight of the Round Table. The *idea behind the Round Table* was that no knight was better than any other knight. Therefore, Sir Herman, you all owe the same amount, three thousand six hundred dollars."

Herman sulked. "That's not fair, Judge, and you know it."

Judge Frerick looked at him pointedly. "It's payable by..." He turned to a man in the crowd. "When are you taking Ione to California, Paul?"

"The Ninth of June, Your Honor."

"Payable by June 9th. And it had better be here by then—or else!" He rapped his gavel to dismiss them.

SPRING

CHAPTER THIRTY-EIGHT

MARCH, 1959

"How do you breed a mink?"
"A male mink breeds her."
"But how does he do it?"
"He bites her in the neck."
"That would make her mad!"
"It *does*."

The two boys were sitting in the screen house in the O'Brian back yard. Lorraine O'Brian had told them to *skedaddle* and sent them outside to play.

"This is mink breeding season," Frankie explained. "It's spring. They only breed in March. You put the female mink into the male mink's cage, and then he bites her in the neck. Pretty soon, they're rolling around in the pen. He's holding on with his teeth; she's trying her darnedest to get away. When that happens, she's not ready. Dad takes her out of the pen and puts her away. Then he grabs another female and puts her in. Sometimes she's ready.

My dad showed me last Saturday. Mom told him he has to give me some sex education before I make my First Confession this month. He's the one who has to give it to me.

Dad said, 'It's a little too early, isn't it?'

Mom said, 'He's at the age of reason. He's been noticing the girls in his class.'

So, Dad showed me. He pointed to a cage with two mink in it. 'That's it. Watch a while.' Then he walked away into the feed room.

Later on, he came out. 'Well?'

'Well what?' I asked. 'Nothing happened.'

He looked at me kind of funny. Then he explained it.

But something *did* happen. He bred her."

"Oh," said Terry Joe. He grinned. "With his *wee wee*?"

"Yeah."

The mink rancher's son continued the lesson. "It takes fifty-one days for the baby mink to be born; they're called kits. Fifty-one days is the gestation period."

"My mom had indigestion with Timmy the whole time. 'Nine long months,' she says."

"Gestation is different. It's shorter for mink," the neighbor boy clarified.

His friend corrected himself. "Indigestation."

"My dad's excited that it's spring; he's rarin' to go. He likes when the kits are born. He bends down and listens at each box. They make a little squeaking sound. When they're born, they're tiny."

"How tiny? Like Tiny Rausch?"

"No, they're smaller than your pinky finger."

The Second Grade children of St. Joseph's Elementary school were tucked neatly into their pews. When they were small, the church had seemed like a large cavity waiting to be filled with their boisterous chatter.

Now the church still seemed large and cavernous, but in a different way. It was a solemn spiritual sanctuary, worthy of whispers only. It was God's house, and today they were begging him for a favor, salvation.

It was Saturday, the day before Palm Sunday. Tomorrow at mass, they would hear a lengthy reading of Our Lord's passion. The members of the congregation would stand or kneel with palm branches in their hands. The following Sunday would be Easter, the most glorious day on the church calendar, according to Sister Bede. The 10:00 o'clock mass would culminate with the Second Graders making their First Holy Communion.

The girls and boys were lined up, elbow to elbow, waiting for their turn in the confessional. The young penitents were busy examining their conscience one last time and practicing their Act of Contrition. Two nuns, Sister Bede and Sister Carmita, watched over them. They tolerated no *funny business* on this day.

Make the sign of the cross. "In the name of the Father, and of the Son, and of the Holy Ghost, Amen. Bless me, Father, for I have sinned. My last confession was… no… no… This is my first confession."

"Say Holy Spirit, not Holy Ghost, Terry Joe," cautioned Sister Bede.

"Won't it still count?" asked the boy.

"Holy Spirit is the modern way. You don't want to sound old-fashioned, do you?" The moment she said it, she knew it was the wrong thing to say. She forced a smile.

He smiled back at her. "Naw, don't worry, Sister. I'll do it your way… this time."

Sister Bede and Sister Carmita had prepared them well. "To make a good confession, you have to feel sorry, truly sorry. Practice feeling sorry whenever you can." The Second Graders felt comfortable with this. In Waite Park feeling sorry was a regular thing to do. "Practice at home, in the car, in the school, and even at church. Say 'I'm sorry' ten times. Then say it again and *mean* it."

Frankie knelt with his hands folded, pretending to pray. He was nervous. Father Thiel had told them that it was dark in the confessional and that his sins were just as dark. Father's remark made him fear purgatory. He needed to have his sins forgiven. The priest would absolve him of them in Christ's name. Then he needn't fear.

When he entered the confessional, he knelt down and waited for God to speak. Was God ready? Should he start first? He stared at the screen that covered the window in front of him. It was pitch dark behind the screen. "Father Thiel?" No one answered; he decided to start.

"Bless me, Father, for I have sinned. This is my first confession." He paused for a response. When none was forthcoming, he continued. "My sins are…" He knew them by heart, and he recited them. He started with the worst ones, the ones that were bothering his conscience the most:

"I cheated. I filled in the magazine subscription forms with Timmy O'Brian. We made up fake names, and we lied about them. I'm sorry. And I lied on the application and played Little League baseball when I was six instead of seven. I'm sorry. P.S. Just for one game. And I stole a chicken at the school bazaar and gave it to Terry Joe because I felt bad for him. I'm sorry. And I scared the young girls from behind the bush in the sisters' yard with Terry Joe and Russell Stein. I'm sorry. And I made our babysitter, Laura Birch, mad when she had to pull me up the stairs, so mad that she swore at me and asked for more money. I'm sorry. And I did not honor my mother. I held her wrists when she tried to spank me with an arrow. I'm sorry. And I hate piano lessons. I'm sorry. And I hooked the bus. I'm sorry."

He paused to catch his breath. He did not say anything about hating the girl in his class with the big head. He wasn't truly sorry for that, so he didn't mention it. An eerie silence met him. "God, are you listening?" he asked. "Are you there? Should I say my Act of Contrition now?" He thought he heard God telling him to do so, so he did. "That's all, God. I'm sorry. Goodbye for this time."

He stood up quickly and pushed the confessional door open. As he exited, he heard the sound of a wooden slat being slid along a window frame. "Come back here, you," he heard God say. But he continued out the door. God knew he had made a bad confession. He had not told him about his intense dislike for Susanne Danbury. Once again, she was at the source of his troubles.

Sister Mary Bede was watching him. He proceeded into the pew to which she had assigned him and knelt down. He folded his hands and bowed his head. "Dear Lord," he prayed, "what have I done now? I'm sorry. Please forgive me. Absolve me of my sins anyway."

He met his best friend, Terry Joe O'Brian, outside the church. The other children were milling around at the base of the steps, feeling cleansed. They were excited and full of sacramental grace.

"Did he dissolve you of your sins?" asked Terry Joe.

"I think so," Frankie replied. "But I'm not sure."

"What penance did he give you?" his best friend asked. "He

gave me three *Our Fathers*, three *Hail Marys* and three *Glory Be's*."

The boy, Frankie, squinted into the afternoon light. "He didn't say nuthin' to me," he stated, hiding what he knew to be true.

His best friend looked at him quizzically. "But he had to say something." Terry Joe was perplexed. "Before he dissolves your sins, he has to give you a penance. Sister said so."

He could not lie to his mother. When she questioned him, he grew evasive. He told her that he had confessed his sins.

"Which priest?" she asked.

"Father Thiel, I think."

"You *think*?"

He lowered his gaze, and then he became sullen. "Terry Joe doesn't think I made a good confession," he admitted.

"Why not? What happened?"

"Nothing happened. The priest never spoke to me."

"Not once?"

The boy shook his head sideways, in the negative.

"Was the window open?" she asked.

"No, it was dark in there."

"He probably didn't have the window open yet," she explained. "He was listening to someone else's confession on the other side. They should have practiced that with you." She looked mystified.

"I missed the practice," said her son. "That was the day I stayed home sick."

"Well, you'll have to go back and make your First Confession." She stood up and brushed off her house dress. She re-tied the bandanna on her head. She was doing housework, vacuuming the floor and dusting furniture. "You still have a week before Easter." She turned the vacuum cleaner on with her foot.

"I'm not going back there," the boy called out loudly. She switched the vacuum cleaner off.

"Yes, you are going back there," said the woman. You can't make your First Holy Communion unless you've already made your First Confession. Grandma's coming over next Sunday, and Uncle Len's family. You're the guest of honor."

"I'm not going back there," the boy persisted.

His mother's face looked angry. "Then go up to your room and think about it!" she ordered. "Come and talk to me when you've come to your senses. Until then, you're grounded. Stay in your room."

The boy turned and left in a huff. He did not come down, and he would not change his mind. His sister, Jeanne, came upstairs and told him that supper was ready, but he told her to "Get away!" He wasn't hungry.

He was angry at his mother, her smug self-assurance. And then an idea struck him. He would teach her a lesson once and for all. He would run away from home!

When he came down into the kitchen, they were almost finished with supper. His father was working late, selling investments up in Melrose with Grandma. He would not be home for supper.

The boy looked at his mother sitting at the end of the table. She was smiling. Then he looked at his brothers and sisters. They were all staring at him, even Baby Chuck.

"I'm running away from home," he announced. Quickly he looked at his mother to gauge her reaction.

There *was* no reaction. She continued to smile, and it made him mad.

But his sisters and brother had heard. They broke into sudden tears. They cried deep, painful sobs. "Oh no, Frankie! Don't do it. Please don't do it. Where will you go? We'll never see you again."

It was all very delightful, except for his mother's unresponsive disregard. She continued to smile. That bothered him. He would show her. He turned on his heels and climbed up the stairs to his room.

In the attic he found three large cardboard boxes. They would serve as suitcases. He began to pack his possessions into them.

Below in the kitchen, his siblings were still crying, but he did not hear the voice of his mother. He would make her cry!

He packed one box with his pants and shirts, underwear and socks. He would need an extra pair of shoes. Those, too, went into the box. There was not enough room for all of his clothes in one box, so he put several articles into the second box.

He planned to be gone a long time, so he packed a jacket and his winter coat, his black stocking cap, a scarf, his gloves, and a pair of boots. He included a thermos for water.

In the third box he put his memorabilia—his shoebox full of baseball cards, his baseball mitt and one ball. He would need a backpack but no school books! And no piano books! He considered putting in his camera but decided against it. He did put in a deck of cards.

On the wall he spied a picture of his family. He took it down and looked at it. The faces of his family stared back at him. Already he was feeling homesick; he put it in the box.

He would need money. The boy had seventeen dollars and forty-two cents in his piggybank. This he extracted by taking the rubber plug out of the hole in the bottom. He stuffed the money into the front pocket of his pants.

Ready to depart, he hoisted the first box of clothes and carried it down the steps. The door opened and the small children ran to him, grasping his legs. "Don't go, Frankie. Don't go. We're sorry!"

"Get away from me," he ordered. "I'm leaving." He would not even show them that he cared. But he noticed that his mother stayed seated at the foot of the table. She was relaxed and calm, and that made him angrier still.

Determined to go, he picked up the first box and stomped out the door and down the steps. It was already dark out; the moon was shining on the lawn. He carried the box far enough away from the house to see the house clearly in the moon's glow. He set the box down on the boulevard; it was heavy.

He marched back into the house for the second box. Again, the children rushed to stop him. He brushed through their arms as if through a thicket of dense undergrowth in the woods, pulling himself along with his hands. The cries of their voices were shrill and full of anguish. Still, however, he heard no sound from his mother.

He picked up the second box. It was heavier than the first. Again, he clambered down the steps and through the tangle of small hands.

His mother sat complacently at the table, picking at her food with a fork. Her lack of concern irritated him. He took the second box out to the boulevard and set it next to the curb.

In a fit of vexation, he returned to the house for the third box. He tramped down the stairs a third time. Again, the children fought to hold him back, to keep him there, to keep the family together.

He stared at his mother. "Well, I'm going. And I'm not coming back!"

"Goodbye, Frankie" was all she said.

As he departed into the night, his feelings seared him. "Goodbye, Frankie." That was all she had said. No tears. No pleas. No anxiety whatsoever. "It's as if she wants me to go," he admitted.

He put his third box down and stared into the night. Where should he go? When would he come back? When would he ever see them again? He took the picture of his family out of the third box and stared at it: a father, a mother, three boys and two girls. And one about to be born in two months! Perhaps he would never see that baby.

Suddenly it dawned on him: he had nowhere to go. This realization struck him like a punch in the gut. He stood and stared at the house, *his* house, *his* family.

He thought it over. In the end he decided that he would give them one more chance.

He lifted one of the heavy boxes and carried it back inside the house and set it on the floor in the back porch. Then he retrieved the second box, and the third.

His mother was still sitting at her place at the kitchen table. The other children were all seated. "Welcome home," said his mother. "If you're hungry, there's still a plate of spaghetti hotdish on the stove." She tried to sound matter-of-fact, and he was glad for that.

He *was* hungry. He should have eaten supper first. "Okay, I'll go to confession," he muttered.

"I told you he would come back," said his sister, Jeanne.

After supper the younger children went upstairs to play. The boy went up with them to his room to unpack. The children went to bed early.

It was late when the boy heard the back door open and his father come in. Frankie crept down the stairs and opened the door just a crack. He heard his mother speak, and then his father let out an uproarious laugh. The boy felt the sting on his face; he was chagrined.

His mother was talking again. He heard only some of her words: "It's her *Give a dog a bone…* method. And it works!"

He stole up the stairs back to bed. The covers were familiar and warm, and he listened to the soft breathing of his brother, Dan, who was asleep beside him.

Easter Sunday! The children arose early and scoured the house for their Easter baskets. They knew that the baskets were filled with sweets. Mr. Easter Bunny's task every year was to hide the containers. He enjoyed the challenge.

Once found, the baskets were open to inspection. The wicker baskets were filled with candies and chocolate eggs. Before their mother could say "no," the children stuffed their mouths with jelly beans and chocolates. The oldest boy liked malted milk chocolate, shaped like miniature footballs, best. In each basket Mrs. Easter Bunny was always sure to include one hard-boiled egg. That contribution was *her* tradition.

"Come, look here!' Mary cried. "Look what Dan found."

The young boy had been looking for his Easter basket and decided to inspect the porch. Now he stood mesmerized by the unexpected sight before him. Inside the porch was a wire cage, and inside the wire cage were two rabbits. They were identical in their appearance, white and furry with cottony tails. Their eyes were pink as were the insides of their ears.

Dan stepped back in horror. He pointed to the cage, but could not talk. *Which one is the Easter bunny*? he wondered.

His sister squealed. "Jeannie, come look! We've caught the Easter Bunny." And then she began to cry, and she wondered how it carried all the candy. With the Easter Bunny a prisoner, did some people in Waite Park not receive any candy? What about elsewhere in Minnesota? What about around the world?

Their father showed up in the doorway. "So, you've found them," he noted.

"How did you catch them?" Mary asked. "Why did you put the Easter Bunny in a cage?" It was all a mystery that her father seemed to be taking in stride.

"Let's name them," said Jeanne.

"They're both females," her father informed them.

"Mopsy and Flopsy," suggested Mary. "Mopsy and Flopsy! Mopsy and Flopsy!"

"Mopsy and Flopsy," echoed her older sister.

"Mopsy and Flopsy," stated their brother, Dan.

"But how do we tell them apart?" inquired Mary. The children looked at them closely.

"You can't tell," said the father, grinning. "It's hard to tell them apart."

"One's fatter than the other one," observed Jeanne. "It doesn't hop around as much."

Their younger brother was pointing at one of the furry animals.

"He's pointing to that one's ear. See how it bends down," explained Mary.

"Yeah, it *flops* down," said Jeanne. The two girls looked at each other with recognition. Simultaneously, they opened their mouths to speak.

"Flopsy," said Dan.

"That one's Flopsy," Mary exclaimed. "Flopsy... Flopsy..."

Her sister mirrored her. "Flopsy... Flopsy... Mopsy's the fatter one... the plumper one," stated Jeanne.

And so, the two rabbits were christened.

The children's mother appeared in the doorway next to their father. "You have to keep them out in the garage. Put your candy away now. It's time to get ready for church. We have to be at the school for pictures by 9:15. Frankie, this is your big day."

In the school's gymnasium-auditorium-lunchroom, a set of risers had been unfolded and set up. Fifty-two children stood ready to climb them and pose for a group picture. This number included six from McKinley Elementary who did not go to Catholic school.

The girls wore white dresses with white anklets and white shoes that buckled on the side. They wore white gloves on their hands and a white veil on their heads, for they, themselves, were symbols—of angelic purity and of the Catholic Church itself. In a way, they represented the Church, and the Church was the bride of Christ. Each of them was clutching a bouquet of flowers.

The boys were dressed in black suits with white shirts and black bow ties at their necks. They were not devils in disguise. They wore black, not because they were less pure than the girls, but to create a contrast—to set the girls apart.

The black shoes on their feet had been polished until they shined, and their hair had been parted and combed. They stood ill-at-ease, waiting to assemble, wanting to be done with it.

At the front of the risers stood Sister Bede and Sister Carmita. They had their hands full, orchestrating the picture-taking. They were busy gesticulating with their hands.

At the back of the auditorium stood the parents, keeping an eye on their sons and daughters. The children's siblings stood at their parents' side, observing the proceedings, afraid to step out of line.

Lorraine O'Brian was watching her son, Terry Joe, carefully for any sign of wayward activity. At the first inkling of rebellion, she was prepared to bolt forward and grab him by the scruff of the neck. She had brought reinforcements along. Her husband, Bill, was standing guard behind her, awaiting orders.

"You look good, Frankie," said Terry Joe as he climbed the riser.

"You too," said his friend. "I hope they hurry up."

In front of him, he spotted a girl with a large head wearing a veil. He tried to ignore her, but she turned around and saw him. She stuck out her tongue at him sweetly, and then she smiled broadly and flashed her white teeth.

"She thinks she looks pretty," growled Jerry Unger, who was standing next to Frankie in the back row. "She's creepy."

There were four rows. "Tall boys in the back; short boys in front of them. Short girls in front; tall girls in back of them—like we practiced," shouted Sister Bede.

"You all look very nice." After we take the group picture, we'll march across the street to the church together, by rows, in single file. Stay together and stay in formation!" Her voice challenged anyone to step out of line. "No shenanigans," she had instructed them at the rehearsal, "or I'll have Sister Anthony speak to you."

For a brief moment Terry Joe weighed her threat, but then he spotted his mother eyeing him. When he saw his father parked behind her, he decided against any *shenanigans*. He waved to her, and she waved back.

The children were restless, antsy. "My collar's strangling me," a boy shouted out. He tugged at his shirt collar.

From the back of the auditorium, his mother called out a warning to him. "Jimmy Holston! Stand still or I'll fry you like a billy goat!" A vein in her forehead was bulging.

"She'll make him a eunuch," whispered Gail Teigen to Irene Pressler, her eyes lively and bright. The girls around her twittered madly.

"My tie's falling off," yelled Ricky Shenker. "I'll just leave it off." But Sister Carmita rushed over to him to clip the tie back on.

CLICK! The photographer snapped a picture.

"Say CHEESE!" yelled Sister Bede.

CLICK! The photographer snapped another picture for posterity.

"The first row may now exit," stated Sister Bede, "over to the door. Stand there and wait for me. Now the second row..."

When the children were all in a line, she opened the door and led them outside. The day was sunny and sparkling. The children paraded to the church, their parents following them.

They climbed the steps, their shoes clicking on the cement. At the door their pace slowed as Sister Anthony handed each of them a small candle. It had a tin funnel around it to catch any wax drippings.

The candle also was a symbol—of Jesus Christ himself, the Light of the World. They would be swallowing his body during the mass to be in communion with him.

They entered the church and walked to the front pews. A communion rail made of white marble lay between them and the sanctuary.

"There's Father Thiel, praying on the kneeler," said a voice to Frankie. It was Jonas Duane. "It's strange not seeing Father Schumacher there."

"I know," said his altar boy partner. "Father Thiel doesn't pray as hard. I wish Father Schumacher could see us now."

At communion the boy closed his eyes and tilted his head back. He opened his mouth and stuck his tongue out, resting it on his bottom teeth and lip. Father Thiel deposited a host on it.

As he walked back to his pew, he saw his sisters staring at him. They were wearing their new Easter bonnets. Next to them sat his mother, holding Baby Chuck in her lap. She just smiled and smiled while his brother, Dan, clung to her arm. His father was seated next to him, eyes closed, either praying or sleeping. The boy could not tell which.

At the end of the pew sat Grandma. She was admiring the procession of girls and boys dressed so nicely in their Sunday finest, making their First Holy Communion. She thought of her oldest granddaughter, Jane, a Lutheran. Grandma scowled. Jane should have been baptized Catholic. Her daughter, Berneda, should never have married Larry Reeder. Two more children had followed, both boys, both Lutherans. Mary Frances Kucher sat discontentedly at the end of the pew. Her oldest granddaughter should have made her First Holy Communion long ago. She would have looked saintly, dressed in a slender white dress and white gloves and a white veil, like a little immaculate angel.

The mass ended and the church bells pealed. The boy's father drove the family home. He parked in the driveway. Immediately the children jumped out of the car. They ran for the garage. The door was open to give the rabbits air to breathe.

"Look at that," said Jeanne. She nudged her sister. "There, in the pen." She pointed to a small white puff ball on the floor of the cage.

There's another one," exclaimed Mary. Dan was pointing to a third.

"They're moving," screamed Mary. Their father came to see. He whistled in surprise. "Well, I'll be..." he stated to himself.

Their mother approached. "Mopsy's having babies," stated Jeanne. "Mom, look!"

"So, it's Mr. and Mrs. Easter Bunny, not two females," stated wife to husband. "How could you get that wrong?"

"With rabbits, it's hard to tell," answered her husband.

"Look at that!" said Mary. She pointed to Mopsy. "In the back there!" The head of a tiny infant rabbit was showing, the newest in a world of newborns. Soon, it too plopped onto the floor of the wire cage.

"Is that how you'll do it, Mom?" Mary asked. Her family looked at the mother's belly.

"More or less," she answered. "Go get a cardboard box, Frankie. We'll have to make a nesting box for them."

"We'll have to cut it down to size," said her husband. "I'll go get my hunting knife." He followed his oldest son into the house.

"Jeanne, get a blanket out of your doll buggy. It'll keep the baby rabbits warm. Mary and Dan, get them some more food and water. Mary, you bring over the hose." The children all moved off to do their tasks.

The woman stood there, looking down at Mopsy. She ran her hand along her own abdomen and felt the bulge in her tummy. "Two more months," she said to herself, "and I'll be giving birth, bringing a baby into the world."

Grandma came up beside her. She, too, had given birth, five times—a long time ago. "He should know better than to bring home two rabbits in the same cage, especially a female and a male."

"Sometimes, men just don't know what they're doing," said her daughter-in-law.

"Yes, and it's the woman who always suffers for it" came the reply.

By noon, Mopsy had given birth thirteen times. "A muffin dozen," stated Jeanne.

"What's that?" asked her older brother.

"You know, doughnuts you get from the bakery—they always give you one more extra."

On April 1st, April Fools' Day, Superintendent Roy Steichel pinned an announcement to the bulletin board in the central plant. It was a terse memo.

NOTICE OF CLOSING

Notice is hereby given that the Great Northern Railway's car shops in Waite Park is closing. It will be relocated in Lincoln, Nebraska, as of July 1, 1959. Management has generously consented to guarantee employment to all full-time employees who relocate at that time. A skeleton crew will be retained until the end of the year or until the relocation is completed.

The superintendent stood back and surveyed the message. He knew that the announcement would hit like a hammer. It was now beyond his control. He alone in Waite Park knew the reason for the closure: Jimmy J. Hill was upset.

When the president of the railroad heard about the attack on Paul Rausch, he bristled in anger. His grandfather had been an abolitionist. He had told his grandson stories of atrocities against Negroes, of slavery and of violence committed by the Ku Klux Klan. "I will never condone men who cloak themselves in white robes and white hoods and who hide their faces behind white masks," his grandfather had preached. "They are nothing more than henchmen for the devil."

His grandson had listened. Neither would he tolerate them. Neither would the Great Northern Railway. The wicked would be punished, like Sodom and Gomorrah!

Roy Steichel shook his head. The many always suffered at the hands of a few. The people of the village would have to brave the decision and fend for themselves. He felt like the captain of a sinking ship, issuing his final decree: "You have done your duty; you can do no more. Now it's *every man for himself.*"

Crew foreman Tommy Stanton was one of the first to read the notice pinned to the bulletin board. The announcement was without emphasis. He thought about his role in the scheme of things, and he felt a certain amount of regret.

Poor Paul! We beat him badly. But he should have told us that it was a setup, that he was a decoy. Now it's come to this. Good old Paul! "I'll have to buy him a beer at Ma's when I see him," he said to himself. It would be his way of apologizing.

CHAPTER THIRTY-NINE

The two boys were keeping each other company in the O'Brian back yard. School had ended for the day, and Terry Joe was busy sharpening his spear, honing the point. The previous day he had tried to burn the wooden point in a fire to harden the wood. That had backfired. Instead of tempering the point, the flames had consumed it. The point had disintegrated in a charred mess.

Undaunted, Terry Joe set out on a new plan of action. In the evening he scoured the basement and came across the answer, a metal point made of iron. It was the ornamental tip of a lampshade, shaped like an arrowhead. He unscrewed the tip from a discarded floor lamp. The bottom end of the metal tip fit perfectly onto the end of the spear. The boy lashed it onto the shaft with a leather shoestring from his father's hunting boot and duck tape.

Terry Joe spent an hour filing the metal to a fine point. Bill O'Brian's electric grindstone on his work bench in the garage expedited the job. The boy put the finishing touches on the spear by hand the following day. His specifications were exacting. When he was satisfied, he jabbed the spear into the air repeatedly to test its weight and balance.

Suddenly he flung it at Val Krause's elm tree toward a gray squirrel that was clinging vertically to the trunk, clutching the bark. The spearhead missed the mark by several inches. The squirrel, a pregnant female, darted around the tree to the other side. There she stopped and chattered profusely, scolding the boys for intruding upon her territory.

The head of the spear struck the trunk of the tree solidly and stuck. The duck tape had held.

"Hey, you killed a tree!" said his friend, who had been watching.

Terry Joe shrugged. "Timmy says I do that every time I pee on one." He went over to retrieve his weapon.

Frankie revealed his news. "We're going to have different teachers in Third Grade next year. Mom asked Sister Anthony to separate us. She says that you are a bad influence on me."

"I know," said Terry Joe. "Us O'Brians have gruff language."

"I don't like it," said his friend. "I told her how it makes me feel—sad... and mad!" The neighbor boy, Frankie, tried to lessen the pain with reason. "We'll still be best friends; we just won't be in the same classroom at school. After school and on weekends, we can play together all we want. I'm going to have Sister Agatha; you're going to have Sister Timothy."

"Watch out for Sister Agatha!" Terry Joe warned. "She likes Indians—better than she likes us. She's short, but she'll twirl that rosary and smack you under the chin with the crucifix. Ask Robbie Stein. She can be mean as hell when she wants to be."

Frankie nodded. He had heard as much.

Just then, the car shops' yard whistle blew. It was precisely 4:30 p.m., the end of the work day. Both boys raised their heads to listen. "We won't be hearing that much longer," said Terry Joe. It was a sobering thought.

Frankie changed the subject to something more distressing. "The railroad's car shops are closing. Do you know who's leaving?" He had heard many rumors.

Terry Joe proved to be a fountain of knowledge. "The Krauses," said Terry Joe. "Lucky got a new job in Minneapolis."

That was shocking news, close to home. Still, losing Norma wasn't a major concern. She ignored him anyway.

"What about Jimmy Holston?"

"He's leaving." That was not good news. Jimmy Holston liked to play football as much as he did.

"What about Ricky Shenker?"

"He's leaving," stated Terry Joe. The girls would not miss Ricky's constant insults. Neither would the boy himself, for that matter.

"What about Gail Teigen? And Irene Pressler? And Jeanie Kovar?"

"They're all staying," said Terry Joe. Hmmm. They would continue to tease John Lewis, but he and his orange bow tie didn't seem to mind their flirtations.

"What about Jonas Duane?"

"He's staying," answered Terry Joe. That was good news. He and Jonas saw eye to eye on many things. They were both deep thinkers. Besides, he wanted to keep his mass-serving partner.

"Jack Kertcher is staying," stated Terry Joe. This is not good news, thought Frankie. He would have to keep an eye on his sister, Jeanne, lest Jack and Jackie Birch turn her into a sinful girl.

"But Lucy Stephens is leaving," added Terry Joe. His friend considered this. It was a shame, but Lucy Stephens would miss Jack Kertcher far more than he would miss her. For some reason, Frankie felt sorry for her.

"What about the Kappases?"

"They're leaving. Howie wants to make a fresh start."

"What about the Johansons and the Brauns?"

"The same thing. Mom figures they'll all be back in a year. She says, 'This is where they grew up. The people of Waite Park will take them back.'

Dad told her, 'They *never* grew up. Nobody else would want them.'" Terry Joe grinned at his father's joke.

"What about the Beckers?"

"She's staying; he's leaving," said Terry Joe. "For five years. Then he'll be back. I don't know why," added Terry Joe. Frankie thought he knew.

"What about the Wojcheskis?"

"He's staying; she's leaving," Terry Joe answered. The neighbor boy knew that his mother would not feel comfortable about his. Perhaps, as his father believed, it was for the best.

"What about Mayor Ryngsmuth and his family? Are they leaving?"

"No," answered Terry Joe. "They're staying. He says this is his home and he'll find other work. My dad says he's a bulldog."

"So does mine. Dad says he's a strong man and a good mayor for Waite Park. For sure, the parade wouldn't be any good without them."

"What about Father Schumacher? Is he coming back?" asked Frankie.

"He's gone," said Terry Joe. "Father Thiel has taken his place. He's the new pastor at St. Joseph's. Father Schumacher is not a priest anymore; he's just a Catholic."

"I wonder why?" thought the other boy aloud. He wondered if his mother would be pleased to hear this news. Probably, he decided.

"But my Uncle Squeak told us that the bishop is gonna write a letter and ask the pope to let Father Schumacher be a priest again. The bishop says that if the pope says 'yes' and if Father Schumacher prays hard enough, he's gonna let Father come back."

Frankie kicked the ground and thought about it. "That's good," he said. "Father Schumacher is good at praying."

A sudden last question came to mind: "What about Susanne Danbury?" inquired Frankie. He held his breath in anticipation.

"Her Dad is old; he's getting a buy-out from the railroad," said Terry Joe. "So, she's staying."

"Oh cripes!" blurted Frankie. He pictured her big head and flashing white teeth.

He tried to calm himself. "At least she lives on the other end of town," he reasoned. "As long as she stays there, things will be normal."

His friend grinned and then prodded, "What if she comes over here to our side?"

"I'll hide" came the swift reply.

"Where will you hide?" was his friend's next question.

The boy's blond head jerked upward. He peered into the sky and squinted into the harsh midday sunlight. His thoughts of escape were flowing freely. "Down in back of the ballpark... behind the fence in left field—by the quicksand pool!"

Terry Joe probed one final time. "What if she finds you there?" He tried to keep a straight face.

His friend looked at him, his face filled with horror. "I'll run away. And this time I won't be coming back!"

Terry Joe's grin was wide and toothy. Suddenly he had an idea. "Hey, it's spring. Let's ride our bikes."

"Yeah, let's," his friend agreed.

"Let's go out to the quarries," said Terry Joe. "Let's see what goes on out there. We're past the age of reason. We should be able to figure it out." Once again, his curiosity was aflame.

His friend, too, had an idea. "After that, I'll race you down Mrs. Beebehauser's hill."

"You mean the one where I broke my arm?"

"Yeah, that one."

Terry Joe thought the proposition over. "You can go first."

"No," answered Frankie. "You're my best friend in the whole wide world. We'll go together."

EPILOGUE

The historic day arrived at last. It was a day of parting, of saying goodbye. The people of Waite Park stood in their front yards, watching those who were preparing to leave. Cars were loaded down, packed and repacked to enhance efficiency. Many had a trailer hooked onto a hitch at the back.

"Take what's essential," ordered the man. "We can take only what's essential." They had already given away what they could.

"No, you can't bring that along."

"But Dad, I have to!"

"I'm sorry, but no. There's no room in the car."

Before they left, their neighbors came over.

"The house is still for sale," commented the owner. "There are no buyers. No work, no buyers."

"We'll keep an eye on it for you."

"Thanks. I appreciate that."

"I'll see that the grass is mowed and the sidewalk's shoveled."

"That's kind of you. You've been a good neighbor."

"It's the least I can do."

In the back yards friends bid farewell to one another. Girls held hands; boys shook hands. At each age, it was difficult to say goodbye.

Those who were a few years older were busy making plans:

"I'll write you one letter a week."

"Heck, I'll *call* you every day."

"You can come visit me."

"Hey, I'd like that. In Nebraska? That's a long way away."

"Just a day in the car… You could take the bus."

"I'll *hook* the bus."

"You always were a silly boy."

The younger boys and girls were feeling their loss:

"Are you going to play football down there, Jimmy?"

"I hope so."

"We'll need to find a new quarterback. No one can throw the old pigskin as far and as straight as you do."

"Who will be my skating partner? I can't skate very well by myself."

"You'll find someone, maybe a *boy*."

"Some *dumb* boy," I suppose.

"You might like him. He could become your boyfriend—and then your husband!"

"I doubt it."

"Stranger things have happened."

And the youngest children swung on the swings and teeter-tottered and played with dump trucks in the sandbox, like they always had. They, as yet, did not know the heartache of separation.

In the front yards fathers and mothers said goodbye to their sons and daughters. They pulled their grandchildren to them, and on this day the grandchildren came willingly and hugged them hard. Grandpa lifted the smaller ones up, and the children saw tears in the man's eyes that they had never seen there before. How strange!

"Let's take a walk, Dad," suggested the son. "We still have a little time."

"Yes, let's," agreed the older man.

And they strolled along the sidewalk eight blocks, along 3rd Street to 10th Avenue, stopping periodically to gaze into the car shops' yard, etching it into their memories.

The gates were locked, and the yard was empty. Trains that needed repair had already been hauled down to Nebraska. On a small tower next to the central plant hung the railroad yard whistle, now silent. "I'll miss 4:30, when the whistle blows," said the dad.

"So will I. There'll be a whistle in Lincoln, but it won't be the same. I'll miss working with you, Dad. You're the one who taught me all I know about working with sheet metal. I followed you over here. I owe you, Dad. Thanks!"

"We'd better head back, son."

And then it was time to go.

"Don't cry, Mom."

"Do you have to go?"

"I have to work, Mom. I need to make money. I have a family to support. The railroad pays us well."

"But I don't *want* you to go."

"We start work on Monday morning, Mom. I have to be there. Some day they may promote me to crew chief."

"I know they will, son. Your father and I will come visit you the first chance we get."

"We'll be home for Christmas, Mom. They give us a week of vacation."

"You take care of him, dear. Feed him well. He likes a good hamburger, medium rare."

"I know."

It was summer once again, and baseballs were flying through the air. Over on the southwest edge of the village, a game was starting. But on this day the family would not watch it.

The car pulled away from the curb, and the people waved. And then they were gone. And those left behind wondered if they would ever see their children and grandchildren again.

The man and woman in the car were younger. They and their children would eventually look at the move as an adventure. As the car sped along the road, the driver was already envisioning the new world that lay ahead of them. It forced a smile from him. He would be up to the challenge.

They were all inhabitants of the same planet. The earth would keep on spinning in circles as it revolved around the sun once every 365 days. Time would keep ticking by in Lincoln, Nebraska, just like it ticked by in Waite Park, Minnesota. As long as he had his family surrounding him, he felt secure. They would adjust. For them the outlook was bright.

But to their parents, it was the end of an era.

"Our lives are going to feel empty without them stopping by all the time."

"I know. I feel it already. But we'll survive."

"Oh, how will we ever cope without them?"

"The railroad's gone, but we're still here. I'll get another job."

"I'm so sad! I don't know if I can go on."

"Heck, we're young yet. We'll find something else to do. It just won't be the same as it was."

"In life, two days are never the same."

"I always thought they were *all* the same."

"Not anymore. "From now on, I'm going to live my life one day at a time."

"That's best."

"I can't stop grieving. I don't know if I ever will stop."

"Neither do I."

"I want to hear his voice *so badly*."

"He'll call tonight when they get there."

"But it's not like he's going off to college. He's gone for good."

"Do you know what our grandson told me this morning? He wants to be an engineer on a train. Can you believe that!"

"I can... Let's eat out tonight. I don't feel like cooking."

"I don't blame you. This whole thing has been a shock to all of us."

"Let's go to the Swan Café for some turtle."

"No."

"No?"

"I'll have the frog legs, a big heaping platter of frog legs."

AUTHOR'S NOTE

Do you believe in omens? On the day I took my book to the printer, a tree fell on our house. "Don't worry; we have more trees," I told my wife.

Her expression soured. "But only one house," she replied. Such is the difference between husbands and wives. I like trees; she likes houses.

In a small community little happens that is without humor. Those that lack that sense are in for a long winter.

Waite Park is a work of entertainment and should be read as nothing more. The names, characters, places, and incidents portrayed in the story are the product of the author's imagination or have been used fictitiously. Any resemblance to actual persons, living or dead, businesses, companies, events, or locales is entirely coincidental.

That having been said, some will say that there's a hint of truth in fiction. But if that's true about this book, it's a fictionalized truth.

The highlights of my life are few, but they are real and rewarding. One of those is writing this book. It reveals much about *who I am*. An old adage says, "If you can't do it, you teach." Hopefully this book will prove that theory wrong.

I grew up in Waite Park back in the 1950s and 1960s at a time when it was good to have an older brother or two to stick up for you. I was fortunate to have five brothers and four sisters, all younger, who looked up to me. After a time they stared down at me. As more time passes, I know they'll watch over me. I tried to tell them my philosophy of life—that something good comes out of something bad. But they seldom believed me. So, I told them stories instead.

Family was important in Waite Park. I had good parents. On Guam in 1944, my dad and his buddy, Louie, were "fed up" with the war in the Pacific. Finally they went to their commanding officer and said, "Sir, send us to the front—to Iwo Jima or Okinawa or even Tokyo itself. We'll get this war over with!"

Now the CO knew that he needed every tinsmith he could find to repair the wings of airplanes, and these two lads were two of the best. He said, "Come with me, boys." And he took them through the back alleys of the camp.

"Where are we going?" asked Dad.

"You're here," said the CO, and he showed them a pile of potatoes. He put them on *kitchen patrol* for a month, peeling spuds.

Occasionally I think about that commanding officer. I owe him a debt; I'm sure of it. I hope to thank him someday—personally.

Parents in Waite Park were the "no-nonsense" type. When I was eighteen, I decided to travel to Europe for three months. On the day I was to leave, I was dragging my heels, delaying my departure. Finally I said to my mother, "Well, Mom, I guess I'll be going."

She looked at me quizzically and said, "Aren't you gone yet?"

I replied, "Well, I guess I'll get my suitcase."

She said, "It's already in the car."

We learned early on that we belonged to an extended family. My Uncle Charley once said to us, "If you don't think I'm funny, then you're not Irish."

"I don't think you're funny at all," said Grandma, "and I'm half-Irish, on my mother's side. It was obvious that she was spoiling for a fight. He just grinned at her. Such is the stock I spring from.

Grandma's blood flows through my veins. I know it's true because I play my cards like she did. It's important what you pass on.

What you didn't learn from your parents (or from your older brothers and sisters), you could learn from your best friend. It was always good to have one because a real best friend was true to you and backed you up and didn't stab you in the back, ever.

In a German Catholic community like Waite Park, the priests and nuns were important. No student wanted one of them to "call home." It made for a long evening.

The rock quarries still exist, but now you have to pay to go into them. That's the government at work. They were, indeed, places where teenagers could gather, away from their parents' watchful eyes.

The Great Northern Railway's car shops is an integral part of this story. In the beginning the car shops was the reason the village existed. It provided employment, and that was a good thing.

As far as I know, the crime in the novel involving the railroad is strictly fiction. Therefore, so is how the crime was solved. The people of Waite Park were good people when I knew them. I'm sure they still are.

Eventually the railroad did relocate the car shops to Lincoln, Nebraska. But that was in 1986. In this novel I have used my literary license to change the year to 1959. At least two of the former mayor's sons continue to live down there.

Waite Park still exists. It has grown so that it is no longer a village but a small city. I prefer to remember it as it was. I remember the elm trees that grew tall and stretched out over the road, their leaves mingling with the leaves of elm trees from across the street. They formed a canopy under which we children played. I remember the neighborhood where we knocked on three doors and two baseball teams spilled out and played until dark, when we switched to another game and ran in the moonlight. And I remember the friendships that we formed. And the lives that we led. Waite Park was our home. Every so often I go back there, looking to see if what I left behind is still there.

FJK

P.S. I waited until my junior year in high school to start dating. My first girlfriend was a girl with a large head and flashing white teeth...

ACKNOWLEDGMENTS

I am indebted to my wife, Mary Gaffrey Knier, for her input into the novel, for her research and her critique of the manuscript. Her attention to detail helped me immensely with the story's authenticity.

I am also indebted to my brother-in-law, John Gaffrey, for his sustained input. It was needed. Although his critique of the manuscript was from a different perspective than his sister's, it, too, was vital. Both critiques were invaluable in shaping the final draft.

I want to express my deep appreciation to my daughter, Alexandra Putzer, for sketching and painting the book's cover. It adds a personal touch.

I wish to thank Corinne Dwyer, editor-in-chief at North Star Press, for her timely instruction regarding the writing of fiction.

I extend my thanks to Father James Ermer for his input at a critical juncture in the novel's development.

I also want to thank Kathy Czeck and her team at Professional Office Services, my printer, for their patience and understanding—and unshakable support—in view of our time constraints. I find it interesting that their office is situated on the very ground where the Great Northern Railway's car shops once stood.

I extend my heartfelt gratitude to those family members and friends who have urged me on by showing an interest in the book and an excitement about it.

Finally, to the people of Waite Park: past, present, and future, I wish you all the best. Hopefully, this book will rekindle memories of days gone by and people that touched our lives. I know it has done so for me. May you find it satisfying.